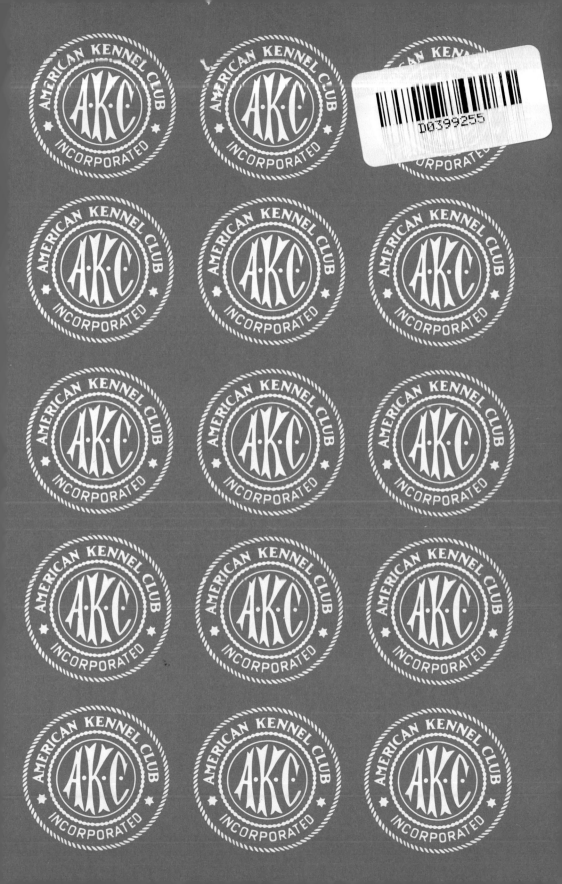

THE COMPLETE DOG BOOK

The English Setter, ADONIS

No. 1 of the American Kennel Club Stud Book, published in Volume 1, 1878, of the National American Kennel Club.

—*Courtesy, New Bedford Standard-Times*

Official Publication
of the American Kennel Club

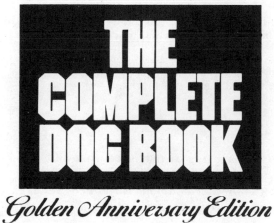

Golden Anniversary Edition

The photograph, history and official standard of every breed admitted to AKC registration, and the selection, training, breeding, care and feeding of pure-bred dogs.

1979
16th Edition - First Printing

HOWELL BOOK HOUSE Inc.
230 Park Avenue, New York, N.Y. 10017

New and revised standards are published when adopted
in the American Kennel Club's official magazine,
Pure-Bred Dogs—American Kennel Gazette.

Library of Congress Cataloging in Publication Data

American Kennel Club.
      The complete dog book.

      "An official publication of the American
Kennel Club."
      Breed standards corr. to May 1, 1979.
      Includes index.
      1. Dogs.   2. Dog breeds.   I. Title.
SF426.A53   1979   636.7   79–1490
ISBN 0–87605–462–9

Contents

GROUP III: WORKING DOGS

GROUP IV: TERRIERS

GROUP V: TOYS

GROUP VI: NON-SPORTING DOGS

CARING FOR YOUR DOG

8

Introduction
to the
Golden Anniversary Edition

THIS is the sixteenth edition, and the fiftieth anniversary year of the American Kennel Club's *The Complete Dog Book.*

Writing in 1929, Dr. John E. DeMund, then AKC president, began his Introduction to the first edition of this book with these words:

> "From time immemorial, the dog—of all the animals—has been most closely associated with man. By his service and devotion, he has earned himself the sobriquet of 'man's best friend,' a title acquired by no other member of the animal kingdom. His loyalty, affection and heroism have been extolled in many tongues in prose and poetry, and scarcely a day passes that some example of his courage, sagacity and devotion to man is not recited in the press."

The dog in all his varied forms has truly been man's best friend as hunter, sentry, shepherd, and above all as companion.

Within these pages you will find a brief history and the official standard of all 124 breeds registered by the American Kennel Club. You will also find a photograph of every breed, as well as an extensive section on "Caring For Your Dog", which provides basic information you need to keep your dog healthy and happy.

A few remarks are in order about *The Complete Dog Book* on this, its fiftieth birthday. The purpose of the book, from the beginning, has been to make available to the public a volume that enables anyone interested to "become better acquainted with the qualifications and appearance of each breed."

Originally, the book contained only a brief history and the standard of each breed. Additions and improvements have been made in each succeeding edition.

In this edition we have for the first time added color photographs of most of the breeds. The purpose of the color pictures is to give a fuller sense of the diversity, quality, and character of that amazing species—*Canis familiaris*.

The Complete Dog Book is something of a publishing phenomenon. It is the greatest selling book on dogs of all time, with sales totaling a million copies. It is universally recognized as the standard reference source on pure-bred dogs, and has been translated into numerous languages. Few books can boast of being in print for fifty consecutive years.

This golden anniversary volume constitutes the most comprehensive and useful edition ever published. Two years in the making, it represents the best efforts of AKC's staff, its member clubs, leading veterinary colleges and other authorities to compile the latest and most helpful knowledge available for pure-bred dog owners. Among the substantial revisions of the previous edition are:

   . . . 35 breed histories changed for greater accuracy

   . . . 21 breed standards updated, including breeds admitted to registration by AKC since the last edition

   . . . Expansion, updating and reorganization of "The Dog Sport" section to include new developments in Obedience and Junior Showmanship

   . . . 94 terms added or revised in the Glossary

   . . . A list is now included of AKC films and services available to dog clubs and owners

The American Kennel Club appreciates the reception you have given *The Complete Dog Book* since its first publication in 1929, and is proud to present this edition.

WILLIAM F. STIFEL, *President*

THE AMERICAN KENNEL CLUB thanks the many who have helped in the creation of this book. We appreciate the cooperation of the many member clubs in helping to make the breed histories as accurate as possible, and the many individuals and professional photographers who have helped in the assemblage of the pictures.

Before You Buy
Your Dog

FOR YOU who are about to purchase a dog, or to receive one as a gift, some considerations are in order, especially if this is to be your first.

To begin with, the family's receptiveness to having the dog must be established. The attitudes, habits and dispositions of all who will have responsibility for the dog must be taken into account. A new puppy is a delight, but there will be need for housebreaking, training to the leash and the obeying of commands, and of course, his daily care. From the time each puppy acquires a master, its health, happiness and welfare are largely determined by the mutual understanding and devotion that develops between them.

Ordinary common sense is important in selecting and caring for a dog. One cares for a dog from the heart, but one must care for a dog from the brain as well. All puppies seem irresistible, but the full grown animal must be visualized. Adult height, length, weight, appetite, disposition, amount of grooming required, must all be carefully considered before bringing home a cuddly ball of fur that can grow up to be a 100-pound terror. Consider, too, any limitations imposed by your environs; if it is to be a city dog, for example, the necessary excursions for exercise and elimination might prove a problem.

What breed is right for you?

In this book you will find a picture, history, and the official standard of the breeds currently accepted for registration by The American Kennel Club. There are dogs of all sizes, shapes and colors. There are old breeds, and relatively new breeds—breeds that have served man as hunter, guard, tracker, shepherd, sled dog, and above all as companion. Studying these pages can be a great aid in choosing the breed whose background inheritance, size and temperament best suits *your* needs and desires.

If you are able to supplement your study with attendance at a dog show, a field trial, an obedience trial, or a visit to a kennel, so much the better. There you will be able to see both puppies and mature adults of the breed that interests you.

Probably the most important consideration in buying a puppy is that it be from someone in whom you can put full confidence. A reliable seller can be of great assistance in the decisions you must make.

For example, one of the questions most frequently asked of sellers is "What is the best breed for a child?". The answer is that it is not so much the breed as it is the individual dog that is the factor, and whether or not the child can properly handle him. The dependable breeder can help a lot in making this determination.

You should determine in advance whether you want a male or a female. Other than the fact that a bitch, unless you have her spayed (which makes her ineligible for conformation showing), comes in season approximately twice a year and at that time must be carefully isolated from males, she is to be considered as desirable a pet as the male, if not more so. She is not as prone to fight with other dogs, and is less liable to stray.

If you are buying your dog with the expectancy of entering it at shows or field trials some day, or if you plan to breed, the pedigree of the puppy you select takes on greater importance, and you should learn as much as you can concerning the dog's ancestry.

A word of caution regarding dogs bought to be watchdogs. It is usually a natural thing for a dog of any breed to sound an alarm when anything strange occurs, or a stranger appears on the premises, and for most homes this is protection enough. However, dogs are available that have been specially trained to be guard or attack dogs, such as are used for professional police work. In acquiring such a dog, be aware that *a dog trained to this extent is safe only in the custody of a person equally well-trained.*

Do not buy a puppy under six weeks of age—eight weeks would probably be better. The important thing is to know that the puppy is fully weaned, and strong enough to be on its own away from the mother.

The puppy should be healthy, normal and alert. Never select from a litter in which disease seems to be present, and certainly never a puppy that seems ill with runny nose, watery eyes or fever. A cowed, trembling, shy puppy, or one that seems snappy and bad-tempered, should be avoided.

From the beginning, you should have a local veterinarian to whom you can turn. He can give you specific recommendations for the area in which you live, and can advise you on the vaccinations that are essential, from the outset, to provide immunity from the diseases that are fatal to so many puppies. The veterinarian will guide and help you in keeping your dog healthy, as well as in caring for him in sickness.

Because it has been subject to past misinterpretation, you should know that the designation "AKC Reg." following the name of a kennel simply means that the kennel's name is thus protected for the sole use of its owner in naming dogs to be registered or shown. It does not signify any special stamp of approval on the kennels—The American Kennel Club does not register or rate kennels as such. Nor does the AKC buy or sell dogs.

The American Kennel Club does register individual dogs, and in buying a pure-bred dog you should assure yourself of the following safeguards:

When you buy a dog that is represented as being eligible for registration with The American Kennel Club, you are entitled to receive an AKC application form properly filled out by the seller, which—when completed by you and submitted to the AKC with the proper fee—will enable you to effect the registration of the dog. (*See Pages 16, 17 and 18.*) When the application has been processed, you will receive an AKC registration certificate.

Under AKC rules, any person who sells dogs that are represented as being AKC registrable, must maintain records that will make it possible to give full identifying information with every dog delivered, even though AKC papers may not yet be available. *Do not accept a promise of later identification.*

The Rules and Regulations of The American Kennel Club stipulate that whenever someone sells or delivers a dog that is said to be registrable with the AKC, the dog must be identified either by putting into the hands of the buyer a properly completed AKC registration application, or by giving the buyer a bill of sale or a written statement, *signed by the seller,* giving the dog's full breeding information as follows:

—**Breed, sex and color of the dog**
—**Date of birth of the dog**
—**Registered names of the dog's sire and dam**
—**Name of the breeder**

If you encounter any problems in acquiring the necessary registration application forms, it is suggested that you write The American Kennel Club, 51 Madison Avenue, New York, N.Y. 10010, *giving full particulars* and the difficulty will be reviewed. All individuals acquiring a dog represented as being AKC registrable should realize it is their responsibility to obtain complete identification of the dog as described above sufficient to identify in AKC records, or THEY SHOULD NOT BUY THE DOG.

APPLICATION FORM FOR REGISTERING DOG WITH AKC (blue). To be filled out by litter owner, and signed by litter owner AND new owner of dog. Fee ($4.) must accompany application. Use this form for recording ORIGINAL transfer only - for subsequent transfers, use Supplemental Transfer Statement (see p. 18).

FEE $4.00	**AKC DOG REGISTRATION APPLICATION**		108
DO NOT SEND CASH	RETURN TO AKC IF NOT USED		
Add $1.00 For Each Supplemental Transfer			

DOG'S NAME →   1ST CHOICE

2ND CHOICE

The person who owns this dog and applies to register it has the right to name it. Limit name to 25 letters. Print one letter per box - skip a box between words. Names are subject to AKC approval. AKC may assign a number suffix.

BREED LABRADOR RETRIEVER

SIRE BUCKINGHAM'S BANDIT SA927543 (4-12)

DAM SAM'S SUNSHINE SB 5983 (3-73)

BREEDER SAM SMITH

LITTER OWNER
SAM SMITH
5229 MAIN ST
DOLTON IL 60419

LITTER NUMBER SL729497

INDICATE DOG'S COLOR
Owner of Litter, circle the one letter below for the color which best describes this dog. If none apply enter color on last line.

A BLACK
B YELLOW
C CHOCOLATE
OTHER

SEX MALE   DATE OF BIRTH NOV 16 1974

JAN 15 1975
ISSUED

®The American Kennel Club Inc. 1972

THE AKC RESERVES THE RIGHT TO CORRECT OR REVOKE OR CAUSE ANY REGISTRATION CERTIFICATE ISSUED. ANY MISREPRESENTATION ON THIS APPLICATION IS USE FOR CANCELLATION AND MAY RESULT IN LOSS OF ALL AKC PRIVILEGES FOR THOSE INDIVIDUALS WHO VIOLATE THE INTEGRITY OF THIS APPLICATION.

SIGNATURE OF OWNER OF KENNEL NAME

IN NAMING
THIS DOG

I hereby give permission to use my AKC registered Kennel Name

Litter owner should indicate color by circling color that most closely resembles PRESENT color of dog.

Litter owner should check sex specified on the face of the application, to be sure it corresponds to sex of dog being transferred.

Person who registers dog has right to name it. Indicate TWO unique name choices. Choices may not contain a Roman or Arabic numeral; AKC reserves right to assign Roman numeral if necessary.

If you own a registered name prefix and are granting permission to use the prefix, complete this section. If your prefix is not registered, leave this section blank.

Reverse side of blue application form. In buying a dog, do not accept an application that has not been properly completed in Section "A" by the litter owner.

INSTRUCTIONS: PLEASE TYPE – OR USE PEN. **NO PENCIL.** Erasures or Corrections may cause return of application for an explanation.

SEC. A

MUST BE COMPLETED IN FULL and SIGNED BY OWNER OF LITTER (AND CO-OWNER, IF ANY) SHOWN ON REVERSE SIDE.

ONE box MUST BE checked
☐ I (we) still own this dog, and I (we) apply to The American Kennel Club to register it and have **ownership** recorded in my (our) name(s).
☒ I (we) certify that this dog was transferred DIRECTLY TO THE FOLLOWING PERSON(S) ON **FEB   4   75**
                                                                                                    mo.   day   year

MUST be filled in by owner(s) of Litter
PRINT NAME(S) OF PERSON(S) TO WHOM   **MR. & MRS. JAMES JOHN⎯⎯N**
DOG WAS DIRECTLY TRANSFERRED
ADDRESS   **631 HARRIS ST. LOU⎯, MO 63120**

Signature   *Sam Smith*   Signature
              OWNER OF LITTER AT BIRTH   CO-OWNER (IF ANY) OF LITTER AT BIRTH

SEC. B

TO BE COMPLE⎯⎯D and SIGNED BY THE PERSON(S) NAMED IN SEC. A A⎯⎯VE, PROVIDED the person(s) owns the dog at the time this application is submitt⎯d to the A.K.C. If th⎯ person(s) named in SEC. A has transferred the dog to some⎯ her person(s). DO NOT COMPLETE SEC. B. Instead - obtain a Supplemental Transfer Statement for⎯ from the A.K.C. Instructions for its completion and use are ⎯⎯ the form.

I apply to Th⎯ American Kennel Club to have Registration Certificate for th⎯ dog issued in my/our name(s), and certify that I/we acquired it DIRECTLY from the person(s) wh⎯ signed Sec. A above, and that I/we still own this dog I agree⎯ o abide by American Kennel Club⎯ules and regulations.

New Owner's Signature   *James Johnson*

New Co-Owner's Signature   *Sam Johnson*

PRINT
Name   **James Johnson**   PRINT   Name   **J⎯an Johnson**
Address **631 Harris**   Address   **631 Harris**
City   **St. Louis**   State **MO** Zip **63120**   City   **⎯t. Louis**   State **MO** Zip **63120**

R⎯GISTRATION FEE MUST ACCOMPANY APPLICATION. MAKE ⎯⎯RS, MONEY O⎯⎯ERS PAYABLE TO THE AMERICAN KENNEL CLUB. DO NOT SEND TAM⎯⎯ ⎯ CASH.

When compl⎯ed and submitted, this Application becomes the property of ⎯e American ⎯ Club

FEE: $4.00 plus $1.00 for each additional transfer of dog repre-sented by Supplemental Transfer Statement.
FEES SUBJECT TO CHANGE WITHOUT NOTICE

Mail to: **THE AMERICAN KENNEL CLUB** 51 Madison A⎯ ⎯ue, **New York, N. Y. 10010**

Litter owner must complete Section "A" by indicating date of transfer and printing name and address of person(s) to whom he is directly transferring the dog.

Litter owner must sign Section "A" verifying details of transfer. Separate and individual signatures of ALL co-owners are required. Husband and wife must sign separately.

If new owner named in Section "A" intends to keep dog and regi⎯er in⎯ his ownership, he should sign and complete Section "B". (Sepa⎯ate and⎯ individual signatures of all co-owners are required.)
If the dog is to be transferred again do not complete Section "⎯". See⎯ page 18 for instructions on completing a supplemental transf⎯ state⎯ ment.

SUPPLEMENTAL TRANSFER STATEMENT (gray). Only the first transfer by the litter owner is to be recorded on the blue application form shown on Pages 16 and 17. If further transfer of the dog is to be made before the application is submitted for registration, the former AND new owner(s) must complete this Supplemental Transfer Statement, and attach it to the completed blue form. A fee of $1. (in addition to $4. fee required with blue form) must accompany each transfer application.

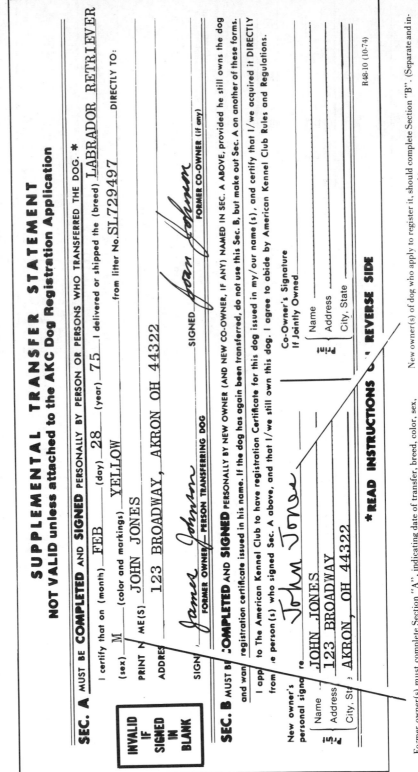

SUPPLEMENTAL TRANSFER STATEMENT
NOT VALID unless attached to the AKC Dog Registration Application

SEC. A MUST BE **COMPLETED** AND **SIGNED** PERSONALLY BY PERSON OR PERSONS WHO TRANSFERRED THE DOG. *

I certify that on (month) FEB (day) 28 (year) 75 I delivered or shipped the (breed) LABRADOR RETRIEVER from litter No. SL729497 DIRECTLY TO:

(sex) M (color and markings) YELLOW

PRINT NAME(S) JOHN JONES

ADDRESS 123 BROADWAY, AKRON OH 44322

SIGN _James Johnson_ SIGNED _Joan Johnson_
FORMER OWNER/PERSON TRANSFERRING DOG   FORMER CO-OWNER (if any)

INVALID IF SIGNED IN BLANK

SEC. B MUST BE **COMPLETED** AND **SIGNED** PERSONALLY BY NEW OWNER (AND NEW CO-OWNER, IF ANY) NAMED IN SEC. A ABOVE, provided he still owns the dog and wants registration certificate issued in his name. If the dog has again been transferred, do not use this Sec. B, but make out Sec. A on another of these forms.

I apply to The American Kennel Club to have registration Certificate for this dog issued in my/our name(s), and certify that I/we acquired it DIRECTLY from the person(s) who signed Sec. A above, and that I/we still own this dog. I agree to abide by American Kennel Club Rules and Regulations.

New owner's personal signature _John Jones_

   Co-Owner's Signature If Jointly Owned

Print { Name JOHN JONES
   Address 123 BROADWAY
   City, State AKRON, OH 44322

Print { Name
   Address
   City, State

***READ INSTRUCTIONS ON REVERSE SIDE**

R48-10 (10-74)

Former owner(s) must complete Section "A", indicating date of transfer, breed, color, sex, and litter number of dog, and must print name and address of *person(s) to whom dog is being directly transferred.* Former owner(s) must sign Section "A" verifying details of transfer. (Separate and individual signatures of all co-owners are required.)

New owner(s) of dog who apply to register it, should complete Section "B". (Separate and individual signatures of all co-owners are required.)

The American Kennel Club

THE AMERICAN KENNEL CLUB, established September 17, 1884, is a non-profit organization devoted to the advancement of pure-bred dogs. It maintains a registry of recognized breeds; adopts and enforces rules and regulations governing dog shows, obedience trials, and field trials; and fosters and encourages interest in, and the health and welfare of, pure-bred dogs.

The AKC does not have individual memberships. Rather, it is comprised of almost 400 autonomous dog clubs throughout the United States. Each club exercises its voting privilege through a representative known as a "delegate". The delegates are the legislative body of the AKC, making the rules, and electing directors from among their number.

The Board of Directors, thus elected, are responsible for the management of the AKC, appointing key staff, and making regulations and policies in conformity with the rules prescribed by the delegates.

The Stud Book, ancestry record of every dog that has been registered since the inception of The American Kennel Club, now represents an enrollment of more than 20,000,000 dogs. Currently close to a million new registrations are being added each year.

The official magazine of the AKC, published monthly, is *Pure-Bred Dogs—American Kennel Gazette*. In addition to articles and photos of every phase of pure-bred dog interest, and news of the various breed clubs, each issue includes official notice of: all forthcoming events approved to be held under AKC rules; listing of all new champions and obedience degree winners; the awards at all dog shows, field trials, and obedience trials; and all actions taken by the club's Board of Directors.

At its headquarters at 51 Madison Avenue, New York, N.Y. 10010, The American Kennel Club maintains a reference library of more than 10,000 volumes. One of the most complete collections of its kind in the world, the Library contains many rare, out-of-print editions (some published as early as 1576). It includes as well the works of modern authorities on the breeds, books and magazines in English and practically all foreign languages. On file are the stud books of many other accredited registration agencies here and abroad. Included in the Library's collection are famous prints and oil paintings by old masters and modern artists, as well as a unique file of pictures for the study of every known breed of dog. The public is invited to use the facilities of the Library, which is open for reference purposes Mondays through Fridays from 10:00 A.M. to 4:00 P.M.

The following booklets, covering AKC rules and regulations, are currently available upon written request to the American Kennel Club, 51 Madison Avenue, New York, N.Y. 10010. There is no charge for individual copies, but when ordered in quantity there is a charge of 25 cents for each copy.

-Rules Applying to Registration and Dog Shows (E 37-17)
-Obedience Regulations (E 36-7)
-Registration and Field Trial Rules (S 55-9)
-Beagle Field Trial Rules (S 56-9)
-Basset Hound Field Trial Rules (S 56 A-9)
-Regulations for Junior Showmanship (E 76-5)
-Match Regulations (E 87)

Various information booklets are also available from AKC, free when ordered individually, but 50 cents each when ordered in quantity. Presently they include booklets on: The Formation of Dog Clubs, Guidelines for Dog Show Judges, Guidelines for Obedience Judges, The Status of a Judge of Licensed Field Trials, Dogs: General Information from the American Kennel Club, et al.

Publications available for a fee include: *The Complete Dog Book* ($10.95); the monthly magazine *Pure-Bred Dogs - American Kennel Gazette* ($2.50 a copy, $15. a year); the monthly Stud Book Register ($2. a copy, $18. a year); a pamphlet covering the Miscellaneous Breeds ($1.), and the Judges Directory ($2.).

In addition, the AKC has 16 mm. films (with sound and color) available for loan to clubs. Reservations must be made on a form obtainable from AKC, and there is a $5. handling charge. These include:

-Inside AKC (28 minutes)
-The Irish Setter . . a Breed Study (30 minutes)
-Gait: Observing Dogs in Motion (37 minutes)
-AKC and the Sport of Dogs (30 minutes)
-200? Covering the fine points of exhibiting
    and judging Obedience. (30 minutes)
-In the Ring with Mr. Wrong. A humorous,
    informative film on dog judging. (20 minutes)

AKC also provides a certified pedigree service for all registered dogs:

3 generations, $7.
4 generations, $15.

The Dog Sport

THE AMERICAN KENNEL CLUB was founded in 1884 by amateur sportsmen interested in establishing a uniform set of rules for the holding of dog shows. From that day to this the Board of Directors, responsible for the operation of AKC, has been made up of dedicated amateur sportsmen.

Each year, more than 8,000 competitive events are held under American Kennel Club rules. These competitions fall into three categories: dog shows, field trials, and obedience trials. In each of these categories, there are formal "licensed" events ("point shows" at which championship points or credit toward field or obedience titles may be earned) and informal events ("match shows" at which no points or credits are earned.)

Dog Shows

Most numerous of the competitive events held under AKC rules are dog shows. At these, the accent is on *conformation*. Judges examine the dogs and place them in accordance with how close (in the judge's opinion) they measure up to the ideal called for in the official standards of their breeds—the standards published in this book.

There are two types of conformation dog shows—specialty and all-breed. Specialty shows are limited to dogs of a designated breed or grouping of breeds; for example, the Poodle Club of America Specialty is for Poodles only. All breed shows, as the name indicates, are for all breeds.

The shows held under AKC rules are put on by individual clubs; the specialty shows by breed clubs, and the all-breed shows by all-breed clubs.

For each breed recognized by AKC, there is a national parent club. (In the case of some rare breeds, however, this parent club may be no longer active.) In addition to the parent club, many breeds have local specialty clubs serving specific geographical areas.

The parent clubs have a unique and vital responsibility. They are the custodians of the official standards of their breeds. Any revision, clarification or addition to a breed standard must come through the parent club. Only after such changes have been approved by the parent club's membership can they be submitted to the AKC's Board of Directors for final approval.

Three phases of the great sport of dogs: *Above:* Final judging at a large show. *Opposite, top:* An Old English Sheepdog competing in Obedience. *Opposite, below:* Competing at a National Open championship field trial.—*Photos by Gilbert, Abrams and Shafer.*

Judging at a conformation show is a process of elimination that ultimately results in one dog being selected as best of breed; if it's an all-breed show, further eliminations climax with one dog being selected best in show.

Most dogs in competition at conformation shows are competing for points toward their championship. To become an official American Kennel Club champion of record, a dog must earn fifteen points. Essentially, these points are based upon the number of dogs in actual competition—the more dogs, the more points. However, the number of dogs required for points varies with the breed, its sex, and the geographical location of the show in accordance with a schedule annually set up by AKC to help equalize competition from breed to breed and area to area.

A dog can earn from one to five points at a show. Wins of three, four or five points are termed "majors." The fifteen points required for championship must be won under at least three different judges, and must include two majors won under different judges.

At a show there are five regular classes in which dogs seeking points compete. (Dogs competing for points are frequently referred to as "class dogs.") These classes are:

Puppy—frequently subdivided into *Puppies—6 to 9 months* and *Puppies—9 to 12 months*
Novice
Bred-by-Exhibitor
American-Bred
Open

Only one male and one female of each breed can win points at each show—as we shall see. There is no intersex competition in these classes—the dogs (males) compete against other dogs, and the bitches (females) against other bitches.

Judging in every breed is the same. The judge begins with the Puppy dog class. In each class the dogs are evaluated and the prime four are placed First, Second, Third and Fourth. However, only the first place winner in each class remains in competition—the others are eliminated.

After the judge has judged the Puppy dogs, Novice dogs, Bred-by-Exhibitor dogs, American-Bred dogs and Open dogs, the winners (first place) from each class are brought back to compete against each other. This is called the Winners class. The dog selected best is the Winners Dog. He is the male who receives the points at the show.

Following selection of the Winners Dog, the dog that placed second

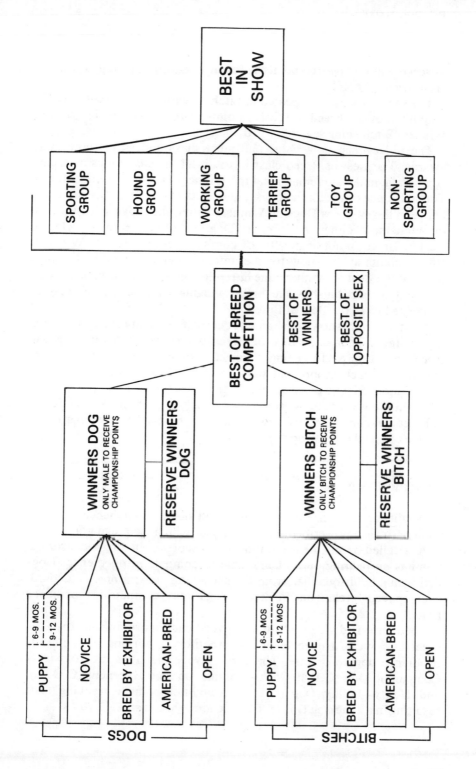

BEST IN SHOW

SPORTING GROUP

HOUND GROUP

WORKING GROUP

TERRIER GROUP

TOY GROUP

NON-SPORTING GROUP

BEST OF BREED COMPETITION

BEST OF WINNERS

BEST OF OPPOSITE SEX

WINNERS DOG
ONLY MALE TO RECEIVE CHAMPIONSHIP POINTS

RESERVE WINNERS DOG

WINNERS BITCH
ONLY BITCH TO RECEIVE CHAMPIONSHIP POINTS

RESERVE WINNERS BITCH

PUPPY
6-9 MOS.
9-12 MOS.

NOVICE

BRED BY EXHIBITOR

AMERICAN-BRED

OPEN

DOGS

PUPPY
6-9 MOS
9-12 MOS

NOVICE

BRED BY EXHIBITOR

AMERICAN-BRED

OPEN

BITCHES

to him in his original class of competition is brought into the ring to compete with the other class winners for Reserve Winners Dog. The Reserve will receive the points if for any reason the Winner's win is disallowed by AKC.

The same process is repeated in bitches, with a Winners Bitch—the only bitch of the breed to receive points at the show—and a Reserve Winners Bitch being selected.

The judge must now judge one more class and make three more awards. The Best of Breed class has in it all the champions of record competing, male and female, and the Winners Dog and Winners Bitch. The judge goes over all the dogs and selects one Best of Breed. Then, between the Winners Dog and Winners Bitch, the judge selects a Best of Winners. If either the Winners Dog or Winners Bitch is selected Best of Breed, it automatically, of course, becomes Best of Winners. (If the points at the show for the defeated Winner were higher than those of the Best of Winners, the latter now gets the same higher total.) The judge then finishes the breed judging by selecting a Best of Opposite Sex to the Best of Breed.

At an all-breed show, this same process of elimination takes place in every breed. Then each Best of Breed winner competes in its group (see Contents pages for listing of dogs by groups). Four placements are awarded in each group, but only the first place winner remains in competition. Finally the six group winners are brought into the ring and a best in show winner is selected. At the largest all-breed shows nearly 4,000 contestants are narrowed down to the best in show winner in the course of one day's judging.

Obedience Trials

Obedience trials are tests of man and dog. In obedience, the dog must perform a prescribed set of exercises which the judge grades or— as it is called by obedience enthusiasts—scores. The dog's conformation has no bearing on its being able to compete in obedience. Dogs that would be disqualified from the show ring under a breed standard, even spayed bitches and neutered dogs, may compete in obedience trials.

Obedience is divided into three levels, each more difficult than the preceding one. At each level a competitor is working for an AKC obedience degree or title. The three levels and titles are: *Novice*— Companion Dog (C.D.); *Open*—Companion Dog Excellent (C.D.X.); and *Utility*—Utility Dog (U.D.). In addition, official tracking tests resulting in a Tracking Dog (T.D.) title are held under AKC rules.

Novice work embraces the basics that all dogs should be taught to make them good companions. The six exercises in Novice work are: heel on leash, stand for examination, heel free, recall, long sit, long down. *Open* work consists of seven exercises: heel free, drop on recall, retrieve on flat, retrieve over the high jump, broad jump, long sit, and long down. *Utility* work consists of: signal exercise, two scent discrimination tests, directed retrieve, directed jumping and group examination.

To receive an obedience title a dog must earn three "legs." To get credit for a leg, a dog must score at least 170 points out of a possible 200 (the passing score and grand total are the same at each level, although the exercises vary), and get more than fifty percent on each exercise.

Only dogs that have earned the Utility Dog title can earn points toward an Obedience Trial Championship. Championship points are recorded for dogs earning a First or Second place in Open B or Utility Class (or Utility B, if divided) according to the schedule of points established by the AKC Board of Directors. To become an Obedience Trial Champion a dog must win 100 points that include a First place in Utility (or Utility B, if divided) with at least 3 dogs in competition, a First place in Open B with at least 6 dogs in competition, and a third First place in either of these competitions. The three First places must be won under three different judges.

Field Trials

Field trials are held (separately) for Basset Hounds, Beagles, Dachshunds, Pointing breeds, Retrievers and English Springer Spaniels. Field trials are analogous to obedience in that they are working tests of man and dog as a team. Important, too, is that field trials expressly test the ability of a breed to continue to perform the function for which it was created.

There are four categories of field trials, each based on the hunting characteristics of the breeds involved:

Hounds pursue the cottontail rabbit or hare at trials, either in packs or in pairs (braces).

The National Beagle Club held its first AKC licensed trial on November 4, 1890 in Hyannis, Massachusetts. Today, AKC annually licenses almost 450 trials for scenting or trailing hounds.

The Pointing breeds assist the hunter in the field by stopping or pointing the moment they scent the presence of a game bird. This style permits the hunter to walk past the dog on point and flush the bird.

The first formal pointing breed trial ever held in the United States, and the first to be recorded in what are now official AKC documents, took place in Memphis, Tennessee on October 8, 1874. Today, AKC licenses some 380 pointing breed field trials each year.

Retrievers do what their name implies—they fetch or retrieve, both from water and land, all game shot by the hunter.

While Retrievers are old breeds, the first field trial for Retrievers under AKC rules was held in December, 1931 in Chester, New York by the Labrador Retriever Club. Today the AKC yearly licenses some 152 trials for Retrievers.

Spaniels (with the notable exception of Brittany Spaniels) are known as the flushing breeds. These dogs are expected to search for feathered game within gunshot range of the hunter. When game is located, they flush the bird into the air, and retrieve on command if the bird is shot.

In 1923, a group of sportsmen organized the English Springer Spaniel Field Trial Association, which held the first trial for Springers in October, 1924 on Fischers Island, New York. The Cocker Spaniel and English Cocker Spaniel have disappeared from the field trial scene in this country. However, AKC licenses forty field trials each year for English Springer Spaniels.

Because of the varying nature of the work expected of field trial breeds, there are different rules for each of the major categories.

Junior Showmanship

A club that is approved to hold a licensed or member all-breed show or a specialty show held apart from an all-breed show, may also be approved to offer Junior Showmanship competition at its show.

Junior Showmanship is judged solely on the ability and skill of the handler. Dogs are handled as in the breed ring although the dog's conformation should not be considered by the judge. Dogs entered in this competition must also be eligible to compete in dog shows or obedience trials.

Junior Showmanship is usually divided by class, age and occasionally by sex. Competition is for Juniors 10 through 16 years inclusive. The Novice class is for those who have not won three (3) first place awards in that class and the Open class is for those who have won three (3) first place awards in the Novice class.

The Dog's Anatomy

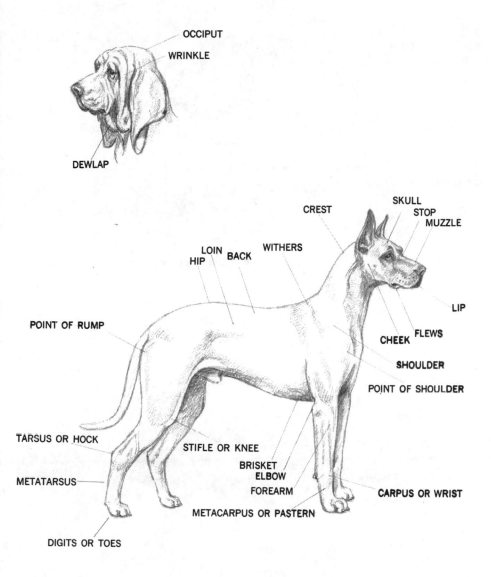

OCCIPUT

WRINKLE

DEWLAP

CREST

SKULL
STOP
MUZZLE

LOIN BACK
HIP

WITHERS

POINT OF RUMP

LIP

FLEWS
CHEEK

SHOULDER

POINT OF SHOULDER

TARSUS OR HOCK

STIFLE OR KNEE

BRISKET
ELBOW

METATARSUS

FOREARM

CARPUS OR WRIST

METACARPUS OR PASTERN

DIGITS OR TOES

A glossary of dog terminology, with some illustrative drawings, is presented on pages 741 to 764.

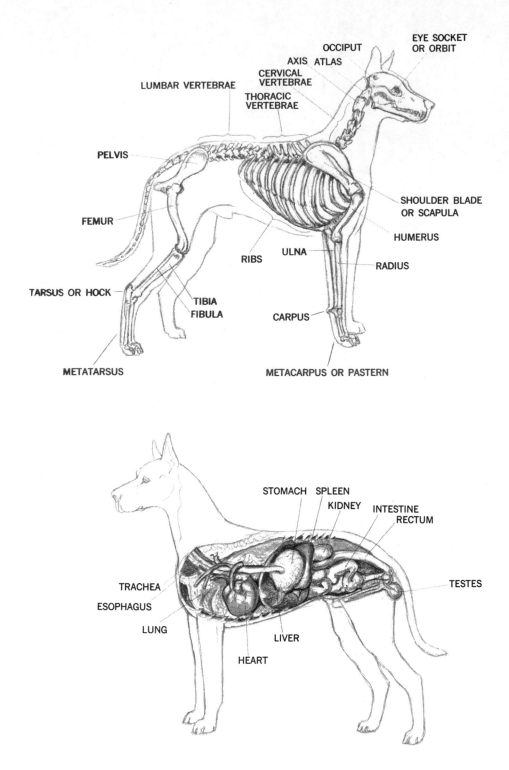

OCCIPUT
EYE SOCKET OR ORBIT
AXIS ATLAS
CERVICAL VERTEBRAE
LUMBAR VERTEBRAE
THORACIC VERTEBRAE
PELVIS
SHOULDER BLADE OR SCAPULA
HUMERUS
FEMUR
ULNA
RIBS
RADIUS
TARSUS OR HOCK
TIBIA
FIBULA
CARPUS
METATARSUS
METACARPUS OR PASTERN

STOMACH   SPLEEN
KIDNEY   INTESTINE
RECTUM
TRACHEA
TESTES
ESOPHAGUS
LUNG
LIVER
HEART

30

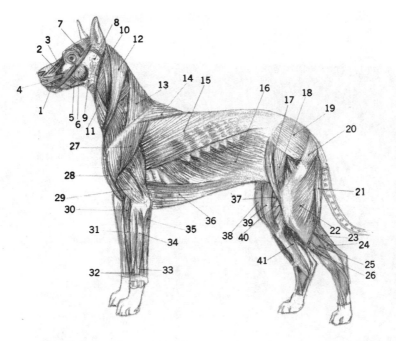

1—DILATOR NARIS LATERALIS
2—LEVATOR NASOLABIALIS
3—LEVATOR LABII SUPERIORIS PROPRIUS
4—OBICULAR ORIS
5—ZYGOMATICUS
6—MASSETER
7—SCUTULARIS
8—PAROTID GLAND
9—SUBMAXILLARY GLAND
10—PAROTIDO-AURICULARIS
11—STERNO-HYOIDEUS
12—BRACHIO-CEPHALICUS
13—TRAPEZIUS
14—TRAPEZIUS
15—LATISSIMUS DORSI
16—OBLIQUUS ABDOMINIS EXTERNUS
17—SARTORIUS
18—TENSOR FASCIAE LATAE
19—GLUTEUS MEDIUS
20—GLUTEUS SUPERFICIALIS
21—SEMITENDINOSUS

22—BICEPS FEMORIS
23—GASTROCNEMIUS
24—SUPERFICIAL DIGITAL FLEXOR
25—DEEP DIGITAL FLEXOR
26—ANTERIOR DIGITAL FLEXOR
27—DELTOID
28—BRACHIO CEPHALICUS
29—TRICEPS
30—EXTENSOR CARPI
31—ANTERIOR DIGITAL EXTENSOR
32—TENDON OF EXTENSOR
    CARPI OBLIQUUS
33—LATERAL DIGITAL EXTENSOR
34—EXTENSOR CARPI ULNARIS
35—FLEXOR CARPI ULNARIS
36—POSTERIOR DEEP PECTORAL
37—VASTUS INTERNUS
38—SARTORIUS
39—SARTORIUS
40—ADDUCTOR
41—DEEP DIGITAL FLEXOR

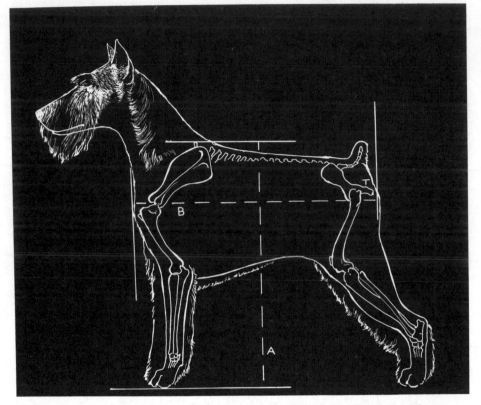

How height and length are measured in the dog. Height is measured from a point horizontal with the withers straight down to the ground (line A). Length is measured from point of shoulder to point of buttock (line B). *Reproduced by permission from "Illustrated Discussion of the Miniature Schnauzer Standard", drawing by Loraine L. Bush.*

Irish Water Spaniel — *Ludwig*

English Cocker Spaniels

Cocker Spaniel — *Ludwig*

Golden Retrievers — *Cumbers*

German Shorthaired Pointers — *Cumbers*

Chesapeake Bay Retrievers — *Cumbers*

Brittany Spaniel — *Conalde*

German Wirehaired Pointer — *Alberts*

English Springer Spaniel — *Ludwig*

Weimaraners — *Cumbers*

Irish Setter puppies

Pointer puppies

Gordon Setter puppy

Gordon Setter — *Cumbers*

Curly-Coated Retriever puppy — *Cumbers*

English Setters — *Cumbers*

Vizsla — *Lyons*

Field Spaniel — Roslin-Williams

Clumber Spaniels - *Cumbers*

Sussex Spaniels — *Cumbers*

Flat-Coated Retrievers — *Cumbers*

Labrador Retrievers — *Cumbers*

Afghan Hound — *Anderson*

Smooth Dachshund — *Anderson*

Wirehaired Dachshunds — *Cumbers*

Miniature Longhaired Dachshund — *Cumbers*

Norwegian Elkhounds

Otter Hounds — *Roslin-Williams*

THE BREEDS

Histories and
Official Standards

ALL OF THE BREEDS currently recognized for registration by The American Kennel Club are presented here in the order (within their Groups) in which they appear in dog show catalogs. A complete listing of the breeds in Group order is included in the Contents, and they are alphabetically identified in the Index at end of the book. The photograph, history and official standard for each breed are on successive pages.

In most instances, the information for the histories has been provided by the parent club of the breed. For the benefit of those unacquainted with dog shows, it should be explained that the official standard for each breed, or revision of the standard, originates with the parent club and not, as many suppose, with The American Kennel Club. The membership of the parent club must approve the standard or revision by vote, and only then can it be submitted to the Board of Directors of The American Kennel Club for approval.

The standard portrays what, in the minds of its compilers, would be the ideal dog of the breed. Ideal in type, in structure, in gait, in temperament—ideal in every aspect.

Thus, the standard is not the representation of any actual dog, but a concept. It is against this concept that a dog show judge must measure every competitor of that breed. The dog most closely approaching that ideal, in the judge's determination, is the dog that wins.

The date shown at end of each standard represents the date of approval of the latest revision. Where no date is shown, it indicates that there has been no change in the standard since the very early editions of *The Complete Dog Book*.

The pictures presented are intended primarily as an aid for the novice. Much care has been taken to select photographs that do credit to the breeds, but it should not be inferred that the dogs pictured are "ideal depictions" of their standards, or entirely without fault. Rare indeed, even among the immortals, is there a dog that measures up 100% in every facet of its standard. In many instances, the pictures were provided by the parent breed clubs.

For convenience in consulting the standards, the disqualifications (for show purposes) specified within a breed standard are presented in italicized type, at the end of the particular standard. It should be noted however, that in addition to these disqualifications, there are the following disqualifications that apply to ALL BREEDS:

A dog which is blind, deaf, castrated, spayed, or which has been changed in appearance by artificial means except as specified in the standard for its breed, or a male which does not have two normal testicles normally located in the scrotum, may not compete at any show and will be disqualified except that a castrated male may be entered as Stud Dog in the Stud Dog Class and a spayed bitch may be entered as Brood Bitch in the Brood Bitch Class. A dog will not be considered to have been changed by artificial means because of removal of dewclaws or docking of a tail, if it is of a breed in which such removal or docking is a regularly approved practice which is not contrary to the standard. (Note: Spayed bitches and monorchid or cryptorchid dogs may compete in obedience trials.)

A dog that is lame at any show may not compete and shall not receive any award at the show. It shall be the judge's responsibility to determine whether the dog is lame.

No dog shall be eligible to compete at any show, and no dog shall receive any award at any show in the event the natural color or shade of natural color, or the natural markings of the dog, have been altered or changed by the use of any substance, whether such substance has been used for cleaning purposes or for any other reason. Such cleaning substances are to be removed before the dog enters the ring.

Any dog whose ears have been cropped or cut in any way shall be ineligible to compete at any show in any state where the laws prohibit the same, except subject to the provisions of such laws.

No dog shall be eligible to compete at any show, no dog shall be brought into the grounds or premises of any dog show, and any dog which may have been brought into the grounds or premises of a dog show shall immediately be removed, if it:
- *(a) shows clinical symptoms of distemper, infectious hepatitis, leptospirosis or other communicable disease, or*
- *(b) is known to have been in contact with distemper, infectious hepatitis, leptospirosis or other communicable disease within thirty days prior to the opening of the show, or*
- *(c) has been kenneled within thirty days prior to the opening of the show on premises on which there existed distemper, infectious hepatitis, leptospirosis, or other communicable disease.*

GROUP I: SPORTING DOGS

Pointer

THE POINTER comes by his name honestly. He was the first dog, so far as we know, used to stand game in the sense in which we use the term today, and was developed as a distinct breed much earlier than any of the setters. For years it was believed the first Pointers used in England were importations from Spain and Portugal, but that theory has been pretty thoroughly disproved and it seems far more likely that Pointers came into general use in Spain, Portugal, throughout eastern Europe and in the British Isles at approximately the same time. Whether or not the dogs from which they sprung were native to all these places no one can say, but it can be stated with confidence that the *development* of the English Pointer took place within the confines of Great Britain, most probably in England itself. Later on Spanish Pointers were brought in, but from the first they were considered as a different strain, if not a different breed, from the English dogs.

The first Pointers of which there is any dependable record appeared in England about 1650, some years before the era of wing-shooting with guns, and the use to which they were put is interesting. Coursing with Greyhounds was a favorite sport of those times and the earliest accounts of Pointers reveal that they were taken afield to locate and point hares. When the hare had been found, the Greyhounds were brought up and unleashed, the game was kicked from cover and the fun began. But early in the eighteenth century, at least by 1711, wing-shooting had come into vogue and, from that day on, the "shorthair" has been considered by the majority of sportsmen the equal, if not the superior, of any of the gun dogs.

As to the Pointer's lineage, as usual we find it something of an enigma, but there is no question that the Foxhound, Greyhound and Bloodhound all had a share in his making. Individuals of the three breeds were probably crossed with the inevitable "setting spaniel," which played such a prominent part in the creation of all our modern bird dogs.

Adherents of the Foxhound cross were especially persistent and active. Even as late as 1868 many English breeders were using it, or at least strongly advocating it, to improve the Pointer. A well-known authority who wrote over the *nom de plume* of "Sixty-one," said that "as far as my experience goes, I consider the Foxhound cross with the Pointer most valuable," and we find Idstone expressing himself as follows: "If the Pointer must be crossed, would it not be advisable to combine Foxhound, Bulldog and Greyhound?" While it is doubtful if any such radical measures were actually used, it was not until the stud book and dog-show era that the idea was definitely discarded. The importance of our official record of breeding and the value of bench shows in establishing and maintaining the correct standards can hardly be over-estimated. Without these two institutions chaos might well have resulted, not only in Pointers, but practically every breed recognized today.

During the first years of the eighteenth century the Spanish Pointer began to appear in England, and he, too, was used for a cross, but as he was exceedingly heavy and very slow in comparison with the English, French, and German Pointers, subsequent breeding operations not only left him out but definitely attempted to correct the faults he had introduced. It appears that his real value was not to improve type but to fix and intensify the pointing instinct, in which, we are told, he was peculiarly strong.

If this was the purpose it seems to have been successful. Remarkable (and incidentally quite unbelievable) stories are to be found in British sporting papers of the early nineteenth century, relating the prodigies performed by certain English Pointers of a former day. Col. Thornton's Pluto and Juno, for example, are said to have held a point on a covey of partridges for an hour and a quarter by the watch. But when we find so solid an authority as Stonehenge telling as gospel truth the now famous yarn of the sportsman who lost his Pointer on the moors, and returning a year later, discovered the skeleton of the dog pointing a skeleton bird, we realize that the statements of these pre-Victorian worthies must be taken with considerably more than a pinch of salt.

During the nineteenth century the English Pointer was repeatedly crossed with the various setters as they came into existence and favor. This, it seems, was partly to improve his disposition, for an old-time writer, commenting on the breed says: "They have a ferocity of temper which will not submit to correction or discipline, unless taken in hand very young." While the Pointer of today is anything but ferocious, it may be that this characteristic, tempered by judicious breeding and in combination with the natural independence that made him object to correction and discipline, has made him the superlative field-trial dog he is today. He certainly possesses the competitive spirit to a greater degree than is usually found in the other bird dogs, a quality that makes him especially suited to public performance.

The modern Pointer is a specialist and looks the part. He is every inch a gun dog. Clean-limbed, lithe, and muscular without being coarse, full of nervous energy and "hunt," put together for speed and endurance, courageous, and with the ability to concentrate on his job, he is an ideal dog for the man or woman who is looking for results when afield. His short hair makes him neat and clean around the house and his disposition makes him adaptable for the kennel. He requires less personal attention than some other gun dogs and he is willing to work satisfactorily for someone other than his own master and handler.

In addition to all this, he has another characteristic—tendency towards early development. As a breed, Pointers seem to acquire the hunting instinct at a tender age, puppies of two months frequently pointing and even backing. For this reason they are especially suited for derby and puppy stakes.

For show purposes, while hardly as attractive in some ways as the Irish Setter, the Pointer is in many respects quite satisfactory. His short coat makes his outline, conformation, and quality easily seen at a glance, and he is a superb poser. His color, usually white with rich liver markings is striking and, like the Irishman, he has an ideal bench temperament. Lemon and white, orange and white, black and white and sometimes solid black are other colorings. Daniel Lambert, an English sportsman, developed a strain of solid blacks as long ago as 1820, and self-colored dogs are still seen in the shows today. But, as already said, the liver and white, lemon and white or black and white specimens are most popular in the ring.

The Pointer is peculiarly fortunate in one all-important respect. He has always been bred for type as well as field ability, hence we have in this case no divergence between the two insofar as appearance goes. From the beginning type has been carefully developed and intelligently preserved. An illustration for Col. Thornton's book *A Tour Through Scotland* shows Captain Fleming of Barochan out hawking. This picture was drawn or painted about 1786, yet a Pointer, which is among the dogs shown, would pass muster today as an excellent specimen. A reprint of this illustration is to be seen in James Watson's *The Dog Book*.

Official Standard for the Pointer

General Appearance—The Pointer is bred primarily for sport afield; he should unmistakably look and act the part. The ideal specimen gives the immediate impression of compact power and agile grace; the head noble, proudly carried; the expression intelligent and alert; the muscular body bespeaking both staying power and dash. Here is an animal whose every movement shows him to be a wide-awake, hard-driving hunting dog possessing stamina, courage, and the desire to go. And in his expression are the loyalty and devotion of a true friend of man.

Temperament—The Pointer's even temperament and alert good sense make him a congenial companion both in the field and in the home. He should be dignified and should never show timidity toward man or dog.

Head—The skull of medium width, approximately as wide as the length of the muzzle, resulting in an impression of length rather than width. Slight furrow between the eyes, cheeks cleanly chiseled. There should be a pronounced stop. From this point forward the muzzle is of good length, with the nasal bone so formed that the nose is slightly higher at the tip than the muzzle at the stop. Parallel plancs of the skull and muzzle are equally acceptable. The muzzle should be deep without pendulous flews. Jaws ending square and level, should bite evenly or as scissors. Nostrils well developed and wide open. *Ears*—Set on at eye level. When hanging naturally, they should reach just below the lower jaw, close to the head, with little or no folding. They should be somewhat pointed at the tip—never round—and soft and thin in leather. *Eyes*—Of ample size, rounded and intense. The eye color should be dark in contrast with the color of the markings, the darker the better.

Neck—Long, dry, muscular and slightly arched, springing cleanly from the shoulders.

Shoulders—Long, thin, and sloping. The top of blades close together.

Front—Elbows well let down, directly under the withers and truly parallel so as to work just clear of the body. Forelegs straight and with oval bone. Knee joint never to knuckle over. Pasterns of moderate length, perceptibly finer in bone than the leg, and slightly slanting. Chest, deep rather than wide, must not hinder free action of forelegs. The breastbone bold, without being unduly prominent. The ribs well sprung, descending as low as the elbow-point.

Back—Strong and solid with only a slight rise from croup to top of shoulders. Loin of moderate length, powerful and slightly arched. Croup falling only slightly to base of tail. Tuck-up should be apparent, but not exaggerated.

Tail—Heavier at the root, tapering to a fine point. Length no greater than to hock. A tail longer than this or docked must be penalized. Carried without curl, and not more than 20 degrees above the line of the back; never carried between the legs.

Hindquarters—Muscular and powerful with great propelling leverage. Thighs long and well developed. Stifles well bent. The hocks clean; the legs straight as viewed from behind. Decided angulation is the mark of power and endurance.

Feet—Oval, with long, closely-set, arched toes, well-padded, and deep. Cat-foot is a fault. Dewclaws on the forelegs may be removed.

Coat—Short, dense, smooth with a sheen.

Color—Liver, lemon, black, orange: either in combination with white or solid-colored. A good Pointer cannot be a bad color. In the darker colors, the nose should be black or brown; in the lighter shades it may be lighter or flesh-colored.

Gait—Smooth, frictionless, with a powerful hindquarters' drive. The head should be carried high, the nostrils wide, the tail moving from side to side rhythmically with the pace, giving the impression of a well-balanced, strongly-built hunting dog capable of top speed combined with great stamina. Hackney gait must be faulted.

Balance and Size—Balance and over-all symmetry are more important in the Pointer than size. A smooth, balanced dog is to be more desired than a dog with strongly contrasting good points and faults. Hound or terrier characteristics are most undesirable. Because a sporting dog must have both endurance and power, great variations in size are undesirable, the desirable height and weight being within the following limits:

```
Dogs:      Height—25-28 inches
           Weight—55-75 pounds
Bitches:   Height—23-26 inches
           Weight—45-65 pounds
```

Approved November 11, 1975

Pointer, German Shorthaired

THE GERMAN SHORTHAIRED POINTER combines in field-dog requirements those qualities which have long popularized the various breeds of hunting dogs. So successfully have keen scenting powers, linked with high intelligence, been fused into the breed through judicious crossing of the descendants of the old Spanish Pointer, English Foxhound, and local German tracking hounds, and so varied are this dog's field accomplishments, that its adaptability has earned it the reputation of being an all-purpose dog. In fact, the term was applied to it by the Germans before U.S. sportsmen started importing the breed to any extent in the early twenties.

It is indeed rare to find wrapped up in one package a staunchly pointing bird dog, a keen-nosed night trailer, a proven duck dog, a natural retriever on land and water, pleasing conformation and markings, great powers of endurance, and an intelligent family watchdog and companion. Indicative of this dog's versatility is its successful work on pheasant, quail, grouse, partridge, jacksnipe, woodcock, duck, rabbits, coon, and possum. It is also used to trail and handle deer. With a water-repellent coat and webbed feet, it retrieves well from rough terrain or icy waters.

The origin of the German Shorthaired Pointer, as indeed with most breeds, cannot be described precisely. Prior to the establishment of the *Klub Kurzhaar* stud book in the 1870s, few records are available, though the German hunting fraternity had already spent many years in attempting to produce a truly versatile utility dog-of-all-work, using of necessity the stock that was locally available. The main source of basic foundation stock seems to have been the German Bird Dog, a not very admirable step down by inheritance from the old Spanish Pointer. Its utility was further improved by introducing local types of scent hounds —track and trail dogs, that were also dependable in water and that were used by the German foresters. These *Schweisshunde (Schweiss—* scent; *Hunde*—dogs) were of many and diverse types. They had originated principally down through the centuries from the hounds introduced from Eastern countries after the Crusades, and had been developed particularly in France, so that they became the forebears of practically all present-day scenting hounds.

The Germans still were not satisfied. Since obedience was of paramount importance, these early dogs were selectively bred for biddability. Steps were taken later to improve stance, style, and, above all, *nose.* Fine Pointers were brought from England and were used to lend elegance to the manner of working—*die höhe nase* (the high nose) being the major aim. This was accomplished, and the breeders then had only the problem of ridding their developing *Kurzhaar* of its unwanted Pointer characteristics—aversion to water and lack of aggressiveness toward predators. These objectives were achieved long before the turn of the century. A dog breeding true to type was developed, giving the world at long last a magnificent utility dog combining these virtues with the good looks, sound temperament, and longevity, that have made the German Shorthaired Pointer a favorite with sportsmen everywhere.

The German Shorthaired Pointer was first admitted to the stud book of the American Kennel Club in March, 1930. The first AKC licensed Specialty Show for German Shorthaired Pointers was held by the German Shorthaired Pointer Club of America at the International Kennel Club show in Chicago on March 29-30, 1941; the first AKC licensed Field Trial for the breed was also held by the Parent Club at Anoka, Minnesota, on May 21, 1944.

Official Standard for the German Shorthaired Pointer

The Shorthair is a versatile hunter, an all-purpose gun dog capable of high performance in field and water. The judgment of Shorthairs in the show ring should reflect this basic characteristic.

General Appearance—The overall picture which is created in the observer's eye is that of an aristocratic, well-balanced, symmetrical animal with conformation indicating power, endurance and agility and a look of intelligence and animation. The dog is neither unduly small nor conspicuously large. It gives the impression of medium size, but is like the proper hunter, "with a short back, but standing over plenty of ground."

Tall leggy dogs, or dogs which are ponderous or unbalanced because of excess substance should be definitely rejected. The first impression is that of a keenness which denotes full enthusiasm for work without indication of nervous or flighty character. Movements are alertly coordinated without waste motion. Grace of outline, clean-cut head, sloping shoulders, deep chest, powerful back, strong quarters, good bone composition, adequate muscle, well-carried tail and taut coat, all combine to produce a look of nobility and an indication of anatomical structure essential to correct gait which must indicate a heritage of purposefully conducted breeding. Doggy bitches and bitchy dogs are to be faulted. A judge must excuse a dog from the ring if it displays extreme shyness or viciousness toward its handler or the judge. Aggressiveness or belligerence toward another dog is not to be considered viciousness.

Symmetry—Symmetry and field quality are most essential. A dog in hard and lean field condition is not to be penalized; however, overly fat or poorly muscled dogs are to be penalized. A dog well-balanced in all points is preferable to one with outstanding good qualities and defects.

Head—Clean-cut, neither too light nor too heavy, in proper proportion to the body. Skull is reasonably broad, arched on side and slightly round on top. Scissura (median line between the eyes at the forehead) not too deep, occipital bone not as conspicuous as in the case of the Pointer. The foreface rises gradually from nose to forehead. The rise is more strongly pronounced in the dog than in the bitch as befitting his sex. The chops fall away from the somewhat projecting nose. Lips are full and deep, never flewy. The chops do not fall over too much, but form a proper fold in the angle. The jaw is powerful and the muscles well developed. The line to the forehead rises gradually and never has a definite stop as that of the Pointer, but rather a stop-effect when viewed from the side, due to the position of the eyebrows. The muzzle is sufficiently long to enable the dog to seize properly and to facilitate his carrying game a long time. A pointed muzzle is not desirable. The entire head never gives the impression of tapering to a point. The depth is in the right proportion to the length, both in the muzzle and in the skull proper. The length of the muzzle should equal the length of skull. A pointed muzzle is a fault. A dish-faced muzzle is a fault. A definite Pointer stop is a serious fault. Too many wrinkles in forehead is a fault.

Ears—Ears are broad and set fairly high, lie flat and never hang away from the head. Placement is just above eye level. The ears, when laid in front without being pulled, meet the lip angle. In the case of heavier dogs, the ears are correspondingly longer. Ears too long or fleshy are to be faulted.

Eyes—The eyes are of medium size, full of intelligence and expression, good humored and yet radiating energy, neither protruding nor sunken. The eye is almond shaped, not circular. The eyelids close well. The best color is dark brown. Light yellow (Bird of Prey) eyes are not desirable and are a fault. Closely set eyes are to be faulted. China or wall eyes are to be disqualified.

Nose—Brown, the larger the better, nostrils well-opened and broad. Spotted nose not desirable. Flesh colored nose disqualifies.

Teeth—The teeth are strong and healthy. The molars intermesh properly. The bite is a true scissors bite. A perfect level bite (without overlapping) is not desirable and must be penalized. Extreme overshot or undershot bite disqualifies.

Neck—Of proper length to permit the jaws reaching game to be retrieved, sloping downwards on beautifully curving lines. The nape is rather muscular, becoming gradually larger towards the shoulders. Moderate houndlike throatiness permitted.

Chest—The chest in general gives the impression of depth rather than breadth; for all that, it should be in correct proportion to the other parts of the body with a fair depth. The chest reaches down to the elbows, the ribs forming the thorax show a rib spring and are not flat or slabsided; they are not perfectly round or barrel-shaped. Ribs that are entirely round prevent the necessary expansion of the chest when taking breath. The back ribs reach well down. The circumference of the thorax immediately behind the elbows is smaller than that of the thorax about a hands-breadth behind elbows, so that the upper arm has room for movement.

Back, Loins and Croup—Back is short, strong and straight with slight rise from root of tail to withers. Loin strong, of moderate length and slightly arched. Tuck-up is apparent. Excessively long, roached or swayed back must be penalized.

Forequarters—The shoulders are sloping, movable, well-covered with muscle. The shoulder blades lie flat and are well laid back nearing a 45° angle. The upper arm (the bones between the shoulder and elbow joints) is as long as possible, standing away somewhat from the trunk so that the straight and closely muscled legs, when viewed from the front appear to be parallel. Elbows which stand away from the body or are too close indicate toes turning inwards or outwards, which must be regarded as faults. Pasterns are strong, short and nearly vertical with a slight spring. Loose, short-bladed or straight shoulders must be faulted. Knuckling over is to be faulted. Down in the pasterns is to be faulted.

Hindquarters—The hips are broad with hip sockets wide apart and fall slightly toward the tail in a graceful curve. Thighs are strong and well-muscled. Stifles well bent. Hock joints are well angulated and strong, straight bone structure from hock to pad. Angulation of both stifle and hock joint is such as to combine maximum combination of both drive and traction. Hocks turn neither in nor out. A steep croup is a fault. Cowhocked legs are a serious fault.

Feet—Are compact, close-knit and round to spoon-shaped. The toes sufficiently arched and heavily nailed. The pads are strong, hard and thick. Dewclaws on the forelegs may be removed. Feet pointing in or out is a fault.

Coat and Skin—The skin is close and tight. The hair is short and thick and feels tough to the hand; it is somewhat longer on the underside of the tail and the back edges of the haunches. It is softer, thinner and shorter on the ears and the head. Any dog with long hair in body coat is to be severely penalized.

Tail—Is set high and firm, and must be docked, leaving 40% of length. The tail hangs down when the dog is quiet, is held horizontally when he is walking. The tail must never be curved over the back toward the head when the dog is moving. A tail curved or bent toward the head is to be severely penalized.

Bones—Thin and fine bones are by no means desirable in a dog which must possess strength and be able to work over any and every country. The main importance is not laid so much on the size of bone, but rather on their being in proper proportion to the body. Bone structure too heavy or too light is a fault. Dogs with coarse bones are handicapped in agility of movement and speed.

Weight and Height—Dogs, 55 to 70 pounds. Bitches, 45 to 60 pounds. Dogs, 23 to 25 inches. Bitches, 21 to 23 inches at the withers. Deviations of one inch above or below the described heights are to be severely penalized.

Color—The coat may be of solid liver or any combination of liver and white, such as liver and white ticked, liver spotted and white ticked, or liver roan. A dog with any area of black, red, orange, lemon or tan, or a dog solid white will be disqualified.

Gait—A smooth lithe gait is essential. It is to be noted that as gait increases from the walk to a faster speed, the legs converge beneath the body. The tendency to single track is desirable. The forelegs reach well ahead as if to pull in the ground without giving the appearance of a hackney gait, and are followed by the back legs which give forceful propulsion. Dragging the rear feet is undesirable.

DISQUALIFICATIONS

China or wall eyes.
Flesh colored nose.
Extreme overshot or undershot.
A dog with any area of black, red, orange, lemon or tan,
  or a dog solid white.

Approved October 14, 1975

Pointer, German Wirehaired

Hunting has been called our earliest sport, but it is more than that. It was a way of life in ancient times when the ax, the club, and the spear were the sole weapons man had with which to find food for himself and his brood. Throughout the course of time he hunted with traps and pitfalls, hawks and falcons, nets and snares, bows and arrows. Later, the princes, the nobles, and the big landowners hunted not for food but for sport, but to the rank and file such privilege was denied.

However, around 1850 the incidence of political revolt, together with improvements in the shotgun and the cartridge, spurred the business of hunting to such degree that everybody, regardless of class distinction, took to the hunt. The number of sportsmen more than doubled as game bird shooting grew popular. More dogs were needed, hence more were bred. And slowly but surely the hunting dog became something of a specialist. One kind grew adept at ranging woods and fields where it pointed birds for the huntsman to shoot, others learned to retrieve from land and from water, and as time went on each attained proficiency in its special department.

Continental sportsmen were hard to please; they were not satisfied with a gun dog that would hunt only one kind of game. They envisioned an all-purpose dog, and so it happened that in various European countries retrieving Pointers began to emerge. One of these, native to Germany, was the *Deutsch-Drahthaar* which, literally translated, means German Wirehair. The dog is known today in America, however, as the German Wirehaired Pointer.

In order to understand the heritage of this breed we must bear in mind that there existed abroad a wide variety of retrieving Pointers, all of them more or less interbred. The early Deutsch-Drahthaar Club, in fact, at first catered to all varieties of wirehaired pointing dogs. Later, however, they thought best to separate their activities into four subdivisions catering to the advancement of the Deutsch-Drahthaar, the Pudelpointer, the Stichelhaar, and the Griffon.

Most of the early wirehaired Pointers represented a combination of Griffon, Stichelhaar, Pudelpointer, and German Shorthair. The Pudelpointer was a cross between a Poodle dog and an English Pointer bitch, while the Griffon and the Stichelhaar were composed of Pointer, Foxhound, Pudelpointer, and a Polish water dog. Thus it is easy to appreciate the different hunting skills incorporated in the wirehaired Pointers of a century or more ago.

Admirable breeders and trainers, the Germans demanded a great deal of their sporting dogs. They had no patience with specialists, preferring instead an extra-rugged hunter capable of working on any kind of game and on any terrain. In the German Wirehaired Pointer, this is exactly what they got, for they molded into the one breed the distinctive traits of Pointer, Foxhound, and Poodle. Through these avenues of diversified accomplishment they created an all-purpose dog approximating their ideal. He pointed and retrieved equally well on land and in water. He was keen-nosed and constitutionally tough. What is more, he had the courage as well as the coat fit to brave any sort of cover.

Coat has always been emphasized throughout the development of the breed, as indicated by a statement made by members of the Drahthaar Club back in 1902, when they said: "The breeding of a correct wire coat is the most important feature." There was ample reason for this emphasis on coat, considering the work that the German Wirehair was called upon to do. In short, he was designed as an all-weather as well as an all-purpose dog, and he had to negotiate underbrush that would have punished severely any dog not so characteristically armored.

The coat is weather-resisting in every sense of the term, and it is to large extent water-repellent. It is straight, harsh, wiry, and quite flat-lying. One and one half to two inches in length, it is long enough to shield the body from rough cover, yet not so long as to hide the outline. A heavy growth on the brow guards the eyes from injury, and a short beard and whiskers combine to save the foreface from laceration by brush and briar. A very dense undercoat insulates the body against the cold of winter, but it sheds out to such a degree as to be almost invisible in summertime.

As history is reckoned, the German Wirehaired Pointer is a comparatively young breed. Developed in Germany from the middle of the previous century on, the dog was recognized as a breed in his native land in 1870, when in just a few short years he supplanted most other breeds of hunting dogs there.

Essentially Pointer in type, he is sturdily built, energetic in action, intelligent and determined in expression. He is friendly but not overfriendly; in fact, he may be aloof to all but his own.

He was brought to America in 1920 and since then has achieved considerable popularity. The breed was accepted for registration and granted separate show classification in 1959. The first championship points were awarded at the International Kennel Club of Chicago show in April of that year.

Official Standard for the German Wirehaired Pointer

The German Wirehaired Pointer is a dog that is essentially Pointer in type, of sturdy build, lively manner, and an intelligent, determined expression. In disposition the dog has been described as energetic, rather aloof but not unfriendly.

Head—*The head* is moderately long, *the skull* broad, the occipital bone not too prominent. *The stop* is medium, *the muzzle* fairly long with nasal bone straight and broad, *the lips* a trifle pendulous but close and bearded. *The nose* is dark brown with nostrils wide open, and *the teeth* are strong with scissors bite. *The ears,* rounded but not too broad, hang close to the sides of the head. *Eyes* are brown, medium in size, oval in contour, bright and clear and overhung with bushy eyebrows. Yellow eyes are not desirable. *The neck* is of medium length, slightly arched and devoid of dewlap; in fact, the skin throughout is notably tight to the body.

Body and Tail—The body is a little longer than it is high, as ten is to nine, with the back short, straight and strong, the entire back line showing a perceptible slope down from withers to croup. The chest is deep and capacious, the ribs well sprung, loins taut and slender, the tuck-up apparent. Hips are broad, with croup nicely rounded and the tail docked, approximately two-fifths of original length.

63

Legs and Feet—Forelegs are straight, with shoulders obliquely set and elbows close. The thighs are strong and muscular. The hind legs are moderately angulated at stifle and hock and as viewed from behind, parallel to each other. Round in outline, the feet are webbed, high arched with toes close, their pads thick and hard, and their nails strong and quite heavy. Leg bones are flat rather than round, and strong, but not so heavy or coarse as to militate against the dog's natural agility.

Coat—The coat is weather-resisting and to some extent water-repellent. The undercoat is dense enough in winter to insulate against the cold but so thin in summer as to be almost invisible. The distinctive outer coat is straight, harsh, wiry and rather flat-lying, from one and one-half to two inches in length; it is long enough to protect against the punishment of rough cover but not so long as to hide the outline. On the lower legs it is shorter and between the toes of softer texture. On the skull it is naturally short and close fitting, while over the shoulders and around the tail it is very dense and heavy. The tail is nicely coated, particularly on the underside, but devoid of feather. These dogs have bushy eyebrows of strong, straight hair and beards and whiskers of medium length.

A short smooth coat, a soft woolly coat, or an excessively long coat is to be severely penalized.

Color—The coat is liver and white, usually either liver and white spotted, liver roan, liver and white spotted with ticking and roaning or sometimes solid liver. The nose is dark brown. The head is brown, sometimes with a white blaze, the ears brown. Any black in the coat is to be severely penalized. Spotted and flesh-colored noses are undesirable and are to be penalized.

Size—Height of males should be from 24 to 26 inches at the withers, bitches smaller but not under 22 inches.

Approved February 7, 1959

Retriever, Chesapeake Bay

WHILE THE CHESAPEAKE BAY RETRIEVER originated in this country, he came from stock destined to sail from England. There is no complete and authentic record of his development; at the same time his breed origin as here described is probably correct and at the present time is the one generally accepted. Theories regarding later development are entirely supposition, lacking, as yet, definite proof.

In the year 1807 an English brig was wrecked off the coast of Maryland and crew and cargo were rescued by the American ship *Canton*. Also rescued were two Newfoundland puppies, a dingy red dog named "Sailor" and a black bitch called "Canton" after the rescuing boat. Presented to the gentlemen who gave hospitality to the sailors of the wrecked brig, the two dogs were found to possess wonderful qualities as retrievers. Many of the nondescript dogs then used for retrieving were bred to them, although we do not know whether Sailor and Canton themselves were ever mated together. Eventually other outcrosses were used, and of these, the English Otter Hound has been claimed as one of the most influential. However, such a cross would probably have produced different results, since the Chesapeake shows no trace of hound. It is more likely that the Flat-Coated and Curly-Coated Retrievers constituted the most important outcrosses, if any were ever purposely made.

By 1885, a definite type of dog was developed. The breed soon became known for its prowess in the rough, icy waters of Chesapeake Bay, where the dogs were often called upon to retrieve 200 or 300 ducks in a day. During World War I continued development was apparent, including the deadgrass color so popular in the Middle West. The Chesapeake of today has improved in appearance, and he is still remarkable in the water.

Official Standard for the Chesapeake Bay Retriever

Head—Skull broad and round with medium stop, nose medium short muzzle, pointed but not sharp. Lips thin, not pendulous, Ears small, set well up on head, hanging loosely and of medium leather. Eyes medium large, very clear, of yellowish or amber color and wide apart.

Neck—Of medium length with a strong muscular appearance, tapering to shoulders.

Shoulder, Chest and Body—Shoulders, sloping and should have full liberty of action with plenty of power without any restrictions of movement. Chest strong, deep and wide. Barrel round and deep. Body of medium length, neither cobby nor roached, but rather approaching hollowness, flanks well tucked up.

Hindquarters and Stifles—Hindquarters should be as high or a trifle higher than the shoulders. They should show fully as much power as the forequarters. There should be no tendency to weakness in either fore or hindquarters. Hindquarters should be especially powerful to supply the driving power for swimming. Back should be short, well-coupled and powerful. Good hindquarters are essential. Stifles should be well-angulated.

Legs, Elbows, Hocks and Feet—Legs should be medium length and straight, showing good bone and muscle, with well-webbed hare feet of good size. The toes well rounded and close, pasterns slightly bent and both pasterns and hocks medium length—the straighter the legs the better, when viewed from front or rear. Dewclaws, if any, must be removed from the hind legs. Dewclaws on the forelegs may be removed. A dog with dewclaws on the hind legs must be disqualified.

Tail—Tail should extend to hock. It should be medium heavy at base. Moderate feathering on stern and tail is permissible. Tail should be straight or slightly curved. Tail should not curl over back or side kink.

Coat and Texture—Coat should be thick and short, nowhere over 1½ inches long, with a dense fine woolly undercoat. Hair on face and legs should be very short and straight with tendency to wave on the shoulders, neck, back and loins only. The curly coat or coat with a tendency to curl not permissible.

The texture of the dog's coat is very important, as the dog is used for hunting under all sorts of adverse weather conditions, often working in ice and snow. The oil in the harsh outer coat and wooly undercoat is of extreme value in preventing the cold water from reaching the dog's skin and aids in quick drying. A Chesapeake's coat should resist the water in the same way that a duck's feathers do. When he leaves the water and shakes himself, his coat should not hold the water at all, being merely moist. Color and coat are extremely important, as the dog is used for duck hunting. The color must be as nearly that of his surroundings as possible and with the fact that dogs are exposed to all kinds of adverse weather conditions, often working in ice and snow, the color of coat and its texture must be given every consideration when judging on the bench or in the ring.

Color—Any color varying from a dark brown to a faded tan or deadgrass. Deadgrass takes in any shade of deadgrass, varying from a tan to a dull straw color. White spot on breast, toes and belly permissible, but the smaller the spot the better. Solid and self-colored dogs are preferred.

Weight—Males, 65 to 80 pounds; females 55 to 70 pounds. **Height**—Males, 23 inches to 26 inches; females, 21 inches to 24 inches. Oversized or undersized dogs are to be severely penalized.

Symmetry and Quality—The Chesapeake dog should show a bright and happy disposition and an intelligent expression, with general outlines impressive and denoting a good worker. The dog should be well proportioned, a dog with a good coat and well balanced in other points being preferable to the dog excelling in some but weak in others.

POSITIVE SCALE OF POINTS

Head, incl. lips, ears & eyes................16	Elbows, legs and feet........12
Neck..............4	Color..............4
Shoulders and body..........12	Stern and tail...................10
Hindquarters and stifles.....12	Coat and texture..............18
	General conformation 12
	TOTAL 100

Note:—The question of coat and general type of balance takes precedence over any scoring table which could be drawn up.

APPROXIMATE MEASUREMENTS

	Inches
Length head, nose to occiput	9½ to 10
Girth at ears	20 to 21
Muzzle below eyes	10 to 10½
Length of ears	4½ to 5
Width between eyes	2½ to 2¾

Girth neck close to shoulder ....20 to 22
Girth at flank ....24 to 25
Length from occiput to tail base ....34 to 35
Girth forearms at shoulders ....10 to 10½
Girth upper thigh ....19 to 20
From root to root of ear, over skull .... 5 to 6
Occiput to top shoulder blades .... 9 to 9½
From elbow to elbow over the shoulders ....25 to 26

DISQUALIFICATIONS

Black.
Dewclaws on hind legs.
White on any part of body, except breast, belly or spots on feet.
Feathering on tail or legs over 1¾ inches long.
Undershot, overshot or any deformity.
Coat curly or tendency to curl all over body.
Specimens unworthy or lacking in breed characteristics.

Approved November 9, 1976

Retriever, Curly-Coated

THE ORIGIN OF THE CURLY-COATED RETRIEVER is one of doubt, but he is popularly believed to be descended from the sixteenth-century English Water Spaniel, and from the retrieving setter. Some maintain the Irish Water Spaniel was his ancestor and it is more than probable that a cross was made with this Spaniel from time to time, the liver color being a recognized color for the Curly as well as the black.

Whichever Spaniel was his progenitor, it is certain that added to the mixture of Water Spaniel and retrieving setter was the small, or St. John's Newfoundland, which, according to records, first arrived in England in 1835 as a ship's dog on board the boats that brought salted cod from Newfoundland. The St. John's dog, curiously enough, is sometimes called a Labrador by early writers, a fact which has given rise to some confusion with respect to the modern Labrador.

In the early eighties the Curly is said to have been crossed again with the Poodle (the one-time retriever of France), this cross taken with the object of giving his coat a tight curl. In the absence of very early records, the correct origin of the Curly must, however, always remain a matter of conjecture, but there appears little doubt that he is one of the oldest of all breeds now classified as Retrievers.

The popular gun dog following the old English Water Spaniel, the Curly was first exhibited in 1860 at England's Birmingham show. In 1889 specimens were exported to New Zealand, where they have long been used for retrieving duck and California quail. In Australia, too, where they are used in the swamps and lagoons of the Murray River on duck, they are much admired as steady and tender-mouthed retrievers quite unsurpassed in the water. A dog and a bitch were exported to the United States about 1907; both were trained to the gun and exhibited successfully at shows. Fairly recently, specimens of the breed have taken part in English field trials open to all types of Retrievers, and they have more than held their own.

In the British Isles in 1896 was formed the Curly Retriever Club which, however, ceased to exist some years before the founding in England of the present Curly Retriever Club in 1933. Its object: "To promote the breeding of pure Curly Retrievers and to foster the interests of the breed particularly as a working gun dog, while preserving the correct type for the dual purpose of the field and the show bench." A special committee was selected to consider and possibly revise the standard of the breed as drawn up by the former club. After considerable deliberation at the March, 1933 meeting, our present standard was approved by a general meeting shortly afterward. The club was fortunate to have as president at that time the noted breed enthusiast, Lord Ashburton, who presented a magnificent silver cup to be competed for at field trials organized by the club for Curly Retrievers.

Many assert that the Curly Retriever is temperamentally easy to train. He is affectionate, enduring, hardy, and will practically live in the water. Moreover, his thick coat enables him to face the most punishing covert. He is a charming and faithful companion and an excellent guard.

Official Standard for the
Curly-Coated Retriever

Head—Long and well proportioned, skull not too flat, jaws long and strong but not inclined to snipiness, nose black, in the black coated variety, with wide nostrils. Teeth strong and level. *Eyes*—Black or brown, but not yellow, rather large but not too prominent. *Ears*—Rather small, set on low, lying close to the head, and covered with short curls.

Coat—Should be one mass of crisp curls all over. A slightly more open coat not to be severely penalized, but a saddle back or patch of uncurled hair behind the shoulder should be penalized, and a prominent white patch on breast is undesirable, but a few white hairs allowed in an otherwise good dog. Color, black or liver.

Shoulders, Chest, Body and Loins—Shoulders should be very deep, muscular and obliquely placed. Chest, not too wide, but decidedly deep. Body, rather short, muscular and well ribbed up. Loin, powerful, deep and firm to the grasp.

Legs and Feet—Legs should be of moderate length, forelegs straight and set well under the body. Quarters strong and muscular, hocks low to the ground with moderate bend to stifle and hock. Feet round and compact with well-arched toes.

Tail—Should be moderately short, carried fairly straight and covered with curls, slightly tapering towards the point.

General Appearance—A strong smart upstanding dog, showing activity, endurance and intelligence.

Retriever, Flat-Coated

WHEN IT BECAME POSSIBLE for man to kill game on the wing many different breeds of dogs were used to find and retrieve it and any such dog was regarded as a retriever. Eventually, by selective breeding for the perfection of this skill, the Retriever Proper, a large black dog, had come into existence in Britain by the early part of the 19th century. It was not accepted as a pure breed, but regarded as a mongrel because of its cross-bred origin from various breeds such as the Large Newfoundland, the setter, the sheepdog and spaniel-like Water dogs.

The last named were invaluable as retrievers to fishermen and were the subjects of trade between Britain and the North American continent, particularly with the cod fishery off Newfoundland during the 19th century. It was at this time that the term "Labrador" dog came into use and was applied indiscriminately to a number of different types of dogs associated with this area. These dogs, found in St. John's, Newfoundland, and called the small Labrador dog, the Lesser Newfoundland or St. John's Newfoundland, contributed towards the Wavy-coated (and subsequently the Flat-coated) retriever, but they must have had considerable British stock as ancestors. They should not be confused with the modern day Labrador Retriever as they differed in coat, size and structure.

The first British dog show was held in 1859, but classification for retrievers, comprising Curly-coated and Wavy or Smooth-coated, was not available until the following year. The winner then was the Wavy-coated retriever, "Wyndham" belonging to Mr. H. Brailsford. Records of awards and pedigrees, if known, were kept from the beginning of shows and published in the Kennel Club Stud Book in 1874. "Wyndham's" pedigree was unknown.

From 1864 on, two bitches of a working strain of retrievers belonging to Mr. J. Hull, a gamekeeper, figured in the awards. These were "Old Bounce", out of his bitch "Boss" and by Blaydon's "Black Sailor", and "Young Bounce", her daughter, by Mr. Chattock's "Cato". It was this stock that produced an important nucleus to the development of the breed.

The greatest credit for the integration of these retrievers into a stable type goes to Mr. E. Shirley, founder of the Kennel Club in 1873. Subsequently the breed gained enormously in popularity and numerous other important breeders made their contribution to the quality and elegance of the Flat-coated retriever as well as to his excellent working abilities.

The breed's most famous patron was Mr. H. R. Cooke, who, for over 70 years, kept the breed in his fabulous "Riverside" kennel—a kennel perhaps unique among those for any breed of dog in numbers, quality and awards won in the field and on the show bench.

Soon after the turn of the century the breed popularity gave way to pressure by the modern Labrador Retriever, and a decade later by the Golden Retriever, and Flatcoat stock has never since risen above its former peak. At times, particularly during the two World Wars, it dwindled to dangerous levels. After World War II it was not easy to pick up the threads of disappearing lines. Mr. S. O'Neill, one of the greatest authorities on the breed, must be credited with a valuable contribution to this end. He showed selfless devotion in putting the breed on as sound a footing as possible and in advising new patrons on correct type. Stock continued to build up gradually until about the mid-sixties when an appreciable increase in number and popularity took place in Britain and a keen demand for the breed appeared in Europe and America.

The parent club in the United States is the Flat-Coated Retriever Society of America, a flourishing and well-integrated club, whose members are very enthusiastic and anxious to further the best interests of the breed.

His fall from popularity has kept the Flatcoat out of the hands of the commercial breeder and under control of those interested in retaining his great natural working abilities. He is unafraid of thick covert and cold water, shows drive and perseverance when out hunting and retrieves tenderly to hand. He has a delightful and inimitable character and temperament, is highly intelligent and companionable and retains his youthful outlook on life into old age, tail-wagging being the hallmark of the breed. Apart from these virtues he is a handsome fellow.

Size was not given in the original standard because sportsmen have a varied preference for this according to the requirements of terrain and conditions of work. What is important is good type and well balanced conformation; otherwise, a fair amount of latitude in size is allowed.

Official Standard for the Flat-Coated Retriever

General Appearance—A bright, active dog of medium size (weighing from 60 pounds to 70 pounds) with an intelligent expression, showing power without lumber and raciness without weediness.

Head—This should be long and nicely molded. The skull flat and moderately broad. There should be a depression or stop between the eyes, slight and in no way accentuated, so as to avoid giving either a down or a dish-faced appearance. The nose of good size with open nostrils. The eyes, of medium size, should be dark brown or hazel, with a very intelligent expression (a round prominent eye is a disfigurement), and they should not be obliquely placed. The jaws should be long and strong, with a capacity of carrying a hare or pheasant. The ears small and well set on close to the side of the head.

Neck, Shoulders and Chest—The head should be well set in the neck, which latter should be long and free from throatiness, symmetrically set and obliquely placed in shoulders, running well into the back to allow of easily seeking for the trail. The chest should be deep and fairly broad, with a well-defined brisket, on which the elbows should work cleanly and evenly. The fore ribs should be fairly flat showing a gradual spring and well arched in the center of the body but rather lighter towards the quarters. Open couplings are to be ruthlessly condemned.

Back and Quarters—The back should be short, square and well ribbed up, with muscular quarters. The stern short, straight and well set on, carried gaily but never much above the level of the back.

Legs and Feet—These are of the greatest importance. The forelegs should be perfectly straight, with bone of good quality carried right down to the feet which should be round and strong. The stifle should not be too straight or too bent and the dog must neither be cowhocked nor move too wide behind; in fact, he must stand and move true all round on legs and feet, with toes close and well arched, the soles being thick and strong. When the dog is in full coat the limbs should be well feathered.

Coat—Should be dense, of fine quality and texture, flat as possible.

Color—Black or liver.

Retriever, Golden

IN THE EARLY 1800s game was plentiful in England and Scotland, and hunting was both a sport and a practical way of obtaining food. Retrievers came into prominence because of the desire for a medium-sized dog that would do well in wild-fowling, both water fowl and upland game.

The most complete records of the development of the Golden Retriever are included in the record books that were kept from 1835 until about 1890 by the gamekeepers at the Guisachan (pronounced Gooeesicun) estate of Lord Tweedmouth at Inverness-Shire, Scotland. These records were released to public notice in *Country Life* in 1952, when Lord Tweedmouth's great-nephew, the sixth Earl of Ilchester, historian and sportsman, published material that had been left by his ancestor. They provided factual confirmation to the stories that had been handed down through generations.

The delightful story that had the "six circus-performing Russian Trackers" as antecedents for Golden Retrievers is only that—a story, one which gained wide circulation but has no basis in fact.

It is known that in developing the Golden Retriever a Tweed Water Spaniel was used. Also, a small, lighter-built Newfoundland. There were other crosses—Irish Setters, other water spaniels. Water retrieving was very important and hunters needed a strong dog that could withstand cold water, would be a good swimmer and could fend with the heavy vegetation in which upland game was found.

Lord Tweedmouth bought his first Yellow Retriever, Nous (i.e. Wisdom) in Brighton in 1865. Nous was said to have been bred by the Earl of Chichester. A photograph of Nous in about 1870 shows a biggish Golden with a wavy coat. Some paintings in the British Museum show dogs similar in type. Portrait painters often painted individuals and families with their favorite dogs.

The location of Guisachan on the Tweed River at Beauly, near Inverness, had a direct bearing on the program pursued by Lord Tweedmouth to produce the characteristics he desired in his Yellow Retrievers. Along the shores of this river was the Tweed Water Spaniel, the hardy type of spaniel used for retrieving. The dog was descended from the ruggedly built water dogs which for years had been used along the British seacoast by families who depended upon the courage, intelligence and ability of these animals to retrieve game under all sorts of conditions. According to Dalziel, author of *British Dogs* (1881), Tweed Water Spaniels were light liver in color, so close in curl as to give the idea that they had originally been a cross from a smooth-haired dog, long in tail, ears heavy in flesh and hard like a hound's—but only slightly feathered, forelegs feathered behind, hind legs smooth, head conical and lips slightly pendulous. "Stonehenge" (John H. Walsh, author of books on dogs and former editor of *The Field* magazine) wrote that Tweed Water Spaniels resembled small ordinary English Retrievers.

Though this variety of water spaniel has long since sunk into obscurity, its influence on the development of Golden Retrievers cannot be overlooked. The gamekeepers' books at Guisachan indicate that Nous was mated to a Tweed Water Spaniel named Belle in about 1867–68.

Belle was liver-colored. At that time, liver was a term to describe any shade of brown to fawn or sand color. Nous and Belle produced four yellow puppies: Crocus, Cowslip, Primrose and Ada. Cowslip proved important in Lord Tweedmouth's plan to develop a Yellow Retriever. She was later bred to a Tweed Water Spaniel and a bitch puppy retained. In time, this dog was bred to a descendant of Ada. Yellow puppies were entered in the records from the breedings, breedings that included an Irish Setter and another Tweed Water Spaniel. It is believed that a Bloodhound was also used. Line breeding, not often used at this time, was a factor in developing the Golden Retriever, as Nous and Cowslip appear several times in the pedigrees.

One researcher who has studied the pictures in the museums

believes that a Yellow Spaniel was also used. The belief was arrived at as much by the type of game that this Spaniel retrieved as by the intense color of the golden coat. However, this particular cross is not recorded in the gamekeepers' books at Lord Tweedmouth's estate.

Occasionally puppies were given to other people who developed their own lines, lines that may or may not have been exchanged in other breedings. The pedigrees of some of the Retrievers of today go back to dogs from Ingestre and Culham strains as well as from those of the Ilchester line at Guisachan. Both Wavy Coats and Labradors may have been used in some of the breeding programs.

Yellow or Golden Retrievers became popular in England toward the end of the 19th century. The first win of a field trial by a Golden Retriever (won by a son of Rust) took place in 1904.

Golden Retrievers were first shown in England at the Crystal Palace show in 1908, and were listed as Flat Coats (Golden). Others (also grouped with other retrievers as Flat Coats) were exhibited in 1909 and 1913. In 1913 they were given separate status by color and shown as Golden or Yellow Retrievers. Some enthusiasts formed the Golden Retriever Club (of England).

Travelers had taken some of the dogs with them on visits to America, and it is known that there were Golden Retrievers in the United States and Canada during the 1890s. Goldens from Great Britain and Canada were brought to both the East and West Coasts of the United States in the 1920s and 1930s.

The first registration of a Golden Retriever by the American Kennel Club was in November 1925. While there had been Goldens registered before that date, they had been registered as Retrievers with some description as to color. In Canada, their first registration as a separate breed was in 1927.

Goldens were furthered in the United States in the 1930s and 1940s. They were predominantly used as hunters, though some were shown on the bench. The owners made a great effort and were conscientious breeders for they wanted sound, good looking dogs as hunters for the game that was then plentiful. More and more of these breeders began exhibiting their dogs in the show ring.

On the whole, the darker dogs were favored but there were some medium gold colors as well. Both dark and light dogs were run in English field trials and seen in the show rings in Scotland and England. The same was true in the United States and Canada, and remains true today. Balance, soundness, gait, trainability and temperament have ever been the first considerations for the knowledgeable fancier.

In England and Scotland the standard was changed in 1936 to allow the lighter as well as the darker colors. As more and more dogs were imported from England and Scotland to fill the American demand, the lighter colors were brought over along with the darker. While there have been some that have won, the very light dog is not well favored in the show rings in the United States, and such winners might have been the exceptions that won because of other qualities. There is a swing away from the very light dog by the American public, and as a rule they have not been favored by field trial people and hunters.

Golden Retriever clubs in the United States and other countries are taking active steps in maintaining the breed at its best. Today, Golden Retrievers are used successfully in field trials, hunting, obedience, as personal companion dogs and as guide dogs for the blind. The excellent nose which makes for good game finding and tracking has been useful in other areas. At least one has been most successful in narcotics detection. However, while Goldens will announce a stranger, they are not generally used for other police work or as guard dogs by commercial firms.

The first three dogs of any breed to achieve the AKC Obedience Champion title, first available in July 1977, were all Golden Retrievers. The first (Ch. Moreland's Golden Tonka) was a bitch, the others were males. Both males and females have done well in field trials and hunting. Their size, their biddable temperament and their desire to please, are all part of why Golden Retrievers have increased so rapidly in popularity.

Official Standard for the Golden Retriever

A symmetrical, powerful, active dog, sound and well put together, not clumsy or long in the leg, displaying a kindly expression and possessing a personality that is eager, alert and self-confident. Primarily a hunting dog, he should be shown in hard working condition. Over-all appearance, balance, gait and purpose to be given more emphasis than any of his component parts.

Size—Males 23-24 inches in height at withers; females 21½–22½. Length from breastbone to buttocks slightly greater than height at withers in ratio of 12–11. Weight for dogs 65–75 pounds; bitches 60–70 pounds.

Head—Broad in skull, slightly arched laterally and longitudinally without prominence of frontal or occipital bones. Good stop. Foreface deep and wide, nearly as long as skull. Muzzle, when viewed in profile, slightly deeper at stop than at tip; when viewed from above, slightly wider at stop than at tip. No heaviness in flews. Removal of whiskers for show purposes optional. *Eyes*—Friendly and intelligent, medium large with dark rims, set well apart and reasonably deep in sockets. Color preferably dark brown, never lighter than color of coat. No white or haw visible when looking straight ahead. *Teeth*—Scissors bite with lower incisors touching inside of upper incisors. *Nose*—Black or dark brown, though lighter shade in cold weather not serious. Dudley nose (pink without pigmentation) to be faulted. *Ears*—Rather short, hanging flat against head with rounded tips slightly below jaw. Forward edge attached well behind and just above eye with rear edge slightly below eye. Low, houndlike ear-set to be faulted.

Neck—Medium long, sloping well back into shoulders, giving sturdy muscular appearance with untrimmed natural ruff. No throatiness.

Body—Well-balanced, short-coupled, deep through the heart. Chest at least as wide as a man's hand, including thumb. Brisket extends to elbows. Ribs long and well sprung but not barrel shaped, extending well to rear of body. Loin short, muscular, wide and deep, with very little tuck-up. Topline level from withers to croup, whether standing or moving. Croup slopes gently. Slabsidedness, narrow chest, lack of depth in brisket, excessive tuck-up, roach or sway back to be faulted.

Forequarters—Forequarters well co-ordinated with hindquarters and capable of free movement. Shoulder blades wide, long and muscular, showing angulation with upper arm of approximately 90 degrees. Legs straight with good bone. Pastern short and strong, sloping slightly forward with no suggestion of weakness.

Hindquarters—Well-bent stifles (angulation between femur and pelvis approximately 90 degrees) with hocks well let down. Legs straight when viewed from rear. Cowhocks and sickle hocks to be faulted.

Feet—Medium size, round and compact with thick pads. Excess hair may be trimmed to show natural size and contour. Open or splayed feet to be faulted.

Tail—Well set on, neither too high nor too low, following natural line of croup. Length extends to hock. Carried with merry action with some upward curve but never curled over back nor between legs.

Coat and Color—Dense and water-repellent with good undercoat. Texture not as hard as that of a shorthaired dog, nor silky as that of a setter. Lies flat against body and may be straight or wavy. Moderate feathering on back of forelegs and heavier feathering on front of neck, back of thighs and underside of tail. Feathering may be lighter than rest of coat. Color lustrous golden of various shades. A few white hairs on chest permissible but not desirable. Further white markings to be faulted.

Gait—When trotting, gait is free, smooth, powerful and well co-ordinated. Viewed from front or rear, legs turn neither in nor out, nor do feet cross or interfere with each other. Increased speed causes tendency of feet to converge toward center line of gravity.

DISQUALIFICATIONS

Deviation in height of more than one inch from standard either way.

Undershot or overshot bite. This condition not to be confused with misalignment of teeth.

Trichiasis (abnormal position or direction of the eyelashes).

Approved September 10, 1963

Retriever, Labrador

THE LABRADOR RETRIEVER did not, as his name implies, come from Labrador, but from Newfoundland, although there is no indication of by what means he reached the latter place. However, in 1822 a traveler in that region reported a number of "small water dogs" and said: "The dogs are admirably trained as retrievers in fowling, and are otherwise useful . . . The smooth or short-haired dog is preferred because in frosty weather the long-haired kind become encumbered with ice on coming out of the water."

Early in the nineteenth century the Earl of Malmesbury reputedly saw one of the dogs that had been carried to England by fishermen and immediately arranged to have some imported. In 1830 the noted British sportsman Colonel Hawker referred to the ordinary Newfoundland and what he called the St. John's breed of water dog, mentioning the former as "very large, strong of limb, rough hair, and carrying his tail high." Referring to what is known now as the Labrador, he said they were "by far the best for any kind of shooting. He is generally black and no bigger than a Pointer, very fine in legs, with short, smooth hair and does not carry his tail so much curled as the other; is extremely quick, running, swimming and fighting . . . and their sense of smell is hardly to be credited. . . ."

The dogs were not at first generally known in England as Labradors. In fact, the origin of the name is shown in a letter written in 1887 by an Earl of Malmesbury in which he said: "We always call mine Labrador dogs, and I have kept the breed as pure as I could from the first I had from Poole, at that time carrying on a brisk trade with Newfoundland. The real breed may be known by its close coat which turns the water off like oil and, above all, a tail like an otter." The Labrador gradually died out in Newfoundland on account of a heavy dog tax which, with the English quarantine law, practically stopped the importations into England. Thereafter many Labradors were interbred with other types of retrievers. Fortunately, however, the Labrador characteristics predominated. And finally fanciers, desiring to stop the interbreeding, drew up a standard so as to discourage crossing with other retrievers.

There is a stud book of the Duke of Buccleuch's Labrador Retrievers which made it possible to work out pedigrees of the two dogs that did most to produce the modern Labrador, Mr. A. C. Butter's Peter of Faskally, and Major Portal's Flapper. These pedigrees go back as far as 1878.

The breed was first recognized by the English Kennel Club as a separate breed in 1903 and has since frequently won the Kennel Club's cup for best in show.

Mr. Leslie Sprake's book *The Labrador Retriever* (published in 1933 by H. F. & G. Witherby, London), deals very fully with the breed and its history. He quotes therein from an article written in 1923 by the Hon. A. Holland Hibbert (the late Lord Knutsford) who, in commenting on the two most important points of the Labrador, the eye and the tail, said:

> *Tail*—The nearer the level carriage and the closer resemblance to an otter tail the better, i.e., short and thick at stump with the hair underneath divided almost as if parted. Otter tails are very rare and straight tails are not common—the more usual carriage being like a Foxhound, except when hunting, and then the tail is almost invariably carried level.
>
> *Eye*—The color of the eye, about which much has been written; when Labradors first came into general notice, the dark eye, which was a great point with the flat coat, was supposed to be necessary also for the Labrador. This was nothing but a show ring opinion, and entirely wrong. Although the very light eye has a startled, and I think disagreeable look, yet the dark eye to my mind is lacking in expression, and looks sulky, hence I welcome what is now generally considered the best color, i.e., light brown, the color of burnt sugar.

In England, no Labrador can become a bench show champion unless he has received a working certificate. In other words, he must qualify in the field as well as on the bench, so that in looking at an English pedigree if a dog is designated as a champion you know that he must have qualified in the field as well as on the bench.

Official Standard for the
Labrador Retriever

General Appearance—The general appearance of the Labrador should be that of a strongly built, short-coupled, very active dog. He should be fairly wide over the loins, and strong and muscular in the hindquarters. The coat should be close, short, dense and free from feather.

Head—The skull should be wide, giving brain room; there should be a slight stop, *i.e.* the brow should be slightly pronounced, so that the skull is not absolutely in a straight line with the nose. The head should be clean-cut and free from fleshy cheeks. The jaws should be long and powerful and free from snipiness; the nose should be wide and the nostrils well developed. Teeth should be strong and regular, with a level mouth. The ears should hang moderately close to the head, rather far back, should be set somewhat low and not be large and heavy. The eyes should be of a medium size, expressing great intelligence and good temper, and can be brown, yellow or black, but brown or black is preferred.

Neck and Chest—The neck should be medium length, powerful and not throaty. The shoulders should be long and sloping. The chest must be of good width and depth, the ribs well sprung and the loins wide and strong, stifles well turned, and the hindquarters well developed and of great power.

Legs and Feet—The legs must be straight from the shoulder to ground, and the feet compact with toes well arched, and pads well developed; the hocks should be well bent, and the dog must neither be cowhocked nor be too wide behind; in fact, he must stand and move true all round on legs and feet. Legs should be of medium length, showing good bone and muscle, but not so short as to be out of balance with rest of body. In fact, a dog well balanced in all points is preferable to one with outstanding good qualities and defects.

Tail—The tail is a distinctive feature of the breed; it should be very thick towards the base, gradually tapering towards the tip, of medium length, should be free from any feathering, and should be clothed thickly all round with the Labrador's short, thick, dense coat, thus giving that peculiar "rounded" appearance which has been described as the "otter" tail. The tail may be carried gaily but should not curl over the back.

Coat—The coat is another very distinctive feature; it should be short, very dense and without wave, and should give a fairly hard feeling to the hand.

Color—The colors are black, yellow, or chocolate and are evaluated as follows:

(a) *Blacks:* All black, with a small white spot on chest permissible. Eyes to be of medium size, expressing intelligence and good temper, preferably brown or hazel, although black or yellow is permissible.

(b) *Yellows:* Yellows may vary in color from fox-red to light cream with variations in the shading of the coat on ears, the underparts of the dog, or beneath the tail. A small white spot on chest is permissible. Eye coloring and expression should be the same as that of the blacks, with black or dark brown eye rims. The nose should also be black or dark brown, although "fading" to pink in winter weather is not serious. A "Dudley" nose (pink without pigmentation) should be penalized.

(c) *Chocolates:* Shades ranging from light sedge to chocolate. A small white spot on chest is permissible. Eyes to be light brown to clear yellow. Nose and eye-rim pigmentation dark brown or liver colored. "Fading" to pink in winter weather not serious. "Dudley" nose should be penalized.

Movement—Movement should be free and effortless. The forelegs should be strong, straight and true, and correctly placed. Watching a dog move towards one, there should be no signs of elbows being out in front, but neatly held to the body with legs not too close together, and moving straight forward without pacing or weaving. Upon viewing the dog from the rear, one should get the impression that the hind legs, which should be well muscled and not cowhocked, move as nearly parallel as possible, with hocks doing their full share of work and flexing well, thus giving the appearance of power and strength.

Approximate Weights of Dogs and Bitches in Working Condition—Dogs—60 to 75 pounds; bitches—55 to 70 pounds.

Height at Shoulders—Dogs—$22^{1}/_{2}$ inches to $24^{1}/_{2}$ inches; bitches—$21^{1}/_{2}$ inches to $23^{1}/_{2}$ inches.

Approved April 9, 1957

Setter, English

FROM the best authorities on the subject, it appears that the English Setter was a trained bird dog in England approximately four hundred years ago. A perusal of some of the old writings leads us to believe that the English Setter had its origin in some of the older of the land spaniels that originated in Spain. We are indebted, however, to Hans Bols, who, in *Partridge Shooting and Partridge Hawking,* written in 1582, presents quite definite pictorial evidence that the setter and the spaniel breeds were quite different in appearance, and even at that time the tails of the spaniels appeared to have been docked as they are today and the tails of setters left as nature intended them.

There is some evidence in the earlier writings of sportsmen that the old English Setter was originally produced from crosses of the Spanish Pointer, the large Water Spaniel, and the Springer Spaniel, and by careful cultivation attained a high degree of proficiency in finding and pointing game in open country. We can see from examination of the sketches in many of the old writings that this setter-spaniel was an extremely handsome dog, many having a head much longer and with a more classical cut than that of the spaniel, while others had the short

spaniel-like head, lacking the well-defined profile of the skull and foreface of the modern dogs. Also most of these older setters had coats
which were quite curly, particularly at the thighs. It can be seen from
this brief review of the origin of the English Setter that even our oldest
authorities were not entirely in accord as to the origin of this breed.

There is little doubt that the major credit for the development of the
modern setter should go to Mr. Edward Laverack, who about 1825
obtained from the Rev. A. Harrison, "Ponto" and "Old Moll." The
Rev. Harrison had apparently kept this breed pure for thirty-five years
or more. From these two Mr. Laverack, through a remarkable process
of inbreeding, produced Prince, Countess, Nellie, and Fairy, which
were marvelous specimens of English Setters. Along about 1874, Mr.
Laverack sold a pair of dogs to Charles H. Raymond of Morris Plains,
N.J. During the next ten years the English Setter became more and
more popular and it was around this time that many Setters bred by
Mr. Llewellin were imported into this country and Canada.

In considering the so-called Llewellin strain, it is recorded in the
writings of Dr. William A. Bruette that about the time the Laverack
strain was at its zenith in England, Mr. R. L. Purcell Llewellin
purchased a number of Mr. Laverack's best show dogs of the pure
Dash-Moll and Dash-Hill Laverack inheritance. The Laveracks he
crossed with some entirely new "blood" which he obtained in the
north of England, represented by Mr. Statter's and Sir Vincent
Corbet's strain, since referred to as the Duke-Rhoebes, the latter being
the two most prominent members of the strain. The result of these
crosses was eminently successful, particularly at field trials; they
swept everything before them. Their reputation spread to America and
many were purchased by sportsmen in different sections of the United
States and Canada, so that this line of breeding soon became firmly
established in this country.

Probably the name that stands out most conspicuously in the
foundation of the field-trial setter in America is Count Noble. This dog
was purchased from Mr. Llewellin by Dave Sanborn of Dowling,
Michigan, who, after trying him out on the prairies, was upon the point
of returning him to England, but was persuaded not to do so by the late
B. F. Wilson of Pittsburgh. On the death of Mr. Sanborn, Count
passed into the hands of Mr. Wilson, who gave him an opportunity to
demonstrate his sterling qualities from coast to coast. The body of this
famous dog was mounted at his death and is now in the Carnegie
Museum at Pittsburgh, where it is visited annually by many sportsmen.

Dr. Walsh in 1878 stated that Mr. Llewellin's dogs were Dan-
Laveracks, because according to him they were all either by Dan out of
Laverack bitches or by a Laverack dog out of a sister of Dan. It is quite
difficult to give a proper definition of a straight-bred Llewellin, but it is

generally accepted that all English Setters may be called Llewellins which trace back in all lines to Duke-Rhoebe-Laverack. This, however, would shut out everything that had Dash II inheritance and this the Llewellin enthusiast does not wish to do, for under such definition it would eliminate a great number of the best known names that appear in the so-called Llewellin pedigrees. R. L. Purcell Llewellin is given credit for making the Duke-Rhoebe-Laverack cross, but in justice to him, according to Mr. A. F. Hochwalt, one of our noted authorities on gun dogs, he is not responsible for the breed being named for him. The name was originated in America by breeders who imported dogs from Mr. Llewellin's kennels and, being great admirers of the man and the dogs he bred, they naturally gave them the name of him from whom they were purchased.

The first show for English Setters was held at Newcastle-on-Tyne on January 28, 1859, and from this time on dog shows flourished throughout England, gradually increasing in popularity. English Setters became increasingly popular, and it is of interest in passing to note that in 1930 for the first time an American was invited abroad to judge English Setters. The expert so honored was none other than the late Benjamin F. Lewis of Lansdowne, Pa., who had been associated with English Setters since his boyhood. His father, B. F. Lewis, born in South Wales, for many years was unquestionably the outstanding handler of all sporting show dogs in America. It is believed that no one will dissent from the opinion that his son, the late Benny, was without an equal as a handler of sporting dogs.

The English Setter has retained its popularity since its introduction to this country primarily because of its usefulness and beauty. There is little doubt that its usefulness has been a prime factor in this respect. As a result of intelligent breeding it has been brought to a high state of perfection and there is always to be found a representative entry at all bench shows and field trials.

The mild, sweet disposition characteristic of this breed along with the beauty, intelligence, and aristocratic appearance it makes in the field and in the home has endeared it both to the sportsman as well as all lovers of a beautiful, active, and rugged outdoor dog. A lovable disposition makes it an ideal companion; it is, however, a dog that requires considerable exercise and therefore is better suited to ownership in the suburbs than in the city.

Official Standard for the
English Setter

Head—Long and lean, with a well-defined stop. The skull oval from ear to ear, of medium width, giving brain room but with no suggestion of coarseness, with but little difference between the width at base of skull and at brows and with a moderately defined occipital protuberance. Brows should be at a sharp angle from the muzzle. Muzzle should be long and square, of width in harmony with the skull, without any fullness under the eyes and straight from eyes to tip of the nose. A dish-face or Roman nose objectionable. The lips square and fairly pendant. Nose should be black or dark liver in color, except in white, lemon and white, orange and white, or liver and white dogs, when it may be of lighter color. Nostrils should be wide apart and large in the openings. Jaws should be of equal length. Overshot or undershot jaw objectionable. Ears should be carried close to the head, well back and set low, of moderate length, slightly rounded at the ends, and covered with silky hair. Eyes should be bright, mild, intelligent and dark brown in color.

Neck—The neck should be long and lean, arched at the crest, and not too throaty.

Shoulders—Shoulders should be formed to permit perfect freedom of action to the forelegs. Shoulder blades should be long, wide, sloping moderately well back and standing fairly close together at the top.

Chest—Chest between shoulder blades should be of good depth but not of excessive width.

Ribs—Ribs, back of the shoulders, should spring gradually to the middle of the body and then taper to the back ribs, which should be of good depth.

Back—Back should be strong at its junction with the loin and should be straight or sloping upward very slightly to the top of the shoulder, the whole forming a graceful outline of medium length, without sway or drop. Loins should be strong, moderate in length, slightly arched, but not to the extent of being roached or wheel-backed. Hipbones should be wide apart without too sudden drop to the root of the tail.

Forelegs—The arms should be flat and muscular, with bone fully developed and muscles hard and devoid of flabbiness; of good length from the point of the shoulder to the elbow, and set at such an angle as will bring the legs fairly under the dog. Elbows should have no tendency to turn either in or out. The pastern should be short, strong and nearly round with the slope from the pastern joint to the foot deviating very slightly forward from the perpendicular.

Hind Legs—The hind legs should have wide, muscular thighs with well developed lower thighs. Stifles should be well bent and strong. Hocks should be wide and flat. The hind pastern or metatarsus should be short, strong and nearly round.

Feet—Feet should be closely set and strong, pads well developed and tough, toes well arched and protected with short, thick hair.

Tail—Tail should be straight and taper to a fine point, with only sufficient length to reach the hocks, or less. The feather must be straight and silky, falling loosely in a fringe and tapering to the point when the tail is raised. There must be no bushiness. The tail should not curl sideways or above the level of the back.

Coat—Coat should be flat and of good length, without curl; not soft or woolly. The feather on the legs should be moderately thin and regular.

Height—Dogs about 25 inches; bitches about 24 inches.

Colors—Black, white and tan; black and white; blue belton; lemon and white; lemon belton; orange and white; orange belton; liver and white; liver belton; and solid white. *Markings*—Dogs without heavy patches of color on the body, but flecked all over preferred.

Symmetry—The harmony of all parts to be considered. Symmetrical dogs will have level backs or be very slightly higher at the shoulders than at the hips. Balance, harmony of proportion, and an appearance of breeding and quality to be looked for, and coarseness avoided.

Movement and Carriage—An easy, free and graceful movement, suggesting rapidity and endurance. A lively tail and a high carriage of head. Stiltiness, clumsiness or a lumbering gait are objectionable.

SCALE OF POINTS

Head
Skull 5		
Ears 5		
Eyes 5		
Muzzle 5	20	

Body
Neck 5		
Chest and shoulders 12		
Back, loin and ribs 10	27	

Running Gear
Forelegs 5		
Hips, thighs and hind legs 12		
Feet 6	23	

Coat
Length and texture 5		
Color and marking 3	8	

Tail
Length and carriage 5	5	

General Appearance and Action
Symmetry, style and movement 12		
Size 5	17	

TOTAL	100

Approved May 8, 1951

Setter, Gordon

BEAUTY, brains and bird sense are the outstanding qualities of the handsome black-and-tan Setter from Scotland whose ancient lineage dates back at least to 1620 when Markham, a writer of the time, praised the "black and fallow setting dog" as "hardest to endure labor." Popular among hunters of Scotland for decades, the black-and-tan (or occasionally black-white-and-tan) Setter came into prominence in the kennels of the fourth Duke of Gordon in the late 1700s. Commenting on these kennels, a writer familiar with the Duke's Gordons describes them much as a sportsman would describe a Gordon of today: "The Gordon Castle Setters are as a rule easy to break and naturally back well. They are not fast dogs but they have good staying powers and can keep on steadily from morning until night. Their noses are first class and they seldom make a false point or what is called at field trials a sensational stand. . . When they stand you may be sure there are birds." A later and illustrious authority, Idstone notes: "I have seen better Setters of the black and tan than of any other breed."

Attracted quite as much by the Gordon's beauty as by his superior hunting ability, George Blunt and Daniel Webster in 1842 imported a brace of the Duke's Gordons to America. In the intervening years other importations from Great Britain and the Scandinavian countries, and the perfecting of the American strains, helped the Gordon achieve great popularity as a pet and faithful gun dog, particularly in the period when game was marketed commercially and a real "meat" dog assured a full bag at the end of the day's shooting.

With the coming of the field-trial form of competition a few decades back, Gordon popularity waned for a time, as the dog's habit of quartering thoroughly and working close to the gun placed him at a disadvantage where flashing speed was demanded, though as a one-man shooting dog the Gordon knows no peer. However, the recent activities of the fast growing Gordon Setter Club of America in sponsoring regular field trials has turned the tide and the Gordon is being encouraged to develop greater range and speed while maintaining his superiority as a methodical, dependable bird finder, consistently placing well up in the ribbons in all-breed field competition.

The Gordon's characteristic eagerness to work for a loving master has never changed over the centuries, nor have his keen intellect and retentive memory, which enable him to improve with age with no need for retraining each season. This consistency of quality is doubtless due to the fact that, unlike fanciers of some other sporting breeds, Gordon breeders, backed by a strong national club, make no distinction between field or show types. As a rule, bench-show champions are used regularly for hunting and give a good account of themselves in the field, as do the field trial winners at the bench show.

The oft-quoted comment that the Gordon's coloring makes him difficult to see in the field has doubtless been made by those who have never seen him there. Against the tan fall sedge grass or early snow, a black dog is highly conspicuous, and when this black dog is difficult to distinguish against his background, it is then too dark to shoot with safety.

A true Setter, the Gordon is distinctive, resembling the English or Irish Setters only in general type. In field-trial competition the smaller, but not light-boned, Gordon has been more favored while the larger dog is preferred for bench work. The official Standard of the breed allows considerable range in sizes primarily because individual sportsmen from various corners of the nation prefer their Gordons of a size to suit their local hunting terrain. There is general agreement, however, on the aristocratic beauty of the Gordon, with his silky black coat, rich mahogany markings, his well-feathered legs and gaily carried tail. The finely chiseled, somewhat heavy head with long, low-set ears is distinctive for its intelligent expression. His good-sized, sturdy build with plenty of bone and substance and his upstanding, stylish gait give him the necessary stamina to match his ardor for the long days in the field. Few dogs, indeed, can match the Gordon's beauty as he quarters the field, tail wagging constantly while busily in quest of a bird, and few can compare with his quiet dignity as he sleeps at the family fireside.

The quality that endears the Gordon to the pet owner or to the sensitive sportsman is his devoted loyalty to members of the household. Wary of the unwanted intruder, the Gordon is not the chum of every passer-by, but lives for the pleasure of being near his owners. This almost fanatical devotion has helped make the Gordon not only a responsive gun dog, but a mannerly, eager-to-please dog in the home. His gentleness with children is a byword with those familiar with the breed. His occasional aggressiveness with other dogs occurs as a result of his jealousy guarding his family's affections.

He who acquires a Gordon Setter owns a rare combination: an aristocrat of ancient lineage and rich beauty, a shooting companion of keen intelligence and inbred hunting ability, a loyal family guard, and, as one authority puts it, "a most pettable dog."

Official Standard for the
Gordon Setter

General Impression—The Gordon Setter is a good-sized, sturdily built, black and tan dog, well muscled, with plenty of bone and substance, but active, upstanding, and stylish, appearing capable of doing a full day's work in the field. He has a strong, rather short back, with well-sprung ribs and a short tail. The head is fairly heavy and finely chiseled. His bearing is intelligent, noble, and dignified, showing no signs of shyness or viciousness. Clear colors and straight or slightly waved coat are correct. He suggests strength and stamina rather than extreme speed. Symmetry and quality are most essential. A dog well-balanced in all points is preferable to one with outstanding good qualities and defects. A smooth, free movement, with high head carriage, is typical.

Size—Shoulder height for males, 24 to 27 inches. For females, 23 to 26 inches.

Weight—Males, 55 to 80 pounds; females, 45 to 70 pounds. Animals that appear to be over or under the prescribed weight limits are to be judged on the basis of conformation and condition. Extremely thin or fat dogs should be discouraged on the basis that under- or overweight hampers the true working ability of the Gordon Setter. The weight-to-height ratio makes him heavier than other setters.

Head—The head is deep, rather than broad, with plenty of brain room; a nicely rounded, good-sized skull, broadest between the ears. The head should have a clearly indicated stop. Below and above the eyes should be lean, and the cheek as narrow as the leanness of the head allows. The muzzle is fairly long and not pointed, either as seen from above or from the side. The flews should not be pendulous. The nose should be broad, with open nostrils and black in color. The muzzle is the same length as the skull from occiput to stop, and the top of the muzzle is parallel to the line of the skull extended. The lip line from the nose to the flews shows a sharp, well-defined, square contour.

Eyes—Of fair size, neither too deep-set, nor too bulging, dark brown, bright, and wise. The shape is oval rather than round. The lids should be tight. *Ears*—Set low on the head approximately on line with the eye, fairly large and thin, well folded and carried close to the head. *Teeth*—The teeth should be strong and white, and preferably should meet in front in a scissors bite, with the upper incisors slightly forward of the lower incisors. A level bite is not to be considered a fault. Pitted teeth from distemper or allied infections should not be penalized.

Neck—Long, lean, arched to the head, and without throatiness.

Shoulders—Should be fine at the points, and lying well back, giving a moderately sloping topline. The tops of the shoulder blades should be close together. When viewed from behind, the neck appears to fit into the shoulders in smooth, flat, lines that gradually widen from neck to shoulder.

Chest—Deep and not too broad in front; the ribs well sprung, leaving plenty of lung room. The chest should reach to the elbows. A pronounced forechest should be in evidence.

Body—The body should be short from shoulder to hips, and the distance from the forechest to the back of the thigh should approximately equal the height from the ground to the withers. The loins should be short and broad and not arched. The croup is nearly flat, with only a slight slope to the tailhead.

Forequarters—The legs should be big-boned, straight, and not bowed, with elbows free and not turned in or out. The angle formed by the shoulder blade and upper arm bone should be approximately 90° when the dog is standing so that the foreleg is perpendicular to the ground. The pasterns should be straight.

Hindquarters—The hind legs from hip to hock should be long, flat, and muscular; from hock to heel, short and strong. The stifle and hock joints are well bent and not turned either in or out. When the dog is standing with the hock perpendicular to the ground, the thigh bone should hang downward parallel to an imaginary line drawn upward from the hock.

Feet—The feet should be formed by close-knit, well-arched toes with plenty of hair between; with full toe pads and deep heel cushions. Feet should not be turned in or out. Feet should be catlike in shape.

Tail—Short and should not reach below the hocks, carried horizontal or nearly so; thick at the root and finishing in a fine point. The feather which starts near the root of the tail should be slightly waved or straight, having triangular appearance, growing shorter uniformly toward the end. The placement of the tail is important for correct carriage. If the croup is nearly flat, the tail must emerge nearly on the same plane as the croup to allow for horizontal carriage. When the angle of the tail bends too sharply at the first coccygeal bone, the tail will be carried too gaily or will droop. The tail placement should be judged in its relationship to the structure of the croup.

Temperament—The Gordon Setter should be alert, gay, interested, and aggressive. He should be fearless and willing, intelligent and capable. He should be loyal and affectionate, and strong-minded enough to stand the rigors of training.

Gait—The action of the Gordon Setter is a bold, strong, driving, free-swinging gait. The head is carried up and the tail "flags" constantly while the dog is in motion. When viewed from the front, the forefeet move up and down in straight lines so that the shoulder, elbow, and pastern joints are approximately in line with each other. When viewed from the rear, the hock, stifle, and hip joints are approximately in line. Thus the dog moves in a straight pattern forward without throwing the feet in or out. When viewed from the side, the forefeet are seen to lift up and reach forward to compensate for the driving hindquarters. The hindquarters reach well forward and stretch far back, enabling the stride to be long and the drive powerful. The over-all appearance of the moving dog is one of smooth-flowing, well-balanced rhythm, in which the action is pleasing to the eye, effortless, economical and harmonious.

Coat—Should be soft and shining, straight or slightly waved, but not curly, with long hair on ears, under stomach and on chest, on back of the fore- and hind legs, and on the tail.

Color and Markings—Black with tan markings, either of rich chestnut or mahogany color. Black penciling is allowed on the toes. The borderline between black and tan colors should be clearly defined. There should not be any tan hairs mixed in the black. The tan markings should be located as follows: (1) Two clear spots over the eyes and not over three quarters of an inch in diameter; (2) On the sides of the muzzle. The tan should not reach to the top of the muzzle, but resembles a stripe around the end of the muzzle from one side to the other; (3) On the throat; (4) Two large clear spots on the chest; (5) On the inside of the hind legs showing down the front of the stifle and broadening out to the outside of the hind legs from the hock to the toes. It must not completely eliminate the black on the back of the hind legs; (6) On the forelegs from the carpus, or a little above, downward to the toes; (7) Around the vent; (8) A white spot on the chest is allowed, but the smaller the better. Predominantly tan, red, or buff dogs which do not have the typical pattern of markings of a Gordon Setter are ineligible for showing and undesirable for breeding.

SCALE OF POINTS:

While not a part of the official breed standard, may be helpful in placing proper emphasis upon qualities desired in the physical make up of the breed.

Head and neck (incl. ears and eyes)	10	Coat	8
Body	15	Color and markings	5
Shoulders, forelegs, forefeet	10	Temperament	10
Hind legs and feet	10	Size, general appearance	15
Tail	5	Gait	12
		TOTAL	100

DISQUALIFICATION

Predominantly tan, red, or buff dogs which do not have the typical pattern of markings of a Gordon Setter.

Approved November 13, 1962

Setter, Irish

THE IRISH SETTER first came into popular notice early in the eighteenth century and less than a hundred years later his reputation was firmly established, not only in his native Ireland but throughout the British Isles. Speculations as to his origin are little more than guesswork, various breeds having been named as his progenitors, but none that can boast a clear title to the honor. Among the conjectures is that he was developed from an Irish Water Spaniel-Irish Terrier cross, but it is far more believable that an English Setter-Spaniel-Pointer combination, with a dash of Gordon thrown in, was the true formula.

The Irish Red Setter was the name originally chosen by the Irish Setter Club of America to designate the breed in this country. His earliest ancestors in the Emerald Isle, on the contrary, were rarely self-colored dogs. By far the larger number were red and white, the white frequently predominating over the red, and even today many individuals across the water are parti-colored. In America, however, solid reds or reds with small and inconspicuous white markings are the only ones accepted as typical, and any large and noticeable white patches are considered blemishes. The Irishman's rich mahogany coat is thoroughly distinctive and has done much to make its wearer the bench-show favorite he is today.

The solid red Setter, as distinguished from the red and white, first appeared in Ireland in the nineteenth century. Mr. Jason Hazzard of Timaskea, County Fermanagh, Sir St. George Gore, and the Earl of Enniskillen all bred self-colored dogs, and it is a matter of record that in 1812 the Earl would have nothing else in his kennels. A few years later Stonehenge wrote: "The blood red, or rich chestnut or mahogany color is the color of an Irish Setter of high mark. This color must be unmixed with black; and studied in a strong light, there must not be black shadows or waves, much less black fringes to the ears, or to the profile of the form." The mention of black in the above is significant as indicating the possibility of the Gordon cross already mentioned. Today this color is absolutely taboo and even a few black hairs are faulted at the shows.

So much for the external appearance of the Irish Setter; now for more important, if less obvious characteristics. The breed is essentially a sporting one, and it is as a gun dog, after all, that this flashy red fellow must stand or fall. The first individuals imported into this country were brought over for use on game and, in spite of the fact that our ruffed grouse, quail, and prairie chicken were new and strange to them, they made good immediately. Elcho, imported in 1875 and one of the first of his breed to make a reputation for himself and his progeny in the United States, was not only a sensational success on the bench, but a thoroughly trained and capable shooting dog. To quote Mr. A. F. Hochwalt, in his book *The Modern Setter,* "All through the early field-trial records we find the Irish Setter holding his own with the 'fashionable blue bloods.' Had the Irish Setter fanciers continued on, their favorite breed would no doubt now be occupying a place as high in field trials as the other two breeds"; by which he means, of course, the English Setter and Pointer.

But the Irish Setter men didn't continue on, insofar as field trials were concerned, with the result that the Llewellin Setter and the Pointer have practically cornered the market in public competition in that field. Yet, in spite of this handicap, the red dog from Erin has lost none of the attributes of the good hunting companion, and given a fair chance, can and does demonstrate his quality as a high-class gun dog on all kinds of game. Strange as it may seem, his good looks have been his undoing in a way. His fatal gift of beauty, together with his gaiety, courage, and personality, have made him an ideal show dog. For this reason many fanciers have yielded to the temptation to breed for the bench only and to sacrifice to this most worthwhile object, field ability equally worthwhile and in no way incompatible with proper color, good size, and correct breed type.

Just a word regarding the characteristic personality of the red dog. First and foremost, he is typically Irish, with a devil-may-care something about him that not only makes him tremendously likable but also adds to his value as a bird dog in rough country and briars. He is bold and at the same time gentle and lovable and loyal. He is tough— good and tough. He can stand continued work in the brush, is almost never stiff or sore, has the best of feet and running gear, and almost never gets "sour" when corrected in his work. He is not an early developer and frequently requires more training than some other breeds, but he is not as a rule headstrong in the sense that he is hard to handle in the brush. His outstanding fault as a field-trial performer is that he is not independent enough and pays too much attention to his handler. In reply to the criticism that he develops slowly, it is only fair to say that, once trained on birds, he is trained for the rest of his life and does not require a repetition of the process every fall. When you own a good Irishman, you own him for many years, every day of which you can be proud of his appearance, his personality, and his performance.

Official Standard for the Irish Setter

General Appearance—The Irish Setter is an active, aristocratic bird-dog, rich red in color, substantial yet elegant in build. Standing over two feet tall at the shoulder, the dog has a straight, fine, glossy coat, longer on ears, chest, tail, and back of legs. Afield he is a swift-moving hunter; at home, a sweet-natured, trainable companion. His is a rollicking personality.

Head—Long and lean, its length at least double the width between the ears. The brow is raised, showing a distinct stop midway between the tip of nose and the well-defined occiput (rear point of skull). Thus the nearly level line from occiput to brow is set a little above, and parallel to, the straight and equal line from eye to nose. The skull is oval when viewed from above or front; very slightly domed when viewed in profile. Beauty of head is emphasized by delicate chiseling along the muzzle, around and below the eyes, and along the cheeks. Muzzle moderately deep, nostrils wide, jaws of nearly equal length. Upper lips fairly square but not pendulous, the underline of the jaws being almost parallel with the top line of the muzzle. The teeth meet in a scissors bite in which the upper incisors fit closely over the lower, or they may meet evenly. *Nose*—Black or chocolate. *Eyes*—Somewhat almond-shaped, of medium size, placed rather well apart; neither deep-set nor bulging. Color, dark to medium brown. Expression soft yet alert. *Ears*—Set well back and low, not above level of eye. Leather thin, hanging in a neat fold close to the head, and nearly long enough to reach the nose.

Neck—Moderately long, strong but not thick, and slightly arched; free from throatiness and fitting smoothly into the shoulders.

Body—Sufficiently long to permit a straight and free stride. Shoulder blades long, wide, sloping well back, fairly close together at the top, and joined in front to long upper arms angled to bring the elbows slightly rearward along the brisket. Chest deep, reaching approximately to the elbows; rather narrow in front. Ribs well sprung. Loins of moderate length, muscular and slightly arched. Top line of body from withers to tail slopes slightly downward without sharp drop at the croup. Hindquarters should be wide and powerful with broad, well-developed thighs.

Legs and Feet—All legs sturdy, with plenty of bone, and strong, nearly straight pastern. Feet rather small, very firm, toes arched and close. Forelegs straight and sinewy, the elbows moving freely. Hind legs long and muscular from hip to hock, short and nearly perpendicular from hock to ground; well angulated at stifle and hock joints, which, like the elbows, incline neither in nor out.

Tail—Strong at root, tapering to fine point, about long enough to reach the hock. Carriage straight or curving slightly upward, nearly level with the back.

Coat—Short and fine on head, forelegs, and tips of ears; on all other parts, of moderate length and flat. Feathering long and silky on ears; on back of forelegs and thighs long and fine, with a pleasing fringe of hair on belly and brisket extending onto the chest. Feet well feathered between the toes. Fringe on tail moderately long and tapering. All coat and feathering as straight and free as possible from curl or wave.

Color—Mahogany or rich chestnut red, with no trace of black. A small amount of white on chest, throat, or toes, or a narrow centered streak on skull, is not to be penalized.

Size—There is no disqualification as to size. The make and fit of all parts and their over-all balance in the animal are rated more important. Twenty-seven inches at the withers and a show weight of about 70 pounds is considered ideal for a dog; the bitch 25 inches, 60 pounds. Variance beyond an inch up or down to be discouraged.

Gait—At the trot the gait is big, very lively, graceful, and efficient. The head is held high. The hindquarters drive smoothly and with great power. The forelegs reach well ahead as if to pull in the ground, without giving the appearance of a hackney gait. The dog runs as he stands: straight. Seen from the front or rear, the forelegs, as well as the hind legs below the hock joint, move perpendicularly to the ground, with some tendency toward a single track as speed increases. But a crossing or weaving of the legs, front or back, is objectionable.

Balance—At his best, the lines of the Irish Setter so satisfy in over-all balance that artists have termed him the most beautiful of all dogs. The correct specimen always exhibits balance whether standing or in motion. Each part of the dog flows and fits smoothly into its neighboring parts without calling attention to itself.

Approved June 14, 1960

Spaniel, American Water

EXACTLY how, when, and where the American Water Spaniel originated is something of a mystery. Nevertheless, the virtues of the breed have long been appreciated by sportsmen in many parts of the United States. It is principally in the Middle West, however, that the present-day specimen evolved, since the dogs from that section had been known to breed true to type for countless generations. Color, coat and conformation combine to suggest the Irish Water Spaniel and the Curly-Coated Retriever, together with the latter's forebear the old English Water Spaniel, as progenitors, although this cannot be advanced categorically.

Prior to recognition as a breed by The American Kennel Club in 1940, the American Water Spaniel had been purely a working gun dog. He had never been introduced to the show ring since his admirers evidently feared that bench shows might damage his prowess as a hunter. But they were soon to learn that selective breeding along with bench show competition actually enhances the value of a dog no matter how well that dog may have been endowed by nature.

As a retriever the American Water Spaniel leaves little to be desired. He will watch the huntsman drop perhaps four or five birds, then work swiftly and merrily until every one is brought in. Rabbits, chickens, grouse, quail, pheasant, ducks—all he handles with unfailing dispatch and tender care. He swims "like a seal," hence few wounded water fowl escape him; his tail serves as a rudder to aid him, especially in turbulent water.

He is as well an all-around shooting dog possessed of an excellent nose; he works thicket, rough ground, or covert depending on body scent for location of game. His enthusiasm and thoroughness are an inspiration to the huntsman, while his desire to please makes him easily taught. He learns quickly to drop to shot and wing, although occasionally his eagerness may render him overanxious. He does not point game, but instead he springs it. In addition to all this, he is an efficient watchdog that fits agreeably into the family circle.

Official Standard for the American Water Spaniel

General Appearance—Medium in size, of sturdy typical spaniel character, curly coat, an active muscular dog, with emphasis placed on proper size and conformation, correct head properties, texture of coat and color. Of amicable disposition; demeanor indicates intelligence, strength and endurance.

Head—Moderate in length, skull rather broad and full, stop moderately defined, but not too pronounced. Forehead covered with short smooth hair and without tuft or topknot. Muzzle of medium length, square and with no inclination to snipiness, jaws strong and of good length, and neither undershot nor overshot, teeth straight and well shaped. Nose sufficiently wide and with well-developed nostrils to insure good scenting power. *Faults*—Very flat skull, narrow across the top, long, slender or snipy muzzle.

Eyes—Hazel, brown or of dark tone to harmonize with coat; set well apart. Expression alert, attractive, intelligent. *Fault*—Yellow eyes to disqualify.

Ears—Lobular, long and wide, not set too high on head, but slightly above the eyeline. Leather extending to end of nose and well covered with close curls.

Neck—Round and of medium length, strong and muscular, free of throatiness, set to carry head with dignity, but arch not accentuated.

Body Structure—Well developed, sturdily constructed but not too compactly coupled. General outline is a symmetrical relationship of parts. Shoulders sloping, clean and muscular. Strong loins, lightly arched, and well furnished, deep brisket but not excessively broad. Well-sprung ribs. Legs of medium length and well boned, but not so short as to handicap for field work.

Legs and Feet—Forelegs powerful and reasonably straight. Hind legs firm with suitably bent stifles and strong hocks well let down. Feet to harmonize with size of dog. Toes closely grouped and well padded. *Fault*—Cowhocks.

Tail—Moderate in length, curved in a slightly rocker shape, carried slightly below level of back; tapered and covered with hair to tip, action lively. *Faults*—Rat or shaved tail.

Coat—The coat should be closely curled or have marcel effect and should be of sufficient density to be of protection against weather, water or punishing cover, yet not coarse. Legs should have medium short, curly feather. *Faults*— Coat too straight, soft, fine or tightly kinked.

Color—Solid liver or dark chocolate, a little white on toes or chest permissible.

Height—15 to 18 inches at the shoulder.

Weight—Males, 28 to 45 pounds; females, 25 to 40 pounds.

DISQUALIFICATION

Yellow eyes.

Spaniel, Brittany

NAMED for the French province in which it originated, the Brittany is the only pointing spaniel officially recognized by the American Kennel Club. Although called a spaniel, its manner of working game is setterlike. In appearance it is smaller than the setters but leggier than most spaniels, with a short tail and a characteristic high ear set.

While it is generally conceded that the basic stock for all bird dogs is the same, most of the actual facts concerning the development and spread of the various breeds are lost in antiquity. Early written records are confusing. Dogs are referred to as being of *Bretagne* or *Brittania*, which may have referred to the British Isles rather than the French province as Brittany was called Armorique until the 5th century. Oppien, who lived about 150 A.D., wrote of the uncivilized people of Brittany (or Britain?) and their dogs, whose sensitiveness of scenting ability surpassed all others, a characteristic many present-day Brittanys retain.

It would seem probable that the dogs of Brittany and Wales had the same progenitors and developed along similar paths, quite possibly interbreeding. The two lands are geographically close and there was much commerce between them. One need only look at today's Welsh Springer and Brittany to recognize their similar physical characteristics.

The first accurate records to pinpoint the actual Brittany-type dog are the paintings and tapestries of the 17th century. The frequency with which this type appears suggests it was fairly common. Oudry (1686–1745) shows a liver and white dog pointing partridge and this same type of dog is common in the Flemish paintings of the school of Jan Steen. Other painters show this same type of dog, so it must have been common along the northern coast of France and in Holland, even stretching into Germany where it developed into the Wachtelhund, a modern breed much like the Brittany in appearance and ability.

Legend has it that the first tailless ancestor of the modern Brittany was bred about the mid-1800s at Pontou, a little town situated in the Valley of Douron, the result of a cross between a white-and-mahogany bitch, owned by an old hunter of the region, and a lemon-and-white dog brought to Brittany by an English sportsman for the woodcock shooting. Of two tailless specimens produced in this litter, only one was considered worth keeping. His work in the field has been described as wonderful and because of it he became a popular stud. All his litters contained puppies either without tails or with short stubs.

There is nothing written before 1850 that can be interpreted unequivocally as referring to the Brittany. In that year the Reverend Davies wrote of hunting in Carhaix with small bob-tailed dogs, not as smooth-coated as the Pointer, that worked well in the brush. They pointed, retrieved their game well and were particularly popular with poachers, as the nature of that profession required that the dogs be easy to handle. The description fits the Brittany to perfection.

It was speculated (and in at least one case confirmed) that matings of the native spaniels of Brittany were made around 1900 with English pointing dogs whose owners vacationed in France primarily for the woodcock shooting. These matings were believed to have been effective in intensifying the pointing qualities of the spaniel while the basic features of the dogs remained essentially Breton.

The Brittanys became a recognized breed when, in 1907, Boy, an orange-and-white, was registered as the first *l'epagneul Breton (queue courte naturelle)*, a nomenclature that was soon shortened to simply *l'epagneul Breton*. Prior to this date, Brittanys had competed in classes for miscellaneous French Spaniels.

The first standard was outlined in 1907. This early standard required that the tail always be short at birth and that, in order to discourage further cross-breeding, black-and-white dogs be disqualified. The requirement for the natural bob-tail was soon dropped.

The breed was first introduced into the United States in 1931 and officially recognized by the American Kennel Club in 1934. The first standard was a direct translation from the French and not particularly comprehensible. The first major accomplishment of the American Brittany Club, upon its formation in 1942, was to replace the original standard with the clear and concise one which, with only minor changes, is still in force today. This standard calls for basically the same dog as the French standard except for color. The French recognize a wider range of colors while the American Kennel Club standard allows only two colors—liver or orange in combination with white, either in clear or roan patterns. There is no preference between the liver and orange nor between the clear and roan factors.

The Brittany's steady gain in popularity in the United States has been due to its merits as a shooting dog. Its smaller size and natural proclivity for hunting close fill the need of the modern American bird hunter. Its superb nose and desire to please are two of its major assets. Its size makes it better adapted to city living than some of the larger bird dogs. Its close range makes it more adaptable to today's hunting areas, crisscrossed with numerous roads and fences.

Many American Brittany breeders have strived to maintain the dual concept, i.e. to breed a dog which is good looking as well as being a good hunter. In the first 30 years of competition in this country, over 150 dogs of the breed have gained the coveted title of "Dual Champion", a champion in both the field and show. The number of Brittany show champions placing in field trials is even larger.

The most popular formal competition has been held in field trials, sponsored by the parent club and its many chapters. Show competition has been, until recently, somewhat limited as most breeders and owners are primarily interested in the field. Prior to 1972 only two Brittanys had been awarded Best in Show. An upsurge of interest took place after that date.

Obedience competition has not attracted many participants, perhaps due to a feeling that too much obedience stifles a dog's initiative in the field. This has been disproved in several instances where dogs have won field trials plus obedience degrees.

A happy, well-adjusted Brittany is one that gets a chance to hunt. Few Brittanys have been raised strictly as house pets and never used for hunting. The Brittany's disposition sets it aside from most of the other pointing breeds. It is quite tractable and has the friendly disposition of the other spaniels. It may be expected to absorb training more easily than some of the other pointing breeds because of an inborn desire to please its master.

Official Standard for the
Brittany Spaniel

General Description—A compact, closely-knit dog of medium size, a leggy spaniel having the appearance, as well as the agility, of a great ground coverer. Strong, vigorous, energetic and quick of movement. Not too light in bone, yet never heavy-boned and cumbersome. Ruggedness, without clumsiness, is a characteristic of the breed. So leggy is he that his height at the withers is the same as the length of his body. He has no tail, or at most, not more than 4 inches.

Weight—Should weigh between 30 and 40 pounds.

Height—$17^1/_2$ to $20^1/_2$ inches—measured from the ground at the highest point of the shoulders. Any Brittany Spaniel measuring under $17^1/_2$ inches or over $20^1/_2$ inches shall be disqualified from bench-show competition.

Coat—Dense, flat or wavy, never curly. Texture neither wiry nor silky. The ears should carry little fringe. The front and hind legs should have some feathering but too little is definitely preferable to too much. Dogs with long or profuse feathering or furnishings shall be so severely penalized as to effectively eliminate them from competition.

Skin—Fine and fairly loose. (A loose skin rolls with briars and sticks, thus diminishing punctures or tearing. But a skin so loose as to form pouches is undesirable.)

Color—Orange and white or liver and white in either clear or roan patterns. Some ticking is desirable. The orange or liver is found in standard parti-color or piebald patterns. Washed out colors are not desirable. Black is a disqualification.

Skull—Medium length (approximately $4^3/_4$ inches). Rounded, very slightly wedge-shaped, but evenly made. Width, not quite as wide as the length (about $4^3/_8$ inches) and never so broad as to appear coarse, or so narrow as to appear racy. Well-defined, but gently sloping stop effect. Median line rather indistinct. The occipital crest only apparent to the touch. Lateral walls well rounded. The Brittany should never be "apple-headed" and he should never have an indented stop. (All measurements of skull are for a $19^1/_2$-inch dog.)

Muzzle—Medium length, about two thirds the length of the skull, measuring the muzzle from the tip to the stop, and the skull from the occipital crest to the stop between the eyes. Muzzle should taper gradually in both horizontal and vertical dimensions as it approaches the nostrils. Neither a Roman nose nor a concave curve (dish-face) is desirable. Never broad, heavy, or snipy.

Nose—Nostrils well open to permit deep breathing of air and adequate scenting while at top speed. Tight nostrils should be penalized. Never shiny. Color, fawn, tan, light shades of brown or deep pink. A black nose is a disqualification. A two-tone or butterfly nose should be penalized.

Eyes—Well set in head. Well protected from briars by a heavy, expressive eyebrow. A prominent, full or pop eye should be heavily penalized. It is a serious fault in a hunting dog that must face briars. Skull well chiseled under the eyes, so that the lower lid is not pulled back to form a pocket or haw for catching seeds, dirt and weed dust. Judges should check by forcing head down to see if lid falls away from the eye. Preference should be for darker-colored eyes, though lighter shades of amber should not be penalized. Light and mean-looking eyes to be heavily penalized.

Ears—Set high, above the level of the eyes. Short and leafy, rather than pendulous, reaching about half the length of the muzzle. Should lie flat and close to the head, with the tip rounded very slightly. Ears well covered with dense, but relatively short hair, and with little fringe.

Lips—Tight to the muzzle, with the upper lip overlapping the lower jaw only sufficiently to cover under lip. Lips dry so that feathers do not stick. Drooling to receive a heavy penalty. Flews to be penalized.

Teeth—Well-joined incisors. Posterior edge of upper incisors in contact with anterior edge of lower incisors, thus giving a true scissors bite. Overshot or undershot jaw to be penalized heavily.

Neck—Medium length. Not quite permitting the dog to place his nose on the ground without bending his legs. Free from throatiness, though not a serious fault unless accompanied by dewlaps. Strong, without giving the impression of being overmuscled. Well set into sloping shoulders. Never concave or ewe-necked.

Body Length—Approximately the same as the height when measured at the withers. Body length is measured from the point of the forechest to the rear of the haunches. A long body should be heavily penalized.

Withers—Shoulder blades should not protrude much. Not too widely set apart with perhaps two thumbs' width or less between the blades. At the withers, the Brittany is slightly higher than at the rump.

Shoulders—Sloping and muscular. Blade and upper arm should form nearly a 90-degree angle when measured from the posterior point of the blade at the withers to the junction of the blade and upper arm, and thence to the point of the elbow nearest the ribs. Straight shoulders do not permit sufficient reach.

Back—Short and straight. Slight slope from highest point of withers to the root of the tail. Never hollow, saddle, sway, or roach-backed. Slight drop from hips to root of tail. Distance from last rib to upper thigh short, about three to four finger widths.

Chest—Deep, reaching the level of the elbow. Neither so wide nor so rounded as to disturb the placement of the shoulder bones and elbows, which causes a paddling movement, and often causes soreness from elbow striking ribs. Ribs well sprung, but adequate heart room provided by depth as well as width. Narrow or slab-sided chests are a fault.

Flanks—Rounded. Fairly full. Not extremely tucked up, nor yet flabby and falling. Loins short and strong. Narrow and weak loins are a fault. In motion the loin should not sway sideways, giving a zigzag motion to the back, wasting energy.

Hindquarters—Broad, strong and muscular, with powerful thighs and well-bent stifles, giving a hip set well into the loin and the marked angulation necessary for a powerful drive when in motion. Fat and falling hindquarters are a fault.

Tail—Naturally tailless, or not over four inches long. (A tail substantially more than 4 inches in length shall disqualify.) Natural or docked. Set on high, actually an extension of the spine at about the same level.

Front Legs—Viewed from the front, perpendicular, but not set too wide as in the case of a dog loaded in shoulder. Elbows and feet turning neither in nor out. Viewed from the side, practically perpendicular to the pastern. Pastern slightly bent to give cushion to stride. Not so straight as in terriers. Falling pasterns, however, are a serious fault. Leg bones clean, graceful, but not too fine. An extremely heavy bone is as much a fault as spindly legs. One must look for substance and suppleness. Height to the elbows should approximately equal distance from elbow to withers.

Hind Legs—Stifles well bent. The stifle generally is the term used for knee joint. If the angle made by the upper and lower leg bones is too straight, the dog quite generally lacks drive, since his hind legs cannot drive as far forward at each stride as is desirable. However, the stifle should not be bent as to throw the hock joint far out behind the dog. Since factors not easily seen by the eye may give the dog his proper drive, a Brittany should not be condemned for straight stifle until the judge has checked the dog in motion from the side. When at a trot, the Brittany's hind foot should step into or beyond the print left by the front foot. The stifle joint should not turn out making a cowhock. The cowhock moves the foot out to the side, thus driving out of line, and losing reach at each stride. Thighs well feathered, but not profusely, halfway to the hock. Hocks, that is, the back pasterns, should be moderately short, pointing neither in nor out; perpendicular when viewed from the side. They should be firm when shaken by the judge.

Feet—Should be strong, proportionately smaller than other spaniels, with close-fitting, well-arched toes and thick pads. The Brittany is not "up on his toes." Toes not heavily feathered. Flat feet, splayed feet, paper feet, etc., are to be heavily penalized. An ideal foot is halfway between the hare- and cat-foot.

A Guide to the Judge—The points below indicate only relative values. To be also taken into consideration are type, gait, soundness, spirit, optimum height, body length and general proportions.

SCALE OF POINTS

Head	25	Running gear	40
Body	35	TOTAL	100

DISQUALIFICATIONS

Any Brittany Spaniel measuring under 17½ inches or over 20½ inches.
Black in the coat, or a black nose.
A tail substantially more than 4 inches in length.

Approved June 14, 1977

Spaniel, Clumber

BECAUSE in type the Clumber Spaniel differs so widely from other members of the great spaniel group, his origin probably will always remain in doubt, as is the case for that matter with many another breed. About all we can do is to ponder the statements of many authorities and then, with the conformation and detail of the breed in mind, resolve the whole into a reasonable supposition, which is that the long, low body resulted from Basset Hound crosses, and the heavy head with noticeable haw from an infusion of the early Alpine Spaniel.

Even within the same litters, the old land spaniels were called by various names—"cockers," "springers," "cock-flushers," and so on, but we do not find the name "Clumber" ascribed at that time. This is not to imply, however, that the Clumber was a later development; indeed, he is believed to be one of the earliest, developed for special uses. The name doubtless arose from Clumber Park, seat of the Duke of Newcastle in Nottingham, to whom the French Duc de Noailles gave several of the dogs which he himself had been breeding carefully for generations.

The year 1859 saw the first class for Clumbers in England and from then on they enjoyed considerable popularity in that country. Due to an abundance of game, there was then no need for a bustling, fast-moving spaniel, consequently the dog was better adapted to foreign shooting conditions than to our own. Nevertheless, he soon made friends in the United States where the breed has been registered since 1883.

He is a dignified, rather slow worker, but a sure finder and a splendid retriever when trained. His most outstanding characteristic, as far as appearances go, is his attractive lemon-and-white coloring.

Official Standard for the
Clumber Spaniel

General Appearance and Size—General appearance, a long, low heavy-looking dog, of a very thoughtful expression, betokening great intelligence. Should have the appearance of great power. Sedate in all movements, but not clumsy. Weight of dogs averaging between 55 and 65 pounds; bitches from 35 to 50 pounds.

Head—Head large and massive in all its dimensions; round above eyes, flat on top, with a furrow running from between the eyes upon the center. A marked stop and large occipital protuberance. Jaw long, broad and deep. Lips of upper jaw overhung. Muzzle not square, but at the same time powerful-looking. Nostrils large, open and flesh-colored, sometimes cherry-colored. *Eyes*—Eyes large, soft, deep-set and showing haw. Hazel in color, not too pale, with dignified and intelligent expression. *Ears*—Ears long and broad at the top, turned over on the front edge; vine-shaped: close to the head; set on low and feathered only on the front edge, and there but slightly. Hair short and silky, without the slightest approach to wave or curl.

Neck and Shoulders—Neck long, thick and powerful, free from dewlap, with a large ruff. Shoulders immensely strong and muscular, giving a heavy appearance in front.

Body—Long, low and well ribbed up. The chest is wide and deep, the back long, broad, and level, with very slight arch over the loin.

Legs and Feet—Forelegs short, straight, and very heavy in bone; elbows close. Hind legs only slightly less heavily boned than the forelegs. They are moderately angulated, with hocks well let down. Quarters well developed and muscular. No feather above the hocks, but thick hair on the back of the legs just above the feet. Feet large, compact, and well filled with hair between the toes.

Coat and Feathers—Coat silky and straight, not too long, extremely dense; feather long and abundant.

Color and Markings—Color, lemon and white, and orange and white. Fewer markings on body the better. Perfection of markings, solid lemon or orange ears, evenly marked head and eyes, muzzle and legs ticked.

Stern—Stern set on a level and carried low.

SCALE OF POINTS

General appearance and size	10	Body and quarters	20
Head	15	Legs and feet	10
Eyes	5	Coat and feather	10
Ears	10	Color and marking	5
Neck and shoulders	15	TOTAL	100

Approved February 6, 1960

Spaniel, Cocker

THE SPANIEL family is a large one, of considerable antiquity. As far back as 1368 we find mention of the *Spanyell*, which came to be divided into two groups, the land spaniel and the water spaniel. A further division separated the land spaniels on a basis of size, when the "cockers" and the very small or toy spaniels were separated from spaniels of larger dimensions. Then, as the cockers and the toys were used for markedly different purposes, these two were once more divided. The toys eventually became the English Toy Spaniels which were maintained principally as pets or comforters, while the Cockers retained their early classification as sporting dogs. That is why the Cocker is called the smallest member of the sporting-dog family.

As a valued helpmeet to the huntsman, this dog was known in his early days by various names, among them "cocker," "cocking spaniel," and finally Cocker Spaniel, the name deriving, according to some authorities, from especial proficiency on woodcock. Not until 1883 were classes provided for him at English bench shows; and not until 1892 was he given breed status in England's Kennel Club stud book. In this country, the Cocker has been exhibited since the early 1880s. Field trials for the breed were started in the United States by the Cocker Spaniel Field Trial Club in 1924. As developed here, the

110

Cocker has evolved somewhat different in type, size, and coloring from the breed now recognized as the English Cocker Spaniel.

The Cocker Spaniel's inherent desire to hunt renders him a capable gun dog when judiciously trained. The usual method of hunting is to let him quarter the ground ahead of the gun, covering all territory within gun range. This he should do at a fast, snappy pace. Upon flushing the game he should stop or preferably drop to a sitting position so as not to interfere with the shot, after which he should retrieve on command only. He should, of course, be so trained that he will be under control at all times. He is likewise valuable for occasional water retrieving and as a rule takes to water readily.

As pet and companion his popularity has been exceptional; he is a great lover of home and family, ordinarily trustworthy and adaptable. Variation in color may have had something to do with the great interest in the breed among which are the solid colors, consisting of black, red, shades of cream or buff and liver, as well as the parti-colors of black and white, black and tan, and combinations of black, tan, and white known as tri-colors. There are, in addition, a few liver-and-whites.

Official Standard for the Cocker Spaniel

General Appearance—The Cocker Spaniel is the smallest member of the Sporting Group. He has a sturdy, compact body and a cleanly chiseled and refined head, with the overall dog in complete balance and of ideal size. He stands well up at the shoulder on straight forelegs with a topline sloping slightly toward strong, muscular quarters. He is a dog capable of considerable speed, combined with great endurance. Above all he must be free and merry, sound, well balanced throughout, and in action show a keen inclination to work; equable in temperament with no suggestion of timidity.

Head—To attain a well-proportioned head, which must be in balance with the rest of the dog, it embodies the following:

Skull—Rounded but not exaggerated with no tendency toward flatness; the eyebrows are clearly defined with a pronounced stop. The bony structure beneath the eyes is well chiseled with no prominence in the cheeks.

Muzzle—Broad and deep, with square, even jaws. The upper lip is full and of sufficient depth to cover the lower jaw. To be in correct balance, the distance from the stop to the tip of the nose is one half the distance from the stop up over the crown to the base of the skull.

Teeth—Strong and sound, not too small, and meet in a scissors bite.

Nose—Of sufficient size to balance the muzzle and foreface, with well-developed nostrils typical of a sporting dog. It is black in color in the blacks and black and tans. In other colors it may be brown, liver or black, the darker the better. The color of the nose harmonizes with the color of the eye rim.

Eyes—Eyeballs are round and full and look directly forward. The shape of the eye rims gives a slightly almond-shaped appearance; the eye is not weak or goggled. The color of the iris is dark brown and in general the darker the better. The expression is intelligent, alert, soft and appealing.

Ears—Lobular, long, of fine leather, well feathered, and placed no higher than a line to the lower part of the eye.

Neck and Shoulders—The neck is sufficiently long to allow the nose to reach the ground easily, muscular and free from pendulous "throatiness". It rises strongly from the shoulders and arches slightly as it tapers to join the head. The shoulders are well laid back forming an angle with the upper arm of approximately 90 degrees which permits the dog to move his forelegs in an easy manner with considerable forward reach. Shoulders are clean-cut and sloping without protrusion and so set that the upper points of the withers are at an angle which permits a wide spring of rib.

Body—The body is short, compact and firmly knit together, giving an impression of strength. The distance from the highest point of the shoulder blades to the ground is fifteen (15%) per cent or approximately two inches more than the length from this point to the set-on of the tail. Back is strong and sloping evenly and slightly downward from the shoulders to the set-on of the docked tail. Hips are wide and quarters well rounded and muscular. The chest is deep, its lowest point no higher than the elbows, its front sufficiently wide for adequate heart and lung space, yet not so wide as to interfere with the straightforward movement of the forelegs. Ribs are deep and well sprung. The Cocker Spaniel never appears long and low.

Tail—The docked tail is set on and carried on a line with the topline of the back, or slightly higher; never straight up like a terrier and never so low as to indicate timidity. When the dog is in motion the tail action is merry.

Legs and Feet—Forelegs are parallel, straight, strongly boned and muscular and set close to the body well under the scapulae. When viewed from the side with the forelegs vertical, the elbow is directly below the highest point of the shoulder blade. The pasterns are short and strong. The hind legs are strongly boned and muscled with good angulation at the stifle and powerful, clearly defined thighs. The stifle joint is strong and there is no slippage of it in motion or when standing. The hocks are strong, well let down, and when viewed from behind, the hind legs are parallel when in motion and at rest.

Feet—Compact, large, round and firm with horny pads; they turn neither in nor out. Dewclaws on hind legs and forelegs may be removed.

Coat—On the head, short and fine; on the body, medium length, with enough undercoating to give protection. The ears, chest, abdomen and legs are well feathered, but not so excessively as to hide the Cocker Spaniel's true lines and movement or affect his appearance and function as a sporting dog. The *texture* is most important. The coat is silky, flat or slightly wavy, and of a texture which permits easy care. Excessive or curly or cottony textured coat is to be penalized.

Color and Markings—*Black Variety* is jet black; shadings of brown or liver in the sheen of the coat is not desirable. A small amount of white on the chest and throat is to be penalized, and white in any other location shall disqualify.

Any Solid Color Other Than Black shall be a uniform shade. Lighter coloring of the feathering is permissible. A small amount of white on the chest and throat is to be penalized, and white in any other location shall disqualify.

Black and Tans, shown under the Variety of Any Solid Color Other than Black, have definite tan markings on a jet black body. The tan markings are distinct and plainly visible and the color of the tan may be from the lightest cream to the darkest red color. The amount of tan markings is restricted to ten (10%) per cent or less of the color of the specimen; tan markings in excess of ten (10%) per cent shall disqualify. Tan markings which are not readily visible in the ring or the absence of tan markings in any of the specified locations shall disqualify. The markings shall be located as follows:

(1) A clear spot over each eye.
(2) On the sides of the muzzle and on the cheeks.
(3) On the undersides of the ears.
(4) On all feet and legs.
(5) Under the tail.
(6) On the chest, optional, presence or absence not penalized.

Tan on the muzzle which extends upward, over and joins, shall be penalized. A small amount of white on the chest and throat is to be penalized, and white in any other location shall disqualify.

Parti-Color Variety—Two or more definite colors appearing in clearly defined markings, distinctly distributed over the body, are essential. Primary color which is ninety (90%) per cent or more shall disqualify; secondary color or colors which are limited solely to one location shall disqualify. Roans are classified as Parti-colors and may be of any of the usual roaning patterns. Tricolors are any of the above colors combined with tan markings. It is preferable that the tan markings be located in the same pattern as for Black and Tans.

Movement—The Cocker Spaniel, though the smallest of the sporting dogs, possesses a typical sporting dog gait. Prerequisite to good movement is balance between the front and rear assemblies. He drives with his strong, powerful rear quarters and is properly constructed in the shoulders and forelegs so that he can reach forward without constriction in a full stride to counterbalance the driving force from the rear. Above all, his gait is co-ordinated, smooth and effortless. The dog must cover ground with his action and excessive animation should never be mistaken for proper gait.

Height—The ideal height at the withers for an adult dog is 15 inches and for an adult bitch 14 inches. Height may vary one-half inch above or below this ideal. A dog whose height exceeds 15½ inches or a bitch whose height exceeds 14½ inches shall be disqualified. An adult dog whose height is less than 14½ inches or an adult bitch whose height is less than 13½ inches shall be penalized.

Note: Height is determined by a line perpendicular to the ground from the top of the shoulder blades, the dog standing naturally with its forelegs and the lower hind legs parallel to the line of measurement.

DISQUALIFICATIONS

Color and Markings—

Blacks—White markings except on chest and throat.

Solid Colors Other Than Black—White markings except on chest and throat. Black and Tans—Tan markings in excess of ten (10%) per cent; tan markings not readily visible in the ring, or the absence of tan markings in any of the specified locations; white markings except on chest and throat.

Parti-Colors—Ninety (90%) per cent or more of primary color; secondary color or colors limited solely to one location.

Height—Males over 15½ inches; females over 14½ inches.

Approved December 12, 1972

Spaniel, English Cocker

ONE OF the oldest types of land spaniel known, the Cocker Spaniel descended from the original spaniels of Spain as one of a family destined to become highly diversified in size, type, coloring, and hunting ability.

Prior to the seventeenth century all members of the group were designated merely as spaniels, whether they were large or small, long-bodied or short, fast or slow on their feet. Gradually the marked difference in size began to impress those who used the dogs for hunting, with the result that the larger dogs were soon springing game and the smaller ones hunting woodcock. The names springer spaniel and cocker, or woodcock spaniel naturally followed, and in 1892 the Kennel Club (England) finally recognized them as separate breeds. This Cocker Spaniel was the English Cocker Spaniel.

It should be remembered that the Springers and Cockers above described, both before and after the date of their official separation in England, appeared in the same litters. Size alone was the dividing line between them. They enjoyed the same heritage, the same colorings, the same hunting skill and much the same general type. Cocker and Springer developed side by side. In fact, the Springer inheritance, naturally incorporated in the Cocker, was a fortunate directive for the success of the English Cocker, for it enabled him to become one of the finest of the smaller hunting dogs.

Exhaustive research disclosed that during the nineteenth century there were two other lines of "cocker" development. One involved the dogs known as "Field or Cocker Spaniels," which eventually branched out into Sussex, Field, and Cocker Spaniels, the latter weighing less than twenty-five pounds and being usually black in color. The other involved the spaniels of the House of Marlborough, of which there were two types—a small, round-headed, short-nosed red-and-white, and a slightly larger dog with shorter ears and longer foreface. The Marlborough "cockers" at long last became the English Toy Spaniels, but before they emerged as a distinct breed, they fused with the smaller cockers of partial Field Spaniel derivation. From these two lines combined came a spaniel approximating the size and type fancied by American importers of that period.

The English Cocker Spaniel Club of America was formed in 1935 to promote the interest of the English Cocker, which had already been recognized as a variety of Cocker Spaniel but not as a breed in its own right. The club's initial specialty show was held the same year on the estate of Mr. E. S. Willing near Bryn Mawr, Pennsylvania, while on May 12, 1936 the standard then operative in England was adopted.

The immediate aim of the club was to discourage the interbreeding of the English and American varieties which English Cocker fanciers considered detrimental to the type they sponsored. Separate classes had been provided at the shows for the English variety; nevertheless, English and American interbred Cockers for some time continued to compete side by side with pure English and pure American specimens. Many an American Cocker, in fact, was entered in the show ring as English on a basis of larger size alone. The resultant confusion militated against the best interests of both varieties, but nothing could be done because no one knew which dogs, genetically, were pure English, which were American, and which a combination of the two.

Under the direction of Mrs. Geraldine R. Dodge, then president of the club, an extensive pedigree search was made of the Cockers of England, Canada, and the United States back to the beginning of official Cocker history abroad in 1892, in order to separate out the pure English lines of descent entirely devoid of American Cocker admixture. When, finally in 1941, this information was obtained, the English Cocker Spaniel Club was in a position to advise authoritatively on the problems of selection and breeding.

Meantime, in 1940 the Canadian Kennel Club recognized the English Cocker Spaniel as a separate breed, as did The American Kennel Club in September, 1946. Not until January, 1947, however, did breed registrations appear in the *Stud Book* under their own heading, for so much had to be done in the interim to comply with the provisions laid down for the official certification of pedigrees.

Official Standard for the
English Cocker Spaniel

General Appearance—The English Cocker Spaniel is an attractive, active, merry sporting dog; with short body and strong limbs, standing well up at the withers. His movements are alive with energy; his gait powerful and frictionless. He is alert at all times, and the carriage of head and incessant action of his tail while at work give the impression that here is a dog that is not only bred for hunting, but really enjoys it. He is well balanced, strongly built, full of quality and is capable of top speed combined with great stamina. His head imparts an individual stamp peculiar to him alone and has that brainy appearance expressive of the highest intelligence; and is in perfect proportion to his body. His muzzle is a most distinctive feature, being of correct conformation and in proportion to his skull.

Character—The character of the English Cocker is of extreme importance. His love and faithfulness to his master and household, his alertness and courage are characteristic. He is noted for his intelligence and merry disposition; not quarrelsome; and is a responsive and willing worker both in the field and as a companion.

Head—The skull and forehead should be well developed with no suggestion of coarseness, arched and slightly flattened on top when viewed both from the stop to the end of the skull as well as from ear to ear, and cleanly chiseled under the eyes. The proportion of the head desirable is approximately one half for the muzzle and one half for the skull. The muzzle should be square with a definite stop where it blends into the skull and in proportion with the width of the skull. As the English Cocker is primarily a sporting dog, the muzzle and jaws must be of sufficient strength and size to carry game; and the length of the muzzle should provide room for the development of the olfactory nerve to insure good scenting qualities, which require that the nose be wide and well developed. Nostrils black in color except in reds, livers, parti-colors and roans of the lighter shades, where brown is permissible, but black preferred. Lips should be square, full and free from flews. Teeth should be even and set squarely. *Faults*—Muzzle too short or snipy. Jaw overshot or undershot. Lips snipy or pendulous. Skull too flat or too rounded, cheeky or coarse. Stop insufficient or exaggerated.

Eyes—The eyes should be of medium size, full and slightly oval shaped; set squarely in skull and wide apart. Eyes must be dark brown except in livers and light parti-colors where hazel is permissible, but the darker the better. The general expression should be intelligent, alert, bright and merry. *Faults*—Light, round or protruding eyes. Conspicuous haw.

Ears—Lobular; set low and close to the head; leather fine and extending at least to the nose, well covered with long, silky, straight or slightly wavy hair. *Faults*—Set or carried too high; too wide at the top; insufficient feathering; positive curls or ringlets.

Neck—Long, clean and muscular; arched towards the head; set cleanly into sloping shoulders. *Faults*—Short; thick; with dewlap or excessive throatiness.

Body—Close coupled, compact and firmly knit, giving the impression of great strength without heaviness. Depth of brisket should reach to the elbow, sloping gradually upward to the loin. Ribs should spring gradually to middle of body, tapering to back ribs which should be of good depth and extend well back. *Faults*—Too long and lacking depth; insufficient spring of rib; barrel rib.

Shoulders and Chest—Shoulders sloping and fine; chest deep and well developed but not too wide and round to interfere with the free action of the forelegs. *Faults*—Straight or loaded shoulders.

Back and Loin—Back short and strong. Length of back from withers to tail-set should approximate height from ground to withers. Height of the dog at the withers should be greater than the height at the hip joint, providing a gradual slope between these points. Loin short and powerful, slightly arched. *Faults*—Too low at withers; long, sway-back or roach back; flat or narrow loin; exaggerated tuck-up.

Forelegs—Straight and strong with bone nearly equal in size from elbow to heel; elbows set close to the body with free action from shoulders; pasterns short, straight, and strong. *Faults*—Shoulders loose; elbows turned in or out; legs bowed or set too close or too wide apart; knees knuckled over; light bone.

Feet—Size in proportion to the legs; firm, round and catlike with thick pads and strong toes. *Faults*—Too large, too small; spreading or splayed.

Hindquarters—The hips should be rounded; thighs broad; well developed and muscular, giving abundance of propelling power. Stifles strong and well bent. Hock to pad moderately short, strong and well let down. *Faults*—Excessive angulation; lightness of bone; stifle too short; hocks too long or turned in or out.

Tail—Set on to conform with the topline of the back. Merry in action. *Faults*—Set too low; habitually carried too high; too short or too long.

Color—Various. In self colors a white shirt frill is undesirable. In particolors, the coloring must be broken on the body and be evenly distributed. No large portion of any one color should exist. White should be shown on the saddle. A dog of any solid color with white feet and chest is not a parti-color. In roans it is desirable that the white hair should be distributed over the body, the more evenly the better. Roans come in various colors: blue, liver, red, orange and lemon. In black and tans the coat should be black; tan spots over the eyes, tan on the sides of the muzzle, on the throat and chest, on forelegs from the knees to the toes and on the hind legs on the inside of the legs, also on the stifle and extending from the hock to the toes. *Faults*—White feet are undesirable in any specimen of self color.

Coat—On head, short and fine; on body, flat or slightly wavy and silky in texture. Should be of medium length with enough undercoating to give protection. The English Cocker should be well feathered but not so profusely as to hide the true lines or interfere with his field work. *Faults*—Lack of coat; too soft, curly or wiry. Excessive trimming to change the natural appearance and coat should be discouraged.

Height—Ideal heights at withers: Males, 16 to 17 inches; females, 15 to 16 inches. Deviations to be severely penalized but not disqualified.

Weight—The most desirable weights: Males, 28 pounds to 34 pounds; females, 26 pounds to 32 pounds. Proper physical conformation and balance should be considered more important than weight alone.

Approved September 13, 1955

Spaniel, English Springer

THE NAME "springing spaniel" included in one classification the ancestral stock from which many of our present-day land spaniels emanated. In 1902 the Kennel Club of England recognized the English Springer Spaniel as a distinct breed.

Though several individuals in America had these spaniels for their shooting, it was not until 1924, when the English Springer Spaniel Field Trial Association was formed, that they became better known. Field trials were inaugurated, and three years later (1927) the English Springer Spaniel Field Trial Association became the parent club of the breed.

This association has aimed to further the English Springer Spaniel both on the bench and in the field. A Standard was approved when the association was formed and later, in 1932, a committee representing the entire breed drew up a new and better Standard, which was adopted by the English Springer Spaniel Field Trial Association and approved by The American Kennel Club. This Standard was made as nearly as possible to foster the natural ability of the Springer Spaniel, a hunting dog that, with training, could do the work required of him. The association has also conducted field trials every year, and it has endeavored to demonstrate to the public just how good the dogs are as shooting dogs. As competition becomes greater, they must of necessity be able to cover their ground rapidly and, if well trained, to obey signals or orders given them.

Unquestionably the present Standard has helped to make the Springer more uniform as a breed, and as a result the dogs as individuals have become much more uniform at bench shows and in field trials. They are admittedly great sporting dogs, hence should not be allowed to lose any of their standard characteristics; that is, they must not become heavy-boned and stocky in type and thus risk any loss of usefulness in the field. Their one purpose is to hunt and find game.

Official Standard for the English Springer Spaniel

General Appearance and Type—The English Springer Spaniel is a medium-size sporting dog with a neat, compact body, and a docked tail. His coat is moderately long and glossy with feathering on his legs, ears, chest and brisket. His pendulous ears, soft gentle expression, sturdy build and friendly wagging tail proclaim him unmistakably a member of the ancient family of spaniels. He is above all a well proportioned dog, free from exaggeration, nicely balanced in every part. His carriage is proud and upstanding, body deep, legs strong and muscular with enough length to carry him with ease. His short level back, well developed thighs, good shoulders, excellent feet, suggest power, endurance, agility. Taken as a whole he looks the part of a dog that can go and keep going under difficult hunting conditions, and moreover he enjoys what he is doing. At his best he is endowed with style, symmetry, balance, enthusiasm and is every inch a sporting dog of distinct spaniel character, combining beauty and utility. *To be penalized:* Those lacking true English Springer type in conformation, expression, or behavior.

Temperament—The typical Springer is friendly, eager to please, quick to learn, willing to obey. In the show ring he should exhibit poise, attentiveness, tractability, and should permit himself to be examined by the judge without resentment or cringing. *To be penalized:* Excessive timidity, with due allowance for puppies and novice exhibits. But no dog to receive a ribbon if he behaves in vicious manner toward handler or judge. Aggressiveness toward other dogs in the ring not to be construed as viciousness.

Size and Proportion—The Springer is built to cover rough ground with agility and reasonable speed. He should be kept to medium size—neither too small nor too large and heavy to do the work for which he is intended. The ideal shoulder height for dogs is 20 inches; for bitches, 19 inches. Length of topline (the distance from top of the shoulders to the root of the tail) should be approximately equal to the dog's shoulder height—never longer than his height—and not appreciably less. The dog too long in body, especially when long in loin, tires easily and lacks the compact outline characteristic of the breed. Equally undesirable is the dog too short in body for the length of his legs, a condition that destroys his balance and restricts the gait.

Weight is dependent on the dog's other dimensions: a 20-inch dog, well proportioned, in good condition should weigh about 49-55 pounds. The resulting appearance is a well-knit, sturdy dog with good but not too heavy bone, in no way coarse or ponderous. *To be penalized:* Over-heavy specimens, cloddy in build. Leggy individuals, too tall for their length and substance. Oversize or undersize specimens (those more than one inch under or over the breed ideal).

Color—May be black or liver with white markings or predominantly white with black or liver markings; tricolor; black and white or liver and white with tan markings (usually found on eyebrows, cheeks, insides of ears and under tail); blue or liver roan. Any white portions of coat may be flecked with ticking. All preceding combinations of colors and markings to be equally acceptable. *To be penalized:* Off colors such as lemon, red or orange not to place.

Coat—On ears, chest, legs and belly the Springer is nicely furnished with a fringe of feathering of moderate length and heaviness. On head, front of forelegs, and below hocks on front of hindlegs the hair is short and fine. The body coat is flat or wavy, of medium length, sufficiently dense to be waterproof, weatherproof and thornproof. The texture fine, and the hair should have the clean, glossy, live appearance indicative of good health. It is legitimate to trim about head, feet, ears; to remove dead hair; to thin and shorten excess feathering particularly from the hocks to the feet and elsewhere as required to give a smart, clean appearance. *To be penalized:* Rough curly coat. Overtrimming, especially of the body coat. Any chopped, barbered or artifical effect. Excessive feathering that destroys the clean outline desirable in a sporting dog.

Head—The head is impressive without being heavy. Its beauty lies in a combination of strength and refinement. It is important that the size and proportion be in balance with the rest of the dog. Viewed in profile the head should appear approximately the same length as the neck and should blend with the body in substance. The skull (upper head) to be of medium length, fairly broad, flat on top, slightly rounded at the sides and back. The occiput bone inconspicuous, rounded rather than peaked or angular. The foreface (head in front of the eyes) approximately the same length as the skull, and in harmony as to width and general character. Looking down on the head the muzzle to appear to be about one half the width of the skull. As the skull rises from the foreface it makes a brow or "stop," divided by a groove or fluting between the eyes. This groove continues upward and gradually disappears as it reaches the middle of the forehead. The amount of "stop" can best be described as moderate. It must not be a pronounced feature; rather it is a subtle rise where the muzzle blends into the upper head, further emphasized by the groove and by the position and shape of the eyebrows which should be well-developed. The stop, eyebrow and the chiseling of the bony structure around the eye sockets contribute to the Springer's beautiful and characteristic expression.

Viewed in profile the topline of the skull and the muzzle lie in two approximately parallel planes. The nasal bone should be straight, with no inclination downward toward the tip of the nose which gives a downfaced look so undesirable in this breed. Neither should the nasal bone be concave resulting in a "dish-faced" profile; nor convex giving the dog a Roman nose. The jaws to be of sufficient length to allow the dog to carry game easily; fairly square, lean, strong, and even, (neither undershot nor overshot). The upper lip to come down full and rather square to cover the line of the lower jaw, but lips not to be pendulous nor exaggerated. The nostrils, well opened and broad, liver color or black depending on the color of the coat. Flesh-colored ("Dudley noses") or spotted ("butterfly noses") are undesirable. The cheeks to be flat, (not rounded, full or thick) with nice chiseling under the eyes. *To be penalized:* Oval, pointed or heavy skull. Cheeks prominently rounded, thick and protruding. Too much or too little stop. Over heavy muzzle. Muzzle too short, too thick, too narrow. Pendulous slobbery lips. Under- or over-shot jaws—a very serious fault, to be heavily penalized.

Teeth—The teeth should be strong, clean, not too small; and when the mouth is closed the teeth should meet in a close scissors bite (the lower incisors touching the inside of the upper incisors). *To be penalized:* Any deviation from above description. Irregularities due to faulty jaw formation to be severely penalized.

Eyes—More than any other feature the eyes contribute to the Springer's appeal. Color, placement, size influence expression and attractiveness. The eyes to be of medium size, neither small, round, full and prominent, nor bold and hard in expression. Set rather well apart and fairly deep in their sockets. The color of the iris to harmonize with the color of the coat, preferably a good dark hazel in the liver dogs and black or deep brown in the black and white specimens. The expression to be alert, kindly, trusting. The lids, tight with little or no haw showing. *To be penalized:* Eyes yellow or brassy in color or noticeably lighter than the coat. Sharp expression indicating unfriendly or suspicious nature. Loose droopy lids. Prominent haw (the third eyelid or membrane in the inside corner of the eye).

Ears—The correct ear-set is on a level with the line of the eye; on the side of the skull and not too far back. The flaps to be long and fairly wide, hanging close to the cheeks, with no tendency to stand up or out. The leather, thin, approximately long enough to reach the tip of the nose. *To be penalized:* Short round ears. Ears set too high or too low or too far back on the head.

Neck—The neck to be moderately long, muscular, slightly arched at the crest, gradually blending into sloping shoulders. Not noticeably upright, nor coming into the body at an abrupt angle. *To be penalized:* Short neck, often the sequence to steep shoulders. Concave neck, sometimes called ewe neck or upside down neck (the opposite of arched). Excessive throatiness.

Body—The body to be well coupled, strong, compact; the chest deep but not so wide or round as to interfere with the action of the front legs; the brisket sufficiently developed to reach to the level of the elbows. The ribs fairly long, springing gradually to the middle of the body then tapering as they approach the end of the ribbed section. The back (section between the withers and loin) to be straight and strong, with no tendency to dip or roach. The loins to be strong, short; a slight arch over loins and hip bones. Hips nicely rounded, blending smoothly into hind legs. The resulting topline slopes *very gently* from withers to tail—the line from withers to back descending without a sharp drop; the back practically level; arch over hips somewhat lower than the withers; croup sloping gently to base of tail; tail carried to follow the natural line of the body. The bottom line, starting on a level with the elbows, to continue backward with almost no up-curve until reaching the end of the ribbed section, then a more noticeable up-curve to the flank, but not enough to make the dog appear small waisted or "tucked up." *To be penalized:* Body too shallow, indicating lack of brisket. Ribs too flat sometimes due to immaturity. Ribs too round (barrel-shaped), hampering the gait. Swayback (dip in back), indicating weakness or lack of muscular development, particularly to be seen when dog is in action and viewed from the side. Roach back (too much arch over loin and extending forward into middle section). Croup falling away too sharply; or croup too high—unsightly faults, detrimental to outline and good movement. Topline sloping sharply, indicating steep withers (straight shoulder placement) and a too low tail-set.

Tail—The Springer's tail is an index both to his temperament and his conformation. Merry tail action is characteristic. The proper set is somewhat low following the natural line of the croup. The carriage should be nearly horizontal, slightly elevated when dog is excited. Carried straight up is untypical of the breed. The tail should not be docked too short and should be well fringed with wavy feather. It is legitimate to shape and shorten the feathering but enough should be left to blend with the dog's other furnishings. *To be penalized:* Tail habitually upright. Tail set too high or too low. Clamped down tail (indicating timidity or undependable temperament, even less to be desired than the tail carried too gaily).

Forequarters—Efficient movement in front calls for proper shoulders, the blades sloping back to form an angle with the upper arm of approximately 90 degrees which permits the dog to swing his forelegs forward in an easy manner. Shoulders (fairly close together at the tips) to lie flat and mold smoothly into the contour of the body. The forelegs to be straight with the same degree of size to the foot. The bone, strong, slightly flattened, not too heavy or round. The knee, straight, almost flat; the pasterns short, strong; elbows close to the body with free action from the shoulders. *To be penalized:* Shoulders set at a steep angle limiting the stride. Loaded shoulders (the blades standing out from the body by overdevelopment of the muscles). Loose elbows, crooked legs. Bone too light or too coarse and heavy. Weak pasterns that let down the feet at a pronounced angle.

Hindquarters—The Springer should be shown in hard muscular condition, well developed in hips and thighs and the whole rear assembly should suggest strength and driving power. The hip joints to be set rather wide apart and the hips nicely rounded. The thighs broad and muscular; the stifle joint strong and moderately bent. The hock joint somewhat rounded, not small and sharp in contour, and moderately angulated. Leg from hock joint to foot pad, short and strong with good bone structure. When viewed from the rear the hocks to be parallel whether the dog is standing or in motion. *To be penalized:* Too little or too much angulation. Narrow, undeveloped thighs. Hocks too short or too long (a proportion of ⅓ the distance from hip joint to foot is ideal). Flabby muscles. Weakness of joints.

Feet—The feet to be round, or slightly oval, compact, well arched, medium size with thick pads, well feathered between the toes. Excess hair to be removed to show the natural shape and size of the foot. *To be penalized:* Thin, open or splayed feet (flat with spreading toes). Hare foot (long, rather narrow foot).

Movement—In judging the Springer there should be emphasis on proper movement, which is the final test of a dog's conformation and soundness. Prerequisite to good movement is balance of the front and rear assemblies. The two must match in angulation and muscular development if the gait is to be smooth and effortless. Good shoulders laid back at an angle that permits a long stride are just as essential as the excellent rear quarters that provide the driving power. When viewed from the front, the dog's legs should appear to swing forward in a free and easy manner, with no tendency for the feet to cross over or interfere with each other. Viewed from the rear, the hocks should drive well under the body following on a line with the forelegs, neither too widely nor too closely spaced. As speed increases there is a natural tendency for the legs to converge toward the center line of gravity or a single line of travel. Seen from the side, the Springer should exhibit a good, long forward stride, without high-stepping or wasted motion. *To be penalized:* Short choppy stride, mincing steps with up and down movement, hopping. Moving with forefeet wide, giving roll or swing to body. Weaving or crossing of fore or hind feet. Cowhocks—hocks turning in toward each other.

In judging the English Springer Spaniel, the over-all picture is a primary consideration. It is urged that the judge look for type which includes general appearance, outline and temperament and also for soundness, especially as seen when the dog is in motion. Inasmuch as the dog with a smooth easy gait must be reasonably sound and well balanced he is to be highly regarded in the show ring; however, not to the extent of forgiving him for not looking like an English Springer Spaniel. A quite untypical dog, leggy, foreign in head and expression, may move well. But he should not be placed over a good all-round specimen that has a minor fault in movement. It should be remembered that the English Springer Spaniel is first and foremost a sporting dog of the spaniel family and he must look and behave and move in character.

Approved June 13, 1978

Spaniel, Field

THE FIELD SPANIEL, to probably greater extent than any variety
within the great spaniel group, has been taken over the hurdles of
man's fancy for exaggerations in type, and as a result the breed
suffered greatly. To Mr. Phineas Bullock of England can be given
credit for perpetuating a dog of tremendous body length and lowness to
the ground, together with phenomenal bone which culminated for a
time in a grotesque caricature of a spaniel.

Apparently the type was established by repeated crosses of the
"Welsh Cocker" with the Sussex Spaniel. Later, largely through the
efforts of Mr. Mortimer Smith, the breed was improved—it took on a
type which all who like sporting spaniels can really admire.

Considerable difficulty was encountered in establishing the modern
Field Spaniel in the United States due to the necessity for introducing
Springer and Cocker crosses in order to eliminate the exaggerations,
and this, of course, rendered many individuals ineligible for registration with The American Kennel Club. In fact, in the early 1880s
when the Cocker was introduced to America, and for many years
thereafter, the sole distinction between the Cockers and the Field
Spaniels for show purposes was one of size.

125

Usually black in color, the Field Spaniel became a useful and handsome breed, sound, straight in the forelegs, and with a height more nearly in balance to length. When built along these lines, he is a dog possessed of endurance, moderate speed and agility. He is level-headed and intelligent, and a dog of great perseverance.

Official Standard for the Field Spaniel

Head—Should be quite characteristic of this grand sporting dog, as that of the Bulldog, or the Bloodhound; its very stamp and countenance should at once convey the conviction of high breeding, character and nobility; skull well developed, with a distinctly elevated occipital tuberosity, which, above all, gives the character alluded to; not too wide across the muzzle, long and lean, never snipy or squarely cut, and in profile curving gradually from nose to throat; lean beneath the eyes—a thickness here gives coarseness to the whole head. The great length of muzzle gives surface for the free development of the olfactory nerve, and thus secures the highest possible scenting powers.

Nose—Well developed, with good open nostrils.

Eyes—Not too full, but not small, receding or overhung, color dark hazel or brown, or nearly black, according to the color of the dog. Grave in expression and showing no haw.

Ears—Moderately long and wide, sufficiently clad with nice setterlike feather and set low. They should fall in graceful folds, the lower parts curling inwards and backwards.

Neck—Long, strong and muscular, so as to enable the dog to retrieve his game without undue fatigue.

Body—Should be of moderate length, well ribbed up to a good strong loin, straight or slightly arched, never slack.

Shoulders and Chest—Former long, sloping and well set back, thus giving great activity and speed; latter deep and well developed, but not too round and wide.

Back and Loin—Very strong and muscular.

Hindquarters—Strong and muscular. The stifles should be moderately bent, and not twisted either in or out.

Stern—Well set on and carried low, if possible below the level of the back, in a straight line or with a slight downward inclination, never elevated above the back, and in action always kept low, nicely fringed with wavy feather of silky texture.

Forelegs—Should be of fairly good length, with straight, clean, flat bone, and nicely feathered. Immense bone is no longer desirable.

Feet—Not too small; round, with short soft hair between the toes; good, strong pads.

126

Coat—Flat or slightly waved, and never curled. Sufficiently dense to resist the weather, and not too short. Silky in texture, glossy and refined in nature, with neither duffleness on the one hand, nor curl or wiriness on the other. On the chest, under belly and behind the legs, there should be abundant feather, but never too much, especially below the hocks, and that of the right sort, *viz.* setterlike. The hindquarters should be similarly adorned.

Color—Black, liver, golden liver, mahogany red, or roan; or any one of these colors with tan over the eyes and on the cheeks, feet, and pasterns. Other colors, such as black and white, liver and white, red or orange and white, while not disqualifying, will be considered less desirable since the Field Spaniel should be clearly distinguished from the Springer Spaniel.

Height—About 18 inches to shoulder.

Weight—From about 35 pounds to 50 pounds.

General Appearance—That of a well-balanced, noble, upstanding sporting dog; built for activity and endurance. A grand combination of beauty and utility, and bespeaking of unusual docility and instinct.

SCALE OF POINTS

Head and jaw	15	Hind legs	10
Eyes	5	Feet	10
Ears	5	Stern	10
Neck	5	Coat and feather	10
Body	10	General appearance	10
Forelegs	10	TOTAL	100

Approved July 14, 1959

Spaniel, Irish Water

THAT THE IRISH WATER SPANIEL is a dog of very ancient lineage is supported by the research made by Alan J. Stern, and reported upon in four articles in *Pure-Bred Dogs-American Kennel Gazette,* January-April, 1965.

The articles noted that a Harvard archaeological expedition to Ireland in 1934–36, excavating a lake dwelling of Lagore near Dunshaughlin, unearthed among other dog remains an Irish Water Spaniel type skull—medium-sized, with clearly defined stop and a more pronounced dome—identified to dogs living in the seventh or eighth century, A.D. The same type of skull was found in the Lake Districts of Central Europe, dating from the later Stone and Bronze ages. Old Roman ruins bear carvings which most resemble the Irish Water Spaniel.

In the late 1100s, before the days of King McCarthy II, dogs found in southern Ireland below the River Shannon were called Shannon Spaniels, Irish Water Spaniels, Rat-Tail Spaniels or Whip-Tail Spaniels. Ireland's Sir Robert Cecil is recorded to have sent the King of France an Irish Water Spaniel in 1598. In 1607, Topsell in his *Historie of the four-footed Beastes* tells of the Water Spagnel with his long, rough, curled hair and a tail somewhat bare and naked. Captain Thomas Brown, in the mid-1700s, remarks on the long ears of the Irish Water Spaniel and the crisp, curly texture of the coat.

These evidences indicate that the dog known as the Southern Irish Water Spaniel was well established centuries before the legendary "Boatswain" (1834–1852), the famous sire of many outstanding gun and show dogs who is often credited as having been the first of the breed as it is known today. Boatswain (pedigree unknown) was bred by Justin McCarthy.

However disputable the breed's development before him, in Boatswain's wake a clear type was bred, exhibited and accepted by kennel club officialdom. In 1849 he sired "Jack", whose name appears in many early pedigrees. The first special class for Irish Water Spaniels was provided in 1859. In 1866, "Doctor" — a great-grandson of Boatswain — won first (Best of Breed) at Birmingham. An oil painting of "Rake", bred in 1864 of Boatswain's bloodlines, shows the contemporary Irish Water Spaniel.

In America, we note that there was an entry of 4 Irish Water Spaniels at the first Westminster Kennel Club show in 1877. One of these was listed as having been imported from Ireland in 1873.

The Irish Water Spaniel is often called the clown of the spaniel family, possibly due to the unique appearance of a characteristic topknot together with a peak of curly hair between the eyes. He is likewise the tallest of our spaniels. Ordinarily he is loyal to those he knows, but forbidding to strangers. He is a grand water dog, not only because he likes water, but because his coat is naturally water-shedding. For this reason he is used in some parts of the country as a duck retriever, although he is not quite as adaptable for upland work because his coat tends to catch on briars.

Official Standard for the
Irish Water Spaniel

Head—Skull rather large and high in dome with prominent occiput; muzzle square and rather long with deep mouth opening and lips fine in texture. Teeth strong and level. The nose should be large with open nostrils, and liver in color. The head should be cleanly chiseled, not cheeky, and should not present a short wedge-shaped appearance. Hair on face should be short and smooth.

Topknot—Topknot, a characteristic of the true breed, should consist of long loose curls growing down into a well-defined peak between the eyes and should not be in the form of a wig; *i.e.* growing straight across.

Eyes—Medium in size and set almost flush, without eyebrows. Color of eyes hazel, preferably of dark shade. Expression of the eyes should be keenly alert, intelligent, direct and quizzical.

Ears—Long, lobular, set low with leathers reaching to about the end of the nose when extended forward. The ears should be abundantly covered with curls becoming longer toward the tips and extending two or more inches below the ends of the leathers.

Neck—The neck should be long, arching, strong and muscular, smoothly set into sloping shoulders.

Shoulders and Chest—Shoulders should be sloping and clean; chest deep but not too wide between the legs. The entire front should give the impression of strength without heaviness.

Body, Ribs and Loins—Body should be of medium length, with ribs well sprung, pear-shaped at the brisket, and rounder toward the hind quarters. Ribs should be carried well back. Loins should be short, wide and muscular. The body should not present a tucked-up appearance.

Hindquarters—The hindquarters should be as high as or a trifle higher than the shoulders and should be very powerful and muscular with well-developed upper and second thighs. Hips should be wide; stifles should not be too straight; and hocks low-set and moderately bent. Tail should be set on low enough to give a rather rounded appearance to the hindquarters and should be carried nearly level with the back. Sound hindquarters are of great importance to provide swimming power and drive.

Forelegs and Feet—Forelegs medium in length, well boned, straight and muscular with elbows close set. Both fore and hind feet should be large, thick and somewhat spreading, well clothed with hair both over and between the toes, but free from superfluous feather.

Tail—The so-called "rat tail" is a striking characteristic of the breed. At the root it is thick and covered for 2 or 3 inches with short curls. It tapers to a fine point at the end, and from the root-curls is covered with short, smooth hair so as to look as if the tail had been clipped. The tail should not be long enough to reach the hock joint.

130

Coat—Proper coat is of vital importance. The neck, back and sides should be densely covered with tight crisp ringlets entirely free from wooliness. Underneath the ribs the hair should be longer. The hair on lower throat should be short. The forelegs should be covered all around with abundant hair falling in curls or waves, but shorter in front than behind. The hind legs should also be abundantly covered by hair falling in curls or waves, but the hair should be short on the front of the legs below the hocks.

Color—Solid liver; white on chest objectionable.

Height and Weight—Dogs, 22 to 24 inches; bitches, 21 to 23 inches. Dogs, 55 to 65 pounds; bitches, 45 to 58 pounds.

General Appearance—That of a smart, upstanding, strongly built but not leggy dog, combining great intelligence and the rugged endurance with a bold, dashing eagerness of temperament.

Gait—Should be square, true, precise and not slurring.

SCALE OF POINTS

Head
Skull and topknot 6
Ears 4
Eyes 4
Muzzle and nose 6 20
Body
Neck 5
Chest, shoulders, back,
   loin and ribs 12 17
Driving Gear
Feet, hips, thighs, stifles
   and continuity of
   hindquarter muscles 14
Feet, legs, elbows and
   muscles of forequarters .. 9 23

Coat
Tightness, denseness
   of curl and general
   texture 16
Color 4 20
Tail
General appearance and
   "set on," length and
   carriage 5 5
General Conformation and Action
Symmetry, style, gait,
   weight and size 15 15

TOTAL 100

Approved June 11, 1940

Spaniel, Sussex

THE SUSSEX SPANIEL doubtless derives his name from Sussex, England, where the first and most important kennel of these dogs belonged to a Mr. Fuller—he it was who developed the rich golden liver color that has long distinguished the breed. Mr. Phineas Bullock, of Field Spaniel fame, also did notable work in furthering the best interests of the Sussex. Specimens of the breed competed in Britain as far back as the Crystal Palace show of 1862.

During his comparatively early days the Sussex was used for certain types of rough shooting in England, where an abundance of game, together with the custom of hunting on foot, rendered the dog satisfactory as a sporting companion. He has not been imported to any great extent to this country, however, probably due to the fact that he has not sufficient speed for the average sportsman, who faces conditions far different from those abroad.

Although he lacks the speed of the Springer and the Cocker, the Sussex has an extremely good nose, and he is a determined hunter, valuable for all forms of upland shooting. He is inclined to give tongue on scent. In disposition he is an entirely normal dog, not too difficult to train, and when properly taught becomes an excellent retriever.

Official Standard for the
Sussex Spaniel

Head—The skull should be moderately long and also wide, with an indention in the middle and a full stop, brows fairly heavy; occiput full, but not pointed, the whole giving an appearance of heaviness without dullness. *Eyes*—Hazel color, fairly large, soft and languishing, not showing the haw overmuch. *Nose* —The muzzle should be about three inches long, square, and the lips somewhat pendulous. The nostrils well developed and liver color. *Ears*— Thick, fairly large and lobe shaped; set moderately low, but relatively not so low as in the black Field Spaniel; carried close to the head and furnished with soft, wavy hair.

Neck—Is rather short, strong and slightly arched, but not carrying the head much above the level of the back. There should not be much throatiness about the skin, but well-marked frill in the coat.

Chest and Shoulders—The chest is round, especially behind the shoulders, deep and wide giving a good girth. The shoulders should be oblique.

Back and Back Rib—The back and loin is long and should be very muscular, both in width and depth; for this development the back ribs must be deep. The whole body is characterized as low, long and level.

Legs and Feet—The arms and thighs must be bony as well as muscular, knees and hocks large and strong; pasterns very short and bony, feet large and round, and with short hair between the toes. The legs should be very short and strong, with great bone, and may show a slight bend in the forearm, and be moderately well feathered. The hind legs should not appear to be shorter than the forelegs, nor be too much bent at the hocks. They should be well feathered above the hocks but should not have much hair below that point. The hind legs are short from the hock to the ground, and wide apart.

Tail—Should be docked from 5 to 7 inches, set low, and not carried above the level of the back, thickly covered with moderately long feather.

Coat—Body coat abundant, flat or slightly waved, with no tendency to curl, moderately well feathered on legs and stern, but clean below the hocks.

Color—Rich golden liver; this is a certain sign of the purity of the breed, dark liver or puce denoting unmistakably a recent cross with the black or other variety of Field Spaniel.

General Appearance—Rather massive and muscular, but with free movements and nice tail action, denoting a cheerful and tractable disposition.

Weight—From 35 pounds to 45 pounds.

POSITIVE POINTS

Head	10	Legs and feet	10
Eyes	5	Tail	5
Nose	5	Coat	5
Ears	10	Color	15
Neck	5	General appearance	15
Chest and shoulders	5		
Back and back ribs	10	TOTAL	100

NEGATIVE POINTS

Light eyes	5	Color, too light or too dark	15
Narrow head	10	Legginess or light of bone	5
Weak muzzle	10	Shortness of body or flat	
Curled ears or set on high	5	sided	5
Curled coat	15	General appearance—sour or	
Carriage of stern	5	crouching	10
Topknot	10		
White on chest	5	TOTAL	100

Approved July 14, 1959

Spaniel, Welsh Springer

THERE appears to be no authentic information as to the approximate date when the Welsh Springer Spaniel first appeared. However, if we examine old writings, old pictures, old prints, we find that when our ancestors took up shooting over dogs, they undoubtedly used a medium-sized spaniel resembling the Welsh Springer of today more than any other variety. These dogs were always red and white, the one and only color distinguishing the breed.

The Welsh Springer is found principally in Wales and the west of England, where he has been known for several hundred years. More recently he went into Scotland and England, while a large number have been exported from England to America, India, Australia, and Siam. The reason for the breed's distribution into such varied climates is an ability to withstand extremes of heat and cold. The Welshman's coat of course helps him, since it is naturally flat and even, with a soft undercoat which prevents injury from thorns and water.

He is, by the way, an excellent water dog; a keen, hard-working dog—no day is too long, no country too rough—and under all circumstances he is a faithful and willing worker for man. He has an excellent nose. He can be used on any kind of game; in fact, there is no better gun dog than the *well-trained* Welshman; as with other flushing spaniels, when not well-trained he may incline to become a lone hunter. However, he is not hard to train. Taken young—say at six months—and taught first obedience and retrieving, he rarely forgets his early lessons.

As a companion, the Welsh Springer is a true pal of handy size, larger and stronger than the Cocker, but smaller than the English Springer. He makes a good guard, too, yet is ordinarily gentle with children and other animals. He is easy to keep and characteristically vigorous. He can live in town and be happy, but to enjoy life at his best, he should work as a gun dog in the country.

Official Standard for the Welsh Springer Spaniel

The "Welsh Spaniel" or "Springer" is also known and referred to in Wales as a "Starter." He is of very ancient and pure origin, and is a distinct variety which has been bred and preserved purely for working purposes.

Head—*Skull*—Proportionate, of moderate length, slightly domed, clearly defined stop, well chiseled below the eyes. *Muzzle*—Medium length, straight, fairly square; the nostrils well developed and flesh colored or dark. *Jaw*—Strong, neither undershot nor overshot. *Eyes*—Hazel or dark, medium size, not prominent, nor sunken, nor showing haw. *Ears*—Set moderately low and hanging close to the cheeks, comparatively small and gradually narrowing towards the tip, covered with nice setterlike feathering. A short chubby head is objectionable.

Neck and Shoulders—*Neck*—Long and muscular, clean in throat, neatly set into long and sloping shoulders. *Forelegs*—Medium length, straight, well boned, moderately feathered.

Body—Not long; strong and muscular with deep brisket, well sprung ribs; length of body should be proportionate to length of leg, and very well balanced; with muscular loin slightly arched and well coupled up. *Quarters*—Strong and muscular, wide and fully developed with deep second thighs. *Hind Legs*—Hocks well let down; stifles moderately bent (neither twisted in nor out), moderately feathered. *Feet*—Round with thick pads. *Stern*—Well set on and low, never carried above the level of the back; lightly feathered and with lively action.

Coat—Straight or flat and thick, of a nice silky texture, never wiry nor wavy. A curly coat is most objectionable. *Color*—Dark rich red and white.

General Appearance—A symmetrical, compact, strong, merry, very active dog; not stilty, obviously built for endurance and activity.

Vizsla

THE ORIGIN of the Vizsla, or Hungarian Pointer, has been obscured by the centuries, but it is fair to assume that its ancestors were the hunters and companions of the Magyar hordes which swarmed over Central Europe more than 1000 years ago and settled in what is now Hungary. Primitive stone etchings of the tenth century show a Magyar huntsman with his falcon and a dog resembling the Vizsla. As far back as the fourteenth century, a manuscript of early Hungarian codes carried a chapter on falconry which was illustrated with a picture of a dog reasonably well identified as a Vizsla. Apparently the breed became a favorite of the early barons and war lords who, either deliberately or by accident, preserved its purity through the years.

The reason for the Vizsla's continued existence, even in that far time, lay in the fact that its innate hunting ability was fostered and developed by the terrain in which it grew, namely, the plains of Hungary.

Here was a section of that country almost entirely agricultural and pastoral; where grains were raised in great abundance; where the growing season was long, the summers hot, the winters tempered by the proximity of water. Here wheat and corn, rye and barley attracted the partridge and other game birds, while the Hungarian hare flourished and grew large. Amid such plenty, it was inevitable that a hunting dog suited to the climatic conditions, and the available game, would be developed. What the huntsman needed and what he eventually got was a dog swift of foot, and cautious so as not to alert quarry in an almost totally uncovered territory; a close-working dog of superior nose and generally high-class hunting ability; a dog, in short, that would combine the duties of the specialists as both pointer and retriever.

The great wars interfered markedly with what otherwise would have been normal breed progress. The close of World War I found the Vizsla all but extinct, and preserved in only a small way by a few of its firmest friends. The years between the two wars were difficult ones, but those who loved the breed refused to let it die out. Hungarians who fled before the Russian occupation in 1945 took their dogs with them into Austria. One of these, it should be noted, Panni IV, has progeny in the United States. Other refugees fled to Italy and Germany, and with them went their favorite Vizslas. Likewise there are some in Czechoslovakia, Turkey, and southern Russia. And now, here in the United States, where the breed was admitted to AKC registry in 1960, Vizslas are giving a good account of themselves as robust and enduring hunters as well as gentle and friendly companions.

Essentially Pointer in type, the Vizsla is a distinguished looking dog of aristocratic bearing, his short coat an attractive rusty-gold. He is powerfully built, but lithe and well balanced, with a light-footed, smooth, and graceful gait. He is a multiple-purpose dog for work on upland game, on rabbits, and for waterfowl retrieving.

Official Standard for the Vizsla

General Appearance—That of a medium-sized hunting dog of quite distinguished appearance. Robust but rather lightly built, his short coat is an attractive rusty-gold, and his tail is docked. He is a dog of power and drive in the field, and a tractable and affectionate companion in the home.

Head—Lean but muscular. The skull is moderately wide between the ears, with a median line down the forehead. Stop moderate. The muzzle is a trifle longer than the skull and, although tapering, is well squared at its end. Jaws strong, with well-developed white teeth meeting in a scissors bite. The lips cover the jaws completely but they are neither loose nor pendulous. Nostrils slightly open, the nose brown. A black or slate-gray nose is objectionable.

Ears—Thin, silky, and proportionately long, with rounded-leather ends; set fairly low and hanging close to the cheeks.

Eyes—Medium in size and depth of setting, their surrounding tissue covering the whites, and the iris or color portion harmonizing with the shade of the coat. A yellow eye is objectionable.

Neck—Strong, smooth, and muscular; moderately long, arched, and devoid of dewlap. It broadens nicely into shoulders which are well laid back.

Body—Strong and well proportioned. The back is short, the withers high, and the topline slightly rounded over the loin to the set-on of the tail. Chest moderately broad and deep, and reaching down to the elbows. Ribs well sprung, and underline exhibiting a slight tuck-up beneath the loin.

Legs and Feet—Forelegs straight, strong, and muscular, with elbows close. The hind legs have well-developed thighs, with moderate angulation at stifles and hocks. Too much angulation at the hocks is as faulty as too little. The hocks, which are well let down, are equidistant from each other from the hock joint to the ground. Cowhocks are faulty. Feet are cat-like, round and compact, with toes close. Nails are brown and short; pads thick and tough. Dewclaws, if any, to be removed. Hare feet are objectionable.

Tail—Set just below the level of the back, thicker at the root, and docked one third off.

Coat—Short, smooth, dense, and close-lying, without woolly undercoat.

Color—Solid. Rusty gold or rather dark sandy yellow in different shades, with darker shades preferred. Dark brown and pale yellow are undesirable. Small white spots on chest or feet are not faulted.

Temperament—That of the natural hunter endowed with a good nose and above-average ability to take training. Lively, gentle-mannered, and demonstratively affectionate. Fearless, and with well-developed protective instinct.

Gait—Far-reaching, light-footed, graceful, smooth.

Size—Males, 22 to 24 inches; females, 21 to 23 inches at the highest point of the shoulders. Any dog measuring over or under these limits shall be considered faulty, the seriousness of the fault depending on the extent of the deviation. Any dog that measures more than 2 inches over or under these limits shall be disqualified.

DISQUALIFICATION

Deviation in height of more than 2 inches from standard either way.

Approved December 10, 1963

Weimaraner
(Vy-mah-rah-ner)

As HISTORY is reckoned, the Weimaraner is a young dog, dating back only to the early nineteenth century. The Bloodhound is believed to be among its ancestors, if not in direct line of descent, then certainly in a collateral way. In their breed investigations, historians stopped when they got as far back as the Red Schweisshund, but it is difficult to imagine that any of the several varieties of Schweisshund did not trace to the Bloodhound, which was well established in Europe at the time of the Crusades. Indeed, the red-tan Schweisshund found in the vicinity of Hanover is described as having "many of the characteristics of the Bloodhound." It was, however, a breed measuring about twenty-one inches at the shoulder, compared with the Bloodhound's maximum of twenty-seven inches and the Weimaraner's top of twenty-seven inches.

The Weimaraner that we know today is the product of selective breeding; of judicious crosses followed by generations of line breeding to fix type and quality. It came from the same general stock which has produced a number of Germany's hunting breeds, one of its cousins being the breed now seen here—the German Shorthaired Pointer. In fact, in its early days, the Weimaraner was known simply as the

Weimar Pointer. Since then height and weight have both been increased, but the distinctive coat color, described as silver grizzle or mouse gray, was approximately the same.

Throughout its early career the Weimaraner was sponsored by the sportsmen nobles in the court of Weimar. Long accustomed to many types of hunting, these men determined to meld into one breed all the qualities they had found worthwhile in their forays against the then abundant game of Germany. In short, the dog had to have good scenting ability, speed, courage, and intelligence.

Formerly the Weimaraner had been a big-game dog used on such quarry as wolves, wild cats, deer, mountain lion, bear, etc. By the time big game in Germany became a rarity, the breed was supported by a club originally started by a few of the men who had drawn up the dog's specifications. They were amateur sportsmen who desired to breed for sport rather than for profit. Accordingly, it was not easy to purchase a Weimaraner in Germany and practically impossible in any foreign country. One had to become a member of the club before purchasing, while gaining admittance to the club meant that the applicant's previous record of sportsmanship must assure proper maintenance of the club's breeding rules. One of these rules demanded that litters resulting from matings deemed unsuitable by a breed survey were not given place in the stud book; another, that specimens, even from approved litters, which did not measure up physically and temperamentally were to be destroyed. Hence there was no chance of a boom in the breed.

America came to know the Weimaraner back in 1929 when an American sportsman and dog breeder, Howard Knight, was made a member of Germany's Weimaraner Club. Permitted to bring back two specimens, he helped found the club in this country and served as its first president. The club has made every effort to carry out the same principles that mapped the career of the breed in its native land.

It should be mentioned in passing that with the demise of big game hunting in Germany, the Weimaraner was trained as a bird dog used on various types of game in upland shooting and as a water retriever noted for its soft mouth. However, both in Germany and in America, the dog has been used more as a personal hunting companion than as a field-trial competitor.

Obedience trials incited the first interest in the breed over here, even before recognition had been granted in 1943 by The American Kennel Club—that was in 1941 when a bitch qualified for her C.D. in three straight shows. Later, another specimen went through all the degrees except the tracking test before reaching his tenth month, while a comparatively young puppy, too, annexed his C.D. Curiously enough, the Weimaraner has seen more actual competition of various kinds in America than it did in all its decades in Germany.

As for temperament, this dog is not happy when relegated to the kennel. He is accustomed to being a member of the family and he accepts the responsibilities which that entails.

Official Standard for the Weimaraner

General Appearance—A medium-sized gray dog, with fine aristocratic features. He should present a picture of grace, speed, stamina, alertness and balance. Above all, the dog's conformation must indicate the ability to work with great speed and endurance in the field.

Height—Height at the withers: dogs, 25 to 27 inches; bitches, 23 to 25 inches. One inch over or under the specified height of each sex is allowable but should be penalized. Dogs measuring less than 24 inches or more than 28 inches and bitches measuring less than 22 inches or more than 26 inches shall be disqualified.

Head—Moderately long and aristocratic, with moderate stop and slight median line extending back over the forehead. Rather prominent occipital bone and trumpets well set back, beginning at the back of the eye sockets. Measurement from tip of nose to stop equal that from stop to occipital bone. The flews should be straight, delicate at the nostrils. Skin drawn tightly. Neck clean-cut and moderately long. Expression kind, keen and intelligent. *Ears*—Long and lobular, slightly folded and set high. The ear when drawn snugly alongside the jaw should end approximately 2 inches from the point of the nose. *Eyes*—In shades of light amber, gray or blue-gray, set well enough apart to indicate good disposition and intelligence. When dilated under excitement the eyes may appear almost black. *Teeth*—Well set, strong and even; well-developed and proportionate to jaw with correct scissors bite, the upper teeth protruding slightly over the lower teeth but not more than $1/16$ of an inch. Complete dentition is greatly to be desired. *Nose*—Gray. *Lips and Gums*—Pinkish flesh shades.

Body—The back should be moderate in length, set in a straight line, strong, and should slope slightly from the withers. The chest should be well developed and deep with shoulders well laid back. Ribs well sprung and long. Abdomen firmly held; moderately tucked-up flank. The brisket should extend to the elbow.

Coat and Color—Short, smooth and sleek, solid color, in shades of mouse-gray to silver-gray, usually blending to lighter shades on the head and ears. A small white marking on the chest is permitted, but should be penalized on any other portion of the body. White spots resulting from injury should not be penalized. A distinctly long coat is a disqualification. A distinctly blue or black coat is a disqualification.

Forelegs—Straight and strong, with the measurement from the elbow to the ground approximately equaling the distance from the elbow to the top of the withers.

Hindquarters—Well-angulated stifles and straight hocks. Musculation well developed.

Feet—Firm and compact, webbed, toes well arched, pads closed and thick, nails short and gray or amber in color. *Dewclaws*—Should be removed.

Tail—Docked. At maturity it should measure approximately 6 inches with a tendency to be light rather than heavy and should be carried in a manner expressing confidence and sound temperament. A non-docked tail shall be penalized.

Gait—The gait should be effortless and should indicate smooth co-ordination. When seen from the rear, the hind feet should be parallel to the front feet. When viewed from the side, the topline should remain strong and level.

Temperament—The temperament should be friendly, fearless, alert and obedient.

FAULTS

Minor Faults—Tail too short or too long. Pink nose.

Major Faults—Doggy bitches. Bitchy dogs. Improper muscular condition. Badly affected teeth. More than four teeth missing. Back too long or too short. Faulty coat. Neck too short, thick or throaty. Low-set tail. Elbows in or out. Feet east and west. Poor gait. Poor feet. Cowhocks. Faulty backs, either roached or sway. Badly overshot, or undershot bite. Snipy muzzle. Short ears.

Very Serious Faults—White, other than a spot on the chest. Eyes other than gray, blue-gray or light amber. Black mottled mouth. Non-docked tail. Dogs exhibiting strong fear, shyness or extreme nervousness.

DISQUALIFICATIONS

Deviation in height of more than one inch from standard either way.
A distinctly long coat. A distinctly blue or black coat.

Approved December 14, 1971

Wirehaired Pointing Griffon

THE ORIGIN of the dog known in America as the Wirehaired Pointing Griffon came in the great period of biological awakening—the last quarter of the nineteenth century. Just a few years before, the Austrian abbot, Mendel, had published his experiments on inheritance, and the youth of Western Europe were anxious to try their skill at breeding.

Thus it was that E. K. Korthals, the son of a wealthy banker at Schooten, near Haarlem, in Holland, began to assemble the dogs from which he was to establish a new sporting breed. His first purchase was Mouche, described as a griffon bitch, gray and brown. She was bought in April of 1874, from M. G. Armand of Amsterdam, for sixty florins, or about twenty-five dollars, and was thought to be about seven years old. It is said of her that she was equally excellent in the woods or in the open. There is considerable doubt regarding her ancestry.

Korthals acquired five other dogs during the next three years—Janus, Hector, Satan, Junon, and Banco. Janus had woolly hair, Junon was short-haired, and the others were rough-coated. The first mating was between Mouche and Janus. The result was a puppy named

Huzaar, apparently the only one in the litter. The next mating was between Mouche and Hector, and this produced a bitch puppy, Madame Augot. The dog Satan was later bred to Madame Augot, resulting in Zampa.

The first breeding of importance was that of Huzaar, son of the rough-coated Mouche and the woolly-coated Janus, to the short-haired bitch, Junon. From this mating came Trouvee, a bitch with a harder coat than any of the others. Trouvee then was bred to Banco, and she whelped Moustache I, Querida, and Lina—three specimens from which, it is agreed, springs the best line in the breed.

Although the origin of the Wirehaired Pointing Griffon is undoubtedly Dutch, it is regarded principally as a French breed, for it was in France that the major portion of the development took place. This is due, in measure, to the fact that Korthals did not remain in Holland. It seemed that the elder Korthals, who was a successful breeder of cattle, could not understand his son's interest in "insignificant animals," as he termed dogs. They evidently had a number of heated discussions of the matter. Finally, rather than give up his interest in dogs, the son left the parental house.

Young Korthals went to Biebesheim, Germany, and soon resumed his breeding activities. Yet Korthals was a man of wide acquaintance among the sporting fraternity of Europe, and invariably he was present at any major field activity connected with dogs. Later he followed the bench shows closely, seeking to popularize the type of griffon—for there had been, for several centuries, dogs called griffons—that he had originated.

Perhaps, though, if any single factor can be credited with the spread of interest in the Wirehaired Pointing Griffon, or Korthals griffon as it is known in France, it was the traveling done by the young breeder during the years he spent as the advance agent of the French nobleman, the Duke of Penthievre. Korthals never forgot his hobby, and whenever he found congenial company he extolled the virtues of the new breed. Admitting that it was a deliberate, even slow, worker, his enthusiasm over its keen nose and its ability to point and retrieve game was infectious. Undoubtedly Korthals had sound reasons, even at that early date, for praising this breed, for it has since gained a wide reputation. It is particularly adapted for swampy country, where its harsh coat—unique in a sporting breed—is a great protection. It also is a strong swimmer and serves as an excellent water retriever. But adherents of the breed claim it can be trained and entered to any game.

When Korthals left Holland for Germany, he disposed of the greater portion of his dogs, and as a consequence found it necessary to replenish his stock to some extent. His first new brood matron in Germany was Donna, which he purchased from Heinrich Freytag in

145

February, 1879. She was of the boulet type, which meant that her coat was rather long. Donna was mated twice to Moustache I, and left two daughters, Augot, and Clairette, both of which showed the characteristics desired. Six years later, Korthals affected a lease for the bitch Vesta, and the breeding from her provided another successful line. Vesta had rough hair, and all her descendants were typical species that carried the right sort of coat.

While there remains some doubt as to the various crosses in the background of the dogs known as the "Korthals patriarchs," it has been suggested by a wide number of authorities that they carried setter, spaniel, and Otter Hound blood. It is known that certain specimens, described in *Livre des Origines du Griffon a poil dur*, as true griffons, trace their ancestry back to the ancient breed called the griffon hound; and it also is known that at least one cross with a Pointer —no doubt the German Shorthair—was effected.

The Wirehaired Pointing Griffon was exhibited in England shortly after it was developed, and it attracted considerable attention. Still, classes were not provided until some years later, the first record of these being at the Barn Elms show in the Jubilee year, 1888. The breed came across the Atlantic twelve years later. The first specimen registered by The American Kennel Club was Zolette, 6773, by Guerre, ex Tambour. The registration appears as a "Russian Setter (Griffon)" in Vol. 4, published in 1887. The sire, Guerre, was a grandson of Donna. So started the American fancy.

Official Standard for the
Wirehaired Pointing Griffon

The Wirehaired Griffon is a dog of medium size, fairly short-backed, rather a little low on his legs. He is strongly limbed, everything about him indicating strength and vigor. His coat is harsh like the bristles of a wild boar and his appearance, notwithstanding his short coat, is as unkempt as that of the long-haired Griffon, but on the other hand he has a very intelligent air.

Head—Long, furnished with a harsh coat, forming a mustache and eyebrows, skull long and narrow, muzzle square. *Eyes*—Large, open, full of expression, iris yellow or light brown. *Ears*—Of medium size, flat or sometimes slightly curled, set rather high, very lightly furnished with hair. *Nose*—Always brown.

Neck—Rather long, no dewlap.

Shoulders—Long, sloping.

Ribs—Slightly rounded.

Forelegs—Very straight, muscular, furnished with rather short wire hair.

Hind Legs—Furnished with rather short stiff hair, and thighs long and well developed.

Feet—Round, firm and well formed.

Tail—Carried straight or gaily, furnished with a hard coat without plume, generally cut to a third of its length.

Coat—Hard, dry, stiff, never curly, the undercoat downy.

Color—Steel gray with chestnut splashes, gray white with chestnut splashes, chestnut, dirty white mixed with chestnut, never black.

Height—$21\frac{1}{2}$ to $23\frac{1}{2}$ inches for males, and $19\frac{1}{2}$ to $21\frac{1}{2}$ inches for females.

GROUP II: HOUNDS

Afghan Hound

THE AFGHAN HOUND was discovered by the Western world in Afghanistan and surrounding regions during the 19th Century. The first specimens of the breed were brought to England in the latter part of that century, and the earliest known pictorial representation of an unmistakable, full-coated Afghan Hound is a drawing reproduced in some copies of a volume of letters written in India in 1809 and published in London in 1813.

Of the breed's origin and its history prior to then, little is known for certain. A vast amount of research, however, has turned up no basis for the once popular belief that the Afghan Hound existed in Egypt thousands of years ago nor for the theory that the breed evolved on the steppes of Asia and represents the original sight hound.

The basic structure of the dog beneath the coat is that of a relatively sturdy coursing hound of a type which might have evolved or been created from other canine types almost anytime, anywhere. The extremely fine, long-haired coat, however, is of a sort found among animals native to high altitudes, and the desired coat pattern of contrasting short hair on the foreface, back and dorsal surface of the tail may also be related to climate.

A problem in any study of the breed is that, like so many other breeds recognized today, the Afghan Hound, as we know and describe it in the standard, represents a blending of dogs of more than one type. Some sources in Afghanistan divide the breed as found there into a half-dozen or more varieties based on locality, color, etc. Although intermediate variations undoubtedly exist, it has been more common to speak in terms of two extremes in type—the hounds of the southern and western desert regions, which tend to be relatively rangy in build, light in color and sparse in outer coat; and the hounds of the northern mountain regions, which tend to be more compact in structure, darker in color and more heavily coated. These and other variations represent logical adaptations to the wide diversity of climate and terrain in the area of Afghanistan.

Among other things, this diversity in the breed—plus the diversity in the Afghan people, their culture and their country—helps explain the apparent conflicts among accounts of how the breed was utilized in its native land. Some tell of Afghan Hounds serving as guard dogs and herd dogs—which are within the capabilities of the breed as we know it.

The major role of these dogs, however, was undoubtedly that of hunting. Indeed, the breed has commonly been sub-titled "The Royal Hunting Dog of Afghanistan", and it is a fact that at the palace in Kabul, the kings of Afghanistan have maintained a kennel of these hounds for many generations. Similar hounds were kept and hunted by the nobles, military officers and others who constituted the leisure class in settled, predominately agricultural regions, while among the pastoral nomads, who make up half of the country's population, possibly all of the men would engage in hunting with their variety of the breed.

The breed is primarily a coursing hound, pursuing its quarry by sight and followed by the huntsman on horseback. Because these dogs tended to outdistance the horses, a good Afghan Hound hunts "on its own", without direction by the huntsman, giving rise to the independence of thought and spirit still typical of the breed.

We are variously told of Afghan Hounds being hunted singly, in dog-and-bitch pairs, in packs, and in a combination with specially trained falcons. Undoubtedly the breed was hunted in all of these ways, but the method would vary according to locality and the nature of the quarry, so that not all Afghan Hounds did all things in all places.

The same principle would apply to the extremely wide variety of game on which they reportedly were used. The Afghan Hound could and quite certainly was employed to hunt whatever animals the locality provided and the huntsman wanted to hunt. In the truest coursing-hound sense, they ran down game such as mountain deer, plains antelopes and hares wherever they might be found. They could also be used to bring to bay such predators as wolves, jackals, wild dogs and snow leopards. They were also used, as a spaniel would be, to flush quail and partridge for the falcon or gun. And they are the equal to any terrier for dispatching marmots, greatly prized by the mountain people for their fur and flesh.

As coursing dogs, Afghan Hounds excel, not so much in straightaway speed—although they have considerable—as in the ability to traverse rough terrain swiftly and sure-footedly. This requires agility in leaping and quickness in turning, plus the stamina to maintain such a strenuous chase for as long as it may take to close on the quarry.

The first recorded appearance of the Afghan Hound in the West was in the latter part of the 19th Century, when British officers and others returning from the Indian-Afghanistan border wars brought dogs from that area back to England, some of which were exhibited at dog shows as "Afghan Hounds". These aroused some interest but no real enthusiasm until 1907, when Captain John Barff brought from Persia via India his dog "Zardin"—a typy, well-coated dog with a dark mask and a great deal of style. This, English dog fanciers decided, was what an Afghan Hound should be! There was some breeding of Afghan Hounds in Great Britain at this time, and some specimens from there or Afghanistan may have reached America prior to World War I.

During that war, however, the breed literally disappeared in the Western world, and the start of the Afghan Hounds we have today dates to 1920, when Major and Mrs. G. Bell Murray and Miss Jean C. Manson brought to Scotland a group of Afghan Hounds they had acquired or bred during an eight year stay in Baluchistan—then an independent state south of Afghanistan, and today a part of Pakistan. Most of these dogs were of the "desert" type—racy, fine headed and light in coat. Breeding from these imports, Miss Manson, the Major and others further developed the "Bell-Murray strain" throughout the '20s.

In 1925, Mrs. Mary Amps shipped to England the first of a group of Afghan Hounds from the kennel she had maintained in Kabul. These were mainly of the "mountain" type—sturdily built, relatively short-coupled and more or less full-coated. From these imports—the most successful of which as a show dog and sire was the English Champion "Sirdar of Ghazni"—Mrs. Amps and others developed what is called, from her kennel name, the "Ghazni strain".

During the '20s, a number of "Bell-Murray" Afghan Hounds were exported to the United States, and when the AKC Stud Book was opened to the breed, some of these were registered, beginning in October, 1926. From two of them came the first registered American-bred Afghan Hound in 1927.

The real start of the breed in this country, however, dates to the first "Ghazni" imports in 1931, when Zeppo Marx and his wife brought from England a bitch, Asra of Ghazni (by Sirdar of Ghazni x Shireen of Ghazni) and a dog, Westmill Omar (Danenda of Ghazni x Surkh of Ghazni). Asra and Omar were later acquired by Q. A. Shaw McKean's "Prides Hill" kennels in Massachusetts. Mr. McKean soon added a young English champion, Badshah of Ainsdart, sired by Sirdar of Ghazni out of Ku Mari of Kaf, a bitch of pure "Bell-Murray" breeding. These three—Asra, Omar and Badshah—formed the cornerstone of the breed in America.

Most of the American breeders of the 1930s came into Afghan Hounds with a background of success in other breeds. As a rule their kennels were founded on Prides Hill stock bred to one or more of the dozens of imports then coming from Great Britain, and the several from India and Afghanistan.

By the late '30s, the breed was off and running in the United States, with annual AKC registrations rising steadily from 20-some per year to over 200 in 1941 and 1942. From the mid-40s to mid-50s registrations settled on a plateau that hovered around 400 to 500 a year, and then began an increasingly accelerated climb that carried to over the 10,000 mark by the mid-70s.

Remarkably, all of the tens of thousands of Afghan Hounds in America today come from a foundation stock of only a couple dozen presumably unrelated individuals. All of the "Bell-Murray" breedings were based on four dogs and four bitches and the "Ghazni" breedings on about nine individuals. In addition to these, there were, prior to 1940, five exports to America from Afghanistan and India which were registered and used for breeding, and a similar number of separate exports to Great Britain. Since World War II, there have been other exports from the East to Great Britain and the Continent, but because these are invariably "short-pedigreed", with their immediate offspring ineligible for AKC registration, the more recent imports remain, at best, a minor factor in American bloodlines.

Although the Afghan Hound was admitted to the AKC Stud Book in 1926, there was no parent club for the breed until a group of leading fanciers met at the 1937 Westminster Kennel Club show and organized what, after a reorganization the following year, became the Afghan Hound Club of America. In 1940 the club was admitted to AKC membership and held its first specialty show.

There being no parent club in 1926, the AKC had adopted a standard which was an expanded version of one then in use by an English breed club. This standard, in turn, was little more than a description of Zardin written some 20 years earlier. One of the first tasks assigned to AHCA, therefore, was the drafting of a "clarified standard". Only a tentative start had been made on the project, however, when the distractions of World War II halted it, and serious work began in early 1946. In England at the same time fanciers were drafting what was to be the first standard approved by The Kennel Club there. After two very different American drafts failed to win approval and an attempt to have a common standard with England was frustrated, a new and quite original standard was drafted and approved by the AHCA membership without dissent in 1948 and adopted by the AKC later that year.

Much of the Afghan Hound's popularity here has been generated by the breed's spectacular qualities as a show dog. In other forms of competition, the Afghan Hound also excels in lure racing and, although its tendency to think for itself makes for something less than perfect precision in executing set exercises and commands, the breed has also done well in obedience work.

Over and beyond their success in such fields, however, Afghan Hounds are prized and loved by their owners as companions and members of the family. With its highly individual personality and with its coat which requires regular care and grooming, it is not the breed for all would-be dog owners, but where the dog and owner combination is right, there is no animal which can equal the Afghan Hound as a pet.

Official Standard for the
Afghan Hound

General Appearance—The Afghan Hound is an aristocrat, his whole appearance one of dignity and aloofness with no trace of plainness or coarseness. He has a straight front, proudly carried head, eyes gazing into the distance as if in memory of ages past. The striking characteristics of the breed —exotic, or "Eastern," expression, long silky topknot, peculiar coat pattern, very prominent hipbones, large feet, and the impression of a somewhat exaggerated bend in the stifle due to profuse trouserings—stand out clearly, giving the Afghan Hound the appearance of what he is, a king of dogs, that has held true to tradition throughout the ages.

Head—The head is of good length, showing much refinement, the skull evenly balanced with the foreface. There is a slight prominence of the nasal bone structure causing a slightly Roman appearance, the center line running up over the foreface with little or no stop, falling away in front of the eyes so there is an absolutely clear outlook with no interference; the underjaw showing great strength, the jaws long and punishing; the mouth level, meaning that the teeth from the upper jaw and lower jaw match evenly, neither overshot nor undershot. This is a difficult mouth to breed. A scissors bite is even more punishing and can be more easily bred into a dog than a level mouth, and a dog having a scissors bite, where the lower teeth slip inside and rest against the teeth of the upper jaw, should not be penalized. The occipital bone is very prominent. The head is surmounted by a topknot of long silky hair. **Ears**—The ears are long, set approximately on level with outer corners of the eyes, the leather of the ear reaching nearly to the end of the dog's nose, and covered with long silky hair. **Eyes**—The eyes are almond-shaped (almost triangular), never full or bulgy, and are dark in color. **Nose**—Nose is of good size, black in color. **Faults**—Coarseness; snipiness; overshot or undershot; eyes round or bulgy or light in color; exaggerated Roman nose; head not surmounted with topknot.

Neck—The neck is of good length, strong and arched, running in a curve to the shoulders which are long and sloping and well laid back. **Faults**—Neck too short or too thick; a ewe neck; a goose neck; a neck lacking in substance.

Body—The back line appearing practically level from the shoulders to the loin. Strong and powerful loin and slightly arched, falling away toward the stern, with the hipbones very pronounced; well ribbed and tucked up in flanks. The height at the shoulders equals the distance from the chest to the buttocks; the brisket well let down, and of medium width. **Faults**—Roach back, sway-back, goose rump, slack loin; lack of prominence of hipbones; too much width of brisket, causing interference with elbows.

Tail—Tail set not too high on the body, having a ring, or a curve on the end; should never be curled over, or rest on the back, or be carried sideways; and should never be bushy.

Legs—Forelegs are straight and strong with great length between elbow and pastern; elbows well held in; forefeet large in both length and width; toes well arched; feet covered with long thick hair; fine in texture; pasterns long and straight; pads of feet unusually large and well down on the ground. Shoulders have plenty of angulation so that the legs are well set underneath the dog. Too much straightness of shoulder causes the dog to break down in the pasterns, and this is a serious fault. All four feet of the Afghan Hound are in line with the body, turning neither in nor out. The hind feet are broad and of good length; the toes arched, and covered with long thick hair; hindquarters powerful and well muscled, with great length between hip and hock; hocks are well let down; good angulation of both stifle and hock; slightly bowed from hock to crotch. **Faults**—Front or back feet thrown outward or inward; pads of feet not thick enough; or feet too small; or any other evidence of weakness in feet; weak or broken down pasterns; too straight in stifle; too long in hock.

Coat—Hindquarters, flanks, ribs, forequarters, and legs well covered with thick, silky hair, very fine in texture; ears and all four feet well feathered; from in front of the shoulders; and also backwards from the shoulders along the saddle from the flanks and the ribs upwards, the hair is short and close, forming a smooth back in mature dogs—this is a traditional characteristic of the Afghan Hound. The Afghan Hound should be shown in its natural state; the coat is not clipped or trimmed; the head is surmounted (in the full sense of the word) with a topknot of long, silky hair—that is also an outstanding characteristic of the Afghan Hound. Showing of short hair on cuffs on either front or back legs is permissible. **Fault**—Lack of shorthaired saddle in mature dogs.

Height—Dogs, 27 inches, plus or minus one inch; bitches, 25 inches, plus or minus one inch.

Weight—Dogs, about 60 pounds; bitches, about 50 pounds.

Color—All colors are permissible, but color or color combinations are pleasing; white markings, especially on the head, are undesirable.

Gait—When running free, the Afghan Hound moves at a gallop, showing great elasticity and spring in his smooth, powerful stride. When on a loose lead, the Afghan can trot at a fast pace; stepping along, he has the appearance of placing the hind feet directly in the foot prints of the front feet, both thrown straight ahead. Moving with head and tail high, the whole appearance of the Afghan Hound is one of great style and beauty.

Temperament—Aloof and dignified, yet gay. **Faults**—Sharpness or shyness.

Approved September 14, 1948

Basenji

(Buh-sen'jee)

THE BASENJI, popularly known as the "barkless dog," is one of the oldest breeds. The first specimens were brought from the source of the Nile as presents to the Pharaohs of ancient Egypt. Later, when the civilization of Egypt declined and fell, the Basenji lapsed into obscurity. However, it was still valued and preserved in its native land of Central Africa, where it was highly prized for its intelligence, speed, hunting power, and silence.

Centuries later an English explorer rediscovered the Basenji and a pair was brought to England in 1895. Unfortunately, these little dogs contracted distemper and shortly thereafter died. Aside from that abortive attempt to make the breed known, the "outside" world in general did not hear of the Basenji until 1937, when it was successfully introduced to England. At the same time, a pair was brought to America by Mrs. Byron Rogers of New York City. Unfortunately for America, this pair and a litter of puppies produced from mating these specimens contracted distemper. All died except the older male dog, Bois.

In 1941 a young female Basenji was brought from Africa to Boston; Alexander Phemister of Kingston, Mass., obtained her and shortly afterward also acquired the male dog, Bois, that Mrs. Rogers had brought into the country in 1937. The young female, Congo, and Bois, both African-bred, were mated, resulting in the first litter of Basenji puppies to be raised to maturity in America. Later other Basenjis were imported from the Canadian kennels of Dr. A. R. B. Richmond, and still others were brought over from England.

Dog lovers all over the country became interested in this breed—so old, yet so new to America—and later purchased young specimens as foundation breeding stock. In 1942 the Basenji Club of America was formed with officers from many parts of the country. Mr. Phemister became the president of the club; Miss Ethelwyn Harrison of Euclid, Ohio, and Dr. Eloise Gerry of Madison, Wis., vice-presidents; George Gilkey of Merrill, Wis., treasurer; and George E. Richards of Lynn, Mass., secretary. The Basenji Club of America accepted the Standard of the breed as drawn up by the Basenji Club of England and in 1943 The American Kennel Club accepted the Standard as official, and the breed for registration in the Stud Book. Within a few months there were fifty-nine Basenjis registered.

The Basenji is about the size and build of a Fox Terrier. The height for a male is seventeen inches at the shoulder, and sixteen inches for a female. The first impression one gets of a Basenji is that he is a proud little dog, and then one is impressed with his beauty, grace, and intelligence. In fact he has often been compared to a little deer.

The coat of the Basenji is one of his most beautiful features. Coming from a tropical climate, the texture is fine and silky and shines like burnished copper in the sun. In colder countries the coat tends to become more coarse, but it never loses its brilliant luster. The color is preferably chestnut red, and then come various shades of red and fawn. There are always white points, including the chest and feet, as well as the tip of the tail, which is tightly curled and lies over to one side of the back.

Several of the breed's most unusual characteristics are: 1) the lack of bark; 2) the broad forehead deeply furrowed with wrinkles; 3) the prick ears, standing straight up from their heads; 4) the dark, intelligent, far-seeing eyes.

The Basenji's intelligence and courage are proved by his hunting ability in his native habitat. The natives use him for pointing, retrieving, for driving game into nets, and hunting wounded quarry. He is also used for hunting the reed rats—vicious long-toothed creatures weighing from twelve to twenty pounds—and here the silence of the Basenji is a particularly great asset. These dogs have wonderful noses, scenting at eighty yards; so together with their keen scent and gift of silence, it is no wonder the natives value them so highly.

Those in America and England who have had the opportunity to know the little Basenji have found him to be all they could hope for in a dog. He is a fascinating, endearing fellow, full of play, yet gentle as a kitten. His fastidious, dainty habits, such as cleaning himself all over—as does a cat—make him an ideal dog for the immaculate housekeeper.

The Basenji's distinctive sound of happiness fairly thrills one, yet this sound he makes is hard to describe. It is somewhere between a chortle and a yodel. However, he is usually very happy when he makes it and one can't help but share the happiness with him.

The breed is tractable and anxious to please and, by nature, an obedient dog. Their sprightly alert manner in obedience show rings and their beautiful gait, resembling a thoroughbred horse's, causes much favorable comment.

The Basenji loves children and is tireless in his play. He has a fascinating manner of teasing one to play. One front paw is brought behind his ear, then down over his nose, and repeated and repeated until he has drawn the desired attention. However, when his owner is ready to call quits, the little Basenji is content to lie right at the feet of his master, just as did his forebears thousands of years ago in the courts of ancient Egypt.

Official Standard for the
Basenji

Characteristics—The Basenji should not bark, but is not mute. The wrinkled forehead and the swift, tireless running gait (resembling a racehorse trotting full out) are typical of the breed.

General Appearance—The Basenji is a small, lightly built, short backed dog, giving the impression of being high on the leg compared to its length. The wrinkled head must be proudly carried, and the whole demeanor should be one of poise and alertness.

Head and Skull—The skull is flat, well chiseled and of medium width, tapering towards the eyes. The foreface should taper from eye to muzzle and should be shorter than the skull. Muzzle, neither coarse, nor snipy but with rounded cushions. Wrinkles should appear upon the forehead, and be fine and profuse. Side wrinkles are desirable, but should never be exaggerated into dewlap. *Nose*—Black greatly desired. A pinkish tinge should not penalize an otherwise first class specimen, but it should be discouraged in breeding. *Eyes*—Dark hazel, almond shaped, obliquely set and far seeing. *Ears*—Small, pointed and erect, of fine texture, set well forward on top of head. *Mouth*—Teeth must be level with scissors bite.

Neck—Of good length, well crested and slightly full at base of throat. It should be well set into flat, laid back shoulders.

Forequarters—The chest should be deep and of medium width. The legs straight with clean fine bone, long forearm and well defined sinews. Pasterns should be of good length, straight and flexible.

Body—The body should be short and the back level. The ribs well sprung, with plenty of heart room, deep brisket, short coupled, and ending in a definite waist.

Hindquarters—Should be strong and muscular, with hocks well let down, turned neither in nor out, with long second thighs.

Feet—Small, narrow and compact, with well-arched toes.

Tail—Should be set on top and curled tightly over to either side.

Coat—Short and silky. Skin very pliant.

Color—Chestnut red (the deeper the better) or pure black, or black and tan, all with white feet, chest and tail tip. White legs, white blaze and white collar optional.

Weight—Bitches 22 pounds approximately. Dogs 24 pounds approximately.

Size—Bitches 16 inches and dogs 17 inches from the ground to the top of the shoulder. Bitches 16 inches and dogs 17 inches from the front of the chest to the farthest point of the hindquarters.

FAULTS

Coarse skull or muzzle. Domed or peaked skull. Dewlap. Round eyes. Low set ears. Overshot or undershot mouths. Wide chest. Wide behind. Heavy bone. Creams, shaded or off colors, other than those defined above, should be heavily penalized.

Approved June 8, 1954

Basset Hound

SINCE THE 1950s the Basset Hound has emerged from relative obscurity to become one of the most publicized and characterized breeds. Actually, the Basset Hound is an old, aristocratic breed. Originally of French lineage, it has flourished for centuries in Europe, primarily in France and Belgium, where it was used chiefly for the slow trailing of rabbits, hares, deer and any other game that can be trailed on foot or taken to ground.

The foremost use of the Basset Hound in the United States is for the hunting of rabbits. However, it is possible to train them for hunting other game such as raccoons and for the trailing, flushing and retrieving of wounded pheasants and other game birds. The Basset is a sturdy, accurate trailer; his tongue is loud and distinctive. The shortness of his legs and his tight, close coat make him particularly useful in dense cover. In trailing ability, the accuracy of his nose makes him second only to the Bloodhound. His slow going ways and appealing clownish appearance belie great intelligence.

Gentle in disposition, the Basset is agreeable to hunting in packs as well as singly. Medium as to size, loyal and devoted to his master and family, not requiring extensive coat care or trimming, considered an "easy keeper"—all makes the Basset an ideal family pet and house-dog.

In general appearance the Basset Hound is a long, low dog, heavier in bone (size considered) than any other breed. His most distinctive feature is his head, which is long and narrow in proportion to its length. His topskull is well domed with a noticeable occipital protuberance. The skin over the head is loose and falls readily into brow wrinkles when the head is lowered. The muzzle is deep with prominent flews and dewlap. The ears are long and lowset, for when the nose is put to ground the ears help cup the scent in trailing. The Basset's eyes are dark, soulful and full of expression. The whole of the head and expression should convey dignity and elegance.

The chest is well developed both in depth and thrust of sternum; the shoulder assembly well muscled and well angulated with elbows laid in tight to a well sprung rib cage. Correct feet are tight and thickly padded. The hindquarters are strong and well angulated to provide rear drive. In short, a Basset is no better than his running gear, for it is that which allows him to fulfil the purpose for which his breed was created—a scenting hound to cover the ground with strength and endurance. The whole dog is the sum of his parts, none of which should be overdone but rather should present a pleasing impression of balance and symmetry.

The first mention of the word "Basset" as applied to a breed of dog appears to have been in an early text on hunting written by Fouilloux in 1585. This book is illustrated with what is considered the first drawing of a Basset, a woodcut showing a sportsman going out in his *charette de chasse* accompanied by his "badger dogs" and Fouilloux gives advice on training the dogs for the purpose of badger hunting.

It is thought that the friars of the French Abbey of St. Hubert were instrumental in selective breeding from various other strains of French hounds to produce a lower set, hence slower moving dog which could be followed on foot. The word "Basset", derived from the French adjective *bas* means a "low thing" or "a dwarf." Since hunting was a classic sport in medieval France, it is not surprising that many of the thoroughly efficient small hounds found their way into the kennels of the aristocracy, only to be dispersed with the changing life style brought on by the Revolution. However, the breed was not lost and we find them mentioned again by M. Blaze is his sporting book *Le Chasseur,* written in 1850. About the same time, in his book *Chiens de Chasse,* M. Robert writes: "The Basset will hunt all animals, even boar and wolf, but he is especially excellent for the *chasse a tir* (shooting with the aid of hounds) of rabbits and hares."

By the mid-nineteenth century the two largest breeders of Bassets in France were producing dogs of slightly different type, especially in head and eye, the two types being identified by the names of their respective breeders. M. Lane's hounds were broader of skull, shorter of ear and with a rounder and more prominent eye. They were generally lemon and white in marking and had a tendency to knuckling.

Count Le Couteulx produced hounds that had more narrow heads, more doming in topskull, a softer, more sunken eye with prominent haw and a down-faced look that created more facial expression. The more glamorous tricolors of the Le Couteulx hounds made them preferred.

In 1886 Lord Galway imported a pair of French Bassets of the Le Couteulx type to England. The following year a mating of these two produced a litter of five pups, but as there was no public exposure of them, no interest in the breed was stirred. It was not until 1874 when Sir Everette Millais imported from France the hound, Model, that real activity with the breed began in England. For his support of the breed and continued drive on a breeding program within his own kennel as well as cooperation with breeding programs established by Lord Onslow and George Krehl, Sir Everette Millais has to be considered the "father of the breed" in England. He first exhibited a Basset at an English dog show in 1875, but it was not until he helped make up a large entry for the Wolverhampton show in 1880 that a great deal of public attention was drawn to the breed. A few years later further interest was created when Queen Alexandra kept Basset Hounds in the royal kennels.

In the United States it is thought that George Washington was the owner of Basset Hounds presented to him as a gift by Lafayette after the American Revolution. In 1883 and 1884 English importations were made by American fanciers of the breed. In 1884 Westminster Kennel Club held a class for the Basset Hound and the English import, Nemours, made his debut before the American public. After subsequent entries at Eastern shows, he completed his championship at Boston in 1886. The first Basset Hounds were registered with The American Kennel Club in 1885.

Gradually the breed began to find favor. By the mid-twenties Gerald Livingston was making multiple importations for his Kilsyth Kennels on Long Island. About the same time Erastus Tefft brought over to his kennels a number of English Bassets, drawing heavily from the Walhampton Pack. Carl Smith imported two French Bassets, one a French champion. Bassets were beginning to be represented regularly at larger shows.

Further attention was drawn to the breed when the February 27, 1928 issue of *Time* magazine carried the picture of a Basset puppy on the cover. The accompanying cover story was carried under the Sport Section heading and was a write-up of the 52nd annual dog show of the Westminster Kennel Club at Madison Square Garden as if it were attended and observed by the puppy, who was instead "at home" in his Kilsyth kennel.

In 1935 a national parent breed club was organized in the United

States, The Basset Hound Club of America. Annual Nationals of the club are held which bring together the various fields of activity for this capable breed: conformation, field trialing, pack hunting, obedience and tracking.

By the 1950s, the Basset Hound was synonymous with TV's "Cleo" for the general public, and in England the cartoonist Graham of the *Daily Mail* had made "Fred Basset" almost human by having him represent Everyman. But the dependable and multi-purpose qualities of the breed can never be completely obscured behind a droll facade.

Official Standard for the Basset Hound

General Appearance—The Basset Hound possesses in marked degree those characteristics which equip it admirably to follow a trail over and through difficult terrain. It is a short-legged dog, heavier in bone, size considered, than any other breed of dog, and while its movement is deliberate, it is in no sense clumsy. In temperament it is mild, never sharp or timid. It is capable of great endurance in the field and is extreme in its devotion.

Head—The head is large and well proportioned. Its length from occiput to muzzle is greater than the width at the brow. In over-all appearance the head is of medium width. *The skull* is well domed, showing a pronounced occipital protuberance. A broad flat skull is a fault. The length from nose to stop is approximately the length from stop to occiput. The sides are flat and free from cheek bumps. Viewed in profile the top lines of the muzzle and skull are straight and lie in parallel planes, with a moderately defined stop. The skin over the whole of the head is loose, falling in distinct wrinkles over the brow when the head is lowered. A dry head and tight skin are faults. *The muzzle* is deep, heavy, and free from snipiness. *The nose* is darkly pigmented, preferably black, with large wide-open nostrils. A deep liver-colored nose conforming to the coloring of the head is permissible but not desirable. *The teeth* are large, sound, and regular, meeting in either a scissors or an even bite. A bite either overshot or undershot is a serious fault. *The lips* are darkly pigmented and are pendulous, falling squarely in front and, toward the back, in loose hanging flews. *The dewlap* is very pronounced. *The neck* is powerful, of good length, and well arched. *The eyes* are soft, sad, and slightly sunken, showing a prominent haw, and in color are brown, dark brown preferred. A somewhat lighter-colored eye conforming to the general coloring of the dog is acceptable but not desirable. Very light or protruding eyes are faults. *The ears* are extremely long, low set, and when drawn forward, fold well over the end of the nose. They are velvety in texture, hanging in loose folds with the ends curling slightly inward. They are set far back on the head at the base of the skull and, in repose, appear to be set on the neck. A high set or flat ear is a serious fault.

Forequarters—*The chest* is deep and full with prominent sternum showing clearly in front of the legs. *The shoulders* and elbows are set close against the sides of the chest. The distance from the deepest point of the chest to the ground, while it must be adequate to allow free movement when working in the field, is not to be more than one-third the total height at the withers of an adult Basset. The shoulders are well laid back and powerful. Steepness in shoulder, fiddle fronts, and elbows that are out, are serious faults. *The forelegs* are short, powerful, heavy in bone, with wrinkled skin. Knuckling over of the front legs is a disqualification. *The paw* is massive, very heavy with tough heavy pads, well rounded and with both feet inclined equally a trifle outward, balancing the width of the shoulders. Feet down at the pastern are a serious fault. *The toes* are neither pinched together nor splayed, with the weight of the forepart of the body borne evenly on each. The dewclaws may be removed.

Body—The rib structure is long, smooth, and extends well back. The ribs are well sprung, allowing adequate room for heart and lungs. Flatsidedness and flanged ribs are faults. The topline is straight, level, and free from any tendency to sag or roach, which are faults.

Hindquarters—The hindquarters are very full and well rounded, and are approximately equal to the shoulders in width. They must not appear slack or light in relation to the over-all depth of the body. The dog stands firmly on its hind legs showing a well-let-down stifle with no tendency toward a crouching stance. Viewed from behind, the hind legs are parallel, with the hocks turning neither in nor out. Cowhocks or bowed legs are serious faults. The hind feet point straight ahead. Steep, poorly angulated hindquarters are a serious fault. The dewclaws, if any, may be removed.

Tail—The tail is not to be docked, and is set in continuation of the spine with but slight curvature, and carried gaily in hound fashion. The hair on the underside of the tail is coarse.

Size—The height should not exceed 14 inches. Height over 15 inches at the highest point of the shoulder blades is a disqualification.

Gait—The Basset Hound moves in a smooth, powerful, and effortless manner. Being a scenting dog with short legs, it holds its nose low to the ground. Its gait is absolutely true with perfect co-ordination between the front and hind legs, and it moves in a straight line with hind feet following in line with the front feet, the hocks well bent with no stiffness of action. The front legs do not paddle, weave, or overlap, and the elbows must lie close to the body. Going away, the hind legs are parallel.

Coat—The coat is hard, smooth, and short, with sufficient density to be of use in all weather. The skin is loose and elastic. A distinctly long coat is a disqualification.

Color—Any recognized hound color is acceptable and the distribution of color and markings is of no importance.

DISQUALIFICATIONS

Height of more than 15 inches at the highest point of the shoulder blades.
Knuckled over front legs.
Distinctly long coat.

Approved January 14, 1964

Beagle

THE ACTUAL ORIGIN of the Beagle is lost in the mists of ancient days and no research, it seems, can ever bring its true history to light. Several well-known beaglers have written their opinions on the origin of the breed, and the following remarks are by Captain Otho Paget of Melton Mowbray, England, who was, perhaps, the dean of all Beaglers.

According to Xenophon there were hounds that hunted by scent in his day and the Romans acquired many of the sports of ancient Greece. There were, however, in England, packs of hounds before the time of the Romans and it is on record that Pwyll, Prince of Wales, a contemporary of King Arthur, had a special breed of white hounds of great excellence. Wales, to this day is still celebrated for its hounds, generally of a light color. Admirers of shooting dogs, setters, spaniels and other kinds, have asserted that these animals were used in building up the hound. By exercise of a little thought it will seem that this must be wrong and that in fact it is the other way about. The hound was the original progenitor of all sporting dogs, and the two distinct breeds would be the "Gaze" or "Greyhound" that hunted by sight alone, and the hound, probably the Bloodhound, that relied entirely on its nose. By the time of good Queen Bess, nearly every country gentleman in England kept a pack of hounds of some sort and hunted the animal of his choice. The fox was not at that time an honored beast of the chase. Hounds in those days seem to have been divided into two classes, the large and the small. The large sort were called "Buck Hounds" and hunted the deer, and the smaller variety were called "Beagles" from the French "Begle" and were hunted on hare.

Coming down to the middle of the eighteenth century, we find fox hunting becoming popular with the younger generations, who wanted something quicker and more exhilarating than watching hounds puzzling out the intricate windings of a hare. The Foxhound was undoubtedly evolved from a mixture of buck hound and Beagle. By this time the vagaries of breeders had produced two distinct types of hare-hunting hounds, one of which was called the Southern hound and the other the North Country Beagle. The former was slow and ponderous, with long ears and deep voice, whilst the other was the exact opposite. According to a writer of that day the "North Country Beagle" was nimble and vigorous and did his business as furiously as Jehu himself could wish him.

In the middle of the nineteenth century Parson Honeywood got together a good pack and showed some excellent sport in Essex. His pack dates as the beginning of the modern Beagle, and nearly every well-known pack of subsequent date owed its origin to that inheritance. The colored engraving "The Merry Beaglers" is as familiar to American sportsmen as it is to anyone in England and will preserve for all time the name of the Reverend Philip Honeywood. We can accept it as true that the Beagle is one of the oldest breeds in history and, with the Bloodhound and perhaps the Otter Hound, closest to the original breed of hounds.

Previous to about 1870 in the United States, the little hunting hounds of the Southern States, then called Beagles, were more of the type of straight-legged Bassets or Dachshunds with weaker heads than the Bassets and were mostly white with few dark markings. They were said to be snappy, tireless hunters, full of vim and quick at a turn, but not handsome in outline. The importations of the late General Rowett of Carlinsville, Illinois, in the sixties marks the turning point in the history of the American strain or strains of Beagle and brought to this country an acquisition of canine beauty little thought of by those who hitherto had hunted with Beagles. From what packs in England General Rowett obtained his hounds is not known.

About 1880 Mr. Arnold of Providence, R.I., imported a pack from the Royal Rock Beagles in the North of England, and this also has had a good deal of influence on the development of American Beagles. In 1896 Mr. James L. Kernochan imported a pack from England and from then on a great many high-class hounds have been brought over.

Among the first sportsmen of note in the Beagle world, whose importations have helped to create the modern Beagle in America, may be mentioned Mr. Harry Peters of Islip, L.I., Mr. George Post of Bernardsville, N.J., Mr. James W. Appleton of Ipswich, Mass., Mr. Eugene Reynal of Millbrook, N.Y., Mr. H. C. Phipps of Westbury, L.I., and many others.

In 1888 The National Beagle Club was formed and held the first field trial. From that time on field trials carrying championship points have sprung up rapidly all over the United States, and as many more clubs sanctioned to hold informal trials. At all these, packs are run in single classes for hounds thirteen to fifteen inches in height and classes for those under thirteen inches, and at the national trials the pack classes are an important feature. There are single classes for young hounds called "derbies" and all-age classes for large and small dogs and bitches. At the national there are, in addition to these single classes, four pack classes which, of course, cannot be run against each other at the same time, as are the hounds in the single classes. Each pack is hunted separately and scored by the judges.

In addition to the regular all-breed American Kennel Club shows, almost all the field-trial clubs conduct specialty shows in connection with their field trials, and in addition to this again, there are hound shows limited to the various breeds of hounds.

Those who are interested in hunting Beagles as a pack generally enjoy hunting the larger hares, rather than cottontail rabbits. Hares do not go to ground and spoil a hunt, and they give much longer, straighter, and faster runs. Kansas jack rabbits have, therefore, been brought to many parts of the East and have bred extensively in each community in which they have been placed. They are only fairly satisfactory. Several experiments have been made in importing English hares, but they have not been very successful, probably due to the fact that the climate and feed in this part of the world do not suit them. Hares have been imported from Germany, however, with great success. They show splendid sport and thrive in this country. The white hare, or snowshoe rabbit, is found in northern swamps and provides excellent sport for a pack, but these hares will not do well when imported to other communities and disappear immediately.

There are thousands of men all over the United States who keep a few Beagles and hunt them individually. In addition, there are many packs recorded with the National Beagle Club. They are all hunted in the legitimate manner with a regular hunt staff, in hunt liveries, with their own distinctive colored collar, etc.

In conclusion, a few remarks as to the modern standard for type may be of interest. The height limit of a Beagle in the United States is fifteen inches and in England sixteen inches. Hounds above this height cannot be entered in field trials or shows. The head should be strong and well proportioned, with a fairly long, clean neck. Sloping shoulders are very important for speed and endurance. The body should be close-coupled and well ribbed up. The front legs should be very straight with as much bone as possible and small, round cat-feet. The quarters should be strong and powerful and the hocks set low to the ground. The stern should be set moderately high with a good brush, but a proud or curly stern is most undesirable. Any true hound color is suitable.

Official Standard for the
Beagle

Head—The skull should be fairly long, slightly domed at occiput, with cranium broad and full. *Ears*—Ears set on moderately low, long, reaching when drawn out nearly, if not quite, to the end of the nose; fine in texture, fairly broad—with almost entire absence of erectile power—setting close to the head, with the forward edge slightly inturning to the cheek—rounded at tip. *Eyes*—Eyes large, set well apart—soft and houndlike—expression gentle and pleading; of a brown or hazel color. *Muzzle*—Muzzle of medium length—straight and square-cut—the stop moderately defined. *Jaws*—Level. Lips free from flews; nostrils large and open. **Defects**—A very flat skull, narrow across the top; excess of dome, eyes small, sharp and terrierlike, or prominent and protruding; muzzle long, snipy or cut away decidedly below the eyes, or very short. Roman-nosed, or upturned, giving a dish-face expression. Ears short, set on high or with a tendency to rise above the point of origin.

Body—*Neck and Throat*—Neck rising free and light from the shoulders strong in substance yet not loaded, of medium length. The throat clean and free from folds of skin; a slight wrinkle below the angle of the jaw, however, may be allowable. **Defects**—A thick, short, cloddy neck carried on a line with the top of the shoulders. Throat showing dewlap and folds of skin to a degree termed "throatiness."

Shoulders and Chest—Shoulders sloping—clean, muscular, not heavy or loaded—conveying the idea of freedom of action with activity and strength. Chest deep and broad, but not broad enough to interfere with the free play of the shoulders. **Defects**—Straight, upright shoulders. Chest disproportionately wide or with lack of depth.

Back, Loin and Ribs—Back short, muscular and strong. Loin broad and slightly arched, and the ribs well sprung, giving abundance of lung room. **Defects**—Very long or swayed or roached back. Flat, narrow loin. Flat ribs.

Forelegs and Feet—*Forelegs*—Straight, with plenty of bone in proportion to size of the hound. Pasterns short and straight. *Feet*—Close, round and firm. Pad full and hard. **Defects**—Out at elbows. Knees knuckled over forward, or bent backward. Forelegs crooked or Dachshundlike. Feet long, open or spreading.

Hips, Thighs, Hind Legs and Feet—Hips and thighs strong and well muscled, giving abundance of propelling power. Stifles strong and well let down. Hocks firm, symmetrical and moderately bent. Feet close and firm. **Defects**—Cowhocks, or straight hocks. Lack of muscle and propelling power. Open feet.

Tail—Set moderately high; carried gaily, but not turned forward over the back; with slight curve; short as compared with size of the hound; with brush. **Defects**—A long tail. Teapot curve or inclined forward from the root. Rat tail with absence of brush.

Coat—A close, hard, hound coat of medium length. **Defects**—A short, thin coat, or of a soft quality.

Color—Any true hound color.

General Appearance—A miniature Foxhound, solid and big for his inches, with the wear-and-tear look of the hound that can last in the chase and follow his quarry to the death.

SCALE OF POINTS

Head

Skull	5	
Ears	10	
Eyes	5	
Muzzle	5	25

Body

Neck	5	
Chest and shoulders	15	
Back, loin and ribs	15	35

Running Gear

Forelegs	10	
Hips, thighs and hind legs	10	
Feet	10	30

Coat	5	
Stern	5	10
TOTAL	100	

Varieties—There shall be two varieties:

Thirteen Inch—which shall be for hounds not exceeding 13 inches in height.

Fifteen Inch—which shall be for hounds over 13 but not exceeding 15 inches in height.

DISQUALIFICATION

Any hound measuring more than 15 inches shall be disqualified.

Packs of Beagles

Hounds—General levelness of pack 40%
        Individual merit of hounds 30%

                                                           70%

Manners 20%
Appointments 10%
    TOTAL 100%

Levelness of Pack—The first thing in a pack to be considered is that they present a unified appearance. The hounds must be as near to the same height, weight, conformation and color as possible.

Individual Merit of the Hounds—Is the individual bench-show quality of the hounds. A very level and sporty pack can be gotten together and not a single hound be a good Beagle. This is to be avoided.

Manners—The hounds must all work gaily and cheerfully, with flags up—obeying all commands cheerfully. They should be broken to heel up, kennel up, follow promptly and stand. Cringing, sulking, lying down to be avoided. Also, a pack must not work as though in terror of master and whips. In Beagle packs it is recommended that the whip be used as little as possible.

Appointments—Master and whips should be dressed alike, the master or huntsman to carry horn—the whips and master to carry light thong whips. One whip should carry extra couplings on shoulder strap.

RECOMMENDATIONS FOR SHOW LIVERY

Black velvet cap, white stock, green coat, white breeches or knickerbockers, green or black stockings, white spats, black or dark brown shoes. Vest and gloves optional. Ladies should turn out exactly the same except for a white skirt instead of white breeches.

Approved September 10, 1957

Black and Tan Coonhound

ALTHOUGH a comparatively recent addition to our roster of pure-breds, the Black and Tan Coonhound is actually an old breed as history is reckoned. In all probability he has descended from the Talbot hound which was known in England during the reign of William I, Duke of Normandy, in the eleventh century; thence down through the Bloodhound and the Foxhound via this country's own Virginia Foxhound, frequently referred to as the "black and tan."

Selectively bred on a basis of color (for there were "cooners" of other colors as well) and for proficiency on possum and raccoon, the black-and-tan strain was carefully developed over a period of years and admitted to registry by The American Kennel Club in 1945.

The Black and Tan Coonhound works his trail with consummate skill and determination, albeit not at a particularly fast pace. In fact, he trails Bloodhound fashion, entirely by scent, with nose to the ground, "barking up" or giving voice the moment his quarry is treed. And despite the fact that the dog has been nurtured as a specialist on coon, he can do equally well in hunting deer, mountain lion, bear, and possibly other big game.

Official Standard for the
Black and Tan Coonhound

The Black and Tan Coonhound is first and fundamentally a working dog, capable of withstanding the rigors of winter, the heat of summer, and the difficult terrain over which he is called upon to work. Judges are asked by the club sponsoring the breed to place great emphasis upon these facts when evaluating the merits of the dog. The general impression should be that of power, agility, and alertness. His expression should be alert, friendly, eager, and aggressive. He should immediately impress one with his ability to cover the ground with powerful rhythmic strides.

Head—The head should be cleanly modeled, with medium stop occurring midway between occiput bone and nose. The head should measure from 9 to 10 inches in males and from 8 to 9 inches in females. Viewed from the profile, the line of the skull is on a practically parallel plane to the foreface or muzzle. *The skin* should be devoid of folds or excess dewlap. *The flews* should be well developed with typical hound appearance. *Nostrils* well open and always black. *Skull* should tend toward oval outline. *Eyes* should be from hazel to dark brown in color, almost round and not deeply set. *The ears* should be low set and well back. They should hang in graceful folds giving the dog a majestic appearance. In length they should extend well beyond the tip of the nose. *Teeth* should fit evenly with slightly scissors bite.

Body—*Neck, Shoulders, and Chest*—The neck should be muscular, sloping, medium length, extending into powerfully constructed shoulders and deep chest. The dog should possess full, round, well-sprung ribs, avoiding flatsidedness. *Back and Tail*—The back should be level, powerful and strong, with a visible slope from withers to rump. Tail should be strong, with base slightly below level of back line, carried free, and when in action at approximately right angle to back.

Legs and Feet—The forelegs should be straight, with elbows well let down, turning neither in nor out; pasterns strong and erect. Feet should be catlike with compact, well-arched toes and thick strong pads. *Hindquarters*—Quarters should be well boned and muscled. From hip to hock long and sinewy, hock to pad short and strong. Stifles and hock well bent and not inclining either in or out. When standing on a level surface the hind feet should set back from under the body, and leg from pad to hock be at right angles to the ground when viewed both from profile and the rear. The stride of the Black and Tan Coonhound should be easy and graceful with plenty of reach in front and drive behind.

Coat and Color—The coat should be short but dense to withstand rough going. As the name implies, the color should be coal black, with rich tan markings above eyes, on sides of muzzle, chest, legs and breeching with black pencil markings on toes.

Size—Measured at the shoulder: males, 25 to 27 inches; females, 23 to 25 inches. Height should be in proportion to general conformation so that dog appears neither leggy nor close to the ground. Dogs oversized should not be penalized when general soundness and proportion are in favor.

Judges should penalize the following defects:

Undersize, elbows out at shoulder, lack of angulation in hindquarters. splay feet, sway- or roach back, flatsidedness, lack of depth in chest, yellow or light eyes, shyness and nervousness.

Faults—Dewclaws; white on chest or other parts of body is highly undesirable and if it exceeds 1½ inches in diameter should be disqualified.

DISQUALIFICATION

White on chest or other parts of the body if it exceeds 1½ inches in diameter.

Approved July 10, 1945

Bloodhound

WHEN Claudius Aelianus, or "Aelian," wrote his famous *Historia Animalium* in the third century A.D., he mentioned in especially glowing terms a breed of hound that was unrivaled for its scenting powers and which was possessed of such great determination that it would not leave the trail until the quarry was located. Thus the early Italian scholar gives us a picture of the dog that is known today as the Bloodhound, a breed that has improved considerably in appearance but which still retains its peculiarly intensified ability to follow the faintest scent.

There has been little evidence to prove how far back the origin of the Bloodhound extends, but it is believed by many authorities that it was known throughout the Mediterranean countries long before the Christian Era. It is called the modern representative of the oldest race of hounds that hunt by scent, indicating, of course, that selective breeding over many centuries has made it outwardly changed from the breed the ancients extolled. Yet its characteristics are so distinctive that cynologists have traced it throughout dog history.

The Bloodhound made its appearance in Europe long before the Crusades, the first specimens being brought from Constantinople. There were two strains, black and white. The blacks were the famed

St. Huberts of the eighth century, while the whiten later became known as the Southern hounds. It was from the black stock that importations were made to England. Both varieties have played big parts in the development of other hounds and hound-type dogs.

In the twelfth century, when even Bishops rode to hounds, dignitaries of the Church were among the foremost in fostering the development of the Bloodhound. A number of high ecclesiastics maintained packs, and the kennel was an important part of every monastery. To them goes a great deal of the credit for keeping the strain clean. In fact, so much care was taken in the breeding of this hound that it came to be called the "blooded hound," meaning aristocratic.

Several centuries later that noted English physician and dog lover, Dr. Johannes Caius, gives a different explanation of the name, but his description of the breed is interesting. It follows:

> . . . The larger class remain to be mentioned; these too have drooping lips and ears, and it is well known that they follow their prey not only while alive but also after death when they have caught the scent of blood. For whether the beasts are wounded alive and slip out of the hunter's hands, or are taken dead out of the warren (but with a profusion of blood in either case), these hounds perceive it at once by smell and follow the trail. For that reason they are properly called Sanguinaraii.
>
> Frequently, however, an animal is stolen, and owing to the cleverness of thieves there is no effusion of blood; but even so they are clever enough to follow dry human footsteps for a huge distance, and can pick a man out of a crowd however large, pressing on through the densest thickets, and they will still go on even though they have to swim across a river. When they arrive at the opposite bank, by a circular movement, they find out which way a man has gone, even if at first they do not hit on the track of the thief. Thus they supplement good luck by artifice and deserve what Aelian says of them in this "Historia Animalium." . . .

Although the Bloodhound reached approximately its modern form in England, the breed has perhaps reached its greatest development in the United States, as far as usefulness is concerned. The breed has been known in America for over a century. Abolitionists once drew touching pictures of poor fugitive slaves pursued by the Bloodhounds, but it is doubted if many of the breed—then fairly numerous in the South—were so employed. Mongrels were frequently called "bloodhounds" and no doubt some of these did harass the slaves.

The pure-bred Bloodhound is one of the most docile of all breeds. His trailing is more for his own sport than for anything else. Unlike the police-trained dog, he does not attack the man he is trailing. The Bloodhound's task ends once he has followed the trail to its termination. But so accurate is he in following a trail that his evidence has been accepted in a court of law.

Some of the great Bloodhounds of the United States have brought about more convictions for police departments than the best human detectives. One dog was credited with more than 600 actual convictions. The famous dog Nick Carter picked up a trail that was 105 hours old and followed it to a subsequent conviction. This record, set in the early 1900s, has since been more than doubled. Owners have proven that a good Bloodhound can be a show champion and a working mantrailer as well; and the lawmen of National Police Bloodhound Association plus the volunteers of Search and Rescue clubs throughout the country increasingly have been putting him back to his traditional work. The breed's stamina and determination are apparent in the great distances it will travel. Several specimens have followed human quarry for more than fifty miles, and one led the detectives 138 miles—all with success.

In obedience, Bloodhounds are quick to learn but may prove obstinate unless taught to enjoy this type of work. In recent years, a growing number have earned their Companion Dog degrees and a few have gone on to get their CDX and Utility degrees.

Bloodhounds have been exhibited in the United States almost from the beginning of organized dog shows in America. The American Bloodhound Club, a national breed organization, has enabled fanciers to conduct Specialty shows from East to West.

Official Standard for the Bloodhound

General Character—The Bloodhound possesses, in a most marked degree, every point and characteristic of those dogs which hunt together by scent (Sagaces). He is very powerful, and stands over more ground than is usual with hounds of other breeds. The skin is thin to the touch and extremely loose, this being more especially noticeable about the head and neck, where it hangs in deep folds.

Height—The mean average height of adult dogs is 26 inches, and of adult bitches 24 inches. Dogs usually vary from 25 inches to 27 inches, and bitches from 23 inches to 25 inches; but, in either case, the greater height is to be preferred, provided that character and quality are also combined.

Weight—The mean average weight of adult dogs, in fair condition, is 90 pounds, and of adult bitches 80 pounds. Dogs attain the weight of 110 pounds, bitches 100 pounds. The greater weights are to be preferred, provided (as in the case of height) that quality and proportion are also combined.

Expression—The expression is noble and dignified, and characterized by solemnity, wisdom, and power.

176

Temperament—In temperament he is extremely affectionate, neither quarrelsome with companions nor with other dogs. His nature is somewhat shy, and equally sensitive to kindness or correction by his master.

Head—The head is narrow in proportion to its length, and long in proportion to the body, tapering but slightly from the temples to the end of the muzzle, thus (when viewed from above and in front) having the appearance of being flattened at the sides and of being nearly equal in width throughout its entire length. In profile the upper outline of the skull is nearly in the same plane as that of the foreface. The length from end of nose to stop (midway between the eyes) should be not less than that from stop to back of occipital protuberance (peak). The entire length of head from the posterior part of the occipital protuberance to the end of the muzzle should be 12 inches, or more, in dogs, and 11 inches, or more, in bitches. *Skull*—The skull is long and narrow, with the occipital peak very pronounced. The brows are not prominent, although, owing to the deep-set eyes, they may have that appearance. *Foreface*—The foreface is long, deep, and of even width throughout, with square outline when seen in profile. *Eyes*—The eyes are deeply sunk in the orbits, the lids assuming a lozenge or diamond shape, in consequence of the lower lids being dragged down and everted by the heavy flews. The eyes correspond with the general tone of color of the animal, varying from deep hazel to yellow. The hazel color is, however, to be preferred, although very seldom seen in red-and-tan hounds. *Ears*—The ears are thin and soft to the touch, extremely long, set very low, and fall in graceful folds, the lower parts curling inward and backward.

Wrinkle—The head is furnished with an amount of loose skin, which in nearly every position appears superabundant, but more particularly so when the head is carried low; the skin then falls into loose, pendulous ridges and folds, especially over the forehead and sides of the face. *Nostrils*—The nostrils are large and open. *Lips, Flews, and Dewlap*—In front the lips fall squarely, making a right angle with the upper line of the foreface; whilst behind they form deep, hanging flews, and, being continued into the pendant folds of loose skin about the neck, constitute the dewlap, which is very pronounced. These characters are found, though in a less degree, in the bitch.

Neck, Shoulders and Chest—The neck is long, the shoulders muscular and well sloped backwards; the ribs are well sprung; and the chest well let down between the forelegs, forming a deep keel.

Legs and Feet—The forelegs are straight and large in bone, with elbows squarely set; the feet strong and well knuckled up; the thighs and second thighs (gaskins) are very muscular; the hocks well bent and let down and squarely set.

Back and Loin—The back and loins are strong, the latter deep and slightly arched. *Stern*—The stern is long and tapering, and set on rather high, with a moderate amount of hair underneath.

Gait—The gait is elastic, swinging and free, the stern being carried high, but not too much curled over the back.

Color—The colors are black and tan, red and tan, and tawny; the darker colors being sometimes interspersed with lighter or badger-colored hair, and sometimes flecked with white. A small amount of white is permissible on chest, feet, and tip of stern.

Borzoi

(Bawr-zoy)

THE BORZOI, known here prior to 1936 as the Russian Wolfhound, is a sight hound dependent on his extreme speed, agility and courage to pursue, overtake and hold the quarry. Today these beautiful and intelligent dogs are as at home in our living rooms as they are in the field.

With a history clouded by the misty past of Czarist Russia, we know the dogs were bred by the Russian aristocracy for hundreds of years. There are, in fact, accounts of hunting expeditions of several Mongol rulers from the time of the conqueror, Genghis Khan, in the thirteenth century in which long hounds were mentioned as principal coursing dogs. In Russia, the precursors of the Borzoi were thought to be of several different types including the long-coated, smooth-faced bearhound of early Russia, the Southern coursing hounds of the Tatars, the Owtchar—a tall Russian sheepdog, as well as other ancient sight-hound types. Whatever the Borzoi origin, by 1260 the coursing of hare for sport is mentioned in connection with the Court of the Grand Duke of Novgorod at the time of the First Czar, and in 1650 the first Borzoi standard was written (reportedly it did not differ greatly from the standard of today.) From the time of the first Czars to the abolition of serfdom in 1861, hunting with Borzois reached the level of the national sport of the aristocracy.

Great rural estates, thousands of acres in extent, with hundreds of serfs, were given over to the breeding and training of, and hunting with, Borzois. In fact, it is difficult today to even imagine the grand scale and magnificence to which the gentle Borzoi is heir. Prior to 1861, and to a lesser extent after that time up to the Russian Revolution in 1917, the time, effort and money expended on these "hunts", as they were called, is surely unequaled in the development of any breed.

During the season, the hunt might have been conducted near its base or it might have traveled from one locale to another seeking out game. Walzoff, writing in his monograph on the Perchino Hunt, says a special hunting train used to transport the people, horses, dogs, tents, kitchens and carriages, etc. to a hunting ground consisted of 40 freight cars, one first and one second-class passenger car, with the Grand Duke and guests arriving on another special train. The hunting party itself would consist of over 100 Borzois, as many foxhounds, and as many people to assist. Often all the horses of a hunt were matched, as well as the leashes of the Borzois and the foxhound packs. Once the team arrived at the spot where wolves were known to be, plans were drawn, preparations made and the hunting commenced. The beaters accompanying a pack of foxhounds would dislodge the game, most notably the wolf, from the forest into the open field where awaiting them at a respectable distance were the mounted huntsmen, each with a trio of Borzois consisting of a bitch and two dogs. When game was sighted, the dogs were slipped by the huntsman. With the Borzois in pursuit of the wolf, and the mounted huntsmen in pursuit of the Borzois, a hair-raising ride ensued and, if the wolf did not escape, the Borzois were required to capture, pin and hold the creature until the arrival of the huntsmen. Arriving full tilt on the scene, the approved style was for the huntsmen to leap headlong into the fray, gag and bind the wolf, after which the wolf was often set free—surely wiser and much more wary for he next time. A moving account of such a hunt can be read in Tolstoy's *War and Peace* (Book II, Part 4, Chapter 3).

From after the Napoleonic Wars to the abolition of serfdom in 1861, there was a period of uncertainty which seemed to result in many experimental outcrosses in the breed. By 1873, only a few Borzois of the old type existed, and in that year the "Imperial Association" was formed to protect and promote this ancient type. This Association is of great interest to the present-day Borzoi fancier as many bloodlines of Borzois in America today, if not most, can be traced back to breeders who were members of this group. Most notable among these was the Grand Duke Nicholas, uncle to the Czar and Field Marshal of the

Russian armies. Second in importance was Artem Boldareff, a wealthy landowner. With these two men in the foreground, members of the Association found, bred and protected the old type Borzoi. And it is to their hunts at Perchino and Woronzova that many of today's Borzois owe their heritage.

As far as is known, the first Borzoi that came to America was brought over from England in 1889 by William Wade of Hulton, Pennsylvania, this hound being purchased from Freeman Lloyd. This was a bitch named Elsie, described in *The English Stockkeeper* as, "Nothing much to look at, being small, light and weedy, with no bone, straight back, very curly tail and too much bent in stifles." C. Steadman Hanks, in the early or middle nineties, imported several Borzois and the records show that some of them were considered very good ones. Mr. Hanks appears to be the only extensive American importer of these hounds who ever visited Russia until 1903, when Joseph B. Thomas went there, with the exception of E. L. Krauss of Pennsylvania, whose importations were of German origin. As somebody wrote, many of them were weedy, although pretty to look at, with good heads and coats, but they had evidently been kennel raised for many generations and seemed to show it in disposition and lack of stamina.

Joseph B. Thomas' importations were made directly from Russia, from the Perchino Kennels, owned by the Grand Duke Nicholas and from the Woronzova Kennels of Artem Boldareff. Many American Borzoi bloodlines rest on these original importations, some in as few as 14 generations; the remaining Borzois trace back through Europe to Russia.

The Borzoi today remains largely unchanged from his Russian ancestors, both in terms of his appearance, his quiet, gentle nature and his abilities. In the West, the dogs are often coursed and throughout the country lure coursing is gaining in popularity. His intelligence and easy training have resulted in many Borzois winning Obedience certificates. While the hunt has been the primary purpose of the Borzoi, his beauty and temperament were also always of prime importance. He was always a companion *par excellence* and the amourment of the salon. Today, this noble breed easily finds its way to the heart of its owner and, while the circumstances of the Borzoi have changed from those of Czarist Russia, they remain true aristocrats.

Official Standard for the
Borzoi

General Appearance—The Borzoi was originally bred for the coursing of wild game on more or less open terrain, relying on sight rather than scent. To accomplish this purpose, the Borzoi needed particular structural qualities to chase, catch and hold his quarry. Special emphasis is placed on sound running gear, strong neck and jaws, courage and agility, combined with proper condition. The Borzoi should always possess unmistakable elegance, with flowing lines, graceful in motion or repose. Males, masculine without coarseness; bitches, feminine and refined.

Head—Skull slightly domed, long and narrow, with scarcely any perceptible stop, inclined to be Roman-nosed. Jaws long, powerful and deep, somewhat finer in bitches but not snipy. Teeth strong and clean with either an even or a scissors bite. Missing teeth should be penalized. Nose large and black.

Ears—Small and fine in quality, lying back on the neck when in repose with the tips when thrown back almost touching behind occiput; raised when at attention.

Eyes—Set somewhat obliquely, dark in color, intelligent but rather soft in expression; never round, full nor staring, nor light in color; eye rims dark; inner corner midway between tip of nose and occiput.

Neck—Clean, free from throatiness; slightly arched, very powerful and well set on.

Shoulders—Sloping, fine at the withers and free from coarseness or lumber.

Chest—Rather narrow, with great depth of brisket.

Ribs—Only slightly sprung, but very deep, giving room for heart and lung play.

Back—Rising a little at the loins in a graceful curve.

Loins—Extremely muscular, but rather tucked up, owing to the great depth of chest and comparative shortness of back and ribs.

Forelegs—Bones straight and somewhat flattened like blades, with the narrower edge forward. The elbows have free play and are turned neither in nor out. Pasterns strong.

Feet—Hare-shaped, with well-arched knuckles, toes close and well padded.

Hindquarters—Long, very muscular and powerful with well bent stifles; somewhat wider than the forequarters; strong first and second thighs; hocks clean and well let down; legs parallel when viewed from the rear.

Dewclaws—Dewclaws, if any, on the hind legs are generally removed; dewclaws on the forelegs may be removed.

Tail—Long, set on and carried low in a graceful curve.

Coat—Long, silky (not woolly), either flat, wavy or rather curly. On the head, ears and front of legs it should be short and smooth; on the neck the frill

181

should be profuse and rather curly. Feather on hindquarters and tail, long and profuse, less so on chest and back of forelegs.

Color—Any color, or combination of colors, is acceptable.

Size—Mature males should be at least 28 inches at the withers and mature bitches at least 26 inches at the withers. Dogs and bitches below these respective limits should be severely penalized; dogs and bitches above the respective limits should not be penalized as long as extra size is not acquired at the expense of symmetry, speed and staying quality. Range in weight for males from 75 to 105 pounds and for bitches from 15 to 20 pounds less.

Gait—Front legs must reach well out in front with pasterns strong and springy. Hackneyed motion with mincing gait is not desired nor is weaving and crossing. However, while the hind legs are wider apart than the front, the feet tend to move closer to the center line when the dog moves at a fast trot. When viewed from the side there should be a noticeable drive with a ground-covering stride from well-angulated stifles and hocks. The over-all appearance in motion should be that of effortless power, endurance, speed, agility, smoothness and grace.

FAULTS

The foregoing description is that of the ideal Borzoi. Any deviation from the above described dog must be penalized to the extent of the deviation keeping in mind the importance of the contribution of the various features toward the basic original purpose of the breed.

Approved June 13, 1972

Dachshund

(Docks-hoond)

THE NAME DACHSHUND *(dachs,* badgers; *hund,* dog) at once reveals and conceals the origin of the breed. In medieval European books on hunting, dogs similar only in possessing the tracking ability of hounds and the proportions and temperament of terriers, because they were used to follow badger to earth, were called badger-dogs or *dachshunds.* A parallel is suggested by the current use of the name "rabbit dog" in various parts of this country for dogs of various breeding, used to hunt rabbits.

Illustrations dating from the fifteenth, sixteenth, and seventeenth centuries show badgers hunted by dogs with elongated bodies, short legs, and hound-type ears—some with the bent front legs of the Basset, some with the heads of terriers, and some with indications of smooth and long coats. It is well to consider that these illustrations were made before the days of photography, that artists capable of depicting dogs with anatomical fidelity have always been rare, and that woodcuts do not lend themselves to fine reproductions of coat distinctions. At best, the pictures and descriptive words can be interpreted with certainty only as defining the functions of the dogs used on badger.

The preponderance of available evidence indicates that smooth and longhaired coats were separated by selective breeding, long prior to recorded registrations; whereas within such recorded history, the wirehaired coat was produced for protection against briar and thorn by crossing in harsh, wiry terrier coats and then breeding out incompatible characteristics of conformation. Early in the seventeenth century the name Dachshund became the designation of a breed type with smooth and longhaired coat varieties, and since 1890 wirehairs have been registered as the third variety. German breeders early learned that crossing between longhairs and either smooths or wirehairs did more harm than good, and barred such crosses from registration. During the early decades of wirehairs, while breeding stock was comparatively rare, crosses with smooths were permitted. Now, with sufficient breeding stock within each of the three varieties to provide any desired characteristics, there is no advantage in coat crossing, with inevitable production of intermediate coats conforming to neither coat standard, and uncertainty of coat texture for several generations.

The badger was a formidable twenty-five to forty-pound adversary. Strength and stamina as well as keenness and courage above and below ground were required of badger dogs. Weights of thirty to thirty-five pounds were not uncommon. Such Dachshunds in packs also were serviceable against wild boar. With this start the breed was adapted to

Smooth Dachshund

Longhaired Dachshund

Wirehaired Dachshund

hunt other game. A smaller sixteen to twenty-two-pound Dachshund proved effective against foxes and to trail wounded deer, and this size has become best known in this country. Still smaller twelve-pound Dachshunds were used on stoat and hare. In the first quarter of the twentieth century, for bolting cottontail rabbits, miniatures with adult weights under five pounds and chest girths under twelve inches, but with plenty of hunting spirit, were produced.

Before the German Dachshund or *Deutscher Teckelklub* was founded in 1888, "racial characteristics," or a standard for the breed had been set up in 1879; and German registration of Dachshunds was included (not always with complete generation data or systematic coat notations) in a general all-breed stud book, the *Deutscher Hunde-Stammbuch,* whose first volume, in 1840, recorded fifty-four Dachshunds and the names of several subsequently prominent breeders, and whose publication continued until officially terminated in 1935. The *Gebrauchsteckel-Klubs,* or hunting Dachshund associations, kept separate stud books, in which were recorded only dogs of demonstrated hunting accomplishment, with scant attention to coat or conformation. From early volumes of the *Deutscher Teckelklub* stud book, first published in 1890, despite meager correlation with older records, pedigrees have been extended back as far as 1860 and 1859. Stud books maintained by clubs devoted to wirehairs, longhairs, and miniatures have waxed and waned. Not until 1915 did the coat-identifying initials *K* for *Kurzhaar,* or smooth, *R* for *Rauhhaar,* or wirehair, and *L* for *Langhaar,* or longhair, become integral components of the *Teckelklub* registration numbers, and later *Z* was added to distinguish *Zwerg* and *Kaninchentechel,* or miniatures, by re-registration after one year on official certification of eligible size. It can be recommended to American Dachshund breeders of longhairs and wirehairs to incorporate the initials L and W, respectively, in names submitted to the AKC for registration of Dachshunds of these coats.

The management of the breed in Germany, as well as the stud books, had been divided. The *Teckelklub* managed the bench shows, while the *Gebrauchsteckel-Klubs* conducted organized hunting activities. In 1935, the nationalized consolidation of all German Dachshund clubs as the *Fachschaft Dachshunde im Reichsverband für das Deutsche Hundewesen (FD-RDH)* unified the breed stud books and co-ordinated the conduct of bench shows with natural-hunting field trials.

Since World War II, management of the Dachshund breed in Germany has reverted to the *Deutscher Teckelklub*—whose registrations are accepted by the AKC—and the *Gebrauchsteckelklub.* The balance of breeding for hunting and symmetry, which advanced the breed for twenty-five years before the war, was altered after the war to stress hunting, with a more terrier-like conformation, whereas in this country the prewar objectives have continued to direct the breed.

Importation of Dachshunds into this country antedates the earliest American dog shows or stud books, and eleven were included in *AKC Stud Book, Volume II* in 1885. Our dogs have found little employment in organized hunting, as we lack the badger and wild boar and do not hunt deer with dogs, nor foxes with pick and shovel. The true character and conformation of the breed have been encouraged by frequent importation of German hunting strains; and to encourage hunting capacity and exemplary conformation and temperament, field trials under AKC rules were instituted in 1935.

The advance of the breed in this country has not been without reverses. Fostered since 1895 by the Dachshund Club of America, by 1913 and 1914 it had gained a place among the ten most numerous breeds at the Westminster Kennel Club shows—to fall in the postwar years to a mere dozen and temporarily translate its name to "badger dog."

After World War I, with replenished breeding stock, there were noteworthy gains. From 1930 to 1940, Dachshunds advanced from twenty-eighth to sixth rank among American registrations, and maintained this average rank through World War II by constructive public relations. Since that time, as the all-breed registration totals have continued to increase year by year, the Dachshund has maintained an important place in the proportionate number of dogs registered and exhibited in the ring.

It is unlikely that one American Dachshund in a thousand is used to hunt, but to understand the functional origin and development of the breed helps us to appreciate its elegant, streamlined proportions, and gives significance to the application of the breed standard.

Specialized characteristics of the breed for its purposes include a long head and well-developed nose; properly angulated shoulder, pelvis, and leg bones; close elbows, and free, straight gait of forelegs and hind legs; long fore-chest and after-chest with well-sprung ribs for ample lung and heart room without excessive width; supple and elastic skin for free action in restricted quarters underground; a remarkably long, powerful jaw with well-fitted teeth; a long, strong neck, capable as a fencer's wrist; powerful legs and sound feet for digging, a well-muscled back for sustained effort; and above all, that fine, high courage which enables it to measure up to every demand of attack or defense without being quarrelsome or undesirably aggressive.

The medium-sized, smooth-haired Dachshund, which predominates in this country is small enough to live in house or apartment, yet large enough for street, suburb, or country. Its short legs insure maximum exercise per mile. Its odorless, sleek, dark, short coat requires no plucking, trimming, brushing, combing, oiling, and no bathing except to remove accidental dirt. Outdoors the Dachshund is hardy, vigorous, and tireless; indoors he is affectionate and responsive, companionable in restful mood, hilarious in play, alert in announcing strangers. The breed offers a range of three coat varieties; standard and miniature sizes; red and black-and-tan and a number of other colors.

Official Standard for the Dachshund

GENERAL FEATURES

General Appearance—Low to ground, short-legged, long bodied, but with compact figure and robust muscular development; with bold and confident carriage of the head and intelligent facial expression. In spite of his shortness of leg, in comparison with his length of trunk, he should appear neither crippled, awkward, cramped in his capacity for movement, nor slim and weasel-like.

Qualities—He should be clever, lively, and courageous to the point of rashness, persevering in his work both above and below ground; with all the senses well developed. His build and disposition qualify him especially for hunting game below ground. Added to this, his hunting spirit, good nose, loud tongue, and small size, render him especially suited for beating the bush. His figure and his fine nose give him an especial advantage over most other breeds of sporting dogs for trailing.

CONFORMATION OF BODY

Head—Viewed from above or from the side, it should taper uniformly to the tip of the nose, and should be clean-cut. The skull is only slightly arched, and should slope gradually without stop (the less stop the more typical) into the finely-formed slightly-arched muzzle (ram's nose). The bridge bones over the eyes should be strongly prominent. The nasal cartilage and tip of the nose are long and narrow; lips tightly stretched, well covering the lower jaw, but neither deep nor pointed; corner of the mouth not very marked. Nostrils well open. Jaws opening wide and hinged well back of the eyes, with strongly developed bones and teeth.

Teeth—Powerful canine teeth should fit closely together, and the outer side of the lower incisors should tightly touch the inner side of the upper. (Scissors bite.)

Eyes—Medium size, oval, situated at the sides, with a clean, energetic, though pleasant expression; not piercing. Color, lustrous dark reddish-brown to brownish-black for all coats and colors. Wall eyes in the case of dapple dogs are not a very bad fault, but are also not desirable.

Ears—Should be set near the top of the head, and not too far forward, long but not too long, beautifully rounded, not narrow, pointed, or folded. Their carriage should be animated, and the forward edge should just touch the cheek.

Neck—Fairly long, muscular, clean-cut, not showing any dewlap on the throat, slightly arched in the nape, extending in a graceful line into the shoulders, carried proudly but not stiffly.

Front—To endure the arduous exertion underground, the front must be correspondingly muscular, compact, deep, long and broad. Forequarters in detail:

Shoulder Blade—Long, broad, obliquely and firmly placed upon the fully developed thorax, furnished with hard and plastic muscles.

Upper Arm—Of the same length as the shoulder blade, and at right angles to the latter, strong of bone and hard of muscle, lying close to the ribs, capable of free movement.

Forearm—This is short in comparison to other breeds, slightly turned inwards; supplied with hard but plastic muscles on the front and outside, with tightly stretched tendons on the inside and at the back.

Joint between forearm and foot (wrists)—These are closer together than the shoulder joints, so that the front does not appear absolutely straight.

Paws—Full, broad in front, and a trifle inclined outwards; compact, with well-arched toes and tough pads.

Toes—There are five of these, though only four are in use. They should be close together, with a pronounced arch; provided on top with strong nails, and underneath with tough toe-pads. Dewclaws may be removed.

Trunk—The whole trunk should in general be long and fully muscled. The back, with sloping shoulders, and short, rigid pelvis, should lie in the straightest possible line between the withers and the very slightly arched loins, these latter being short, rigid, and broad.

Chest—The breastbone should be strong, and so prominent in front that on either side a depression (dimple) appears. When viewed from the front, the thorax should appear oval, and should extend downward to the mid-point of the forearm. The enclosing structure of ribs should appear full and oval, and when viewed from above or from the side, full-volumed, so as to allow by its ample capacity, complete development of heart and lungs. Well ribbed up, and gradually merging into the line of the abdomen. If the length is correct, and also the anatomy of the shoulder and upper arm, the front leg when viewed in profile should cover the lowest point of the breast line.

Abdomen—Slightly drawn up.

Hindquarters—The hindquarters viewed from behind should be of completely equal width.

Croup—Long, round, full, robustly muscled, but plastic, only slightly sinking toward the tail.

Pelvic Bones—Not too short, rather strongly developed, and moderately sloping.

Thigh Bone—Robust and of good length, set at right angles to the pelvic bones

Hind Legs—Robust and well-muscled, with well-rounded buttocks.

Knee Joint—Broad and strong.

Calf Bone—In comparison with other breeds, short; it should be perpendicular to the thigh bone, and firmly muscled.

The bones at the base of the foot (tarsus) should present a flat appearance, with a strongly prominent hock and a broad tendon of Achilles.

The central foot bones (metatarsus) should be long, movable toward the calf bone, slightly bent toward the front, but perpendicular (as viewed from behind).

Hind Paws—Four compactly closed and beautifully arched toes, as in the case of the front paws. The whole foot should be posed equally on the ball and not merely on the toes; nails short.

Tail—Set in continuation of the spine, extending without very pronounced curvature, and should not be carried too gaily.

Note—Inasmuch as the Dachshund is a hunting dog, scars from honorable wounds shall not be considered a fault.

SPECIAL CHARACTERISTICS OF THE THREE COAT-VARIETIES

The Dachshund is bred with three varieties of coat: (1) Shorthaired (or *Smooth*); (2) Wirehaired; (3) Longhaired. All three varieties should conform to the characteristics already specified. The longhaired and shorthaired are old, well-fixed varieties, but into the wirehaired Dachshund, the blood of other breeds has been purposely introduced; nevertheless, in breeding him, the greatest stress must be placed upon conformity to the general Dachshund type. The following specifications are applicable separately to the three coat-varieties, respectively:

(1) SHORTHAIRED (or SMOOTH) DACHSHUND

Hair—Short, thick, smooth and shining; no bald patches. Special faults are: Too fine or thin hair, leathery ears, bald patches, too coarse or too thick hair in general.

Tail—Gradually tapered to a point, well but not too richly haired, long, sleek bristles on the underside are considered a patch of strong-growing hair, not a fault. A brush tail is a fault, as is also a partly or wholly hairless tail.

Color of Hair, Nose and Nails:

One-Colored Dachshund—This group includes red (often called tan), red-yellow, yellow, and brindle, with or without a shading of interspersed black hairs. Nevertheless a clean color is preferable, and red is to be considered more desirable than red-yellow or yellow. Dogs strongly shaded with interspersed black hairs belong to this class, and not to the other color groups. A small white spot is admissible, but not desirable. Nose and Nails—Black; brown is admissible, but not desirable.

Two-Colored Dachshund—These comprise deep black, chocolate, gray (blue), and white; each with tan markings over the eyes, on the sides of the jaw and underlip, on the inner edge of the ear, front, breast, inside and behind the front legs, on the paws and around the anus, and from there to about one-third to one-half of the length of the tail on the under side. The most common two-colored Dachshund is usually called black-and-tan. A small white spot is admissible but not desirable. Absence, undue prominence or extreme lightness of tan markings is undesirable. Nose and Nails—In the case of black dogs, black; for chocolate, brown (the darker the better); for gray (blue) or white dogs, gray or even flesh color, but the last named color is not desirable; in the case of white dogs, black nose and nails are to be preferred.

Dappled Dachshund—The color of the dappled Dachshund is a clear brownish or grayish color, or even a white ground, with dark irregular patches of dark-gray, brown, red-yellow or black (large areas of one color not desirable). It is desirable that neither the light nor the dark color should predominate. Nose and Nails—As for One- and Two-Colored Dachshund.

(2) WIREHAIRED DACHSHUND

The general appearance is the same as that of the shorthaired, but without being long in the legs, it is permissible for the body to be somewhat higher off the ground.

Hair—With the exception of jaw, eyebrows, and ears, the whole body is covered with a perfectly uniform tight, short, thick, rough, hard coat, but with finer, shorter hairs (undercoat) everywhere distributed between the coarser hairs, resembling the coat of the German Wirehaired Pointer. There should be a beard on the chin. The eyebrows are bushy. On the ears the hair is shorter than on the body; almost smooth, but in any case conforming to the rest of the coat. The general arrangement of the hair should be such that the wirehaired Dachshund, when seen from a distance should resemble the smooth-haired. Any sort of soft hair in the coat is faulty, whether short or long, or wherever found on the body; the same is true of long, curly, or wavy hair, or hair that sticks out irregularly in all directions; a flag tail is also objectionable.

Tail—Robust, as thickly haired as possible, gradually coming to a point, and without a tuft.

Color of Hair, Nose and Nails—All colors are admissible. White patches on the chest, though allowable, are not desirable.

(3) LONGHAIRED DACHSHUND

The distinctive characteristic differentiating this coat from the short-haired, or smooth-haired Dachshund is alone the rather long silky hair.

Hair—The soft, sleek, glistening, often slightly wavy hair should be longer under the neck, on the underside of the body, and especially on the ears and behind the legs, becoming there a pronounced feather; the hair should attain its greatest length on the underside of the tail. The hair should fall beyond the lower edge of the ear. Short hair on the ear, so-called "leather" ears, is not desirable. Too luxurious a coat causes the longhaired Dachshund to seem coarse, and masks the type. The coat should remind one of the Irish Setter, and should give the dog an elegant appearance. Too thick hair on the paws, so-called "mops," is inelegant, and renders the animal unfit for use. It is faulty for the dog to have equally long hair over all the body, if the coat is too curly, or too scrubby, or if a flag tail or overhanging hair on the ears are lacking; or if there is a very pronounced parting on the back, or a vigorous growth between the toes.

Tail—Carried gracefully in prolongation of the spine; the hair attains here its greatest length and forms a veritable flag.

Color of Hair, Nose and Nails—Exactly as for the smooth-haired Dachshund, except that the red-with-black (heavily sabled) color is permissible and is formally classed as a red.

MINIATURE DACHSHUNDS

Note—Miniature Dachshunds are bred in all three coats. Within the limits imposed, symmetrical adherence to the general Dachshund conformation, combined with smallness, and mental and physical vitality, should be the outstanding characteristics of Miniature Dachshunds. They have not been given separate classification but are a division of the Open Class for "under 10 pounds, and 12 months old or over."

GENERAL FAULTS

Serious Faults—Over- or undershot jaws, knuckling over, very loose shoulders.

Secondary Faults—A weak, long-legged, or dragging figure; body hanging between the shoulders; sluggish, clumsy, or waddling gait; toes turned inwards or too obliquely outwards; splayed paws; sunken back, roach (or carp) back; croup higher than withers; short-ribbed or too weak chest; excessively drawn-up flanks like those of a Greyhound; narrow, poorly-muscled hindquarters; weak loins; bad angulation in front or hindquarters; cowhocks; bowed legs; wall eyes, except for dappled dogs; bad coat.

Minor Faults—Ears wrongly set, sticking out, narrow or folded; too marked a stop; too pointed or weak a jaw; pincer teeth; too wide or too short a head; goggle eyes, wall eyes in the case of dappled dogs, insufficiently dark eyes in the case of all other coat-colors; dewlaps; short neck; swan neck; too fine or too thin hair; absence of, or too profuse or too light tan markings in the case of two-colored dogs.

Approved January 12, 1971

Foxhound, American

ACCORDING to well-known authorities on the American Hound, the first mention that we have of hound importations to America appears in a diary of one of De Soto's retainers. It is further mentioned that hounds were utilized to hunt Indians instead of foxes and hare.

From this same good authority we learn that in 1650 Robert Brooke sailed for the Crown Colony in America, taking his pack of hounds with him, which according to this authority were the taproot of several strains of American Hounds and remained in the family for nearly three hundred years. Then Mr. Thomas Walker of Albemarle County, Virginia, imported hounds from England in 1742; in 1770 George Washington subscribed to the importation of hounds from England, and in 1785 received some French Hounds from Lafayette, their voices being "like the bells of Moscow." These importations formed the foundation from which have developed some of the strains of the present-day Virginia hounds.

In 1808 the Gloucester Foxhunting Club imported some of the "best English Hounds," and the Baltimore Hunt Club made many importations from England. Then followed the Rosseau importations from France, and the Irish importations of 1830. The latter are the taproot of the Henry-Birdsong and Trigg strains. Around 1857 General Maupin got from east Tennessee the dog, Tennessee Lead, which, crossed on English importations, produced the "Maupin dog" now known as the Walker hound, another well-known strain of American Hound.

The Foxhound in this country is used for four purposes, all of them quite different from each other, and thus calling for hounds of a different characteristic.

1. The field trial hound which is run competitively at field trials where speed and a rather jealous nature are important.
2. A hound for hunting a fox with a gun. Here a slow-trailing hound with a good voice is needed.
3. "Trail" hounds, or drag hounds, which are raced or hunted on a drag, speed alone counting.
4. Hounds to hunt in large numbers (say fifteen to twenty or more) in a pack. This latter class is, of course, the type used by the hunt clubs and hunting farmers.

The types of American hounds have varied widely in different localities, but in the last few years the American Foxhound Club and the hunts which are members of the Masters of Foxhounds Association have made great strides in developing a more standard type.

Official Standard for the American Foxhound

Head—*Skull*—Should be fairly long, slightly domed at occiput, with cranium broad and full. ***Ears*—**Ears set on moderately low, long, reaching when drawn out nearly, if not quite, to the tip of the nose; fine in texture, fairly broad, with almost entire absence of erectile power—setting close to the head with the forward edge slightly inturning to the cheek—round at tip. ***Eyes*—**Eyes large, set well apart—soft and houndlike—expression gentle and pleading; of a brown or hazel color. ***Muzzle*—**Muzzle of fair length—straight and square-cut —the stop moderately defined.

Defects—A very flat skull, narrow across the top; excess of dome; eyes small, sharp and terrierlike, or prominent and protruding; muzzle long and snipy, cut away decidedly below the eyes, or very short. Roman-nosed, or upturned, giving a dish-face expression. Ears short, set on high, or with a tendency to rise above the point of origin.

Body—*Neck and Throat*—Neck rising free and light from the shoulders, strong in substance yet not loaded, of medium length. The throat clean and free from folds of skin, a slight wrinkle below the angle of the jaw, however, is allowable.

Defects—A thick, short, cloddy neck carried on a line with the top of the shoulders. Throat showing dewlap and folds of skin to a degree termed "throatiness."

Shoulders, Chest and Ribs—Shoulders sloping—clean, muscular, not heavy or loaded—conveying the idea of freedom of action with activity and strength. Chest should be deep for lung space, narrower in proportion to depth than the English hound—28 inches (*girth*) in a 23-inch hound being good. Well-sprung ribs—back ribs should extend well back—a three-inch flank allowing springiness.

Back and Loins—Back moderately long, muscular and strong. Loins broad and slightly arched.

Defects—Very long or swayed or roached back. Flat, narrow loins.

Forelegs and Feet—*Forelegs*—Straight, with fair amount of bone. Pasterns short and straight.

Feet—Foxlike. Pad full and hard. Well-arched toes. Strong nails.

Defects—Straight, upright shoulders, chest disproportionately wide or with lack of depth. Flat ribs. Out at elbow. Knees knuckled over forward, or bent backward. Forelegs crooked. Feet long, open or spreading.

Hips, Thighs, Hind Legs and Feet—Hips and thighs, strong and muscled, giving abundance of propelling power. Stifles strong and well let down. Hocks firm, symmetrical and moderately bent. Feet close and firm.

Defects—Cowhocks, or straight hocks. Lack of muscle and propelling power. Open feet.

Tail—Set moderately high; carried gaily, but not turned forward over the back; with slight curve; with very slight brush.

Defects—A long tail, Teapot curve or inclined forward from the root. Rat tail, entire absence of brush.

Coat—A close, hard, hound coat of medium length.

Defects—A short thin coat, or of a soft quality.

Height—Dogs should not be under 22 or over 25 inches. Bitches should not be under 21 or over 24 inches measured across the back at the point of the withers, the hound standing in a natural position with his feet well under him.

Color—Any color.

SCALE OF POINTS

Head			*Running Gear*		
Skull	5		Forelegs	10	
Ears	5		Hips, thighs and hind		
Eyes	5		legs	10	
Muzzle	5	20	Feet	15	35
Body			*Coat and Tail*		
Neck	5		Coat	5	
Chest and shoulders	15		Tail	5	10
Back, loins and ribs	15	35	TOTAL		100

Foxhound, English

FOXHUNTING in the United States is almost contemporaneous with the sport in Great Britain. The Foxhound with which we are dealing is known in the United States in dog shows and elsewhere as the *English* Foxhound, though why it should be designated by that name any more than a Fox Terrier should be called an *English* Fox Terrier, is hard to understand. The English Foxhound has been bred along careful lines for over one hundred and fifty years, the stud books published by the Masters of Foxhounds Association (of England) dating back before 1800; it is an easy matter for any owner of an English Foxhound to trace its pedigree back. The breeding of Foxhounds in England has always been in the hands of masters of hounds, who kept the most careful records of their breeding operations.

For the benefit of those who may be interested in knowing how long the English Foxhound in his pure state has been in the United States, we find that there are records which established the fact that the first Lord Fairfax imported hounds from England in 1738, and there are unauthenticated records of even earlier importations. The *English Foxhound Stud Book of America*, published by the Masters of Foxhounds Association of America, dates its earliest entries back to 1890, but there are earlier records which would incline one to the belief that there were many earlier importations and certainly the blood of the Genesee Valley pack must date at least twenty years before that time, records having been kept of it with fair accuracy ever since.

In England as in America these hounds have always been used for foxhunting as followed in the English fashion of riding to hounds. There have been over two hundred and fifty packs of hounds in Great Britain, all of which used English Hounds, while in America we have over a hundred packs, of which not over 10 per cent use hounds which would be eligible for the *English Foxhound Stud Book*, although the blood has been freely mixed with the American Foxhound.

In appearance the English Hound is far stouter than his American cousin, and perhaps no better description of his general appearance can be given than to quote a passage from Mr. Cuthbert Bradley's *Reminiscences of Frank Gillard,* in which he describes Belvoir Gambler '85, one of the greatest Foxhounds that was ever bred. He says:

Although Belvoir Gambler cannot be bred from rule of thumb, the proportions of this remarkable Foxhound are worth preserving as an example of what symmetry should be. Standing twenty-three inches at the shoulder, from the extreme point of his shapely shoulders to the outer curve of his well-turned quarters, he measured twenty-seven and a half inches in length whilst from elbow to ground his height was only twelve inches. Possessing great depth of rib and room round the heart, he girthed thirty-one inches, and his arm below was eight and a quarter inches round. Below the knee he measured eight and a quarter inches of solid bone, while round the thigh he spanned full nine and a quarter inches. The extended neck was ten inches from cranium to shoulder and the head ten inches and a half long. His color was of the richest, displaying all of the beautiful "Belvoir tan," and his head had that brainy appearance expressive of the highest intelligence. Gambler might have inspired that earnest poet, Cannon Kingsley, when he described the modern Foxhound, "The result of nature not limited, but developed by high civilization. Next to an old Greek statue there are few such combinations of grace and strength as in a fine Foxhound."

Although the tendency today is to breed hounds a little bigger, the above description cannot be equaled.

Official Standard for the English Foxhound

Head—Should be of full size, but by no means heavy. Brow pronounced, but not high or sharp. There should be a good length and breadth, sufficient to give in a dog hound a girth in front of the ears of fully 16 inches. The nose should be long (4½ inches) and wide, with open nostrils. Ears set on low and lying close to the cheeks. Most English hounds are "rounded" which means that about 1¼ inches is taken off the end of the ear. The teeth must meet squarely, either a *pig-mouth* (overshot) or undershot being a disqualification.

Neck—Must be long and clean, without the slightest throatiness, not less than 10 inches from cranium to shoulder. It should taper nicely from shoulders to head, and the upper outline should be slightly convex.

The Shoulders should be long and well clothed with muscle, without being heavy, especially at the points. They must be well sloped, and the true arm between the front and the elbow must be long and muscular, but free from fat or lumber. **Chest and Back Ribs**—The chest should girth over 31 inches in a 24-inch hound, and the back ribs must be very deep.

Back and Loin—Must both be very muscular, running into each other without any contraction between them. The couples must be wide, even to raggedness, and the topline of the back should be absolutely level, the **Stern** well set on and carried gaily but not in any case curved *over* the back like a squirrel's tail. The end should taper to a point and there should be a fringe of hair below. The **Hindquarters** or propellers are required to be very strong, and as endurance is of even greater consequence than speed, straight stifles are preferred to those much bent as in a Greyhound. **Elbows** set quite straight, and neither turned in nor out are a *sine qua non*. They must be well let down by means of the long true arm above mentioned.

Legs and Feet—Every Master of Foxhounds insists on legs as straight as a post, and as strong; size of bone at the ankle being especially regarded as all important. The desire for straightness had a tendency to produce knuckling-over, which at one time was countenanced, but in recent years this defect has been eradicated by careful breeding and intelligent adjudication, and one sees very little of this trouble in the best modern Foxhounds. The bone cannot be too large, and the feet in all cases should be round and catlike, with well-developed knuckles and strong horn, which last is of the greatest importance.

Color and Coat—Not regarded as very important, so long as the former is a good "hound color," and the latter is short, dense, hard, and glossy. Hound colors are black, tan, and white, or any combination of these three, also the various "pies" compounded of white and the color of the hare and badger, or yellow, or tan. The **Symmetry** of the Foxhound is of the greatest importance, and what is known as "quality" is highly regarded by all good judges.

SCALE OF POINTS

Head	5	Elbows	5
Neck	10	Legs and feet	20
Shoulders	10	Color and coat	5
Chest and back ribs	10	Stern	5
Back and loin	15	Symmetry	5
Hindquarters	10	TOTAL	100

DISQUALIFICATION

Pig-mouth (overshot) or undershot.

Greyhound

SWIFT AS a ray of light, graceful as a swallow, and wise as a Solomon, there is some basis for the prediction that the Greyhound is a breed that will never die. His fame, first written in the hot sands of Egypt, can be traced in the varying terrains of almost every country, on every continent on the globe. His was the type the ancients knew, and from time immemorial he has been a symbol of the aristocracy. Yet the Greyhound is a dog that needs no fanfare to herald his approach, no panoply to keep him in the public eye. His innate qualities give him admittance to any circles, high or low.

The first knowledge of the Greyhound comes from the Tomb of Amten, in the Valley of the Nile, regarded by Egyptologists as belonging to the fourth dynasty, which in modern chronology would be between 2900 and 2751 B.C. The carvings in this old tomb show dogs of unmistakable Greyhound type in three separate scenes. In two they are attacking a deer, while in the other an animal with horns, somewhat similar to the American mountain goat. The dogs have ring tails.

The origin of the name "Greyhound" is somewhat open to dispute, and a number of suppositions have been advanced. One is that it is derived from *Graius*, meaning Grecian, because the dog was in high esteem among the ancient Greeks. Another conjecture is that it derives from the old British *grech* or *greg*, meaning a dog. Also, some say that it came to use because gray was once the prevailing color in the breed.

While the old Egyptian scenes establish the Greyhound as a recognizable type at a very early date, it is from a Roman source that there has come the first complete description of the breed. This was written by Ovid, who lived from 43 B.C. to A.D. 17. Reading this, one can have little doubt that the dog of ancient times is the same as the one of today. With certain allowances, it fits perfectly.

The Greyhound always has had a cultural and aristocratic background. He was the favorite of royalty in Egypt, and he was bred and raised in such luxurious surroundings that there was every reason for the oppressed races and the common people of those times to hate this dog. Yet the disposition of the dog was just as lovable and tractable then as it is today. Had the common people been allowed to own specimens of this dog, the story would have been entirely different, but his ownership was restricted to the ruling classes.

The ancient traditions connected with the Greyhound have come down throughout history. He is found in England at a very early date. In fact, a manuscript from the ninth century A.D. is illustrated with a picture of Elfric, Duke of Mercia; and beside this old Saxon chieftain stands his huntsman with a brace of Greyhounds. Just how many centuries before the time of Elfric the Greyhound was known in England is not known, but there is every reason to suppose that the breed had been there a long time.

The famous Canute Laws, written in Danish—for at that time the Danes had conquered much of what is now England—and enacted in a Parliament held at Winchester in 1016, give further evidence as to the status of the Greyhound. No. 31 of these Canute Laws states:

> No meane person may keepe any greihounds, but freemen may keepe greihounds, so that their knees may be cut before the verderons of the forest, and without cutting of their knees also, if he does not abide 10 miles from the bounds of the forest. But if they doe come any nearer to the forest, they shall pay 12 pence for every mile; but if the greihound be found within the forest, the master or owner of the dog shall forfeit the dog and ten shillings to the King.

The Greyhound has been used on practically all kinds of small game from time to time, including deer, stags, foxes, and so forth, but the hare is his natural quarry, and coursing the sport with which he has been associated for centuries. In fact, coursing has been done on an organized basis in England for nearly two centuries.

The famous Waterloo Cup Meet was instituted in England in 1836, and it has been held continuously ever since—with the exception of the war years 1917 and 1918. On the other hand, two meetings were held in

199

1887, so actually the 1936 event was the one-hundredth. At the beginning this was an eight-dog stake, but in 1837 the number was double, and the next year it was double again to thirty-two dogs. In 1857 it became a sixty-four-dog stake, and it has remained that way ever since.

More than half a century before the Waterloo Cup event, there was organized one of the most colorful clubs in the sporting history of England. This was known as the Swaffham Coursing Society, and it came into being in 1776, organized by the Earl of Orford. It was limited to twenty-five members, using all but one letter of the alphabet, each member being assigned a letter and colors. Still, coursing did not assume uniformity until the Duke of Norfolk drew up a set of rules, some years later, that have been accepted as the standard procedure ever since.

The Greyhound came to America long before 1776. Laurel Drew, a historian of the breed, has traced Greyhounds that were brought to this country (along with Mastiffs) by Spanish explorers in the early 1500s "to guard, hunt, intimidate and punish their enemies—in this case, the Indians." The reports tell of Greyhound hunting prowess, of how they "went into the woods that were near and returned bringing hares and rabbits."

The Greyhound figures prominently in the journals of George Cartwright, an English explorer to Labrador in 1770. And Baron Freidrich von Steuben, the German professional soldier who was so helpful to General Washington in the American Revolutionary War, was always accompanied by a huge Greyhound named Azor.

One of the most celebrated of many Greyhound owners in history was General George A. Custer. Custer was especially fond of coursing breeds—Greyhounds and "staghounds"—and traveled with a hound pack that numbered about forty. One book reports that Custer's dogs were about to run a matched race the day before he left on his fatal expedition to Big Horn River in 1876.

Greyhounds were among the earliest at American dog shows, too. The catalog of the first Westminster Kennel Club show in 1877 includes the entry of 18 Greyhounds. And the breed was in the second edition of the AKC stud book (in 1885) with listings of three males and five bitches.

The invention of the mechanical lure by O. P. Smith in 1912, leading to the introduction of track racing for Greyhounds in the 1920s, added another—and sizeable—dimension to interest in the breed. This interest is as strong as ever today.

Official Standard for the Greyhound

Head—Long and narrow, fairly wide between the ears, scarcely perceptible stop, little or no development of nasal sinuses, good length of muzzle, which should be powerful without coarseness. Teeth very strong and even in front.

Ears—Small and fine in texture, thrown back and folded, except when excited, when they are semipricked.

Eyes—Dark, bright, intelligent, indicating spirit.

Neck—Long, muscular, without throatiness, slightly arched, and widening gradually into the shoulder.

Shoulders—Placed as obliquely as possible, muscular without being loaded.

Forelegs—Perfectly straight, set well into the shoulders, neither turned in nor out, pasterns strong.

Chest—Deep, and as wide as consistent with speed, fairly well-sprung ribs.

Back—Muscular and broad.

Loins—Good depth of muscle, well arched, well cut up in the flanks.

Hindquarters—Long, very muscular and powerful, wide and well let down, well-bent stifles. Hocks well bent and rather close to ground, wide but straight fore and aft.

Feet—Hard and close, rather more hare than cat-feet, well knuckled up with good strong claws.

Tail—Long, fine and tapering with a slight upward curve.

Coat—Short, smooth and firm in texture.

Color—Immaterial.

Weight—Dogs, 65 to 70 pounds; bitches, 60 to 65 pounds.

SCALE OF POINTS

General symmetry and quality	10	
Head and neck	20	
Chest and shoulders	20	
Back	10	
Quarters	20	
Legs and feet	20	
TOTAL	**100**	

Harrier

Probably the oldest work on hare hunting is the famous essay penned by the ancient Greek historian Xenophon about 400 B.C., and with that as a basis, hare hunting has been a favorite subject of the greatest authorities on the dog for the past 2300 years. Regardless of that, there is a striking unanimity of doubt concerning the direct ancestors of this old breed of scent hound.

The Harrier, as he exists today, was unknown in Xenophon's time, although he describes two types of hound that were used with equal success in the early hunting of the hare. One he calls "the Castorean," which was reputed to be the favorite of the demi-god Castor. The other is designated as "the fox-breed," which is explained as a product of the fox and the dog. On the other hand, Xenophon has listed the qualities of a hound suitable for the purposes, and they bear amazing similarity to the desirable points of modern times.

This early treatise on hunting is no fragmentary remnant of a scholarly mind, but one of the most definite and minute portrayals of a sport that ever has been written. Perhaps the only real difference between the way the Greeks hunted the hare and the manner accepted in England and other countries is that in 400 B.C. the hares were driven into nets. This practice would bring great censure on hunters of today. Still, sportsmanship was given some consideration in ancient times, for Xenophon says: "In tracking the hare, no delay should be made, for it is sportsmanlike, as well as a proof of fondness for exertion, to use every means to capture the animal speedily."

Even the great English authority on all breeds, Stonehenge, was a little mystified by the origin of the Harrier. The theory he advances rather cautiously is that it springs from the old Southern hound, with an infusion of a little Greyhound blood.

Undoubtedly the Southern hound has played a great part in the development of all scent hound breeds in the British Isles, yet there is little or no mention of the origin of this basic breed. The most logical supposition appears to be that it was brought to England by the Normans, for hunting is of great antiquity on the Continent.

The first pack of Harriers in England was the Penistone, which was established by Sir Elias de Midhope in 1260. These Harriers were held together for at least five centuries, and it is recorded that in the fourteenth, the seventeenth, and the eighteenth centuries, the masters were supplied by the Wilsons of Broomhead Hall. Hunting the hare has always had great popularity throughout the British Isles, and in some ways enjoyed greater favor than foxhunting. One great cause of its popularity was that a pack of Harriers could be followed on foot. This enlisted the interest of many, and among the hundred odd packs that hunted regularly in England half a century ago, many were scratch packs. A scratch pack was made up of hounds owned by various individuals—thus bringing the sport down to the level of the poorer man. However, horses are used in most cases today.

In support of the Norman origin of this and other hound breeds, there has been an interesting bit of information supplied by Wynn in regard to the name *harrier*. He shows that this may have come from the Norman word *harier*, denoting Saxon raches, or hounds. Further, *harier* was used down to 1750 for all hounds, not necessarily hare-hounds. And back in 1570, Dr. Caius mentioned stag- and fox-harriers.

Despite all stories of the ancient origin of Harriers, it is the general belief that the dog of today is merely a smaller edition of the Foxhound, and that he has been bred down from the larger hound by selective breeding. Save in size, the Harrier is the external replica of the Foxhound. Some specimens of the Harrier bear a unique, blue mottle color, which is not recognized in English Foxhounds, but in the majority of cases their colors are the same. It also is said that some Harriers are somewhat heavier in the head, in proportion, than is the Foxhound.

Harriers have been known in the United States as long as any of the scent-hound breeds, and they have been used for hunting since Colonial times. In later times, the Harrier proved a great favorite of the drag hunt, in which his slower pace is no detriment.

Official Standard for the
Harrier

The points of the modern Harrier are very similar to those of the English Foxhound. The Harrier, however, is smaller than the English Foxhound and the most popular size is 19 to 21 inches. They should be active, well balanced and full of strength and quality, with shoulders sloping into the muscles of the back, clean and not loaded on the withers or point.

The back level and muscular, and not dipping behind the withers or arching over the loin. The elbow's point set well away from the ribs, running parallel with the body and not turning outwards. Deep, well-sprung ribs, running well back, with plenty of heart room, and a deep chest.

Good straight legs with plenty of bone running well down to the toes, but not overburdened, inclined to knuckle over very slightly but not exaggerated in the slightest degree. Round catlike feet, and close toes turning inwards. Hind legs and hocks stand square, with a good sweep and muscular thigh to take the weight off the body.

The head should be of a medium size with good bold forehead, and plenty of expression; head must be well set up on a neck of ample length, and not heavy; stern should be set well up, long and well controlled.

Ibizan Hound

IBIZAN HOUND history is traceable back to approximately 3400 B.C. The glory that was ancient Egypt was a most fitting setting for this regal hound, which was owned and hunted by the Pharaohs.

Numerous artifacts found in the tombs of the Pharaohs now reinforce the existence of such a dog in those long past times. Hemako, who reigned in the period of the 1st Dynasty (3100 to 2700 B.C.) was buried in a tomb near Saggara. When this site was unearthed many artifacts were uncovered, one of which was a carved dish bearing the image of the Ibizan. These dogs, which are also referred to as Galgo Hounds, are quite distinct in their appearance; therefore, no other could be mistaken as being represented. Nevermat, of the 4th Dynasty, who lived at approximately 2600 B.C., Tutankhamen of the 14th century B.C. and the Ptolemies of the 30th and final Dynasty, all have tombs which have yielded further proof of the hound's ancient and proud heritage. Cleopatra was an ardent devotee of the Galgo, and her reign was the twilight of the Pharaohs' time in Egypt.

The tomb of Tutankhamen proved a treasure trove when discovered in 1922. Anubis, "The Watchdog of the Dead", a long honored deity, was well represented by a full sized true to life statue, which is the identical duplicate of the Ibizan Hound of today. This marvelously preserved piece of carved statuary was coated with resins and varnishes. The eyes are of obsidian (a volcanic variety of rock which has a very glassy look and is deep black) and are rimmed with gold leaf, as are the insides of the ears. Anubis also bears a beautiful collar of gold, but time had not deteriorated his beauty nor the fact that the original model could only have been the greyhound-type, prick eared, sickle tailed dog now known as the Ibizan. It was originally thought that the jackal had been the original model, this miscalculation due to the fact that the Ibizan was extinct in its land of origin at the time of these numerous discoveries.

We can but surmise the movement of the breed from Egypt to the island from which it now derives its name. The hardy sea-traders of Phoenicia were well traveled in those days and had entrée to many lands. It is thought that they are basically responsible for the survival of this breed. It was the Phoenicians who discovered the island now known as Ibiza in the 8th or 9th century B.C. Now belonging to Spain, Ibiza has been ruled and conquered by many — Egyptians, Chaldeans, Carthaginians, Romans, Vandals and Arabs. Roman coins bear the head of an Ibizan Hound, and Hasdrubal once ruled this land. Conejera, a member of this Balearic grouping was a small off island also which claims historical fame by being the birthplace of the famed Hannibal. It is said that the Ibizan Hound was the dog whch accompanied him with his mighty elephants on that long trek across the Alps.

This breed has survived even the hard life that the Ibizan group of islands has imposed on it. Only the fittest could survive, as food is scarce, and the natives used these dogs to assist in providing the necessary food to sustain their lives. As a result these dogs have learned to hunt with great skill, tenacity, and patience. The owners of these hounds also culled their litters diligently, for only the strongest and most perfect specimens could survive the hardships. We must give our thanks to those early owners and breeders, for through their dedication we have seen a breed travel through centuries unmarked by numerous problems evident in many other breeds. These animals are as strong, fit and vigorous today as they were in the days of the Pharaohs.

The first Ibizans reached the United States in mid-1956, imported by Colonel and Mrs. Seoane of Rhode Island. Hannibal (Stop) and Certera (Tanit) created quite a stir and soon it was known that the first litter would arrive in the fall. Eight pups were the result of the first breeding and the 4 males and 4 females (Asuncion, Malchus V, Denia, Heulalia, Granada, Mago, Gisco and Sertorius), along with several other imports and their parents, form the foundations of the breed here.

Over the years the breed has flourished in this county and they are respected by all who have come into intimate contact with them as lively companions, pets, watchdogs, hunters, and friends. They lend themselves well to family life and the ever-changing American life-styles. Their temperament is excellent, and their health has proven superior. Structurally they are extremely strong and resilient. The Ibizan Hound Club of the United States has been most stringent in impressing upon the owners and breeders of this hound the importance of fully retaining the fine qualities of this dog first and foremost, and has kept its pledge to preserve it true to form.

The Ibizan Hound was admitted to AKC stud book registration effective October 1, 1978, and became eligible for show competition January 1, 1979.

Official Standard for the Ibizan Hound

Head—Long and narrow, in the form of a sharp cone truncated at its base; extremely dry-fleshed. *Skull*–Long and flat, prominent occipital bone, little defined stop; narrow brow. *Ears*–Prominent prick ears, always rigid; erect on alert, but highly mobile and at times pointed forward, sideways, or backward, according to mood. The center of the base is at the level of the eyes, and in the form of an enlarged rhomboid truncated at a third of its longer diagonal. Thin, with texture of fine leather; no hair in interior. *Eyes*–Oblique and small, ranging in color from clear amber to caramel; aspect intelligent and unpredictable. *Muzzle*–Elongated, fine, and slender, sometimes snipy; very light Roman convex. Length from eyes to point of nose equal to distance from eyes to occiput. *Nose*–Prominent, extending beyond lower jaw; flesh color tending to harmonize with that of coat; nostrils open. *Jaws*–Exceptionally strong, lean. *Lips*–Thin and tight. *Teeth*–Level mouth; teeth perfectly opposed in scissors bite; white and well-set.

Neck—Long, slender, slightly arched; strong, yet flat-muscled.

Withers—Loose and detached.

Shoulders—Sloping.

Back—Level and straight; taut yet elastic.

Loins—Medium breadth; slightly arched.

Rump—Very slight sloping.

Tail—Long, set rather low; highly mobile, and carried in sickle, ring, otter or saber positions according to mood and individual specimen.

Chest—Deep and long; breastbone sharply angled and very prominent; flat ribs, protruding when dog is in top working condition.

Belly—Underbelly retracted, but not so deeply as Greyhound.

Forequarters—Straight front; forearms very long, strong, straight and close, lying flat on chest and continuing in straight line to ground. Clean fine bone; well-developed sinews; pasterns straight and flexible.

Hindquarters—Relatively vertical; strong but flat-muscled; hocks strong and close to ground.

Feet—Hare-foot; toes long and closed, very strong; interdigital spaces well protected by hair; durable pads.

Coat—*Short:* Shortest on head and ears and longest at back of thighs and under tail. *Wire-haired:* Can be from one to three inches in length with a possible generous mustache, more hair on back, back of thighs and tail. Both types of coat are always hard in texture. Neither coat is preferable to the other.

Color—Red and white, red with white, white with red, lion and white, lion with white, white with lion; solid white, solid red; all other colors excluded. The preponderant pattern is predominantly red, with white feet and "socks," tail tip, chest, and muzzle, with blaze on forehead. The solid colors are desirable but relatively rare.

Height—Height of dogs at withers ranges from 23½ to 27½ inches; height of bitches at withers ranges from 22½ to 26 inches. Sizes somewhat over or under norms not to be regarded as demerits when other qualities are good.

Weight—Average weight of dogs, 50 pounds; bitches, 42 to 49 pounds.

Gait—A trot in suspension; elegant and graceful in the manner of the Afghan. In speed the Ibizan is in the same class as other coursing breeds, and is without equal in agility and high-jumping and broad-jumping ability, being capable of springing to great heights from a standstill.

Approved October 10, 1978
Effective January 1, 1979

Irish Wolfhound

EARLY IRISH LITERATURE abounds in references to these large dogs which are called, interchangeably, "Irish dogs", "Big Dogs of Ireland", "Greyhounds (or Grehounds) of Ireland", "Wolfdogs of Ireland", "Great Hounds of Ireland". Irish Wolfhound is the more modern name.

By the year 391 A.D., the breed was known in Rome, when the first authentic mention of it was written by the Roman Consul Quintus Aurelius, who had received seven of them as a gift which "all Rome viewed with wonder." Through the ensuing centuries the Irish Wolfhound has inspired poets and authors. In 1790 it was written, "The Irish Greyhound is the largest of dogkind and its appearance the most beautiful. He is about 3 feet high, somewhat like a Greyhound but more robust. His aspect is mild, his disposition is peaceable, yet his strength so great that in combat the Mastiff or Bulldog is far from being equal to him."

In the following century another wrote of the Irish Wolfhound, "This noble animal is similar in shape to the Greyhound, larger than the Mastiff, tractable as the Spaniel."

He was coveted for his hunting prowess, particularly in the pursuit of the gigantic Irish elk which stood six feet at the shoulders, and the wolf. With the disappearance from Ireland of these animals, and the excessive exportation of the dwindling ranks of Wolfhounds, the breed was allowed to become almost extinct.

It was at this point that Captain George A. Graham, a Scot in the British Army, gathered the remaining specimens and restored the breed. His work began in 1862 and 23 years later, under his supervision, the first breed standard was set forth. To meet the requirements of this standard remains the goal which every bona fide breeder strives to attain.

The Irish Wolfhound is a large rough-coated, shaggy-browed hound, built on galloping lines. Even as he lies by a modern hearth or romps about an enclosed lawn, gallops in a meadow or along a beach, it is easy to imagine him as the prominent figure he once was in the feudal life of the Middle Ages.

Because of his great size and the amount of exercise essential to his well-being, the Irish Wolfhound is not a dog to be acquired without serious forethought. His ideal home is one which provides fenced property of sufficient size to accomodate the galloping natural to this athletic sight hound. Hunting by sight and chase is what he was bred and historically used for; the length of leg and back, the deep chest, the power of his limbs and body attest to the heritage and needs of the Irish Wolfhound.

His ideal owner is one who has the capacity to respond to the gentle nature which dwells within his great frame; who discerns the intelligence which manifests itself in his response to everyday situations as they occur. The Irish Wolfhound does best when human companionship is the core of his daily life. At maturity, despite his space-eating size, he is a calm presence within a family circle, dignified and responsive, providing no harshness of attitude or deed is directed his way. A sensitive dog, the Irish Wolfhound's development is thwarted when his environment is ungiving.

His nature and temperament make him totally unsuitable as guard dog, watch dog, or patrol dog, in country, town or city. Though alert he is not suspicious; though courageous he is not aggressive.

City dwellers and those in closely populated suburbs frequently are seeking guard or watch dogs, and frequently today, these are working couples who want a dog to be on solitary duty in an apartment or house from morning to night. Emphatically, the Irish Wolfhound is not a satisfactory choice. As an incidental function, by his very appearance, he is a formidable deterrent to intruders, but he is more likely to serenade the moon than bark at noises and people. To confine a mature dog of this size as his way of life is foolhardy; subjecting a puppy to such circumstances should be unthinkable. Wolfhound puppyhood lasts a year or more and left alone a puppy can demolish a room per hour and injure himself in the process. A six-month-old Irish Wolfhound puppy weighs about 100 pounds, is not yet through teething; nor are his body functions ready for prolonged containment.

An occasional Irish Wolfhound is raised and kept successfully under less than ideal conditions by owners who have not only the wish, but the will and the stamina to provide very extensive leash walking and to cope with sidewalks and traffic, close neighbors and pedestrians. The hygienic responsibility incumbent upon owners of giant breeds of dogs is awesome.

Irish Wolfhounds have only the kindest intentions toward children. Common sense, however, precludes the mingling of a small child with a young Wolfhound; the child is no match for an affectionate, playful puppy weighing 50 to 100 pounds, a toss of whose head or a running sideswipe of whose body can have bruising consequences.

A completely natural breed, the Wolfhound's ears are uncropped, his tail undocked. Clippers and trimmers are enemies to his coat: no part of him, particularly his head, should appear styled.

Irish Wolfhounds compete in dog shows from coast to coast, though he is seen in greater number at those held outdoors, which better suit him. No stranger to obedience competition and coursing trials, he has won degrees and titles in both.

The habitat of most Irish Wolfhounds bred in this century has been the private home where his quiet manners, gentle nature and comfortable sense of companionship have made it a natural one. Although the chase is not his preoccupation, we must never forget it is his natural sport and the sight of him in characteristic gallop, swiftly covering the ground beneath him, is exhilarating and leaves no doubt of his need to exercise this birthright.

Official Standard for the
Irish Wolfhound

General Appearance—Of great size and commanding appearance, the Irish Wolfhound is remarkable in combining power and swiftness with keen sight. The largest and tallest of the galloping hounds, in general type he is a rough-coated, Greyhoundlike breed; very muscular, strong though gracefully built; movements easy and active; head and neck carried high, the tail carried with an upward sweep with a slight curve towards the extremity. The minimum height and weight of dogs should be 32 inches and 120 pounds; of bitches, 30 inches and 105 pounds; these to apply only to hounds over 18 months of age. Anything below this should be debarred from competition. Great size, including height at shoulder and proportionate length of body, is the desideratum to be aimed at, and it is desired to firmly establish a race that shall average from 32 to 34 inches in dogs, showing the requisite power, activity, courage and symmetry.

Head—Long, the frontal bones of the forehead very slightly raised and very little indentation between the eyes. Skull, not too broad. Muzzle, long and moderately pointed. Ears, small and Greyhoundlike in carriage.

Neck—Rather long, very strong and muscular, well arched, without dewlap or loose skin about the throat.

Chest—Very deep. Breast, wide.

Back—Rather long than short. Loins arched.

Tail—Long and slightly curved, of moderate thickness, and well covered with hair.

Belly—Well drawn up.

Forequarters—Shoulders, muscular, giving breadth of chest, set sloping. Elbows well under, neither turned inwards nor outwards.

Leg—Forearm muscular, and the whole leg strong and quite straight.

Hindquarters—Muscular thighs and second thigh long and strong as in the Greyhound, and hocks well let down and turning neither in nor out.

Feet—Moderately large and round, neither turned inwards nor outwards. Toes, well arched and closed. Nails, very strong and curved.

Hair—Rough and hard on body, legs and head; especially wiry and long over eyes and underjaw.

Color and Markings—The recognized colors are gray, brindle, red, black, pure white, fawn, or any other color that appears in the Deerhound.

FAULTS

Too light or heavy a head, too highly arched frontal bone; large ears and hanging flat to the face; short neck; full dewlap; too narrow or too broad a chest; sunken or hollow or quite straight back; bent forelegs; overbent fetlocks; twisted feet; spreading toes; too curly a tail; weak hindquarters and a general want of muscle; too short in body. Lips or nose liver-colored or lacking pigmentation.

LIST OF POINTS IN ORDER OF MERIT

1. *Typical.* The Irish Wolfhound is a rough-coated Greyhoundlike breed, the tallest of the coursing hounds and remarkable in combining power and swiftness.
2. *Great size* and commanding appearance.
3. Movements easy and active.
4. Head, long and level, carried high.
5. Forelegs, heavily boned, quite straight; elbows well set under.
6. Thighs long and muscular; second thighs, well muscled, stifles nicely bent.
7. Coat, rough and hard, specially wiry and long over eyes and under jaw.
8. Body, long, well ribbed up, with ribs well sprung, and great breadth across hips.
9. Loins arched, belly well drawn up.
10. Ears, small, with Greyhoundlike carriage.
11. Feet, moderately large and round; toes, close, well arched.
12. Neck, long, well arched and very strong.
13. Chest, very deep, moderately broad.
14. Shoulders, muscular, set sloping.
15. Tail, long and slightly curved.
16. Eyes, dark.

Note—The above in no way alters the "Standard of Excellence," which must in all cases be rigidly adhered to; they simply give the various points in order of merit. If in any case they appear at variance with Standard of Excellence, it is the latter which is correct.

Approved September 12, 1950

Norwegian Elkhound

COMRADE to the vikings, guardian of lonely farms and *saeters*, herder of flocks and defender from wolves and bear, a hunter always and a roamer with hardy men, the Norwegian Elkhound comes down to us through more than six millennia with all his Nordic traits untainted, a fearless dog and friendly, devoted to man and the chase. We read of him in sagas, we find his remains by the side of his viking-master along with the viking's weapons—sure proof of the esteem in which he was held; and in the Viste Cave at Jaeren, in western Norway, his skeleton was uncovered among the stone implements in a stratum dating from 4000 to 5000 B.C.

Selected and bred for his ability to accomplish a definite purpose, the Elkhound achieved his distinctive type by natural methods. No form was imposed upon him; he was not squeezed into a preconceived standard; his structure and rare beauty, like those of the thoroughbred horse, were evolved from the tests of performance. Every physical characteristic is the expression of a need. His compactness, his muscled robustness, his squareness, his width and depth are true expressions of nature's requirements for a dog that would hunt day after day and all day long in rugged country, where stamina rather than extreme speed is called for.

For, though the Elkhound in foreign countries has become known and loved chiefly, perhaps, for his engaging and sensitive qualities as a comrade of man, his reliability and quickness to learn and adapt himself to any circumstances and conditions, it should never be forgotten that, from first to last, he has been at all times the peerless hunter of big game.

Many years ago, bear were still common in Norway, but today they are almost extinct, and the native dog's main use is the hunting of elk. (*Elk* is incorrectly used in the United States for the Wapiti, *Cervus Canadensis,* and our *moose* is a true elk.) A century ago, Captain Lloyd, an English sportsman, a mighty hunter, and a fascinating writer, devoted his leisure to the description of bear hunting in Norway; and from that time on, everyone that has seen the Elkhound work in the forests of his native land has added to his praise. Space forbids adequate treatment of the subject here; but those who wish to pursue the matter further and who cannot obtain a copy of Captain Lloyd's books, now long out of print, will find an excellent substitute in Frantz Rosenberg's *Big Game Shooting,* published in England in 1928.

The Elkhound's highly developed senses amount almost to intuition, and it is common to read of, or, if one is fortunate, experience, such incidents as seeing a seasoned dog take body scent at from two to three miles or to hear him indicating to his master by a slight whimpering that the elk has become alarmed and has begun to run, at a time when no human senses can apprehend any sign by which the hound ascertains this fact. Equally subtle is his method of engaging a bull. Knowing well that an elk can outfoot him, he holds the animal by just enough barking to attract his attention. Even with a skillful dog, however, the elk often moves on before the hunter can get up over the steep countryside; and in that case, the dog, aware that the bull, if not excited by sound or scent, will soon pause, works silently and very carefully up wind until he is once more with his quarry.

After a while, the bull, becoming angry at the small beast annoying him, begins to attack with a wide sweeping movement of the great antlers and by striking with his deadly forefeet; but now, the Elkhound, short-backed so that he can, to use Herr Aarflot's apt expression, bounce like a rubber ball, jumps nimbly in and out, while giving full and furious tongue so that his high-pitched voice will reach his master.

The Elkhound is well adapted to the hunting of any other four-footed game and soon becomes expert on lynx, mountain lion, and raccoon; and Sir Henry Pottinger declares that he is also an excellent tracker of fox. The same authority states: "There is no more deadly way of approaching capercailzie, black game, and other forest birds than with a dog of the breed under discussion held or fastened to the belt by a long leash and allowed to precede the hunter."

The Elkhound, then, is an exceedingly versatile dog developed through constant contact with man in pursuit of game. It was not until

1877 that he began to be considered from an exhibition point of view. In that year the Norwegian Hunters' Association held its first show, and shortly thereafter pedigrees, which had been handed down, were checked and traced as far back as feasible, a stud book (*Norsk Hundestambok*) was published, and a standard drawn up. Before that time, there had been some confusion of type owing to different developments in different parts of the country; but if we study the photograph of such a grand dog as that pillar of the stud book, known to fame as Gamle Bamse Gram (Old Bamse that belonged to Consul Gram), we shall see that all the essential elements of the modern show dog were already there, needing only a little refinement, a little emphasis.

At any rate, by the turn of the century, the breed was making very rapid progress, and, though there were few or no really large kennels, there were many expert breeders devoted to the Elkhound's improvement; and when the Norwegian Kennel Club (Norsk Kennelklub) inaugurated its annual shows at Oslo, the Elkhound came into his own as Norway's great contribution to dogdom. Since then he has been exported in ever-increasing numbers; and his friendly disposition, his intelligence, his staunchness, his absolute dependability and trustworthiness, his eagerness to praise, his sensitivity and his fearless confidence have gained for him everywhere a popularity based even more on his comradely character than on his unsurpassed abilities as a sporting hound.

Official Standard for the Norwegian Elkhound

General Description—The Norwegian Elkhound is a hardy gray hunting dog. In appearance, a typical northern dog of medium size and substance, square in profile, close coupled and balanced in proportions. The head is broad with prick ears, and the tail is tightly curled and carried over the back. The distinctive gray coat is dense and smooth-lying. In temperament, the Norwegian Elkhound is bold and energetic, an effective guardian yet normally friendly, with great dignity and independence of character. As a hunter, the Norwegian Elkhound has the courage, agility and stamina to hold moose and other big game at bay by barking and dodging attack, and the endurance to track for long hours in all weather over rough and varied terrain.

In the show ring, presentation in a natural, unaltered condition is essential.

Head—Broad at the ears, wedge-shaped, strong, and dry (without loose skin). Viewed from the side, the forehead and back of the skull are only slightly arched; the stop not large, yet clearly defined. The bridge of the nose is straight, parallel to and about the same length as the skull. The muzzle is thickest at the base and, seen from above or from the side, tapers evenly without being pointed. Lips are tightly closed and teeth meet in a scissors bite.

Ears—Set high, firm and erect, yet very mobile. Comparatively small; slightly taller than their width at the base with pointed (not rounded) tips. When the dog is alert, the orifices turn forward and the outer edges are vertical.

Eyes—Very dark brown, medium in size, oval, not protruding.

Neck—Of medium length, muscular, well set up with a slight arch and with no loose skin on the throat.

Body—Square in profile and close coupled. Distance from brisket to ground appears to be half the height at the withers. Distance from forechest to rump equals the height at the withers. Chest deep and moderately broad; brisket level with points of elbows; and ribs well sprung. Loin short and wide with very little tuck-up. The back is straight and strong from its high point at the withers to the root of the tail.

Forequarters—Shoulders sloping with elbows closely set on. Legs well under body and medium in length; substantial, but not coarse, in bone. Seen from the front, the legs appear straight and parallel. Single dewclaws are normally present.

Hindquarters—Moderate angulation at stifle and hock. Thighs are broad and well-muscled. Seen from behind, legs are straight, strong and without dewclaws.

Feet—Paws comparatively small, slightly oval with tightly-closed toes and thick pads. Pasterns are strong and only slightly bent. Feet turn neither in nor out.

Tail—Set high, tightly curled, and carried over the centerline of the back. It is thickly and closely haired, without brush, natural and untrimmed.

Coat—Thick, hard, weather-resisting and smooth-lying; made up of soft, dense, woolly undercoat and coarse, straight covering hairs. Short and even on head, ears, and front of legs; longest on back of neck, buttocks and underside of tail. The coat is not altered by trimming, clipping or artificial treatment. Trimming of whiskers is optional.

Color—Gray, medium preferred, variations in shade determined by the length of black tips and quantity of guard hairs. Undercoat is clear light silver as are legs, stomach, buttocks, and underside of tail. The gray body color is darkest on the saddle, lighter on the chest, mane and distinctive harness mark (a band of longer guard hairs from shoulder to elbow). The muzzle, ears, and tail tip are black. The black of the muzzle shades to lighter gray over the forehead and skull. Yellow or brown shading, white patches, indistinct or irregular markings, "sooty" coloring on the lower legs and light circles around the eyes are undesirable. Any overall color other than gray as described above, such as red, brown, solid black, white or other solid color, disqualifies.

Gait—Normal for an active dog constructed for agility and endurance. At a trot the stride is even and effortless; the back remains level. As the speed of the trot increases, front and rear legs converge equally in straight lines toward a center line beneath the body so that the pads appear to follow in the same tracks (single-track). Front and rear quarters are well balanced in angulation and muscular development.

Size—The height at the withers for dogs is 20$^{1}/_{2}$ inches, for bitches 19$^{1}/_{2}$ inches. Weight for dogs about 55 pounds; for bitches about 48 pounds.

DISQUALIFICATIONS

Any overall color other than gray as described above, such as red, brown, solid black, white or other solid color.

Approved February 13, 1973

Otter Hound

WHILE THERE are allusions to otter hunting and Otter Hounds in the time of King John, who reigned in England from 1199 to 1216, it is not until Edward II (1307-1327) that there is any sort of a description of the kind of dogs that made up a pack of Otter Hounds. This record has been left, fortunately, by William Twici, the huntsman. He makes mention of them as a "rough sort of dog, between a hound and a terrier."

The hunting of the otter never was a so-called major sport in England, but it appears to have existed from very early times. It first was practiced because the otters were preying on the fish in the rivers and streams to an annoying extent. Later it enjoyed a considerable vogue because it was the only kind of hunting possible from April to September.

The undoubted heyday of the Otter Hound in England extended from the middle to the end of the nineteenth century. During many of those years there were eighteen to twenty packs hunting regularly through the season. Most famous, for its record of killing otters, was the Hawkstone pack of the Hon. Geoffrey Hill. From 1870 to 1890 this pack disposed of 704 otters, in 1881, alone, killing sixty-two.

Still, all authorities agree that the best trained pack of Otter Hounds ever hunted in England was that of Squire Lomax of Clitheroe. This was at the peak of its perfection about 1868. The Squire was a stickler for the fine points of the game, and, while results interested him, his major concern was the manner in which his pack worked. It is said that they were trained so well that his signals could be given with the most casual wave of the hand. But then, Squire Lomax had spent the greater part of his life developing this pack; and when the majority of them died in one season, he did not attempt to replace them, believing that enough years did not remain for him to train a new pack as well as the first.

The origin of the Otter Hound is shrouded in mystery, but the earliest writers advance a number of logical opinions as to its origin. According to Stonehenge, its ancestors are the Southern hound and the Welsh Harrier. This is supported by the fact that there were large numbers of Otter Hounds to be found in Devonshire, the chief stronghold of the Southern hound, and in Wales.

A somewhat less acceptable opinion is that of E. Buckley, who ascribes the coat of the Otter Hound to the Water Spaniel—a somewhat different type from the breed known today—and credits the hardiness to the Bulldog. Other writers mention the Bloodhound, supporting this by the domed shape of the skull, and the length of the ears. In fact, writing as early as 1575, Turberville makes no distinction between the Bloodhound and the Otter Hound in describing the hunting of the otter.

The French origin of the Otter Hound appears to be one of the most reasonable. This is the opinion of Marples, who, describing the Otter Hound, says it is the almost exact duplicate of the old Vendee hound of France. The two breeds are alike in both coat and bodily formation.

The Otter Hound is a big dog, ranging from 24 to 27 inches, and weighing from 75 to 115 pounds. He has a hard, crisp and close coat of an oily nature that can stand any amount of immersion in water. The most desired combination of colors always has been the blue and white, but the breed ranges through many shades to black and tan. It is a peer among swimmers, its progress through the water being aided greatly by its webbed feet.

The working qualities of the Otter Hound always have been emphasized to such an extent that it never has been popularly known as a bench-show specimen in England. Still, it usually was the custom for some of the great packs to send a few couple apiece to the major shows. The Carlisle and Kendal packs were noted for their show dogs.

Otter Hounds first made their appearance in the United States about the year 1900, and they made their bench-show debut in 1907 at shows in Claremont, Okla., and registrations are recorded. These are of Hartland Mosstrooper, 135,335, and Hartland Statesman, 135,334, both owned by H.S. Wardner of New York City. Incidentally, Mr. Wardner was one of the two exhibitors of 1907, and he undoubtedly was America's first breeder.

While the Otter Hound never has grown to wide popularity in the United States, its sagacity and character have retained for it many steadfast friends. What it lacks in smartness of appearance is compensated by its working qualities and its unfailing devotion to its master.

Official Standard for the Otter Hound

General Appearance—The Otter Hound is a large, rough-coated, squarely symmetrical hound. The length of a dog's body from withers to base of tail is approximately equal to its height at the withers. However, a bitch is not to be faulted if her length of body is slightly greater than her height. The Otter Hound is amiable and boisterous. It has an extremely sensitive nose, and is inquisitive and persevering in investigating scents. The Otter Hound should be shown on a loose lead. The Otter Hound hunts its quarry on land and water and requires a combination of characteristics unique among hounds—most notably a rough, double coat and webbed feet.

Head—The head is large, fairly narrow, and well covered with hair. The length from tip of nose to occiput is 11 to 12 inches in a hound 26 inches at the withers. This proportion should be maintained in larger and smaller hounds.

The *skull* (cranium) is long, fairly narrow under the hair, and only slightly domed. The muzzle is long and square in cross-section with powerful jaws and deep flews. The *stop* is not pronounced. The *nose* is large, dark, and completely pigmented. The *ears* are long, pendulous, and folded. They are set low and hang close to the head. They are well covered and fringed with hair. The tips of the *ear* leather reach at least to the tip of the nose. The *eyes* are deeply set. The haw shows only slightly. The eyes are dark, but may vary with the color of the hound. The *jaws* are powerful and capable of a crushing grip. A scissors bite is preferred. **Faults**—Bite grossly undershot or overshot.

Neck and Body—The *neck* looks shorter than it really is because of the abundance of hair on it. The neck blends smoothly into the trunk. The *chest* is deep; the *ribs* extend well toward the rear of the trunk. The *topline* is level. The *tail* is fairly long, reaching at least to the hock. It is well feathered (covered and fringed with hair). It is carried sickle-fashion (not over the back) when a dog is moving or alert, but may droop when the dog is at rest.

Forequarters—*Shoulders* clean, powerful, and well-sloped. *Legs* heavy-boned and straight.

Hindquarters—Thighs large and well-muscled. *Legs* moderately angulated. Legs parallel when viewed from the rear. *Feet* large, broad, compact, and well padded, with membranes connecting the toes (web-footed). *Dewclaws*, if any, on the hind legs are generally removed; dewclaws on the forelegs may be removed.

Coat—The rough outer coat is three to six inches long on the back, shorter on the extremities. It must be hard (coarse and crisp). A water-resistant inner coat of short woolly hair is an essential feature of the breed. A naturally stripped coat lacking length and fringes is correct for an Otter Hound that is being worked. A proper hunting coat will show the hard outer coat and woolly undercoat. **Faults**—A soft outer coat is a very serious fault as is a woolly-textured top coat. Lack of undercoat is a serious fault. An outer coat much longer than six inches becomes heavy when wet and is a fault.

Color—Any color or combination of colors is acceptable. The nose should be darkly pigmented, black or liver, depending on the color of the hound.

Gait—The Otter Hound moves freely with forward reach and drive. The gait is smooth and effortless and capable of being maintained for many miles. Otter Hounds single-track at slower speed than light-bodied hounds. Because they do not lift their feet high off the ground, Otter Hounds may shuffle when they walk or move at a slow trot.

Size—Males range from 24 to 27 inches at the withers, and weigh from 75 to 115 pounds, depending on the height and condition of the hound. Bitches are 22 to 26 inches at the withers and 65 to 100 pounds. A hound in hard working condition may weigh as much as 15 pounds less than one of the same height that is not being worked. Otter Hounds should not be penalized for being shown in working condition (lean, well-muscled, naturally stripped coat).

Approved October 12, 1971

Rhodesian Ridgeback

THE RHODESIAN RIDGEBACK, sometimes referred to as the African Lion Hound, is a native of South Africa having been bred by the Boer farmers to fill their specific need for a serviceable hunting dog in the wilds.

The Dutch, Germans, and Huguenots who emigrated to South Africa in the sixteenth and seventeenth centuries brought with them Danes, Mastiffs, Greyhounds, Bloodhounds, Terriers, and other breeds. For one hundred years from 1707, European immigration was closed, and the native dogs played an important part in the development and ultimate character of the Ridgeback.

The Hottentots, a native race living within range of these early settlers, had a hunting dog that was half wild with a ridge on his back formed by the hair growing forward. There was interbreeding between these dogs and those of the settlers, and this crossbreeding, in due course, established the foundation stock of our present-day Ridgeback.

Good hunting dogs were hard to come by in those days and their value was high. The Boer settler needed a dog that could flush a few partridge, pull down a wounded buck, guard the farm from marauding animals and prowlers at night. He also needed a dog that could withstand the rigors of the African Bush, hold up under the drastic changes in temperature from the heat of the day to nights below freezing, and go a full twenty-four hours or more without water. He required a shorthaired dog that would not be eaten by ticks. In addition, he needed a companion that would stay by him while he slept in the Bush and that would be devoted to his wife and children. These were the qualities that the early settlers needed in a dog. Of necessity, then, the Boer farmer developed, by selective breeding, a distinct breed of the African Veldt—the Ridgeback.

In 1877, the Reverend Helm introduced two Ridgebacks into Rhodesia where the big game hunters, Selons, Upcher, Van Rooyen, and others, found them outstanding in the sport of hunting lions on horseback. They raised and bred these dogs with an appreciation of their exceptional hunting qualities, the ridge on their back becoming a unique trademark. In 1922, a group of Rhodesian breeders set up a standard for Ridgebacks which has remained virtually unchanged ever since.

Some outstanding specimens were imported in 1950, and the breed was admitted to registry by the AKC in 1955.

The Ridgeback, in a comparatively short space of time, has won himself many admirers in the United States for his innate qualities. He is clean, an easy keeper and never noisy or quarrelsome. Because of his heritage, obedience training comes readily to him and his desire to please his master, coupled with his general good nature and liking for children, is making him new friends each year.

Official Standard for the
Rhodesian Ridgeback

The peculiarity of this breed is the *ridge* on the back, which is formed by the hair growing in the opposite direction to the rest of the coat. The ridge must be regarded as the characteristic feature of the breed. The ridge should be clearly defined, tapering and symmetrical. It should start immediately behind the shoulders and continue to a point between the prominence of the hips, and should contain two identical crowns opposite each other. The lower edges of the crown should not extend further down the ridge than one third of the ridge.

General Appearance—The Ridgeback should represent a strong muscular and active dog, symmetrical in outline, and capable of great endurance with a fair amount of speed.

Head—Should be of a fair length, the skull flat and rather broad between the ears and should be free from wrinkles when in repose. The stop should be reasonably well defined. *Muzzle*—Should be long, deep and powerful, jaws level and strong with well-developed teeth, especially the canines or holders. The lips clean, closely fitting the jaws. *Eyes*—Should be moderately well apart, and should be round, bright and sparkling, with intelligent expression, their color harmonizing with the color of the dog. *Ears*—Should be set rather high, of medium size, rather wide at base, and tapering to a rounded point. They should be carried close to the head. **Nose**—Should be black, or brown, in keeping with the color of the dog. No other colored nose is permissible. A black nose should be accompanied by dark eyes, a brown nose by amber eyes.

Neck and Shoulders—The neck should be fairly strong and free from throatiness. The shoulders should be sloping, clean and muscular, denoting speed.

Body, Back, Chest and Loins—The chest should not be too wide, but very deep and capacious; ribs moderately well sprung, never rounded like barrel hoops (which would indicate want of speed), the back powerful, the loins strong, muscular and slightly arched.

Legs and Feet—The forelegs should be perfectly straight, strong and heavy in bone; elbows close to the body. The feet should be compact, with well-arched toes, round, tough, elastic pads, protected by hair between the toes and pads. In the hind legs the muscles should be clean, well defined, and hocks well down.

Tail—Should be strong at the insertion, and generally tapering towards the end, free from coarseness. It should not be inserted too high or too low, and should be carried with a slight curve upwards, never curled.

Coat—Should be short and dense, sleek and glossy in appearance, but neither woolly nor silky.

Color—Light wheaten to red wheaten. A little white on the chest and toes permissible but excessive white there and any white on the belly or above the toes is undesirable.

Size—A mature Ridgeback should be a handsome, upstanding dog; dogs should be of a height of 25 to 27 inches, and bitches 24 to 26 inches.

Weight—(Desirable) dogs 75 pounds, bitches 65 pounds.

SCALE OF POINTS

Ridge	20	Coat	5
Head	15	Tail	5
Neck and shoulders	10	Size, symmetry, general	
Body, back, chest, loins	10	appearance	20
Legs and feet	15	TOTAL	100

Approved November, 1955

Saluki

THE SALUKI, royal dog of Egypt, is perhaps the oldest known breed of domesticated dog, "a distinct breed and type as long ago as 329 B.C. when Alexander the Great invaded India." He is said to be as old as the earliest known civilization, the claim being based on the fact that the hounds shown on the earliest carvings look more like Salukis than any other breed: they have a Greyhound body with feathered ears, tail, and legs. Exactly the same hound appears on the Egyptian tombs of 2100 B.C. and more recent excavations of the still older Sumerian empire, estimated at 7000-6000 B.C., have produced carvings of striking resemblance to the Saluki.

"Whenever one sees the word 'dog' in the Bible it means the Saluki." As the Mohammedan religion classes the dog as unclean, the Moslem declared the Saluki sacred and called him "the noble one" given them by Allah for their amusement and benefit. This permitted them to eat of the meat brought down in the chase. The Saluki was the only dog of the time allowed to sleep on the carpet of the Sheikh's tent. So great was the esteem in which the dog was held that his body was often mummified like the bodies of the Pharaohs themselves. The remains of numerous specimens have thus been found in the ancient tombs of the Upper Nile region.

As the desert tribes are nomadic, the habitat of the Saluki comprised all the region stretching from the Caspian Sea to the Sahara, including Egypt, Arabia, Palestine, Syria, Mesopotamia, Anatholia, and Persia. Naturally the types varied somewhat in this widely scattered area. However, this difference was mostly in size and coat. Thus we find the Arabian-bred Saluki of a smaller type with less feathering on the legs and ears than the Persian variety.

Salukis were first brought into England in 1840: a bitch owned by Sir Hamilton Smith, a dog in Regents Park Zoological Gardens, and one owned by the Duke of Devonshire at Chatsworth. They were then known as Persian Greyhounds, since these three came from Persia. Evidently there was no real interest, however, in Salukis until the Hon. Florence Amherst imported the first Arabian Salukis in 1895, from the kennels of Prince Abdulla in Transjordania. It is greatly to her credit that the breed has made such headway among European countries.

England later learned more about the Saluki from her army officers stationed in the East during the Great War. Other specimens, either prizes of war or the gifts of friendly tribes, were brought home. Mr. Mervyn Herbert brought back several fine specimens from Egypt while Mr. Vereker-Cowley imported Malik-el-Zobair and Zobeida-el-Zobair. These, with Ch. Sarona Kelb and Sarona-Sarona, imported from Mesopotamia by Brigadier General Lance in 1920, figure prominently in the pedigrees of most of our present-day Salukis.

Having tremendous speed, the Saluki was used by the Arabs principally in bringing down the gazelle, that fastest of antelopes. It is recorded that the Pharaohs rode to the chase with their hawks on their wrists and Salukis on the lead. We also believe the Saluki was used on jackals, foxes, and hares. A cut published in 1852 shows a wild boar hunt in Algeria with Salukis tackling the boar. In England, the dog is used largely on hares, and regular coursing meets are held, with the judging based on ability to turn quickly and overtake the hare in the best possible time. The Saluki hunts largely by sight, although he has a fair nose. The sport of racing Salukis is much enjoyed in England and on the Continent, where a special track with a mechanical rabbit and hurdles at intervals is used.

The Saluki's sight is remarkable, and his hereditary traits often crop out—he loves to lie on the sand and watch an eagle soaring for his prey while paying no attention to the gull. Sarona Dhole, a son of Sarona Kalb, soon after his arrival in America, chased a fox and registered a kill within a few seconds after sighting the quarry.

On his native heath the Saluki gets no pampering. He lives hard, and it is a case of survival of the fittest—one reason for his strong constitution and sturdy frame, enabling him to stand any climate in unheated kennels. His feet are hard and firm, and the hair between the toes is a great protection. In all his running and dodging over the roughest kind of ground and rocky country, he never damages pads or toes.

His beauty is that of the thoroughbred horse; grace and symmetry of form; clean-cut and graceful; short silky hair except on the ears, legs, and tail; slender, well-muscled neck, shoulders, and thighs; arched loins; long tail carried naturally in a curve with silky hair hanging from the underside; the arched toes; the rather long head with deep, far-seeing eyes—an expression of dignity mixed with gentleness.

Salukis come in a wide variety of colors, including white, cream, fawn, golden, red, grizzle and tan, tri-color (white, black and tan), and black and tan.

In disposition he shows great attachment to his master. He is affectionate without being demonstrative, a good watchdog but not aggressive.

The Saluki was a well-established breed in England for a number of years before he began to come into his own in this country. It was not until November, 1927, that the breed was officially recognized by The American Kennel Club. In July, 1927, the Saluki Club of America was formed, with only seven or eight fanciers among its members, and since that time interest has been steadily growing.

At the Westminster Show of 1927 there were two Salukis entered in the Miscellaneous Class. The following year regular classes were provided, and there were ten. In 1929 there was a further increase in entries, with much more interest shown by the public. Since the breed was officially recognized by The American Kennel Club, there have been regular classes at all the principal shows. So now, instead of being looked upon as something of a curiosity, the Saluki is a familiar sight in the dog world and is becoming more popular year by year.

Official Standard for the Saluki

Head—Long and narrow, skull moderately wide between the ears, not domed, stop not pronounced, the whole showing great quality. Nose black or liver. **Ears**—Long and covered with long silky hair hanging close to the skull and mobile. **Eyes**—Dark to hazel and bright; large and oval, but not prominent. **Teeth**—Strong and level.

Neck—Long, supple and well muscled.

Chest—Deep and moderately narrow. **Forequarters**—Shoulders sloping and set well back, well muscled without being coarse. **Forelegs**—Straight and long from the elbow to the knee.

Hindquarters—Strong, hipbones set well apart and stifle moderately bent, hocks low to the ground, showing galloping and jumping power.

Loin and Back—Back fairly broad, muscles slightly arched over loin.

Feet—Of moderate length, toes long and well arched, not splayed out, but at the same time not cat-footed; the whole being strong and supple and well feathered between the toes.

Tail—Long, set on low and carried naturally in a curve, well feathered on the underside with long silky hair, not bushy.

Coat—Smooth and of a soft silky texture, slight feather on the legs, feather at the back of the thighs and sometimes with slight woolly feather on the thigh and shoulder.

Colors—White, cream, fawn, golden, red, grizzle and tan, tricolor (white, black and tan) and black and tan.

General Appearance—The whole appearance of this breed should give an impression of grace and symmetry and of great speed and endurance coupled with strength and activity to enable it to kill gazelle or other quarry over deep sand or rocky mountains. The expression should be dignified and gentle with deep, faithful, far-seeing eyes. Dogs should average in height from 23 to 28 inches and bitches may be considerably smaller, this being very typical of the breed.

The Smooth Variety—In this variety the points should be the same with the exception of the coat, which has no feathering.

Scottish Deerhound

THE ORIGIN of the Deerhound breed is of such antiquity and the earliest descriptive names bestowed on it so inextricably mixed that no sound conclusion can be arrived at as to whether the Deerhound was at one time identical with the ancient Irish Wolfdog and, in the course of centuries, bred to a type better suited to hunt deer, or whether, as some writers claim, he is the descendant of the hounds of the Picts. Very early descriptive names were used to identify the purpose of the dog rather than to identify species. We find such names as "Irish Wolf Dog," "Scotch Greyhound," "Rough Greyhound," "Highland Deerhound." Dr. Caius, in his book *Of Englishe Dogges* (1576) speaking of Greyhounds, relates: "Some are of a greater sorte, some of a lesser; some are smoothe skynned and some curled, the bigger therefore are appointed to hunt the bigger beastes, the duck, the hart, the doe."

All this is relatively unimportant when we can definitely identify the breed as Deerhounds as early as the sixteenth and seventeenth centuries. From there on the term Deerhound has been applied to the breed, which of all dogs has been found best suited for the pursuit and killing of the deer.

At all times great value has been set on the Deerhound. The history of the breed teems with romance increasing in splendor right down through the Age of Chivalry when no one of rank lower than an earl might possess these dogs. A leash of Deerhounds was held the fine whereby a noble lord condemned to death might purchase his reprieve. Records of the Middle Ages allude repeatedly to the delightful attributes of this charming hound, his tremendous courage in the chase, his gentle dignity in the home.

So highly has the Deerhound been esteemed that the desire for exclusive ownership has at many times endangered the continuance of the breed. As the larger beasts of the chase became extinct, or rare, in England and southern Scotland, the more delicate, smooth Greyhound took the place of the larger Deerhound. The Highlands of Scotland, last territory wherein the stag remained numerous in a wild state, became, as might be expected, the last stronghold of this breed. Here again the Highland Chieftains assumed exclusive proprietorship to such an extent that it was rare to find a good specimen south of the River Forth. So severely was this policy pursued that in 1769 the breed physically and numerically ran very low. This, of course, must be attributed in a great measure to the collapse of the clan system after Culloden 1745. It was not until about 1825, when the restoration of the breed was undertaken very successfully by Archibald and Duncan McNeill (the latter afterwards Lord Colonsay), that the Deerhound regained his place of pre-eminence and former perfection. The Great War, in later times, had considerable effect on the breed when so many of the large estates in Scotland and England were broken up. Although this "Royal Dog of Scotland" is represented at English shows in good numbers and to a considerable extent at shows in the Eastern States of this country, the Deerhound remains a rare dog of such historical interest and character that ownership should give anyone great pride of possession.

The high valuation of the Deerhound is not the result of rarity so much as the fact that as a hunter he is pre-eminent, with a high aggregate of desirable characteristics. He has a keen scent, which may be used in tracking, but it is that combination of strength and speed necessary to cope with the large Scottish deer (often weighing 250 pounds) that is most valued. The hounds are usually hunted singly or in pairs. Centuries of hunting as the companions and guards of Highland Chieftains have given the Deerhound an insatiable desire for human companionship. For this reason the best Deerhounds are seldom raised as kennel dogs. In character the Deerhound is quiet and dignified, keen and alert, and although not aggressive, has great persistence and indomitable courage when necessary. While it might savor of boasting to claim that the Deerhound of today is identical with the dog of early history, descriptions of which are mostly legendary, it is nevertheless a well-established fact that in type, size, and character he closely conforms to authentic records of the eighteenth and nineteenth centuries.

The hunting of antlered game with dogs is not permitted in the United States, but the Deerhound has been used very successfully on wolves, coyotes, and rabbits, and is keen to match his speed with anything that runs. As a companion the Deerhound is ideal, being tractable and easy to train and possessing the most dependable loyalty and utmost devotion to his master. The most authentic and complete work on the breed is *Scotch Deerhounds and their Masters* written by George Cupples. Much has also been written about the Deerhound by Scrope in *Days of Deerstalking* and other works. The best descriptions of the breed are found in nineteenth-century British dog books.

The grace, dignity and beauty of the Deerhound have been faithfully depicted in many of Landseer's paintings and drawings, and Sir Walter Scott, who owned the famous Deerhound Maida, makes many enthusiastic allusions to the breed, which he describes as "The most perfect creature of Heaven."

Official Standard for the Scottish Deerhound

Head—Should be broadest at the ears, narrowing slightly to the eyes, with the muzzle tapering more decidedly to the nose. The muzzle should be pointed, but the teeth and lips level. The head should be long, the skull flat rather than round with a very slight rise over the eyes but nothing approaching a stop. The hair on the skull should be moderately long and softer than the rest of the coat. The nose should be black (in some blue fawns—blue) and slightly aquiline. In lighter colored dogs the black muzzle is preferable. There should be a good mustache of rather silky hair and a fair beard.

Ears—Should be set on high; in repose, folded back like a Greyhound's, though raised above the head in excitement without losing the fold, and even in some cases semierect. A prick ear is bad. Big thick ears hanging flat to the head or heavily coated with long hair are bad faults. The ears should be soft, glossy, like a mouse's coat to the touch and the smaller the better. There should be no long coat or long fringe, but there is sometimes a silky, silvery coat on the body of the ear and the tip. On all Deerhounds, irrespective of color of coat, the ears should be black or dark colored.

Neck and Shoulders—The neck should be long—of a length befitting the Greyhound character of the dog. Extreme length is neither necessary nor desirable. Deerhounds do not stoop to their work like the Greyhounds. The mane, which every good specimen should have, sometimes detracts from the apparent length of the neck. The neck, however, must be strong as is necessary to hold a stag. The nape of the neck should be very prominent where the head is set on, and the throat clean cut at the angle and prominent. Shoulders should be well sloped; blades well back and not too much width between them. Loaded and straight shoulders are very bad faults.

Tail—Should be tolerably long, tapering and reaching to within 1 1/2 inches of the ground and about 1 1/2 inches below the hocks. Dropped perfectly down or curved when the Deerhound is still, when in motion or excited, curved, but in no instance lifted out of line of the back. It should be well covered with hair, on the inside, thick and wiry, underside longer and towards the end a slight fringe is not objectionable. A curl or ring tail is undesirable.

Eyes—Should be dark—generally dark brown, brown or hazel. A very light eye is not liked. The eye should be moderately full, with a soft look in repose, but a keen, far-away look when the Deerhound is roused. Rims of eyelids should be black.

Body—General conformation is that of a Greyhound of larger size and bone. Chest deep rather than broad but not too narrow or slab-sided. Good girth of chest is indicative of great lung power. The loin well arched and drooping to the tail. A straight back is not desirable, this formation being unsuited for uphill work, and very unsightly.

Legs and Feet—Legs should be broad and flat, and good broad forearms and elbows are desirable. Forelegs must, of course, be as straight as possible. Feet close and compact, with well-arranged toes. The hindquarters drooping, and as broad and powerful as possible, the hips being set wide apart. A narrow rear denotes lack of power. The stifles should be well bent, with great length from hip to hock, which should be broad and flat. Cowhocks, weak pasterns, straight stifles and splay feet are very bad faults.

Coat—The hair on the body, neck and quarters should be harsh and wiry, about 3 or 4 inches long; that on the head, breast and belly much softer. There should be a slight fringe on the inside of the forelegs and hind legs but nothing approaching the "feather" of a Collie. A woolly coat is bad. Some good strains have a mixture of silky coat with the hard which is preferable to a woolly coat. The climate of the United States tends to produce the mixed coat. The ideal coat is a thick, close-lying ragged coat, harsh or crisp to the touch.

Color—is a matter of fancy, but the dark blue-gray is most preferred. Next come the darker and lighter grays or brindles, the darkest being generally preferred. Yellow and sandy red or red fawn, especially with black ears and muzzles, are equally high in estimation. This was the color of the oldest known strains—the McNeil and Chesthill Menzies. White is condemned by all authorities, but a white chest and white toes, occurring as they do in many of the darkest-colored dogs, are not objected to, although the less the better, for the Deerhound is a self-colored dog. A white blaze on the head, or a white collar, should entirely disqualify. The less white the better but a slight white tip to the stern occurs in some of the best strains.

Height—*Height of Dogs*—From 30 to 32 inches, or even more if there be symmetry without coarseness, which is rare.

Height of Bitches—From 28 inches upwards. There is no objection to a bitch being large, unless too coarse, as even at her greatest height she does not approach that of the dog, and therefore could not be too big for work as overbig dogs are.

Weight—From 85 to 110 pounds in dogs, and from 75 to 95 pounds in bitches.

POINTS OF THE DEERHOUND
ARRANGED IN ORDER OF IMPORTANCE

1. *Typical*—A Deerhound should resemble a rough-coated Greyhound of larger size and bone.
2. *Movements*—Easy, active and true.
3. As tall as possible consistent with quality.
4. *Head*—Long, level, well balanced, carried high.
5. *Body*—Long, very deep in brisket, well-sprung ribs and great breadth across hips.
6. *Forelegs*—Strong and quite straight, with elbows neither in nor out.
7. *Thighs*—Long and muscular, second thighs well muscled, stifles well bent.
8. *Loins*—Well arched, and belly well drawn up.
9. *Coat*—Rough and hard, with softer beard and brows.
10. *Feet*—Close, compact, with well-knuckled toes.
11. *Ears*—Small (dark) with Greyhoundlike carriage.
12. *Eyes*—Dark, moderately full.
13. *Neck*—Long, well arched, very strong with prominent nape.
14. *Shoulders*—Clean, set sloping.
15. *Chest*—Very deep but not too narrow.
16. *Tail*—Long and curved slightly, carried low.
17. *Teeth*—Strong and level.
18. *Nails*—Strong and curved.

DISQUALIFICATION

White blaze on the head, or a white collar.

Approved March, 1935

Whippet

THE WHIPPET, an English Greyhound in miniature, is a sporting dog of the first flight as well as a very charming, affectionate, and intelligent pet. He is the fastest domesticated animal of his weight, capable of speeds up to thirty-five miles per hour. Though his main forte is as a racedog, he is a rabbit courser of great ability. His rat-killing feats, too, are nearly equal to those of the most hard-bitten terriers. As an animal of beauty, grace of outline, and smoothness of action, he stands near the top in the realm of dogdom.

He is extraordinarily keen when racing or on game, though in the living room he is quiet, dignified, unobtrusive, and above all, highly decorative. His intelligence, when treated as a member of the family, compares favorably with most terriers. He is never snappy or "barky," though as a watchdog he is excellent. Contrary to external appearances, he is by no means delicate and difficult to care for. All in all, he makes an ideal dual-purpose small dog for an owner of discrimination.

As a breed the Whippet is not one of our oldest, having been evolved in England a hundred and some years ago, though it was not until 1891 that official recognition was given by the English Kennel Club.

It is said that when such barbaric pastimes as bull- and bearbaiting and dogfighting began to lose favor, the sporting gentry of that period originated the Whippet for the milder (to them) entertainment of coursing rabbits in an enclosure. The early specimens differed a great deal from our best present-day dogs. These were crosses of small English Greyhounds and various terriers, both smooth and rough-coated. It was not until a much later date that fanciers added an infusion of Italian Greyhound blood which aided so materially in improving type.

At first the breed was known as "snap-dog," and the so-called sport was termed "snap-dog coursing." This was because the dog that caught or snapped-up the greatest number of rabbits during a match was declared winner. It will be noted that this ignoble pastime, in which the rabbit had absolutely no chance of escape, differed greatly from legitimate coursing in the open with Greyhounds and was purely a gambling proposition. Later the Whippet was used primarily for straight racing. This sport had its inception, and still flourishes for that matter, in Lancashire and Yorkshire. Here the colliers nicknamed the Whippet, "the poor man's race horse."

The standard course is 200 yards straightaway, and the method of racing unique. Each dog has two attendants—a slipper and a handler. All dogs are held on their handicap marks by their slippers while their handlers trot up the track and across the finish line, all the while yelling encouragement and frantically waving towels or rags (which the Whippets are trained from puppyhood to run to) to their charges. At the "Get set!" command of the starter, each slipper picks his dog up by the tail and the skin of the neck and when the pistol cracks the animals are literally thrown into their stride. They then race at top speed up the track and grab the waving rags of their handlers, who are some twenty yards behind the actual finish. Different-colored wool collars are worn to distinguish the entries.

As Whippets vary in weight, from ten to twenty-eight pounds, a rather elaborate system of handicapping was evolved. This is based upon the fact that the heavier the dog, everything else being equal, the faster he should be. Times as fast as eleven and one-half seconds have been recorded, but any dog that can do twelve flat from his handicap mark is considered excellent. Generally speaking, bitches are slightly faster and are usually handicapped accordingly.

Whippets appear first to have been brought to America by English mill operatives of Massachusetts. Lawrence and Lowell, for many years, were the center of Whippet racing in this country. Later, however, the sport moved South when Maryland, particularly in the neighborhood of Baltimore, held the spotlight. Many refinements have been made that have improved racing immensely. Electric starting boxes are used, steeplechases inaugurated, and the entire establishments patterned after the best of horse tracks. The very latest thing in Maryland was a circular track with an electric hare.

From the standpoint of the fancier, Whippets make an ideal exhibition dog. With their small size (around twenty pounds) and smooth coat they are neither difficult to transport nor keep in condition. Their quiet deportment in the ring makes them comparatively easy to show, as is attested by the winnings of numerous novices who handle their own entries.

Official Standard for the
Whippet

General Appearance—A moderate size sight hound giving the appearance of elegance and fitness, denoting great speed, power, and balance without coarseness. A true sporting hound that covers a maximum of distance with a minimum of lost motion.

Head—Long and lean, fairly wide between the ears, scarcely perceptible stop, good length of muzzle which should be powerful without being coarse. Nose entirely black.

Ears—Small, fine in texture, thrown back and folded. Semipricked when at attention. Gay ears are incorrect and should be severely penalized.

Eyes—Large, dark, with keen intelligent alert expression. Lack of pigmentation around eyelids is undesirable. Yellow or dilute-colored eyes should be strictly penalized. Blue or china-colored eyes shall disqualify. Both eyes must be of the same color.

Muzzle—Muzzle should be long and powerful denoting great strength of "bite" without coarseness. Teeth should be white and strong. Teeth of upper jaw should fit closely over teeth of lower jaw creating a strong scissors bite. Extremely short muzzle or lack of underjaw should be strictly penalized. An even bite is extremely undesirable. Undershot shall disqualify. Overshot one-quarter inch or more shall disqualify.

Neck—Long, clean and muscular, well arched with no suggestion of throatiness, widening gracefully into the top of the shoulder. A short thick neck, or concave curvature of the top neckline sometimes called ewe (opposite of arched), should be penalized.

Shoulders—Long, well laid back, with flat muscles, allowing for moderate space between shoulder blades at the peak of withers. The length of the shoulder blade equals the length of the upper arm. A straight shoulder blade, short upper arm, a heavily muscled or loaded shoulder, or a very narrow shoulder, all restricting low free movement, should be strictly penalized.

Brisket—Very deep and strong, reaching as nearly as possible to the point of the elbow. Ribs well sprung but with no suggestion of barrel shape. Should fill in the space between the forelegs so that there is no appearance of a hollow between them.

Back and Loin—The back broad, firm and well muscled, having length and a strong natural arch over the loin, creating a definite tuck-up of the underline. A short loin creating a cramped stance should be penalized.

Topline and Croup—The topline runs smoothly from the withers with a graceful and not too accentuated arch beginning over the loin and carrying through over the croup, with the arch being continuous without flatness. A wheelback, flat back, dip behind shoulder blades, or a back that falls away sharply creating a cut-away appearance should be penalized. A steep or flat croup should be penalized.

Forelegs—Straight, giving appearance of strength and substance of bone. The points of the elbows should point neither in nor out, but straight back. When the dog moves, the joints allow free movement from the point of the shoulder to give a long low reach. Pasterns strong, slightly bent and flexible. Bowed legs, tied-in elbows, legs lacking substance, legs set far under the body so as to create a forechest, weak or straight pasterns should be strictly penalized.

Feet—Feet must be well formed with hard, thick pads and strong nails. Nails naturally short or of moderate length. Toes should be long, close and well arched. Feet more hare than cat, but both are acceptable. Flat, open, or soft feet without thick hard pads, should be strictly penalized.

Hindquarters—Long and powerful, stifles well bent, hocks well let down and close to the ground. Thighs broad and muscular. The muscles are long and flat and carry well down toward the hock. Sickle or cowhocks should be strictly penalized.

Tail—The tail long and tapering, reaching to the hipbone when drawn through between the hind legs. When the dog is in motion, the tail is carried low with a gentle upward curve; tail should not be carried higher than top of back. A curled tail should be penalized.

Coat and Color—Close, smooth and firm in texture, A coarse, or wooly coat should be penalized. Color immaterial.

Gait—Low, free moving and smooth, with reach in the forequarters and strong drive in the hindquarters. The dog has great freedom of action when viewed from the side; the forelegs reach forward close to the ground; the hindlegs have strong propelling power. Lack of front reach or rear drive, a short, mincing gait with high knee action should be strictly penalized. When moving and viewed from front or rear, legs should turn neither in nor out, nor should feet cross or interfere with each other. Crossing in front or moving too close should be strictly penalized.

N.B. Old scars and injuries, the result of work or accident should not be allowed to prejudice the dog's chance in the show ring, unless they interfere with its movement or ability to perform.

Size—Ideal height for dogs, 19 to 22 inches; for bitches, 18 to 21 inches, measured across the shoulders at the highest point. One-half inch above or below the above stated measurements will disqualify.

DISQUALIFICATIONS
Blue or china-colored eyes.
Undershot.
Overshot one-quarter inch or more.
A dog one-half inch above or below the measurements specified under "Size."

Approved March 9, 1976

Borzoi — *Ashbey*

Harriers — *Roslin-Williams*

English Foxhounds — *Cumbers*

Saluki — *Cumbers*

Basenjis — *Cumbers*

Irish Wolfhounds

Bloodhound — *Brisbin*

Rhodesian Ridgeback — *Megginson*

Scottish Deerhounds — *Arnold*

Basset Hounds — *Cumbers*

Beagle — *Cumbers*

Greyhound — *Thompson*

Whippets — *Roslin-Williams*

Alaskan Malamutes — *Munger*

Belgian Sheepdog — *Thornton*

Belgian Malinois puppy - *Cumbers*

Belgian Tervuren — *Thompson*

Doberman Pinschers — *Bergman*

Shetland Sheepdogs — *Krook*

German Shepherd Dogs — *Troy*

Old English Sheepdog — *Van Rensselaer*

Bearded Collies — *Thompson*

St. Bernard

Siberian Husky — *Anderson*

Bernese Mountain Dog — *Cumbers*

Great Pyrenees — *Pook*

GROUP III: WORKING DOGS

Akita
(A-keé-ta)

THE AKITA is designated as a national monument in his native country of Japan. The breed is a wonderful combination of dignity with good nature, alert courage and docility. The Akita is very affectionate with family members and friends and thrives on human companionship. Since times long past, Japanese mothers have left their children in the trusted care of the family Akita. Typically reserved in demeanor, the Akita will stand to the defense of his family whenever a threatening stranger or animal arouses his protective instinct. Bred as a versatile hunting dog in the rugged mountains of Northern Japan, he has been successfully used to drive large game and retrieve waterfowl.

The Akita today is the modern-day, large-sized descendant of the ancient Japanese dog whose likeness has been found carved in the tombs of the early Japanese people. The upright ears and tail curled over the back are unmistakable.

There is a spiritual significance attached to the Akita. In Japan they are affectionately regarded as loyal companions and pets, protectors of the home and a symbol of good health. When a child is born, the proud family will usually receive a small statue of an Akita signifying health, happiness and a long life. If a person is ill, friends will send a small statue of an Akita to express their wish for a speedy recovery.

Historical records cite the breed's development early in the seventeenth century. A famous nobleman was exiled to Akita Prefecture, the northernmost province of the island of Honshu, Japan, and ordered to live out his days as a provincial ruler. The nobleman had an ardent interest in dogs and encouraged the land barons in his domain to compete in the breeding of a large, versatile, intelligent hunting dog. Through generations of selective breeding there evolved the Akita, a dog of superior size and frame, endowed with keen hunting abilities, powerful working attributes and a fearless spirit.

Once ownership was restricted to the Imperial family and the ruling aristocracy. Care and feeding of the Akita were detailed in elaborate ceremony and special leashes were used to denote the Akita's rank and the standing of his owner. A special vocabulary was used to address the Akita and in speaking about them. Each Akita became the charge of a specially appointed caretaker who wore an ornate costume commensurate with the esteem in which the individual Akita was held.

Several times during the next three hundred years the breed suffered near extinction, as interest in the continuity of selective breeding surged and waned, depending on the inclination of the current ruling class. Fortunately periodic favor managed to perpetuate the breed through the Meiji and Taisho eras. As the twentieth century drew near and Japan was exposed to other societies, being a dog-devotee became very fashionable in emulation of the European culture.

In 1927, the Akitainu Hozankai society of Japan was established to preserve the purity of the Akita breed. In July 1931, the government of Japan designated the Akita breed as a national monument and as one of Japan's national treasures. So highly regarded is the breed that the Japanese government will subsidize the care and feeding of an Akita champion if the owner is unable to do so.

An ancient Japanese word *matagi* means esteemed hunter, an honor applied to the men of a village having the best hunting skills. The northern Prefecture of Akita is a rugged mountainous area with cold snowy winters. There the Akita was known as *Matagiinu,* esteemed dog hunter, and used to hunt bear, deer and wild boar. The Yezo, largest and fiercest of old world bears, was held at bay by a team of Akitas, a male and a female, awaiting the arrival of the hunter with arrow or spear.

The Akita's hunting abilities include great strength, keen eye and nose, silence and speed in a resoundingly durable, sturdy body, suitable for hunting in deep snows. His hard, intelligent, never-give-in attitude in the field was prized by his masters. The Akita's soft mouth enabled him to retrieve waterfowl after they had been brought down by the hunter's arrow. The breed is said to have been used to drive fish at sea into the fisherman's nets.

The renowned Helen Keller is credited with bringing the first Akitas into the United States. While visiting the Prefecture of Akita in June 1937, she was presented with a two month old puppy by the Ministry of Education. Later, after the death of the puppy, the Ministry forwarded a second Akita to Miss Keller. In the summer of 1947, Miss Keller returned to Akita Prefecture while on a speaking engagement and visited with Mr. Ichiro Ogasawara, the senior official of Akitainu Hozankai, responsible for obtaining the Akitas for Miss Keller.

The breed's popularity in the United States, following World War II, may be attributed to American servicemen of the occupational forces, who so admired the noble dogs that they took them home to their families. They were attracted to the Akita because of the breed's intelligence and adaptability to different situations.

Each year there is a solemn ceremony in Tokyo's Shibuya railroad station. Hundreds of dog lovers do homage to the loyalty and devotion of the Akita dog, Hachiko, faithful pet of Dr. Eisaburo Ueno, a professor at Tokyo University.

It was the daily habit for Hachiko to accompany his master to the train station to see him off. Every afternoon Hachiko would return to the station to greet his master. On a May evening in 1925, Professor Ueno did not return; he had died that afternoon at the university. Hachiko, the loyal Akita, waited at the station until midnight. The next day and for the next nine years Hachiko returned to the station and waited for his beloved master before walking home, alone. Nothing and no one could discourage Hachiko from maintaining his nightly vigil. It was not until he followed his master in death, in March 1934, that Hachiko failed to appear in his place at the railroad station.

The fidelity of Hachiko was known throughout Japan. Upon his demise, newspaper stories led to the suggestion that a statue be erected in the station. Contributions from the United States and other countries were received. Today the statue of the Akita, Hachiko, pays silent tribute to the breed's faithfulness and loyalty.

The Akita Club of America was founded in 1956. The breed was admitted to registration in the American Kennel Club Stud Book in October, 1972, and to regular show classification in the Working Group at AKC shows beginning April 4, 1973.

Official Standard for the
Akita

General Appearance—Large, powerful, alert, with much substance and heavy bone. The broad head, forming a blunt triangle, with deep muzzle, small eyes and erect ears carried forward in line with back of neck, is characteristic of the breed. The large, curled tail, balancing the broad head, is also characteristic of the breed.

Head—Massive but in balance with body; free of wrinkle when at ease. Skull flat between ears and broad; jaws square and powerful with minimal dewlap. Head forms a blunt triangle when viewed from above. *Fault*—Narrow or snipy head.

Muzzle—Broad and full. Distance from nose to stop is to distance from stop to occiput as 2 is to 3. *Stop*—Well defined, but not too abrupt. A shallow furrow extends well up forehead.

Nose—Broad and black. Liver permitted on white Akitas, but black always preferred. *Disqualification*—Butterfly nose or total lack of pigmentation on nose.

Ears—The ears of the Akita are characteristic of the breed. They are strongly erect and small in relation to rest of head. If ear is folded forward for measuring length, tip will touch upper eye rim. Ears are triangular, slightly rounded at tip, wide at base, set wide on head but not too low, and carried slightly forward over eyes in line with back of neck. *Disqualification*—Drop or broken ears.

Eyes—Dark brown, small, deep-set and triangular in shape. Eye rims black and tight.

Lips and Tongue—Lips black and not pendulous; tongue pink.

Teeth—Strong with scissors bite preferred, but level bite acceptable. *Disqualification*—Noticeably undershot or overshot.

Neck and Body—

Neck—Thick and muscular; comparatively short, widening gradually toward shoulders. A pronounced crest blends in with base of skull.

Body—Longer than high, as 10 is to 9 in males; 11 to 9 in bitches. Chest wide and deep; depth of chest is one-half height of dog at shoulder. Ribs well sprung, brisket well developed. Level back with firmly-muscled loin and moderate tuck-up. Skin pliant but not loose. *Serious Faults*—Light bone, rangy body.

Tail—Large and full, set high and carried over back or against flank in a three-quarter, full, or double curl, always dipping to or below level of back. On a three-quarter curl, tip drops well down flank. Root large and strong. Tail bone reaches hock when let down. Hair coarse, straight and full, with no appearance of a plume. *Disqualification*—Sickle or uncurled tail.

Forequarters and Hindquarters—

Forequarters—Shoulders strong and powerful with moderate layback. Forelegs heavy-boned and straight as viewed from front. Angle of pastern 15 degrees forward from vertical. *Faults*—Elbows in or out, loose shoulders.

Hindquarters—Width, muscular development and comparable to forequarters. Upper thighs well developed. Stifle moderately bent and hocks well let down, turning neither in nor out.

Dewclaws—On front legs generally not removed; dewclaws on hind legs generally removed.

Feet—Cat feet, well knuckled up with thick pads. Feet straight ahead.

Coat—Double-coated. Undercoat thick, soft, dense and shorter than outer coat. Outer coat straight, harsh and standing somewhat off body. Hair on head, legs and ears short. Length of hair at withers and rump approximately two inches, which is slightly longer than on rest of body, except tail, where coat is longest and most profuse. *Fault*—Any indication of ruff or feathering.

Color—Any color including white; brindle; or pinto. Colors are brilliant and clear and markings are well balanced, with or without mask or blaze. White Akitas have no mask. Pinto has a white background with large, evenly placed patches covering head and more than one-third of body. Undercoat may be a different color from outer coat.

Gait—Brisk and powerful with strides of moderate length. Back remains strong, firm and level. Rear legs move in line with front legs.

Size—Males 26 to 28 inches at the withers; bitches 24 to 26 inches. *Disqualification*—Dogs under 25 inches; bitches under 23 inches.

Temperament—Alert and responsive, dignified and courageous. Aggressive toward other dogs.

DISQUALIFICATIONS

Butterfly nose or total lack of pigmentation on nose.
Drop or broken ears.
Noticeably undershot or overshot.
Sickle or uncurled tail.
Dogs under 25 inches; bitches under 23 inches.

Approved December 12, 1972

Alaskan Malamute

(Mahla-myoot)

THE ALASKAN MALAMUTE, one of the oldest Arctic sled dogs, was named after the native Innuit tribe called Mahlemuts, who settled along the shores of Kotzebue Sound in the upper western part of Alaska. Long before Alaska became a possession of the United States, this Arctic region was called by the Russians, who were the discoverers, "Alashak" or "Alyeska," meaning "vast country." Native people were already living in Alyeska land when these Asiatic sailors visited the shores, having been forced by storms when whaling in Bering Strait to land in this North country opposite Siberia. Returned to their homeland, they told stories about seeing "native people using dogs to haul sledges."

The origin of these people and also the dogs has never been ascertained. We do know that they had been in Alaska for generations; where they came from is as indefinite as it is with any of the other Arctic natives, either of Greenland in the east of North America or the Samoyed tribe of Russia. The same is true about the origin of all Arctic dogs.

The tribe of Mahlemuts, now spelled Malamutes, were called "high-type" Innuits. Many writers of Alaska, in translations from Russian explorers and records left by Englishmen who traveled the Alaskan coast, all give similar accounts about these fine Innuits. *Innuit* means "people" in the Orarian language. Never are the Mahlemuts mentioned without reference to their dogs. One writer, who went to Alaska in the early days of exploration after it had become a possession of the United States, gives interesting references about the Innuits and especially about the Mahlemuts. He uses the original spelling, so that we know the records were taken at an early date.

> Upon arriving at Unalakleet, I found that a party of Mahlemuts had arrived the day before by dog teams. They had carried mail from Point Barrow down along the coast wherever White Men were living. They had also been runners for the Russian Muscovy Whaling Company when they had landed in this Arctic region. These Mahlemuts were wonderful looking natives . . . taller than their Greenland cousins. They were industrious, skilled in hunting and fishing, made perfect sledges, and had dogs of . . . beauty and endurance. These dogs had traveled . . . hundreds of miles and being better cared for by their drivers than is the usual lot of Arctic dogs . . . [they] were affectionate and seemed tireless . . .

This description differs from tales told by people who have seen other native dogs in the Arctic, whose dispositions perhaps resulted from the environment in which they lived. The usual treatment of sledge dogs in the North has been harsh, owing to the uncivilized tribes who wandered from place to place until white men invaded their villages.

Another Alaskan traveler, a missionary who journeyed thousands of miles by dog team, writes:

> These Malamutes, now spelled *Malamute*, a corruption of the original word Mahlemut (Mahle meaning name of the Innuit tribe and Mut meaning Village in Orarian vocabulary of the Mahlemut dialect), are a high type people. They are peaceful, happy, hard workers, believe in one wife, are able guides and have wonderful dogs. Even though uncivilized, they have realized that it is important to have fine animals to pull sledges; that without them, means of travel in this sort of country would be impossible at times. The dogs are powerful looking, have thick dense double coats (outer coat of thick coarse fur and inner coat a fuzzy down lying close to skin) called weather coats, erect ears, magnificent bushy tails carried over their backs like waving plumes, tough feet, colors varying but mostly wolf grey or black and white. The dogs have remarkable endurance and fortitude. The Malamute people and their dogs are much respected among other Innuits.

A book entitled *Researches of Alaska* includes several references with these Malamute dogs being called the native dogs of Alaska. "Natives recognized in their crude way the importance of the dogs, as they were considered indispensable for transportation in the North."

Later another reference says: "Dogs were two and two, side by side (gang hitch), leader in front, harnessed to a sledge, colors varying from grey to black and white, and carrying a heavy load. The dogs were powerful looking . . . and did not appear vicious. The natives, called Malamutes, were not Indians but perhaps related to the Asiatic Arctic natives of the Chukchis. [This is a suggestion of their ancestry, but not confirmed.] The Mahlemut dialect is simple to understand and the natives themselves a happy tribe. They are fond of their children and their dogs. The dogs work hard and have wonderful endurance."

A Russian translation gives another reference about the "Mahlemuts found over the sea in the Vast Land" called the "stopping-off" place by the Russian sailors. This writer referred to the workmanship of the Mahlemuts and the sledges, and admitted the "Mahlemut dogs and sledges are better than those of the Russians for interior travel."

It is confirmed that these Alaskan Malamute sledge dogs were used as draught animals and they have never lost their identity. When Alaska became settled by white men, it is true that the Arctic breed was mingled with that of outside dogs, just as they have been in Greenland, Labrador, Siberia, or any of the other Arctic countries. During the Alaskan Sweepstakes, the lure of racing became so popular that many drivers tried all sorts of experiments in mixing the Arctic breed with some outside strain, and this period from 1909 to 1918 was the age of "decay of the Arctic sledge dog." Fortunately, the sport of sled-dog racing became popular in the United States, and interest in developing the pure strain of the native Alaskan Malamute started in 1926 after a careful study of all types of Northern breeds had been made. Malamutes still hold many racing records. During World War I, several Malamutes were among the dogs sent across by A. A. Allen, who assembled 150 dogs for this purpose, 100 coming from Alaska. These Malamutes also made remarkable records for hauling and were distinctive in their appearance. The two recent Byrd Antarctic Expeditions have used Malamutes as well as other Arctic breeds, and again the records have been outstanding.

The word *husky*, as sometimes applied to the Malamute, is a misnomer; it was originally a term of disrespect used by the Indians or Aleuts who invaded Alaska and were hostile to the Innuits, calling them "huskies." This word has gradually been used in the North to describe working dogs of mixed breeds used to pull sledges. No pure breed of Arctic dog is called "husky" except the Siberian Husky. The

Alaskan Malamute is the native Alaskan Arctic breed, cousin to the Samoyed of Russia, Siberian Husky (Kolyma River Region), and the Eskimo dogs of Greenland and Labrador.

Well-informed Arctic writers who have made a study of Arctic formations seem to disagree about the origin of the Arctic peoples. Some believe that during the Glacier Age there was land connecting Asia and Alaska, and also Greenland and Labrador. Perhaps our Alaskan natives and Labrador Eskimos came into these countries by dog power. Others claim immigration spread from the Hudson Bay country, east and west; others that Greenland was originated by Norwegians who went "native" and likewise, Alaska by Asiatic people. This happened many generations ago—all we know today is that Arctic breeds were found and that the Alaskan Arctic sledge dog native to that country is the breed now called the Malamute.

In the United States, Alaskan Malamutes are being shown on the bench. As pets they have become popular sled dogs among sportspeople who enjoy this winter recreation. They are very fond of people and especially children, who enjoy driving them to sleds.

Official Standard for the
Alaskan Malamute

General Appearance and Characteristics—The Alaskan Malamute is a powerful and substantially built dog with a deep chest and strong, compact body, not too short coupled, with a thick, coarse guard coat of sufficient length to protect a dense, woolly undercoat, from 1 to 2 inches in depth when dog is in full coat. Stands well over pads, and this stance gives the appearance of much activity, showing interest and curiosity. The head is broad, ears wedge-shaped and erect when alerted. The muzzle is bulky with only slight diminishing in width and depth from root to nose, not pointed or long, but not stubby. The Malamute moves with a proud carriage, head erect and eyes alert. Face markings are a distinguishing feature. These consist of either cap over head and rest of face solid color, usually grayish white, or face marked with the appearance of a mask. Combinations of cap and mask are not unusual. The tail is plumed and carried over the back, not like a fox brush, or tightly curled, more like a plume waving.

Malamutes are of various colors, but are usually wolfish gray or black and white. Their feet are of the "snowshoe" type, tight and deep, with well-cushioned pads, giving a firm and compact appearance. Front legs are straight with big bone. Hind legs are broad and powerful, moderately bent at stifles, and without cowhocks. The back is straight, gently sloping from shoulders to hips. The loin should not be so short or tight as to interfere with easy, tireless movement. Endurance and intelligence are shown in body and expression. The eyes have a "wolf-like" appearance by their position, but the expression is soft and indicates an affectionate disposition.

Temperament—The Alaskan Malamute is an affectionate, friendly dog, not a "one-man" dog. He is a loyal, devoted companion, playful on invitation, but generally impressive by his dignity after maturity.

Head—The head should indicate a high degree of intelligence, and is broad and powerful as compared with other "natural" breeds, but should be in proportion to the size of the dog so as not to make the dog appear clumsy or coarse. *Skull*—The skull should be broad between the ears, gradually narrowing to eyes, moderately rounded between ears, flattening on top as it approaches the eyes, rounding off to cheeks, which should be moderately flat. There should be a slight furrow between the eyes, the topline of skull and topline of the muzzle showing but little break downward from a straight line as they join. *Muzzle*—The muzzle should be large and bulky in proportion to size of skull, diminishing but little in width and depth from junction with skull to nose; lips close fitting; nose black; upper and lower jaws broad with large teeth, front teeth meeting with a scissors grip but never overshot or undershot.

Eyes—Brown, almond shaped, moderately large for this shape of eye, set obliquely in skull. Dark eyes preferred.

Ears—The ears should be of medium size, but small in proportion to head. The upper halves of the ears are triangular in shape, slightly rounded at tips, set wide apart on outside back edges of the skull with the lower part of the ear joining the skull on a line with the upper corner of the eye, giving the tips of the ears the appearance, when erect, of standing off from the skull. When erect, the ears point slightly forward, but when the dog is at work the ears are sometimes folded against the skull. High-set ears are a fault.

Neck—The neck should be strong and moderately arched.

Body—The chest should be strong and deep; body should be strong and compactly built but not short coupled. The back should be straight and gently sloping to the hips. The loins should be well muscled and not so short as to interfere with easy, rhythmic movement with powerful drive from the hindquarters. A long loin which weakens the back is also a fault. No excess weight.

Shoulders, Legs and Feet—Shoulders should be moderately sloping; forelegs heavily boned and muscled, straight to pasterns, which should be short and strong and almost vertical as viewed from the side. The feet should be large and compact, toes, tight-fitting and well arched, pads thick and tough, toenails short and strong. There should be a protective growth of hair between toes. Hind legs must be broad and powerfully muscled through thighs; stifles moderately bent, hock joints broad and strong, moderately bent and well let down. As viewed from behind, the hind legs should not appear bowed in bone, but stand and move true in line with movement of the front legs, and not too close or too wide. The legs of the Malamute must indicate unusual strength and tremendous propelling power. Any indication of unsoundness in legs or feet, standing or moving, is to be considered a serious fault. Dewclaws on the hind legs are undesirable and should be removed shortly after pups are whelped.

Tail—Moderately set and following the line of the spine at the start, well furred and carried over the back when not working—not tightly curled to rest on back—or short furred and carried like a fox brush, a waving plume appearance instead.

Coat—The Malamute should have a thick, coarse guard coat, not long and soft. The undercoat is dense, from 1 to 2 inches in depth, oily and woolly. The coarse guard coat stands out, and there is thick fur around the neck. The guard coat varies in length, as does the undercoat; however, in general, the coat is moderately short to medium along the sides of the body with the length of the coat increasing somewhat around the shoulders and neck, down the back and over the rump, as well as in the breeching and plume. Malamutes usually have shorter and less dense coats when shed out during the summer months.

Color and Markings—The usual colors range from light gray through the intermediate shadings to black, always with white on underbodies, parts of legs, feet, and part of mask markings. Markings should be either caplike and/or mask-like on face. A white blaze on forehead and/or collar or spot on nape is attractive and acceptable, but broken color extending over the body in spots or uneven splashings is undesirable. One should distinguish between mantled dogs and splash-coated dogs. The only solid color allowable is the all-white.

Size—There is a natural range in size in the breed. The desirable freighting sizes are:

Males—25 inches at the shoulders—85 pounds.

Females—23 inches at the shoulders—75 pounds.

However, size consideration should not outweigh that of type, proportion, and functional attributes, such as shoulders, chest, legs, feet, and movement. When dogs are judged equal in type, proportion, and functional attributes, the dog nearest the desirable freighting size is to be preferred.

IMPORTANT.—In judging Alaskan Malamutes their function as a sledge dog for heavy freighting must be given consideration above all else. The judge must bear in mind that this breed is designed primarily as the working sledge dog of the North for hauling heavy freight, and therefore he should be a heavy-boned, powerfully built, compact dog with sound legs, good feet, deep chest, powerful shoulders, steady, balanced, tireless gait, and the other physical equipment necessary for the efficient performance of his job. He isn't intended as a racing sled dog designed to compete in speed trials with the smaller Northern breeds.

The Malamute as a sledge dog for heavy freighting is designed for strength and endurance and any characteristic of the individual specimen, including temperament, which interferes with the accomplishment of this purpose is to be considered the most serious of faults. Faults under this provision would be splayfootedness, any indication of unsoundness or weakness in legs, cowhocks, bad pasterns, straight shoulders, lack of angulation, stilted gait or any gait which isn't balanced, strong, and steady, ranginess, shallowness, ponderousness, lightness of bone, poor over-all proportion, and similar characteristics.

SCALE OF POINTS

General Appearance	20	Feet	10
Head	15	Coat and Color	10
Body	20	Tail	5
Legs and Movement	20	TOTAL	100

Approved April 12, 1960

268

Bearded Collie

SOMETIMES known as the Highland Collie, the Mountain Collie, or the Hairy Mou'ed Collie, the Bearded Collie is one of Britain's oldest breeds. While some have theorized that the Beardie was around to greet the Romans when they first invaded Britain, the current theory is that like most shaggy haired herding dogs, the Bearded Collie descends from the Magyar Komondor of central Europe.

As with most breeds not used by the nobility, there are few early records on this humble herdsman's dog. The earliest known pictures of Bearded Collies are a 1771 Gainsborough portrait of the Duke of Buccleigh and a 1772 Reynolds portrait of that peer's wife and daughter accompanied by two dogs. With Reinagle's more easily recognizable "Sheepdog" published in Taplin's 1803 *Sportsman's Cabinet,* and a description of the breed published in an 1818 edition of *Live Stock Journal,* the existence of the breed as we know it is firmly established.

At the end of the Victorian era, Beardies were fairly popular in southern Scotland, both as working and as show dogs. When Bearded

Collies classes were offered at shows, usually in the area about Peebleshire, they were well supported. However, there was then no official standard, since no breed club existed to establish one and each judge had to adopt his own criteria. The lack of a strong breed club proved quite a misfortune. The local popularity of the breed continued until World War I, during which there were few dog shows. By the 1930s there was no kennel breeding Bearded Collies for show purposes.

That Beardies did not die out rests on their ability as workers and the devotion of the Peebleshire shepherds and drovers to the breed. They are still highly valued as a sheepdog, due to their ability to turn in a good day's work in south Scotland's misty, rainy and cold climate, and their adeptness on the rough, rocky ground.

The Bearded Collie's other major use is as a drover. They work with little direction from the butchers and drovers who find them very valuable in moving troublesome cattle. The shepherds and drovers have valued Beardies to such an extent that they have been more than reluctant to sell any puppies (especially bitches) unless they could be sure the puppies would actually be worked.

After World War II, Mrs. G. O. Willison, owner of the Bothkennar Kennels, saved the Beardie from further chance of extinction when she began to breed them for show purposes. She spearheaded the establishment of the Bearded Collie Club in Britain in 1955. After much travail, in 1959 the Kennel Club in England allowed Bearded Collies to be eligible for Challenge Certificates and championships and the popularity of the breed began to steadily increase.

Bearded Collies were introduced into the United States in the late 1950s, but none of these dogs were bred. It wasn't until 1967 that the first litter of Bearded Collies was born in this country. By July 1969, there was enough interest for the Bearded Collie Club of America to be founded.

The breed became eligible to be shown in the Miscellaneous Class as of June 1, 1974. The AKC Stud Book was opened to Bearded Collie registrations on October 1, 1976, and the breed became eligible to compete in the Working Group on February 1, 1977.

Official Standard for the
Bearded Collie

Characteristics—The Bearded Collie is hardy and active, with an aura of strength and agility characteristic of a real working dog. Bred for centuries as a companion and servant of man, the Bearded Collie is a devoted and intelligent member of the family. He is stable and self-confident, showing no signs of shyness or aggression. This is a natural and unspoiled breed.

General Appearance—The Bearded Collie is a medium sized dog with a medium length coat that follows the natural lines of the body and allows plenty of daylight under the body. The body is long and lean, and though strongly made, does not appear heavy. A bright inquiring expression is a distinctive feature of the breed. The Bearded Collie should be shown in a natural stance.

Head—The head is in proportion to the size of the dog. The skull is broad and flat; the stop is moderate; the cheeks are well filled beneath the eyes; the muzzle is strong and full; the foreface is equal in length to the distance between the stop and occiput. The nose is large and squarish. A snipy muzzle is to be penalized. *(See Color section for pigmentation.)*

Eyes: The eyes are large, expressive, soft and affectionate, but not round nor protruding, and are set widely apart. The eyebrows are arched to the sides to frame the eyes and are long enough to blend smoothly into the coat on the sides of the head. *(See Color section for eye color.)*

Ears: The ears are medium sized, hanging and covered with long hair. They are set level with the eyes. When the dog is alert, the ears have a slight lift at the base.

Teeth: The teeth are strong and white, meeting in a scissors bite. Full dentition is desirable.

Neck—The neck is in proportion to the length of the body, strong and slightly arched, blending smoothly into the shoulders.

Forequarters—The shoulders are well laid back at an angle of approximately forty-five degrees; a line drawn from the highest point of the shoulder blade to the forward point of articulation approximates a right angle with a line from the forward point of articulation to the point of the elbow. The top of the shoulder blades lie in against the withers, but they slope outwards from there sufficiently to accommodate the desired spring of ribs. The legs are straight and vertical, with substantial, but not heavy, bone and are covered with shaggy hair all around. The pasterns are flexible without weakness.

Body—The body is longer than it is high in an approximate ratio of five to four, length measured from point of chest to point of buttocks, height measured at the highest point of the withers. The length of the back comes from the length of the ribcage and not that of the loin. The back is level. The ribs are well sprung from the spine but are flat at the sides. The chest is deep, reaching at least to the elbows. The loins are strong. The level back line blends smoothly into the curve of the rump. A flat croup or a steep croup is to be severely penalized.

Hindquarters—The hind legs are powerful and muscular at the thighs with well bent stifles. The hocks are low. In normal stance, the bones below the hocks are perpendicular to the ground and parallel to each other when viewed from the rear; the hind feet fall just behind a perpendicular line from the point of buttocks when viewed from the side. The legs are covered with shaggy hair all around.

Tail: The tail is set low and is long enough for the end of the bone to reach at least the point of the hocks. It is normally carried low with an upward swirl at the tip while the dog is standing. When the dog is excited or in motion, the curve is accentuated and the tail may be raised but is never carried beyond a vertical line. The tail is covered with abundant hair.

Feet—The feet are oval in shape with the soles well padded. The toes are arched and close together, and well covered with hair including between the pads.

Coat—The coat is double with the undercoat soft, furry and close. The outercoat is flat, harsh, strong and shaggy, free from wooliness and curl, although a slight wave is permissible. The coat falls naturally to either side but must never be artificially parted. The length and density of the hair are sufficient to provide a protective coat and to enhance the shape of the dog, but not so profuse as to obscure the natural lines of the body. The dog should be shown as naturally as is consistent with good grooming but the coat must not be trimmed in any way. On the head, the bridge of the nose is sparsely covered with hair which is slightly longer on the sides to cover the lips. From the cheeks, the lower lips and under the chin, the coat increases in length towards the chest, forming the typical beard. An excessively long, silky coat or one which has been trimmed in any way must be severely penalized.

Color—

Coat: All Bearded Collies are born either black, blue, brown or fawn, with or without white markings. With maturity, the coat color may lighten, so that a born black may become any shade of gray from black to slate to silver, a born brown from chocolate to sandy. Blues and fawns also show shades from dark to light. Where white occurs, it only appears on the foreface as a blaze, on the skull, on the tip of the tail, on the chest, legs and feet and around the neck. The white hair does not grow on the body behind the shoulder nor on the face to surround the eyes. Tan markings occasionally appear and are acceptable on the eyebrows, inside the ears, on the cheeks, under the root of the tail, and on the legs where the white joins the main color.

Pigmentation: Pigmentation on the Bearded Collie follows coat color. In a born black, the eye rims, nose and lips are black, whereas in the born blue, the pigmentation is a blue-gray color. A born brown dog has brown pigmentation and born fawns a correspondingly lighter brown. The pigmentation is completely filled in and shows no sign of spots.

Eyes: Eye color will generally tone with the coat color. In a born blue or fawn, the distinctively lighter eyes are correct and must not be penalized.

Size—The ideal height at the withers is 21 - 22 inches for adult dogs and 20 - 21 inches for adult bitches. Height over and under the ideal is to be severely penalized. The express objective of this criterion is to insure that the Bearded Collie remains a medium sized dog.

Gait—Movement is free, supple and powerful. Balance combines good reach in forequarters with strong drive in hindquarters. The back remains firm and level. The feet are lifted only enough to clear the ground, giving the impression that the dog glides along making minimum contact. Movement is lithe and flexible to enable the dog to make the sharp turns and sudden stops required of the sheep dog. When viewed from the front and rear, the front and rear legs travel in the same plane from the shoulder and hip joint to pads at all speeds. Legs remain straight, but feet move inward as speed increases until the edges of the feet converge on a center line at a fast trot.

Serious faults:
—snipy muzzle
—flat croup or steep croup
—excessively long, silky coat
—trimmed or sculptured coat
—height over or under the ideal

Note: A first standard for the Bearded Collie was approved October 12, 1976. The revised standard shown above was approved August 9, 1978.

Belgian Malinois

THE BELGIAN MALINOIS is one of the three types of Belgian sheepherding dogs registered in Belgium and France as the *Chien de Berger Belge*. It derives from the same stock described in the history of the Belgian Sheepdog which follows, but is traced back in Belgium only to 1898 when a specimen of this breed, a dog named Tomy, was the first to attract attention.

The breed has proven truly adaptable to training, and many Belgian Malinois have won the award of working champion in Belgium.

Except for the coat and color, the Belgian Malinois is identical in conformation to the Belgian Sheepdog and Belgian Tervuren. It is distinguished from these other breeds by its short coat, which is especially short on the head and ears, with somewhat longer hair around the neck and on the tail and the back of the thighs. In color it is similar to the Belgian Tervuren.

In 1948 some Belgian Malinois were imported to the United States from Belgium. These dogs, as well as the Belgian Tervuren, were registered and shown as Belgian Sheepdogs up to July 1, 1959, when the AKC established them as three separate breeds. The Belgian Malinois has been registered as a separate breed since that date. Separate show classification for the Belgian Malinois has been provided since June 30, 1965.

Official Standard for the
Belgian Malinois

General Appearance—The Belgian Malinois is a well-balanced, square dog, elegant in appearance, with an exceedingly proud carriage of the head and neck. The dog is strong, agile, well-muscled, alert and full of life. It stands squarely on all fours and viewed from the side, the topline, forelegs and hind legs closely approximate a square. The whole conformation gives the impression of depth and solidity without bulkiness. The expression indicates alertness, attention and readiness for activity, and the gaze is intelligent and questioning. The male is usually somewhat more impressive and grand than its female counterpart, which has a distinctly feminine look.

Size and Substance—Males, 24 to 26 inches in height; females, 22 to 24 inches, measured at the withers. The length, measured from point of breastbone to point of rump, should equal the height, but bitches may be slightly longer. Bone structure is moderately heavy in proportion to height so that the dog is well balanced throughout and neither spindly or leggy nor cumbersome and bulky.

Coat—Comparatively short, straight, with dense undercoat. Very short hair on the head, ears and lower legs. The hair is somewhat longer around the neck where it forms a collarette, and on the tail and the back of the thighs.

Color—Rich fawn to mahogany, with black overlay. Black mask and ears. The under parts of the body, tail, and breeches are lighter fawn, but washed-out fawn color on the body is a fault. The tips of the toes may be white and a small white spot on the chest is permitted.

Head—Clean-cut and strong, over-all size in proportion to the body. *Skull*—Top flattened rather than rounded, the width approximately the same as the length but no wider. *Stop*—Moderate. *Muzzle, Jaws, Lips*—Muzzle moderately pointed, avoiding any tendency to snipiness, and approximately equal in length to that of the topskull. The jaws are strong and powerful. The lips tight and black, with no pink showing on the outside. *Ears*—Triangular in shape, stiff, erect and in proportion to the head in size. Base of the ear should not come below the center of the eye. *Eyes*—Brown, preferably dark brown, medium size, slightly almond shaped, not protruding. *Nose*—Black, without spots or discolored areas. *Teeth*—A full complement of strong, white teeth, evenly set and meeting in an even bite or a scissors bite, neither overshot nor undershot.

Torso—*Neck*—Round and rather outstretched, tapered from head to body, well muscled with tight skin. *Topline*—The withers are slightly higher and slope into the back, which must be level, straight and firm from withers to hip joints. The loin section, viewed from above, is relatively short, broad and strong, but blending smoothly into the back. The croup is medium long, sloping gradually. *Tail*—Strong at the base, bone to reach hock. At rest it is held low, the tip bent back level with the hock. In action it is raised with a curl, which is strongest toward the tip, without forming a hook. *Chest*—Not broad, but deep. The lowest point reaches the elbow, forming a smooth ascendant curve to the abdomen, which is moderately developed, neither tucked-up nor paunchy.

Forequarters—*Shoulders*—Long and oblique, laid flat against the body, forming a sharp angle (approximately 90°) with the upper arm. ***Legs*—**Straight, strong and paralleled to each other. Bone oval rather than round. Length and substance well proportioned to the size of the dog. Pastern: Medium length, strong and very slightly sloped. Dewclaws may be removed. ***Feet*—**Round (cat-footed), toes curved close together, well padded. Nails strong and black except that they may be white to match white toe tips.

Hindquarters—*Thighs*—Broad and heavily muscled. The upper and lower thigh bones approximately parallel the shoulder blade and upper arm respectively, forming a relatively sharp angle at stifle joint. ***Legs*—**Length and substance well proportioned to the size of the dog. Bone oval rather than round. Legs are parallel to each other. The angle at the hock is relatively sharp, although the Belgian Malinois does not have extreme angulation. Metatarsus medium length, strong and slightly sloped. Dewclaws, if any, should be removed. ***Feet*—**Slightly elongated, toes curved close together, well padded. Nails strong and black except that they may be white to match white toe tips.

Gait—Smooth, free and easy, seemingly never tiring, exhibiting facility of movement rather than a hard driving action. The dog tends to single-track at a fast gait, the legs, both front and rear, converging toward the center line of gravity of the dog, while the backline remains firm and level, parallel to the line of motion with no crabbing. The Belgian Malinois shows a marked tendency to move in a circle rather than a straight line.

FAULTS

Any deviation from these specifications is a fault, the degree to which a dog is penalized depending on the extent to which the dog deviates from the standard and the extent to which the particular fault would actually affect the working ability of the dog.

DISQUALIFICATIONS

Ears hanging, as on a hound.

Tail—cropped or stump.

Males under 22¹/₂ or over 27¹/₂ inches in height. Females under 20¹/₂ or over 25¹/₂ inches in height.

Approved April 13, 1965

Belgian Sheepdog

THE TERM *Chien de Berger* many years ago was loosely applied to any European dog used for herding sheep. Holland, France, and Belgium all had sheepdogs which varied in coat—there were longhaired, shorthaired, and roughhaired kinds. Anatomically their structure was identical. Some even said that if the dogs were shaved and but casually observed, one could not be distinguished from the other.

However much or little truth there is in this assertion, the fact remains that prior to the year 1891 the Belgian Sheepdog was the genuine shepherd's dog, fairly common throughout the greater part of Europe. It was a potpourri of all sizes, all hairs, all colors, all types. Some of the dogs were cropped. Certain of them had long tails, some naturally short tails, while others were docked. And they reproduced themselves with little if any consistency as regards general appearance and special attributes. Such results were inevitable, since the dogs were bred on a basis of herding aptitude without regard for coat, color, or conformation.

Also inevitable was the fact that gradually a semblance of type did develop, due to the isolation of locality and the way of life; then subsequently the emerging types were named for the districts to which they were native. Such nomenclature of course is not unique in any breed or country, for many of our present-day breed names are geographic.

The modern history of the Belgian Sheepdog begins at the close of the nineteenth century, its most vital development taking place between the years 1891 and 1898, or thereabouts. In 1891 one Professor Reul assembled a group of shepherd dogs for the purpose of studying the different types then existing in Belgium. Sheep raising at that time was in a decline. The dogs had been bred indiscriminately and fed as economically as possible; therefore they tended to be rather slight in frame and quite varied in type, coat, and color. There were, in fact, six varieties—the Belgians called them breeds. The Belgian Kennel Club never wished to recognize them all, but the Royal Society of St. Hubert did deem them deserving of championships.

In his survey, Professor Reul noticed three kinds which did exhibit a certain similarity: a longhaired black, a shorthaired fawn and charcoal, and a shaggy-haired, dark ash-gray. He recommended breeding together only those of similar coat. A small group of devotees, who then formed the Belgian Kennel Club, did not immediately go along with Professor Reul's suggestion, and so for a short period fanciers continued to interbreed long-coated and shaggy, or tough-coated, fawns. However, in 1897 the Belgian Kennel Club decided to admit only three kinds of coats: the black for long hair, the blackened fawn for short hair, and the ash-gray for tough hair. Since the edict ruled on color as well as coat length and texture, this was a notable step forward in keeping the varieties distinct.

Besides Professor Reul, there was another farsighted pioneer who deserves mention for the part he played in the development of the Belgian Sheepdog, namely, M. Rose of the village of Groenendael. Years before Professor Reul's survey, M. Rose had been breeding longhaired blacks with some success. In 1885 he had found in one of his litters a longhaired black bitch, which he named Petite, presumably a sport, to which he was so attracted that he determined to establish a strain. Blacks were rare in those days, but after a year's search he located Piccard D'Uccle, a black male of similar type, which he purchased from its owner, M. Bernaert, for mating with his female. This pair produced a litter whose individual names are engraved on pedigrees of the past as pillars of the breed—Duc, Pitt, Baronne, Margot, and Bergere, all of Groenendael. Duc made his show debut in 1898; he was subsequently mated to several females, and the best of these were used to carry on the strain.

Thus the Groenendael, which took its name from the village of its birth and early development, was started on its way. Its beauty, symmetry and sturdy structure contributed to its growing popularity, which extended before many years to the United States.

The first Belgians came to America in 1907 when five specimens were imported. A few more crossed the sea in 1912 to make their home in Englewood, New Jersey, where they were used in police work. Two years later, Mr. Auguste de Conti imported a pair which worked with the Brooklyn police force. Mr. H. Persson, of Staten Island, brought over two from the kennels of M. Madoux, a prominent breeder of Groenendaels.

The Belgian Sheepdog bred in the United States between World War I and World War II was almost exclusively the Groenendael, and this longhaired black dog became generally known as the Belgian Sheepdog in this country.

In 1948 some Malinois, or shorthaired fawn-and-black dogs, were imported from Belgium. In 1954 and the years immediately following, a number of Tervuren, or longhaired fawn-and-black dogs, were imported, and these have gained some popularity here. All of these different types were registered and shown as Belgian Sheepdogs up to July 1, 1959, when the AKC established them as three separate breeds, dogs of the Groenendael type alone being registered and shown as Belgian Sheepdogs. The other types are now registered as separate breeds, the Belgian Malinois and the Belgian Tervuren, and separate show classification is provided for each breed.

As for imported dogs, Groenendaels are eligible for registration in the United States only if they have at least three generations of pure Groenendael ancestors.

Fanciers are rich in praise of the Belgian Sheepdog's many good qualities, particularly those having to do with devoted companionship. Scientific breeders are equally enthusiastic concerning its intelligence and value as a worker. It has long been used overseas as a police dog; in fact, some authorities credit it as the first breed to be thoroughly trained for such exacting duties. During World War I, thousands were trained as messengers between outflung sectors where human messengers would have met certain death. Many of these dogs gave their lives.

Official Standard for the
Belgian Sheepdog

Personality—The Belgian Sheepdog should reflect the qualities of intelligence, courage, alertness, and devotion to master. To his inherent aptitude as guardian of flocks should be added protectiveness of the person and property of his master. He should be watchful, attentive, and always in motion when not under command. In his relationship with humans he should be observant and vigilant with strangers but not apprehensive. He should not show fear or shyness. He should not show viciousness by unwarranted or unprovoked attack. With those he knows well, he is most affectionate and friendly, zealous of their attention, and very possessive.

General Appearance—The first impression of the Belgian Sheepdog is that of a well-balanced, square dog, elegant in appearance, with an exceedingly proud carriage of the head and neck. He is a strong, agile, well-muscled animal, alert and full of life. His whole conformation gives the impression of depth and solidity without bulkiness. The male dog is usually somewhat more impressive and grand than his female counterpart. The bitch should have a distinctly feminine look.

Size and Substance—Males should be 24–26 inches in height and females 22–24 inches, measured at the withers. The length, measured from point of breastbone to point of rump, should equal the height. Bitches may be slightly longer. Bone structure should be moderately heavy in proportion to his height so that he is well balanced throughout and neither spindly or leggy nor cumbersome and bulky. **Stance**—The Belgian Sheepdog should stand squarely on all fours. Side view: the topline, front legs, and back legs should closely approximate a square.

Expression—Indicates alertness, attention, readiness for activity. Gaze should be intelligent and questioning.

Coat—The guard hairs of the coat must be long, well-fitting, straight, and abundant. They should not be silky or wiry. The texture should be a medium harshness. The undercoat should be extremely dense, commensurate, however, with climatic conditions. The Belgian Sheepdog is particularly adaptable to extremes of temperature or climate. The hair is shorter on the head, outside of the ears, and lower part of the legs. The opening of the ear is protected by tufts of hair. **Ornamentation**—Especially long and abundant hair, like a collarette, around the neck; fringe of long hair down the back of the forearm; especially long and abundant hair trimming the hindquarters, the breeches; long, heavy, and abundant hair on the tail.

Color—Black. May be completely black or may be black with white, limited as follows: Small to moderate patch or strip on forechest. Between pads of feet. On *tips* of hind toes. On chin and muzzle (frost—may be white or gray). On *tips* of front toes—allowable but a fault.

Head—Clean-cut and strong, over-all size should be in proportion to the body. **Skull**—Top flattened rather than rounded. The width approximately the same, but not wider, than the length. **Stop**—Moderate. **Muzzle, Jaws, Lips**—Muzzle moderately pointed, avoiding any tendency to snipiness, and approximately equal in length to that of the topskull. The jaws should be strong and powerful. The lips should be tight and black, with no pink showing on the outside. *Ears*—Triangular in shape, stiff, erect, and in proportion to the head in size. Base of the ear should not come below the center of the eye. *Eyes*— Brown, preferably dark brown. Medium size, slightly almond shaped, not protruding. *Nose*—Black, without spots or discolored areas. *Teeth*—A full complement of strong, white teeth, evenly set. Should not be overshot or undershot. Should have either an even bite or a scissors bite.

Torso—Neck—Round and rather outstretched, tapered from head to body, well muscled, with tight skin. *Topline*—The withers are slightly higher and slope into the back which must be level, straight, and firm from withers to hip joints. The loin section, viewed from above, is relatively short, broad and strong, but blending smoothly into the back. The croup is medium long, sloping gradually. *Tail*—Strong at the base, bone to reach hock. At rest the dog holds it low, the tip bent back level with the hock. When in action he raises it and gives it a curl, which is strongest toward the tip, without forming a hook. *Chest*—Not broad, but deep. The lowest point should reach the elbow, forming a smooth ascendant curve to the abdomen. *Abdomen*—Moderate development. Neither tuck-up nor paunchy.

Forequarters—Shoulder—Long and oblique, laid flat against the body, forming a sharp angle (approximately 90°) with the upper arm. *Legs*—Straight, strong, and parallel to each other. Bone oval rather than round. Development (length and substance) should be well proportioned to the size of the dog. Pastern: Medium length, strong, and very slightly sloped. *Feet*—Round (cat-footed), toes curved close together, well padded. Nails strong and black except that they may be white to match white toe tips.

Hindquarters—Thighs—Broad and heavily muscled. The upper and lower thigh bones approximately parallel the shoulder blade and upper arm respectively, forming a relatively sharp angle at stifle joint. *Legs*—Length and substance well proportioned to the size of the dog. Bone oval rather than round. Legs are parallel to each other. The angle at the hock is relatively sharp, although the Belgian Sheepdog does not have extreme angulation. Metatarsus medium length, strong, and slightly sloped. Dewclaws, if any, should be removed. *Feet*—Slightly elongated. Toes curved close together, well padded. Nails strong and black except that they may be white to match white toe tips.

Gait—Motion should be smooth, free and easy, seemingly never tiring, exhibiting facility of movement rather than a hard driving action. He tends to single-track on a fast gait; the legs, both front and rear, converging toward the center line of gravity of the dog. The backline should remain firm and level, parallel to the line of motion with no crabbing. He shows a marked tendency to move in a circle rather than a straight line.

FAULTS

Any deviation from these specifications is a fault. In determining whether a fault is minor, serious, or major, these two factors should be used as a guide: 1. The extent to which it deviates from the Standard. 2. The extent to which such deviation would actually affect the working ability of the dog.

DISQUALIFICATIONS

Viciousness.
Color—any color other than black, except for white in specified areas.
Ears—hanging (as on a hound).
Tail—cropped or stump.
Males under 22 1/2 or over 27 1/2 inches in height.
Females under 20 1/2 or over 25 1/2 inches in height.

Approved June 9, 1959

Belgian Tervuren

THE BELGIAN TERVUREN is one of the Belgian types of shepherd dog registered in Belgium and France as the *Chien de Berger Belge*. It is of common origin with the Groenendael and other types. The Tervuren resembles the Groenendael strikingly in conformation, but differs as strikingly in color.

The close relationship between the two breeds grows out of the fact that the earliest of Belgium's sheepdogs incorporated several different kinds or varieties: Some had long hair, some short hair, others tough or shaggy hair, while colors included black, ash-gray, and blackened fawn as well as other shades not so easily identifiable. All were bred together indiscriminately.

A century or more ago, when sheepherding abroad was an important part of rural life, the shepherd's dog was bred solely on a basis of proficiency in herding. The dog's appearance meant nothing to the herdsmen, whose livelihood depended upon the safety and well-being of their sheep. All that mattered was a strong and rugged body, together with superior herding ability. This, without a doubt, the Belgian herdsmen got, but at the same time, by interbreeding, they played havoc with the inheritable factors involved in coat length, color, and texture.

The advent of dog shows in the 1880s coincided with a decline in sheepherding. The wolf menace was on the way out; fences and corrals were coming into greater use, and growing rail facilities helped to obviate the need for quite so much protracted trailing to the markets. Dog shows, however primitive they may have been then as compared with now, tended to direct attention to the dog as an attractive animal in its own right, rather than a mere shepherd's assistant.

From the start of selective breeding, which may be said to have begun with the institution of dog shows, gradually more or less definite types began to emerge from the previous hodgepodge of coat and color.

This volume's history of the Belgian Sheepdog breed explains the evolution of the Groenendael, which began about 1885. The evolution of the Tervuren began in much the same manner, and from identical stock on the sire's side, but exactly when is not clear.

One M. F. Corbeel, of the town of Tervuren, owned Tom and Poes, a pair of sheepdogs with long, black-tipped fawn hair. From this mating came Miss, a female which fortunately came into the possession of M. Danhieux, a breeder as astute as M. Rose, which in its way is high praise. M. Danhieux proceeded to mate Miss with the longhaired black, Piccard D'Uccle, the very same dog that was progenitor of the Groenendaels. This union produced the justly famed Milsart, a blackened fawn dog acknowledged to be the best Tervuren whelped in the era before 1900. In 1907 Milsart became the first Tervuren champion.

In the aforementioned discussion of the Groenendael, black was cited as dominant. In view of Milsart's ancestry, this statement would cause confusion in the minds of those conversant with Mendelian inheritance unless it were explained further that the longhaired black, Piccard D'Uccle, harbored the fawn factor in his make-up.

Owing to the similarity of the Tervuren with the Groenendael, it is obvious that the major difference between the two, that of color, should assume importance. In texture, the hair of the Tervuren is medium harsh, neither silky nor wiry. In color, it is a rather light fawn at first, but by the age of eighteen months it takes on a depth and richness approximating warm mahogany overlaid with black. Actually only the tips of the fawn hairs are black. The blackening extends over the dog like a veil, much as if it had been stroked with a hand covered with charcoal or soot. The black is especially pronounced on shoulders and back, face, ears, and tail tip. The chief consideration is that the coat have sufficient black, but not too much, since the ground color is a deep rich fawn.

As regards the breeding potentialities of the Tervuren, the factor for fawn is a recessive, so despite ancestry two fawns bred together cannot produce a black. This is the reason the customary three-generation proof of pure Tervuren ancestry is not required for registration of acceptable imports.

The first Tervuren apparently came to the United States early in the 1940s, brought over by Europeans of unknown nationality. One of the unregistered progeny of the pair was Wolf, a blackened fawn owned by the William McGees of Toledo. Wolf lived a long and useful life of fifteen years. Rudy Robinson imported the first registered Tervuren in 1954. Strangely, although the Tervuren originated in Belgium, almost all of our imports have come from France.

The breed has not been slow to make its presence felt here; in fact it has proved especially adept at obedience work. The first American-bred litter of Tervuren, whelped in 1954, has for its sire and dam two CD titleholders—Cheri du Clos St. Jacques and Crigga du Clos St. Jacques—both of which won their degrees before they were a year old. A few years later, Nightwatch Russet Cavalier earned his tracking degree in Canada at approximately the same age. D'Jimmy du Clos St. Clair, owned by Betty C. Hinckley of Chicago, in 1958 became the first champion of the breed in this country.

Previously the Belgian Tervuren was registered and shown as one of the types of Belgian Sheepdog. In 1959, however, it was granted registration as a separate breed with separate classification at the shows.

Official Standard for the
Belgian Tervuren

Personality—The Belgian Tervuren should reflect the qualities of intelligence, courage, alertness and devotion to master. To his inherent aptitude as guardian of flocks should be added protectiveness of the person and property of his master. He should be watchful, attentive and usually in motion when not under command. In his relationship with humans he should be observant and vigilant with strangers but not apprehensive. He should not show fear or shyness. He should not show viciousness by unwarranted or unprovoked attack. With those he knows well, he is most affectionate and friendly, zealous for their attention and very possessive.

General Appearance—The first impression of the Belgian Tervuren is that of a well-balanced square dog, elegant in appearance, with proud carriage of the head and neck. He is a strong, agile, well-muscled animal, alert and full of life. His whole conformation gives the impression of depth and solidity without bulkiness. The male is usually somewhat more impressive and grand than the female. The female should have a distinctly feminine look. Because of frequent comparisons between the Belgian Tervuren and the German Shepherd Dog, it is to be noted that these two breeds differ considerably in size, substance and structure, the difference being especially noticeable in the formation of the topline and the hindquarters.

Size and Substance—Males 24–26 inches in height, and females 22–24 inches, measured at the withers. The length, measured from point of breastbone to point of rump, should equal the height. Bone structure medium in proportion to height so that he is well balanced throughout and neither spindly or leggy nor cumbersome and bulky. *Stance*—The Belgian Tervuren should stand squarely on all fours. Viewed from the side, the topline, ground level, front legs, and back legs should closely approximate a perfect square.

Expression—Intelligent and questioning, indicating alertness, attention and readiness for action.

Coat—The guard hairs of the coat must be long, well-fitting, straight and abundant. They should not be silky or wiry. The texture should be a medium harshness. The undercoat should be very dense, commensurate, however, with climatic conditions. The Belgian Tervuren is particularly adaptable to extremes of temperature or climate. The hair is shorter on the head, outside the ears and on the lower part of the legs. The opening of the ear is protected by tufts of hair. *Ornamentation*—Especially long and abundant hair, like a collarette, around the neck; fringe of long hair down the back of the forearm; especially long and abundant hair trimming the hindquarters—the breeches; long, heavy and abundant hair on the tail.

Color—Rich fawn to russet mahogany with black overlay. The coat is characteristically double pigmented, wherein the tip of each fawn hair is blackened. On mature males, this blackening is especially pronounced on the shoulders, back and rib section. The chest color is a mixture of black and gray. The face has a black mask, and the ears are mostly black. The tail typically has a darker or black tip. The underparts of the body, tail and breeches are light beige. A small white patch is permitted on the chest, not to extend to the neck or breast. The tips of the toes may be white. White or gray hair (frost) on chin or muzzle is normal. Although some allowance is to be made for dogs under 18 months of age, when the true color is attained, washed-out color or color too black resembling the Belgian Sheepdog is undesirable.

Head—Well chiseled, dry, long without exaggeration. *Skull and muzzle,* measuring from the stop, should be of equal length. Over-all size should be in proportion to the body. Top of skull flattened rather than rounded, the width approximately the same but not wider than the length. Stop moderate. Muzzle moderately pointed, avoiding any tendency to snipiness. *The jaws* should be strong and powerful. *The lips* should be tight and black, with no pink showing on the outside. *Ears* are equilateral triangles in shape, well cupped, stiff, erect, not too large. Set high, the base of the ear should not come below the center of the eye. *Eyes* brown, preferably dark brown, medium size, slightly almond shaped, not protruding. Light or yellow eyes are a fault. *Nose* black, without spots or discolored areas. Nostrils well defined. There should be a full complement of *strong white teeth* evenly set. Either a scissors or even bite is acceptable. Should not be overshot or undershot. Teeth broken by accident should not be severely penalized, but worn teeth, especially incisors, are often indicative of the lack of proper bite, although some allowance should be made for age. Discolored (distemper) teeth are not to be penalized.

Torso—Neck round, muscular, rather outstretched, slightly arched and tapered from head to body. Skin well-fitting with no loose folds. Topline horizontal, straight and firm from withers to hip joints. The loin section, viewed from above, is relatively short, broad and strong, but blending smoothly into the back. The croup is medium long, sloping gradually. *Tail*—Strong at the base, the last vertebra to reach the hock. At rest the dog holds it low, the tip bent back level with the hock. When in action he raises it and gives it a curl, which is strongest toward the tip, without forming a hook. Tail should not be carried too high nor turned to one side. *Chest*—Not broad but deep, the lowest point should reach the elbow, forming a smooth ascendant curve to the abdomen. *Abdomen*—Moderately developed, neither tucked-up nor paunchy.

Forequarters—Legs straight, parallel, perpendicular to the ground. Shoulders long and oblique, laid flat against the body, forming a sharp angle (approximately 90°) with the upper arm. Top of the shoulder blades should be roughly a thumb's width apart. Arms should move in a direction exactly parallel to the axis of the body. Forearms long and well muscled. Bone flat rather than round. Pasterns short and strong, slightly sloped. Feet round (cat-footed), toes curved close together, well padded, strong nails. Nail color can vary from black to transparent.

Hindquarters—Legs powerful without heaviness, moving in the same pattern as the limbs of the forequarters. Thighs broad and heavily muscled. Stifles clearly defined, with upper shank at right angles to the hip bones. Bone flat rather than round. Hocks moderately bent. Metatarsi short, perpendicular to the ground, parallel to each other when viewed from the rear. Dewclaws, if any, should be removed. Feet slightly elongated, toes curved close together, heavily padded, strong nails. Nail color may vary from black to transparent.

Gait—The gait is lively and graceful, covering the maximum of ground. Always in motion, seemingly never tiring, he shows facility of movement rather than a hard driving action. He tends to single-track at a fast gait, the legs both front and rear converging toward the center line of gravity of the dog. The back line should remain firm and level, parallel to the line of motion with no crabbing. His natural tendency is to move in a circle rather than a straight line.

DISQUALIFICATIONS

Ears—hanging, as on a hound.

Tail—cropped or stump.

Color—white markings anywhere except as specified.

Teeth—pronounced undershot.

Size—males under 22$\frac{1}{2}$ or over 27$\frac{1}{2}$ inches in height; females under 20$\frac{1}{2}$ or over 25$\frac{1}{2}$ inches in height.

Approved May 12, 1959

Bernese Mountain Dog

ARISTOCRATIC IN APPEARANCE, ancient in lineage, the Bernese Mountain Dog has long been at home on the farms in the middle land of Switzerland. One of the four varieties of Swiss Mountain Dogs, the Bernese shares similar distinctive coloring with the other varieties, but is the only one of the four to have a long, silky coat. These dogs worked as drovers and draft dogs as well as watch dogs in the farmyards mainly in the Canton of Berne.

The ancestors of these dogs were brought into Switzerland over two thousand years ago by the invading Roman soldiers. But until a few years before World War I, they had been almost forgotten by all save the oldest inhabitants of Berne. They were still found in the area of Duerrbach, but the breed had degenerated to such an extent as to be practically unrecognizable. When in 1892 the Swiss fancier Franz Schertenleib attempted to find good specimens to be used as breeding stock, his search was a long one. However, he was successful, and several other fanciers became interested as well. The rehabilitation was started, and succeeded under the knowledgeable leadership of the great geologist, canine researcher and judge Professor Albert Heim. In 1907, a specialty club was formed and the breed found favor with many Swiss, who developed them as house pets and companions, although their old role on farms still continued.

A handsome, long haired, sturdily built dog, the Bernese is jet black in color, with rich russet markings on his legs, cheeks, spots over each eye, and on either side of the snowy white chest markings. A white blaze adorns its muzzle and forehead, and it is highly desirable that the dogs have white feet, white tail tip and that the white chest marking forms a Swiss cross. The coat is of medium length and silky with a slight wave, but it must not be curly. An impressive looking dog, 23 to 27½ inches in height for dogs, with bitches slightly smaller, the Bernese is characterized by dark eyes, V-shaped ears hanging close to the head in repose, but brought slightly forward and raised at the base when alert. His short-backed, compact, and well-ribbed-up body, with broad chest, deep brisket, and strong muscular loins show that he is well suited to hard work.

The Bernese is an extremely hardy dog, thriving in cold weather. He needs only a small amount of daily grooming to look well kept. For his emotional development and well being he needs human companion-ship, and he is a willing and quick learner. He is self-confident and exceptionally faithful.

Official Standard for the
Bernese Mountain Dog

General Appearance—A well-balanced dog, active and alert; a combination of sagacity, fidelity and utility.

Height—Dogs, 23 inches to 27½ inches; bitches, 21 inches to 26 inches at shoulder.

Head—Skull flat, defined stop and strong muzzle. Dewlaps very slightly developed, flews not too pendulous, jaw strong with good, strong teeth. *Eyes*— dark, hazel-brown, full of fire. *Ears*—V-shaped, set on high, not too pointed at tips and rather short. When in repose, hanging close to head; when alert, brought slightly forward and raised at base.

Body—Rather short than too long in back, compact and well ribbed up. Chest broad with good depth of brisket. Loins strong and muscular.

Legs and Feet—Forelegs perfectly straight and muscular, thighs well developed and stifles well bent. Feet round and compact. Dewclaws should be removed.

Tail—Of fair thickness and well covered with long hair, but not to form a flag; moderate length. When in repose, should be carried low, upward swirl permissible; when alert, may be carried gaily, but may never curl or be carried over back.

Coat—Soft and silky with bright, natural sheen; long and slightly wavy but may never curl.

Color and Markings—Jet-black with russet-brown or deep tan markings on all four legs, a spot just above forelegs, each side of white chest markings and spots over eyes, which may never be missing. The brown on the forelegs must always be between the black and white. *Preferable, but not a condition, are—* White feet, tip of tail, pure white blaze up foreface, a few white hairs on back of neck, and white star-shaped markings on chest. When the latter markings are missing, it is not a disqualification.

FAULTS

Too massive in head; light or staring eyes; too heavy or long ears; too narrow or snipy muzzle; undershot or overshot mouth; pendulous dewlaps; too long or Setterlike body; splay or hare feet; tail curled or carried over back; cowhocks; and white legs.

SCALE OF POINTS

General appearance	15	Tail	10
Size and height	5	Coat	10
Head	15	Color and markings	15
Body	15		
Legs and feet	15	TOTAL	100

Approved April 13, 1937

Bouvier des Flandres

(Boo-vyay duh Flawn-druh)

DR. REUL, of the Veterinary School of Brussels, was the first to call the attention of breeders to the many good qualities of the Bouvier. At that time, the Bouvier was a dog of great size (about twenty-six inches high at the shoulder), with a heavy cylindrical body, rough gray, dark hair, and a rough appearance. It was found in Southwest Flanders and on the French northern plain. As a rule, it was owned by people who occupied themselves with cattle, for the dog's chief aptitude seemed to be cattle-driving.

Most of the early Bouvier breeders were farmers, butchers, or cattle merchants not particularly interested in breeding pedigreed dogs. All they wanted was help in their work. No one is surprised that the first Bouviers were not absolutely uniform in size, weight, and color. Nevertheless, they all had enough characteristics in common to be recognized as Bouviers. They had different names—*Vuilbaard* (dirty beard), *koehond* (cow dog), *toucheur de boeuf* or *pic* (cattle driver).

The Societe Royale St. Hubert took cognizance of the breed when it appeared on the show benches at the International dog show of May, 1910, in Brussels. The two Bouviers shown there were Nelly and Rex, belonging to a Mr. Paret of Ghent. However, a Standard of the Bouvier type was not adopted until 1912. That was accomplished by a Frenchman, Mr. Fontaine, vice-president of the Club St. Hubert du Nord. At that time a society of Bouvier breeders, founded in Roulers (West) Flanders, invited many of the most famous Belgian experts to a meeting in August of that year. Among those who attended were A. Houtart, J. Levita, Baron van Zuylen of Nyefelt and Dr. van Herreweghe, veterinarian of Scharlaken, and others who promulgated a Standard of perfection which became the first official Standard to be recognized by the Societe Royale St. Hubert.

From then on, the Bouvier des Flandres grew to be more and more appreciated, and several dogs, such as Ch. Bella, Ch. Picard, Ch. Zola of Mr. De Rycker (Roulers); Pickzwart of Dr. van Herreweghe; Jim and Maerten de lu Wornaffe Domicent, Anna de l'Yperlei and Amie of Mr. Lapierre (Ypres), were enlisted in the L.O.S.H. (the stud book of the Societe Royale St. Hubert).

The breed was making rapid progress when World War I broke out. Those parts of the country where the Bouvier was most largely bred, and where it was becoming popular, were entirely destroyed; the people left the country, and most of the dogs were lost. Many were abandoned and died, others were acquired by the Germans. Nevertheless, a few men succeeded in keeping their dogs all through the war, so Sultan (owned by Messrs. Van der Vennet and Gryson), Picko (owned by Mr. De Poorter) Bella and Kiss de Ramillies (owner, Mr. Mottoule) escaped. The dog whose progeny afterwards did much to revive the Bouvier in Belgium lived in the Belgian Army as the property of Veterinarian Captain Barbry. This dog, Ch. Nic de Sottegem, was shown in 1920 at the Olympic show in Antwerp, where the judge, Charles Huge, said: "Nic is the ideal type of Bouvier. He has a short body, with well developed ribs, short flanks, strong legs, good feet, long and oblique shoulders. His head is of a good shape, with somber eyes and an ideal courageous expression. His hair is dry and dark. The tail should not have been cut so short. I hope that this dog will have numerous progeny."

Mr. Huge's hope was realized. When Nic died in 1926, he left many descendants whose names appear in almost every pedigree. Among those worthy of mention are Prince D'Or, Ch. Draga, Coralie de Sottegem, Goliath de la Lys, Lyda, Nora, Ch. Dragon de la Lys, etc. From these dogs, gathered together one day at Ghent, a group of experts, including Charles Huge, V. Tenret, V. Taeymans, Count de Hemptinne, Captain Binon and A. Gevaert, after examining and measuring each one carefully, established a more comprehensive Standard.

Since then Bouviers have attained even greater success abroad, especially in Holland and Belgium. The average number at the shows was thirty, which is relatively large, but so popular did Bouviers become that often this number was exceeded.

Breeders do not forget that the Bouvier is first of all a working dog, and although they try to standardize its type, they do not want it to lose the early qualities which first called attention to its desirability. For that reason, in Belgium a Bouvier cannot win the title of champion unless he has also won a prize in a work-competition as a police, defense, or army dog.

Official Standard for the
Bouvier des Flandres

The Bouvier des Flandres is a powerfully built, compact, short-coupled, rough-coated dog of notably rugged appearance. He gives the impression of great strength without any sign of heaviness or clumsiness in his overall makeup. He is agile, spirited and bold, yet his serene, well-behaved disposition denotes his steady, resolute and fearless character. His gaze is alert and brilliant, depicting his intelligence, vigor and daring. By nature he is an equable dog.

His origin is that of a cattle herder and general farmer's helper, including cart pulling. He is an ideal farm dog. His harsh coat protects him in all weather, enabling him to perform the most arduous tasks. The coat may be trimmed slightly only to accent the body line. Overtrimming which alters the natural rugged appearance is to be avoided.

He has been used as an ambulance and messenger dog. Modern times find him as a watch and guard dog as well as a family friend, guardian and protector. His physical and mental characteristics and deportment, coupled with his olfactory abilities, his intelligence and initiative enable him to also perform as a tracking dog and a guide dog for the blind.

Head—The head is impressive in scale, accentuated by beard and mustache. It is in proportion to body and build.

Skull—Well developed and flat, slightly less wide than long. When viewed from the side, the top lines of the skull and the muzzle are parallel. It is wide between the ears, with the frontal groove barely marked. The stop is more apparent than real, due to upstanding eyebrows. The proportions of length of skull to length of muzzle are 3 to 2.

Eyes—The expression is bold and alert. They neither protrude nor are sunken in the sockets. Their shape is oval with the axis on a horizontal plane, when viewed from the front. Their color is a dark nut brown. The eye rims are black without lack of pigment and the haw is barely visible. Yellow or light eyes are to be strongly penalized, along with a walleyed or staring expression.

Ears—Placed high and alert. They are rough-coated. If cropped, they are to be a triangular contour and in proportion to the size of the head. The inner corner of the ear should be in line with the outer corner of the eye. Ears that are too low or too closely set are serious faults.

Muzzle—Broad, strong, well filled out, tapering gradually toward the nose without ever becoming snipy or pointed. The cheeks are flat and lean. with the lips being dry and tight fitting. A narrow, snipy muzzle is faulty.

Nose—Large, black, well developed, round at the edges, with flared nostrils. A brown, pink or spotted nose is a serious fault.

Jaws and Teeth—The jaws are powerful and of equal length. The teeth are strong, white and healthy, with the incisors meeting in a scissors bite. Overshot or undershot bites are to be severely penalized.

Neck—The neck is strong and muscular, widening gradually into the shoulders. When viewed from the side, it is gracefully arched with upright carriage. A short, squatty neck is faulty. No dewlap.

Body or Trunk—Powerful, broad and short. The length from the point of the shoulder to the tip of the buttocks is equal to the height from the ground to the highest point of the withers. The chest is broad, with the brisket extending to the elbow in depth. A long-lined, rangy dog should be faulted.

Ribs—The ribs are deep and well sprung. The first ribs are slightly curved, the others well sprung and very sloped nearing the rear, giving proper depth to the chest. Flat ribs or slabsidedness is to be strongly penalized.

Back—Short, broad, well muscled with firm level topline. It is supple and flexible with no sign of weakness.

Flanks and Loins—Short, wide and well muscled, without weakness. The abdomen is only slightly tucked up.

Croup or Rump—The horizontal line of the back should mold unnoticeably into the curve of the rump, which is characteristically wide. A sunken or slanted croup is a serious fault.

Tail—Is to be docked, leaving 2 or 3 vertebrae. It must be set high and align normally with the spinal column. Preferably carried upright in motion. Dogs born tailless should not be penalized.

Forequarters—Strong boned, well muscled and straight.

Shoulders and Upper Arms—The shoulders are relatively long, muscular but not loaded, with good layback. The shoulder blade and humerus are approximately the same length, forming an angle slightly greater than 90 degrees when standing. Straight shoulders are faulty.

Elbows—Close to the body and parallel. Elbows which are too far out or in are faults.

Forearms—Viewed either in profile or from the front are perfectly straight, parallel to each other and perpendicular to the ground. They are well muscled and strong boned.

Wrists—Exactly in line with the forearms. Strong boned.

Pasterns—Quite short, slightly sloped forward. Dewclaws may be removed.

Feet—Both forefeet and hind feet are rounded and compact turning neither in nor out; the toes close and well arched; strong black nails; thick tough pads.

Hindquarters—Firm, well muscled with large, powerful hams. They should be parallel with the front legs when viewed from either front or rear.

Thighs—Wide and muscular. The upper thigh must be neither too straight nor too sloping. There is moderate angulation at the stifle.

Legs—Moderately long, well muscled, neither too straight nor too inclined.

Hocks—Strong, rather close to the ground. When standing and seen from the rear, they will be straight and perfectly parallel to each other and perpendicular to the ground. In motion, they must turn neither in nor out. There is a slight angulation at the hock joint. Sickle or cowhocks are serious faults.

Metatarsi—Hardy and lean, rather cylindrical and perpendicular to the ground when standing. If born with dewclaws, they are to be removed.

Coat—A tousled, double coat capable of withstanding the hardest work in the most inclement weather. The outer hairs are rough and harsh, with the undercoat being fine, soft and dense.

Topcoat—Must be harsh to the touch, dry, trimmed, if necessary, to a length of approximately $2^1/2$ inches. A coat too long or too short is a fault, as is a silky or woolly coat. It is tousled without being curly. On the skull, it is short, and on the upper part of the back, it is particularly close and harsh always, however, remaining rough.

Undercoat—A dense mass of fine, close hair, thicker in winter. Together with the topcoat, it will form a water-resistant covering. A flat coat, denoting lack of undercoat is a serious fault.

Mustache and Beard—Very thick, with the hair being shorter and rougher on the upper side of the muzzle. The upper lip, with its heavy mustache and the chin with its heavy and rough beard gives that gruff expression so characteristic of the breed.

Eyebrows—Erect hairs accentuating the shape of the eyes without ever veiling them.

Color—From fawn to black, passing through salt and pepper, gray and brindle. A small white star on the chest is allowed. Other than chocolate brown, white, or parti-color, which are to be severely penalized, no one color is to be favored.

Height—The height as measured at the withers—Dogs, from $24^1/2$ to $27^1/2$ inches; bitches, from $23^1/2$ to $26^1/2$ inches. In each sex, the ideal height is the median of the two limits, i.e., 26 inches for a dog and 25 inches for a bitch. Any dog or bitch deviating from the minimum or maximum limits mentioned shall be severely penalized.

Gait—The whole of the Bouvier des Flandres must be harmoniously proportioned to allow for a free, bold and proud gait. The reach of the forequarters must compensate for and be in balance with the driving power of the hindquarters. The back, while moving in a trot, will remain firm and flat. In general, the gait is the logical demonstration of the structure and build of the dog. It is to be noted that while moving at a fast trot, the properly built Bouvier will tend to single-track.

Temperament—As mentioned under general description and characteristics, the Bouvier is an equable dog, steady, resolute and fearless. Viciousness or shyness is undesirable.

Faults—The foregoing description is that of the ideal Bouvier des Flandres. Any deviation from this is to be penalized to the extent of the deviation.

Approved June 10, 1975

Boxer

ALTHOUGH it has reached its greatest perfection in Germany during the past hundred years, the Boxer springs from a line of dogs known throughout the whole of Europe since the sixteenth century. Prior to that time, ancestors of the breed would hardly be recognized as Boxers could they be placed beside modern specimens. Still, evidence points to the Boxer as one of the many descendants of the old fighting dog of the high valleys of Tibet.

The Boxer is cousin to practically all recognized breeds of the Bulldog type, and these all go back to basic Molossus blood. Few other strains can claim such courage and stamina; and from this line emanates the attractive fawn color that has recurred throughout the centuries.

Flemish tapestries of the sixteenth and seventeenth centuries show scenes of stag and boar hunting; the dogs are the same as the Spanish Alano, found in great numbers in Andalusia and Estramadura, and the Matin de Terceira or Perro do Presa, from the Azores. The Alano and the Matin have been regarded as the same breed—they are either ancestors of the Boxer or they trace back to a common ancestor.

In France, there is a breed known as the Dogue de Bordeaux that is very close, both in appearance and size to the old Tibetan Mastiff, and it is from this massive dog that the Bouldogue du Mida was developed.

The Bouldogue du Mida, found principally in the South of France, possesses many of the points of the Boxer.

While all the European breeds mentioned are related to the Boxer, this favorite of Germany has been developed along scientific lines that not only have succeeded in retaining all his old qualities, but have resulted in a much more attractive appearance. Besides Bulldog blood, the Boxer carries a certain heritage from a terrier strain. There is also some reason to believe that English Bulldogs were at one time imported into Germany. Indeed, Reinagle's noted Bulldog, done in 1803, is not unlike the Boxer, and pictures of some English specimens of 1850 are almost identical with the German dog.

Until dogfighting and bullbaiting were outlawed by most civilized peoples in the middle of the nineteenth century, the Boxer, like all dogs of his type, was used for this purpose. Today he has become an accredited member of society, but he still has the same degree of courage and the ability to defend, as well as aggressiveness when needed. Withal, he is devoted to his master.

The quality of the Boxer is best emphasized, perhaps, when we remember that he was one of the first selected in Germany for police training. This work demands intelligence, fearlessness, agility, and strength.

Considering that the entire modern history of the Boxer is wrapped up with Germany, it seems rather curious that he bears a name obviously English. Yet the name fits him. It arises from his manner of fighting, for invariably he begins a fight with his front paws, somewhat like a man boxing.

The Boxer has been bred and exhibited sporadically in the United States since the early days of the twentieth century, but it was not until about 1940 that the public began to take an interest in the breed. This came about because of the consistent Group winning of certain outstanding dogs.

The first Boxer was registered in 1904; the first championship by a specimen of the breed was finished in 1915.

Official Standard for the
Boxer

General Appearance—The Boxer is a medium-sized, sturdy dog, of square build, with short back, strong limbs, and short, tight-fitting coat. His musculation, well developed, should be clean, hard and appear smooth (not bulging) under taut skin. His movements should denote energy. The gait is firm yet elastic (springy), the stride free and ground-covering, the carriage proud and noble. Developed to serve the multiple purposes of guard, working and escort-dog, he must combine elegance with substance and ample power, not alone for beauty but to ensure the speed, dexterity and jumping ability essential to arduous hike, riding expedition, police or military duty. Only a body whose individual parts are built to withstand the most strenuous efforts, assembled as a complete and harmonious whole, can respond to these combined demands. Therefore, to be at his highest efficiency he must never be plump or heavy, and, while equipped for great speed, he must never be racy.

The head imparts to the Boxer a unique individual stamp, peculiar to him alone. It must be in perfect proportion to the body, never small in comparison to the over-all picture. The muzzle is his most distinctive feature, and great value is to be placed on its being of correct form and in absolute proper proportion to the skull.

In judging the Boxer, first consideration should be given to general appearance; next, over-all balance, including the desired proportions of the individual parts of the body to each other, as well as the relation of substance to elegance—to which an attractive color or arresting style may contribute. Special attention is to be devoted to the head, after which the dog's individual components are to be examined for their correct construction and function, and efficiency of gait evaluated.

General Faults—Head not typical, plump, bulldoggy appearance, light bone, lack of balance, bad condition, lack of noble bearing.

Head—The beauty of the head depends upon the harmonious proportion of the muzzle to the skull. The muzzle should always appear powerful, never small in its relationship to the skull. The head should be clean, not showing deep wrinkles. Folds will normally appear upon the forehead when the ears are erect, and they are always indicated from the lower edge of the stop running downward on both sides of the muzzle. The dark mask is confined to the muzzle and is in distinct contrast to the color of the head. Any extension of the mask to the skull, other than dark shading around the eyes, creates a somber, undesirable expression. When white replaces any of the black mask, the path of any upward extension should be between the eyes. The muzzle is powerfully developed in length, width and depth. It is not pointed, narrow, short or shallow. Its shape is influenced first through the formation of both jawbones, second through the placement of the teeth, and third through the texture of the lips.

The Boxer is normally undershot. Therefore, the lower jaw protrudes beyond the upper and curves slightly upward. The upper jaw is broad where attached to the skull and maintains this breadth except for a very slight tapering to the front. The incisor teeth of the lower jaw are in a straight line, the canines preferably up front in the same line to give the jaw the greatest possible width. The line of incisors in the upper jaw is slightly convex toward the front. The upper corner incisors should fit snugly back of the lower canine teeth on each side, reflecting the symmetry essential to the creation of a sound, non-slip bite.

The lips, which complete the formation of the muzzle, should meet evenly. The upper lip is thick and padded, filling out the frontal space created by the projection of the lower jaw. It rests on the edge of the lower lip and, laterally, is supported by the fangs (canines) of the lower jaw. Therefore, these fangs must stand far apart, and be of good length so that the front surface of the muzzle is broad and squarish and, when viewed from the side, forms an obtuse angle with the topline of the muzzle. Over-protrusion of the overlip or underlip is undesirable. The chin should be perceptible when viewed from the side as well as from the front without being over-repandous (rising above the bite line) as in the Bulldog. The Boxer must not show teeth or tongue when the mouth is closed. Excessive flews are not desirable.

The top of the skull is slightly arched, not rotund, flat, nor noticeably broad, and the occiput not too pronounced. The forehead forms a distinct stop with the topline of the muzzle, which must not be forced back into the forehead like that of a Bulldog. It should not slant down (down-faced), nor should it be dished, although the tip of the nose should lie somewhat higher than the root of the muzzle. The forehead shows just a slight furrow between the eyes. The cheeks, though covering powerful masseter muscles compatible with the strong set of teeth, should be relatively flat and not bulge, maintaining the clean lines of the skull. They taper into the muzzle in a slight, graceful curve. The ears are set at the highest points of the sides of the skull, cut rather long without too broad a shell, and are carried erect. The dark brown eyes, not too small, protruding or deep-set, are encircled by dark hair, and should impart an alert, intelligent expression. Their mood-mirroring quality combined with the mobile skin furrowing of the forehead gives the Boxer head its unique degree of expressiveness. The nose is broad and black, very slightly turned up; the nostrils broad, with the nasolabial line running between them down through the upper lip, which, however, must not be split.

Faults—Lack of nobility and expression, somber face, unserviceable bite. Pinscher or Bulldog head, sloping topline of muzzle, muzzle too light for skull, too pointed a bite (snipy). Teeth or tongue showing with mouth closed, driveling, split upper lip. Poor ear carriage, light ("Bird of Prey") eyes.

Neck—Round, of ample length, not too short; strong, muscular and clean throughout, without dewlap; distinctly marked nape with an elegant arch running down to the back. *Fault*—Dewlap.

Body—In profile, the build is of square proportions in that a horizontal line from the front of the forechest to the rear projection of the upper thigh should equal a vertical line dropped from the top of the withers to the ground.

Chest and Forequarters—The brisket is deep, reaching down to the elbows; the depth of the body at the lowest point of the brisket equals half the height of the dog at the withers. The ribs, extending far to the rear, are well arched but not barrel-shaped. Chest of fair width and forechest well defined, being easily visible from the side. The loins are short and muscular; the lower stomach line, lightly tucked up, blends into a graceful curve to the rear. The shoulders are long and sloping, close-lying and not excessively covered with muscle. The upper arm is long, closely approaching a right angle to the shoulder blade. The forelegs, viewed from the front, are straight, stand parellel to each other, and have strong, firmly joined bones. The elbows should not press too closely to the chest wall or stand off visibly from it. The forearm is straight, long and firmly muscled. The pastern joint is clearly defined but not distended. The pastern is strong and distinct, slightly slanting, but standing almost perpendicular to the ground. The dewclaws may be removed as a safety precaution. Feet should be compact, turning neither in nor out, with tightly arched toes (cat feet) and tough pads. *Faults*—Chest too broad, too shallow or too deep in front; loose or overmuscled shoulders; chest hanging between shoulders; tied-in or bowed-out elbows; turned feet; hare feet; hollow flanks; hanging stomach.

Back—The withers should be clearly defined as the highest point of the back; the whole back short, straight and muscular with a firm topline. *Faults*—Roach back, sway back, thin lean back, long narrow loins, weak union with croup.

Hindquarters—Strongly muscled with angulation in balance with that of forequarters. The thighs broad and curved, the breech musculature hard and strongly developed. Croup slightly sloped, flat and broad. Tail attachment high rather than low. Tail clipped, carried upward. Pelvis long and, in females especially, broad. Upper and lower thigh long, leg well angulated with a clearly defined, well-let-down hock joint. In standing position, the leg below the hock joint (metatarsus) should be practically perpendicular to the ground, with a slight rearward slope permissible. Viewed from behind, the hind legs should be straight, with the hock joints leaning neither in nor out. The metatarsus should be short, clean and strong, supported by powerful rear pads. The rear toes just a little longer than the front toes, but similar in all other respects. Dewclaws, if any, may be removed. *Faults*—Too rounded, too narrow, or falling off of croup; low-set tail; higher in back than in front; steep, stiff, or too slightly angulated hindquarters; light thighs; bowed or crooked legs; cowhocks; overangulated hock joints (sickle hocks); long metatarsus (high hocks); hare feet; hindquarters too far under or too far behind.

Gait—Viewed from the side, proper front and rear angulation is manifested in a smoothly efficient, level-backed, ground-covering stride with powerful drive emanating from a freely operating rear. Although the front legs do not contribute impelling power, adequate "reach" should be evident to prevent interference, overlap or "side-winding" (crabbing). Viewed from the front, the shoulders should remain trim and the elbows not flare out. The legs are parallel until gaiting narrows the track in proportion to increasing speed, then the legs come in under the body but should never cross. The line from the shoulder down through the leg should remain straight, although not necessarily perpendicular to the ground. Viewed from the rear, a Boxer's breech should not roll. The hind feet should "dig in" and track relatively true with the front. Again, as speed increases, the normally broad rear track will become narrower. *Faults*—Stilted or inefficient gait, pounding, paddling or flailing out of front legs, rolling or waddling gait, tottering hock joints, crossing over or interference—front or rear, lack of smoothness.

Height—Adult males—22¹/₂ to 25 inches; females—21 to 23¹/₂ inches at the withers. Males should not go under the minimum nor females over the maximum.

Coat—Short, shiny, lying smooth and tight to the body.

Color—The colors are fawn and brindle. Fawn in various shades from light tan to dark deer red or mahogany, the deeper colors preferred. The brindle variety should have clearly defined black stripes on fawn background. White markings on fawn or brindle dogs are not to be rejected and are often very attractive, but must be limited to one third of the ground color and are not desirable on the back of the torso proper. On the face, white may replace a part or all of the otherwise essential black mask. However, these white markings should be of such distribution as to enhance and not detract from true Boxer expression.

Character and Temperament—These are of paramount importance in the Boxer. Instinctively a "hearing" guard dog, his bearing is alert, dignified and self-assured, even at rest. In the show ring, his behavior should exhibit constrained animation. With family and friends, his temperament is fundamentally playful, yet patient and stoical with children. Deliberate and wary with strangers, he will exhibit curiosity, but, most importantly, fearless courage and tenacity if threatened. However, he responds promptly to friendly overtures when honestly rendered. His intelligence, loyal affection and tractability to discipline make him a highly desirable companion. *Faults*—Lack of dignity and alertness, shyness, cowardice, treachery and viciousness (belligerency toward other dogs should not be considered viciousness).

DISQUALIFICATIONS

Boxers with white or black ground color, or entirely white or black, or any color other than fawn or brindle. (White markings, when present, must not exceed one third of the ground color.)

Approved December 12, 1967

Briard

(Bree-arrd)

THE BRIARD is a very old breed of French working dog. Depicted in eighth century tapestries and mentioned in records of the twelfth century, the breed is accurately described in the fourteenth and sixteenth centuries. In early times, Briards were used to defend their charges against wolves and poachers, but the dividing up of the land and the increase in population which followed the French Revolution gradually transformed their work into the more peaceful tasks of herding the flocks, keeping the sheep within the unfenced boundaries of the pastures and guarding their masters' property.

In an article written in 1809, these dogs were referred to as the *Chien Berger de Brie* (Shepherd Dog of Brie) and they were entered as such in dog shows in the latter part of the century. Briards do not necessarily originate in the Province of Brie, as the name may imply. Many authorities claim that *Chien de Brie* is a distortion of the name *Chien d'Aubry* from the fourteenth century legend of "Aubry of Montdidier". In that legend, the principal role was played by Aubry's dog, believed to be a Briard.

The first known standard for the Briard was written in 1897 by a club of shepherd dog breeders. Then, in 1909, a French society called *Les*

Amis du Briard was founded. Although this club disbanded during World War I, it was formed again in 1923 and established a more precise standard for the Briard in 1925. This standard, with slight modification, was adopted by the Briard Club of America, founded in 1928. Although a more descriptive version of this standard was approved by the American Kennel Club in 1975, it has remained essentially unchanged.

The history of the Briard in the Americas is not well documented. Some credit the Marquis de Lafayette with the introduction of the breed to this country. However, writings of Thomas Jefferson indicate that he also brought representatives of the breed to this continent about the same time. It was not until 1922 that a litter of Briards was registered with the American Kennel Club. Barbara Danielson of Groton, Massachusetts, bred this litter.

The many remarkable qualities which have helped the Briard to withstand the test of time have been passed down through the centuries. The French shepherd, being a practical and frugal man, kept only the dogs with superior abilities and the Briard breeders of today carefully strive to preserve these highly valued traits. Intelligent, loyal and obedient, even the companion Briard will display the instinct to herd whatever is at hand, often pushing his master with his head to direct him; alerting his people to anything unusual; and enthusiastically carrying out any task he thinks has been delegated to him. The Briard is still not inclined to wander away from his property and he may decide that the young children in the family must also remain within these boundaries. The breed is prized in the United States, as well as in France, by those who use them for herding, although this occupation is now less common on both continents.

Distinctive in appearance, the Briard has eyebrows and beard, which give the typical expression of the breed and the tail has a small hook at the end, called a *crochet*. The correct coat is slightly wavy, of moderate length and the texture is such that mud and dirt do not cling to it. Another distinctive characteristic is that two dewclaws are required on each rear foot, a traditional trait on most French sheepdogs.

Briards learn readily and training should begin at a young age. Trainers familiar with the breed insist that the dog should not have severe punishment, as harsh training methods never accomplish their purpose with a Briard. Instead, consistency, verbal reproof and much praise are all that are needed, for the dog will do his best to please his master if he understands what is expected of him. Briards have an excellent memory and once a lesson (good or bad) is learned, it is never forgotten.

304

Although Briards have been used primarily as guarding and herding dogs, they are unusually versatile. They also have served successfully as tracking and hunting dogs and they have a splendid record as war dogs. In this capacity, they served as sentries at advanced posts, where their acute hearing proved to be invaluable. They accompanied patrols, carried food, supplies and even munitions to the front. Reports from the medical corps tell of the Briard's excellent ability to lead corpsmen to the wounded on the battlefield and it is said that they would pass by those beyond hope. They were also used for pulling carts, but this type of work is not suited to the Briard. Their eagerness to please causes them to overwork to the point of exhaustion and they do not seem to sense any physical limitations. This and other occupations in war service severely reduced their numbers and threatened the breed's existence. Credit must be given to the devoted breeders, who saved the Briard from extinction, carefully preserving the breed's many fine qualities.

Admirable dog that he is, the Briard is not the ideal dog for every home. The remarkable character of the breed can only be developed by a willingness on the part of the owner to devote time and affection to the dog. His coat requires regular grooming or the hair that is shed will cause matting, which is difficult to remove. He is likely to view himself more as a companion than a servant and can be somewhat independent. Those, who desire an instantly obedient dog should not choose a Briard. Most important, the Briard is by nature, reserved with strangers. For this reason, the young Briard puppy must be introduced to varied situations and people, if he is to grow into the calm, self-assured adult he is meant to be. He is a dog that must have the close companionship of man to reach his full potential and he only reaches his full objective in life when he is at the side (or sitting on the feet) of the people he loves.

The Briard has been described as "a heart wrapped in fur", a companion who understands every mood and wish, one who will spend his lifetime trying to please his master. For those who have time and love to give, he is a loyal and unselfish friend, who returns every kindness given to him, many times over.

Official Standard for the
Briard

General Appearance—Vigorous and alert, powerful without coarseness, strong in bone and muscle, exhibiting the strength and agility required of the herding dog. Dogs lacking these qualities, however concealed by the coat, are to be penalized.

Character—A dog of handsome form. He is a dog at heart, with spirit and initiative, wise and fearless with no trace of timidity. Intelligent, easily trained, faithful, gentle and obedient, the Briard possesses an excellent memory and an ardent desire to please his master. He retains a high degree of his ancestral instinct to guard home and master. Although he is reserved with strangers, he is loving and loyal to those he knows. Some will display a certain independence.

Head—The head of a Briard always gives the impression of length, having sufficient width without being cumbersome. The correct length of a good head, measured from the occiput to the tip of the nose, is about forty (40%) per cent of the height of the dog at the withers. There is no objection to a slightly longer head, especially if the animal tends to a longer body line. The width of the head, as measured across the skull, is slightly less than the length of the skull from the occiput to the stop. Viewed from above, from the front or in profile, the fully-coated silhouette gives the impression of two rectangular forms, equal in length but differing in height and width, blending together rather abruptly. The larger rectangle is the skull and the other forms the muzzle. The topline of the muzzle is parallel to the topline of the skull, and the junction of the two forms a well-marked stop, which is midway between the occiput and the tip of the nose, and on a level with the eyes. The muzzle with mustache and beard is somewhat wide and terminates in a right angle. The muzzle must not be narrow or pointed. Although not clearly visible on the fully-coated head, the occiput is prominent and the forehead is very slightly rounded. The head joins the neck in a right angle and is held proudly alert. The head is sculptured in clean lines, without jowls or excess flesh on the sides, or under the eyes or temples. The lips are of medium thickness, firm of line and fitted neatly, without folds or flews at the corners. The lips are black. The head is well covered with hair which lies down, forming a natural part in the center. The eyebrows do not lie flat but, instead, arch up and out in a curve that lightly veils the eyes. The hair is never so abundant that it masks the form of the head or completely covers the eyes.

Nose—Square rather than round, always black with nostrils well opened. *Disqualification*—Any color other than black.

Teeth—Strong, white and adapting perfectly in a scissors bite.

Eyes—Eyes set well apart with the inner corners and outer corners on the same level. Large, well opened and calm, they must never be narrow or slanted. The gaze is frank, questioning and confident. The color must be black or black-brown with very dark pigmentation of the rim of the eyelids, whatever the color of the coat. *Disqualification*—Yellow eyes or spotted eyes.

Ears—The ears should be attached high, have thick leather and be firm at the base. Low-set ears cause the head to appear to be too arched. The length of the natural ear should be equal to or slightly less than one-half the length of the head, always straight and covered with long hair. The natural ear must not lie flat against the head and, when alert, the ears are lifted slightly, giving a square look to the top of the skull. The ears when cropped should be carried upright and parallel, emphasizing the parallel lines of the head; when alert, they should face forward, well open with long hair falling over the opening. The cropped ear should be long, broad at the base, tapering gradually to a rounded tip.

Neck—Strong and well constructed, the neck is in the shape of a truncated cone, clearing the shoulders well. It is strongly muscled and has good length.

BODY:

Chest—The chest is broad and deep with moderately curved ribs, egg-shaped in form, the ribs not too rounded. The breastbone is moderately advanced in front, descending smoothly to the level of the elbows and shaped to give good depth to the chest. The abdomen is moderately drawn up but still presents good volume.

Topline—The Briard is constructed with a very slight incline, downward from the prominent withers to the back which is straight, to the broad loin and the croup which is slightly inclined. The topline is strong, never swayed nor roached.

Proportions—The Briard is not cobby in build. In males the length of the body, measured from the point of the shoulder to the point of the buttock, is equal to or slightly more than his height at the withers. The female may be a little longer.

Tail—Uncut, well feathered, forming a crook at the extremity, carried low and not deviating to the right or to the left. In repose, the bone of the tail descends to the joint of the hock, terminating in the crook, similar in shape to the printed letter "J" when viewed from the dog's right side. In action, the tail is raised in a harmonious curve, never going above the level of the back, except for the terminal crook. *Disqualification*—Tail non-existent or cut.

Legs—The legs are powerfully muscled with strong bone. Viewed from the front or rear, the legs are straight and parallel to the median line of the body, never turned inward or outward. The distance between the front legs is equal to the distance between the rear legs. The construction of the legs is of utmost importance, determining the dog's ability to work and his resistance to fatigue. The hindquarters are powerful, providing flexible, almost tireless movement.

Forequarters—Shoulder blades are long and sloping forming a 45-degree angle with the horizontal, firmly attached by strong muscles and blending smoothly with the withers. The forelegs are vertical when viewed from the side except the pasterns are very slightly inclined.

Hindquarters—The croup is well muscled and slightly sloped to give a well-rounded finish. The pelvis slopes at a 30-degree angle from the horizontal and forms a right angle with the upper leg bone. Viewed from the side, the legs are well angulated with the metatarsus slightly inclined, the hock making an angle of 135 degrees.

Feet—Strong and rounded, being slightly oval in shape. The feet travel straight forward in the line of movement. If the rear toes turn out very slightly when the hocks and metatarsus are parallel, then the position of the feet is correct. The nails are always black and hard. The pads are well developed, compact and elastic, covered with strong tissue. The toes are strong, well arched and compact.

Dewclaws—Two dewclaws are required on each rear leg, placed low on the leg, giving a wide base to the foot. Occasionally the nail may break off completely. The dog shall not be penalized for the missing nail so long as the digit itself is present. Ideally the dewclaws form additional functioning toes. Dewclaws on the forelegs may or may not be removed. *Disqualification*— Anything less than two dewclaws on each rear leg.

Coat—The outer coat is coarse, hard and dry (making a dry rasping sound between the fingers). It lies down flat, falling naturally in long, slightly waving locks, having the sheen of good health. On the shoulders the length of hair is generally six inches or more. The undercoat is fine and tight on all the body.

Color—All uniform colors are permitted except white. The colors are black, various shades of gray and various shades of tawny. The deeper shades of each color are preferred. Combinations of two of these colors are permitted, provided there are no marked spots and the transition from one color to another takes place gradually and symmetrically. The only permissible white: white hairs scattered throughout the coat and/or a white spot on the chest not to exceed one inch in diameter at the root of the hair. *Disqualification*—White coat. Spotted coat. White spot on chest exceeding one inch in diameter.

Gait—The well-constructed Briard is a marvel of supple power. His movement has been described as "quicksilver," permitting him to make abrupt turns, springing starts and sudden stops required of the sheepherding dog. His gait is supple and light, almost like that of a large feline. The gait gives the impression that the dog glides along without touching the ground. Strong, flexible movement is essential to the sheep dog. He is above all a trotter, single-tracking, occasionally galloping and he frequently needs to change his speed to accomplish his work. His conformation is harmoniously balanced and strong to sustain him in the long day's work. Dogs with clumsy or inelegant gait must be penalized.

Size—Males 23 to 27 inches at the withers; bitches 22 to 25½ inches at the withers. *Disqualification*—All dogs and bitches under the minimum.

DISQUALIFICATIONS

Nose any color other than black.
Yellow eyes or spotted eyes.
Tail non-existent or cut.
Less than two dewclaws on each rear leg.
White coat.
Spotted coat.
White spot on chest exceeding one inch in diameter.
All dogs or bitches under the minimum size limits.

Approved February 8, 1975

Bullmastiff

THE KNOWN history of the Bullmastiff begins about the year 1860 in England. It is probable that the story of the breed is really centuries old, but proof is difficult.

In the latter part of the nineteenth century in England, the problem of keeping large estates and game preserves free from the depredations of poachers was an acute one. Penalties were severe, yet poaching seemed impossible to eradicate by mere laws. Accordingly, the game-keeper's life was anything but safe. Poachers would often prefer to shoot it out with the keeper on the chance of escape rather than accept the penalties which they would incur upon apprehension.

It is not surprising, therefore, that the gamekeepers decided to enlist the aid of the greatest protector nature has given to man—the dog. These men cared nothing for the looks of a dog as long as he served them well. Numerous breeds were therefore tried. The Mastiff, while courageous and powerful, was not fast enough and not sufficiently aggressive. The Bulldog, big, strong and active in those days, was a trifle too ferocious and not large enough for their needs. These men wanted dogs that would remain silent at the approach of poachers. They needed fearless dogs that would attack on command. They wanted the poachers thrown and held, but not mauled. For these needs, they crossed Mastiff and Bulldog, and the dog they wanted was produced.

From this utilitarian birth, the breed was founded. Inevitably, came the rivalry between keepers as to the quality of their dogs. Inevitably, also, came the breeding to and from outstanding performers of their time—a true survival of the fittest. For many years, then, after the birth of the breed, its history was wholly a utilitarian one. The only contests in which Bullmastiffs engaged were against man, either on the moor or in demonstrations, when they were muzzled and the man was allowed a club, restricted in size to certain weights and measurements. In these contests no man was ever able to hold his feet against a dog of proven worth. In those days the Bullmastiff was known sometimes by his present name, but more usually as the "Gamekeeper's Night-Dog."

During the breed's early years, we find interesting references by contemporary writers. One appears in General William Hutchinson's book *Dog Breaking,* published in London in 1885:

> Bulldogs have good noses. I have known of the cross between them and the Mastiff being taught to follow the scent of a man almost as truly as a Bloodhound.

In 1900, the Westminster *Gazette* reports that Major Crowe of the War Office visited an exhibition of these dogs with a view to reporting on their possible usefulness as an aid to sentries. In *The Field,* August 20, 1901, we find the following:

> Mr. Burton of Thorneywood Kennels brought to the show one Night-Dog (not for competition) and offered any person one pound who could escape from it while securely muzzled. One of the spectators who had had experience with dogs volunteered and amused a large assembly of sportsmen and keepers who had gathered there. The man was given a long start and the muzzled dog slipped after him. The animal caught him immediately and knocked down his man the first spring. The latter bravely tried to hold his own, but was floored every time he got on his feet, ultimately being kept to the ground until the owner of the dog released him. The man had three rounds with the powerful canine, but was beaten each time and was unable to escape.

For this type of work, dogs of a dark brindle color were preferred owing to their lack of visibility. It was inevitable, however, that as the breed gained in popularity and true Mastiff blood was used, a large number of light fawns should appear. With the gradual disappearance of poaching and the continued demand for Bullmastiffs as guards and watchdogs, this color became popular. The black mask and densely colored ears were often inherited from the Mastiff.

Finally, owing to the increasing popularity of the breed, a number of pioneers started, on a scientific basis, to breed to type in an effort to set a goal which pure-bred dog breeders might seek. This type finally became sufficiently distinct for the English Kennel Club to grant recognition of the Bullmastiff as a pure-bred dog in 1924. At this time the Kennel Club differentiated between the Bullmastiff, crossbred, and the Bullmastiff, pure-bred, the latter being, of necessity, the descendant of three generations of dogs which were neither pure Mastiff nor pure Bulldog. Classes were then provided at a few shows and the dogs were finally awarded Challenge Certificates in 1928. In time the breed became known in many countries, having been exported from England to Siam, India, the Federated Malay States, Africa, and America. The short coat has proved convenient in warm climates, and yet the dog can live in the open in inclement weather.

In October, 1933, The American Kennel Club granted recognition to the Bullmastiff, and since that time the breed has made numerous friends in this country.

Official Standard for the
Bullmastiff

General Appearance—That of a symmetrical animal, showing great strength; powerfully built but active. The dog is fearless yet docile, has endurance and alertness. The foundation breeding was 60% Mastiff and 40% Bulldog.

Head—Skull large, with a fair amount of wrinkle when alert; broad, with cheeks well developed. Forehead flat. Muzzle broad and deep; its length, in comparison with that of the entire head, approximately as 1 is to 3. Lack of foreface with nostrils set on top of muzzle is a reversion to the Bulldog and is very undesirable. Nose black with nostrils large and broad. Flews not too pendulous, stop moderate, and the mouth (bite) preferably level or slightly undershot. Canine teeth large and set wide apart. A dark muzzle is preferable.

Eyes—Dark and of medium size.

Ears—V-shaped and carried close to the cheeks, set on wide and high, level with occiput and cheeks, giving a square appearance to the skull; darker in color than the body and medium in size.

Neck—Slightly arched, of moderate length, very muscular, and almost equal in circumference to the skull.

Body—Compact. Chest wide and deep, with ribs well sprung and well set down between the forelegs. *Forequarters*—Shoulders muscular but not loaded, and slightly sloping. Forelegs straight, well boned and set well apart; elbows square. Pasterns straight, feet of medium size, with round toes well arched. Pads thick and tough, nails black. *Back*—Short, giving the impression of a well balanced dog. *Loins*—Wide, muscular and slightly arched, with fair depth of flank. *Hindquarters*—Broad and muscular with well developed second thigh denoting power, but not cumbersome. Moderate angulation at hocks. Cowhocks and splay feet are bad faults. *Tail*—Set on high, strong at the root and tapering to the hocks. It may be straight or curved, but never carried hound fashion.

Coat—Short and dense, giving good weather protection.

Color—Red, fawn or brindle. Except for a very small white spot on the chest, white marking is considered a fault.

Size—Dogs, 25 to 27 inches at the shoulder, and 110 to 130 pounds weight. Bitches, 24 to 26 inches at the shoulder, and 100 to 120 pounds weight. Other things being equal, the heavier dog is favored.

Approved February 6, 1960

Collie

THERE ARE two varieties of Collie, the rough-coated being by far the more familiar. During the 1960s and '70s, however, many fanciers have increased their breeding of the smooth-coated variety and many smooths of excellent type are now being exhibited.

Although the exact origin of the Collie remains an enigma, both varieties existed long ago in the unwritten history of the herding dogs of Scotland and northern England.

Since sheepherding is one of the world's oldest occupations, the Collie's ancestors date far back in the history of dogs. The smooth Collie, which for as long as there have been written standards for the breed has been bred to the same standard except for coat, was considered principally as a drover's dog used for guiding cows and sheep to market, not for standing over and guarding them at pasture. Until the last two centuries, both varieties were strictly working dogs without written pedigrees. Their untutored masters saw no need for pedigrees, if indeed they were capable of keeping stud books.

The earliest illustrations known to bear a resemblance to both varieties are found as woodcuts in *The History of Quadrupeds* by Thomas Bewick, antedating 1800. The rough dog was described as a "Shepherd's Dog" and the smooth as a "ban dog". The rough was described as being only 14 inches at the shoulder and the smooth was said to be much larger and descended from the Mastiff. (Mastiff in this sense does not refer to the breed we know today by that name but was something of a generic term used basically to describe a common type dog.) It is well established that the roughs at that time were not only much smaller but had shorter, broader heads and were usually black or black and white in color.

From early in the 19th century, when some dog fanciers began to take interest in these dogs, and the keeping of written pedigrees began, the breed progressed rapidly, becoming not only larger in stature but also more refined. The dog "Old Cockie" was born in 1867 and he is credited with not only stamping characteristic type on the rough Collie but he is believed by usually reliable authorities to be responsible for introducing to the breed the factors which led to the development of the sable coat color in the Collie. A short time later Collies were seen of almost every imaginable color, including red, buff, mottle of various shades and a few sables. At that time the most frequently seen colors were black, tan and white, black and white (without tan) and what are

313

Collie (Rough)

Collie (Smooth)

now called blue merles, but which were known then as "tortoise shell".

The early pedigrees were very much abbreviated, as compared with our present breed records. In fact, the first volume of the English stud book showed 78 "sheep dogs and Scotch Collies" registered up to 1874. Fifteen of them had written pedigrees but only three extended beyond sire and dam. Proof that pride of ownership was given priority over written records is found in the fact that it was in 1860 that the first classes for "Scotch Sheep Dogs" were offered at the second dog show ever held in England, that of the Birmingham Dog Society. Both varieties competed in the same classes.

Shortly thereafter, Queen Victoria visited Balmoral and saw her first Collies. As Collies have been doing ever since, they captivated her heart and she enthusiastically began to sponsor them. There was a marked surge in the popularity of the breed which found itself not only the indispensable helpmate of the humble shepherd but the treasure and the playmate of the royal and the rich.

Collie type was well enough "fixed" by 1886 so that the English breeders have never seen fit to change the height and weight established in their standard at that time. Numerous clarifying changes have taken place in the United States standard over the ensuing years but except for recognizing that the Collie has become slightly larger and heavier on this side of the Atlantic there is no fundamental difference, even today, from that 1886 description of the ideal Collie.

Many of the early settlers in the new world brought dogs with them to herd their sheep and cattle in the Colonies but it was not until May of 1877, 17 years after their show ring debut in England, that they were shown here, at the second show of the Westminster Kennel Club in New York. Classes were offered for "Shepherd Dogs, or Collie Dogs" and a few were entered. The next year, however, was to see great interest and excitement. Two Collies imported from Queen Victoria's Royal Balmoral Kennel had been entered! Soon Collies were to be found as prized possessions of the wealthy and socially elite. Kennels were established by the well-known fancier J. P. Morgan and his financial contemporaries, and many fashionable estates up the Hudson River and on Long Island had Collie kennels. English dogs were imported for what were then considered to be exorbitant prices. It is interesting to note that about a half century later almost the reverse situation was occurring. The Collie became a highly desired breed in Japan and there was great persuasion to convince some of the American breeders to export some of their top dogs. By this time, the importation of Collies from England had become exceedingly rare.

Being no longer in great demand as a herder, today's Collie has transferred these abilities to serving as a devoted family dog where he shows a particular affinity for small children. For many years his general popularity has placed him among the top dozen of the favorite dogs registered by the American Kennel Club. Elegant and beautiful in appearance, loyal and affectionate in all his actions, self-appointed guardian of everything he can see or hear, the Collie represents, to his many admirers, the ideal family companion.

The Collie has been the beneficiary of a "good press". Its parent Club, The Collie Club of America, Inc. was organized in 1886, two years after the establishment of the American Kennel Club and was the second parent club to join the AKC. Very active in promoting the interest of the breed, the parent Club now has a membership numbering well over 3500 and its annual specialty show attracts over 400 Collies from all over the United States. Great impetus to the breed's popularity was provided by the famous Collie stories of Albert Payson Terhune. His "Lad: A Dog" was followed by many more volumes that have been eagerly read by several generations of Americans. More recently the television exploits of "Lassie" have brought to children and their parents a strong desire to have, for their very own "a lovely dog like that."

Official Standard for the Collie

ROUGH

General Character—The Collie is a lithe, strong, responsive, active dog, carrying no useless timber, standing naturally straight and firm. The deep, moderately wide chest shows strength, the sloping shoulders and well-bent hocks indicate speed and grace, and the face shows high intelligence. The Collie presents an impressive, proud picture of true balance, each part being in harmonious proportion to every other part and to the whole. Except for the technical description that is essential to this Standard and without which no Standard for the guidance of breeders and judges is adequate, it could be stated simply that no part of the Collie ever seems to be out of proportion to any other part. Timidity, frailness, sullenness, viciousness, lack of animation, cumbersome appearance and lack of over-all balance impair the general character.

Head—The head properties are of great importance. When considered in proportion to the size of the dog the head is inclined to lightness and never appears massive. A heavy-headed dog lacks the necessary bright, alert, full-of-sense look that contributes so greatly to expression. Both in front and profile view the head bears a general resemblance to a well-blunted lean wedge, being smooth and clean in outline and nicely balanced in proportion. On the sides it tapers gradually and smoothly from the ears to the end of the black nose, without being flared out in backskull ("cheeky") or pinched in muzzle ("snipy"). In profile view the top of the backskull and the top of the muzzle lie in two approximately parallel, straight planes of equal length, divided by a very slight but perceptible stop or break. A mid-point between the inside corners of the eyes (which is the center of a correctly placed stop) is the center of balance in length of head.

The end of the smooth, well-rounded muzzle is blunt but not square. The underjaw is strong, clean-cut and the depth of skull from the brow to the under part of the jaw is not excessive. The teeth are of good size, meeting in a scissors bite. *Overshot or undershot jaws are undesirable, the latter being more severely penalized.* There is a very slight prominence of the eyebrows. The backskull is flat, without receding either laterally or backward and the occipital bone is not highly peaked. The proper width of backskull necessarily depends upon the combined length of skull and muzzle and the width of the backskull is less than its length. Thus the correct width varies with the individual and is dependent upon the extent to which it is supported by length of muzzle. Because of the importance of the head characteristics, *prominent head faults are very severely penalized.*

Eyes—Because of the combination of the flat skull, the arched eyebrows, the slight stop and the rounded muzzle, the foreface must be chiseled to form a receptacle for the eyes and they are necessarily placed obliquely to give them the required forward outlook. Except for the blue merles, they are required to be matched in color. They are almond-shaped, of medium size and never properly appear to be large or prominent. The color is dark and the eye does not show a yellow ring or a sufficiently prominent haw to affect the dog's expression. The eyes have a clear, bright appearance, expressing intelligent inquisitiveness, particularly when the ears are drawn up and the dog is on the alert. In blue merles, dark brown eyes are preferable, but either or both eyes may be merle or china in color without specific penalty. A large, round, full eye seriously detracts from the desired "sweet" expression. *Eye faults are heavily penalized.*

Ears—The ears are in proportion to the size of the head and, if they are carried properly and unquestionably "break" naturally, are seldom too small. Large ears usually cannot be lifted correctly off the head, and even if lifted, they will be out of proportion to the size of the head. When in repose the ears are folded lengthwise and thrown back into the frill. On the alert they are drawn well up on the backskull and are carried about three-quarters erect, with about one-fourth of the ear tipping or "breaking" forward. *A dog with prick ears or low ears cannot show true expression and is penalized accordingly.*

Neck—The neck is firm, clean, muscular, sinewy and heavily frilled. It is fairly long, carried upright with a slight arch at the nape and imparts a proud, upstanding appearance showing off the frill.

Body—The body is firm, hard and muscular, a trifle long in proportion to the height. The ribs are well-rounded behind the well-sloped shoulders and the chest is deep, extending to the elbows. The back is strong and level, supported by powerful hips and thighs and the croup is sloped to give a well-rounded finish. The loin is powerful and slightly arched. *Noticeably fat dogs, or dogs in poor flesh, or with skin disease, or with no undercoat are out of condition and are moderately penalized accordingly.*

Legs—The forelegs are straight and muscular, with a fair amount of bone considering the size of the dog. A cumbersome appearance is undesirable. *Both narrow and wide placement are penalized.* The forearm is moderately fleshy and the pasterns are flexible but without weakness. The hind legs are less fleshy, muscular at the thighs, very sinewy and the hocks and stifles are well bent. *A cowhocked dog or a dog with straight stifles is penalized.* The comparatively small feet are approximately oval in shape. The soles are well padded and tough, and the toes are well arched and close together. When the Collie is not in motion the legs and feet are judged by allowing the dog to come to a natural stop in a standing position so that both the forelegs and the hind legs are placed well apart, with the feet extending straight forward. Excessive "posing" is undesirable.

Gait—Gait is sound. When the dog is moved at a slow trot toward an observer its straight front legs track comparatively close together at the ground. The front legs are not out at the elbows, do not "cross over", nor does the dog move with a choppy, pacing or rolling gait. When viewed from the rear the hind legs are straight, tracking comparatively close together at the ground. At a moderate trot the hind legs are powerful and propelling. Viewed from the side the reasonably long, "reaching" stride is smooth and even, keeping the back line firm and level.

As the speed of the gait is increased the Collie single tracks, bringing the front legs inward in a straight line from the shoulder toward the center line of the body and the hind legs inward in a straight line from the hip toward the center line of the body. The gait suggests effortless speed combined with the dog's herding heritage, requiring it to be capable of changing its direction of travel almost instantaneously.

Tail—The tail is moderately long, the bone reaching to the hock joint or below. It is carried low when the dog is quiet, the end having an upward twist or "swirl." When gaited or when the dog is excited it is carried gaily but not over the back.

Coat—The well-fitting, proper-textured coat is the crowning glory of the rough variety of Collie. It is abundant except on the head and legs. The outer coat is straight and harsh to the touch. *A soft, open outer coat or a curly outer coat, regardless of quantity is penalized.* The undercoat, however, is soft, furry and so close together that it is difficult to see the skin when the hair is parted. The coat is very abundant on the mane and frill. The face or mask is smooth. The forelegs are smooth and well feathered to the back of the pasterns. The hind legs are smooth below the hock joints. Any feathering below the hocks is removed for the show ring. The hair on the tail is very profuse and on the hips it is long and bushy. The texture, quantity and the extent to which the coat "fits the dog" are important points.

Color—The four recognized colors are "Sable and White," "Tri-color," "Blue Merle" and "White." There is no preference among them. The "Sable and White" is predominantly sable (a fawn sable color of varying shades from light gold to dark mahogany) with white markings usually on the chest, neck, legs, feet and the tip of the tail. A blaze may appear on the foreface or backskull or both. The "Tri-color" is predominantly black, carrying white markings as in a "Sable and White" and has tan shadings on and about the head and legs. The "Blue Merle" is a mottled or "marbled" color predominantly blue-gray and black with white markings as in the "Sable and White" and usually has tan shadings as in the "Tri-color." The "White" is predominantly white, preferably with sable, tri-color or blue-merle markings.

Size—Dogs are from 24 to 26 inches at the shoulder and weigh from 60 to 75 pounds. Bitches are from 22 to 24 inches at the shoulder, weighing from 50 to 65 pounds. *An undersize or an oversize Collie is penalized according to the extent to which the dog appears to be undersize or oversize.*

Expression—Expression is one of the most important points in considering the relative value of Collies. *Expression,* like the term "character" is difficult to define in words. It is not a fixed point as in color, weight or height and it is something the uninitiated can properly understand only by optical illustration. In general, however, it may be said to be the combined product of the shape and balance of the skull and muzzle, the placement, size, shape and color of the eye and the position, size and carriage of the ears. An expression that shows sullenness or which is suggestive of any other breed is entirely foreign. The Collie cannot be judged properly until its expression has been carefully evaluated.

SMOOTH

The Smooth Variety of Collie is judged by the same Standard as the Rough Variety, except that the references to the quantity and the distribution of the coat are not applicable to the Smooth Variety, which has a short, hard, dense, flat coat of good texture, with an abundance of undercoat.

Approved May 10, 1977

Doberman Pinscher

WITH ITS racial roots somewhat obscure, the Doberman Pinscher became within a comparatively short time a dog of fixed type, whose characteristics of both body and spirit have extended its popularity in many lands. Originating in Apolda, in Thueringen, Germany, around 1890, the breed was officially recognized in 1900. Since that date the Doberman Pinscher has made fast friends in Europe, in the Orient, and the Americas. It takes its name from Louis Dobermann of Apolda.

Of medium size and clean-cut appearance, the dog at first glance does not give evidence of its great muscular power. So compact is its structure, so dense the laying on of muscle under the short coat, and so elegant and well chiseled the outline, that the novice would probably underestimate the weight by fifteen to twenty pounds. Weight is the only particular, however, in which the Doberman is deceptive. Its qualities of alertness, agility, muscular and temperamental fire stand patent for any eye to see. It is an honest dog, uncamouflaged by superfluous coat or the wiles of the artful conditioner. One gains at once the impression of sinewy nimbleness, of the quick co-ordination of the well-trained athlete.

There is also an air of nobility about the Doberman Pinscher which is part of its birthright. More than most other breeds, it gives the impression of a blue-blooded animal, or aristocrat. From the strong muzzle and wedge-shaped head to the clearly defined stifle, the outline is definite and sharply etched. The fearless and inquisitive expression of the dark eye is in harmony with the bodily characteristics. The Doberman looks upon the stranger boldly and judges him with unerring instinct. He is ready, if need be, to give prompt alarm and to back his warning with defense of his master and his master's goods. Yet, he is affectionate, obedient, and loyal.

Traditionally compounded of the old shorthaired shepherd-dog stock, with admixtures of Rottweiler, Black and Tan Terrier, and smooth-haired German Pinscher, the Doberman has been fortunate, with the aid of selective breeding, to have absorbed the good qualities of the races which have contributed to its heritage. It has been from the beginning a working dog devoted to the service of mankind.

At first, the Doberman was used almost exclusively as a guard and home watchdog. As it developed, its qualities of intelligence and ability to absorb and retain training brought it into demand as police and war dog. In this service its agility and courage made it highly prized. An excellent nose adapted the dog to criminal trailing; it has also led to its use as a hunting dog.

Among the endearing qualities of the Doberman has come to be its devotion to hearth and home, and its discriminating service as friend and guardian of the whole family. The properly bred and trained specimen has a sane mind and a sound body; the heart and spirit of a gentleman.

In the United States the breed has been fostered, and its popularity has reached out into every state through The Doberman Pinscher Club of America, which was founded in February, 1921. Through the efforts of this organization, keen interest has been maintained in the breed, further evidenced by the increasing number of breeders and exhibitors.

Official Standard for the
Doberman Pinscher

General Conformation and Appearance—The appearance is that of a dog of medium size, with a body that is square; the height, measured vertically from the ground to the highest point of the withers, equalling the length measured horizontally from the forechest to the rear projection of the upper thigh.

Height—at the withers—**Dogs**—26 to 28 inches, ideal about 27$\frac{1}{2}$ inches; **Bitches**—24 to 26 inches, ideal about 25$\frac{1}{2}$ inches. Length of head, neck and legs in proportion to length and depth of body. Compactly built, muscular and powerful, for great endurance and speed. Elegant in appearance, of proud carriage, reflecting great nobility and temperament. Energetic, watchful, determined, alert, fearless, loyal and obedient.

The judge shall dismiss from the ring any shy or vicious Doberman.

Shyness—A dog shall be judged fundamentally shy if, refusing to stand for examination, it shrinks away from the judge; if it fears an approach from the rear; if it shies at sudden and unusual noises to a marked degree.

Viciousness—A dog that attacks or attempts to attack either the judge or its handler, is definitely vicious. An aggressive or belligerent attitude towards other dogs shall not be deemed viciousness.

Head—Long and dry, resembling a blunt wedge in both frontal and profile views. When seen from the front, the head widens gradually toward the base of the ears in a practically unbroken line. Top of skull flat, turning with slight stop to bridge of muzzle, with muzzle line extending parallel to top line of skull. Cheeks flat and muscular. Lips lying close to jaws. Jaws full and powerful, well filled under the eyes.

Eyes—Almond shaped, moderately deep set, with vigorous, energetic expression. Iris, of uniform color, ranging from medium to darkest brown in black dogs; in reds, blues, and fawns the color of the iris blends with that of the markings, the darkest shade being preferable in every case.

Teeth—Strongly developed and white. Lower incisors upright and touching inside of upper incisors—a true scissors bite. *42 correctly placed teeth*, 22 in the lower, 20 in the upper jaw. Distemper teeth shall not be penalized. ***Disqualifying Faults***—Overshot more than $3/16$ of an inch. Undershot more than $1/8$ of an inch. Four or more missing teeth.

Ears—Normally cropped and carried erect. The upper attachment of the ear, when held erect, is on a level with the top of the skull.

Neck—Proudly carried, well muscled and dry. Well arched, with nape of neck widening gradually toward body. Length of neck proportioned to body and head.

Body—Back short, firm, of sufficient width, and muscular at the loins, extending in a straight line from withers to the *slightly* rounded croup. ***Withers*** —pronounced and forming the highest point of the body. ***Brisket***—reaching deep to the elbow. ***Chest***—broad with forechest well defined. ***Ribs***—well sprung from the spine, but flattened in lower end to permit elbow clearance. ***Belly***— well tucked up, extending in a curved line from the brisket. ***Loins***—wide and muscled. ***Hips***—broad and in proportion to body, breadth of hips being approximately equal to breadth of body at rib cage and shoulders.

Tail—Docked at approximately second joint, appears to be a continuation of the spine, and is carried only slightly above the horizontal when the dog is alert.

Forequarters—*Shoulder Blade*—sloping forward and downward at a 45-degree angle to the ground meets the upper arm at an angle of 90 degrees. Length of shoulder blade and upper arm are equal. Height from elbow to withers approximately equals height from ground to elbow. ***Legs***—seen from front and side, perfectly straight and parallel to each other from elbow to pastern;

muscled and sinewy, with heavy bone. In normal pose and when gaiting, the elbows lie close to the brisket. *Pasterns*—firm and almost perpendicular to the ground. *Feet*—well arched, compact, and catlike, turning neither in nor out. Dewclaws may be removed.

Hindquarters—The angulation of the hindquarters balances that of the forequarters. *Hip Bone*—falls away from spinal column at an angle of about 30 degrees, producing a slightly rounded, well-filled-out croup. *Upper Shanks*—at right angles to the hip bones, are long, wide, and well muscled on both sides of thigh, with clearly defined stifles. Upper and lower shanks are of equal length. While the dog is at rest, hock to heel is perpendicular to the ground. Viewed from the rear, the legs are straight, parallel to each other, and wide enough apart to fit in with a properly built body. *Cat Feet*—as on front legs, turning neither in nor out. Dewclaws, if any, are generally removed.

Gait—Free, balanced, and vigorous, with good reach in the forequarters and good driving power in the hindquarters. When trotting, there is strong rear-action drive. Each rear leg moves in line with the foreleg on the same side. Rear and front legs are thrown neither in nor out. Back remains strong and firm. When moving at a fast trot, a properly built dog will single-track.

Coat, Color, Markings—*Coat,* smooth-haired, short, hard, thick and close lying. Invisible gray undercoat on neck permissible. *Allowed Colors*—Black, red, blue, and fawn (Isabella). *Markings*—Rust, sharply defined, appearing above each eye and on muzzle, throat and forechest, on all legs and feet, and below tail. *Nose*—Solid black on black dogs, dark brown on red ones, dark gray on blue ones, dark tan on fawns. White patch on chest, not exceeding $1/2$ square inch, permissible.

FAULTS

The foregoing description is that of the ideal Doberman Pinscher. Any deviation from the above described dog must be penalized to the extent of the deviation.

DISQUALIFICATIONS

Overshot more than $3/16$ of an inch; undershot more than $1/8$ of an inch. Four or more missing teeth.

Approved October 14, 1969

German Shepherd Dog

DERIVED FROM the old breeds of herding and farm dogs, and associated for centuries with man as servant and companion, the German Shepherd Dog has been subject to intensive development. Sponsored by the *Verein für Deutsche Schäferhunde,* the parent club of the breed, founded in 1899 in Germany, the cult of the Shepherd spread rapidly from about 1914 onward in many parts of the world. Interest in the breed has been fostered by specialty clubs in many lands as it has been in the United States by the German Shepherd Dog Club of America.

First, last and all the time a working dog, the German Shepherd Dog has been developed both temperamentally and structurally through selective breeding, through judging which, on the whole, has been of a constructive character, and through specialized training.

Considering first the more important side of the dog—its character— the Shepherd is distinguished for loyalty, courage, and the ability to assimilate and retain training for a number of special services. He should be of equable disposition, poised, unexcitable, and with well-controlled nerves. For his typical work as a herding sheep dog, he must not be gun-shy and must have courage to protect his flock from attacks, either animal or human. For his work as a police dog, a development which followed upon a natural aptitude for training, he must have this courage also, but, in addition, must be able to make use of the excellent nose which he usually possesses. In his work as a leader of the blind, the Shepherd must and does exhibit a high order of intelligence and discrimination involving the qualities of observation, patience, faithful watchfulness, and even, to a certain degree, the exercise of judgment.

These qualities, which have endeared the German Shepherd Dog to a wide public in practically every country of the globe, are those of the companion, protector, and friend. The German Shepherd is not a pugnacious brawler, but a bold and punishing fighter if need be. In his relation to man he does not give affection lightly; he has plenty of dignity and some suspicion of strangers, but his friendship, once given, is given for life.

On the physical side, the German Shepherd Dog has been developed to a point of almost ideal fitness for the work he is called upon to do. He is a dog of middle size with enough weight to be effective as herder or patrolman, but not enough to be cumbersome or unwieldy.

By careful selective breeding, the naturally easy trot of the German Shepherd Dog has been brought to a high pitch of nearly effortless motion. Essentially a trotting animal, his structure has been modified so as to increase the power, elasticity and length of his gait. Other things being equal, the best-moving Shepherd is the one which covers the maximum amount of ground with the minimum expenditure of energy. So well co-ordinated and harmonious is this gait when properly exemplified that the dog seems to glide forward without visible effort, suspended, one might almost think, from the firm beam of his back.

The impression of the dog as a whole is one of ruggedness combined with nobility, of power combined with agility. There should be a sense of balance, forequarter and hindquarter compensating each other in their development. The outline should be smooth and flowing, and the top line of the dog, from the ear to the tip of the full tail, a single sweeping succession of unbroken curves. The German Shepherd Dog is a natural dog, unchanged for any whim of the show ring.

Official Standard for the
German Shepherd Dog

General Appearance—The first impression of a good German Shepherd Dog is that of a strong, agile, well-muscled animal, alert and full of life. It is well balanced, with harmonious development of the forequarter and hindquarter. The dog is longer than tall, deep-bodied, and presents an outline of smooth curves rather than angles. It looks substantial and not spindly, giving the impression, both at rest and in motion, of muscular fitness and nimbleness without any look of clumsiness or soft living. The ideal dog is stamped with a look of quality and nobility—difficult to define, but unmistakable when present. Secondary sex characteristics are strongly marked, and every animal gives a definite impression of masculinity or femininity, according to its sex.

Character—The breed has a distinct personality marked by direct and fearless, but not hostile, expression, self-confidence and a certain aloofness that does not lend itself to immediate and indiscriminate friendships. The dog must be approachable, quietly standing its ground and showing confidence and willingness to meet overtures without itself making them. It is poised, but when the occasion demands, eager and alert; both fit and willing to serve in its capacity as companion, watchdog, blind leader, herding dog, or guardian, whichever the circumstances may demand. The dog must not be timid, shrinking behind its master or handler; it should not be nervous, looking about or upward with anxious expression or showing nervous reactions, such as tucking of tail, to strange sounds or sights. Lack of confidence under any surroundings is not typical of good character. Any of the above deficiencies in character which indicate shyness must be penalized as very serious faults and any dog exhibiting pronounced indications of these must be excused from the ring. It must be possible for the judge to observe the teeth and to determine that both testicles are descended. Any dog that attempts to bite the judge must be disqualified. The ideal dog is a working animal with an incorruptible character combined with body and gait suitable for the arduous work that constitutes its primary purpose.

Head—The head is noble, cleanly chiseled, strong without coarseness, but above all not fine, and in proportion to the body. The head of the male is distinctly masculine, and that of the bitch distinctly feminine. The muzzle is long and strong with the lips firmly fitted, and its topline is parallel to the topline of the skull. Seen from the front, the forehead is only moderately arched, and the skull slopes into the long, wedge-shaped muzzle without abrupt stop. Jaws are strongly developed. *Ears*—Ears are moderately pointed, in proportion to the skull, open toward the front, and carried erect when at attention, the ideal carriage being one in which the center lines of the ears, viewed from the front, are parallel to each other and perpendicular to the ground. A dog with cropped or hanging ears must be disqualified. *Eyes*—Of medium size, almond shaped, set a little obliquely and not protruding. The color is as dark as possible. The expression keen, intelligent and composed. *Teeth*—42 in number—20 upper and 22 lower—are strongly developed and meet in a scissors bite in which part of the inner surface of the upper incisors meet and engage part of the outer surface of the lower incisors. An overshot jaw or a level bite is undesirable. An undershot jaw is a disqualifying fault. Complete dentition is to be preferred. Any missing teeth other than first premolars is a serious fault.

Neck—The neck is strong and muscular, clean-cut and relatively long, proportionate in size to the head and without loose folds of skin. When the dog is at attention or excited, the head is raised and the neck carried high; otherwise typical carriage of the head is forward rather than up and but little higher than the top of the shoulders, particularly in motion.

Forequarters—The shoulder blades are long and obliquely angled, laid on flat and not placed forward. The upper arm joins the shoulder blade at about a right angle. Both the upper arm and the shoulder blade are well muscled. The forelegs, viewed from all sides, are straight and the bone oval rather than round. The pasterns are strong and springy and angulated at approximately a 25-degree angle from the vertical.

Feet—The feet are short, compact, with toes well arched, pads thick and firm, nails short and dark. The dewclaws, if any, should be removed from the hind legs. Dewclaws on the forelegs may be removed, but are normally left on.

Proportion—The German Shepherd Dog is longer than tall, with the most desirable proportion as 10 to 8½. The desired height for males at the top of the highest point of the shoulder blade is 24 to 26 inches; and for bitches, 22 to 24 inches. The length is measured from the point of the prosternum or breastbone to the rear edge of the pelvis, the ischial tuberosity.

Body—The whole structure of the body gives an impression of depth and solidity without bulkiness. *Chest*—Commencing at the prosternum, it is well filled and carried well down between the legs. It is deep and capacious, never shallow, with ample room for lungs and heart, carried well forward, with the prosternum showing ahead of the shoulder in profile. *Ribs*—Well sprung and long, neither barrel-shaped nor too flat, and carried down to a sternum which reaches to the elbows. Correct ribbing allows the elbows to move back freely when the dog is at a trot. Too round causes interference and throws the elbows out; too flat or short causes pinched elbows. Ribbing is carried well back so that the loin is relatively short. *Abdomen*—Firmly held and not paunchy. The bottom line is only moderately tucked up in the loin.

Topline—*Withers*—The withers are higher than and sloping into the level back. *Back*—The back is straight, very strongly developed without sag or roach, and relatively short. The desirable long proportion is not derived from a long back, but from over-all length with relation to height, which is achieved by length of forequarter and length of withers and hindquarter, viewed from the side. *Loin*—Viewed from the top, broad and strong. Undue length between the last rib and the thigh, when viewed from the side, is undesirable. *Croup*—Long and gradually sloping.

Tail—Bushy, with the last vertebra extended at least to the hock joint. It is set smoothly into the croup and low rather than high. At rest, the tail hangs in a slight curve like a saber. A slight hook—sometimes carried to one side—is faulty only to the extent that it mars general appearance. When the dog is excited or in motion, the curve is accentuated and the tail raised, but it should never be curled forward beyond a vertical line. Tails too short, or with clumpy ends due to ankylosis, are serious faults. A dog with a docked tail must be disqualified.

Hindquarters—The whole assembly of the thigh, viewed from the side, is broad, with both upper and lower thigh well muscled, forming as nearly as possible a right angle. The upper thigh bone parallels the shoulder blade while the lower thigh bone parallels the upper arm. The metatarsus (the unit between the hock joint and the foot) is short, strong and tightly articulated.

Gait—A German Shepherd Dog is a trotting dog, and its structure has been developed to meet the requirements of its work. *General Impression*—The gait is outreaching, elastic, seemingly without effort, smooth and rhythmic, covering the maximum amount of ground with the minimum number of steps. At a walk it covers a great deal of ground, with long stride of both hind legs and forelegs. At a trot the dog covers still more ground with even longer stride, and moves powerfully but easily, with co-ordination and balance so that the gait appears to be the steady motion of a well-lubricated machine. The feet travel close to the ground on both forward reach and backward push. In order to achieve ideal movement of this kind, there must be good muscular development and ligamentation. The hindquarters deliver, through the back, a powerful forward thrust which slightly lifts the whole animal and drives the body forward. Reaching far under, and passing the imprint left by the front foot, the hind foot takes hold of the ground; then hock, stifle and upper thigh come into play and sweep back, the stroke of the hind leg finishing with the foot still close to the ground in a smooth follow-through. The over-reach of the hindquarter usually necessitates one hind foot passing outside and the other hind foot passing inside the track of the forefeet, and such action is not faulty unless the locomotion is crabwise with the dog's body sideways out of the normal straight line.

Transmission—The typical smooth, flowing gait is maintained with great strength and firmness of back. The whole effort of the hindquarter is transmitted to the forequarter through the loin, back and withers. At full trot, the back must remain firm and level without sway, roll, whip or roach. Unlevel topline with withers lower than the hip is a fault. To compensate for the forward motion imparted by the hindquarters, the shoulder should open to its full extent. The forelegs should reach out close to the ground in a long stride in harmony with that of the hindquarters. The dog does not track on widely separated parallel lines, but brings the feet inward toward the middle line of the body when trotting in order to maintain balance. The feet track closely but do not strike or cross over. Viewed from the front, the front legs function from the shoulder joint to the pad in a straight line. Viewed from the rear, the hind legs function from the hip joint to the pad in a straight line. Faults of gait, whether from front, rear or side, are to be considered very serious faults.

Color—The German Shepherd Dog varies in color, and most colors are permissible. Strong rich colors are preferred. Nose black. Pale, washed-out colors and blues or livers are serious faults. A white dog or a dog with a nose that is not predominantly black, must be disqualified.

Coat—The ideal dog has a double coat of medium length. The outer coat should be as dense as possible, hair straight, harsh and lying close to the body. A slightly wavy outer coat, often of wiry texture, is permissible. The head, including the inner ear and foreface, and the legs and paws are covered with short hair, and the neck with longer and thicker hair. The rear of the forelegs and hind legs has somewhat longer hair extending to the pastern and hock, respectively. Faults in coat include soft, silky, too long outer coat, woolly, curly, and open coat.

DISQUALIFICATIONS

Cropped or hanging ears.
Undershot jaw.
Docked tail.
White dogs.
Dogs with noses not predominantly black.
Any dog that attempts to bite the judge.

Approved February 11, 1978

Giant Schnauzer

F EW RACES have been more prolific in their development of new breeds of dog than the Germanic peoples. Not only have they evinced rare patience in tracing ancestries, but they have proved their ability to fix type. One of the most notable examples of their breeding skill is the Schnauzer, for here is a dog not only brought to splendid physical conformation and keen mental development, but reproduced in three distinct sizes. The one under consideration here is the Riesenschnauzer—the Giant.

It is important to realize that the Miniature, the Standard, and the Giant Schnauzers are three separate and distinct breeds. Schnauzer breeding has been remarkable in that it has produced, from various sources that intermingled only in rare instances, if at all, three breeds which have developed toward one comparable standard of perfection.

Of the three, the dog now known in America as the Standard Schnauzer, which is the medium-sized specimen, is without doubt the oldest. He is the one apparently portrayed in paintings by Dürer, dating from 1492, and he is also the one of the ''Nachtwächter-Brunnen,'' the statue of a night watchman and his dog erected in a square in Stuttgart, Württemberg, in 1620. These instances are important only as they indicate the antiquity of the type of dog perfected at those dates and still retained today.

In unearthing the history of this breed it must be remembered that occupations of men had a great deal to do with all development in dogs. There were no bench shows in those days, and when a new breed was produced, it was aimed at a specific work. Also, its characteristics were governed to large extent by weather and living conditions.

All Schnauzers had their origin in the neighboring kingdoms of Württemberg and Bavaria. These are agricultural sections where the raising of sheep, cattle, and other livestock has been a major occupation for years. Since railroads were not known, sheep and cattle had to be driven to market, which meant that dogs were necessary to help the shepherds.

There is little doubt that when Bavarian cattlemen went to Stuttgart they came across the medium-sized Schnauzer. Here was a dog to catch anyone's attention, for even then it was sound, while it showed power throughout its trim lines. The Bavarians liked the dog, but they were not satisfied with its size. The sheepmen could use this size of dog, but the drovers needed a larger specimen for cattle.

The first attempts to produce a drover's dog on terrier lines, with a wiry coat, were no doubt by crossings between the medium-sized Schnauzer and some of the smooth-coated driving and dairymen's dogs then in existence. Later there were crossings with the rough-haired sheep dogs, and much later, with the black Great Dane. There is also reason to believe that the Giant Schnauzer is closely related to the Bouvier des Flandres, which was the driving dog of Flanders.

For many years the Giant Schnauzer was called the Münchener, and it was widely known as a great cattle and driving dog. Von Stephanitz places its origin as Swabia—in the south of Bavaria, and it was found in a state of perfection in the region between Munich and Augsburg.

The Giant Schnauzer was practically unknown outside of Bavaria until nearly the end of the first decade of this century. Cattle-driving was then a thing of the past, but the breed was still found in the hands of butchers, at stockyards, and at breweries. The breweries maintained the dogs as guards, at which duty they are pre-eminently successful.

Not until just before World War I did the Giant Schnauzer begin to come to nationwide attention in Germany as a suitable subject to receive police training at the schools in Berlin and other principal cities. He proved such an intelligent pupil that police work has been his main occupation since that time. His progress in the United States has been very slow. Making his appearance here at the time when the German Shepherd was reaching its peak, the Bavarian dog had little chance to make headway against such well-established, direct competition.

Official Standard for the
Giant Schnauzer

General Description—The Giant Schnauzer should resemble, as nearly as possible, in general appearance, a larger and more powerful version of the Standard Schnauzer, on the whole a bold and valiant figure of a dog. Robust, strongly built, nearly square in proportion of body length to height at withers, active, sturdy, and well muscled. Temperament which combines spirit and alertness with intelligence and reliability. Composed, watchful, courageous, easily trained, deeply loyal to family, playful, amiable in repose, and a commanding figure when aroused. The sound, reliable temperament, rugged build, and dense weather-resistant wiry coat make for one of the most useful, powerful, and enduring working breeds.

Head—Strong, rectangular in appearance, and elongated; narrowing slightly from the ears to the eyes, and again from the eyes to the tip of the nose. The total length of the head is about one-half the length of the back (withers to set-on of tail). The head matches the sex and substance of the dog. The top line of the muzzle is parallel to the top line of the skull; there is a slight stop which is accentuated by the eyebrows.

Skull—(Occiput to Stop). Moderately broad between the ears; occiput not too prominent. Top of skull flat; skin unwrinkled.

Cheeks—Flat, but with well-developed chewing muscles; there is no "cheekiness" to disturb the rectangular head appearance (with beard).

Muzzle—Strong and well filled under the eyes; both parallel and equal in length to the topskull; ending in a moderately blunt wedge. The nose is large, black, and full. The lips are tight, and not overlapping, black in color.

Bite—A full complement of sound white teeth (6/6 incisors, 2/2 canines, 8/8 premolars, 4/6 molars) with a scissors bite. The upper and lower jaws are powerful and well formed. *Disqualifying Faults*—Overshot or undershot.

Ears—When cropped, identical in shape and length with pointed tips. They are in balance with the head and are not exaggerated in length. They are set high on the skull and carried perpendicularly at the inner edges with as little bell as possible along the other edges. When uncropped, the ears are V-shaped button ears of medium length and thickness, set high and carried rather high and close to the head.

Eyes—Medium size, dark brown, and deep-set. They are oval in appearance and keen in expression with lids fitting tightly. Vision is not impaired nor eyes hidden by too long eyebrows.

Neck—Strong and well arched, of moderate length, blending cleanly into the shoulders, and with the skin fitting tightly at the throat; in harmony with the dog's weight and build.

Body—Compact, substantial, short-coupled, and strong, with great power and agility. The height at the highest point of the withers equals the body length from breastbone to point of rump. The loin section is well developed, as short as possible for compact build.

Forequarters—The forequarters have flat, somewhat sloping shoulders and high withers. Forelegs are straight and vertical when viewed from all sides with strong pasterns and good bone. They are separated by a fairly deep brisket which precludes a pinched front. The elbows are set close to the body and point directly backwards.

Chest—Medium in width, ribs well sprung but with no tendency toward a barrel chest; oval in cross section; deep through the brisket. The breastbone is plainly discernible, with strong forechest; the brisket descends at least to the elbows, and ascends gradually toward the rear with the belly moderately drawn up. The ribs spread gradually from the first rib so as to allow space for the elbows to move close to the body.

Shoulders—The sloping shoulder blades (scapulae) are strongly muscled, yet flat. They are well laid back so that from the side the rounded upper ends are in a nearly vertical line above the elbows. They slope well forward to the point where they join the upper arm (humerus), forming as nearly as possible a right angle. Such an angulation permits the maximum forward extension of the forelegs without binding or effort. Both shoulder blades and upper arm are long, permitting depth of chest at the brisket.

Back—Short, straight, strong, and firm.

Tail—The tail is set moderately high and carried high in excitement. It should be docked to the second or not more than the third joint (approximately one and one-half to about three inches long at maturity).

Hindquarters—The hindquarters are strongly muscled, in balance with the forequarters; upper thighs are slanting and well bent at the stifles, with the second thighs (tibiae) approximately parallel to an extension of the upper neckline. The legs from the hock joint to the feet are short, perpendicular to the ground while the dog is standing naturally, and from the rear parallel to each other. The hindquarters do not appear over-built or higher than the shoulders. Croup full and slightly rounded.

Feet—Well-arched, compact and catlike, turning neither in nor out, with thick tough pads and dark nails.

Dewclaws—Dewclaws, if any, on hind legs should be removed; on the forelegs, may be removed.

Gait—The trot is the gait at which movement is judged. Free, balanced and vigorous, with good reach in the forequarters and good driving power in the hindquarters. Rear and front legs are thrown neither in nor out. When moving at a fast trot, a properly built dog will single-track. Back remains strong, firm, and flat.

Coat—Hard, wiry, very dense; composed of a soft undercoat and a harsh outer coat which, when seen against the grain, stands slightly up off the back, lying neither smooth nor flat. Coarse hair on top of head; harsh beard and eyebrows, the Schnauzer hallmark.

Color—Solid black or pepper and salt.

Black—A truly pure black. A small white spot on the breast is permitted.

Pepper and Salt—Outer coat of a combination of banded hairs (white with black and black with white) and some black and white hairs, appearing gray from a short distance. *Ideally:* an intensely pigmented medium gray shade with "peppering" evenly distributed throughout the coat, and a gray undercoat. *Acceptable:* all shades of pepper and salt from dark iron-gray to silver-gray.

Every shade of coat has a dark facial mask to emphasize the expression; the color of the mask harmonizes with the shade of the body coat. Eyebrows, whiskers, cheeks, throat, chest, legs, and under tail are lighter in color but include "peppering."

Height—The height of the withers of the male is 25½ to 27½ inches, and of the female, 23½ to 25½ inches, with the mediums being desired. Size alone should never take precedence over type, balance, soundness, and temperament. It should be noted that too small dogs generally lack the power and too large dogs, the agility and maneuverability, desired in a working dog.

FAULTS

The foregoing description is that of the ideal Giant Schnauzer. Any deviation from the above described dog must be penalized to the extent of the deviation.

The judge shall dismiss from the ring any shy or vicious Giant Schnauzer.
Shyness—A dog shall be judged fundamentally shy if, refusing to stand for examination, it repeatedly shrinks away from the judge; if it fears unduly any approach from the rear; if it shies to a marked degree at sudden and unusual noises.
Viciousness—A dog that attacks or attempts to attack either the judge or its handler, is definitely vicious. An aggressive or belligerent attitude towards other dogs shall not be deemed viciousness.

DISQUALIFICATIONS

Overshot or undershot.

Approved February 13, 1971

Great Dane

IN APPEARANCE and nature the Great Dane is one of the most elegant and distinguished varieties of giant-type dog.

Accurate canine history is limited to but little longer than the last half century. The first dog show was held as recently as 1859 in England, where the "dog game" was born. Before that time, there were occasional records of different sorts of dogs over a period of more than three thousand years; but the items are so few, incomplete, and inaccurate that a student of the dogs of antiquity can "prove" almost anything he cares to imagine.

The name of the breed (in the English language) is a translation of an old French designation, *grand Danois*, meaning "big Danish." This was only one of half a dozen names which had been used for centuries in France. Why the English adopted the name "Great Dane" from the French is a mystery. At the same time the French were also calling it *dogue allemand* or "German Mastiff." "Mastiff" in English, *dogge* in the Germanic, *dogue* or *dogo* in the Latin languages, all meant the same thing: a giant dog with heavy head for fighting or hunting purposes. It was one of the dozen varieties of dog recognized as distinctive enough at that time to have a name of its own.

There is no known reason for connecting Denmark with either the origin or the development of the breed. It was "made in Germany," and it is German fanciers who have led the world in breeding most of the finest specimens.

If the reader is susceptible to the charms of antiquity, he will be interested in Cassel's claim that on Egyptian monuments of about 3000 B.C. there are drawings of dogs much like the Great Dane. Also, the earliest written description of a dog resembling the breed may be found in Chinese literature of 1121 B.C. (an article by Dr. G. Ciaburri, Great Dane Club of Italy publication, 1929).

Eminent zoologists like Keller and Kraemer believe that the Mastiff breeds originated in Asia. They think the modern Tibetan Mastiff, occasionally shown in England, is the most direct descendant of the prototype.

The great naturalist Buffon (1707–1788) claimed the Irish Wolfhound as the principal ancestor of our Great Dane. The comparative anatomist Cuvier (1769–1832) found more evidence in favor of the old English Mastiff as the root from which it sprang. Both Irish and English breeds are known to have been carefully bred for 1300 years and more. Today most students favor the idea that the Great Dane, or Deutsche Dogge, resulted from a mixture of both these ancient types.

This is not to say that the German Mastiff or Great Dane is a new breed. It is, indeed, a very old one which has been cultivated as a distinct type for probably 400 years, if not longer. Like all old varieties of dog, it was developed for a useful purpose. The Germans used the Great Dane as a boar hound. Europe's erstwhile boar was one of the most savage, swift, powerful, and well-armed of all big game on the Continent. To tackle the wild boar required a superdog, and that is precisely what the Germans developed. We who fancy him speak of him as the king of dogs.

In common with all other breeds, the Great Dane's history of and development to a modern standard type began in the latter nineteenth century. In 1880 at Berlin, Dr. Bodinus called a meeting of Great Dane judges who declared that the breed should be known as *Deutsche dogge* and that all other designations, especially the term "Great Dane," should be abolished thereafter. So far as the German people are concerned this declaration has been observed, but English-speaking people have paid no heed. The Italians, who have a large Great Dane fancy, have also failed to give Germany credit for the name selected: *alano*. This word means "a mastiff," consequently the name of their organization means "Mastiff Club of Italy." This, however, has not prevented close co-operation between fanciers of the two countries.

The leading Italian breeders have based their operation on nothing but German imported stock or its descendants.

In 1891 the Great Dane Club of Germany adopted a precise standard, or official description of the ideal specimen. In 1885, there was a Great Dane Club in England, and in 1889 at Chicago the German Mastiff or Great Dane Club of America was founded with G. Muss-Arnoldt as first delegate. Two years later the club reorganized as the Great Dane Club of America. At that time, its membership was mostly of Eastern fanciers.

The American standard of the Great Dane has always been based on the German standard as adopted by the Deutsche Doggen Club. In fact, all nations have recognized the authority of Germany in this matter. The English, French, Italian, Indian, and Dutch standards are almost exact translations from the German. The world over there is a single ideal of excellence in Great Danes. If a Dane rates high in Germany, he will rate high anywhere. This is not true of several breeds which have seen local fads take hold, so that there is a diversity of types in the same breed from country to country. This causes confusion in judging and breeding, since a "flyer" in one country might be considered quite undesirable in another.

The Great Dane has developed steadily in popularity. He was never the rage outside of Germany in Bismarck's day; nevertheless, year after year all over the world he has slowly increased in numbers. The Germans have kept before them the stern business the boar hound must engage in. A merely "pretty" dog has not been enough. He must have size and weight, nobility and courage, speed and endurance. What more can one ask for in a dog?

Official Standard for the
Great Dane

1. GENERAL CONFORMATION

(a) General Appearance—The Great Dane combines in its distinguished appearance dignity, strength and elegance with great size and a powerful, well-formed, smoothly muscled body. He is one of the giant breeds, but is unique in that his general conformation must be so well balanced that he never appears clumsy and is always a unit—the Apollo of dogs. He must be spirited and courageous—never timid. He is friendly and dependable. This physical and mental combination is the characteristic which gives the Great Dane the majesty possessed by no other breed. It is particularly true of this breed that there is an impression of great masculinity in dogs as compared to an impression of femininity in bitches. The male should appear more massive throughout than the bitch, with larger frame and heavier bone. In the ratio between length and height, the Great Dane should appear as square as possible. In bitches, a somewhat longer body is permissible. **Faults**—Lack of unity; timidity; bitchy dogs; poor musculature; poor bone development; out of condition; rickets; doggy bitches.

(b) Color and Markings
    (i) **Brindle Danes.** Base color ranging from light golden yellow to deep golden yellow always brindled with strong black cross stripes; deep-black mask preferred. Black may or may not appear on the eyes, ears and tail tip. The more intensive the base color and the more distinct the brindling, the more attractive will be the color. Small white marks at the chest and toes are not desirable. **Faults**—Brindle with too dark a base color; silver-blue and grayish-blue base color; dull (faded) brindlings; white tail tip. Black fronted, dirty colored brindles are not desirable.
    (ii) **Fawn Danes.** Light golden yellow to deep golden yellow color with a deep black mask. Black may or may not appear on the eyes, ears, and tail tip. The deep golden yellow color must always be given the preference. Small white spots at the chest and toes are not desirable. **Faults**—Yellowish-gray, bluish-yellow, grayish-blue, dirty yellow color (drab color), lack of black mask. Black fronted, dirty colored fawns are not desirable.
    (iii) **Blue Danes.** The color must be a pure steel blue, as far as possible without any tinge of yellow, black or mouse gray. Small white marks at the chest and toes are not desirable. **Faults**—Any deviation from a pure steel-blue coloration.
    (iv) **Black Danes.** Glossy Black. **Faults**—Yellow-black, brown-black or blue-black. White markings, such as stripes on the chest, speckled chest and markings on the paws are permitted but not desirable.
    (v) **Harlequin Danes.** Base color: pure white with black torn patches irregularly and well distributed over the entire body; pure white neck preferred. The black patches should never be large enough to give the appearance of a blanket nor so small as to give a stippled or dappled effect. (Eligible, but less desirable,

are a few small gray spots; also pointings where instead of a pure white base with black spots, there is a white base with single black hairs showing through which tend to give a salt and pepper or dirty effect.) **Faults**—White base color with a few large spots; bluish-gray pointed background.

(c) Size—The male should not be less than 30 inches at the shoulders, but it is preferable that he be 32 inches or more, providing he is well proportioned to his height. The female should not be less than 28 inches at the shoulders, but it is preferable that she be 30 inches or more, providing she is well proportioned to her height.

(d) Condition of Coat—The coat should be very short and thick, smooth, and glossy. **Faults**—Excessively long hair (stand-off coat); dull hair (indicating malnutrition, worms and negligent care).

(e) Substance—Substance is that sufficiency of bone and muscle which rounds out a balance with the frame. **Faults**—Lightweight whippety Danes; coarse, ungainly proportioned Danes—always there should be balance.

2. MOVEMENT

(a) Gait—Long, easy, springy stride with no tossing or rolling of body. The back line should move smoothly, parallel to the ground, with minimum rise and fall. The gait of the Great Dane should denote strength and power showing good driving action in the hindquarters and good reach in front. As speed increases, there is a natural tendency for the legs to converge toward the center line of balance beneath the body and there should be no twisting in or out at the joints. **Faults**—Interference of crossing; twisting joints; short steps; stilted steps; the rear quarters should not pitch; the forelegs should not have a hackney gait. When moving rapidly, the Great Dane should not pace for the reason that it causes excessive side-to-side rolling of the body and thus reduces endurance.

(b) Rear End (Croup, Legs, Paws)—The croup must be full, slightly drooping and must continue imperceptibly to the tail root. **Faults**—A croup which is too straight; a croup which slopes downward too steeply; and too narrow a croup.

Hind legs, the first thighs (from hip joint to knee) are broad and muscular. The second thighs (from knee to hock joint) are strong and long. Seen from the side, the angulation of the first thigh with the body, of the second thigh with the first thigh, and the pastern root with the second thigh should be very moderate, neither too straight nor too exaggerated. Seen from the rear, the hock joints appear to be perfectly straight, turned neither towards the inside nor towards the outside. **Faults**—Hind legs: Soft flabby, poorly muscled thighs; cowhocks which are the result of the hock joint turning inward and the hock and rear paws turning outward; barrel legs, the result of the hock joints being too far apart; steep rear. As seen from the side, a steep rear is the result of the angles of the rear legs forming almost a straight line; overangulation is the result of exaggerated angles between the first and second thighs and the hocks and is very conducive to weakness. The rear legs should never be too long in proportion to the front legs.

Paws—Round and turned neither toward the inside nor toward the outside. Toes short, highly arched and well closed. Nails short, strong and as dark as possible. **Faults**—Spreading toes (splay foot); bent, long toes (rabbit paws); toes turned toward the outside or toward the inside. Furthermore, the fifth toe on the hind legs appearing at a higher position and with wolf's claw or spur; excessively long nails; light-colored nails.

(c) Front End (Shoulders, Legs, Paws)—Shoulders— The shoulder blades must be strong and sloping and seen from the side must form as nearly as possible a right angle in its articulation with the humerus (upper arm) to give a long stride. A line from the upper tip of the shoulder to the back of the elbow joint should be as nearly perpendicular as possible. Since all dogs lack a clavicle (collar bone) the ligaments and muscles holding the shoulder blade to the rib cage must be well developed, firm and secure to prevent loose shoulders. **Faults**—Steep shoulders, which occur if the shoulder blade does not slope sufficiently; overangulation; loose shoulders which occur if the Dane is flabby muscled, or if the elbow is turned toward the outside; loaded shoulders.

Forelegs—The upper arm should be strong and muscular. Seen from the side or front, the strong lower arms run absolutely straight to the pastern joints. Seen from the front, the forelegs and the pastern roots should form perpendicular lines to the ground. Seen from the side, the pastern root should slope only very slightly forward. **Faults**—Elbows turned toward the inside or toward the outside, the former position caused mostly by too narrow or too shallow a chest, bringing the front legs too closely together and at the same time turning the entire lower part of the leg outward; the latter position causes the front legs to spread too far apart, with the pastern roots and paws usually turned inwards. Seen from the side, a considerable bend in the pastern toward the front indicates weakness and is in most cases connected with stretched and spread toes (splay foot); seen from the side, a forward bow in the forearm (chair leg); an excessively knotty bulge in the front of the pastern joint.

Paws—Round and turned neither toward the inside nor toward the outside. Toes short, highly arched and well closed. Nails short, strong and as dark as possible. **Faults**—Spreading toes (splay foot), bent, long toes (rabbit paws); toes turned toward the outside or toward the inside; light-colored nails.

3. HEAD

(a) Head Conformation— Long, narrow, distinguished, expressive, finely chiseled, especially the part below the eyes (which means that the skull plane under and to the inner point of the eye must slope without any bony protuberance in a pleasing line to the full square jaw), with strongly pronounced stop. The masculinity of the male is very pronounced in the expression and structure of head (this subtle difference should be evident in the dog's head through massive skull and depth of muzzle); the bitch's head may be more delicately formed. Seen from the side, the forehead must be sharply set off from the

bridge of the nose. The forehead and the bridge of the nose must be straight and parallel to one another. Seen from the front, the head should appear narrow, the bridge of the nose should be as broad as possible. The cheek muscles must show slightly, but under no circumstances should they be too pronounced (cheeky). The muzzle part must have full flews and must be as blunt vertically as possible in front; the angles of the lips must be quite pronounced. The front part of the head, from the tip of the nose up to the center of the stop should be as long as the rear part of the head from the center of the stop to the only slightly developed occiput. The head should be angular from all sides and should have definite flat planes and its dimensions should be absolutely in proportion to the general appearance of the Dane. **Faults**—Any deviation from the parallel planes of skull and foreface; too small a stop; a poorly defined stop or none at all; too narrow a nose bridge; the rear of the head spreading laterally in a wedgelike manner (wedge head); an excessively round upper head (apple head); excessively pronounced cheek musculature; pointed muzzle; loose lips hanging over the lower jaw (fluttering lips) which create an illusion of a full deep muzzle. The head should be rather shorter and distinguished than long and expressionless.

(b) Teeth—Strong, well developed and clean. The incisors of the lower jaw must touch very lightly the bottoms of the inner surface of the upper incisors (scissors bite). If the front teeth of both jaws bite on top of each other, they wear down too rapidly. **Faults**—Even bite; undershot and overshot; incisors out of line; black or brown teeth; missing teeth.

(c) Eyes—Medium size, as dark as possible, with lively intelligent expression; almond-shaped eyelids, well-developed eyebrows. **Faults**—Light-colored, piercing, amber-colored, light blue to a watery blue, red or bleary eyes; eyes of different colors; eyes too far apart; Mongolian eyes; eyes with pronounced haws; eyes with excessively drooping lower eyelids. In blue and black Danes, lighter eyes are permitted but are not desirable. In harlequins, the eyes should be dark. Light-colored eyes, two eyes of different color and walleyes are permitted but not desirable.

Nose—The nose must be large and in the case of brindled and "single-colored" Danes, it must always be black. In harlequins, the nose should be black; a black spotted nose is permitted; a pink-colored nose is not desirable.

Ears—Ears should be high, set not too far apart, medium in size, of moderate thickness, drooping forward close to the cheek. Top line of folded ear should be about level with the skull. **Faults**—Hanging on the side, as on a Foxhound.

Cropped ears: high set, not set too far apart, well pointed but always in proportion to the shape of the head and carried uniformly erect.

4. TORSO

(a) Neck—The neck should be firm and clean, high-set, well arched, long, muscular and sinewy. From the chest to the head, it should be slightly tapering, beautifully formed, with well-developed nape. **Faults**—Short, heavy neck, pendulous throat folds (dewlaps).

(b) Loin and Back—The withers forms the highest part of the back which slopes downward slightly toward the loins which are imperceptibly arched and strong. The back should be short and tensely set. The belly should be well shaped and tightly muscled, and, with the rear part of the thorax, should swing in a pleasing curve (tuck-up). **Faults**—Receding back; sway back; camel or roach back; a back line which is too high at the rear; an excessively long back; poor tuck-up.

(c) Chest—Chest deals with that part of the thorax (rib cage) in front of the shoulders and front legs. The chest should be quite broad, deep and well muscled. **Faults**—A narrow and poorly muscled chest; strong protruding sternum (pigeon breast).

(d) Ribs and Brisket—Deals with that part of the thorax back of the shoulders and front legs. Should be broad, with the ribs sprung well out from the spine and flattened at the side to allow proper movement of the shoulders extending down to the elbow joint. **Faults**—Narrow (slab-sided) rib cage; round (barrel) rib cage; shallow rib cage not reaching the elbow joint.

5. TAIL

Should start high and fairly broad, terminating slender and thin at the hock joint. At rest, the tail should fall straight. When excited or running, slightly curved (saberlike). **Faults**—A too high, or too low set tail (the tail set is governed by the slope of the croup); too long or too short a tail; tail bent too far over the back (ring tail); a tail which is curled; a twisted tail (sideways); a tail carried too high over the back (gay tail); a brush tail (hair too long on lower side). Cropping tails to desired length is forbidden.

DISQUALIFICATIONS

Danes under minimum height.

White Danes without any black marks (albinos).

Merles, a solid mouse-gray color or a mouse-gray base with black or white or both color spots or white base with mouse-gray spots.

Harlequins and solid-colored Danes in which a large spot extends coatlike over the entire body so that only the legs, neck and the point of the tail are white.

Brindle, fawn, blue and black Danes with white forehead line, white collars, high white stockings and white bellies.

Danes with predominantly blue, gray, yellow or also brindled spots.

Any color other than those described under "Color and Markings."

Docked tails.

Split noses.

Approved August 10, 1976

Great Pyrenees

PERHAPS no other breed can boast such a colorful history of association with, and service to, mankind through as many centuries as can the Great Pyrenees, Le Grand Chien des Montagnes, Le Chien des Pyrenees, or, as he is known in England and on the Continent, the Pyrenean Mountain Dog, the dog of French royalty and nobility and working associate of the peasant shepherds high on the slopes of the Pyrenees Mountains. His remains are found in the fossil deposits of the Bronze Age, which roughly dates his appearance in Europe between 1800 and 1000 B.C., although it is believed that he came originally from Central Asia or Siberia and followed the Aryan migration into Europe. It is also generally accepted that he is a descendant of the mastiff type whose remains are found in the kitchen-middens of the Baltic and North Sea coasts in the oldest strata containing evidence of the domestic dog, and which appear in Babylonian art about the close of the third millennium B.C. in a size and general appearance resembling the Great Pyrenees.

Once in Europe, the Great Dog of the Mountains developed under climatic conditions similar to those of his habitat and there remained isolated in the high mountainous areas until medieval times, when we find him gracing bas-reliefs at Carcassone, bearing the royal arms of

France approximately some five hundred years before his adoption as the court dog in the seventeenth century. As early as 1407 the historian Mons. Bourdet describes the regular guard of Pyrenees dogs owned by the Chateau of Lourdes. These dogs were given a special place in the sentry boxes along with the armed guards; they also accompanied the gaolers on their daily rounds. Their use for these purposes became very general and each large chateau boasted its band of Great Pyrenees. It was not until the young Dauphin, accompanied by Mme. de Maintenon in 1675 on a visit to Barreges, fell in love with a beautiful *Patou* (a generic name for the breed meaning "shepherd") and insisted on taking it back to the Louvre with him, and not until the Marquis de Louvois also succumbed to their charm, that the dog of the shepherd of the Pyrenees became the companion and pet of nobility. Once accepted at court, every noble wanted one, and the breed gained prominence.

It was, however, in the isolation of the lonely mountain pastures that the Pyrenean Mountain Dog developed his inherent traits of devotion, fidelity, sense of guardianship, and intelligent understanding of mankind. Here, in the days when packs of wild animals roamed the mountain slopes freely, he was the official guardian of the flocks. Having a precocious sense of smell and keen sight, he was an invaluable companion of the shepherd, his worth being counted equal to that of two men. Armed by nature with a long, heavy coat which rendered him invulnerable against attack except for the point of the chin and the base of the brain, and armed by his masters with a broad iron collar from which protruded spikes an inch and a half long, the Pyrenees dog was an almost unbeatable foe which won such glory and fame as a vanquisher of wolves and bears that he became known as the Pyrenean wolf dog or hound, and the Pyrenean bearhound.

By disposition and profession, no better dog could have been chosen to assume the role of protector and friend of the early settlements of the Biscay fisherfolk on Newfoundland Island. By 1662, when their first permanent colony at Rougnoust was made, it was the Great Pyrenees dog which had become the companion of the people. Here he was crossed with the black English Retriever, brought over by the English settlers, and from this cross resulted the Newfoundland. The old Landseer type, with its black and white coat, showed the cross far more markedly because of his coloring than the black Newfoundland, although the resemblance in general type is quite noticeable in both.

With the diminution of the wild beasts in the Pyrenees, the breed seemed destined to extinction for a while. Moreover, it was eagerly sought after by breeders in Continental Europe and great numbers were exported from France. However, thanks to the efforts of some gentlemen sportsmen, as well as to the fact that dogs were of use about the peasants' farms in winter (when their services were not required on the mountain slopes), they were bred in increasing numbers until today the breed is well established in its habitat once again. The dogs are not infrequently referred to as "mat-dogs" because of their habit of lying outside the cottage doors when not busying themselves with menial chores such as pulling carts.

The Great Pyrenees has come into general prominence only since its recognition by The American Kennel Club in February, 1933. It seems hard to realize that the first pair were brought over by General Lafayette for his friend, Mr. J. S. Skinner, in 1824, being "recommended by him from personal experience as of inestimable value to wool-growers in all regions exposed to the depredations of wolves and sheepkilling dogs." Thus writes Mr. Skinner in his book *The Dog and the Sportsman.* Since that date a few scattered specimens have been imported, but not until 1933 was the actual breeding of the dogs launched in America. In the years that have elapsed since their recognition here, champions have been crowned, litters raised and distributed throughout the country, and new dogs imported.

Pre-eminently a watchdog and companion, the Great Pyrenees holds promise also as a dog suited for the sportsman. His love of pulling carts makes him amenable to sled work in winter, and his instinct for feeling out soft places in the snow makes him ideal for pack and guide work on ski trips. He was used during World War I for pack service and for many years for running contraband goods over the Franco-Spanish border by similar methods. Taking dangerous byways impossible for man to travel, he ran the circuit regularly, successfully avoiding the customs officials. His beauty also recommends him for use in the moving picture industry, especially as he has already been used with success for this purpose in France. Certainly no more picturesque animal could be found; he has been aptly called, "an animated snowdrift of the Pyrenees Mountains." The nearer his appearance approaches that of the brown bear, except for the color and the drooping ears, the closer he is to the perfect type.

Official Standard for the
Great Pyrenees

General Appearance—A dog of immense size, great majesty, keen intelligence, and kindly expression of unsurpassed beauty and a certain elegance, all white or principally white with markings of badger, gray, or varying shades of tan. In the rolling, ambling gait it shows unmistakably the purpose for which it has been bred, the strenuous work of guarding the flocks in all kinds of weather on the steep mountain slopes of the Pyrenees. Hence soundness is of the greatest importance and absolutely necessary for the proper fulfillment of his centuries' old task.

Size—The average height at the shoulder is 27 inches to 32 inches for dogs, and 25 inches to 29 inches for bitches. The average length from shoulder blades to root of tail should be the same as the height in any given specimen. The average girth is 36 inches to 42 inches for dogs and 32 inches to 36 inches for bitches. The weight for dogs runs 100 to 125 pounds and 90 to 115 pounds for bitches. A dog heavily boned; with close cupped feet; double dewclaws behind and single dewclaws in front.

Head—Large and wedge-shaped, measuring 10 inches to 11 inches from dome to point of nose, with rounding crown, furrow only slightly developed and with no apparent stop. *Cheeks*—Flat. *Ears*—V-shaped, but rounded at the tips, of medium size, set parallel with the eyes, carried low and close to the head except when raised at attention. *Eyes*—Of medium size, set slightly obliquely, dark rich brown in color with close eyelids, well pigmented. *Lips*—Close-fitting, edged with black. *Dewlaps*—Developed but little. The head is in brief that of a brown bear, but with the ears falling down. *Neck*—Short, stout and strongly muscular.

Body—Well-placed shoulders set obliquely, close to the body. *Back and Loin*—Well coupled, straight and broad. *Haunches*—Fairly prominent. *Rump*—Sloping slightly. *Ribs*—Flat-sided. *Chest*—Deep. *Tail*—Of sufficient length to hang below the hocks, well plumed, carried low in repose, and curled high over the back, "making the wheel" when alert.

Coat—Created to withstand severe weather, with heavy fine white undercoat and long flat thick outer coat of coarser hair, straight or slightly undulating.

Qualities—In addition to his original age-old position in the scheme of pastoral life as protector of the shepherd and his flock, the Great Pyrenees has been used for centuries as a guard and watchdog on the large estates of his native France, and for this he has proven ideal. He is as serious in play as he is in work, adapting and molding himself to the moods, desires and even the very life of his human companions, through fair weather and foul, through leisure hours and hours fraught with danger, responsibility and extreme exertion; he is the exemplification of gentleness and docility with those he knows, of faithfulness and devotion for his master even to the point of self-sacrifice; and of courage in the protection of the flock placed in his care and of the ones he loves.

SCALE OF POINTS

Head
    Shape of skull 5
    Ears 5
    Eyes 5
    Muzzle 5
    Teeth 5 25
General Conformation
    Neck 5

    Chest 5
    Back 5
    Loins 5
    Feet 5 25
Coat 10
Size and Soundness 25
Expression and General
    Appearance 15
    TOTAL 100

Approved February 13, 1935

Komondor

OF THE THREE breeds of working dog native for ten centuries to the sheep and cattle countries of Hungary, there seems little doubt that the king of them all is the Komondor. This heavily coated dog is an almost direct descendant of the Aftscharka, which the Huns found on the southern steppes when they passed through Russia. Many of today's Komondorok (plural) bear striking resemblance to the massive, long-legged Russian herdsman's dog, but the breed generally has become more compact.

The Komondor is a mighty fellow. His head is impressive in its generous formation, and his general appearance is commanding. At first sight he is likely to create fear. Strangers of evil intent have reason to be fearful, but he is a devoted companion to his master and readily mingles with friends of the master.

One often sees pictures of the Komondor that show him with a heavily matted coat and with his head covered all over with long hair. The dog thus seems unkempt, and this is the way he is found in his habitat, where he lives in the open practically all the time. Under such circumstances, it would be impossible for the Komondor to have a well-groomed appearance, but he responds readily to care. When reared in kennels and prepared for shows, he is a handsome dog.

The Komondor is the chief of the herdsman's dogs, but he is not often utilized for rounding up the herds. He merely accompanies the flocks and herds in exceptional cases, and then more in the capacity of protector than as herder. His vigilance and courage have earned him a rather enviable position of trust, and much of the routine work is left to the smaller dogs.

The Magyars who have bred the Komondor for more than a thousand years attend principally to their herds and flocks and do not concern themselves with keeping pedigrees of their dogs. However, there is no need of pedigrees for them, as the dogs are not permitted to mate outside their own race.

It is doubtful if any dogs with pedigrees could be found in the so-called "Puszta," for the shepherds and herdsmen do not look upon dog breeding either as a commercial venture or as a hobby. Still, the crossing of a Komondor and a Kuvasz would be unimaginable, and also practically impossible. The Komondor still resides in the Puszta, while the Kuvasz has become, in recent times, more the watchdog of the village.

The history of pure-bred dog breeding in Hungary is not unlike that of any other country in the world. Definite records go back hardly a century, but those in existence are soundly attested by reliable parties. The Hungarian Kennel Club and the Hungarian Komondor Club maintain a strong control over the interests of the Komondor, these organizations having accepted the Standard of the breed as drawn up by a committee made up of members of the two clubs. The American Kennel Club's Standard of the breed is a translation of the Hungarian.

In reading the Standard, it should be noted that its salient points denote the strength and the protective features that have been bred into the Komondor for centuries, and these should be maintained. Today there is not perhaps as pressing a need for such a self-reliant dog, as there was in the past. In times of old he had to be ready at any moment to fight all manner of beasts of prey, many of which were his superior in size and weight. When the odds were against him, he could depend to some extent on that heavy coat to cover his most vulnerable points, and could call, too, upon an intelligence far superior to that of his wild adversaries.

Official Standard for the
Komondor

General Appearance—The Komondor is characterized by imposing strength, courageous demeanor and pleasing conformation. In general, it is a big muscular dog with plenty of bone and substance, covered with an unusual, heavy, white coat.

Nature and Characteristics—An excellent houseguard. It is wary of strangers. As a guardian of herds, it is, when grown, an earnest, courageous, and very faithful dog. The young dog, however, is as playful as any other puppy. It is devoted to its master and will defend him against attack by any stranger. Because of this trait, it is not used for driving the herds, but only for guarding them. The Komondor's special task is to protect the animals. It lives during the greater part of the year in the open, without protection against strange dogs and beasts of prey.

Head—The head looks somewhat short in comparison to the seemingly wide forehead. The skull is somewhat arched when viewed from the side. Stop is moderate. The muzzle somewhat shorter than the length of the skull. The top of the muzzle is straight and about parallel with the line of the top of the skull. The muzzle is powerful, bite is scissors; level bite is acceptable. Any missing teeth is a serious fault. Distinctly undershot or overshot bite is a serious fault.

Ears—Medium set, hanging and V-shaped. Erect ears or ears that move toward an erect position are faults.

Eyes—Medium-sized and almond-shaped, not too deeply set. The edges of the eyelids are gray. The iris of the eyes is dark brown, light color is not desirable. Blue-white eyes are disqualifying.

Muzzle—In comparison to the length given in the head description, the muzzle is wide, coarse and not pointed. Nostrils are wide. Color of the nose is black. A dark gray or dark brown nose is not desirable but is acceptable. Flesh colored noses are disqualifying.

Neck—Muscular, of medium length, moderately arched. The head erect. Any dewlap is a fault.

Body—Characterized chiefly by the powerful, deep chest which is muscular and proportionately wide. Shoulders are moderately sloping. The back is level. Rump is wide, muscular, slightly sloping towards the root of the tail. The body is rectangular, only slightly longer than the height at the withers. The belly is somewhat drawn up at the rear.

Tail—A straight continuation of the rumpline, and reaches down to the hocks. Slightly curved upwards at its end. When the dog is excited, the tail is raised up to the level of the back. The tail is not to be docked. A short or curly tail is a fault. Bobtails are disqualifying.

Forelegs—Straight, well boned and muscular. Viewed from any side, the legs are like vertical columns. The upper arms join the body closely, without loose elbows.

Hindquarters and Legs—The steely, strong bone structure is covered with highly developed muscles. The legs are straight as viewed from the rear. Stifles well bent. Dewclaws must be removed.

Feet—Strong, rather large and with close, well-arched toes. Nails are black or gray. Pads are hard, elastic and dark.

Movement—Light, leisurely and balanced. Takes long strides.

Coat—Characteristic of the breed is the dense, weather-resisting double coat. The puppy coat is relatively soft, but it shows a tendency tc fall into cords. In the mature dog the coat consists of a dense, soft, woolly undercoat, much like the puppy coat, and a coarser outer coat that is wavy or curly. The coarser hairs of the outer coat trap the softer undercoat forming permanent strong cords that are felty to the touch. A grown dog is covered with a heavy coat of these tassel-like cords, which form themselves naturally, and once formed, require no care other than washing. Too curly a coat is not desired. Straight or silky coat is a serious fault. Short, smooth hair on the head and legs is a disqualification. Failure of the coat to cord by two years of age is a disqualification.

The coat is longest at the rump, loins and tail. It is of medium length on the back, shoulders and chest. Shorter on the cheeks, around the eyes, ears, neck, and on the extremities. It is shortest around the mouth and lower part of the legs up to the hocks.

Color—Color of the coat is white. Any color other than white is disqualifying.

In the ideal specimen the skin is gray. Pink skin is less desirable but is acceptable if no evidence of albinism. The nose, lips, outlines of eyelids and pads are dark or gray. It is good if the gums and palate are also dark.

Size—Dogs, 25½ inches and upward at the withers; bitches, 23½ inches and upward at withers. While size is important, type, character, symmetry, movement and ruggedness are of the greatest importance, and are on no account to be sacrificed for size alone.

Faults—Size below limit. Short or too curly coat. Straight or silky coat. Any missing teeth. Distinctly undershot or overshot bite. Looseness or slackness. Short or curly tail. Light-colored eyes. Erect ears or ears that move toward an erect position. Dewlaps on the neck.

DISQUALIFICATIONS

Blue-white eyes.
Color other than white.
Bobtails.
Flesh-colored nose.
Short, smooth hair on head and legs.
Failure of the coat to cord by two years of age.

Approved February 13, 1973

Kuvasz

From Tibet, that strange high-flung domain of the lamas, came the ancestors of the breed that today is known as the Kuvasz (plural, Kuvaszok). Yet this is not a new name for the breed. It is merely a corrupted spelling of Turkish and Arabian words that signified the unexcelled guarding instincts of this big dog.

The Turkish word is *kawasz*, which means "armed guard of the nobility." In the Arabian this appears as *kawwasz*, which signifies "archer," an expression that probably was a mere figure of speech to denote the high esteem in which the dog was held, since many centuries ago an archer was regarded with great respect. Words with nearly the same spelling and meaning are found throughout all the countries whose languages originate in Tibet.

There is little doubt of the part that the Kuvasz played in the history of the kingdoms and empires which flourished throughout Europe five to eight centuries ago. Dogs of this breed were the constant companions of many a ruler of a turbulent country; indeed, none but those within the favor of the royal circles were permitted to own specimens of the Kuvasz.

Known in many countries, it was in Hungary that the Kuvasz developed into the form in which he is seen today. He still is a big dog, but he is not the giant of ancient times. At present he measures approximately twenty-eight inches at the shoulder, but there is every reason to believe that the dog which issued from Tibet stood considerably higher. He was a dog of which the common people stood in awe; his appearance alone was enough to discourage attacks on noblemen by the populace.

The first great period in the Hungarian history of the Kuvasz seemed to reach a climax during the second half of the fifteenth century. His renown reached far and wide. There were numerous big estates that bred the dog and kept their own stud books. Many were trained for hunting, and they proved very successful on the big game of those times.

King Matthias I, who reigned from 1458 to 1490, had at least one Kuvasz with him whenever he traveled, and there were numerous specimens about his palace and the surrounding grounds. Few other rulers have had to strive so hard to hold their domains together. Plots and political intrigue were the rule rather than the exception, while assassinations were not uncommon. It is said that King Matthias was reluctant to place any great trust in even the members of his own household, and his court was filled with ambitious noblemen.

It is no wonder that King Matthias relied more upon his dogs than upon his human guards. He knew that in this big, sturdy fellow he had, perhaps, the only true security that was possible. Often, when the tumultuous day was over—and he waged wars almost continually—the king would retire to his study and spend half the night poring over his books and his maps, preparing his orders for the following day, and while he worked, a big white Kuvasz sprawled just inside the door.

King Matthias became so impressed with the Kuvasz that he developed a large pack to be used for hunting purposes. His kennels on his large estates in Siebenbuergen were among the most impressive in Europe, and the scope of his breeding did a great deal toward perpetuating a splendid strain of the breed. Surplus puppies were presented only to the noblemen and to visiting dignitaries.

Eventually, many specimens got into the hands of the commoners, but this was long after the time of King Matthias I, when herders found them suitable for work with sheep and cattle. It was in this later period that the name of the breed was corrupted to its present spelling. Incidentally, this spelling is rather unfortunate, because it changes the meaning rather ridiculously to that of "mongrel."

According to von Stephanitz, the great German authority on all Central European breeds, the Kuvasz is related to the Komondor, which had been brought from the Russian steppes by the Huns. He ventures the opinion that the *kawasz* or *kawwasz* was crossed with the indigenous country dog of Hungary. While this is something of a conjecture, there is strong evidence that points to truth. At any rate, the original type has proved dominant, and the Kuvasz of today— perhaps a little smaller—is very similar to his earliest progenitors.

Official Standard for the
Kuvasz

General Characteristics—A spirited dog of keen intelligence, determination, courage and curiosity. Very sensitive to praise and blame. Primarily a one-family dog. Devoted, gentle and patient without being overly demonstrative. Always ready to protect loved ones even to the point of self-sacrifice. Extremely strong instinct to protect children. Polite to accepted strangers, but rather suspicious and very discriminating in making new friends. Unexcelled guard, possessing ability to act on his own initiative at just the right moment without instruction. Bold, courageous and fearless. Untiring ability to work and cover rough terrain for long periods of time. Has good scent and has been used to hunt game.

General Appearance—A working dog of larger size, sturdily built, well balanced, neither lanky nor cobby. White in color with *no markings*. Medium boned, well muscled, without the slightest hint of bulkiness or lethargy. Impresses the eye with strength and activity combined with light-footedness, moves freely on strong legs. Trunk and limbs form a horizontal rectangle slightly deviated from the square. Slightly inclined croup. Hindquarters are particularly well developed. Any tendency to weakness or lack of substance is a decided fault.

Movement—Easy, free and elastic. Feet travel close to the ground. Hind legs reach far under, meeting or even passing the imprints of the front legs. Moving toward an observer, the front legs do not travel parallel to each other but rather close together at the ground. When viewed from the rear, the hind legs (from the hip joint down) also move close at the ground. As speed increases, the legs gradually angle more inward until the pads are almost single-tracking. Unless excited, the head is carried rather low at the level of the shoulders. Desired movement cannot be maintained without sufficient angulation and firm slimness of body.

Height—Measured at the withers: dogs, 28 to 30 inches; bitches, 26 to 28 inches.
Weight—Dogs, approximately 100 to 115 pounds; bitches, approximately 70 to 90 pounds.

Color—White.

354

Head—Proportions are of great importance as the head is considered to be the most beautiful part of the Kuvasz. Length of head measured from tip of nose to occiput is slightly less than half the height of the dog at the withers. Width is half the length of the head. The skull is elongated but not pointed. The stop is defined, never abrupt, raising the forehead gently above the plane of the muzzle. The longitudinal midline of the forehead is pronounced, widening as it slopes to the muzzle. Cheeks flat, bony arches above the eyes. The skin dry, no excess flews.

Muzzle—Length in proportion to the length of the head, top straight, not pointed, underjaw well developed. Inside of the mouth preferably black.

Nose—Large, black, nostrils well opened.

Lips—Black, closely covering the teeth. The upper lip covers tightly the upper jaw only. Lower lip tight and not pendulous.

Bite—Dentition full, scissors bite preferred. Level bite acceptable.

Eyes—Almond-shaped, set well apart, somewhat slanted. In profile, the eyes are set slightly below the plane of the muzzle. Lids tight, haws should not show. Dark brown, the darker the better.

Ears—V-shaped, tip is slightly rounded. Rather thick, they are well set back between the level of the eye and the top of the head. When pulled forward the tip of the ear should cover the eye. Looking at the dog face to face, the widest part of the ear is about level to the eye. The inner edge of the ear lies close to the cheek, the outer edge slightly away from the head forming a V. In the relaxed position, the ears should hold their set and are not cast backward. The ears should not protrude above the head.

Neck—Muscular, without dewlap, medium length, arched at the crest.

Forequarters—Shoulders muscular. The scapula and humerus form a right angle, are long and of equal length. Legs are medium boned, straight and well muscled. Elbows neither in nor out. When viewed from the side, the forechest protrudes slightly in front of the shoulders. The joints are dry, hard. Dewclaws on the forelegs should not be removed.

Body—Forechest is well developed, chest deep with long well-sprung ribs reaching almost to the elbows. Shoulders long with withers higher than back. Back is of medium length, straight, firm and quite broad. The loin is short, muscular and tight. The croup well muscled, slightly sloping. The brisket is deep, well developed and runs parallel to the ground. The stomach is well tucked up.

Bone—In proportion to size of body. Medium, hard. Never heavy or coarse.

Hindquarters—The portion behind the hip joint is moderately long producing wide, long and strong muscles of the upper thigh. The femur is long, creating well-bent stifles. Lower thigh is long, dry, well muscled. Metatarsus is short, broad and of great strength. Dewclaws, if any, are removed.

Tail—Carried low, natural length reaching at least to the hocks. In repose it hangs down resting on the body, the end but slightly lifted. In state of excitement, the tail may be elevated to the level of the loin, the tip slightly curved up. Ideally there should not be much difference in the carriage of the tail in state of excitement or in repose.

Feet—Well padded. Pads resilient, black. Feet are closed tight forming round "cat feet". The rear paws somewhat longer, some hair between the toes, the less the better. Dark nails are preferred.

Skin—The skin is heavily pigmented. The more slate gray or black pigmentation the better.

Coat—The Kuvasz has a double coat formed by a guard hair and fine undercoat. The texture of the coat is medium coarse. The coat ranges from quite wavy to straight. Distribution follows a definite pattern over the body regardless of coat type. The head, muzzle, ears and paws are covered with short, smooth hair. The neck has a mane that extends to and covers the chest. Coat on the front of the forelegs up to the elbows and the hind legs below the thighs is short and smooth. The backs of the forelegs are feathered to the pastern with hair 2 to 3 inches long. The body and sides of the thighs are covered with a medium length coat. The back of the thighs and the entire tail is covered with hair 4 to 6 inches long. It is natural for the Kuvasz to lose most of the long coat during hot weather. Full luxuriant coat comes in seasonably, depending on climate. Summer coat should not be penalized.

FAULTS

The foregoing description is that of the ideal Kuvasz. Any deviation from the above-described dog must be penalized to the extent of the deviation.

DISQUALIFICATIONS

Overshot bite. Undershot bite.
Dogs smaller than 26 inches. Bitches smaller than 24 inches.
Any color other than white.

Approved July 9, 1974

Mastiff

THE BREED commonly called "Mastiff" in English speaking countries is more properly described as the *Old English* Mastiff. It is a giant short-haired dog, with heavy head and short muzzle, which has been bred in England for over two thousand years as a watchdog. The term "mastiff" describes a group of giant varieties of dog rather than a single breed. They are supposed to have originated in Asia.

So little is known about dogs of any sort prior to a century ago that almost all theories of ancestry are of small importance. Every partisan would like to claim the greatest antiquity for his particular sort of Mastiff as well as to say that the other sorts sprang from it. There is very little proof one way or the other.

Cassel finds drawings on Egyptian monuments of typical Mastiffs dating about 3000 B.C. In literature, the earliest reference is in Chinese about 1121 B.C. So much for the undoubted antiquity of the Mastiff group's ancestry.

So far as the Mastiff is concerned, it has a longer history than most. Caesar describes them in his account of invading Britain in 55 B.C., when they fought beside their masters against the Roman legions with such courage and power as to make a great impression. Soon afterward we find several different accounts of the huge British fighting dogs brought back to Rome where they defeated all other varieties in combat at the Circus. They were also matched against human gladiators as well as against bulls, bears, lions, and tigers.

Today we are likely to think of such cruel spectacles as belonging only to the dim ages of the past, but this is not true. Dog fights, bullbaiting, and bearbaiting were respectable and popular forms of amusement in England and America little more than a century ago. Such brutalizing events were patronized by nobility and clergy in England, while public-spirited citizens left legacies so that the common folk might be entertained in this way on holidays.

Dogfighting and animal-baiting were made illegal in England in 1853, due to Queen Victoria's insistence, but for twenty years longer the law was little obeyed. American dog fanciers are interested in the word *fancier,* which was synonymous with *bettor*—meaning especially a bettor on a dog or prize fight—and are interested also in the name of one of the most fashionable sporting establishments in London, over a hundred years ago, called the "Westminster Pit," with 300 seats. *Westminster* meant "dogs" even then—but fighting dogs!

While the Mastiff was always in front rank as a fighting dog, this does not account for his popularity in England for two thousand years. It was as bandogs, or tiedogs (tied by day but loose at night) that they were found everywhere. In fact, long ago, keeping of these Mastiffs was compulsory for the peasants. During Anglo Saxon times there had to be kept at least one Mastiff for each two villeins. By this means wolves and other savage game were kept under control. They were also used in hunting packs by the nobility. It was as protectors of the home, however, that they were most used, and probably as a result of centuries of such service the Mastiff has acquired unique traits as a family dog.

That the Mastiff has long been numerous is indicated by the development of the English language itself. The ancient word in Anglo-Saxon and in over a score of kindred languages for a member of the canine race is *hound* or something very similar. A rather modern word coming from the Latin languages is like *dog,* but it means one certain *type* of dog in all languages but English. In all but English it means a *Mastiff* sort. So we can believe that when the Normans conquered the Anglo-Saxons in 1066 and made Norman-French the official language of England, *dogues* (or Mastiffs) were so plentiful that people forgot eventually there was any other name for a canine creature. This is the only explanation a dog man can offer for such a peculiar change in a language.

Anecdotes extolling the power and agility of Mastiffs as well as their devotion to their masters would fill a large volume of marvels. Herodotus tells of Cyrus the Great, founder of the Persian Empire about 550 B.C., who received a Mastiff as a gift from the King of Albania. Cyrus matched the dog against another and also set it against a bull. But the Mastiff was meek, so Cyrus in disgust had it killed. News of this reception of his gift came back to the King of Albania. He sent messengers with another Mastiff—a bitch—to Cyrus, telling him that a Mastiff was no ordinary cur and that it scorned to notice such common creatures as a Persian dog or a bull. He urged him to select a worthy opponent such as a lion or even an elephant. The King of Albania concluded by saying Mastiffs were rare and royal gifts and that he would not send Cyrus another. Whereupon, says Herodotus, the Mastiff bitch was set to attack an elephant and did so with such fury and efficiency that she worried the elephant down to the ground and would have killed it.

That is one of the oldest and probably the tallest Mastiff tale on record! However, it gives proof of the reputation of Mastiffs as powerful, agile, and courageous dogs. It is even more interesting to know that Albania was the land of the people known as Alani, an Asiatic race. Also that similar names stand for "mastiffs," *e.g. Alano, Alan,* and *Alaunt.*

The story of Sir Peers Legh, Knight of Lyme Hall, (near Stockport, Cheshire) at the Battle of Agincourt, October 25, 1415, is well-known. He had brought his favorite Mastiff—also a bitch—to France, and when he fell, she stood over and defended him many hours until he was picked up by English soldiers and carried to Paris, where he died of his wounds. The faithful Mastiff was returned to England and from her is descended the famous Lyme Hall strain which the family has bred to this day—a period of over five centuries. In the drawing room of the castle is still to be seen an old stained-glass window portraying the gallant Sir Peers and his devoted Mastiff.

The present-day English Mastiff is based on the strains of Lyme Hall and that of the Duke of Devonshire's Kennels at Chatsworth. Chaucer wrote in Middle English (a language resulting from a cross between old Anglo-Saxon and Norman-French) 300 years after the Norman Conquest, describing the Old English Mastiff in his "Knight's Tale." He tried to use the Italian-French word for Mastiff, *Alan,* which is still used in English heraldry to describe the figure of "a Mastiff with cropped ears" on a coat of arms.

Chaucer wrote sometime before his death in 1400:

> Aboute his char ther wenten white *Alaunts*
> Twenty and mo, as gret as any stere
> To hunten at the leon or the dere.

So here is proof that 600 years ago Mastiffs were hunted in packs in England on such different game as lion or deer. Chaucer says they were as large as a steer! Even though cattle were much smaller in those days, this is hard to credit. The white color is authentic. We have plenty of pictures and descriptions of white and piebald Mastiffs, often with long coats, of about a century ago.

Official Standard for the Mastiff

General Character and Symmetry—Large, massive, symmetrical and well-knit frame. A combination of grandeur and good nature, courage and docility.

General Description of Head—In general outline giving a massive appearance when viewed from any angle. Breadth greatly to be desired. *Skull*—Broad and somewhat rounded between the ears, forehead slightly curved, showing marked wrinkles which are particularly distinctive when at attention. Brows (superciliary ridges) moderately raised. Muscles of the temples well developed, those of the cheeks extremely powerful. Arch across the skull a flattened curve with a furrow up the center of the forehead. This extends from between the eyes to halfway up the skull. *Ears*—Small, V-shaped, rounded at the tips. Leather moderately thin, set widely apart at the highest points on the sides of the skull continuing the outline across the summit. They should lie close to the cheeks when in repose. Ears dark in color, the blacker the better, conforming to the color of the muzzle. *Eyes*—Set wide apart, medium in size, never too prominent. Expression alert but kindly. The stop between the eyes well marked but not too abrupt. Color of eyes brown, the darker the better and showing no haw.

Face and Muzzle—Short, broad under the eyes and running nearly equal in width to the end of the nose. Truncated, *i.e.* blunt and cut off square, thus forming a right angle with the upper line of the face. Of great depth from the point of the nose to underjaw. Underjaw broad to the end and slightly rounded. Canine teeth healthy, powerful and wide apart. Scissors bite preferred but a moderately undershot jaw permissible providing the teeth are not visible when the mouth is closed. Lips diverging at obtuse angles with the septum and sufficiently pendulous so as to show a modified square profile. Nose broad and always dark in color, the blacker the better, with spread flat nostrils (not pointed or turned up) in profile. Muzzle dark in color, the blacker the better. Muzzle should be half the length of the skull, thus dividing the head into three parts—one for the foreface and two for the skull. In other words, the distance from tip of nose to stop is equal to one-half the distance between the stop and the occiput. Circumference of muzzle (measured midway between the eyes and nose) to that of the head (measured before the ears) as 3 is to 5.

Neck—Powerful and very muscular, slightly arched, and of medium length. The neck gradually increases in circumference as it approaches the shoulder. Neck moderately "dry" (not showing an excess of loose skin).

360

Chest and Flanks—Wide, deep, rounded and well let down between the forelegs, extending at least to the elbow. Forechest should be deep and well defined. Ribs extremely well rounded. False ribs deep and well set back. There should be a reasonable, but not exaggerated, cuf-up.

Shoulder and Arm—Slightly sloping, heavy and muscular. No tendency to looseness of shoulders.

Forelegs and Feet—Legs straight, strong and set wide apart, heavy-boned. Elbows parallel to body. Feet heavy, round and compact with well-arched toes. Pasterns strong and bent only slightly. Black nails preferred.

Hind Legs—Hindquarters broad, wide and muscular. Second thighs well developed, hocks set back, wide apart and parallel when viewed from the rear.

Back and Loins—Back muscular, powerful and straight. Loins wide and muscular, slightly rounded over the rump.

Tail—Set on moderately high and reaching to the hocks or a little below. Wide at the root, tapering to the end, hanging straight in repose, forming a slight curve but never over the back when dog is in action.

Coat—Outer coat moderately coarse. Undercoat, dense, short and close lying.

Color—Apricot, silver fawn or dark fawn-brindle. Fawn-brindle should have fawn as a background color which should be completely covered with very dark stripes. In any case muzzle, ears and nose must be dark in color, the blacker the better, with similar color tone around the orbits, extending upwards between them.

Size—Dogs, minimum, 30 inches at the shoulder; bitches, minimum, $27\frac{1}{2}$ inches at the shoulder.

SCALE OF POINTS

General character and symmetry 10	Chest and ribs 10
Height and substance 10	Forelegs and feet 10
Skull 10	Back, loins and flanks 10
Face and muzzle 12	Hind legs and feet 10
Ears 5	Tail 3
Eyes 5	Coat and color 5
	TOTAL 100

Approved July 8, 1941

Newfoundland

THERE IS much uncertainty about the origin of the Newfoundland. Some say that his ancestors are the white Great Pyrenees, dogs brought to the coast of Newfoundland by the Basque fishermen; others that he descended from a "French hound" (probably the Boarhound); but all agree that he originated in Newfoundland and that his ancestors were undoubtedly brought there by fishermen from the European Continent. Many old prints of Newfoundlands show apparent evidence of a Husky ancestor, while other traits can be traced to other breeds. At any rate, a dog evolved which was particularly suited to the island of his origin.

He was a large dog, with size and strength to perform the tasks required of him. He had a heavy coat to protect him from the long winters and the icy waters surrounding his native island. His feet were large, strong, and webbed so that he might travel easily over marshes and shores. Admired for his physical powers and attractive disposition, he was taken to England where he was extensively bred until most of the Newfoundlands of pedigree, even in Newfoundland, today are descended from forebears born in England.

At the present time, the Newfoundland is admired and bred in many different countries including, besides his native land, England, France, Holland, Germany, Switzerland, Italy, Canada, and the United States.

The breed standard was written for a working dog, essentially a dog as much at home in the water as on dry land. Canine literature gives us stories of brave Newfoundlands which have rescued men and women from watery graves; stories of shipwrecks made less terrible by dogs which carried life lines to stricken vessels; of children who have fallen into deep water and have been brought safely ashore by Newfoundlands; and of dogs whose work was less spectacular but equally valuable as they helped their fishermen owners with their heavy nets and performed other tasks necessary to their occupations. Although he is a superior water dog, the Newfoundland has been used and is still used in Newfoundland and Labrador as a true working dog, dragging carts, or more often carrying burdens as a pack horse.

In order to perform these duties the Newfoundland must be a large dog—large enough to bring ashore a drowning man. He must have powerful hindquarters and a lung capacity which enables him to swim for great distances. He must have the heavy coat which protects him from the icy waters. In short, he must be strong, muscular, and sound so that he may do the work for which he has become justly famous. Above all things, the Newfoundland must have the intelligence, the loyalty, and the sweetness which are his best-known traits. He must be able and willing to help his master perform his necessary tasks at command, and also have the intelligence to act on his own responsibility when his rescue work demands it.

In this country, where the Newfoundland is kept, not as an active worker, but as a companion, guard, and friend, we appreciate particularly the sterling traits of the true Newfoundland disposition. Here we have the great size and strength which makes him an effective guard and watchdog combined with the gentleness which makes him a safe companion. For generations he has been the traditional children's protector and playmate. He is not easily hurt by small tugging fingers (as is a smaller dog) and he seems to undertake the duties of nursemaid of his own accord without training. We know of no better description of the character of the Newfoundland dog than the famous epitaph which reads:

Near this Spot
are deposited the Remains of one
who possessed Beauty without Vanity,
Strength without Insolence,
Courage without Ferocity,
and all the Virtues of Man without his Vices.

363

This Praise, which would be unmeaning Flattery
if inscribed over human Ashes,
is but a just tribute to the Memory of
BOATSWAIN, a DOG,
who was born in Newfoundland May 1803
and died at Newstead Nov. 18th, 1808.

Official Standard for the Newfoundland

General Appearance—The Newfoundland is large, strong, and active, at home in water and on land, and has natural life-saving instincts. He is a multipurpose dog capable of heavy work as well as of being a devoted companion for child and man. To fulfill its purposes the Newfoundland is deep bodied, well muscled, and well coordinated. A good specimen of the breed has dignity and proud head carriage. The length of the dog's body, from withers to base of tail, is approximately equal to the height of the dog at the withers. However, a bitch is not to be faulted if the length of her body is slightly greater than her height. The dog's appearance is more massive throughout than the bitch's, with larger frame and heavier bone. The Newfoundland is free moving with a loosely slung body. When he moves, a slight roll is perceptible. Complete webbing between the toes is always present. Large size is desirable but never at the expense of gait, symmetry, balance, or conformation to the Standard herein described.

Head—The head is massive with a broad skull, slightly arched crown, and strongly developed occipital bone. The slope from the top of the skull to the tip of the muzzle has a definite but not steep stop. The forehead and face is smooth and free of wrinkles; the muzzle is clean cut and covered with short, fine hair. The muzzle is square, deep, and fairly short; its length from stop to tip of nose is less than from stop to occiput. The nostrils are well developed. The bitch's head follows the same general conformation as the dog's but is feminine and less massive. A narrow head and a snipy or long muzzle are to be faulted.

The eyes are dark brown, relatively small, and deep-set; they are spaced wide apart and have no haw showing. Round, protruding, or yellow eyes are objectionable.

The ears are relatively small and triangular with rounded tips. They are set well back on the skull and lie close to the head. When the ear is brought forward it reaches to the inner corner of the eye on the same side.

The teeth meet in a scissors or level bite.

The Newfoundland's expression is soft and reflects the character of the breed; benevolent, intelligent, dignified, and of sweet disposition. The dog never looks or acts either dull or ill-tempered.

Neck—The neck is strong and well set on the shoulders. It is long enough for proud head carriage.

Body—The Newfoundland's chest is full and deep with the brisket reaching at least down to the elbows. The back is broad, and the topline is level from the withers to the croup, never roached, slack, or swayed. He is broad at the croup, is well muscled, and has very strong loins. The croup slopes at an angle of about 30 degrees. Bone structure is massive throughout but does not give a heavy, sluggish appearance.

Forequarters—When the dog is not in motion, the forelegs are perfectly straight and parallel with the elbows close to the chest. The layback of the shoulders is about 45 degrees, and the upper arm meets the shoulder blade at an angle of about 90 degrees. The shoulders are well muscled. The pasterns are slightly sloping.

Hindquarters—Because driving power for swimming, pulling loads, or covering ground efficiently is dependent on the hindquarters, the rear assembly of the Newfoundland is of prime importance. It is well muscled, the thighs are fairly long, the stifles well bent, and the hocks wide and straight. Cowhocks, barrel legs, or pigeon toes are to be seriously faulted.

Feet—The feet are proportionate to the body in size, cat-foot in type, well-rounded and tight with firm, arched toes, and with webbing present. Dewclaws on the rear legs are to be removed.

Tail—The tail of the Newfoundland acts as a rudder when he is swimming. Therefore, it is broad and strong at the base. The tail reaches down a little below the hocks. When the dog is standing the tail hangs straight down, possibly a little bent at the tip; when the dog is in motion or excited, the tail is carried straight out or slightly curved, but it never curls over the back. A tail with a kink is a serious fault.

Gait—The Newfoundland in motion gives the impression of effortless power, has good reach, and strong drive. A dog may appear symmetrical and well balanced when standing, but, if he is not structurally sound, he will lose that symmetry and balance when he moves. In motion, the legs move straight forward; they do not swing in an arc nor do the hocks move in or out in relation to the line of travel. A slight roll is present. As the dog's speed increases from a walk to a trot, the feet move in under the center line of the body to maintain balance. Mincing, shuffling, crabbing, too close moving, weaving, hackney action, and pacing are all faults.

Size—The average height for dogs is 28 inches, for bitches 26 inches. The average weight for dogs is 150 pounds, for bitches 120 pounds. Large size is desirable but is not to be favored over correct gait, symmetry, and structure.

Coat—The Newfoundland has a water-resistant double coat. The outer coat is moderately long and full but not shaggy. It is straight and flat with no curl, although it may have a slight wave. The coat, when rubbed the wrong way, tends to fall back into place. The undercoat, which is soft and dense, is often less dense during summer months or in tropical climates but is always found to some extent on the rump and chest. An open coat is to be seriously faulted. The hair on the head, muzzle, and ears is short and fine, and the legs are feathered all the way down. The tail is covered with long dense hair, but it does not form a flag.

Color—*Black*—A slight tinge of bronze or a splash of white on chest and toes is not objectionable. Black dogs that have only white toes and white chest and white tip to tail should be exhibited in the classes provided for "black."

***Other than black*—**Should in all respects follow the black except in color, which may be almost any, so long as it disqualifies for the black class, but the colors most to be encouraged are bronze or white and black (Landseer) with black head marked with narrow blaze, even marked saddle and black rump extending on to tail. Beauty in markings to be taken greatly into consideration.

DISQUALIFICATIONS

Markings other than white on a solid-colored dog.

Approved June 9, 1970

Old English Sheepdog

WHILE as compared with some other kinds of dogs the Old English Sheepdog cannot boast the same antiquity, there is nevertheless ample evidence that it can trace its origin to the early nineteenth century or at least 150 years back, thus proving that among recognized breeds it is no mere upstart. As to its real origin, there are conflicting ideas based on premises obscured by the passage of time. A painting by Gainsborough of a Duke of Buccleuch, from which engravings were struck off in 1771, shows the peer with his arms clasped about the neck of what appears to be a fairly good specimen of present-day Old English Sheepdog. This is the earliest picture known that in any manner depicts the breed. What, however, the pictured dog was supposed to be at that period is not certain.

In all probability the breed was first developed in the west of England, in the counties of Devon and Somerset and the Duchy of Cornwall, although from what breeds it was produced is a matter of conjecture. Some maintain that the Scotch Bearded Collie had a large part in its making; others claim for one of its progenitors the Russian Owtchar.

At all events, in the beginning of the eighteenth century, we read of a "drover's dog" which was used largely for driving sheep and cattle into the markets of the metropolis. These drover's dogs were exempt from taxes and, to prove their occupation, they were docked. Some believe that the nicknames "bob" and "bobtail" trace to this custom. It is not true, of course, that the practice of removing the tail has produced a breed naturally bobtailed or tailless. In fact, few specimens of the breed are whelped without tails, or with tails long or comparatively short. According to the Standard, the tail should be removed at the first joint, when the puppy is three or four days old, and it should never be longer than one and one-half or two inches in length at maturity. Seldom is an Old English Sheepdog seen in the show ring today with more than a mere thickening of the skin where the tail has been removed. Since this dog has been used more for driving than for herding, the lack of a tail to serve as a rudder, so to speak, has in no wise affected its working ability with heavier kinds of sheep and cattle.

For years after the breed's introduction into this country, fanciers did considerable harm by misinterpreting "profuseness" of coat as "excessiveness." This misled the public into believing that the Old English Sheepdog was difficult to care for, when as a matter of fact a dog with typical coat of the right texture is no harder to keep in shape than is any other longhaired dog. Furthermore, it is homeloving, not given to roaming and fighting, and it is extremely agile; because of its intelligence, affection, and lack of boisterousness, it makes an ideal house dog. It has a tender mouth and can be trained as a retriever; it makes a first-class sledge dog, and is satisfactory as a companion equally at home in apartment, large house, drawing room, and practically anywhere else.

In seeking a good representative of the breed, points to look for include a body practically square; good bone, deep brisket, chest, and spring of rib; strong foreface, dark or walleyes, level teeth; straight forelegs, well-let-down hocks; and a hard coat with good underjacket. Markings are not important. The dogs do well under almost any climatic conditions, their coats serving as insulation against heat, cold, and dampness. A marked characteristic of the breed is its gait, which is quite like the shuffle of a bear.

Official Standard for the
Old English Sheepdog

Skull—Capacious and rather squarely formed, giving plenty of room for brain power. The parts over the eyes should be well arched and the whole well covered with hair. **Jaw**—Fairly long, strong, square and truncated. The stop should be well defined to avoid a Deerhound face. (The attention of judges is particularly called to the above properties, as a long, narrow head is a deformity.) **Eyes**—Vary according to the color of the dog. Very dark preferred, but in the glaucous or blue dogs a pearl, walleye or china eye is considered typical. (A light eye is most objectionable.) **Nose**—Always black, large and capacious. **Teeth**—Strong and large, evenly placed and level in opposition. **Ears**—Medium-sized, and carried flat to side of head, coated moderately.

Legs—The forelegs should be dead straight, with plenty of bone, removing the body a medium height from the ground, without approaching legginess, and well coated all around. **Feet**—Small, round; toes well arched, and pads thick and hard.

Tail—It is preferable that there should be none. Should never, however, exceed 1½ or 2 inches in grown dogs. When not natural-born bobtails however, puppies should be docked at the first joint from the body and the operation performed when they are from three to four days old.

Neck and Shoulders—The neck should be fairly long, arched gracefully and well coated with hair. The shoulders sloping and narrow at the points, the dog standing lower at the shoulder than at the loin.

Body—Rather short and very compact, ribs well sprung and brisket deep and capacious. *Slabsidedness highly undesirable.* The loin should be very stout and gently arched, while the hindquarters should be round and muscular and with well-let-down hocks, and the hams densely coated with a thick, long jacket in excess of any other part.

Coat—Profuse, but not so excessive as to give the impression of the dog being overfat, and of a good hard texture; not straight, but shaggy and free from curl. *Quality and texture of coat to be considered above mere profuseness.* Softness or flatness of coat to be considered a fault. The undercoat should be a waterproof pile, when not removed by grooming or season.

Color—Any shade of gray, grizzle, blue or blue-merled with or without white markings or in reverse. *Any shade of brown or fawn to be considered distinctly objectionable and not to be encouraged.*

Size—Twenty-two inches and upwards for dogs and slightly less for bitches. Type, character and symmetry are of the greatest importance and are on no account to be sacrificed to size alone.

General Appearance and Characteristics—A strong, compact-looking dog of great symmetry, practically the same in measurement from shoulder to stern as in height, absolutely free from legginess or weaselness, very elastic in his gallop, but in walking or trotting he has a characteristic ambling or pacing movement, and his bark should be loud, with a peculiar "pot-casse" ring in it. Taking him all round, he is a profusely, but not *excessively* coated, thick-set, muscular, able-bodied dog with a most intelligent expression, free from all Poodle or Deerhound character. *Soundness should be considered of greatest importance.*

SCALE OF POINTS

Skull	5	Body and loins	10
Eyes	5	Hindquarters	10
Ears	5	Legs	10
Teeth	5	Coat (texture, quality and	
Nose	5	condition)	15
Jaw	5	General appearance and	
Foreface	5	movement	15
Neck and shoulders	5	TOTAL	100

Approved October 13, 1953

Puli
(Poo-lee)

THE PULI (plural Pulik), or driver, has been an integral part of the lives of Hungarian shepherds for more than 1000 years. When the Magyars came into Hungary they brought their sheepdogs with them. There were larger kinds similar to the Komondor and the Kuvasz, and a smaller kind which resembled the Puli. Except in color, the Puli was quite similar to the Tibetan Terrier, which may well have been its foundation stock.

Color and size both played a part in the development of Hungary's sheepdogs, each for its particular type of work. The more easily seen, lighter-colored kinds guarded herds and flocks from robbers and wild animals at night, while the smaller, darker-colored Puli was used to drive and herd the sheep during the day. There was ample reason for this, since sheep take direction more certainly from dark dogs than from light-colored ones. Moreover the dark dog was more distinctive to the shepherd's eye, as it worked among the flocks rounding them up and even, so it is claimed, jumping on them or running over their backs to cut off or turn back a runaway.

The dark color has always been recognized as truly characteristic of the Puli. Ordinarily it is called black, but it is a black so unlike that of any other breed as to warrant explanation. It is dull; in some cases bronze-tinged, in others just barely grayed like a weather-worn old coat faded by the sun. An out-of-door life on the hillside, in all weathers but particularly under a constant and glaring sun, robbed the black of its intensity and its sheen. This was the black prized as typical of the breed in its homeland. There are, in addition, Pulik both gray and white. Any shade of gray is allowed so long as it is solid gray. The Puli is first and last a solid-colored dog. There may be some intermixture of hair of different colors usually present in the grays, and this is acceptable if the general appearance of solid color is maintained.

The Puli coat, too, is unique. There is nothing exactly like it in all dogdom. The undercoat is soft, woolly, very dense; the outer coat long and profuse. The puppy coat is tufted, but with growth the undercoat tangles with the top coat in such a manner as to form long cords. This matting and cording is the natural protector of the working Puli, with the over-all effect, as in other Hungarian sheepdogs, best described as unkempt.

Of course in this country more dogs are kept as guards, watchdogs, and companions than as sheepherders, hence we may find the groomed coat preferred to the uniquely corded coat which is the Puli's rightful heritage. But whatever the style of his hair, the Puli's vigor, versatility, and intelligence fit him as well for the home as for the hills.

He is a medium-sized dog averaging seventeen inches height and thirty pounds or so weight, and so striking in appearance that it would be impossible to confuse him with any other kind of dog. His shaggy hair covers his head like an umbrella, and falls all over his body to the very tip of his upcurled tail in such profusion that he seems larger than he actually is. He is keen and quick, and he moves with a gait as springy, almost, as a bouncing ball, this trait a hand-me-down, perhaps, from those dogs of long ago whose dazzling footwork was the admiration of the shepherd boy with his sheep.

Official Standard for the Puli

General Appearance—A dog of medium size, vigorous, alert, and extremely active. By nature affectionate, he is a devoted and home-loving companion, sensibly suspicious of strangers and therefore an excellent guard. Striking and highly characteristic is the shaggy coat which centuries ago fitted him for the strenuous work of herding the flocks on the plains of Hungary.

Head—Of medium size, in proportion to the body. The skull is slightly domed and not too broad. **Stop**—clearly defined but not abrupt, neither dished nor downfaced, with a strong muzzle of medium length ending in a nose of good size. **Teeth** are strong and comparatively large, and the bite may be either level or scissors. Flews tight. **Ears**—Hanging and set fairly high, medium size, and V-shaped. **Eyes**—Deep-set and rather large, should be dark brown, but lighter color is not a serious fault.

Neck and Shoulders—Neck strong and muscular, of medium length, and free of throatiness. Shoulders clean-cut and sloping, with elbows close.

Body—The chest is deep and fairly broad with ribs well sprung. Back of medium length, straight and level, the rump sloping moderately. Fairly broad across the loins and well tucked up.

Tail—Occasionally born bobtail, which is acceptable, but never cut. The tail is carried curled over the back when alert, carried low with the end curled up when at rest.

Legs and Feet—Forelegs straight, strong, and well boned. Feet round and compact with thick-cushioned pads and strong nails. Hindquarters well developed, moderately broad through the stifle which is well bent and muscular. Dewclaws, if any, may be removed from both forelegs and hind legs.

372

Puli (Groomed coat)

Puli (Corded coat)

Coat—Characteristic of the breed is the dense, weather-resisting double coat. The outer coat, long and of medium texture, is never silky. It may be straight, wavy, or slightly curly, the more curly coat appearing to be somewhat shorter. The undercoat is soft, woolly, and dense. The coat mats easily, the hair tending to cling together in bunches, giving a somewhat corded appearance even when groomed. The hair is profuse on the head, ears, face, stifles, and tail, and the feet are well haired between the toes. Usually shown combed, but may also be shown uncombed with the coat hanging in tight, even cords.

Color—Solid colors, black, rusty-black, various shades of gray, and white. The black usually appears weathered and rusty or slightly gray. The inter-mixture of hair of different colors is acceptable and is usually present in the grays, but must be uniform throughout the coat so that the over-all appearance of a solid color is maintained. Nose, flews, and eyelids are black.

Height—Males about 17 inches, and should not exceed 19 inches. Females about 16 inches, and should not exceed 18 inches.

Serious Faults—Overshot or undershot. Lack of undercoat, short or sparse coat. White markings such as white paws or spot on chest. Flesh color on nose, flews, or eyelids. Coat with areas of two or more colors at the skin.

Approved April 12, 1960

Rottweiler
(Rott-why-lurr)

THE ORIGIN of the Rottweiler is not a documented record. Once this is recognized, actual history tempered by reasonable supposition indicates the likelihood he is descended from one of the drover dogs indigenous to Ancient Rome. This drover dog has been described by various accredited sources to have been of the Mastiff type, possessing great intelligence, dependable, rugged, willing to work and with a strong guarding instinct.

The transition from Roman herding dog to the dog we know today as the Rottweiler can be attributed to the ambitions of the Roman Emperors to conquer Europe. Very large armies were required for these expeditions and the logistics of feeding that number of men became a major consideration. No means of refrigeration existed which meant the meat for the soldiers accompanied the troops "on the hoof." Understandably, the services of a dog capable of keeping the herd intact during the long march were needed. The above described "Mastiff type" was admirably suited to both that job and the additional responsibility of guarding the supply dumps at night.

Campaigns of the Roman Army varied in scope, but the one concerning us took place approximately 74 A.D. Its route was across the Alps terminating in what is now Southern Germany. Arae Flaviae, as the new territory was called, had natural advantages of climate, soil and central location. There is much evidence pointing to the vital role of the fearless Roman drover dog on this trek from Rome to the banks of the Neckar River.

We have no reason to doubt that descendants of the original Roman drover dogs continued to guard the herds through the next two centuries. Circa 260 A.D. the Swabians ousted the Romans from Arae Flaviae, taking over the city. Agriculture and the trading of cattle remained their prime occupations, insuring the further need for the dogs.

About 700 A.D. the local Duke ordered a Christian church built on the site of the former Roman Baths. Excavations unearthed the red tiles of Roman villas. To distinguish the town from others, it was then named "das Rote Wil" (the red tile), which of course is recognizable as the derivation of the present Rottweil.

Rottweil's dominance as a cultural and trade center increased unabated and in the middle of the 12th Century further fame and fortune came to it. An all new town with elaborate fortification was built on the heights above the river. The security, thus provided, attracted yet increased commerce in cattle. Butchers concentrated in the area and inevitably more dogs were needed to drive the cattle to and from the markets.

The descendants of the Roman drover dog plied their trade without interruption until the middle of the 19th Century at which time the driving of cattle was outlawed. In addition the donkey and the railroad replaced the dog cart.

The Rottweiler Metzgerhund (butcher dog) as he came to be called then fell on hard times. His function had been severely curtailed and in those days, dogs earned their keep or there was no reason for their existence. The number of Rottweilers declined so radically that in 1882 the dog show in Heilbronn, Germany reported one poor example of the breed present.

The annals of cynology make no further mention of the breed until 1901 when a combined Rottweiler and Leonberger Club was formed. This Club was short lived but notable because the first Rottweiler standard appeared under its auspices. It is of value for us to know that the general type advocated has not changed substantially and the character called for, not at all.

In these years (1901 - 1907) the Rottweiler again found favor as a police dog. Several clubs were organized as dissension was most common until 1921 when it was agreed to form the *Allgemeiner*

Deutscher Rottweiler Klub (ADRK). By that time 3400 Rottweilers had been registered by three or four clubs. Duplications and confusion ended when the ADRK published its first stud book in 1924.

Since its inception, despite the difficulties encountered during and in the aftermath of World War II, the ADRK remained intact and through its leadership enlightened, purposeful breeding programs have been promoted both in Germany and abroad.

The first Rottweiler was admitted to the American Kennel Club Stud Book in 1931. The standard was adopted in 1935. The first obedience title awarded an American Rottweiler was in 1939 and the first championship nine years later in 1948.

There are at this writing in 1978 three Rottweiler Clubs across the United States eligible to hold a Specialty Show. Two of the three are qualified to hold Obedience Trials.

Perhaps he has departed physically from his Roman ancestor, but assuredly the characteristics for which he was so admired in Roman times have been preserved and are the very attributes for which the Rottweiler is held in such high esteem today.

Official Standard for the Rottweiler

General Appearance and Character—The Rottweiler is a good-sized, strongly built, active dog. He is affectionate, intelligent, easily trained to work, naturally obedient and extremely faithful. While not quarrelsome, he possesses great courage and makes a splendid guard. His demeanor is dignified and he is not excitable.

Head—Is of medium length, the skull broad between the ears. Stop well pronounced as is also the occiput. Muzzle is not very long. It should not be longer than the distance from the stop to the occiput. Nose is well developed, with relatively large nostrils and is always black. Flews which should not be too pronounced are also black. Jaws should be strong and muscular; teeth strong—incisors of lower jaw must touch the inner surface of the upper incisors. Eyes are of medium size, dark brown in color and should express faithfulness, good humor and confidence. The ears are comparatively small, set high and wide and hang over about on a level with top of head. The skin on head should not be loose. The neck should be of fair length, strong, round and very muscular, slightly arched and free from throatiness.

Forequarters—Shoulders should be well placed, long and sloping, elbows well let down, but not loose. Legs muscular and with plenty of bone and substance, pasterns straight and strong. Feet strong, round and close, with toes well arched. Soles very hard, toe nails dark, short and strong.

Body—The chest is roomy, broad and deep. Ribs well sprung. Back straight, strong and rather short. Loins strong and deep, and flanks should not be tucked up. Croup short, broad, but not sloping.

Hindquarters—Upper thigh is short, broad and very muscular. Lower thigh very muscular at top and strong and sinewy at the bottom. Stifles fairly well bent, hocks strong. The hind feet are somewhat longer than the front ones, but should be close and strong with toes well arched. There should be no dewclaws.

Tail—Should be short, placed high (on level with back) and carried horizontally. Dogs are frequently born with a short stump tail and when tail is too long it must be docked close to body.

Coat—Hair should be short, coarse and flat. The undercoat which is absolutely required on neck and thighs should not show through outer coat. The hair should be a little longer on the back of front and hind legs and on tail.

Color—Black, with clearly defined markings on cheeks, muzzle, chest and legs, as well as over both eyes. Color of markings: tan to mahogany brown. A small spot of white on chest and belly is permissible but not desirable.

Height—Shoulder height for males is $23^3/_4$ to 27 inches, for females, $21^3/_4$ to $25^3/_4$ inches, but height should always be considered in relation to the general appearance and conformation of the dog.

FAULTS

Too lightly built or too heavily built. Swayback. Roach back. Too long body. Lack of spring of ribs. Head too long and narrow, or too short and plump. Lack of occiput, snipy muzzle, cheekiness, top line of muzzle not straight. Light or flesh-colored nose. Hanging flews. Overshot or undershot. Loose skin on head. Ears set too low, or ears too heavy. Long or narrow or rose ear, or ears uneven in size. Light, small or slanting eyes, or lack of expression. Neck too long, thin or weak, or very noticeable throatiness. Lack of bone and muscle. Short or straight shoulders. Front legs too close together or not straight. Weak pasterns. Splay feet, light nails, weak toes. Flat ribs. Sloping croup. Too heavy or plump body. Flanks drawn up. Flat thighs. Cowhocks or weak hocks. Dewclaws. Tail set too high or too low, or that is too long or too thin. Soft, too short, too long or too open coat. Wavy coat or lack of undercoat. White markings on toes, legs, or other parts of body. Markings not too well defined or smudgy. The one-color tan Rottweiler with either black or light mask, or with black streak on back as well as other colors such as brown or blue, are not recognized and are believed to be crossbred, as is also a longhaired Rottweiler. Timid or stupid-appearing animals are to be positively rejected.

Approved April 9, 1935

Saint Bernard

SHROUDED IN LEGEND and the mists of time, the origin of the Saint Bernard is subject to many theories.

It seems most probable that the Saint Bernard developed from stock that resulted from the breeding of heavy Asian "Molosser" (*Canis molossus*), brought to Helvetia (Switzerland) by Roman armies during the first two centuries A.D., with native dogs which undoubtedly existed in the region at the time of the Roman invasions.

During the following centuries, these dogs were widely used in the valley farms and Alpine dairies for a variety of guarding, herding, and drafting duties. Referred to as *Talhund* (Valley Dog) or *Bauernhund* (Farm Dog), they were apparently well established by 1050 A.D., when Archdeacon Bernard de Menthon founded the famous Hospice in the Swiss Alps as a refuge for travelers crossing the treacherous passes between Switzerland and Italy.

Just when dogs were first brought to the Hospice is debatable, since the Hospice was destroyed by fire in the late sixteenth century, and, soon after, a large part of the Hospice archives were lost. Apparently, the Hospice was still without dogs during the first part of the sixteenth century. Earlier records mention nothing about such animals.

The first notation concerning the dogs was not until 1707. This, however, was merely a casual reference to dogs at the Hospice and carried the implication that their rescue work at the St. Bernard Pass was a fact well known at the time. From a digest of early references, it appears that the dogs were first brought to the Hospice sometime between 1660 and 1670. It is likely that large dogs were recruited from the valley areas below to serve as watchdogs for the Hospice and companions for the Monks during the long winter months when the Hospice was almost completely isolated.

This isolation of the Hospice no doubt resulted in inbreeding of the original stock which soon produced the distinctive strain of "Hospice Dog". It also follows that only those animals with the strongest instincts for survival in the extremely adverse conditions at the Hospice were to leave their genetic imprint upon the breed during those early years.

The lonely Monks, who took the dogs along on their trips of mercy, soon discovered the animals were excellent pathfinders in the drifting snow, and the dogs' highly developed sense of smell made them invaluable in locating helpless persons overcome during storms. Thus began this working together of Monk and dog which made many of the world's most romantic pages of canine history.

379

St. Bernard (Longhaired)

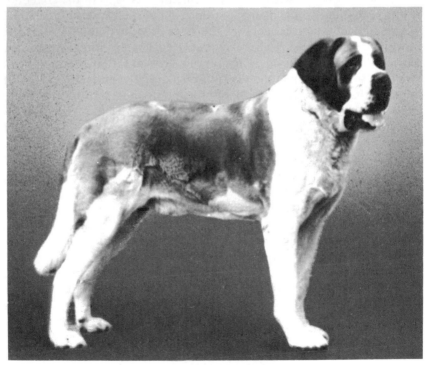

St. Bernard (Shorthaired)

380

During the three centuries that Saint Bernards have been used in rescue work at the Hospice, it is estimated that they have been responsible for the saving of well over 2,000 human lives. Although the building of railroad tunnels through the Alps has lessened foot and vehicular travel across the St. Bernard Pass, the Monks have continued to maintain these fine dogs for companionship and in honor of the Hospice tradition.

We are told that Saint Bernards required no training for their work since generations of service in this capacity seemed to have stamped the rescuing instinct indelibly upon their character. It would be more accurate to say that the dogs' rescue instincts were used as the basis for training by the Monks. In the company of the Monks, young dogs were taken on patrols with a pack of older dogs in search of possible traveler casualties. When the dogs came upon a victim, they would lie down beside him to provide warmth for their bodies, and lick the person's face to restore consciousness. In the meantime, one of the patrol dogs would be on his way back to the Hospice to give the alarm and guide a rescue party to the scene.

In addition to their pathfinding capabilities and keen sense of smell which enables them to locate human beings buried under the snow, the dogs are reputed to possess an uncanny sixth sense which warns them of approaching avalanches. Instances have been reported where a dog would suddenly change position for no apparent reason a few seconds before an avalanche came hurtling down across the spot where he had stood, burying it under tons of snow and ice.

Although it was well known that a special type of dog did rescue work at the Hospice by 1800, the breed at that time had been given no name other than "Hospice Dogs". Between 1800 and 1810, Barry, perhaps the most celebrated dog in history, lived at the Hospice. For fully half a century after his death, the Hospice dogs in certain parts of Switzerland were called "Barryhund" (Barry dog) in his honor.

Barry is credited with saving forty lives. Although legend has it that he was killed by the forty-first person he attempted to rescue, who mistook his bulk for that of a wolf, this tale is only an interesting story. As a matter of fact, Barry was given a painless death in Berne, Switzerland, in 1814, after he had attained a ripe old age. His likeness in mounted form is now preserved in the Natural History Museum in Berne.

The years 1816 to 1818 were seasons of uncommonly severe weather at the Hospice, and, as a result, many of the leading Hospice strains perished. It was easy at that time, however, to get good animals of like breeding from the lower valleys, and within a few years, the dog situation at the Hospice was again satisfactory.

Confronted by a similar situation in 1830, coupled with the fact that their breed was considerably weakened by inbreeding and disease, the Monks resorted to an outcross to give added size and new vigor to their dogs. The Newfoundland, which at that time was larger than the Saint Bernard and shared strong rescuing instincts, was the breed decided upon to give the new blood. Results of this crossing showed all of the desired objectives and, at the same time, did not destroy the Saint Bernard type and characteristics. Due to this crossing, however, the first longhaired Saint Bernards appeared—prior to 1830, all the Saint Bernards were shorthaired dogs.

At first it was believed that the longhaired variety might have an advantage in the snow and icy conditions existing at the Hospice. Unfortunately, ice clung to the coat and made the longhaired dogs unsuited to the tasks of the rescue dogs. After this was determined, the Monks gave the longhaired dogs as gifts to friends and benefactors in the valley areas, and only the shorthaired dogs were kept at the Hospice.

The English, who as early as 1810, imported some of the Hospice dogs to replenish their Mastiff blood, referred to the breed for a number of years as "Sacred Dogs". In Germany, around 1828, the name of "Alpendog" was proposed. In 1833, a writer, Daniel Wilson, first spoke of the so-called Saint Bernard dog, but it was not until 1865 that this name definitely appeared, and only since 1880 has it been recognized as the official designation for the breed.

During the last half of the 1800s, breeding of both the longhaired and shorthaired Saint Bernards continued in the valleys of Switzerland, and eventually the breed spread across Germany and other continental European countries and England.

In 1887, an International Congress was held in Zurich which was guided by Swiss authorities on the breed. At this Congress, an International Standard for the perfection of the breed was developed.

The Saint Bernard Club of America was organized in 1888, the year following the Zurich Congress, and the International Standard was adopted by it. This club continues to function for the interests of the Saint Bernard and is one of the oldest specialty clubs in the United States.

Official Standard for the
Saint Bernard

SHORTHAIRED

General—Powerful, proportionately tall figure, strong and muscular in every part, with powerful head and most intelligent expression. In dogs with a dark mask the expression appears more stern, but never ill-natured.

Head—Like the whole body, very powerful and imposing. The massive skull is wide, slightly arched and the sides slope in a gentle curve into the very strongly developed, high cheek bones. Occiput only moderately developed. The supra-orbital ridge is very strongly developed and forms nearly a right angle with the horizontal axis of the head. Deeply imbedded between the eyes and starting at the root of the muzzle, a furrow runs over the whole skull. It is strongly marked in the first half, gradually disappearing toward the base of the occiput. The lines at the sides of the head diverge considerably from the outer corner of the eyes toward the back of the head. The skin of the forehead, above the eyes, forms rather noticeable wrinkles, more or less pronounced, which converge toward the furrow. Especially when the dog is in action, the wrinkles are more visible without in the least giving the impression of morosity. Too strongly developed wrinkles are not desired. The slope from the skull to the muzzle is sudden and rather steep.

The muzzle is short, does not taper, and the vertical depth at the root of the muzzle must be greater than the length of the muzzle. The bridge of the muzzle is not arched, but straight; in some dogs, occasionally, slightly broken. A rather wide, well-marked, shallow furrow runs from the root of the muzzle over the entire bridge of the muzzle to the nose. The flews of the upper jaw are strongly developed, not sharply cut, but turning in a beautiful curve into the lower edge, and slightly overhanging. The flews of the lower jaw must not be deeply pendant. The teeth should be sound and strong and should meet in either a scissors or an even bite; the scissors bite being preferable. The undershot bite, although sometimes found with good specimens, is not desirable. The overshot bite is a fault. A black roof to the mouth is desirable.

Nose (Schwamm)—Very substantial, broad, with wide open nostrils, and, like the lips, always black.

Ears—Of medium size, rather high set, with very strongly developed burr (Muschel) at the base. They stand slightly away from the head at the base, then drop with a sharp bend to the side and cling to the head without a turn. The flap is tender and forms a rounded triangle, slightly elongated toward the point, the front edge lying firmly to the head, whereas the back edge may stand somewhat away from the head, especially when the dog is at attention. Lightly set ears, which at the base immediately cling to the head, give it an oval and too little marked exterior, whereas a strongly developed base gives the skull a squarer, broader and much more expressive appearance.

Eyes—Set more to the front than the sides, are of medium size, dark brown, with intelligent, friendly expression, set moderately deep. The lower eyelids, as a rule, do not close completely and, if that is the case, form an angular wrinkle toward the inner corner of the eye. Eyelids which are too deeply pendant and show conspicuously the lachrymal glands, or a very red, thick haw, and eyes that are too light, are objectionable.

Neck—Set high, very strong and in action is carried erect. Otherwise horizontally or slightly downward. The junction of head and neck is distinctly marked by an indentation. The nape of the neck is very muscular and rounded at the sides which makes the neck appear rather short. The dewlap of throat and neck is well pronounced: too strong development, however, is not desirable.

Shoulders—Sloping and broad, very muscular and powerful. The withers are strongly pronounced.

Chest—Very well arched, moderately deep, not reaching below the elbows.

Back—Very broad, perfectly straight as far as the haunches, from there gently sloping to the rump, and merging imperceptibly into the root of the tail.

Hindquarters—Well-developed. Legs very muscular.

Belly—Distinctly set off from the very powerful loin section, only little drawn up.

Tail—Starting broad and powerful directly from the rump is long, very heavy, ending in a powerful tip. In repose it hangs straight down, turning gently upward in the lower third only, which is not considered a fault. In a great many specimens the tail is carried with the end slightly bent and therefore hangs down in the shape of an "*f*". In action all dogs carry the tail more or less turned upward. However it may not be carried too erect or by any means rolled over the back. A slight curling of the tip is sooner admissible.

Forearms—Very powerful and extraordinarily muscular.

Forelegs—Straight, strong.

Hind Legs—Hocks of moderate angulation. Dewclaws are not desired; if present, they must not obstruct gait.

Feet—Broad, with strong toes, moderately closed, and with rather high knuckles. The so-called dewclaws which sometimes occur on the inside of the hind legs are imperfectly developed toes. They are of no use to the dog and are not taken into consideration in judging. They may be removed by surgery.

Coat—Very dense, short-haired (stockhaarig), lying smooth, tough, without however feeling rough to the touch. The thighs are slightly bushy. The tail at the root has longer and denser hair which gradually becomes shorter toward the tip. The tail appears bushy, not forming a flag.

Color—White with red or red with white, the red in its various shades; brindle patches with white markings. The colors red and brown-yellow are of entirely equal value. Necessary markings are: white chest, feet and tip of tail, noseband, collar or spot on the nape; the latter and blaze are very desirable. Never of one color or without white. Faulty are all other colors, except the favorite dark shadings on the head (mask) and ears. One distinguishes between mantle dogs and splash-coated dogs.

Height at Shoulder—Of the dog should be 27½ inches minimum, of the bitch 25½ inches. Female animals are of finer and more delicate build.

Considered as faults—are all deviations from the Standard, as for instance a swayback and a disproportionately long back, hocks too much bent, straight hindquarters, upward growing hair in spaces between the toes, out at elbows, cowhocks and weak pasterns.

LONGHAIRED

The longhaired type completely resembles the shorthaired type except for the coat which is not shorthaired (stockhaarig) but of medium length plain to slightly wavy, never rolled or curly and not shaggy either. Usually, on the back, especially from the region of the haunches to the rump, the hair is more wavy, a condition, by the way, that is slightly indicated in the shorthaired dogs. The tail is bushy with dense hair of moderate length. Rolled or curly hair on the tail is not desirable. A tail with parted hair, or a flag tail, is faulty. Face and ears are covered with short and soft hair; longer hair at the base of the ear is permissible. Forelegs only slightly feathered; thighs very bushy.

Approved May 12, 1959

Samoyed

(Sam-a-yed)

DOG OF THE AGES, with a history and tradition as fascinating as the breed itself! The legend runs that, from the plateau of Iran, man's first earthly habitat, as the sons of man multiplied, the mightier tribes drove the lesser ones, with their families, their herds, and their dogs, farther and farther away in order that the natural food found there might be ample for those remaining. Onward and still farther northward through Mongolia, then the center of the world's culture, on and on, went the lesser tribes, until eventually the Samoyed peoples, primitives of the family of Sayantsi, reliably described as a race in the "transition stages between the Mongol pure and the Finn," found themselves safely entrenched behind bulwarks of snow and ice in the vast sketches of tundra reaching from the White Sea to the Yenisei River. Here for generations they have lived a nomadic life, dependent upon their reindeer herd and upon their dogs as reindeer shepherds, sledge dogs, and household companions.

Here, through the centuries, the Samoyed has bred true. Of all modern breeds, the Samoyed is most nearly akin to the primitive dog—

no admixture of wolf or fox runs in the Samoyed strain. The Arctic suns and snows have bleached the harsh stand-off coat and tipped the hairs with an icy sheen. The constant companionship with man through the years has given an almost uncanny "human" understanding, while generations of guarding reindeer, requiring always a protector, never a killer, has developed through the ages in the breed a disposition unique in the canine world. Something of the happy childlike air of these primitive peoples is found as well in every Samoyed.

Nor has the long human association made of the stalwart Samoyed a pampered pet. As work dogs Samoyeds of the great Arctic and Antarctic expeditions have a record of achievement unexcelled in the canine world. The sledge dogs of early polar explorer Fridtjof Nansen (19 males, averaging 58.7 pounds each, and 9 bitches averaging 50.5 pounds), working day after day under conditions of utmost hardship, drew one and a half times their own weight of supplies, and worked with the joyous abandon and carefree air typical of the breed. Each new expedition—Jackson-Harmsworth, the Duc d'Abruzzi, Borch-grevink, Shackleton, Scott, and most notably, Roald Amundsen in his successful reach of the South Pole in 1911—added new luster to the breed's history.

Introduced into England less than a hundred years ago, practically every show sees the Samoyeds in the forefront. Queen Alexandra was an ardent fancier, and the descendants of her dogs are found today in many English and American kennels. The dog is found in every region—Samoyeds born in northern Siberia have safely crossed the equator and remained in healthy condition to work in Antarctic snows. Dogs from Antarctic expeditions have survived the suns of Australia to return to England and start great kennels there.

Beautiful, eye-arresting, perhaps the most beautiful breed in existence; gentle and companionable; an excellent watchdog; never a troublemaker, yet able to hold its own when forced into a fight; with an independence born of unusual intelligence, yet marked with a loyalty to a loved owner which wins hearts; the big, white dog with the "smiling" face and dark, intelligent eyes, and the strong, sturdy muscular body, with legs built for speed—that is the Samoyed.

As puppies, "little white teddy bears," the Samoyed characteristics are strongly shown: guardians always, gentle, kindly, sturdy, adaptable, the "big white dog carries in its face and heart the spirit of Christmas the whole year through."

Official Standard for the
Samoyed

General Conformation:

(a) General Appearance—The Samoyed, being essentially a working dog, should present a picture of beauty, alertness and strength, with agility, dignity and grace. As his work lies in cold climates, his coat should be heavy and weather-resistant, well groomed, and of good quality rather than quantity. The male carries more of a "ruff" than the female. He should not be long in the back as a weak back would make him practically useless for his legitimate work, but at the same time, a close-coupled body would also place him at a great disadvantage as a draft dog. Breeders should aim for the happy medium, a body not long but muscular, allowing liberty, with a deep chest and well-sprung ribs, strong neck, straight front and especially strong loins. Males should be masculine in appearance and deportment without unwarranted aggressiveness; bitches feminine without weakness of structure or apparent softness of temperament. Bitches may be slightly longer in back than males. They should both give the appearance of being capable of great endurance but be free from coarseness. Because of the depth of chest required, the legs should be moderately long. A very short-legged dog is to be deprecated. Hindquarters should be particularly well developed, stifles well bent and any suggestion of unsound stifles or cowhocks severely penalized. General appearance should include movement and general conformation, indicating balance and good substance.

(b) Substance—Substance is that sufficiency of bone and muscle which rounds out a balance with the frame. The bone is heavier than would be expected in a dog of this size but not so massive as to prevent the speed and agility most desirable in a Samoyed. In all builds, bone should be in proportion to body size. The Samoyed should never be so heavy as to appear clumsy nor so light as to appear racy. The weight should be in proportion to the height.

(c) Height—Males—21 to 23½ inches; females—19 to 21 inches at the withers. An oversized or undersized Samoyed is to be penalized according to the extent of the deviation.

(d) Coat (Texture & Condition)—The Samoyed is a double-coated dog. The body should be well covered with an undercoat of soft, short, thick, close wool with longer and harsh hair growing through it to form the outer coat, which stands straight out from the body and should be free from curl. The coat should form a ruff around the neck and shoulders, framing the head (more on males than on females). Quality of coat should be weather resistant and considered more than quantity. A droopy coat is undesirable. The coat should glisten with a silver sheen. The female does not usually carry as long a coat as most males and it is softer in texture.

(e) Color—Samoyeds should be pure white, white and biscuit, cream, or all biscuit. Any other colors disqualify.

Movement:

(a) Gait—The Samoyed should trot, not pace. He should move with a quick agile stride that is well timed. The gait should be free, balanced and vigorous, with good reach in the forequarters and good driving power in the hindquarters. When trotting, there should be a strong rear action drive.

Moving at a slow walk or trot, they will not single-track, but as speed increases the legs gradually angle inward until the pads are finally falling on a line directly under the longitudinal center of the body. As the pad marks converge the forelegs and hind legs are carried straight forward in traveling, the stifles not turned in nor out. The back should remain strong, firm and level. A choppy or stilted gait should be penalized.

(b) Rear End—Upper thighs should be well developed. Stifles well bent—approximately 45 degrees to the ground. Hocks should be well developed, sharply defined and set at approximately 30 per cent of hip height. The hind legs should be parallel when viewed from the rear in a natural stance, strong, well developed, turning neither in nor out. Straight stifles are objectionable. Double-jointedness or cowhocks are a fault. Cowhocks should only be determined if the dog has had an opportunity to move properly.

(c) Front End—Legs should be parallel and straight to the pasterns. The pasterns should be strong, sturdy and straight, but flexible with some spring for proper let-down of feet. Because of depth of chest, legs should be moderately long. Length of leg from the ground to the elbow should be approximately 55 per cent of the total height at the withers—a very short-legged dog is to be deprecated. Shoulders should be long and sloping, with a layback of 45 degrees and be firmly set. Out at the shoulders or out at the elbows should be penalized. The withers separation should be approximately 1–1½ inches.

(d) Feet—Large, long, flattish—a hare-foot, slightly spread but not splayed; toes arched; pads thick and tough, with protective growth of hair between the toes. Feet should turn neither in nor out in a natural stance but may turn in slightly in the act of pulling. Turning out, pigeon-toed, round or cat-footed or splayed are faults. Feathers on feet are not too essential but are more profuse on females than on males.

Head:

(a) Conformation—Skull is wedge-shaped, broad, slightly crowned, not round or apple-headed, and should form an equilateral triangle on lines between the inner base of the ears and the center point of the stop. **Muzzle**— Muzzle of medium length and medium width, neither coarse nor snipy; should taper toward the nose and be in proportion to the size of the dog and the width of skull. The muzzle must have depth. **Stop**—Not too abrupt, nevertheless well defined. **Lips**—Should be black for preference and slightly curved up at the corners of the mouth, giving the "Samoyed smile." Lip lines should not have the appearance of being coarse nor should the flews drop predominately at corners of the mouth.

Ears—Strong and thick, erect, triangular and slightly rounded at the tips; should not be large or pointed, nor should they be small and "bear-eared." Ears should conform to head size and the size of the dog; they should be set well apart but be within the border of the outer edge of the head; they should be mobile and well covered inside with hair; hair full and stand-off before the ears. Length of ear should be the same measurement as the distance from inner base of ear to outer corner of eye.

Eyes—Should be dark for preference; should be placed well apart and deep-set; almond shaped with lower lid slanting toward an imaginary point approximating the base of ears. Dark eye rims for preference. Round or protruding eyes penalized. Blue eyes disqualifying.

Nose—Black for preference but brown, liver, or Dudley nose not penalized. Color of nose sometimes changes with age and weather.

Jaws and Teeth—Strong, well-set teeth, snugly overlapping with scissors bite. Undershot or overshot should be penalized.

(b) Expression—The expression, referred to as "Samoyed expression," is very important and is indicated by sparkle of the eyes, animation and lighting up of the face when alert or intent on anything. Expression is made up of a combination of eyes, ears and mouth. The ears should be erect when alert; the mouth should be slightly curved up at the corners to form the "Samoyed smile."

Torso:

(a) Neck—Strong, well muscled, carried proudly erect, set on sloping shoulders to carry head with dignity when at attention. Neck should blend into shoulders with a graceful arch.

(b) Chest—Should be deep, with ribs well sprung out from the spine and flattened at the sides to allow proper movement of the shoulders and freedom for the front legs. Should not be barrel-chested. Perfect depth of chest approximates the point of elbows, and the deepest part of the chest should be back of the forelegs—near the ninth rib. Heart and lung room are secured more by body depth than width.

(c) Loin and Back—The withers forms the highest part of the back. Loins strong and slightly arched. The back should be straight to the loin, medium in length, very muscular and neither long nor short-coupled. The dog should be "just off square"—the length being approximately 5 per cent more than the height. Females allowed to be slightly longer than males. The belly should be well shaped and tightly muscled and, with the rear of the thorax, should swing up in a pleasing curve (tuck-up). Croup must be full, slightly sloping, and must continue imperceptibly to the tail root.

Tail—The tail should be moderately long with the tail bone terminating approximately at the hock when down. It should be profusely covered with long hair and carried forward over the back or side when alert, but sometimes dropped when at rest. It should not be high or low set and should be mobile and loose—not tight over the back. A double hook is a fault. A judge should see the tail over the back once when judging.

Disposition—Intelligent, gentle, loyal, adaptable, alert, full of action, eager to serve, friendly but conservative, not distrustful or shy, not overly aggressive. Unprovoked aggressiveness to be severely penalized.

DISQUALIFICATIONS

Any color other than pure white, cream, biscuit, or white and biscuit. Blue eyes.

Approved April 9, 1963

Shetland Sheepdog

THE SHETLAND SHEEPDOG, as its name implies, is a working Collie in miniature. There is little doubt that the small working Collie, from which came the modern show Collie evolving on larger lines, was likewise the progenitor of the Shetland Sheepdog evolving on smaller ones. It was assisted in the process by the environment of the Islands, which produced diminutiveness in all its stock, and by crosses with other small breeds residing in, if not indigenous to, the Islands.

The Shetland Islands themselves are not conducive to abundance of fodder or flocks, made up as they are of rugged rocks on which only meager vegetation can survive and surrounded by the sea, which brews frequent and severe storms. Small wonder that only the hardiest of both man and beast, and the smallest, could find subsistence. The actual origin of the breed cannot be traced by reference to records, as none were ever written. Tradition makes the dogs as old as the working Collies of Scotland, which frequently came to Shetland as the breed's forebears, and as old as the Islands themselves.

As the Islands were isolated from the trend of travel, the little dogs were a long time coming to the ken of dog-loving folk. Thus the breed did not take its place on the show bench until well along in the present century. The year 1909 marked the initial recognition of the Sheltie by the English Kennel Club. Not until 1914 did the breed obtain separate classification as Shetland Sheepdogs, and not Shetland Collies, because of pressure brought to bear by the Collie breeders. The first Challenge Certificate was awarded to the breed in 1915, after which World War I put a stop to all progress for the next few years.

The history of the several clubs catering to the breed has been one of ups and downs centering around the variations in size and type which still linger in a refined form today. The Shetland Sheepdog Club in the Islands, founded in 1908, was, of course, the oldest. They asked for a rough Collie in miniature, height not exceeding 15 inches. The Scottish Shetland Sheepdog Club, a year later, asked for first an "ordinary Collie in miniature" and finally a "modern show Collie in miniature," ideal height 12 inches, and eventually 13^{1}/$_{2}$. The English Shetland Sheepdog Club, founded in 1914, was an offshoot of the Scottish requiring "approximately a show Collie in miniature," height (ideal) first 12 inches and finally from 12 to 15, the ideal being 13^{1}/$_{2}$. The British Breeders' Association came into being for a time as the offspring of the English Club and asked for a "show Collie in miniature," maintaining the same heights. In 1930 the Scottish and English Clubs revised their standards jointly to read "should resemble a Collie (Rough) in miniature." The American Shetland Sheepdog Association, youngest in years, tried to profit by the experience of its predecessors by combining the best of each in its standard. The current standard specifies height from 13 to 16 inches.

The club controversy was reflected by the struggle of breeders to fix and perpetuate the proper type and size. The smaller breeds intermingling with the working Collies brought in faults quite contradictory to true Collie type. Small spaniels were undoubtedly responsible for contributing undesirable wavy coats, low ears, large round eyes, gay tails, long bodies, and desirable calm, devoted dispositions. Little yellow Iceland dogs with smutty muzzles and pricked ears made their mark on the breed.

To offset these influences, crosses with modern Collies were resorted to—this introduced a new set of faults along with an undeniable set of virtues derived from long generations of breeding for perfection in Collie points. The chief drawbacks, whose results we are reaping today, were legginess, loss of substance, excess size, and imbalance. At the same time, the breed was given great impetus in the improvement of head properties, especially in type, skull, and expression. While the breed is still suffering somewhat from this inescapable method of its improvement, it is likewise reaping the reward of now having within the breed all the points inseparable from the correct Collie, enabling breeders to produce substantial, beautifully balanced little dogs, with weather-resisting Collie coats, Collie type and expression, and Sheltie size, charm, and character.

The breed characteristics common to all Shelties can be used for two purposes pertaining to their working propensities or their companionship qualities. It is their nature to obey, willingly and naturally, with few or no lessons needed, an instinct coming no doubt from the many generations of obediently trained dogs behind them. The instinct to guard property or places and to give watchdog warning makes them invaluable for work as farm helpers or home protectors, a heritage of the constant vigilance required to protect the crofters' cottages, flocks, and herds from invaders of all kinds. Their ability to run swiftly and gracefully, and jump with agility over obstacles, makes them a delight in fields and woods as well as in farm work. But what most endears them to everybody is their devoted, docile natures and their keen and all but human intelligence and understanding.

Official Standard for the
Shetland Sheepdog

Preamble—The Shetland Sheepdog, like the Collie, traces to the Border Collie of Scotland, which, transported to the Shetland Islands and crossed with small, intelligent, longhaired breeds, was reduced to miniature proportions. Subsequently crosses were made from time to time with Collies. This breed now bears the same relationship in size and general appearance to the Rough Collie as the Shetland Pony does to some of the larger breeds of horses. Although the resemblance between the Shetland Sheepdog and the Rough Collie is marked, there are differences which may be noted.

General Description—The Shetland Sheepdog is a small, alert, rough-coated, longhaired working dog. He must be sound, agile and sturdy. The outline should be so symmetrical that no part appears out of proportion to the whole. Dogs should appear masculine; bitches feminine.

Size—The Shetland Sheepdog should stand between 13 and 16 inches at the shoulder. Note: Height is determined by a line perpendicular to the ground from the top of the shoulder blades, the dog standing naturally, with forelegs parallel to line of measurement. *Disqualification*—Heights below or above the desired size range are to be disqualified from the show ring.

Coat—The coat should be double, the outer coat consisting of long, straight, harsh hair; the undercoat short, furry, and so dense as to give the entire coat its "stand-off" quality. The hair on face, tips of ears and feet should be smooth. Mane and frill should be abundant, and particularly impressive in males. The forelegs well feathered, the hind legs heavily so, but smooth below the hock joint. Hair on tail profuse. Note: Excess hair on ears, feet, and on hocks may be trimmed for the show ring. *Faults*—Coat short or flat, in whole or in part; wavy, curly, soft or silky. Lack of undercoat. Smooth-coated specimens.

Color—Black, blue merle, and sable (ranging from golden through mahogany); marked with varying amounts of white and/or tan. *Faults*—Rustiness in a black or a blue coat. Washed out or degenerate colors, such as pale sable and faded blue. Self-color in the case of blue merle, that is, without any merling or mottling and generally appearing as a faded or dilute tri-color. Conspicuous white body spots. Specimens with more than 50 per cent white shall be so severely penalized as to effectively eliminate them from competition. *Disqualification*—Brindle.

Temperament—The Shetland Sheepdog is intensely loyal, affectionate, and responsive to his owner. However, he may be reserved toward strangers but not to the point of showing fear or cringing in the ring. *Faults*—Shyness, timidity, or nervousness. Stubbornness, snappiness, or ill temper.

Head—The head should be refined and its shape, when viewed from top or side, be a long, blunt wedge tapering slightly from ears to nose, which must be black. *Skull and Muzzle*—Top of skull should be flat, showing no prominence at nuchal crest (the top of the occiput). Cheeks should be flat and should merge smoothly into a well-rounded muzzle. Skull and muzzle should be of equal length, balance point being inner corner of eye. In profile the top line of skull should parallel the top line of muzzle, but on a higher plane due to the presence of a slight but definite stop. Jaws clean and powerful. The deep, well-developed under-jaw, rounded at chin, should extend to base of nostril. Lips tight. Upper and lower lips must meet and fit smoothly together all the way around. Teeth level and evenly spaced. Scissors bite. *Faults*—Two-angled head. Too prominent stop, or no stop. Overfill below, between, or above eyes. Prominent nuchal crest. Domed skull. Prominent cheekbones. Snipy muzzle. Short, receding, or shallow under-jaw, lacking breadth and depth. Overshot or undershot, missing or crooked teeth. Teeth visible when mouth is closed.

Eyes—Medium size with dark, almond-shaped rims, set somewhat obliquely in skull. Color must be dark, with blue or merle eyes permissible in blue merles only. *Faults*—Light, round, large or too small. Prominent haws.

Ears—Small and flexible, placed high, carried three-fourths erect, with tips breaking forward. When in repose the ears fold lengthwise and are thrown back into the frill. *Faults*—Set too low. Hound, prick, bat, twisted ears. Leather too thick or too thin.

Expression—Contours and chiseling of the head, the shape, set and use of ears, the placement, shape and color of the eyes, combine to produce expression. Normally the expression should be alert, gentle, intelligent and questioning. Toward strangers the eyes should show watchfulness and reserve, but no fear.

Neck—Neck should be muscular, arched, and of sufficient length to carry the head proudly. *Faults*—Too short and thick.

Body—In over-all appearance the body should appear moderately long as measured from shoulder joint to ischium (rearmost extremity of the pelvic bone), but much of this length is actually due to the proper angulation and breadth of the shoulder and hindquarter, as the back itself should be comparatively short. Back should be level and strongly muscled. Chest should be deep, the brisket reaching to point of elbow. The ribs should be well sprung, but flattened at their lower half to allow free play of the foreleg and shoulder. Abdomen moderately tucked up. *Faults*—Back too long, too short, swayed or roached. Barrel ribs. Slab-side. Chest narrow and/or too shallow.

Forequarters—From the withers the shoulder blades should slope at a 45-degree angle forward and downward to the shoulder joints. At the withers they are separated only by the vertebra, but they must slope outward sufficiently to accommodate the desired spring of rib. The upper arm should join the shoulder blade at as nearly as possible a right angle. Elbow joint should be equidistant from the ground or from the withers. Forelegs straight viewed from all angles, muscular and clean, and of strong bone. Pasterns very strong, sinewy and flexible. Dewclaws may be removed. *Faults*—Insufficient angulation between shoulder and upper arm. Upper arm too short. Lack of outward slope of shoulders. Loose shoulders. Turning in or out of elbows. Crooked legs. Light bone.

Feet (front and hind)—Feet should be oval and compact with the toes well arched and fitting tightly together. Pads deep and tough, nails hard and strong. *Faults*—Feet turning in or out. Splay-feet. Hare-feet. Cat-feet.

Hindquarters—There should be a slight arch at the loins, and the croup should slope gradually to the rear. The hipbone (pelvis) should be set at a 30-degree angle to the spine. The thigh should be broad and muscular. The thighbone should be set into the pelvis at a right angle corresponding to the angle of the shoulder blade and upper arm. Stifle bones join the thighbone and should be distinctly angled at the stifle joint. The over-all length of the stifle should at least equal the length of the thighbone, and preferably should slightly exceed it. Hock joint should be clean-cut, angular, sinewy, with good bone and strong ligamentation. The hock (metatarsus) should be short and straight viewed from all angles. Dewclaws should be removed. Feet (*see* Forequarters). *Faults*—Croup higher than withers. Croup too straight or too steep. Narrow thighs. Cowhocks. Hocks turning out. Poorly defined hock joint. Feet (*see* Forequarters).

Tail—The tail should be sufficiently long so that when it is laid along the back edge of the hind legs the last vertebra will reach the hock joint. Carriage of tail at rest is straight down or in a slight upward curve. When the dog is alert the tail is normally lifted, but it should not be curved forward over the back. *Faults*—Too short. Twisted at end.

Gait—The trotting gait of the Shetland Sheepdog should denote effortless speed and smoothness. There should be no jerkiness, nor stiff, stilted, up-and-down movement. The drive should be from the rear, true and straight, dependent upon correct angulation, musculation, and ligamentation of the entire hindquarter, thus allowing the dog to reach well under his body with his hind foot and propel himself forward. Reach of stride of the foreleg is dependent upon correct angulation, musculation and ligamentation of the forequarters, together with correct width of chest and construction of rib cage. The foot should be lifted only enough to clear the ground as the leg swings forward. Viewed from the front, both forelegs and hind legs should move forward almost perpendicular to ground at the walk, slanting a little inward at a slow trot, until at a swift trot the feet are brought so far inward toward center line of body that the tracks left show two parallel lines of footprints actually touching a center line at their inner edges. *There should be no crossing of the* *feet nor throwing of the weight from side to side.* **Faults**—Stiff, short steps, with a choppy, jerky movement. Mincing steps, with a hopping up and down, or a balancing of weight from side to side (often erroneously admired as a "dancing gait" but permissible in young puppies). Lifting of front feet in hackney-like action, resulting in loss of speed and energy. Pacing gait.

SCALE OF POINTS

General Appearance
Symmetry 10
Temperament 10
Coat 5   25
Head
Skull and stop 5
Muzzle 5
Eyes, ears and expression
.... 10   20
Body
Neck and back 5
Chest, ribs and brisket 10
Loin, croup, and tail 5   20

Forequarters
Shoulder 10
Forelegs and feet 5   15
Hindquarters
Hip, thigh and stifle
.... 10
Hocks and feet 5   15
Gait
Gait—smoothness and
   lack of waste motion
   when trotting
.... 5   5
TOTAL 100

DISQUALIFICATIONS

Heights below or above the desired range, i.e. 13-16 inches.
Brindle color.

Approved May 12, 1959

Siberian Husky

THE SIBERIAN HUSKY was originated by the Chukchi people of northeastern Asia as an endurance sled dog. When changing conditions forced these semi-nomadic natives to expand their hunting grounds, they responded by developing a unique breed of sled dog, which met their special requirements and upon which their very survival depended. The Chukchis needed a sled dog capable of traveling great distances at a moderate speed, carrying a light load in low temperatures with a minimum expenditure of energy. Research indicates that the Chukchis maintained the purity of their sled dogs through the 19th century and that these dogs were the sole and direct ancestors of the breed known in the United States today as the Siberian Husky.

Shortly after 1900 Americans in Alaska began to hear accounts of this superior strain of sled dog in Siberia. The first team of Siberian Huskies made its appearance in the All Alaska Sweepstakes Race of 1909. The same year a large number of them were imported to Alaska by Charles Fox Maule Ramsay, and his team, driven by John "Iron Man" Johnson, won the grueling 400-mile race in 1910. For the next decade Siberian Huskies, particularly those bred and raced by Leonhard Seppala, captured most of the racing titles in Alaska, where the rugged terrain was ideally suited to the endurance capabilities of the breed.

In 1925 the city of Nome, Alaska was stricken by a diphtheria epidemic and supplies of anti-toxin were urgently needed. Many sled dog drivers, including Leonhard Seppala, were called upon to relay the life-saving serum to Nome by dog team. This heroic Serum Run focused attention upon Siberian Huskies, and Seppala brought his dogs to the United States on a personal appearance tour. While here, he was invited to compete in sled dog races in New England, where the sport had already been introduced. The superior racing ability and delightful temperament of Seppala's Siberian Huskies won the respect and the hearts of sportsmen from Alaska to New England. It was through the efforts of these pioneer fanciers that the breed was established in the United States and that AKC recognition was granted in 1930. Many Siberian Huskies were assembled and trained at Chinook Kennels in New Hampshire for use on the Byrd Antarctic Expeditions. Dogs of the breed also served valiantly in the Army's Arctic Search and Rescue Unit of the Air Transport Command during World War II.

The Siberian Husky is naturally friendly and gentle in temperament. He possesses at times an independent nature, and although very alert, in many cases he lacks the aggressive or protective tendencies of a watch dog. He is by nature fastidiously clean and free from the body odors that many dense-coated breeds have. Although remarkable for his adaptability to all kinds of living conditions, his natural desire to roam makes a measure of control necessary at all times. The understanding owner will find the Siberian Husky an enjoyable companion in country or city. He has endeared himself to dog fanciers everywhere by his versatility, striking beauty, and amiable disposition.

Official Standard for the Siberian Husky

General Appearance—The Siberian Husky is a medium-sized working dog, quick and light on his feet and free and graceful in action. His moderately compact and well-furred body, erect ears and brush tail suggest his Northern heritage. His characteristic gait is smooth and seemingly effortless. He performs his original function in harness most capably, carrying a light load at moderate speed over great distances. His body proportions and form reflect this basic balance of power, speed and endurance. The males of the Siberian Husky breed are masculine but never coarse; the bitches are feminine but without weakness of structure. In proper condition, with muscle firm and well-developed, the Siberian Husky does not carry excess weight.

Head:

Skull—Of medium size and in proportion to the body; slightly rounded on top and tapering gradually from the widest point to the eyes. *Faults*—Head clumsy or heavy; head too finely chiseled.

Muzzle—Of medium length; that is, the distance from the tip of the nose to the stop is equal to the distance from the stop to the occiput. The stop is well-defined and the bridge of the nose is straight from the stop to the tip. The muzzle is of medium width, tapering gradually to the nose, with the tip neither pointed nor square. The lips are well-pigmented and close fitting; teeth closing in a scissors bite. *Faults*—Muzzle either too snipy or too coarse; muzzle too short or too long; insufficient stop; any bite other than scissors.

Ears—Of medium size, triangular in shape, close fitting and set high on the head. They are thick, well-furred, slightly arched at the back, and strongly erect, with slightly rounded tips pointing straight up. *Faults*—Ears too large in proportion to the head; too wide-set; not strongly erect.

Eyes—Almond shaped, moderately spaced and set a trifle obliquely. The expression is keen, but friendly; interested and even mischievous. Eyes may be brown or blue in color; one of each or parti-colored are acceptable. *Faults*—Eyes set too obliquely; set too close together.

Nose—Black in gray, tan or black dogs; liver in copper dogs; may be flesh-colored in pure white dogs. The pink-streaked "snow nose" is acceptable.

Body:

Neck—Medium in length, arched and carried proudly erect when dog is standing. When moving at a trot, the neck is extended so that the head is carried slightly forward. *Faults*—Neck too short and thick; neck too long.

Shoulders—The shoulder blade is well laid back at an approximate angle of 45 degrees to the ground. The upper arm angles slightly backward from point of shoulder to elbow, and is never perpendicular to the ground. The muscles and ligaments holding the shoulder to the rib cage are firm and well-developed. *Faults*—Straight shoulders; loose shoulders.

Chest—Deep and strong, but not too broad, with the deepest point being just behind and level with the elbows. The ribs are well-sprung from the spine but flattened on the sides to allow for freedom of action. *Faults*—Chest too broad; "barrel ribs"; ribs too flat or weak.

Back—The back is straight and strong, with a level topline from withers to croup. It is of medium length, neither cobby nor slack from excessive length. The loin is taut and lean, narrower than the rib cage, and with a slight tuck-up. The croup slopes away from the spine at an angle, but never so steeply as to restrict the rearward thrust of the hind legs. In profile, the length of the body from the point of the shoulder to the rear point of the croup is slightly longer than the height of the body from the ground to the top of the withers. *Faults*—Weak or slack back; roached back; sloping topline.

Legs and Feet:

Forelegs—When standing and viewed from the front, the legs are moderately spaced, parallel and straight, with elbows close to the body and turned neither in nor out. Viewed from the side, pasterns are slightly slanted, with pastern joint strong, but flexible. Bone is substantial but never heavy. Length of the leg from elbow to ground is slightly more than the distance from the elbow to the top of withers. Dewclaws on forelegs may be removed. *Faults*—Weak pasterns; too heavy bone; too narrow or too wide in the front; out at the elbows.

Hindquarters—When standing and viewed from the rear, the hind legs are moderately spaced and parallel. The upper thighs are well-muscled and powerful, the stifles well-bent, the hock joint well-defined and set low to the ground. Dewclaws, if any, are to be removed. *Faults*—Straight stifles, cow-hocks, too narrow or too wide in the rear.

Feet—Oval in shape, but not long. The paws are medium size, compact and well-furred between the toes and pads. The pads are tough and thickly cushioned. The paws neither turn in nor out when dog is in natural stance. *Faults*—Soft or splayed toes; paws too large and clumsy; paws too small and delicate; toeing in or out.

Tail—The well-furred tail of fox-brush shape is set on just below the level of the topline, and is usually carried over the back in a graceful sickle curve when the dog is at attention. When carried up, the tail does not curl to either side of the body, nor does it snap flat against the back. A trailing tail is normal for the dog when working or in repose. Hair on the tail is of medium length and approximately the same length on top, sides and bottom, giving the appearance of a round brush. *Faults*—A snapped or tightly curled tail; highly plumed tail; tail set too low or too high.

Gait—The Siberian Husky's characteristic gait is smooth and seemingly effortless. He is quick and light on his feet, and when in the show ring should be gaited on a loose lead at a moderately fast trot, exhibiting good reach in the forequarters and good drive in the hindquarters. When viewed from the front to rear, while moving at a walk the Siberian Husky does not single-track, but as the speed increases the legs gradually angle inward until the pads are falling on a line directly under the longitudinal center of the body. As the pad marks converge, the forelegs and hind legs are carried straight forward, with neither elbows nor stifles turned in or out. Each hind leg moves in the path of the foreleg on the same side. While the dog is gaiting, the topline remains firm and level. *Faults*—Short, prancing or choppy gait, lumbering or rolling gait; crossing; crabbing.

Coat—The coat of the Siberian Husky is double and medium in length, giving a well-furred appearance, but is never so long as to obscure the clean-cut outline of the dog. The undercoat is soft and dense and of sufficient length to support the outer coat. The guard hairs of the outer coat are straight and somewhat smooth-lying, never harsh nor standing straight off from the body. It should be noted that the absence of the undercoat during the shedding season is normal. Trimming of the whiskers and fur between the toes and around the feet to present a neater appearance is permissible. Trimming of the fur on any other part of the dog is not to be condoned and should be severely penalized. *Faults*—Long, rough or shaggy coat; texture too harsh or too silky; trimming of the coat, except as permitted above.

Color—All colors from black to pure white are allowed. A variety of markings on the head is common, including many striking patterns not found in other breeds.

Temperament—The characteristic temperament of the Siberian Husky is friendly and gentle, but also alert and outgoing. He does not display the possessive qualities of the guard dog, nor is he overly suspicious of strangers or aggressive with other dogs. Some measure of reserve and dignity may be expected in the mature dog. His intelligence, tractability, and eager disposition make him an agreeable companion and willing worker.

Size—*Height*—Dogs, 21 to 23½ inches at the withers. Bitches, 20 to 22 inches at the withers. *Weight*—Dogs, 45 to 60 pounds. Bitches, 35 to 50 pounds. Weight is in proportion to height. The measurements mentioned above represent the extreme height and weight limits, with no preference given to either extreme. **Disqualification**—Dogs over 23½ inches and bitches over 22 inches.

Summary—The most important breed characteristics of the Siberian Husky are medium size, moderate bone, well-balanced proportions, ease and freedom of movement, proper coat, pleasing head and ears, correct tail, and good disposition. Any appearance of excessive bone or weight, constricted or clumsy gait, or long, rough coat should be penalized. The Siberian Husky never appears so heavy or coarse as to suggest a freighting animal; nor is he so light and fragile as to suggest a sprint-racing animal. In both sexes the Siberian Husky gives the appearance of being capable of great endurance. In addition to the faults already noted, obvious structural faults common to all breeds are as undesirable in the Siberian Husky as in any other breed, even though they are not specifically mentioned herein.

DISQUALIFICATION

Dogs over 23½ inches and bitches over 22 inches.

Approved November 9, 1971

Standard Schnauzer

OF THE THREE Schnauzers: Miniature, Standard, and Giant, all of which are bred and registered as distinct breeds, the medium, or Standard, is the prototype. He is a German breed of great antiquity, which in the fifteenth and sixteenth centuries must have been in high favor as a household companion, for his portrait appears in many paintings of the period. Albrecht Dürer is known to have owned one for at least twelve years, as the portrait of the same dog occurs several times in works of that artist between the years 1492 and 1504. Rembrandt painted several Schnauzers, Lucas Cranach the Elder shows one in a tapestry dated 1501, and in the eighteenth century one appears in a canvas of the English painter Sir Joshua Reynolds. At Mechlinburg, Germany, in the market place there is a statue of a hunter dating from the fourteenth century, with a Schnauzer crouching at his feet which conforms very closely to the present-day show standard.

The general impression of the Schnauzer is that of a compact, sinewy, square-built dog, sturdy and alert, with stiff wiry coat and bristling eyebrows and whiskers. His nature combines high-spirited temperament with unusual intelligence and reliability. He occupies the midway position between the large breeds and the toys.

As far as can be determined, the Schnauzer originated in the crossing of black German Poodle and gray wolf spitz upon wirehaired Pinscher stock. From the Pinscher element derives the tendency to fawn-colored undercoat, and from the wolf spitz is inherited the typical pepper and salt coat color and its harsh wiry character. Solid black specimens of the breed, while fairly common in Germany, are still rather unusual in this country. Several breeders, however, have taken them up and are endeavoring to correct the tendency shown by the blacks to revert to the soft coat of their Poodle ancestry.

The breed in America was originally classed as a terrier, whereas German breeders have always regarded the Schnauzer principally as a working dog. His principal vocation was that of rat catcher, yard dog, and guard. Before World War I in Germany, fully 90 per cent of the dogs, used to guard the carts of farm produce in the market places while the farmers rested themselves and their teams at the inns, were of strong Schnauzer blood. It was the extraordinary qualities of these dogs that led to further inquiries as to their breed, resulting in the discovery that the land of their origin holds the Schnauzer second to none for sagacity and fearlessness. Owing to these characteristics, the "dogs with the human brain" (as their owners proudly call them) were much used by the army during the war as dispatch carriers and Red Cross aides; they are also employed in Germany in police work.

German breeders are anxious that the Schnauzer shall not deteriorate into a mere show dog. To this end, most of the "Verein von Schnauzern" (Schnauzer Clubs) hold periodic ratting trials. Rats are placed in a large ring surrounded by wire netting, the floor of which is covered with straw or brushwood; two or more dogs are turned in, and the dog which noses out and kills the most rats in the shortest time is declared the winner. Ratting trials have also been held occasionally at some of the larger dog shows in Germany and have proved a great attraction to the public, as well as a telling advertisement for the breed. Schnauzers are also proving themselves apt pupils for obedience tests, which are a feature of so many of the present-day shows.

In this country and in England, they are used mainly as personal guards and companions, for which purpose their devotion and bravery, coupled with an uncanny perception of approaching danger, renders them suitable. They are good water dogs and are easily taught to retrieve; and, on at least one western sheep ranch, Schnauzers have proved themselves the most efficient of various breeds tried as protection for the flocks against marauding coyotes.

Schnauzers were first exhibited in Germany as Wire-Haired Pinschers in 1879 at the Third German International Show at Hanover; they came from the Württemberg Kennels of Burger Leonburg, and a dog named Schnauzer won first prize. Württemberg is the cradle of many of the German breeds, and one of the most important of the early Schnauzer breeders was a Württemberger, Herr Max Hartenstein of the Plavia Kennels.

A standard was published in 1880 and the breed made rapid progress as a show dog. The first specialty show was held at Stuttgart in 1890 with the remarkable entry of ninety-three dogs. The Pinscher Club was founded at Cologne in 1895 and the Bavarian Schnauzer Club at Munich in 1907. In 1918 the Pinscher and Schnauzer Clubs united to become the official representative of the breed in the German Kennel Club—it is known as the Pinscher-Schnauzer Club. There are today clubs devoted to the breed in Holland, Austria, Switzerland, Czechoslovakia, England, and America.

From a breeding point of view, there are two major male lines of descent, tracing back to two unregistered dogs, one the above-mentioned Schnauzer and the other called Seppel, while the two most famous basic bitches are Settchen and Jette von Enz. Settchen traces back to Schnauzer and was bred to a dog of the Seppel line called Prinz Harttmuth; by this mating she became the dam of Sieger Rex von Den Gunthersburg. Rex in turn became the sire of Sieger Rigo Schnauzerlust, and these two dogs, Rex and Rigo, have had a greater influence on the breed than any others in the stud book. Jette von Enz was the dam of Rigo, and her line traces back to Seppel. A litter-brother of Rigo, named Rex von Egelsee, also figures prominently in the early breeding records; both these dogs were used extensively and with excellent results for inbreeding. Demonstrative of the stamina and virility of Schnauzers is the fact that both Rigo and Rex were successfully serving as studs when they were twelve years old.

Schnauzers have become widely known in this country only since World War I, but one is said to have been shown at the Westminster Kennel Club Show in the Miscellaneous Class in 1899. The first recorded importation was Fingal, brought over by Mr. Leisching of Rochester, N.Y., in 1905. Fingal died in 1914, at the age of ten. The Schnauzer Club of America was formed in 1925. The first Schnauzer to become an American champion was the Swiss bitch, Resy Patricia, imported by Mrs. Maurice Newton, who bred from her the first American-bred champion, Fracas Franconia. The first dog to make the American title was Holm von Egelsee, which was also the first Sieger to come to this country. He was imported by William D. Goff, the president of the Standard Schnauzer Club of America.

All Schnauzers in Germany have their ears cropped, but since cropping in this country is governed by the separate laws of the different states, the American Schnauzer Club Standard permits both the cropped and the natural ear.

Official Standard for the
Standard Schnauzer

General Appearance—The Standard Schnauzer is a robust, heavy-set dog, sturdily built with good muscle and plenty of bone; square-built in proportion of body-length to height. His nature combines high-spirited temperament with extreme reliability. His rugged build and dense harsh coat are accentuated by the hallmark of the breed, the arched eyebrows, bristly mustache, and luxuriant whiskers.

Head—Strong, rectangular, and elongated; narrowing slightly from the ears to the eyes and again to the tip of the nose. The total length of the head is about one half the length of the back measured from the withers to the set-on of the tail. The head matches the sex and substance of the dog. The top line of the muzzle is parallel with the top line of the skull. There is a slight stop which is accentuated by the wiry brows. *Skull (Occiput to Stop)*—Moderately broad between the ears with the width of the skull not exceeding two thirds the length of the skull. The skull must be flat; neither domed nor bumpy; skin unwrinkled. *Cheeks*—Well-developed chewing muscles, but not so much that "cheekiness" disturbs the rectangular head form. *Muzzle*—Strong, and both parallel and equal in length to the topskull; it ends in a moderately blunt wedge with wiry whiskers accenting the rectangular shape of the head. Nose is large, black and full. The lips should be black, tight and not overlapping. *Eyes*—Medium size; dark brown; oval in shape and turned forward; neither round nor protruding. The brow is arched and wiry, but vision is not impaired nor eyes hidden by too long an eyebrow. *Bite*—A full complement of white teeth, with a strong, sound scissors bite. The canine teeth are strong and well developed with the upper incisors slightly overlapping and engaging the lower. The upper and lower jaws are powerful and neither overshot nor undershot. (**Faults**—A level bite is considered undesirable but a lesser fault than an overshot or undershot mouth.) *Ears*—Evenly shaped, set high and carried erect when cropped. If uncropped, they are small, V-shaped button ears of moderate thickness and carried rather high and close to the head.

Neck—Strong, of moderate thickness and length, elegantly arched and blending cleanly into the shoulders. The skin is tight, fitting closely to the dry throat with no wrinkles or dewlaps.

Shoulders—The sloping shoulder blades are strongly muscled, yet flat and well laid back so that the rounded upper ends are in a nearly vertical line above the elbows. They slope well forward to the point where they join the upper arm, forming as nearly as possible a right angle when seen from the side. Such an angulation permits the maximum forward extension of the forelegs without binding or effort.

Chest—Of medium width with well-sprung ribs, and if it could be seen in cross-section would be oval. The breastbone is plainly discernible. The brisket must descend at least to the elbows and ascend gradually to the rear with the belly moderately drawn up.

Body—Compact, strong, short-coupled and substantial so as to permit great flexibility and agility. The height at the highest point of the withers equals the length from breastbone to point or rump. *Faults*—Too slender or shelly; too bulky or coarse; excessive tuck-up.

Back—Strong, stiff, straight and short, with a well-developed loin section; the distance from the last rib to the hips as short as possible. The top line of the back should not be absolutely horizontal, but should have a slightly descending slope from the first vertebra of the withers to the faintly curved croup and set-on of the tail.

Forelegs—Straight, vertical, and without any curvature when seen from all sides; set moderately far apart; with heavy bone; elbows set close to the body and pointing directly to the rear.

Hindquarters—Strongly muscled, in balance with the forequarters, never appearing higher than the shoulders. Croup full and slightly rounded. Thighs broad with well-bent stifles. The second thigh, from knee to hock, is approximately parallel with an extension of the upper-neck line. The legs, from the clearly defined hock joint to the feet, are short and perpendicular to the ground and when viewed from the rear are parallel to each other.

Feet—Small and compact, round with thick pads and strong black nails. The toes are well closed and arched (cat's paws) and pointing straight ahead. *Dewclaws*—Dewclaws, if any, on the hind legs are generally removed. Dewclaws on the forelegs may be removed.

Tail—Set moderately high and carried erect. It is docked to not less than 1 inch nor more than 2 inches. *Faults*—Squirrel tail.

Height—Ideal height at the highest point of the shoulder blades, $18^{1}/_{2}$ to $19^{1}/_{2}$ inches for males and $17^{1}/_{2}$ inches to $18^{1}/_{2}$ inches for females. Dogs measuring over or under these limits must be faulted in proportion to the extent of the deviation. Dogs measuring more than one half inch over or under these limits must be disqualified.

Coat—Tight, hard, wiry and as thick as possible, composed of a soft, close undercoat and a harsh outer coat which, when seen against the grain, stands up off the back, lying neither smooth nor flat. The outer coat (body coat) is trimmed (by plucking) only to accent the body outline. When in show condition, the outer coat's proper length is approximately $1^{1}/_{2}$ inches, except on the ears, head, neck, chest, belly and under the tail where it may be closely trimmed to give the desired typical appearance of the breed.

On the muzzle and over the eyes the coat lengthens to form luxuriant beard and eyebrows; the hair on the legs is longer than that on the body. These "furnishings" should be of harsh texture and should not be so profuse so as to detract from the neat appearance or working capabilities of the dog. *Faults*—Soft, smooth, curly, wavy or shaggy; too long or too short; too sparse or lacking undercoat; excessive furnishings; lack of furnishings.

Color—Pepper and salt or pure black.

Pepper and Salt—The typical pepper and salt color of the topcoat results from the combination of black and white hairs, and white hairs banded with black. Acceptable are all shades of pepper and salt from dark iron-gray to silver gray. Ideally, pepper and salt Standard Schnauzers have a gray undercoat, but a tan or fawn undercoat is not to be penalized. It is desirable to have a darker facial mask that harmonizes with the particular shade of coat color. Also, in pepper and salt dogs, the pepper and salt mixture may fade out to light gray or silver white in the eyebrows, whiskers, cheeks, under throat, across chest, under tail, leg furnishings, under body, and inside legs.

Black—Ideally the black Standard Schnauzer should be a true rich color, free from any fading or discoloration or any admixture of gray or tan hairs. The undercoat should also be solid black. However, increased age or continued exposure to the sun may cause a certain amount of fading and burning. A small white smudge on the chest is not a fault. Loss of color as a result of scars from cuts and bites is not a fault.

Faults—Any colors other than specified, and any shadings or mixtures thereof in the topcoat such as rust, brown, red, yellow or tan; absence of peppering; spotting or striping; a black streak down the back; or a black saddle without typical salt and pepper coloring—and gray hairs in the coat of a black; in blacks, any undercoat color other than black.

Gait—Sound, strong, quick, free, true and level gait with powerful, well-angulated hindquarters that reach out and cover ground. The forelegs reach out in a stride balancing that of the hindquarters. At a trot, the back remains firm and level, without swaying, rolling or roaching. When viewed from the rear, the feet, though they may appear to travel close when trotting, must not cross or strike. Increased speed causes feet to converge toward the center line of gravity. **Faults**—Crabbing or weaving; paddling, rolling, swaying; short, choppy, stiff, stilted rear action; front legs that throw out or in (East and West movers); hackney gait, crossing over, or striking in front or rear.

FAULTS

Any deviation from the specifications in the Standard is to be considered a fault and should be penalized in proportion to the extent of the deviation. In weighing the seriousness of a fault, greatest consideration should be given to deviation from the desired alert, highly intelligent, spirited, reliable character of the Standard Schnauzer, and secondly to any deviation that detracts from the Standard Schnauzer's desired general appearance of a robust, active, square-built, wire-coated dog. Dogs that are shy or appear to be highly nervous should be seriously faulted and dismissed from the ring. Vicious dogs shall be disqualified.

DISQUALIFICATIONS

Vicious dogs.
Males under 18 inches or over 20 inches in height. Females under 17 inches or over 19 inches in height.

Approved May 14, 1968

Welsh Corgi, Cardigan

THE CARDIGAN WELSH CORGI is one of the oldest breeds in the British Isles, yet even in England the breed has come to be a show specimen only in very recent times. The apparent mystery surrounding its origin has been due to the absence of any previously written history, and to the simple fact that the poor hillmen of Wales saw no reason to publicize dogs that had been so useful to them for centuries.

The data upon which this summarized history of the breed is written was collected over a period of twenty years by W. Lloyd-Thomas of Mabws Hall, Llanrhystyd, Cardiganshire, South Wales.

In the beginning, the Corgi came to the high country now known as Cardiganshire with the tall, tawny-headed Celts from Central Europe. The migration of this warrior tribe to Wales is placed, roughly, at about 1200 B.C., which means that the Corgi has been known in the land whence its name comes for more than 3000 years. The dog was a member of the same family that has produced the Dachshund.

The village of Bronant, in Mid-Cardiganshire, became the especial stronghold of those early Celts, for the place is rich in remains of the old fortifications—indeed, Bronant is ringed round with them. The inhabitants, too, give evidence of that early settlement, for considerable numbers of them are tall and auburn-haired. They are said to be the direct descendants of the hard-pressed, fiery race that threw up these mounds.

The vigilance and intelligence of the Corgi must have been a great asset to the Celts from earliest times, and tales handed down from father to son for generations identify him always as a valued member of the family circle. His uses were many and varied, not the least of which were his guardianship of the children and his aid in beating out game, in those times of more than ordinary importance.

Still, the occupation which made the Corgi worth his weight in gold to those Welsh hillmen came at a much later period, but still hundreds of years ago. This was when the Crown owned practically all land, and the tenant farmers, or crofters, were permitted to fence off only a few acres surrounding their dooryards. The rest was open country, known as common land, on which the crofter was permitted to graze his cattle, one of the chief sources of his meager income. It can be imagined that there was great competition among the crofters to secure as much as possible of this pasture land for their own uses, and the task would have been difficult had it not been for the Corgi. The little dog which had been with this Celtic people so long, and which had come to be of almost human intelligence, was trained to perform a service the opposite of that done by the herding dog.

Instead of herding the cattle, the Corgi would nip at their heels and drive them as far afield as desired. Often the crofter called upon his dog to clear "his" ground of the neighbor's cattle. The dog worked the same way in either case. The crofter would stand by his gate and give a soft whistle of two notes, one high, one low. Many times the dog could not see the cattle he was to chase, but he would keep going as long as he could hear that whistle. His speed was remarkable, considering his short legs with their out-turned feet, but the length of his back gave him added spring. When the dog had scattered the cattle by biting their hocks—avoiding death only by ducking close to the ground when they kicked—the crofter would give the recall signal, a shrill, long-drawn-out whistle made by placing the fingers in the mouth. The dog would return at once.

The division of the Crown lands, their subsequent sale to the crofters, and the appearance of fences, removed the usefulness of the Corgi. He was still retained as guard and companion by some of the hillmen, but to most he was a luxury they could not afford. In many instances he was succeeded by the red herder and by the brindle herder. The original type of Corgi known in Bronant since time immemorial became very scarce, and it is due only to the greatest care on the part of modern breeders that the old strains have been preserved.

Needless to say, stud books were unknown to the Celts and to the early Welsh farmer-descendants of the old warrior tribe. But if there were no records, there was a rigid policy of selective breeding unsurpassed in this present day. The original Corgis had to be proficient workers, and no mating was consummated without due consideration.

After the breaking up of the Crown lands, and the introduction of the new breeds, there was a certain amount of experimentation with crosses. The ancient dog of Bronant was crossed with the red herder, but it did not prove very successful and was not attempted many times. The brindle herder, however, made a rather fortuitous cross. The progeny followed the dominant characteristics of the Corgi, and gained a little through the finer coat and the color of the brindle herder. Crossed later with the Collie, there was produced the breed known as the heeler.

The principal strains of the Cardigan Welsh Corgi of today go back to the old Bronant Corgi with a slight infusion of brindle herder blood. This dog approximates as nearly as possible the dog that enjoyed his greatest popularity in Cardiganshire a century and more ago.

Official Standard for the Cardigan Welsh Corgi

General Appearance—Low-set, sturdily built, with heavy bone and deep chest. Over-all silhouette long in proportion to height, culminating in low tail-set and foxlike brush. Expression alert and foxy, watchful yet friendly.

General Impression—A handsome, powerful, small dog, capable of both speed and endurance, intelligent, sturdy, but not coarse.

Head and Skull—Skull moderately wide and flat between the ears, with definite though moderate stop. *Muzzle* to measure about 3 inches in length, or in proportion to the skull as 3 to 5. Muzzle medium, *i.e.* neither too pointed nor too blunt but somewhat less fine than the Pembroke. *Nose*—Black. Nostrils of moderate size. Under-jaw clean-cut and strong. *Eyes*—Medium to large, and rather widely set, with distinct corners. Color dark to dark amber but clear. Blue eyes, or one dark and one blue eye, permissible in blue merles. *Mouth*—Teeth strong and regular, neither overshot nor undershot. Pincer (level) bite permissible but scissors bite preferred, *e.g.*, the inner side of the front teeth resting closely over the front of the lower front teeth. *Ears*—Large and prominent in proportion to size of dog. Slightly rounded at the tips, moderately wide at the base, and carried erect, set well apart and well back, sloping slightly forward when erect. Flop ears a serious fault.

Neck—Muscular, well developed, especially in males, and in proportion to dog's build; fitting into strong, well-shaped shoulders.

Forequarters—Chest broad, deep, and well let down between forelegs. Forelegs short, strong, and slightly bowed around chest, and with distinct but not exaggerated crook below the carpus. Elbows close to side. A straight, terrier-like front is a fault.

Body—Long and strong, with deep brisket, well-sprung ribs with moderate tuck-up of loin. Topline level except for slight slope of spine above tail.

Hindquarters—Strong, with muscular thighs. Legs short and well boned.

Feet—Round and well padded. Hind dewclaws, if any, should be removed. Front dewclaws may be removed.

Tail—Long to moderately long, resembling a fox brush. Should be set fairly low on body line, carried low when standing or moving slowly, streaming out when at a dead run, lifted when tracking or excited, but never curled over the back. A rat tail or a whip tail are faults.

Coat—Medium length but dense. Slightly harsh texture, but neither wiry nor silky. Weather-resistant. An overly short coat or a long and silky and/or curly coat are faults. Normal grooming and trimming of whiskers is permitted. Any trimming that alters the natural length of the coat is not permitted and is a serious fault. A distinctly long coat is a disqualification.

Size—Height approximately 12 inches at the highest point of the shoulder blades. Length usually between 36 and 44 inches from nose to tip of tail. In considering the height, weight, and length of a dog, over-all balance is a prime factor.

Accepted Colors—All shades of red. Sables. All shades of brindle. Black with or without tan or brindle points. The above colors usually with white flashings on chest, neck, feet, face or tail tip. No preference in above colors. *Disqualifications:* Any merlization other than blue. Excessive (over 50%) white.

DISQUALIFICATIONS

A distinctly long coat.
Any merlization other than blue.
Excessive (over 50%) white.

Approved December 14, 1976

Welsh Corgi, Pembroke

ALTHOUGH all evidence seems to point to the fact that the Pembroke Welsh Corgi is a much younger dog than the Cardigan Welsh Corgi, it is still true that the Corgi from Pembrokeshire is a breed of considerable antiquity. No breed that traces its origin back to A.D. 1107 can be regarded as an especially new type of dog.

In modern times there has been an effort to link the two types of Corgi under the heading of a single breed. This is far from the truth, according to W. Lloyd-Thomas, the Welsh authority who has spent so many years digging out the history of these small cattle dogs. He has given some interesting information, that, while it tends to divorce the two Corgis definitely, still gives the Pembroke a colorful past.

The direct ancestors of the Pembroke were brought across the Channel by the Flemish weavers who were induced by Henry I of England and took up their abode in Wales. This occurred in 1107, and it stands as a sturdy cornerstone upon which the development of a breed has been built. While weaving was one of their occupations, these Flemish people were also of an agrarian nature, and they soon had transferred to the southwest corner of Wales, at Haverfordwest, the replicas of the model homes and farms in their native land. The dog fitted into this scheme.

This early progenitor of the Pembroke Welsh Corgi of today has been described as having a noticeable resemblance to the old Schipperkes. It sprang from the same family that includes the

Keeshond, the Pomeranian, the Samoyed, the Chow Chow, the Norwegian Elkhound, and the Finnish Spitz. It has little or nothing of the Dachshund characteristics.

In relation to the Cardigan, the Pembroke is shorter in body; the legs are straighter and lighter-boned, while the coat is of finer texture. Two of the most noticeable differences are in the ears and the tail. Cardigan ears are rounded, while the Pembroke's are pointed at the tip and stand erect. The Cardigan has a long tail, and the Pembroke a short one. In disposition, the Pembroke is more restless, more easily excited. If one could see specimens of the early members of both breeds at the same time, the differences would be very marked. In modern times they have become more similar. The whole development of the Pembroke evinces a desire on the part of its breeders to produce a lower, stockier dog. It also may be noted that the head has grown stronger, while, in these times, good sized, round-tipped ears are not unusual.

The manner in which the Pembroke and the Cardigan have approached each other in appearance is not merely a matter of chance or of selective breeding. It is known, rather definitely that the two were crossed before the middle of the nineteenth century.

The story comes direct from one of the old crofters, a man of nearly ninety years, who spent his whole lifetime in Bronant. It seemed that in his youth, many of the young people in that village found a manner of increasing their pocket money. There were always plenty of the Cardigan puppies; in fact, the majority were a burden on the poor tenant farmers. If these puppies were retained, they would cost money to feed. One day an enterprising young man tucked a couple of Corgi puppies under his arm and set forth into a neighboring shire. When he returned there was the jingle of coins in his pocket. Thereafter, other young men followed the example. The old hillman who relates this incident says that he sold puppies to the farmers in Carmarthenshire and in Pembrokeshire.

It is not known whether any Cardigan Corgis had gone into Pembrokeshire at an earlier date, but it is quite possible, and it is only logical that if the two breeds were in the same section they would be bred together at some time. So far as known, the Pembroke was not taken into Cardiganshire up to the time of World War I, although since then there have been many instances of inter-matings.

The two breeds of Corgi were mated together frequently at the time when these dogs first came to the consciousness of the bench-show fanciers. Little was known about either dog, and crossings were common. This practice has been stopped, or practically so, since more information has become available, and all breeders of today are determined to keep the Pembroke distinct from the Cardigan.

The Pembroke is one of the most agreeable of small house dogs. It has an affectionate nature, but does not force its attentions upon those unwilling to accept them. Its intelligence is undoubted, and it is a remarkably alert, ever-vigilant guard of the fireside.

Official Standard for the Pembroke Welsh Corgi

General Appearance—Low-set, strong, sturdily built and active, giving an impression of substance and stamina in a small space. Should not be so low and heavy-boned as to appear coarse or overdone, nor so light-boned as to appear racy. Outlook bold, but kindly. Expression intelligent and interested. Never shy nor vicious.

Size and Proportions—Moderately long and low. The distance from the withers to base of tail should be approximately 40 per cent greater than the distance from the withers to the ground. *Height* (from ground to highest point on withers) should be 10 to 12 inches. *Weight* is in proportion to size, not exceeding 30 pounds for dogs and 28 pounds for bitches. In show condition, the preferred medium-size dog of correct bone and substance will weigh approximately 27 pounds, with bitches approximately 25 pounds. Obvious oversized specimens and diminutive toylike individuals must be very seriously penalized.

Head and Skull—Head to be foxy in shape and appearance, but not sly in expression. Skull to be fairly wide and flat between the ears. Moderate amount of stop. Very slight rounding of cheek, and not filled in below the eyes, as foreface should be nicely chiseled to give a somewhat tapered muzzle. Distance from the occiput to center of stop to be greater than the distance from stop to nose tip, the proportion being five parts of total distance for the skull and three parts for the foreface. Muzzle should be neither dish-faced nor Roman-nosed. *Nose*—Black and fully pigmented.

Eyes—Oval, medium in size, not round nor protruding, nor deep-set and piglike. Set somewhat obliquely. Variations of brown in harmony with coat color. Eye rims dark, preferably black. While dark eyes enhance the expression, true black eyes are most undesirable, as are yellow or bluish eyes.

Ears—Erect, firm, and of medium size, tapering slightly to a rounded point. Ears are mobile, and react sensitively to sounds. A line drawn from the nose tip through the eyes to the ear tips, and across, should form an approximate equilateral triangle. Bat ears, small catlike ears, overly large weak ears, hooded ears, ears carried too high or too low, are undesirable. Button, rose or drop ears are very serious faults.

Mouth—Scissors bite, the inner side of the upper incisors touching the outer side of the lower incisors. Level bite is acceptable. Lips should be tight, with little or no fullness, and black. Overshot or undershot bite is a very serious fault.

Neck—Fairly long, of sufficient length to provide over-all balance of the dog. Slightly arched, clean and blending well into the shoulders. A very short neck giving a stuffy appearance, and a long, thin or ewe neck, are faulty.

Body—Rib cage should be well sprung, slightly egg-shaped, and moderately long. Deep chest, well let down between forelegs. Exaggerated lowness interferes with the desired freedom of movement and should be penalized. Viewed from above, the body should taper slightly to end of the loin. Loin short. Firm level topline, neither riding up to nor falling away at the croup. A slight depression behind the shoulders caused by heavier neck coat meeting the shorter body coat is permissible. Round or flat rib cage, lack of brisket, extreme length or cobbiness, are undesirable.

Forequarters—Legs short; forearms turned slightly inward, with the distance between the wrists less than between the shoulder joints, so that the front does not appear absolutely straight. Ample bone carried right down into the feet. Pasterns firm and nearly straight when viewed from the side. Weak pasterns and knuckling over are serious faults. Shoulder blades long and well laid back along the rib cage. Upper arms nearly equal in length to shoulder blades. Elbows parallel to the body, not prominent, and well set back to allow a line perpendicular to the ground to be drawn from the tip of the shoulder blade through to elbow.

Hindquarters—Ample bone, strong and flexible, moderately angulated at stifle and hock. Exaggerated angulation is as faulty as too little. Thighs should be well muscled. Hocks short, parallel, and when viewed from the side are perpendicular to the ground. Barrel hocks or cowhocks are most objectionable. Slipped or double-jointed hocks are very faulty.

Tail—Docked as short as possible without being indented. Occasionally a puppy is born with a natural dock, which if sufficiently short, is acceptable. A tail up to two inches in length is allowed, but if carried high tends to spoil the contour of the topline.

Feet—Oval, with the two center toes slightly in advance of the two outer ones. Turning neither in nor out. Pads strong and feet arched. Nails short. Dewclaws on both forelegs and hind legs usually removed. Too round, long and narrow, or splayed feet are faulty.

Movement—Free and smooth. Forelegs should reach well forward, without too much lift, in unison with the driving action of hind legs. The correct shoulder assembly and well-fitted elbows allow the long, free stride in front. Viewed from the front, legs do not move in exact parallel planes, but incline slightly inward to compensate for shortness of leg and width of chest. Hind legs should drive well under the body and move on a line with the forelegs, with hocks turning neither in nor out. Feet must travel parallel to the line of motion with no tendency to swing out, cross over, or interfere with each other. Short, choppy movement, rolling or high-stepping gait, close or overly wide coming or going, are incorrect. This is a herding dog which must have the agility, freedom of movement, and endurance to do the work for which he was developed.

Color—The outer coat is to be of self colors in red, sable, fawn, black and tan, with or without white markings. White is acceptable on legs, chest, neck (either in part or as a collar), muzzle, underparts, and as a narrow blaze on head.

Very Serious Faults—

Whitelies—Body color white with red or dark markings.

Mismarks—Self colors with any area of white on back between withers and tail, on sides between elbows and back of hindquarters, or on ears. Black with white markings and no tan present.

Blues—Colored portions of the coat have a distinct bluish or smoky cast. This coloring is associated with extremely light or blue eyes and liver or gray eye rims, nose and lip pigment.

Coat—Medium length; short, thick, weather-resistant undercoat with a coarser, longer outer coat. Over-all length varies, with slightly thicker and longer ruff around neck, chest and on the shoulders. The body coat lies flat. Hair is slightly longer on back of forelegs and underparts, and somewhat fuller and longer on rear of hindquarters. The coat is preferably straight, but some waviness is permitted. This breed has a shedding coat, and seasonal lack of undercoat should not be too severely penalized, providing the hair is glossy, healthy, and well groomed. A wiry, tightly marcelled coat is very faulty, as is an overly short, smooth and thin coat.

Very Serious Fault—

Fluffies—A coat of extreme length with exaggerated feathering on ears, chest, legs and feet, underparts and hindquarters. Trimming such a coat does not make it any more acceptable.

The Corgi should be shown in its natural condition, with no trimming permitted except to tidy the feet, and, if desired, remove the whiskers.

OVER-ALL PICTURE

Correct type, including general balance and outline, attractiveness of head-piece, intelligent outlook and correct temperament, is of primary importance. Movement is especially important, particularly as viewed from the side. A dog with smooth and free gait has to be reasonably sound and must be highly regarded. A minor fault must never take precedence over the above desired qualities.

A dog must be very seriously penalized for the following faults, regardless of whatever desirable qualities the dog may present:

Whitelies, Mismarks or Blues; Fluffies; Button, Rose or Drop Ears; Overshot or Undershot Bite; Oversize or Undersize.

The judge shall dismiss from the ring any Pembroke Welsh Corgi that is vicious or excessively shy.

Approved June 13, 1972.

416

Samoyed — *Ludwig*

Collies — *Cumbers*

Boxers — *Allen*

Kuvasz — *Allen*

Pulik — *Cumbers*

Bullmastiff — *Anderson*

Mastiff — *Thompson*

Komondor — *Ludwig*

Pembroke Welsh Corgi puppies — *Callea*

Cardigan Welsh Corgi — *McInnes*

Great Danes — *Allen*

Newfoundland

Rottweiler — *Cumbers*

Airedale Terrier — *Ludwig*

Bull Terrier (white) — *Thompson*

Bull Terrier (colored)

Bedlington Terrier — *Allen*

Border Terrier — *Roslin-Williams*

Fox Terriers (smooth) — *Allen*

Fox Terriers (wire) — *Cumbers*

Miniature Schnauzer — *Allen*

Kerry Blue Terrier — *Ashbey*

Norfolk Terrier — *Thompson*

Norwich Terrier — *Thompson*

Irish Terriers — *Cumbers*

Soft-Coated Wheaten Terriers — *Cumbers*

Sealyham Terriers — *Cumbers*

Scottish Terriers — *Cumbers*

GROUP IV: TERRIERS

Airedale Terrier

THE ORIGIN of the Airedale Terrier is enveloped in the same veil of theory and conjecture which shrouds the origin of all species in man's attempt to retrace the stages in evolution. Antique art records the existence of English dogs having a distinct resemblance to the terriers of later days and from which undoubtedly sprang the Broken-haired or Old English Terrier.

This extinct black and tan tyke is thought by some authorities to have been the common progenitor of the Irish, Fox, Welsh, and Airedale Terrier. At all events, an admixture of his varying types and sizes from seventeen to thirty pounds in weight formed the roots, so to speak, of the genealogical tree of the breed fostered by sporting Yorkshiremen for hunting the fox, badger, weasel, foumart, otter, water rat, and small game in the valleys of the rivers Colne, Calder, Warfe, and Aire. These constant companions and guardians, while excelling in agility, eyesight, hearing, and untiring courage, lacked the keen nose and swimming ability of the rough-coated Otter Hound, with which they competed in the chase, and was the wise reason for crossing the two breeds in the constructive attempt to embody the virtues of both in a better breed of larger and stronger terriers.

From 1864 on, the earlier whelps were called Working, Waterside, and Bingley Terriers. They were shown in increasing numbers at local agricultural shows at the time dog shows were in their early growth.

In 1879 classes were first provided for Airedale Terriers at the Airedale Agricultural Society's show held at Bingley, Yorkshire. Welsh Terriers received classification at shows in 1883, and the Smooth Fox Terrier received separate classifications at Birmingham in 1862. The towns of Skipton, Bradford, Keighley, and Otley followed Bingley with classifications, and some years later the competition for the Otley gold medal became the premier win in the breed.

Champion Master Briar (1897–1906) is conceded to be the patriarch of the breed. He may be likened to the trunk of the family tree whose branches grew in many directions. His great sons, Ch. Clonmel Monarch and Crompton Marvel, carried on his prepotency. The former was exported to Philadelphia, where ardent fanciers molded the breed in this hemisphere.

Present-day winners in most of the countries which breed, exhibit, and support the breed with Airedale Terrier clubs all now trace to the founders of the modern king of terriers. This honor goes to Ch. Warland Ditto (1919–1927), the Cragsman King family, and the celebrated Warland Kennels, which bred their foundation bitches to Ch. Rhosddu Royalist. His daughter, International Champion Warland Strategy, produced the key sire, which when bred to her sister, Warland Wingate, produced the great sire Ch. Warland Whatnot. He in turn sired Clonmel Monarque, whose sons Ch. Clee Courtier and Clee Brigand are responsible for the greater number of the 1928–1935 champions when bred to bitches by the record sire of champions, Ch. Flornell Mixer, a Warland Ditto grandson by Moorehead Marquis, whose grandam also owned Ch. Rhosddu Royalist as sire. Warland Ditto, his sire Cragsman Dictator, his dam, Ch. Warland Strategy, and her sire, Ch. Rhosddu Royalist, were all exported to the U.S.A.

Nearly all of the male lines of former families here and in Great Britain have disappeared, leaving few collateral sires for an outcross. We still have a few in descendants of Ch. Ridgewood Rocket, Ch. Geelong Cadet and Ch. Briarcroft Perfection—dogs which held their own in competition with imported champions at the large shows.

434

The degree of perfection of type attained in the breed by those who have carried on the idea of their standard is attested by the frequency with which Airedales have been judged best of all breeds in the most important all-breed shows of England and America. They shine, however, greatest in the minds of their many fond owners who value the faithful attachment, companionship, and protection of their families as a priceless possession.

Airedale Terriers are used on great game in Africa, India, Canada, and our game lands. They were among the first breeds used for police duty in Germany and Great Britain. They have also been used in several wars as dependable dispatch bearers due to their ability to suffer wounds, without faltering at the next order for duty. Their sweet disposition, possibly inherited from the hound blood, has endeared them to many of the best breeders and owners of leading kennels, many of whom are women who take a pride in showing their own stock. The correct temperament in puppyhood is one of discretion, and when mature, a certain dignified aloofness both with strangers and their kind. Their disposition can be molded by the patience of their masters in any environment, but when trained for defense and attack they are usually unbeatable for their weight.

Official Standard for the Airedale Terrier

Head—Should be well balanced with little apparent difference between the length of skull and foreface. *Skull* should be long and flat, not too broad between the ears and narrowing very slightly to the eyes. Scalp should be free from wrinkles, stop hardly visible and cheeks level and free from fullness. *Ears* should be V-shaped with carriage rather to the side of the head, not pointing to the eyes, small but not out of proportion to the size of the dog. The topline of the folded ear should be above the level of the skull. *Foreface* should be deep, powerful, strong and muscular. Should be well filled up before the eyes. *Eyes* should be dark, small, not prominent, full of terrier expression, keenness and intelligence. *Lips* should be tight. *Nose* should be black and not too small. *Teeth* should be strong and white, free from discoloration or defect. Bite either level or vise-like. A slightly overlapping or scissors bite is permissible without preference.

Neck—Should be of moderate length and thickness gradually widening towards the shoulders. Skin tight, not loose.

Shoulders and Chest—Shoulders long and sloping well into the back. Shoulder blades flat. From the front, chest deep but not broad. The depth of the chest should be approximately on a level with the elbows.

Body—Back should be short, strong and level. Ribs well sprung. Loins muscular and of good width. There should be but little space between the last rib and the hip joint.

Hindquarters—Should be strong and muscular with no droop.

Tail—The root of the tail should be set well up on the back. It should be carried gaily but not curled over the back. It should be of good strength and substance and of fair length.

Legs—*Forelegs* should be perfectly straight, with plenty of muscle and bone. *Elbows* should be perpendicular to the body, working free of sides. *Thighs* should be long and powerful with muscular second thigh, stifles well bent, not turned either in or out, hocks well let down parallel with each other when viewed from behind. *Feet* should be small, round and compact with a good depth of pad, well cushioned; the toes moderately arched, not turned either in or out.

Coat—Should be hard, dense and wiry, lying straight and close, covering the dog well over the body and legs. Some of the hardest are crinkling or just slightly waved. At the base of the hard very stiff hair should be a shorter growth of softer hair termed the undercoat.

Color—The head and ears should be tan, the ears being of a darker shade than the rest. Dark markings on either side of the skull are permissible. The legs up to the thighs and elbows and the under-part of the body and chest are also tan and the tan frequently runs into the shoulder. The sides and upper parts of the body should be black or dark grizzle. A red mixture is often found in the black and is not to be considered objectionable. A small white blaze on the chest is a characteristic of certain strains of the breed.

Size—Dogs should measure approximately 23 inches in height at the shoulder; bitches, slightly less. Both sexes should be sturdy, well muscled and boned.

Movement—Movement or action is the crucial test of conformation. Movement should be free. As seen from the front the forelegs should swing perpendicular from the body free from the sides, the feet the same distance apart as the elbows. As seen from the rear the hind legs should be parallel with each other, neither too close nor too far apart, but so placed as to give a strong well-balanced stance and movement. The toes should not be turned either in or out.

FAULTS

Yellow eyes, hound ears, white feet, soft coat, being much over or under the size limit, being undershot or overshot, having poor movement, are faults which should be severely penalized.

SCALE OF POINTS

Head	10	Color	5
Neck, shoulders and chest	10	Size	10
Body	10	Movement	10
Hindquarters and tail	10	General characteristics and	
Legs and feet	10	expression	15
Coat	10	TOTAL	100

Approved July 14, 1959

American Staffordshire Terrier

ORIGINALLY accepted for registration in The American Kennel Club stud book in 1935 as Staffordshire Terrier, the name of the breed was changed January 1, 1972, to American Staffordshire Terrier.

To give correctly the origin and history of the American Staffordshire Terrier, it is necessary to comment briefly on two other dogs, namely the Bulldog and the terrier.

Until the early part of the nineteenth century, the Bulldog was bred with great care in England for the purpose of baiting bulls. The Bulldog of that day was vastly different from our present-day "sourmug". Pictures from as late as 1870 represent the Bulldog as agile and as standing straight on his legs—his front legs in particular. In some cases he was even possessed of a muzzle, and long rat tails were not uncommon. The Bulldog of that day, with the exception of the head, looked more like the present-day American Staffordshire Terrier than like the present-day Bulldog.

Some writers contend it was the white English Terrier, or the Black-and-Tan Terrier, that was used as a cross with the Bulldog to perfect the Staffordshire Terrier. It seems easier to believe that any game terrier, such as the Fox Terrier of the early 1800s, was used in this cross, since some of the foremost authorities on dogs of that time state that the Black-and-Tan and the white English Terrier were none too game, but these same authorities go on to stress the gameness of the Fox Terrier. It is reasonable to believe that breeders who were attempting to perfect a dog that would combine the spirit and agility of the terrier with the courage and tenacity of the Bulldog, would not use a terrier which was not game. In analyzing the three above-mentioned terriers at that time, we find that there was not a great deal of difference in body conformation, the greatest differences being in color, aggressiveness, and spirit.

In any event, it was the cross between the Bulldog and the terrier that resulted in the Staffordshire Terrier, which was originally called the Bull-and-Terrier Dog, Half and Half, and at times Pit Dog or Pit Bullterrier, later assuming the name in England of Staffordshire Bull Terrier. As early as 1870, these dogs began to find their way into this country, where they became known as Pit Dog, Pit Bull Terrier, later American Bull Terrier, and still later, as Yankee Terrier.

They were recognized by the American Kennel Club under the name Staffordshire Terrier in 1935, with the name revised January 1, 1972 to American Staffordshire Terrier. The name Staffordshire Bull Terrier was originally applied to this dog in England.

Breeders in this country developed a type which is heavier in weight than the Staffordshire Bull Terrier of England, the latter now being considered a different breed in the United States, thus the name American Staffordshire Terrier. While the weight may vary, it should be in proportion to size. The American Staffordshire Terrier's chief requisites should be strength unusual for his size, soundness, balance, a strong, powerful head, a well-muscled body, and courage that is proverbial.

To clarify the confusion that may exist, even in the minds of dog fanciers, concerning the difference between the Bull Terrier and the American Staffordshire Terrier, it is advisable to comment briefly upon Bull Terriers. The Bull Terrier was introduced by Mr. James Hinks of Birmingham, who had been experimenting for several years with the old bull-and-terrier dog, now known as Staffordshire. It is generally conceded that he used the Staffordshire, crossed with the white English Terrier, and some writers contend that a dash of Pointer and Dalmatian blood was also used to help perfect the all-white Bull Terrier.

In mentioning the gameness of the Staffordshire, it is not the intention to tag him as a fighting machine, or to praise this characteristic. These points are discussed because they are necessary in giving the correct origin and history of the breed. The good qualities of the dogs are many, and it would be difficult for anyone to overstress them. In appearance, they are flashy-looking and they attract much attention on the show bench. As to character, they exceed being dead game; nevertheless, they should not be held in ill repute merely because man has been taking advantage of this rare courage to use them in the pit as gambling tools. These dogs are docile, and with a little training are even tractable around other dogs. They are intelligent, excellent guardians, and they protect their masters' property with an air of authority that counts; they easily discriminate between strangers who mean well and those who do not. They have another characteristic that is unusual: when they are sold, or change hands, they accept their new master in a comparatively short time.

Official Standard for the American Staffordshire Terrier

General Impression—The American Staffordshire Terrier should give the impression of great strength for his size, a well put-together dog, muscular, but agile and graceful, keenly alive to his surroundings. He should be stocky, not long-legged or racy in outline. His courage is proverbial.

Head—Medium length, deep through, broad skull, very pronounced cheek muscles, distinct stop; and ears are set high. *Ears*—Cropped or uncropped, the latter preferred. Uncropped ears should be short and held half rose or prick. Full drop to be penalized. *Eyes*—Dark and round, low down in skull and set far apart. No pink eyelids. *Muzzle*—Medium length, rounded on upper side to fall away abruptly below eyes. Jaws well defined. Underjaw to be strong and have biting power. Lips close and even, no looseness. Upper teeth to meet tightly outside lower teeth in front. Nose definitely black.

Neck—Heavy, slightly arched, tapering from shoulders to back of skull. No looseness of skin. Medium length.

Shoulders—Strong and muscular with blades wide and sloping.

Back—Fairly short. Slight sloping from withers to rump with gentle short slope at rump to base of tail. Loins slightly tucked.

Body—Well-sprung ribs, deep in rear. All ribs close together. Forelegs set rather wide apart to permit of chest development. Chest deep and broad.

Tail—Short in comparison to size, low set, tapering to a fine point; not curled or held over back. Not docked.

Legs—The front legs should be straight, large or round bones, pastern upright. No resemblance of bend in front. Hindquarters well-muscled, let down at hocks, turning neither in nor out. Feet of moderate size, well-arched and compact. Gait must be springy but without roll or pace.

Coat—Short, close, stiff to the touch, and glossy.

Color—Any color, solid, parti, or patched is permissible, but all white, more than 80 per cent white, black and tan, and liver not to be encouraged.

Size—Height and weight should be in proportion. A height of about 18 to 19 inches at shoulders for the male and 17 to 18 inches for the female is to be considered preferable.

Faults—Faults to be penalized are: Dudley nose, light or pink eyes, tail too long or badly carried, undershot or overshot mouths.

Approved, June 10, 1936

Australian Terrier

AS THE HISTORY of breeds is reckoned, the Australian Terrier is of comparatively recent origin. It is believed that its ancestors first appeared on the show bench in the years 1872 to 1876, included with (or as) Broken-haired Terriers, though there is record of an entry of a Rough-haired Terrier at the Queensland Royal Show in 1868. In 1885 there was the first entry for an Australian Rough at Melbourne. By 1899 it was exhibited as an Australian Terrier, rough coated, at the Sydney Royal Easter show.

In those years in Australia this type of dog was casually known by these several names, noting a far-flung stock of many terrier breeds. The Broken-hair or Rough-coat Terrier most resembled the old Scotch, not to be confused with the later Scottish Terrier. However, as breeders came to discover, these early dogs could not compete successfully with the more modern Scotties and other like Terriers being imported from Britain. So, as has been the case with many breeds during their inception, crosses were resorted to for improvement and the dog was molded to a type in keeping with what Australian fanciers thought it should be.

Several Terriers entered into the composition of the Australian Terrier, although few agree as to exactly which ones. The Cairn (though not imported to Australia until the 1914 era), the Dandie Dinmont, the Irish Terrier, the Black-and-Tan (today known as the Manchester Terrier), the Yorkshire and the prick-eared Skye have all been given credit for participation by different people at different times.

But, what is just as likely, the qualities attributed to these breeds may have been handed down by way of a common related ancestry with all the short-legged sporting Terriers originating in the British Isles.

There is sufficient evidence from references in Terrier history to be confident that the Australian Terrier is a composite of several of those considered best for a "three-way" small sporting-working Terrier: (1) For the home—companionable, affectionate, intelligent, protective, and not high-strung. (2) Sturdy—with a pleasing general appearance that is without physical structure handicaps, and owning an easy-to-care-for coat and a history for longevity. (3) Possessing a body able to go to ground; with a strong jaw, good nose and eyesight above average. Also, a protective ruff for the throat in combat with snakes and vermin, and a topknot to shield the eyes. All mark the Aussie as a truly desirable dog for the purposes required.

Being a true pioneer and colonist, each of these little Terriers possesses the virtue of originality of character, bringing constant new interest and joy to its family as it develops its own amusing and endearing characteristics. The Aussie can be keenly alert or he can lapse into a soft mood that has you wondering if he is daydreaming of the gorse-heather covered moors or the eucalyptus-wattle tree scenes of his origin.

The first of the many world-wide Australian Terrier clubs was formed in Melbourne in 1889, and the Standard established in 1896. The breed was not long in gathering to itself an enthusiastic coterie of admirers, not only because of its gratifying individuality of appearance (which was displayed proudly riding in carriages owned by the more prosperous pioneers) but also because of its adaptability as a useful small hunter and protector in the Australian bushland.

The Australian Terrier was granted breed status in England in 1933, and is currently recognized in Canada, Ireland, India, South Africa, South America, Mexico, Europe and of course, Australasia. Aussies were introduced into the United States during the first quarter of the century and were admitted to registry by the AKC in 1960. The standard approved then has not changed except to make a proper correction so that Blue-Tans and Sandy-Reds are equally acceptable. In 1977, the parent Australian Terrier Club of America became a member club of the AKC.

Here is one of the smallest working Terriers—about 10" shoulder height and 12 to 14 lbs. in weight—but all dog and ready to go. His courage, his spirit, and his constant air of assurance and intelligence are in-born qualities, dating back to the days in his native land when he guarded the mines and tended the sheep. He is a welcome protector, seeming to accept responsibility for home and household—in city or country—and ever ready to alert and guard his family. Withal he is not aggressive, but rather quiet for one of his kind and extremely affectionate. His harsh coat is good for any weather, and its slight or gradual shedding is only one point of many in his favor as both an indoor and outdoor companion.

Official Standard for the Australian Terrier

General Appearance—Small, sturdy, rough-coated terrier of spirited action and self-assured manner.

Head—Long, flat-skulled, and full between the eyes, with the stop moderate. The muzzle is no longer than the distance from the eyes to the occiput. Jaws long and powerful, teeth of good size meeting in a scissors bite, although a level bite is acceptable. **Nose**—Black. **Ears**—Set high on the skull and well apart. They are small and pricked, the leather either pointed or slightly rounded and free from long hairs. **Eyes**—Small, dark, and keen in expression; not prominent. Light-colored and protruding eyes are faulty.

Neck—Inclined to be long, and tapering into sloping shoulders; well furnished with hair which forms a protective ruff.

Body—Low-set and slightly longer from the withers to the root of the tail than from the withers to the ground. **Chest**—Medium wide, and deep, with ribs well sprung but not round. Topline level.

Tail—Set on high and carried erect but not too gay; docked leaving two fifths.

Legs and Feet—Forelegs straight and slightly feathered to the carpus or so-called knee; they are set well under the body with elbows close and pasterns strong. Hindquarters strong and well muscled but not heavy; legs moderately angulated at stifles and hocks, with hocks well let down. Bone medium in size. Feet are small, clean, and catlike, the toes arched and compact, nicely padded and free from long hair. Nails strong and black.

Coat—Outer coat harsh and straight, and about two and one half inches all over the body. Undercoat short and soft. The topknot, which covers only the top of the skull, is of finer texture and lighter color than the body coat.

Color—May be blue-black or silver-black, with rich tan markings on head and legs, sandy color or clear red. The blue-black is bluish at the roots and dark at the tips. In the silver-blacks each hair carries black and silver alternating with black at the tips. The tan is rich and deep, the richer the better. In the sandies, any suggestion of smuttiness is undesirable.

Gait—Straight and true; sprightly, indicating spirit and assurance.

Temperament—That of a hard-bitten terrier, with the aggressiveness of the natural ratter and hedge hunter, but as a companion, friendly, affectionate, and biddable.

Size—Shoulder height, about 10 inches. Average weight 12 to 14 pounds.

Approved October 13, 1970

Bedlington Terrier

THE BEDLINGTON TERRIER takes his name from the mining shire of that name, in the County of Northumberland, England. Purely a Northumbrian production, he first came to be known as the Rothbury Terrier, having originated in the Hannys hills, where the sporting squires loved a game terrier.

The origin of the breed remains a mystery. However, going back to 1820, we find that a Joseph Ainsley of Bedlington acquired a bitch, Phoebe, from a friend at Alnwick. This bitch was known as Coates Phoebe, since she found her home at the vicarage where young Coates, the vicar's son, had sporting proclivities. In 1825 Phoebe was mated to a Rothbury dog, Andersons Piper, also acquired by Ainsley of Bedlington, and the fruit of this union was the Bedlington Terrier in question.

About this time there flourished in Bedlington a colony of nailers who took to the breed and became noted for their plucky terriers. Of this dog's gameness there was not the slightest doubt—he never shirked at any kind of vermin and could more than hold his own at drawing a badger or at ratting in or out of Wales.

Although many crosses were introduced, there was always a band of enthusiastic admirers who kept to the original breed, and it was not until 1877 that the National Bedlington Terrier Club (England) was formed by a few influential fanciers who made themselves responsible for bringing him to the notice of the public by exhibiting him on the show bench. Since then the Bedlington has made vast improvement in type.

Many tales have been told by the older generation of matches made by the miners and nailers of that period, where large sums were at stake on the result of a fight between terriers of their respective fancies. The Bedlington was never a mischief seeker, but once he started fighting, it was to the death.

As time went on, he was taken into the homes of the elite, who found him a tractable and first-class companion. He was not long in developing into a pet, his great heart and lovable nature endearing him to all fortunate enough to own him.

There are two distinct colors, liver and blue, and it is only a question of fancy as to which is preferred. In the early days the liver was much in evidence, and some great dogs were of that color; in fact, the liver dog was preferred to the blue which is now so fashionable. Whether the former shade has become rarer from a change of tastes on the part of Bedlington breeders, or whether it is merely a coincidence that so few good liver-colored specimens happen to be shown at the present time, we are unable to say, but the fact remains that of late high-class blue Bedlingtons far outnumber good liver specimens. While there have been many good specimens of both colors, it is noticeable that the mother of the celebrated Piper was a blue-black bitch, possessing a light-colored topknot, a characteristic which has been meticulously preserved.

Both Piper and his mother, Phoebe, were considerably lighter in weight and smaller in stature than the dogs of the present day. But it is on record that Piper was set on a badger at eight months old and was constantly at work, more or less on badgers, foxes, otters and other vermin. He drew a badger after he was fourteen years old, when toothless and nearly blind, after several other terriers had failed.

There are not many today that would face a badger, owing no doubt to the fact that women have adopted the Bedlington and he is becoming more of a pet. However, the old fire is latent within him, for when his jealous nature is aroused, he will fight for his place in one's affection.

One reason there were fewer Bedlingtons at one time than their desirability warranted was the trimming necessary for exhibition in the show ring. Known only to a few so-called experts, this trimming seemed difficult. Gradually, however, the knack was mastered, so that now most owners trim their own dogs and find it quite easy. It is only necessary to see it done by someone who knows how, after which, with a little practice, the novice becomes expert. The dog is hardy and not difficult to raise, and his feeding is the same as that required for other terriers of like weight.

Official Standard for the
Bedlington Terrier

General Appearance—A graceful, lithe, well-balanced dog with no sign of coarseness, weakness or shelliness. In repose the expression is mild and gentle, not shy or nervous. Aroused, the dog is particularly alert and full of immense energy and courage. Noteworthy for endurance, Bedlingtons also gallop at great speed, as their body outline clearly shows.

Head—Narrow, but deep and rounded. Shorter in skull and longer in jaw. Covered with a profuse topknot which is lighter than the color of the body, highest at the crown, and tapering gradually to just back of the nose. There must be no stop and the unbroken line from crown to nose end reveals a slender head without cheekiness or snipiness. Lips are black in the blue and tans and brown in all other solid and bi-colors. *Eyes*—Almond-shaped, small, bright and well sunk with no tendency to tear or water. Set is oblique and fairly high on the head. Blues have dark eyes; blues and tans, less dark with amber lights; sandies, sandies and tans, light hazel; liver, livers and tans, slightly darker. Eye rims are black in the blue and blue and tans, and brown in all other solid and bi-colors. *Ears*—Triangular with rounded tips. Set on low and hanging flat to the cheek in front with a slight projection at the base. Point of greatest width approximately 3 inches. Ear tips reach the corners of the mouth. Thin and velvety in texture, covered with fine hair forming a small silky tassel at the tip. *Nose*—Nostrils large and well defined. Blues and blues and tans have black noses. Livers, livers and tans, sandies, sandies and tans have brown noses. *Jaws*—Long and tapering. Strong muzzle well filled up with bone beneath the eye. Close-fitting lips, no flews. *Teeth*—Large, strong and white. Level or scissors bite. Lower canines clasp the outer surface of the upper gum just in front of the upper canines. Upper premolars and molars lie outside those of the lower jaw.

Neck and Shoulders—Long, tapering neck with no throatiness, deep at the base and rising well up from the shoulders which are flat and sloping with no excessive musculature. The head is carried high.

Body—Muscular and markedly flexible. Chest deep. Flat-ribbed and deep through the brisket, which reaches to the elbows. Back has a good natural arch over the loin, creating a definite tuck-up of the underline. Body slightly greater in length than height. Well-muscled quarters are also fine and graceful.

Legs and Feet—Lithe and muscular. The hind legs are longer than the forelegs, which are straight and wider apart at the chest than at the feet. Slight bend to pasterns which are long and sloping without weakness. Stifles well angulated. Hocks strong and well let down, turning neither in nor out. Long hare feet with thick, well-closed-up, smooth pads. Dewclaws should be removed.

446

Coat—A very distinctive mixture of hard and soft hair standing well out from the skin. Crisp to the touch but not wiry, having a tendency to curl, especially on the head and face. When in show trim must not exceed 1 inch on body; hair on legs is slightly longer.

Tail—Set low, scimitar-shaped, thick at the root and tapering to a point which reaches the hock. Not carried over the back or tight to the underbody.

Color—Blue, sandy, liver, blue and tan, sandy and tan, liver and tan. In bicolors the tan markings are found on the legs, chest, under the tail, inside the hindquarters and over each eye. The topknots of all adults should be lighter than the body color. Patches of darker hair from an injury are not objectionable, as these are only temporary. Darker body pigmentation of all colors is to be encouraged.

Height—The preferred Bedlington Terrier dog measures 16^1/$_2$ inches at the withers, the bitch 15^1/$_2$ inches. Under 16 inches or over 17^1/$_2$ inches for dogs and under 15 inches or over 16^1/$_2$ inches for bitches are serious faults. Only where comparative superiority of a specimen outside these ranges clearly justifies it, should greater latitude be taken.

Weight—To be proportionate to height within the range of 17 to 23 pounds.

Gait—Unique lightness of movement. Springy in the slower paces, not stilted or hackneyed. Must not cross, weave or paddle.

Approved September 12, 1967

Border Terrier

AS THE NAME suggests, the Border Terrier has its origin on either side of the Cheviot Hills which form the Border country, and may be regarded as one of the oldest kinds of terriers in Great Britain. As a purely "working terrier," Border farmers, shepherds, and sportsmen for generations carefully preserved a particular strain of this dog which could be found in almost every Border homestead.

With the hills at their disposal and miles from habitation, stock was subjected to the ravages of the powerful hill foxes, and to hunt and kill them the Border farmer and shepherd required a game terrier with length of leg sufficient to follow a horse, yet small enough to follow a fox to ground. The dogs had to be active, strong, and tireless; they had to have weather-resisting coats in order to withstand prolonged exposure to drenching rains and mists in the hills.

The Border Terrier is a tireless, hard worker for his size, and he is full of pluck. There is no wall he cannot get over or wire entanglement he cannot scramble through. Should the fox run to earth, he will bolt him every time, or stay the night in the earth until the matter is settled from his point of view. It may therefore be gathered that in order to meet these requirements the Border Terrier, as now known, was evolved by a process of judicious selection from the native hill terriers.

448

Until the English Kennel Club recognition was given, the Border Terrier was unknown to the great majority, but he was always exhibited in considerable numbers at most of the Agricultural Societies' shows in the Border country. Following recognition by the English Kennel Club and the formation of the Border Terrier Club in 1920, the breed has been catered to at many of the important shows in the British Isles, but few specimens are as yet seen at shows in the United States.

Official Standard for the Border Terrier

Since the Border Terrier is a working terrier of a size to go to ground and able, within reason, to follow a horse, his conformation should be such that he be ideally built to do his job. No deviations from this ideal conformation should be permitted, which would impair his usefulness in running his quarry to earth and in bolting it therefrom. For this work he must be alert, active and agile, and capable of squeezing through narrow apertures and rapidly traversing any kind of terrain. His head, "like that of an otter," is distinctive, and his temperament ideally exemplifies that of a terrier. By nature he is good-tempered, affectionate, obedient, and easily trained. In the field he is hard as nails, "game as they come" and driving in attack. It should be the aim of Border Terrier breeders to avoid such over-emphasis of any point in the Standard as might lead to unbalanced exaggeration.

General Appearance—He is an active terrier of medium bone, strongly put together, suggesting endurance and agility, but rather narrow in shoulder, body and quarter. The body is covered with a somewhat broken though close-fitting and intensely wiry jacket. The characteristic "otter" head with its keen eye, combined with a body poise which is "at the alert," gives a look of fearless and implacable determination characteristic of the breed. The proportions should be that the height at the withers is slightly greater than the distance from the withers to the tail, *i.e.* by possibly 1-1½ inches in a 14-pound dog.

Weight—Dogs, 13-15½ pounds, bitches, 11½-14 pounds, are appropriate weights for Border Terriers in hard-working condition.

Head—Similar to that of an otter. Moderately broad and flat in skull with plenty of width between the eyes and between the ears. A slight, moderately broad curve at the stop rather than a pronounced indentation. Cheeks slightly full. *Ears*—Small, V-shaped and of moderate thickness, dark preferred. Not set high on the head but somewhat on the side, and dropping forward close to the cheeks. They should not break above the level of the skull. *Eyes*—Dark hazel and full of fire and intelligence. Moderate in size, neither prominent nor small and beady. *Muzzle*—Short and "well filled." A dark muzzle is characteristic and desirable. A few short whiskers are natural to the breed. *Teeth*—Strong, with a scissors bite, large in proportion to size of dog. *Nose*—Black, and of a good size.

Neck—Clean, muscular and only long enough to give a well-balanced appearance. It should gradually widen into the shoulder. *Shoulders*—Well laid back and of good length, the blades converging to the withers gradually from a brisket not excessively deep or narrow.

Forelegs—Straight and not too heavy in bone and placed slightly wider than in a Fox Terrier. *Feet*—Small and compact. Toes should point forward and be moderately arched with thick pads.

Body—Deep, fairly narrow and of sufficient length to avoid any suggestions of lack of range and agility. Deep ribs carried well back and not oversprung in view of the desired depth and narrowness of the body. The body should be capable of being spanned by a man's hands behind the shoulders. Back strong but laterally supple, with no suspicion of a dip behind the shoulder. Loin strong and the underline fairly straight.

Tail—Moderately short, thick at the base, then tapering. Not set on too high. Carried gaily when at the alert, but not over the back. When at ease, a Border may drop his stern.

Hindquarters—Muscular and racy, with thighs long and nicely molded. Stifles well bent and hocks well let down.

Coat—A short and dense undercoat covered with a very wiry and somewhat broken top coat which should lie closely, but it must not show any tendency to curl or wave. With such a coat a Border should be able to be exhibited almost in his natural state, nothing more in the way of trimming being needed than a tidying-up of the head, neck and feet. *Hide*—Very thick and loose fitting.

Movement—Straight and rhythmical before and behind, with good length of stride and flexing of stifle and hock. The dog should respond to his handler with a gait which is free, agile and quick.

Color—Red, grizzle and tan, blue and tan, or wheaten. A small amount of white may be allowed on the chest but white on the feet should be penalized.

SCALE OF POINTS

Head, ears, neck and teeth	20	Back and loin	10
Legs and feet	15	Hindquarters	10
Coat and skin	10	Tail	5
Shoulders and chest	10	General appearance	10
Eyes and expression	10	TOTAL	100

Approved March 14, 1950

Bull Terrier

THERE ARE two varieties of the Bull Terrier breed, the white and the colored. The breed dates back to about 1835. It is almost unanimously believed that it was established by mating a Bulldog to a white English Terrier, which breed is now extinct. The results were known as the "bull and terrier." Some few years later, to gain size, this dog was crossed with the Spanish Pointer, and even to this day evidence of Pointer inheritance is seen occasionally.

Then about the year 1860 fanciers decided that an entirely white dog would be more attractive, so James Hinks produced an all white one which was taken up enthusiastically by young bloods of the day as the most fashionable dog.

It was a dog for sportsmen in times when life in general was more strenuous and of rougher, coarser fiber—when dog fights were allowed and well attended. As fighting dog, or "gladiator," of the canine world, such a dog had to be of great strength, agility, and courage. Withal, he was bred by gentlemen, for gentlemen, for those who had a great sense of fair play, and who scorned the liar and the deceiver in any game. The dog was taught to defend himself and his master courageously, yet he was not to seek or provoke a fight—and so the white variety became known as "the white cavalier," a title which he bears with distinction to this day.

Contrary to the opinion of those who do not know him, the Bull Terrier is an exceedingly friendly dog; he thrives on affection, yet is always ready for a fight and a frolic. The preference in this country is for a well-balanced animal, not freaky in any particular, but well-put-together, active and agile—a gladiator of perfect form.

There is also the Colored Bull Terrier which, in accordance with its Standard, must be any color other than white, or any color with white just so long as the white does not predominate. The "Colored" was voted a separate variety of Bull Terrier in 1936.

Official Standard for the
Bull Terrier

WHITE

The Bull Terrier must be strongly built, muscular, symmetrical and active, with a keen determined and intelligent expression, full of fire but of sweet disposition and amenable to discipline.

The Head should be long, strong and deep right to the end of the muzzle, but not coarse. Full face it should be oval in outline and be filled completely up giving the impression of fullness with a surface devoid of hollows or indentations, *i.e.*, egg shaped. In profile it should curve gently downwards from the top of the skull to the tip of the nose. The forehead should be flat across from ear to ear. The distance from the tip of the nose to the eyes should be perceptibly greater than that from the eyes to the top of the skull. The underjaw should be deep and well defined. *The Lips* should be clean and tight. *The Teeth* should meet in either a level or in a scissors bite. In the scissors bite the upper teeth should fit in front of and closely against the lower teeth, and they should be sound, strong and perfectly regular.

The Ears should be small, thin and placed close together. They should be capable of being held stiffly erect, when they should point upwards. *The Eyes* should be well sunken and as dark as possible, with a piercing glint and they should be small, triangular and obliquely placed; set near together and high up on the dog's head. Blue eyes are a disqualification. *The Nose* should be black, with well-developed nostrils bent downward at the tip.

The Neck should be very muscular, long, arched and clean, tapering from the shoulders to the head and it should be free from loose skin. *The Chest* should be broad when viewed from in front, and there should be great depth from withers to brisket, so that the latter is nearer the ground than the belly.

The Body should be well rounded with marked spring of rib, the back should be short and strong. The back ribs deep. Slightly arched over the loin. The shoulders should be strong and muscular but without heaviness. The shoulder blades should be wide and flat and there should be a very pronounced backward slope from the bottom edge of the blade to the top edge. Behind the shoulders there should be no slackness or dip at the withers. The underline from the brisket to the belly should form a graceful upward curve.

The Legs should be big boned but not to the point of coarseness; the forelegs should be of moderate length, perfectly straight, and the dog must stand firmly upon them. The elbows must turn neither in nor out, and the pasterns should be strong and upright. The hind legs should be parallel viewed from behind. The thighs very muscular with hocks well let down. Hind pasterns short and upright. The stifle joint should be well bent with a well-developed second thigh. *The Feet* round and compact with well-arched toes like a cat.

The Tail should be short, set on low, fine, and ideally should be carried horizontally. It should be thick where it joins the body, and should taper to a fine point.

The Coat should be short, flat, harsh to the touch and with a fine gloss. The dog's skin should fit tightly. *The Color* is white though markings on the head are permissible. Any markings elsewhere on the coat are to be severely faulted. Skin pigmentation is not to be penalized.

Movement—The dog shall move smoothly, covering the ground with free, easy strides, fore and hind legs should move parallel each to each when viewed from in front or behind. The forelegs reaching out well and the hind legs moving smoothly at the hip and flexing well at the stifle and hock. The dog should move compactly and in one piece but with a typical jaunty air that suggests agility and power.

FAULTS

Any departure from the foregoing points shall be considered a fault, and the seriousness of the fault shall be in exact proportion to its degree, *i.e.* a very crooked front is a very bad fault; a rather crooked front is a rather bad fault; and a slightly crooked front is a slight fault.

DISQUALIFICATION

Blue eyes.

COLORED

The Standard for the Colored Variety is the same as for the White except for the sub-head "Color" which reads: *Color.* Any color other than white, or any color with white markings. Other things being equal, the preferred color is brindle. A dog which is predominantly white shall be disqualified.

DISQUALIFICATIONS

Blue eyes.
Any dog which is predominantly white.

Approved July 9, 1974

Cairn Terrier

THE HISTORY of the Cairn Terrier is enhanced by the fact that the modern Cairn is an attempt to preserve in typical form the old-time working terrier of the Isle of Skye. The fancier, for a proper appreciation of the Cairn, should know what the uses and appearance of these terriers were. Fortunately weights, engravings, measurements, descriptions of their appearance, and accounts of the use of these terriers exist.

From Martin's *History of the Dog* in 1845, Capt. McDonald's description and measurements of the ideal Cairn in 1876, from Ross's *Cairn Terrier*, Darley Matheson's *Terriers*, and many other writers, it is plain that these were working terriers, with courage for the bolting of otter, foxes, and other vermin from among rocks, cliffs, and ledges on the wild shores of their misty isle.

Variation in appearance existed in these early times, as each breeder had his own fancies. But continued selection for a definite purpose soon resulted in the production of a rather definite type. This was a terrier weighing from fourteen to sixteen pounds, with the bitches two pounds or so less; a dog active, game, rather longish in body, short on the leg, with short, pointed muzzle, broad head; ears short, erect, pointed, and set wide apart; large, expressive dark eyes; with hard coat not over an inch and a half long and soft furry undercoat.

The Cairn's sporting instincts and vermin-killing ability made him a useful member of the laird's and crofter's households. Becoming popular with those who desired a sporting terrier capable of hunting in all weather, he was taken up by fanciers and admitted to the English Kennel Club *Stud Book* as a recognized breed.

To retain the best old-working type was the ideal aimed at by the English Cairn Terrier Club on its formation. The Cairn Terrier Club of America has the same object. Both clubs have the same ideal weight for dogs—fourteen pounds or a stone. The two standards with only slight differences in wording describe the same dog—the old-time terrier of the Isle of Skye and the West Highlands of Scotland.

The Cairn has characteristics in common with other breeds of terriers. He should have a level back with tail set on at back level, a straight front, well-sloped shoulders, deep brisket, strong loins and hindquarters, compact feet with thick pads, and he should move easily and freely on a loose lead with terrier smartness and style. But, while these points of contact with other breeds of terriers exist, there are also marked differences which are of great importance to the continuation of the Cairn's distinctive qualities.

In head, the Cairn differs from all other terriers. Short and broad-headed, his foreface should be little, if any, longer than the distance from stop to occiput. The muzzle should be rather pointed and not too heavy or deep. He should have a well-defined stop and a slight indentation between the eyes, flattening out into his broad skull. The ears should be set wide apart, neither too far down on the side nor too high up on the head. They should be small, short, pointed, erect, and free from long hairs. The expression should be keen, alert, varminty. He should have a medium-sized, dark hazel eye, distinct eyelashes, and shaggy protecting brows. He should have plenty of head furnishings, which may be softer than his body coat. Lack of these spoils the characteristic appearance of the head, which is, perhaps, the most important feature of the breed. A Cairn with a good head is half through in the show ring.

The height of the Cairn, which differs from that of other terriers, is important in giving the breed the distinctive conformation which the late Mr. Glynn called "Cairnishness." He is not so low to ground, and in proportion to his size, is slightly longer in back than the Sealyham and the Scottish Terrier.

The Cairn's typical coat is double with a harsh outer jacket and a soft furry undercoat. Any color except white is permissible, and dark points—muzzle, ears, and tail—are desirable. He is not trimmed, only a certain amount of "tidying up" being allowable. He should always be shown in good coat and with plenty of head furnishings, for a proper coat is one of the breed's distinctive features. There is one, and only one, correct size for the Cairn Terrier—fourteen pounds for dogs, thirteen pounds for bitches, and the dogs should be in proper proportion to those weights.

The modern Cairn should have the hardiness to meet the performance of his old-time prototype. Utility should be the aim of the fancier, since the expressed object of the Cairn Terrier Clubs is to preserve the breed in its best old-working type. If the breed is to resist passing fads and the inroads of modernization, the first consideration in judging should be given to those qualities which are unique in the Cairn.

Official Standard for the Cairn Terrier

General Appearance—That of an active, game, hardy, small working terrier of the short-legged class; very free in its movements, strongly but not heavily built, standing well forward on its forelegs, deep in the ribs, well coupled with strong hindquarters and presenting a well-proportioned build with a medium length of back, having a hard, weather-resisting coat; head shorter and wider than any other terrier and well furnished with hair giving a general foxy expression.

Head:
Skull—Broad in proportion to length with a decided stop and well furnished with hair on the top of the head, which may be somewhat softer than the body coat. *Muzzle*—Strong but not too long or heavy. *Teeth*—Large, mouth neither overshot nor undershot. *Nose*—Black. *Eyes*—Set wide apart, rather sunken, with shaggy eyebrows, medium in size, hazel or dark hazel in color, depending on body color, with a keen terrier expression. *Ears*—Small, pointed, well carried erectly, set wide apart on the side of the head. Free from long hairs.

Tail—In proportion to head, well furnished with hair but not feathery. Carried gaily but must not curl over back. Set on at back level.

Body—Well muscled, strong, active body with well-sprung, deep ribs, coupled to strong hindquarters, with a level back of medium length, giving an impression of strength and activity without heaviness.

Shoulders, Legs and Feet—A sloping shoulder, medium length of leg, good but not too heavy bone; forelegs should not be out at elbows, and be perfectly straight, but forefeet may be slightly turned out. Forefeet larger than hind feet. Legs must be covered with hard hair. Pads should be thick and strong and dog should stand well up on its feet.

Coat—Hard and weather-resistant. Must be double-coated with profuse harsh outer coat and short, soft, close furry undercoat.

Color—May be of any color except white. Dark ears, muzzle and tail tip are desirable.

Ideal Size—Involves the weight, the height at the withers and the length of body. Weight for bitches, 13 pounds; for dogs, 14 pounds. Height at the withers—bitches, 9½ inches; dogs, 10 inches. Length of body from 14¼ to 15 inches from the front of the chest to back of hindquarters. The dog must be of balanced proportions and appear neither leggy nor too low to ground; and neither too short nor too long in body. Weight and measurements are for matured dogs at two years of age. Older dogs may weigh slightly in excess and growing dogs may be under these weights and measurements.

Condition—Dogs should be shown in good hard flesh, well muscled and neither too fat or thin. Should be in full good coat with plenty of head furnishings, be clean, combed, brushed and tidied up on ears, tail, feet and general outline. Should move freely and easily on a loose lead, should not cringe on being handled, should stand up on their toes and show with marked terrier characteristics.

FAULTS

1. **Skull**—Too narrow in skull.
2. **Muzzle**—Too long and heavy a foreface; mouth overshot or undershot.
3. **Eyes**—Too large, prominent, yellow, and ringed are all objectionable.
4. **Ears**—Too large, round at points, set too close together, set too high on the head; heavily covered with hair.
5. **Legs and Feet**—Too light or too heavy bone. Crooked forelegs or out at elbow. Thin, ferrety feet; feet let down on the heel or too open and spread. Too high or too low on the leg.
6. **Body**—Too short back and compact a body, hampering quickness of movement and turning ability. Too long, weedy and snaky a body, giving an impression of weakness. Tail set on too low. Back not level.
7. **Coat**—Open coats, blousy coats, too short or dead coats, lack of sufficient undercoat, lack of head furnishings, lack of hard hair on the legs. Silkiness or curliness. A slight wave permissible.
8. **Nose**—Flesh or light-colored nose.
9. **Color**—White on chest, feet or other parts of body.

Approved May 10, 1938

Dandie Dinmont Terrier

THE DANDIE DINMONT TERRIER was bred from selected specimens of the rough native terrier of the Border hunters in the Cheviot Hills between England and Scotland and was first recorded as a distinct type of breed about 1700. He was distinguished by his pre-eminence in hunting the otter and the badger. A direct line of these dogs descended to the farmers in the Teviotdale Hills, where Sir Walter Scott in his travels chanced upon them and made them famous in his *Guy Mannering,* published in 1814. His character Dandie Dinmont, a farmer, supposed to have been a Mr. James Davidson of Hindlee, near Hawick, kept the immortal six, Auld Pepper, Auld Mustard, Young Pepper, Young Mustard, Little Pepper, and Little Mustard. Sir Walter gives an excellent description of their pluck: "I have them a' regularly entered, first wi' rottens, then wi' stots or weasels, and then wi' the tods and brocks, and now they fear naething that ever cam' wi' a hairy skin on't." From the time of the popularity of *Guy Mannering* to the present day, the breed has been known as "Dandie Dinmont's Terriers."

Terriers recognizable as Dandies appear in paintings by Ansdell and Landseer made before 1850. King Louis Philippe of France owned a pair of the breed in 1845.

Today the hunting qualities of the Dandie are not so often required, but his other qualities make him an excellent house dog. He is intelligent, fond of children, and an excellent guard. He has a will of his own and will sometimes obey a command reluctantly, with a look of "I'll do it, but please don't make me."

The points of a Dandie are quite the opposite of the average terrier—there are no straight lines. Head, large with a full, domed skull; eyes, large, full, of a very deep hazel and luminous, the darker the better; jaw, strong, deep and punishing; body, long, back rather low at the shoulder with a corresponding arch over the loins and slight drop to the root of the tail, combined with a broad, deep, and powerful chest; front legs, short, with paws slightly outcurved for digging; hind legs, longer and not so heavy; tail, set low, slightly curved and carried at an angle of about forty-five degrees—it should come up like a scimitar. There are two distinct colors: pepper—blue gray to light silver with light tan or silver points and very light gray or white topknot; and mustard—dark ochre color to cream with white points and topknot. The intermediate shades in each color are the more desirable. The Dandie has a rough double coat, made up of hard and soft hair in the proportion of about double the amount of hard hair to that of soft. This forms a thorough watershed which feels crisp to the touch, but does not have the harsh feel of the wire-coated dog. The head is covered with soft, silky hair, which should not be confined to a mere topknot. When groomed and properly shaped, this forms one of the characteristic features of the "show" Dandie.

Regular coat care is necessary for a Dandie. Frequent plucking will improve the texture and color of the coat. Only the longest hairs should be removed to keep the double coat and pencilled appearance. If the coat is neglected for a long period, it may be necessary to strip it down close to the skin. This will leave only undercoat and the Dandie may appear white. It can take months for the coat to grow in to proper length and texture after stripping.

Dandies fit in anywhere, either in a rough-and-tumble out-of-doors life or in the confines of a city apartment. They are an ideal size, between eighteen and twenty-four pounds, small enough to fit a small apartment and yet a dog big in character.

Official Standard for the
Dandie Dinmont Terrier

Head—Strongly made and large, not out of proportion to the dog's size, the muscles showing extraordinary development, more especially the maxillary. *Skull* broad between the ears, getting gradually less towards the eyes, and measuring about the same from the inner corner of the eye to back of skull as it does from ear to ear. The forehead well domed. The head is *covered* with very soft silky hair, which should not be confined to a mere topknot, and the lighter in color and silkier it is the better. The **Cheeks,** starting from the ears proportionately with the skull have a gradual taper towards the muzzle, which is deep and strongly made, and measures about three inches in length, or in proportion to skull as 3 is to 5. The **Muzzle** is covered with hair of a little darker shade than the topknot, and of the same texture as the feather of the forelegs. The top of the muzzle is generally bare for about an inch from the back part of the nose, the bareness coming to a point towards the eye, and being about one inch broad at the nose. The nose and inside of **Mouth** black or dark-colored. The **Teeth** very strong, especially the canines, which are of extraordinary size for a small dog. The canines mesh well with each other, so as to give the greatest available holding and punishing power. The incisors in each jaw are evenly spaced and six in number, with the upper incisors overlapping the lower incisors in a tight, scissors bite.

Eyes—Set wide apart, large, full, round, bright, expressive of great determination, intelligence and dignity; set low and prominent in front of the head; color, a rich dark hazel. **Ears**—Pendulous, set well back, wide apart, and low on the skull, hanging close to the cheek, with a very slight projection at the base, broad at the junction of the head and tapering almost to a point, the forepart of the ear tapering very little—the tapering being mostly on the back part, the forepart of the ear coming almost straight down from its junction with the head to the tip. They should harmonize in color with the body color. In the case of a Pepper dog they are covered with a soft straight brownish hair (in some cases almost black). In the case of a Mustard dog the hair should be mustard in color, a shade darker than the body, but not black. All should have a thin feather of light hair starting about 2 inches from the tip, and of nearly the same color and texture as the topknot, which gives the ear the appearance of a *distinct point*. The animal is often 1 or 2 years old before the feather is shown. The cartilage and skin of the ear should not be thick, but rather thin. Length of ear from 3 to 4 inches.

Neck—Very muscular, well-developed and strong, showing great power of resistance, being well set into the shoulders.

Body—Long, strong and flexible; ribs well sprung and round, chest well developed and let well down between the forelegs; the back rather low at the shoulder, having a slight downward curve and a corresponding arch over the loins, with a very slight gradual drop from top of loins to root of tail; both sides of backbone well supplied with muscle.

Tail—Rather short, say from 8 to 10 inches, and covered on the upper side with wiry hair of darker color than that of the body, the hair on the under side being lighter in color and not so wiry, with nice feather about 2 inches long, getting shorter as it nears the tip; rather thick at the root, getting thicker for about 4 inches, then tapering off to a point. It should not be twisted or curled in any way, but should come up with a curve like a scimitar, the tip, when excited, being in a perpendicular line with the root of the tail. It should neither be set on too high nor too low. When not excited it is carried gaily, and a little above the level of the body.

Legs—The forelegs short, with immense muscular development and bone, set wide apart, the chest coming well down between them. The feet well formed *and not flat*, with very strong brown or dark-colored claws. Bandy legs and flat feet are objectionable. The hair on the forelegs and feet of a Pepper dog should be tan, varying according to the body color from a rich tan to a pale fawn; of a Mustard dog they are of a darker shade than its head, which is a creamy white. In both colors there is a nice feather, about 2 inches long, rather lighter in color than the hair on the forepart of the leg. The hind legs are a little longer than the forelegs, and are set rather wide apart but not spread out in an unnatural manner, while the feet are much smaller; the thighs are well developed, and the hair of the same color and texture as the forelegs, but having no feather or dewclaws; the whole claws should be dark; but the claws of all vary in shade according to the color of the dog's body.

Coat—This is a very important point; the hair should be about 2 inches long; that from skull to root of tail, a mixture of hardish and soft hair, which gives a sort of crisp feel to the hand. The hard should not be wiry; the coat is what is termed piley or penciled. The hair on the under part of the body is lighter in color and softer than on the top. The skin on the belly accords with the color of dog.

Color—The color is pepper or mustard. The pepper ranges from a dark bluish black to a light silvery gray, the intermediate shades being preferred, the body color coming well down the shoulder and hips, gradually merging into the leg color. The mustards vary from a reddish brown to a pale fawn, the head being a creamy white, the legs and feet of a shade darker than the head. The claws are dark as in other colors. (Nearly all Dandie Dinmont Terriers have some white on the chest, and some have also white claws.)

Size—The height should be from 8 to 11 inches at the top of shoulder. Length from top of shoulder to root of tail should not be more than twice the dog's height, but preferably 1 or 2 inches less. **Weight**—The preferred weight from 18 to 24 pounds. These weights are for dogs in good working condition.

The relative value of the several points in the standard are apportioned as follows:

SCALE OF POINTS

Head	10	Legs and feet	10
Eyes	10	Coat	15
Ears	10	Color	5
Neck	5	Size and weight	5
Body	20	General appearance	5
Tail	5	TOTAL	100

Approved June 10, 1969

462

Fox Terrier

Smooth Fox Terrier

Wire Fox Terrier

THE FOX TERRIER is one of the best known and most widely distributed of pure-bred dogs. You may find one wherever the English language is spoken. Clubs have been formed in Belgium, France, Germany, Italy, and other European countries to promote the interests of the breed, which comes in two varieties, the smooth and the wire.

The Fox Terrier is an ancient breed of English origin. In 1790 Colonel Thornton's Pitch, a smooth-coated white terrier with markings, was recorded both in print and on canvas. It is probable that the Smooth and the Wire sprang from widely different sources. A profound student of the related breeds claims that the ancestor of the Wire was the old rough-coated black-and-tan working terrier of Wales, Derbyshire, and Durham, and that the more important ancestors of the Smooth were the smooth-coated black-and-tan, the Bull Terrier, the Greyhound, and the Beagle.

The Smooth antedated the Wire by some fifteen or twenty years in the show ring, and at first was classified among the sporting breeds. This was a tribute to his keen nose, remarkable eyesight, and staying powers in accomplishing his work of driving the fox from his hole or the drain in which he had taken refuge when too closely pursued by the hounds.

Wires were liberally crossed with Smooths in the earlier days of breeding in order to give to the Wire the predominating white pigmentation, the cleaner-cut head, and more classical outline of the Smooth. For this reason no extended pedigree of a Wire Fox Terrier will be found without many Smooth ancestors. On the other hand, the Wire outcross appears only in the pedigrees of such of the modern Smooths as descend in the T-line, so called, from Dusky D'Orsay, bred by Mr. Francis Redmond in England in 1915 in a deliberate attempt, it is alleged, to improve the Smooth. It is believed that the T-line now exists only in Australia.

The practice of interbreeding the Smooth with the Wire and vice versa has been almost universally discontinued for some years.

An English writer has described the ideal Fox Terrier well as follows:

He should be strong and gay, with a brave, wise way with him in the fields or at home. His head should be long and lean, with much strength in front of his eyes; these should be small and dark and full of the pride of life. His ears should be small, set high on his head, and in shape like a V. His neck should be long with a slight arch. The bones from which the forelegs spring should slope well back and be nice and long; these forelegs must be straight and round and thick; his hind legs strong with good reach, and his hocks should be near the ground; his feet should be small and round, and his pads thick. He should have a deep, but not at all a broad, chest; and his ribs should spring well out, so as to make a deep but not a flat side. His back should appear straight, or with but a slight curve; and his loins should be firm and strong. His tail must spring from the top and not from the back of the dog; it should be stout and stand straight up. His coat should be smooth, and straight, and hard, and dense. He should be white, but his marks, black or tan or both, may be of all shapes and on all parts of the dog, but there must be more white than black or tan; he must not have red or blue or liver marks. A dog or bitch should weigh at least a stone (fourteen pounds), and a dog may have up to four more pounds, and a bitch up to two more; much more than this does not help. He should move in a way that shows his limbs are sound and straight and free; but it is hard to make this clear in ink, and if a man can find no guide to help him in this, it will be well to ask a good judge of a horse to show him. In brief, when the dog comes to you or when he goes from you, his legs should seem to be straight and free and not too far each from each, nor yet too near; one's eye must learn to judge this with care.

The original Fox Terrier Standard was so well drawn in 1876 by the Fox Terrier Club (England) that no change has been found necessary except the reducing of the weight of a male dog in show condition from twenty pounds to eighteen pounds.

The American Fox Terrier Club, which is the parent club in this country, adopted this Standard when the club was founded in 1885, and later enlarged upon it only to the extent of giving amplifying measurements to supplement the provisions as to weight.

Official Standard for the
Fox Terrier

The following shall be the standard of the Fox Terrier, amplified in part in order that a more complete description of the Fox Terrier may be presented. The standard itself is set forth in ordinary type, the amplification in italics.

Head—The skull should be flat and moderately narrow, gradually decreasing in width to the eyes. Not much stop should be apparent, but there should be more dip in the profile between the forehead and the top jaw than is seen in the case of a Greyhound. The cheeks must not be full. The ears should be V-shaped and small, of moderate thickness, and drooping forward close to the cheek, not hanging by the side of the head like a Foxhound. *The top line of the folded ear should be well above the level of the skull.* The jaws, upper and lower, should be strong and muscular and of fair punishing strength, but not so as in any way to resemble the Greyhound or modern English Terrier. There should not be much falling away below the eyes. This part of the head should, however, be moderately chiseled out, so as not to go down in a straight slope like a wedge. The nose, toward which the muzzle must gradually taper, should be black. *It should be noticed that although the foreface should gradually taper from eye to muzzle and should tip slightly at its juncture with the forehead, it should not "dish" or fall away quickly below the eyes, where it should be full and well made up, but relieved from "wedginess" by a little delicate chiseling.* The eyes and the rims should be dark in color, *moderately* small and rather deep-set, full of fire, life and intelligence and as nearly as possible circular in shape. *Anything approaching a yellow eye is most objectionable.* The teeth should be as nearly as possible together, *i.e. the points* of the upper (*incisors*) teeth on the outside of or *slightly overlapping* the lower teeth. *There should be apparent little difference in length between the skull and foreface of a well-balanced head.*

Neck—Should be clean and muscular, without throatiness, of fair length, and gradually widening to the shoulders.

Shoulders—Should be long and sloping, well laid back, fine at the points, and clearly cut at the withers.

Chest—Deep and not broad.

Back—Should be short, straight (*i.e. level*), and strong, with no appearance of slackness. *Brisket should be deep, yet not exaggerated.*

Loin—Should be very powerful, *muscular* and very slightly arched. The foreribs should be moderately arched, the back ribs deep *and well sprung*, and the dog should be well ribbed up.

Hindquarters—Should be strong and muscular, quite free from droop or crouch; the thighs long and powerful; *stifles well curved and turned neither in nor out*; hocks *well bent* and near the ground *should be perfectly upright and parallel each with the other when viewed from behind*, the dog standing well up

466

on them like a Foxhound, and not straight in the stifle. *The worst possible form of hindquarters consists of a short second thigh and a straight stifle.*

Stern—Should be set on rather high and carried gaily, but not over the back or curled. It should be of good strength, anything approaching a "pipe-stopper" tail being especially objectionable.

Legs—The forelegs viewed from any direction must be straight with bone strong right down to the feet, showing little or no appearance of ankle in front, and being short and straight in pasterns. Both forelegs and hind legs should be carried straight forward in traveling, the stifles not turning outward. The elbows should hang perpendicularly to the body, working free of the sides. **Feet**—Should be round, compact and not large; the soles hard and tough; the toes moderately arched and turned neither in nor out.

Coat—Should be smooth, flat, but hard, dense and abundant. The belly and under side of the thighs should not be bare.

Color—White should predominate; brindle, red, or liver markings are objectionable. Otherwise this point is of little or no importance.

Symmetry, Size and Character—The dog must present a generally gay, lively and active appearance; bone and strength in a small compass are essentials, but this must not be taken to mean that a Fox Terrier should be cloddy, or in any way coarse—speed and endurance must be looked to as well as power, and the symmetry of the Foxhound taken as a model. The terrier, like the hound, must on no account be leggy, nor must he be too short in the leg. He should stand like a cleverly made hunter, covering a lot of ground, yet with a short back, as before stated. He will then attain the highest degree of propelling power, together with the greatest length of stride that is compatible with the length of his body. Weight is not a certain criterion of a terrier's fitness for his work—general shape, size and contour are the main points; and if a dog can gallop and stay, and follow his fox up a drain, it matters little what his weight is to a pound or so. *According to present-day requirements, a full-sized, well-balanced dog should not exceed 15¹/₂ inches at the withers, the bitch being proportionately lower—nor should the length of back from withers to root of tail exceed 12 inches, while, to maintain the relative proportions, the head should not exceed 7¹/₄ inches or be less than 7 inches. A dog with these measurements should scale 18 pounds in show condition—a bitch weighing some 2 pounds less—with a margin of 1 pound either way.*

Balance—*This may be defined as the correct proportions of a certain point, or points, when considered in relation to a certain other point or points. It is the keystone of the terrier's anatomy. The chief points for consideration are the relative proportions of skull and foreface; head and back; height at withers and length of body from shoulder-point to buttock—the ideal of proportion being reached when the last two measurements are the same. It should be added that, although the head measurements can be taken with absolute accuracy, the height at withers and length of back and coat are approximate, and are inserted for the information of breeders and exhibitors rather than as a hard and fast rule.*

Movement—*Movement, or action, is the crucial test of conformation. The terrier's legs should be carried straight forward while traveling, the forelegs hanging perpendicular and swinging parallel with the sides, like the pendulum of* *a clock. The principal propulsive power is furnished by the hind legs, perfection of action being found in the terrier possessing long thighs and muscular second thighs well bent at the stifles, which admit of a strong forward thrust or "snatch" of the hocks. When approaching, the forelegs should form a continuation of the straight line of the front, the feet being the same distance apart at the elbows. When stationary, it is often difficult to determine whether a dog is slightly out at shoulder, but, directly he moves, the defect—if it exists— becomes more apparent, the forefeet having a tendency to cross, "weave" or "dish." When, on the contrary, the dog is tied at the shoulder, the tendency of the feet is to move wider apart, with a sort of paddling action. When the hocks are turned in—cowhock—the stifles and feet are turned outwards, resulting in a serious loss of propulsive power. When the hocks are turned outwards the tendency of the hind feet is to cross, resulting in an ungainly waddle.*

N.B.—Old scars or injuries, the result of work or accident, should not be allowed to prejudice a terrier's chance in the show ring, unless they interfere with its movement or with its utility for work or stud.

WIRE

This variety of the breed should resemble the smooth sort in every respect except the coat, which should be broken. The harder and more wiry the texture of the coat is, the better. On no account should the dog look or feel woolly; and there should be no silky hair about the poll or elsewhere. The coat should not be too long, so as to give the dog a shaggy appearance, but, at the same time, it should show a marked and distinct difference all over from the smooth species.

SCALE OF POINTS

Head and ears	15	Stern	5
Neck	5	Legs and feet	15
Shoulders and chest	10	Coat	15
Back and loin	10	Symmetry, size and	
Hindquarters	15	character	10
		TOTAL	100

DISQUALIFICATIONS

Nose—White, cherry or spotted to a considerable extent with either of these colors.

Ears—Prick, tulip or rose.

Mouth—Much undershot, or much overshot.

Irish Terrier

THE IRISH TERRIER had been established in his native country and elsewhere and truly bred long before entering the show ring in 1879. His origin has been much debated, but there is indisputable evidence that he is one of the oldest of the terrier breeds. In his beautiful red jacket, alert and trim, his piercing eyes reflecting a rare intelligence, he is a gallant picture of authentic terrier type and character.

The outline and conformation of this terrier of Erin are peculiar to the breed and differ markedly from those of any other in the terrier group. The body is longer, proportionately, than the Fox Terrier's, for example, with a much more decided trend to racing lines, but with no lack of substance or sturdiness of bone structure; indeed, the difference in size and shape between the Irish Terrier and the Fox Terrier has been likened to that between hunter and cob. The hunterlike raciness of build and greater freedom of action in the Irish Terrier is alien to the Fox Terrier, in which variety cobbiness is desired. Another comparison may be helpful: the similarity in outline of the Irish Terrier to the grand old Irish Wolfhound is unmistakable; the drawing of one is almost a miniature of the other, and there are equally striking similarities of character.

The Irish Terrier is an incomparable pal, and the loyal, unyielding protector of those he loves. None is hardier or more adaptable. He is equally at home on the country estate, in the city apartment, or in camp; he thrives in the northland or in the tropics. He is the interested playmate and protector of children, eager to join in their fun and frolic. In their service, as in his master's, he challenges whatever may menace. He is a born guardsman.

The Irish Terrier is an accomplished sportsman. In this country he will catch and kill woodchucks and other small game, and rates with any dog in hunting rabbits. He is death on vermin. A natural water dog, and not apt to be gun-shy, he may be trained to retrieve in water as well as on land. Indeed, the Irish Terrier has many of the sporting gifts and talents of the Chesapeake Bay Retriever, the Beagle, and the Spaniel. He has hunted big game successfully in the far north and in the tropics.

The Irish Terrier scored as a war dog in World War I. He was "over there," and not inconsiderably in evidence. As messenger and sentinel he did his bit with that incomparable spirit and disregard of danger for which he has always been justly famed.

The following is a brief excerpt from an article written by Lt. Col. E. H. Richardson, later Commandant of the British War-Dog School, reviewing the Irish Terrier's services:

> I can say with decided emphasis that the Irish Terriers of the service more than did their part. Many a soldier is alive today through the effort of one of these very Terriers. Isolated with his unit in some advanced position, entirely cut off from the main body by a wall of shells, and thus prevented communicating his position or circumstance by telephone or runner so that help might follow, this messenger dog was often the only means his officers had of carrying the dispatch which eventually would bring relief. My opinion of this breed is indeed a high one. They are highly sensitive, spirited dogs of fine mettle, and those of us who respect and admire the finer qualities of mind will find them amply reflected in these terriers. They are extraordinarily intelligent, faithful, and honest, and a man who has one of them as a companion will never lack a true friend.

In the show ring the Irish Terrier's style and deportment are peculiarly his own. Alert and grim when challenged, the threatening demeanor of his challenger means nothing at all to him. His fearlessness and disregard of danger have won him the nickname of "daredevil."

In fine, the Irish Terrier is a peerless pal; the playmate and protector of children; a consummate sportsman; and a war dog with the saving of human lives to his credit. In competition he is an impressive picture of intrepid terrier character. He has been styled the D'Artagnan of the show ring.

Official Standard for the
Irish Terrier

Head—Long, but in nice proportion to the rest of the body; the skull flat, rather narrow between the ears, and narrowing slightly toward the eyes; free from wrinkle, with the stop hardly noticeable except in profile. The jaws must be strong and muscular, but not too full in the cheek, and of good punishing length. The foreface must not fall away appreciably between or below the eyes; instead, the modeling should be delicate. An exaggerated foreface, or a noticeably short foreface, disturbs the proper balance of the head and is not desirable. The foreface and the skull from occiput to stop should be approximately equal in length. Excessive muscular development of the cheeks, or bony development of the temples, conditions which are described by the fancier as "cheeky", or "strong in head", or "thick in skull" are objectionable. The "bumpy" head, in which the skull presents two lumps of bony structure above the eyes, is to be faulted. The hair on the upper and lower jaws should be similar in quality and texture to that on the body, and of sufficient length to present an appearance of additional strength and finish to the foreface. Either the profuse, goat-like beard, or the absence of beard, is unsightly and undesirable.

Teeth—Should be strong and even, white and sound; and neither overshot nor undershot.

Lips—Should be close and well-fitting, almost black in color.

Nose—Must be black.

Eyes—Dark brown in color; small, not prominent; full of life, fire and intelligence, showing an intense expression. The light or yellow eye is most objectionable, and is a bad fault.

Ears—Small and V-shaped; of moderate thickness; set well on the head, and dropping forward closely toward the outside corner of the eye. The top of the folded ear should be well above the level of the skull. A "dead" ear, hound-like in appearance, must be severely penalized. It is not characteristic of the Irish Terrier. The hair should be much shorter and somewhat darker in color than that on the body.

Neck—Should be of fair length and gradually widening toward the shoulders; well and proudly carried, and free from throatiness. Generally there is a slight frill in the hair at each side of the neck, extending almost to the corner of the ear.

Shoulders and Chest—Shoulders must be fine, long, and sloping well into the back. The chest should be deep and muscular, but neither full nor wide.

Body—The body should be moderately long. The short back is not characteristic of the Irish Terrier, and is extremely objectionable. The back must be strong and straight, and free from an appearance of slackness or "dip" behind the shoulders. The loin should be strong and muscular, and slightly arched, the ribs fairly sprung, deep rather than round, reaching to the level of the elbow. The bitch may be slightly longer than the dog.

Hindquarters—Should be strong and muscular; thighs powerful; hocks near the ground; stifles moderately bent.

Stern—Should be docked, taking off about one quarter. It should be set on rather high, but not curled. It should be of good strength and substance; of fair length and well covered with harsh, rough hair.

Feet and Legs—The feet should be strong, tolerably round, and moderately small; toes arched and turned neither out nor in, with dark toenails. The pads should be deep, and must be perfectly sound and free from corns. Cracks alone do not necessarily indicate unsound feet. In fact, all breeds have cracked pads occasionally, from various causes.

Legs moderately long, well set from the shoulders, perfectly straight, with plenty of bone and muscle; the elbows working clear of the sides; pasterns short, straight, and hardly noticeable. Both fore and hind legs should move straight forward when traveling; the stifles should not turn outwards. "Cowhocks"—that is, the hocks turned in and the feet turned out—are intolerable. The legs should be free from feather and covered with hair of similar texture to that on the body to give proper finish to the dog.

Coat—Should be dense and wiry in texture, rich in quality, having a broken appearance, but still lying fairly close to the body, the hairs growing so closely and strongly together that when parted with the fingers the skin is hardly visible; free of softness or silkiness, and not so long as to alter the outline of the body, particularly in the hindquarters. On the sides of the body the coat is never as harsh as on the back and quarters, but it should be plentiful and of good texture. At the base of the stiff outer coat there should be a growth of finer and softer hair, lighter in color, termed the undercoat. Single coats, which are without any undercoat, and wavy coats are undesirable; the curly and the kinky coats are most objectionable.

Color—Should be whole-colored: bright red, golden red, red wheaten, or wheaten. A small patch of white on the chest, frequently encountered in all whole-colored breeds, is permissible but not desirable. White on any other part of the body is most objectionable. Puppies sometimes have black hair at birth, which should disappear before they are full grown.

Size—The most desirable weight in show condition is 27 pounds for the dog and 25 pounds for the bitch. The height at the shoulder should be approximately 18 inches. These figures serve as a guide to both breeder and judge. In the show ring, however, the informed judge readily identifies the oversized or undersized Irish Terrier by its conformation and general appearance. Weight is not the last word in judgment. It is of the greatest importance to select, insofar as possible, terriers of moderate and generally accepted size, possessing the other various characteristics.

General Appearance—The over-all appearance of the Irish Terrier is important. In conformation he must be more than a sum of his parts. He must be all-of-a-piece, a balanced vital picture of symmetry, proportion and harmony. Furthermore, he must convey character. This terrier must be active, lithe and wiry in movement, with great animation; sturdy and strong in substance and bone structure, but at the same time free from clumsiness, for speed, power and endurance are most essential. The Irish Terrier must be neither "cobby" nor "cloddy", but should be built on lines of speed with a graceful, racing outline.

Temperament—The temperament of the Irish Terrier reflects his early background: he was family pet, guard dog, and hunter. He is good tempered, spirited and game. It is of the utmost importance that the Irish Terrier show fire and animation. There is a heedless, reckless pluck about the Irish Terrier which is characteristic, and which, coupled with the headlong dash, blind to all consequences, with which he rushes at his adversary, has earned for the breed the proud epithet of "Daredevil". He is of good temper, most affectionate, and absolutely loyal to mankind. Tender and forebearing with those he loves, this rugged, stout-hearted terrier will guard his master, his mistress and children with utter contempt for danger or hurt. His life is one continuous and eager offering of loyal and faithful companionship and devotion. He is ever on guard, and stands between his home and all that threatens.

Approved December 10, 1968

Kerry Blue Terrier

THE KERRY BLUE TERRIER originated in Ireland, having been noticed first in the mountainous regions of County Kerry, hence the name. The dogs had been pure-bred in that section for over a hundred years.

Gentle, lovable, and intelligent, the Kerry is an all-round working and utility terrier, used in Ireland and England for hunting small game and birds, and for retrieving from land and water. He is used quite successfully, too, for herding sheep and cattle.

These dogs were always considered as working and sporting terriers, no thought being given to them as a bench-show dog. However, after the formation of the Republic, they began to appear on the bench and met with quick favor. The first few came out at the Dublin show. English fanciers were quick to realize their possibilities if properly groomed, and the Kennel Club there provided regular classification for them. Their rise to popularity was almost instant, and each show brought out increasing numbers of entries.

The Kerry in Ireland is fostered by the Irish Blue Terrier Club of Dublin, organized by H. G. Fotterell. The principal variance in standard is that the Irish will not permit the trimming of coat. Dogs must be shown in the rough.

The Blue Terrier Club of England, organized by Captain Watts Williams, is the supporting organization back of the Blues for England. The English Standard is with a few minor exceptions identical with the American Standard in that coats must be trimmed.

There is more or less conjecture as to who imported the first Kerry and where it was first shown in this country. However, it appears that the first important show at which Kerries appeared was at Westminster in 1922. For two years following their initial exhibition at Madison Square Garden, they were relegated to the Miscellaneous Class, but in 1924 they were officially recognized by The American Kennel Club as a breed and given championship rating.

During the Westminster show of 1926, a group of fanciers met in the Waldorf-Astoria, New York City, when they organized a specialty club known as the Kerry Blue Terrier Club of America. Among the objects of the club were to encourage the breeding of Kerries and to assist its fanciers; to adopt a standard and to foster both the utilitarian and the sporting qualities of the dog with an aim toward field trials as well as dog shows.

The Kerry is a dog of many-sided accomplishment. He is an instinctive trailer and retrieves well. He is adaptable to all manner of farmwork, for which he is easily trained. He is an indomitable foe and cannot be surpassed as a watchdog and companion. In some instances in England he has even been used for police work. With proper treatment, food, and exercise, the Kerry Blue Terrier is very long-lived and will usually retain his activeness until the end; in fact, Kerries at six and eight years of age might be taken for young dogs.

Official Standard for the Kerry Blue Terrier

Head—Long, but not exaggerated and in good proportion to the rest of the body. Well-balanced, with little apparent difference between the length of the skull and foreface. (*20 points*)

Skull—Flat, with very slight stop, of but moderate breadth between the ears, and narrowing very slightly to the eyes. *Cheeks*—Clean and level, free from bumpiness. *Ears*—V-shaped, small but not out of proportion to the size of the dog, of moderate thickness, carried forward close to the cheeks with the top of the folded ear slightly above the level of the skull. A "dead" ear houndlike in appearance is very undesirable. *Foreface*—Jaws deep, strong and muscular. Foreface full and well made up, not falling away appreciably below the eyes but moderately chiseled out to relieve the foreface from wedginess. *Nose*—Black, nostrils large and wide. *Teeth*—Strong, white and either level or with the upper (incisors) teeth slightly overlapping the lower teeth. An undershot mouth should be strictly penalized. *Eyes*—Dark, small, not prominent, well placed and with a keen terrier expression. Anything approaching a yellow eye is very undesirable.

Neck—Clean and moderately long, gradually widening to the shoulders upon which it should be well set and carried proudly. (*5 points*)

Shoulders and Chest—Shoulders fine, long and sloping, well laid back and well knit. Chest deep and of but moderate breadth. (*10 points*)

Legs and Feet—Legs moderately long with plenty of bone and muscle. The forelegs should be straight from both front and side view, with the elbows hanging perpendicularly to the body and working clear of the sides in movement, the pasterns short, straight and hardly noticeable. Both forelegs and hind legs should move straight forward when traveling, the stifles turning neither in nor out. (*10 points*) Feet should be strong, compact, fairly round and moderately small, with good depth of pad free from cracks, the toes arched, turned neither in nor out, with black toenails.

Body—Back short, strong and straight (*i.e.* level), with no appearance of slackness. Loin short and powerful with a slight tuck-up, the ribs fairly well sprung, deep rather than round. (*10 points*)

Hindquarters and Stern—Hindquarters strong and muscular with full freedom of action, free from droop or crouch, the thighs long and powerful, stifles well bent and turned neither in nor out, hocks near the ground and, when viewed from behind, upright and parallel with each other, the dog standing well up on them. Tail should be set on high, of moderate length and carried gaily erect, the straighter the tail the better. (*10 points*)

Color—The correct mature color is any shade of blue gray or gray blue from deep slate to light blue gray, of a fairly uniform color throughout except that distinctly darker to black parts may appear on the muzzle, head, ears, tail and feet. (*10 points*) Kerry color, in its process of "clearing" from an apparent black at birth to the mature gray blue or blue gray, passes through one or more transitions—involving a very dark blue (darker than deep slate), shades or tinges of brown, and mixtures of these, together with a progressive infiltration of the correct mature color. Up to 18 months such deviations from the correct mature color are permissible without preference and without regard for uniformity. Thereafter, deviation from it to any significant extent must be severely penalized. Solid black is never permissible in the show ring. Up to 18 months any doubt as to whether a dog is black or a very dark blue should be resolved in favor of the dog, particularly in the case of a puppy. Black on the muzzle, head, ears, tail and feet is permissible at any age.

Coat—Soft, dense and wavy. A harsh, wire or bristle coat should be severely penalized. In show trim the body should be well covered but tidy, with the head (except for the whiskers) and the ears and cheeks clear. (*15 points*)

General Conformation and Character—The typical Kerry Blue Terrier should be upstanding, well knit and in good balance, showing a well developed and muscular body with definite terrier style and character throughout. A low-slung Kerry is not typical. (*10 points*)

Height—The ideal Kerry should be 18½ inches at the withers for a dog, slightly less for a bitch. In judging Kerries, a height of 18–19½ inches for a dog, and 17½–19 inches for a bitch should be given primary preference. Only where the comparative superiority of a specimen outside of the ranges noted clearly justifies it, should greater latitude be taken. In no case should it extend to a dog over 20 inches or under 17½ inches, or to a bitch over 19½ inches or under 17 inches. The minimum limits do not apply to puppies.

Weight—The most desirable weight for a fully developed dog is from 33–40 pounds, bitches weighing proportionately less.

DISQUALIFICATIONS

Solid black.
Dewclaws on hind legs.

Approved September 15, 1959

Lakeland Terrier

THE LAKELAND TERRIER is one of the oldest working terrier breeds still known today. It was bred, raised, and worked in the lake districts of England long before there was a kennel club or an official stud book. The fact that it has been outstripped by many younger terrier breeds is not so much a reflection on its quality as a tribute to the scope of its working ability. The name "Lakeland," indeed, is a modern acquisition. In olden times the breed was known as the Patterdale Terrier.

It is related that long before the days of the great John Peel, or before any packs of hounds were formed, the Lakeland was kept by the farmers in the mountain districts, who, at that time, would form a hunt with a couple of hounds and these terriers. Their work was to destroy the foxes found raiding the sheepfolds. There was sport, but it was not sport for sport's sake alone. It was a very practical matter.

The color of these dogs did not matter to their owners; they bred principally for gameness at first. The color was quite secondary as long as the dogs were game enough to withstand the punishment meted out by the foxes in their rocky mountain lairs. Later came the packs of hounds, but there was not a single pack in the lake district that did not have one or two game old terriers that had continually shown their courage with fox or otter. These were coveted as breeding material.

None of their puppies were ever destroyed. They were given out among various friends and followers of the hunt, later to be tried and the best workers retained to carry on the traditions of the older dogs.

So great was the courage of the native Lakeland Terriers that they would follow underground for tremendous distances. It is told that, in 1871, Lord Lonsdale had one which crawled twenty-three feet under rock after an otter. In order to extricate the dog it was necessary to undertake extensive blasting operations. Finally, after three days' work, they reached the dog, and he was gotten out, none the worse for his experience. Still other dogs have been known to be locked underground for ten or twelve days and have been taken out alive. Others have paid the penalty.

Classes for the likeliest-looking terrier, suitable for fox or otter, were judged in connection with agricultural shows throughout the lake district about 1896, when more interest was evinced in this game old breed. They were judged by masters of hounds or other experienced hunting men. At that time, the color ranged from grizzle to blue and tan, red or wheaten, with a sprinkling of white terriers. Later these classes were divided in color; for white working terriers and for colored working terriers. Always working ability was taken into consideration.

Usually the white terriers were found working with the Otter Hounds, as in many cases a dark terrier got severely mauled in the muddy waters due to the excitement of the younger hounds when the otter had been dislodged from under tree roots and drains.

It is believed by experienced terrier men that the somewhat remote ancestors of the Lakeland Terrier are similar to the progenitor of the Border Terrier. In fact, there is sound evidence that the Lakeland is an offshoot of the breed that became known later as the Bedlington, which was closely related to the Dandie Dinmont.

A hundred-odd years ago—in 1830, or thereabouts—these northern counties of England, Northumberland, Cumberland, and West-moreland, had many varieties of terrier, each named after the small locality in which it was found in greatest numbers. Many of the old names have been lost since the breeds have gained recognition. This changing of names usually took place when specialist clubs were formed, with breeders unwilling to agree on any of the older names; and, of course, there were cases where the same dog might have been known by half a dozen different names.

Cumberland was the birthplace of the Lakeland Terrier. This is a particularly beautiful country, richly studded with lakes, particularly in the southern part. The Bedlington is attributed to neighboring Northumberland County, but it is not difficult to suppose that there was certain traffic in dogs at that time.

The first organized effort to promote the interest of this Cumberland County breed came at the Kersurck show in 1912, when a terrier club was formed. The new club made considerable headway for two years, and then came the outbreak of World War I. Naturally, all civilian activities were under a damper, and little or nothing was heard of the Lakeland Terrier again until 1921. That year fanciers met at Whitehaven, in Cumberland. According to Thomas Hosking, who later came to the United States and who was one of the nine fanciers who attended, the name Lakeland Terrier was chosen at that meeting. The Standard was drawn up at that time, and shortly afterward the breed was made eligible for registration in the stud book of the Kennel Club (England).

Although a worker for generations, the Lakeland makes a very good appearance in the ring. He has a dense, weather-resisting coat, strong jaws of moderate length, powerful hindquarters, and good legs and feet on a short, strong back. Despite his gameness and courage, he has an attractive, quiet disposition.

Official Standard for the
Lakeland Terrier

General Appearance—The Lakeland Terrier is a small, workman-like dog of square, sturdy build and gay, friendly, self-confident demeanor. He stands on his toes as if ready to go, and he moves, lithe and graceful, with a straight-ahead, free stride of good length. His head is rectangular in contour, ears V-shaped, and wiry coat finished off with fairly long furnishings on muzzle and legs.

Head—Well balanced, rectangular, the length of skull equaling the length of the muzzle when measured from occiput to stop, and from stop to nosetip. *The skull* is flat on top and moderately broad, the cheeks almost straightsided, and the stop barely perceptible. *The muzzle* is broad with straight nose bridge and good fill-in beneath the eyes. *The nose* is black, except that liver-colored noses shall be permissible on liver-coated dogs. *Jaws* are powerful. *The teeth*, which are comparatively large, may meet in either a level, edge-to-edge bite, or a slightly overlapping scissors bite. Specimens with teeth overshot or undershot are to be disqualified. *The ears* are small, V-shaped, their fold just above the top of the skull, the inner edge close to the cheeks, and the flap pointed down. *The eyes,* moderately small and somewhat oval in outline, are set squarely in the skull, fairly wide apart. Their normally dark color may be a warm brown or black. *The expression* depends upon the dog's mood of the moment; although typically alert, it may be intense and determined, or gay and even impish.

Neck—Reachy and of good length; refined but strong; clean at the throat, slightly arched, and widening gradually into the shoulders. The withers, that point at the back of the neck where neck and body meet, are noticeably higher than the level of the back.

Body—In over-all length-to-height proportion, the dog is approximately square. The moderately narrow *chest* is deep; it extends to elbows which are held close to the body. Shoulder blades are sloping, that is, well laid back, their musculature lean and almost flat in outline. *The ribs* are well sprung and moderately rounded. *The back* is short and level in topline. *Loins* are taut and short, although they may be a trifle longer in bitches than in dogs. *Quarters* are strong, broad, and muscular.

Legs and Feet—*Forelegs* are strongly boned, clean, and absolutely straight as viewed from the front or side, and devoid of appreciable bend at the pasterns. *Hind legs* too are strong and sturdy, the second thighs long and nicely angulated at the stifles and the hocks. *Hocks* are well let down, with the bone from hock to toes straight and parallel to each other. The small *feet* are round, the toes compact and well padded, the nails strong. Dewclaws, if any, are to be removed.

Tail—Set high on the body, the tail is customarily docked so that when the dog is set up in show position, the tip of the docked tail is on an approximate level with the skull. In carriage it is gay or upright, although a slight curve in the direction of the head is considered desirable. The tail curled over the back is faulty.

Coat and Color—Two-ply or double, the outer coat is hard and wiry in texture, the undercoat soft. Furnishings on muzzle and legs are plentiful as opposed to profuse. *The color* may be blue, black, liver, black and tan, blue and tan, red, red grizzle, grizzle and tan, or wheaten. Tan as desirable in the Lakeland Terrier, is a light wheaten or straw color, with rich red or mahogany tan to be penalized. Otherwise, colors, as specified, are equally acceptable. Dark-saddled specimens (whether black grizzle or blue) are nearly solid black at birth, with tan points on muzzle and feet. The black recedes and usually turns grayish or grizzle at maturity, while the tan also lightens.

Size—The ideal *height* of the mature dog is 14½ inches from the withers to the ground, with up to a ½-inch deviation either way permissible. Bitches may measure as much as one inch less than dogs. The *weight* of the well-balanced, mature specimen in hard, show condition, averages approximately 17 pounds, those of other heights proportionately more or less.

Size is to be considered of lesser importance than other qualities, that is, when judging dogs of equal merit, the one nearest the ideal size is to be preferred. Symmetry and proportion, however, are paramount in the appraisal, since all qualities together must be considered in visualizing the ideal.

Movement—Straight and free, with good length of stride. Paddling, moving close, and toeing-in are faulty.

Temperament—The typical Lakeland Terrier is bold, gay, and friendly, with a self-confident, cock-of-the-walk attitude. Shyness, especially shy-sharpness, in the mature specimen is to be heavily penalized.

SCALE OF POINTS

Head	15	Legs and feet	10
Eyes, ears, expression	15	Size and symmetry	10
Neck	5	Movement	10
Body	10	Temperament	10
Coat	15	TOTAL	100

DISQUALIFICATION

The front teeth overshot or undershot.

Approved May 14, 1963

Manchester Terrier

GENERATIONS AGO, before the days of dog shows, there was in England a Black-and-Tan Terrier, less graceful in outline and coarser in type than those of today. Those early dogs did not have penciled toes and dotted brows, and their tan was smutty; nevertheless they were sound, game, and useful. They were accomplished rat killers, whether in the pits or along the watercourses. In fact their value was reckoned not at all upon any consideration of make and shape but solely upon the number of rats they had killed.

The Black-and-Tan Terrier was one of the breeds mentioned by Dr. Caius in the famous letter concerning the dogs of England that was sent to Gesner for inclusion in his encyclopedic work on the dogs of all nations. Dr. Caius completed his survey in 1570. He described the breed as carrying the essential colors and characteristics, but as being rougher in coat and shorter on the leg.

The Manchester district of England was a noted center for two "poor men's sports," rat killing and rabbit coursing. A fancier by the name of John Hulme, with the idea of producing a dog that could be used at both contests, mated a Whippet bitch with a celebrated rat-killing dog, a crossbred terrier dark brown in color. On this basis the roached back, seldom found in a terrier, is explained. The dogs proved useful, other fanciers took to breeding them, and the Manchester school of terriers was launched.

The name Manchester, however, was regarded as somewhat misleading, for similar dogs were known in many parts of England. Designation of the new breed did not take place until 1860 or thereabouts, at which time the city for which the dog was named had become a breed center. Manchesters soon spread over the British Isles and eventually came to this country in considerable numbers, but years were to pass before the name was stabilized. Actually it was dropped for a time as being too restricted in designation, and the dog was once again known as the Black-and-Tan Terrier. In 1923, however, the newly formed Manchester Terrier Club of America changed the name back to Manchester Terrier, and there it has remained.

Whippet, Greyhound, and Italian Greyhound have all been mentioned (with how much accuracy none can say) as partners of more or less importance in the creation of the Manchester. But supposition regarding heritage does not end there. That extensive investigator, Ash, surmised a bit regarding a Dachshund ancestor. He said it would be interesting to know not whether the Dachshund is related, but how closely it is related to the Manchester Terrier. In substantiation of this conjecture is the description by Whitaker in 1771 of the dog of Manchester as a "short-legged, crooked-legged dog." Such a relationship seems fantastic; even so it is not an impossibility, since the Dachshund's forebears were not so exaggerated as are the dogs of this day.

As a sagacious, intelligent house pet and companion, no breed is superior to the well-bred Manchester. There is a sleek, breedy look about him that no other dog presents. His long, clean head, keen expression, glossy coat, whip tail, and smart, wide-awake appearance always command attention, while his clean habits and short coat admit him to homes which might shut out his rough-haired brothers. Moreover his weight leaves nothing to be desired, for there is a medium-sized type weighing over twelve and not exceeding twenty-two pounds, and a toy weighing twelve pounds or under.

Up until 1959 the Manchester Terrier and the Toy Manchester Terrier were registered as two separate breeds, although interbreeding between the two breeds was permitted. Since that date they have been registered as a single breed, the Manchester Terrier, with two varieties, the Toy and the Standard, for dog-show purposes.

Development of the Toy from the larger dog was first a matter of chance and later a matter of selective breeding. It came about in this manner: Two of the larger specimens would produce a litter in which all but one puppy attained the same size as the parents. As has happened again and again in the breeding of dogs, the tiny prototype attracted attention to such a degree as to create a demand for more. So naturally the breeders tried to produce more puppies of the smaller size. It had been claimed that the Toy was so highly prized as to prompt surreptitious matings with Italian Greyhounds in order to keep the dog small. Fortunately these crosses were not perpetuated.

At this point excessive inbreeding took its toll. As can be readily understood, there were few toy-sized dogs to breed from, so inbreeding became the order of the day. In Victorian times size diminished alarmingly to around two and one-half pounds, and the tiny ones were admittedly delicate. Realizing their mistake, breeders endeavored to correct their technique; they aimed for, and got, more normal toy weight together with renewed vigor.

When the anti-cropping edict was passed in England, many of the older fanciers grew discouraged after trying for a time to produce an attractive-looking dog with small button ears, and consequently many ceased breeding. A few staunch devotees, however, kept the breed alive. They loved the game little fellow, whether his ears were up or down, trimmed or untrimmed, and they stayed with him through lean times and good.

No longer are extremes of any sort favored or fostered within the breed, for "the gentleman's terrier," as he was known long ago, has come into his own. He exhibits that true Manchester type, with its flat skull, triangular eyes, accented kiss marks, and sleek ebony coat with clearly delineated markings. The sole difference between the larger dog and the Toy is concerned with the ears. Both varieties have moderately small, thin ears, narrow at the base and pointed at the tips. They are set high on the skull and quite close together. In the Standard variety, ears may be erect or button; if cropped, they are long and carried straight up. In the Toy variety, however, cropping disqualifies. The Toy ear is carried naturally erect, without sidewise flare.

Official Standard for the Manchester Terrier

Head—Long, narrow, tight-skinned, almost flat, with a slight indentation up the forehead; slightly wedge-shaped, tapering to the nose, with no visible cheek muscles, and well filled up under the eyes; tight-lipped jaws, level in mouth, and functionally level teeth, or the incisors of the upper jaw may make a close, slightly overlapping contact with the incisors of the lower jaw.

Eyes—Small, bright, sparkling and as near black as possible; set moderately close together; oblong in shape, slanting upwards on the outside; they should neither protrude nor sink in the skull.

Nose—Black.

Ears (*Toy Variety*)—Of moderate size; set well up on the skull and rather close together; thin, moderately narrow at base; with pointed tips; naturally erect carriage. Wide, flaring, blunt-tipped or "bell" ears are a serious fault; cropped or cut ears shall disqualify.

Ears (*Standard Variety*)—Erect, or button, small and thin; smaller at the root and set as close together as possible at the top of the head. If cropped, to a point, long and carried erect.

Neck and Shoulders—The neck should be a moderate length, slim and graceful; gradually becoming larger as it approaches, and blend smoothly with the sloping shoulders; free from throatiness; slightly arched from the occiput.

Chest—Narrow between the legs; deep in the brisket.

Body—Moderately short, with robust loins; ribs well sprung out behind the shoulders; back slightly arched at the loin, and falling again to the tail to the same height as the shoulder.

Legs—Forelegs straight, of proportionate length, and well under body. Hind legs should not turn in or out as viewed from the rear; carried back; hocks well let down. **Feet**—Compact, well arched, with jet black nails; the two middle toes in the front feet rather longer than the others; the hind feet shaped like those of a cat.

Tail—Moderately short, and set on where the arch of the back ends; thick where it joins the body, tapering to a point, not carried higher than the back.

Coat—Smooth, short, thick, dense, close and glossy; not soft.

Color—Jet black and rich mahogany tan, which should not run or blend into each other but abruptly forming clear, well-defined lines of color division. A small tan spot over each eye; a very small tan spot on each cheek; the lips of the upper and lower jaws should be tanned, extending under the throat, ending in the shape of the letter V; the inside of the ears partly tanned. Tan spots, called "rosettes", on each side of the chest above the front legs, more pronounced in puppies than in adults. There should be a black "thumb mark" patch on the front of each foreleg between the pastern and the knee. There should be a distinct black "pencil mark" line running lengthwise on the top of each toe on all four feet. The remainder of the forelegs to be tan to the knee. Tan on the hind legs should continue from the penciling on the feet up the inside of the legs to a little below the stifle joint; the outside of the hind legs to be black. There should be tan under the tail, and on the vent, but only of such size as to be covered by the tail. White in any part of the coat is a serious fault, and shall disqualify whenever the white shall form a patch or stripe measuring as much as $1/2$-inch in its longest dimension.

Weight (*Toy Variety*)—Not exceeding 12 pounds. It is suggested that clubs consider dividing the American-bred and open classes by weight as follows: 7 pounds and under, over 7 pounds and not exceeding 12 pounds.

Weight (*Standard Variety*)—Over 12 pounds and not exceeding 22 pounds. Dogs weighing over 22 pounds shall be disqualified. It is suggested that clubs consider dividing the American-bred and open classes by weight as follows: over 12 pounds and not exceeding 16 pounds, over 16 pounds and not exceeding 22 pounds.

486

DISQUALIFICATIONS

Color—White in any part of the coat, forming a patch or stripe measuring as much as ¹/₂ inch in its longest dimension.

Weight (Standard Variety)—Over 22 pounds.

Ears (Toy Variety)—Cropped or cut ears.

Approved June 12, 1962

Miniature Schnauzer

THE SCHNAUZER is of German origin, said to be recognizable in pictures of the fifteenth century. The Miniature Schnauzer is derived from the Standard Schnauzer and is said to have come from mixing of Affenpinschers and Poodles with small Standards. The Miniature Schnauzer was exhibited as a distinct breed as early as 1899.

Today's Miniature Schnauzer in the United States is an elegant dog of the Terrier Group. While the breed resembles other dogs in this group, almost all of which were bred in the British Isles to "go to ground" to attack vermin of all kinds, his origin and blood are quite different, giving the Miniature Schnauzer a naturally happy temperament.

The breed is characterized by its stocky build, wiry coat and abundant whiskers and leg furnishings. A Miniature Schnauzer may be of several colors with salt and pepper (gray) being the most common, although blacks and black and silvers are now seen in increasing numbers. The salt and pepper color is the result of unique light and dark banding of each hair instead of a mixing of light and dark hairs. The correct coat can be retained only by stripping and is lost when the coat is clipped. The breed has a soft undercoat which can range from black and dark gray to very light gray or beige. If the animal is clipped, in time only the undercoat will remain.

The breed is hardy, healthy, intelligent and fond of children. It was developed as a small farm dog, used as a ratter. His size (12-14 inches at the withers) has permitted him to adapt easily to small city quarters. On the other hand, he is still at home in the country and can cover a substantial amount of ground without tiring. As a rule a Miniature Schnauzer is not a fighter, although he will stand up for himself if necessary.

There is no standard weight for the breed, but a grown bitch of about 13 inches should weigh about 14 pounds, with a dog weighing somewhat more. The weight depends, to a great extent, on the amount of bone.

The Miniature Schnauzer is now viewed primarily as a charming and attractive companion. He is seldom addicted to wandering. He is devoted to his home and family and functions very well as a guard dog in that he can give an alarm as well as a larger dog. His good health, good temperament and attractive appearance combine to fit him admirably for his role as family pet.

Miniature Schnauzers have been bred in the United States since 1925 and have gained steadily in popular favor. The American Miniature Schnauzer Club began its independent operation in August 1933.

Official Standard for the
Miniature Schnauzer

General Appearance—The Miniature Schnauzer is a robust, active dog of terrier type, resembling his larger cousin, the Standard Schnauzer, in general appearance, and of an alert, active disposition. He is sturdily built, nearly square in proportion of body length to height, with plenty of bone, and without any suggestion of toyishness. *Faults:* Type—Toyishness, raciness or coarseness.

Temperament—The typical Miniature Schnauzer is alert and spirited, yet obedient to command. He is friendly, intelligent and willing to please. He should never be over-agressive or timid. *Faults:* Temperament—Shyness or viciousness.

Head—Strong and rectangular, its width diminishing slightly from ears to eyes, and again to the tip of the nose. The forehead is unwrinkled. The topskull is flat and fairly long. The foreface is parallel to the topskull, with a slight stop, and is at least as long as the topskull. The muzzle is strong in proportion to the skull; it ends in a moderately blunt manner, with thick whiskers which accentuate the rectangular shape of the head. *Faults:* Head coarse and cheeky. *Teeth*—The teeth meet in a scissors bite. That is, the upper front teeth overlap the lower front teeth in such a manner that the inner surface of the upper incisors barely touches the outer surface of the lower incisors when the mouth is closed. *Faults:* Bite—Undershot or overshot jaw. Level bite. *Eyes*—Small, dark brown and deep-set. They are oval in appearance and keen in expression. *Faults:* Eyes—Light and/or large and prominent in appearance. *Ears*—When cropped the ears are identical in shape and length, with pointed tips. They are in balance with the head and not exaggerated in length. They are set high on the skull and carried perpendicularly at the inner edges, with as little bell as possible along the outer edges. When uncropped, the ears are small and V-shaped, folding close to the skull.

Neck—Strong and well arched, blending into the shoulders, and with the skin fitting tightly at the throat.

Body—Short and deep, with the brisket extending at least to the elbows. Ribs are well sprung and deep, extending well back to a short loin. The underbody does not present a tucked-up appearance at the flank. The topline is straight; it declines slightly from the withers to the base of the tail. The over-all length from chest to stern bone appears to equal the height at the withers. *Faults:* Chest too broad or shallow in brisket. Sway or roach back.

Forequarters—The forequarters have flat, somewhat sloping shoulders and high withers. Forelegs are straight and parallel when viewed from all sides. They have strong pasterns and good bone. They are separated by a fairly deep brisket which precludes a pinched front. The elbows are close, and the ribs spread gradually from the first rib so as to allow space for the elbows to move close to the body. *Faults:* Loose elbows.

Hindquarters—The hindquarters have strong-muscled, slanting thighs: they are well bent at the stifles and straight from hock to so-called heel. There is sufficient angulation so that, in stance, the hocks extend beyond the tail. The hindquarters never appear overbuilt or higher than the shoulders. *Faults:* Bowed or cowhocked hindquarters.

Feet—Short and round (cat-feet) with thick, black pads. The toes are arched and compact.

Movement—The trot is the gait at which movement is judged. When approaching, the forelegs, with elbows close to the body, move straight forward, neither too close nor too far apart. Going away, the hind legs are straight and travel in the same planes as the forelegs. *Note: It is generally accepted that when a full trot is achieved, the rear legs continue to move in the same planes as the forelegs, but a very slight inward inclination will occur. It begins at the point of the shoulder in front and at the hip joint in the rear. Viewed from the front or rear, the legs are straight from these points to the pads. The degree of inward inclination is almost imperceptible in a Miniature Schnauzer that has correct movement. It does not justify moving close, toe-ing in, crossing, or moving out at the elbows.* Viewed from the side, the forelegs have good reach, while the hind legs have strong drive, with good pick-up of hocks. The feet turn neither inward nor outward. *Faults:* Single tracking. Sidegaiting. Paddling in front, or high hackney knee action. Weak rear action.

Tail—Set high and carried erect. It is docked only long enough to be clearly visible over the topline of the body when the dog is in proper length of coat. *Fault:* Tail set low.

Coat—Double, with hard, wiry, outer coat and close undercoat. Head, neck and body coat must be plucked. When in show condition the body coat should be of sufficient length to determine texture. Close covering on neck, ears and skull. Furnishings are fairly thick but not silky. *Faults:* Coat—too soft or too smooth and slick in appearance.

Size—From 12 to 14 inches. Ideal size 13½ inches. *(See disqualifications.)*

Color—The recognized colors are salt and pepper, black and silver, and solid black. The typical color is salt and pepper in shades of gray, tan shading is permissible. The salt and pepper mixture fades out to light gray or silver white in the eyebrows, whiskers, cheeks, under throat, across chest, under tail, leg furnishings, under body, and inside legs. The light under-body hair is not to rise higher on the sides of the body than the front elbows.

The black and silvers follow the same pattern as the salt and peppers. The entire salt-and-pepper section must be black.

Black is the only solid color allowed. It must be a true black with no gray hairs and no brown tinge except where the whiskers may have become discolored. A small white spot on the chest is permitted.

DISQUALIFICATIONS

Dogs or bitches under 12 inches or over 14 inches.
Color solid white or white patches on the body.

Approved March 13, 1979

Norfolk Terrier

THE NORFOLK TERRIER is small and sturdy, alert and fearless, with sporting instincts and an even temperament. Good natured and gregarious, the Norfolk has proved adaptable under a wide variety of conditions.

In England at the turn of the century working terriers from stables in Cambridge, Market Harborough, and Norwich, were used by Frank "Roughrider" Jones to develop a breed recognized by the English Kennel Club in 1932 as the Norwich Terrier. In the early days there was a diversity in type, size, color, coat and ear carriage. Correct color and ear carriage were constantly argued. When the Norwich breed standard was drawn up the drop ear and the prick ear terriers remained one breed. The English Kennel Club, in 1964, recognized them as two breeds — the drop ear variety as the Norfolk and the prick ear as the Norwich.

The year that the breed divided in England an article in *The Field* stated: "Actually there is nothing new about the Norfolk Terrier, but simply the name under which it is registered. The Eastern Counties have always produced these principally wheaten, red and otherwise black and tan or grizzle good-ribbed short-legged terriers, built on the generally accepted lines of a hunt terrier. They go to ground readily and are famous ratters.''

In the United States those who remember the ''Roaring Twenties'' still refer to the Norwich as a ''Jones Terrier'' after Frank Jones, from whom many American sportsmen traveling abroad bought their first little red terriers. In 1936, thanks to the efforts of Gordon Massey (who registered the first Norwich Terrier in this country) and Henry Bixby, then Executive Vice President of the American Kennel Club, the Norwich Terrier was accepted as a breed by the AKC. They remained one breed until 1979 when division by ear carriage became official. The drop ears are now recognized as the Norfolk, while the prick ears remain Norwich.

Visually there appears to be a distinct difference between the two breeds, resulting in two slightly different breed standards. In England each breed has developed with success since separation and we look forward to the future of the American bred Norfolk Terrier.

Today, although as many live in cities as in foxhunting country, the Norfolk should still conform to the standard. The characteristic coat requires regular grooming but trimming is heavily penalized. The ears should be neatly dropped, slightly rounded at the tip, carried close to the cheek and not falling lower than the outer corner of the eye.

The Norfolk Terrier is essentially a sporting terrier—not a Toy. His chief attributes are gameness, hardiness, loyalty to his master, and great charm. He is affectionate and reasonably obedient. He must be kept small enough to conform with the standard. Above all, the outstanding personality, characteristic of this breed, must never be subordinated for the sake of appearance and conformation.

Official Standard for the
Norfolk Terrier

Characteristics—The Norfolk Terrier is one of the smallest of the terriers, but a "demon" for its size. Of a lovable disposition, not quarrelsome, and with a hardy constitution. Temperament: steady and fearless.

General Appearance—A small, low, keen dog, strong with good substance and bone.

Head—Skull wide (good width between the ears) and slightly rounded. Muzzle strong; length about one-third less than a measurement from the occiput to the bottom of the stop, which should be well defined.

Eyes—Dark, intelligent, full of expression, bright and keen.

Ears—Neatly dropped, small, with break just above the skull line; carried close to the cheek and not falling lower than the outer corner of the eye; slightly rounded at the tip.

Mouth—Tight lipped. Jaws clean and strong. Teeth strong, rather large; scissors bite.

Neck—Medium length and strong.

Forequarters—Clean and powerful shoulders; short, powerful legs, as straight as consistently possible.

Body—Moderately short and compact, with well sprung ribs.

Hindquarters—Sound and well muscled, good turn of stifle, hocks well let down and straight when viewed from the rear, with great powers of propulsion.

Feet—Round, with thick pads.

Tail—Medium docked, carriage not excessively gay.

Coat—Hard, wiry and straight, lying close to the body. It is longer and rougher on the neck and shoulders, in full coat forming almost a mane. Hair on the head, ears and muzzle, short and smooth, except for slight eyebrows and slight whiskers.

Color—All shades of red, red wheaten, black and tan or grizzle. White marks or patches are undesirable but shall not disqualify.

Size—Ideal height 10 inches at withers. Ideal weight 10 to 12 lbs.

Faults—A mouth over- or undershot; a long narrow head. Trimming is not desirable. Honorable scars from fair wear and tear shall not count against.

- Approved August 9, 1978
- Effective January 1, 1979

Norwich Terrier

THE ROOTS of the Norwich were firmly planted in East Anglia, England. By the 1880s owning a small ratting terrier was a fad among the sporting undergraduates of Cambridge University. A popular strain developed of very small red and black and tan working crossbreds from native, Yorkshire, and Irish den stock.

By the turn of the century one of these Trumpington Terriers moved to a stable near the city of Norwich. "Rags" was sandy colored, short of leg, stocky, with cropped ears. A notorious ratter and dominant sire, he is the modern breed's progenitor. For the next two decades various horsemen bred other game terrier types to "Rags" and his descendants, including a half-sized brindle Staffordshire. So from companions and barnyard ratters there gradually developed a line of excellent fox bolters, and one of these introduced the breed to America in 1914.

Bred in Market Harborough by the noted "Roughrider" Frank Jones, "Willum" became the inseparable companion of a Philadelphia sportsman, Robert Strawbridge. This Jones' terrier was also low legged, cropped and docked but his very hard coat had black shadings and his head showed a marked resemblance to a Bull Terrier. "Willum" proved a charming muscular 12 pound ambassador, and a prolific sire of M.F.H. Hunt Terriers in Vermont, New York, Pennsylvania and Virginia. He died at 14 years of age defending his hearth from a vicious canine intruder, just a few years before the breed was recognized in England in 1932. Though the AKC made Norwich Terriers official in 1936, there are still some Americans who associate Norwich with "Willum's" breeder and steadfastly call them Jones' Terriers.

In 1964 England recognized the drop ear Norwich as a separate breed, terming them the Norfolk Terrier. The American Kennel Club has now taken the same step, effective as of January 1, 1979. The recognition of the two varieties as separate breeds is now the rule in all English speaking countries, in Europe and in Scandinavia.

Norwich are hardy, happy-go-lucky, weatherproof companions. Though game on vermin, they are unusually gregarious with children, adults and other domestic animals. Today they still weigh about 12 pounds, are short legged, sturdy and can be any shade from wheaten to dark red, black and tan or grizzle. They are very loyal, alert and have a sensitive intelligence.

Their body lengths and breadths vary, but their docked tails should be long enough to firmly grasp. Smooth coated and wedge shaped, their heads should have plenty of brain room with ears spaced well apart. A delineated stop between the wide set eyes should be just nearer the muzzle than the top of the skull. The small dark almond eyes coupled with a slightly foxy muzzle give Norwich their typical impish expression.

Most Norwich owners prefer a terrier of sagacious character with a harsh carefree coat, large close fitting teeth and tolerate the variations of color and conformation which befit its heritage. Its unique standard employs horsemens' terms and the breed's characteristic mane calls for coarser, longer protective hair on neck and shoulders. Breeders must remain watchful and guard against show fads, exaggerations, excessive coats or fancy trimming. To keep personality a priority factor, the parent club rewards working abilities, obedience and racing competitions along with show ring events.

Official Standard for the
Norwich Terrier

Head—Skull wide, slightly rounded with good width between the ears. Muzzle strong but not long or heavy, with slightly "foxy" appearance. Length about one-third less than the measurement from the occiput to the bottom of the stop, which should be well defined. *Faults*–A long narrow head; over square muzzle; highly rounded dome.

Ears—Small, pointed, erect and set well apart. *Faults*–Oversize; poor carriage.

Eyes—Very bright, dark and keen. Full of expression. *Faults*–Light or protruding eyes.

Jaw—Clean, strong, tight lipped, with strong, large, closely-fitting teeth; scissors bite. *Faults*–A mouth over- or undershot.

Neck—Short and strong, well set on clean shoulders.

Body—Moderately short, compact and deep with level topline, ribs well sprung. *Faults*–A long weak back, loaded shoulders.

Legs—Short and powerful and as straight as is consistent with the short legs for which we aim. Sound bone, round feet, thick pads. *Faults*–Out at elbow, badly bowed, knuckled over. Too light in bone.

Quarters—Strong, rounded, with great powers of propulsion. *Faults*–Cowhocks.

Tail—Medium docked, carriage not excessively gay.

Color—All shades of red, wheaten, black and tan and grizzle. White markings on chest, though allowable, are not desirable. *Faults*–White markings elsewhere or to any great extent on the chest.

Coat—As hard and wiry as possible, lying close to the body, with a definite undercoat. Top coat absolutely straight; in full coat forming almost a mane on shoulders and neck. Hair on head, ears and muzzle, except for slight eyebrows and whiskers, is absolutely short and smooth. These dogs should be shown with as nearly a natural coat as possible. A minimum of tidying is permissible but excessive trimming, shaping and clipping shall be heavily penalized by the judge. *Faults*–Silky or curly coat.

Weight—Ideal, 11 to 12 pounds.

Height—Ideal, 10 inches at the withers.

General Appearance—A small, low rugged terrier, tremendously active. A perfect demon, yet not quarrelsome, and of a lovable disposition, and a very hardy constitution. Honorable scars from fair wear and tear shall not count against.

DISQUALIFICATION

Cropped ears shall disqualify.

Approved August 9, 1978
Effective January 1, 1979

497

Scottish Terrier

MOST LOVERS of the Scottish Terrier have a deep and abiding belief that this breed is the most ancient of any of the Highland terriers; that the other breeds are only offshoots from this, the parent stem, and that the Scottie is the original, dyed-in-the-wool, simon-pure Highland terrier. They will tell you that the Skye Terrier mentioned in early histories and chronicles was not the Skye as we know it today, but the forerunner of our favorite and similar in type to it. They will refer you to such early writers as Jacques du Fouilloux, who published *La Venerie* in 1561, Turberville and Dr. Stevens, whose books *The Noble Art of Venerie* and *The Maison Rustique* appeared in 1575 and 1572, respectively. All of these works described an "earth dog used in hunting the fox and the brocke," and these descriptions fit closely to what might have been the forerunner of our present-day Scottie.

In the seventeenth century, when King James VI of Scotland became James I of England, he wrote to Edinburgh to have a half dozen terriers sent to France as a present and addressed the letter to the Laird of Caldwell, naming the Earl of Montieth as having good ones. Later, the great English authority, Rawdon B. Lee, wrote as follows:

> The Scottie is the oldest variety of the canine race indigenous to Britain.
> . . . For generations he had been a popular dog in the Highlands where,
> strangely enough, he was always known as the Skye Terrier, although he

is different from the long-coated, unsporting-like creature with which that name is now associated.

While all this is very interesting and quite possibly true, the fact remains that it is neither definite nor conclusive.

Leaving the realm of speculation and inference and coming down to history and known facts, we do know that the Scottish Terrier as we find it today has been bred in purity for many years. The first show to have a class for Scottish Terriers was at Birmingham in England, in 1860. Later, a number of other shows carried this classification, but the dogs shown in these classes were not Scottish Terriers, but Skyes, Dandie Dinmonts, and Yorkshires.

All the while, however, Scotchmen who saw these dogs winning as Scottish Terriers were indignant, and about 1877 they broke into print in the *Live Stock Journal* with a series of letters protesting the situation and discussing the points and character of the true Scottish Terrier. The discussion waxed so furious that the editors finally called a halt with the statement, "We see no use in prolonging this discussion unless each correspondent describes the dog which he holds to be the true type." This challenge was taken up by Captain Gordon Murray, who in a letter to the "Stock Keeper" under the *nom de plume* of "Strathbogie," described in detail his conception of a proper Scottish Terrier. This quieted the warring factions and about 1880 J. B. Morrison was persuaded to draw up a standard. This was accepted by all parties.

The essentials of this standard have been retained in all the later standards, only minor changes having been introduced. In 1882 the Scottish Terrier Club was organized, with joint officers for England and Scotland. Later, as interest in the breed grew, the two countries organized separate clubs, although they have always worked harmoniously together. A joint committee revamped the Morrison standard and in 1933 the English club again revised this standard. The present American Standard was adopted in 1925, Messrs. Bixby, Cadwalader, and Megargee being the committee who made the revisions. In most essentials these standards are identical, the chief difference between the American and the foreign standards being in the weight requirements.

John Naylor is credited with being the first to introduce the Scottish Terrier to this country, his initial importation in 1883 consisting of a dog and a bitch, Tam Glen and Bonnie Belle. He showed extensively and continued importing, among his later importations being his famous dogs Glenlyon and Whinstone. The first Scottish Terrier registered in America was Dake (3688), a brindle dog whelped September 15, 1884, bred by O. P. Chandler of Kokomo, Indiana. His sire was Naylor's Glenlyon. This was in the *American Kennel Register,* published by *Forest and Stream,* and about the time The American Kennel Club was being organized. In December, 1887, a bitch Lassie was registered, bred by W. H. Todd of Vermillion, Ohio. Her sire was Glencoe, by Imp. Whinstone *ex.* Imp. Roxie. Here we find Whinstone figuring as a sire. Now Whinstone was by Allister, which together with Dundee formed the two great fountainheads of the breed. Whinstone sired Ch. Bellingham Baliff which was acquired by J. J. Little, founder of the famous Newcastle Kennels. Whinstone therefore was the forerunner and progenitor of the Scottish Terrier in this country today.

Since those days there have been thousands of importations and many notable breeders have carried on the work. Probably very little if any of the early blood is to be found today. Nevertheless, these early dogs must take their place in history; and to that pioneer breeder and missionary of the breed, John Naylor, the great popularity of this staunch little breed today stands as an enduring monument.

Official Standard for the Scottish Terrier

Skull *(5 points)*—Long, of medium width, slightly domed and covered with short, hard hair. It should not be quite flat, as there should be a slight stop or drop between the eyes.

Muzzle *(5 points)*—In proportion to the length of skull, with not too much taper toward the nose. Nose should be black and of good size. The jaws should be level and square. The nose projects somewhat over the mouth, giving the impression that the upper jaw is longer than the lower. The teeth should be evenly placed, having a scissors or level bite, with the former being preferable.

Eyes *(5 points)*—Set wide apart, small and of almond shape, not round. Color to be dark brown or nearly black. To be bright, piercing and set well under the brow.

Ears *(10 points)*—Small, prick, set well up on the skull, rather pointed but not cut. The hair on them should be short and velvety.

Neck *(5 points)*—Moderately short, thick and muscular, strongly set on sloping shoulders, but not so short as to appear clumsy.

Chest *(5 points)*—Broad and very deep, well let down between the forelegs.

Body *(15 points)*—Moderately short and well ribbed up with strong loin, deep flanks and very muscular hindquarters.

Legs and Feet *(10 points)*—Both forelegs and hind legs should be short and very heavy in bone in proportion to the size of the dog. Forelegs straight or slightly bent with elbows close to the body. Scottish Terriers should not be out at the elbows. Stifles should be well bent and legs straight from hock to heel. Thighs very muscular. Feet round and thick with strong nails, forefeet larger than the hind feet. *Note*—The gait of the Scottish Terrier is peculiarly its own and is very characteristic of the breed. It is not the square trot or walk that is desirable in the long-legged breeds. The forelegs do not move in exact parallel planes—rather in reaching out incline slightly inward. This is due to the shortness of leg and width of chest. The action of the rear legs should be square and true and at the trot both the hocks and stifles should be flexed with a vigorous motion.

Tail *(2½ points)*—Never cut and about 7 inches long, carried with a slight curve but not over the back.

Coat *(15 points)*—Rather short, about 2 inches, dense undercoat with outer coat intensely hard and wiry.

Size and Weight *(10 points)*—Equal consideration must be given to height, length of back and weight. Height at shoulder for either sex should be about 10 inches. Generally, a well-balanced Scottish Terrier dog of correct size should weigh from 19 to 22 pounds and a bitch, from 18 to 21 pounds. The principal objective must be symmetry and balance.

Color *(2½ points)*—Steel or iron gray, brindled or grizzled, black, sandy or wheaten. White markings are objectionable and can be allowed only on the chest and that to a slight extent only.

General Appearance *(10 points)*—The face should wear a keen, sharp and active expression. Both head and tail should be carried well up. The dog should look very compact, well muscled and powerful, giving the impression of immense power in a small size.

Penalties—Soft coat, round, or very light eye, overshot or undershot jaw, obviously oversize or undersize, shyness, timidity or failure to show with head and tail up are faults to be penalized. No judge should put to Winners or Best of Breed any Scottish Terrier not showing real terrier character in the ring.

SCALE OF POINTS

Skull	5	Legs and feet	10
Muzzle	5	Tail	2½
Eyes	5	Coat	15
Ears	10	Size	10
Neck	5	Color	2½
Chest	5	General appearance	10
Body	15	TOTAL	100

Approved June 10, 1947

Sealyham Terrier

THE SEALYHAM TERRIER derives its name from Sealyham, Haverfordwest, Wales, the estate of Captain John Edwardes who, between 1850 and 1891, developed from obscure ancestry a strain of dogs noted for prowess in quarrying badger, otter, and fox. The requisite qualities were extreme gameness and endurance with as much substance as could be encompassed in a dog small and quick enough to dig and battle underground.

As the working ability of Sealyham Terriers drew public interest, they began to take their places with other terrier breeds in prominent homes and on the show bench. Their first recorded appearance at a dog show was at Haverfordwest, Wales, in October, 1903. In January, 1908, a group of Welsh fanciers founded the Sealyham Terrier Club of Haverfordwest and at their first meeting drew up the original standard of points for the breed. The first championship show at which Sealyhams appeared was at the English Kennel Club Show in October, 1910. The breed was recognized on March 8, 1911, by The Kennel Club, which offered the first Challenge Certificates for Sealyham Terriers at the Great Joint Terrier Show, London, June 10, 1911.

There are three clubs that sponsor the breed in Great Britain: the Sealyham Terrier Club of Haverfordwest, which holds an annual show in Wales; the Sealyham Terrier Breeders' Association, which holds an annual championship show near London; and the Midland

Sealyham Terrier Club, which holds an annual championship show at Rugby.

The breed was recognized by the American Kennel Club in 1911, shortly after its original importation into the United States. Since its American show debut at San Mateo, California, in September 1911, its popularity as a show dog has remained fairly constant and in recent years it has not been uncommon for the Sealyham to be awarded first in the Terrier Group and Best in Show at all-breed fixtures.

The American Sealyham Terrier Club was founded on May 15, 1913, to promote the interests of the breed in the United States and to encourage exhibition and working trials. The latter have succumbed to suburban sprawl and a more humane feeling among Sealyham owners. However, a new interest is rising in the more controlled All-Terrier trials. The club offers, for club members, annual trophies for the most Bests in Show, most Group firsts, and most Bests of Breed won during the year. Annual specialty shows are held in an Eastern state during the winter, in the Midwest in late spring, and as part of the Montgomery County Kennel Club Terrier show in Pennsylvania in the fall.

The Sealyham Terrier Club of Southern California is a very active group of breeders in that state offering their specialty in June near Los Angeles.

The Sealyham of today is chiefly a companion, but when given the opportunity makes a very good working terrier. He is very outgoing, friendly yet a good house watchdog whose big-dog bark discourages intruders. He is easily trained but more often than not will add his own personal touch to the exercise or trick being taught. With proper care, food, and training, a Sealyham is very long-lived, 12 to 16 years not being uncommon, and active to the end.

Sealyhams require coat care at regular intervals. They do not shed which means that the dead hair must be pulled or combed out to prevent the formation of hair mats. Regular plucking of the dead hair, trimming of the head, neck, tail, and feet, will keep a smart looking, clean terrier which is a joy to own.

Official Standard for the
Sealyham Terrier

The Sealyham should be the embodiment of power and determination, ever keen and alert, of extraordinary substance, yet free from clumsiness.

Height—At withers about 10¹/₂ inches.

Weight—23-24 pounds for dogs; bitches slightly less. It should be borne in mind that size is more important than weight.

Head—Long, broad and powerful, without coarseness. It should, however, be in perfect balance with the body, joining neck smoothly. Length of head roughly, three-quarters height at withers, or about an inch longer than neck. Breadth between ears a little less than one-half length of head. *Skull*—Very slightly domed, with a shallow indentation running down between the brows, and joining the muzzle with a moderate stop. *Cheeks*—Smoothly formed and flat, without heavy jowls. *Jaws*—Powerful and square. Bite level or scissors. Overshot or undershot bad faults. *Teeth*—Sound, strong and white, with canines fitting closely together. *Nose*—Black, with large nostrils. White, cherry or butterfly bad faults. *Eyes*—Very dark, deeply set and fairly wide apart, of medium size, oval in shape with keen terrier expression. Light, large or protruding eye bad faults. Lack of eye rim pigmentation not a fault. *Ears*—Folded level with top of head, with forward edge close to cheek. Well rounded at tip, and of length to reach outer corner of eye. Thin, not leathery, and of sufficient thickness to avoid creases. Prick, tulip, rose or hound ears bad faults.

Neck—Length slightly less than two-thirds of height of dog at withers. Muscular without coarseness, with good reach, refinement at throat, and set firmly on shoulders.

Shoulders—Well laid back and powerful, but not over-muscled. Sufficiently wide to permit freedom of action. Upright or straight shoulder placement highly undesirable.

Legs—Forelegs strong, with good bone; and as straight as is consistent with chest being well let down between them. Down on pasterns, knuckled over, bowed, and out at elbow, bad faults. Hind legs longer than forelegs and not so heavily boned. *Feet*—Large but compact, round with thick pads, strong nails. Toes well arched and pointing straight ahead. Forefeet larger, though not quite so long as hind feet. Thin, spread or flat feet bad faults.

Body—Strong, short-coupled and substantial, so as to permit great flexibility. Brisket deep and well let down between forelegs. Ribs well sprung.

Back—Length from withers to set-on of tail should approximate height at withers, or 10¹/₂ inches. Topline level, neither roached nor swayed. Any deviations from these measurements undesirable. *Hindquarters*—Very powerful, and protruding well behind the set-on of tail. Strong second thighs, stifles well bent, and hocks well let down. **Cowhocks bad fault.**

Tail—Docked and carried upright. Set on far enough forward so that spine does not slope down to it.

Coat—Weather-resisting, comprised of soft, dense undercoat and hard, wiry top coat. Silky or curly coat bad fault.

Color—All white, or with lemon, tan or badger markings on head and ears. Heavy body markings and excessive ticking should be discouraged.

Action—Sound, strong, quick, free, true and level.

SCALE OF POINTS

General character, balance and size	15	Shoulders and brisket 10	
		Body, ribs & loin 10	
Head 5		Hindquarters 10	
Eyes 5		Legs and feet 10	
Mouth 5		Coat 10	50
Ears 5		Tail 5	
Neck 5	25	Color (body marking & ticking) 5	10
		TOTAL	100

Approved February 9, 1974

Skye Terrier

THE MAJORITY of terriers have attained something of their present-day form within the last century. The Skye Terrier of nearly four centuries ago was like the specimens of today.

One may find mention of the Skye Terrier in that historic volume called *Of Englishe Dogges*, which was penned, strangely, by Dr. John Caius, master of Gonville and Caius College, Cambridge University, and court physician to Edward VI, Queen Mary, and Queen Elizabeth. He was a man of broad education aside from the sciences, and also a great traveler and sportsman. Referring to the breed, he says it was "brought out of barbarous borders fro' the uttermost countryes northward," ... "which, by reason of the length of heare, makes showe neither of face nor of body."

Thus we find the Skye Terrier of today. His flowing coat is the same as the one that proved such a grand protection in the days when his only occupation was to challenge vicious animals that otherwise might have crippled him at a single bite. Perhaps this long coat has been a handicap, for all followers of this game old working terrier have witnessed him surpassed in popularity by one after another of the newer breeds. Still they are reluctant to change him in any manner. Indeed, they stand by the motto of the Skye Club of Scotland —"Wha daur meddle wi' me."

The breed takes its name from the chief of those northwestern islands of Scotland that, as far back as he can be traced, formed his native home, and in which he was found in greatest perfection. He is the only terrier distinctively belonging to the northwestern islands that is not common to the whole of Scotland. Those who have the best practical knowledge of the Skye maintain that he is without rival in his own peculiar domain, and that wherever there are rocks, dens, burrows, cairns, or covers to explore, or waters to take to, his services should be called.

From the nature of Dr. Caius' allusion to him, it is evident that the Skye Terrier had become known in the cities of England, especially in the royal palace. The kings and queens of England have always set the styles in that country, and as soon as the Skye had been accepted in court—evidently in the middle of the sixteenth century when Dr. Caius penned the historic work—he was soon the fashionable pet of all degrees of nobility, and after that of the commoners.

No other definite terrier breed has yet existed long enough to rival the duration of the Skye's popularity, for he still was the most widely known of all the terriers down to the end of the nineteenth century. He was kept in all the English-speaking countries. Since then he has slipped quietly into the background, yet his admirers in England and Scotland—where he has maintained his greatest foothold—are happy to point to the time when "a duchess would almost be ashamed to be seen in the park unaccompanied by her long-coated Skye."

The Skye Terrier was one of the most important breeds at American bench shows before the turn of the century, and the rivalry among the leading kennels was exceptionally keen. Although the frontiers of his activities have been somewhat curtailed, the true value of the Skye Terrier is evinced by the tenacious grasp which he has on those who have come in contact with him. Thus, entries may sometimes be small at bench shows today, but seldom does one find a major show without some specimens of this old terrier breed.

Official Standard for the
Skye Terrier

General Appearance—The Skye Terrier is a dog of style, elegance, and dignity; agile and strong with sturdy bone and hard muscle. Long, low, and lank—he is twice as long as he is high—he is covered with a profuse coat that falls straight down either side of the body over oval-shaped ribs. The hair well feathered on the head veils forehead and eyes to serve as protection from brush and briar as well as amid serious encounters with other animals. He stands with head high and long tail hanging, and moves with a seemingly effortless gait. Of suitable size for his hunting work, strong in body, quarters, and jaw.

Temperament—That of the typical working terrier capable of overtaking game and going to ground, displaying stamina, courage, strength, and agility. Fearless, good-tempered, loyal and canny, he is friendly and gay with those he knows and reserved and cautious with strangers.

Head—Long and powerful, strength being deemed more important than extreme length. Moderate width at the back of the skull tapers gradually to a strong muzzle. The stop is slight. The dark muzzle is just moderately full as opposed to snipy, and the nose is always black. A Dudley, flesh-colored, or brown nose shall disqualify. Powerful and absolutely true jaws and mouth with the incisor teeth closing level, or with the upper teeth slightly overlapping the lower. *Eyes*—Brown, preferably dark brown, medium in size, close-set, and alight with life and intelligence. *Ears*—Symmetrical and gracefully feathered. They may be carried prick or drop. When prick, they are medium in size, placed high on the skull, erect at their outer edges, and slightly wider apart at the peak than at the skull. Drop ears, somewhat larger in size and set lower, hang flat against the skull.

Neck—Long and gracefully arched, carried high and proudly.

Body—Pre-eminently long and low. The backline is level, the chest deep, with oval-shaped ribs. The sides appear flattish due to the straight falling and profuse coat.

Legs and Feet—*Forequarters*—Legs short, muscular, and straight as possible. "Straight as possible" means straight as soundness and chest will permit; it does not mean "terrier straight." Shoulders well laid back, with tight placement of shoulder blades at the withers, and elbows should fit closely to the sides and be neither loose nor tied. Forearm should curve slightly around the chest. *Hindquarters*—Strong, full, well developed, and well angulated. Legs short, muscular, and straight when viewed from behind. *Feet*—Large harefeet preferably pointing forward, the pads thick and nails strong and preferably black.

Movement—The legs proceed straight forward when traveling. When approaching, the forelegs form a continuation of the straight line of the front, the feet being the same distance apart as the elbows. The principal propelling power is furnished by the hind legs, which travel straight forward. Forelegs should move well forward, without too much lift. The whole movement may be termed free, active, and effortless and give a more or less fluid picture.

Tail—Long and well feathered. When hanging, its upper section is pendulous, following the line of the rump, its lower section thrown back in a moderate arc without twist or curl. When raised, its height makes it appear a prolongation of the backline. Though not to be preferred, the tail is sometimes carried high when the dog is excited or angry. When such carriage arises from emotion only, it is permissible. But the tail should not be constantly carried above the level of the back nor hang limp.

Coat—Double. Undercoat short, close, soft, and woolly. Outer coat hard, straight, and flat, $5^{1}/_{2}$ inches long without extra credit granted for greater length. The body coat hangs straight down each side, parting from head to tail. The head hair, which may be shorter and softer, veils forehead and eyes and forms a moderate beard and apron. The long feathering on the ears falls straight down from the tips and outer edges, surrounding the ears like a fringe and outlining their shape. The ends of the hair should mingle with the coat at the sides of the neck.

Color—The coat must be of one over-all color at the skin but may be of varying shades of the same color in the full coat, which may be black, blue, dark or light gray, silver platinum, fawn, or cream. The dog must have no distinctive markings except for the desirable black points of ears, muzzle, and tip of tail, all of which points are preferably dark even to black. The shade of head and legs should approximate that of the body. There must be no trace of pattern, design, or clear-cut color variations, with the exception of the breed's only permissible white which occasionally exists on the chest not exceeding 2 inches in diameter.

The puppy coat may be very different in color from the adult coat. As it is growing and clearing, wide variations of color may occur; consequently this is permissible in dogs under 18 months of age. However, even in puppies there must be no trace of pattern, design, or clear cut variations with the exception of the black band of varying width frequently seen encircling the body coat of the cream-colored dog, and the only permissible white which, as in the adult dog, occasionally exists on the chest not exceeding 2 inches in diameter.

Size—Dogs: Shoulder height, 10 inches. Length, chest bone over tail at rump, 20 inches. Head, $8^{1}/_{2}$ inches. Tail, 9 inches. Bitches: Shoulder height, $9^{1}/_{2}$ inches. Length, chest bone over tail at rump, 19 inches. Head, 8 inches. Tail, $8^{1}/_{2}$ inches. A slightly higher or lower dog of either sex is acceptable, providing body, head, and tail dimensions are proportionately longer or shorter. The ideal ratio of body length to shoulder height is 2 to 1, which is considered the correct proportion.

Measurements are taken with the Skye standing in natural position with feet well under. A box caliper is used vertically and horizontally. For the height, the top bar should rest on the withers. The head is measured from the tip of the nose to the back of the occipital bone, and the tail from the root to tip. Dogs 8 inches or less at the withers and bitches $7^{1}/_{2}$ inches or less at the withers are to be penalized.

DISQUALIFICATIONS

A Dudley, flesh-colored or brown nose.

Approved May 8, 1973

Soft-Coated Wheaten Terrier

THE ACTUAL ORIGIN of the Soft-Coated Wheaten Terrier cannot be found in printed record. Recurring reference to a terrier soft in coat, wheaten in color, and of a size to fit the Wheaten of today, lends credence to the belief that the history of the Soft-Coated Wheaten began long before records were kept and when the challenge of "best dog" was most often settled in a "fists up" confrontation between the owners.

Known for more than 200 years in Ireland, the Soft-Coated Wheaten Terrier is believed by some to be an important ancestor of the Kerry Blue. Legend tells us that when the Spanish Armada was sunk off the shores of Ireland, the blue dogs who swam ashore found terriers with a soft, wheaten coat waiting to welcome them.

Bits of information show us a hardy dog who hunted small game cleverly and silently, guarded stock and garden with courage and tenacity, and was both companion and protector to his owners.

Of necessity these early dogs were bred for their working qualities, with shade of coat or exact measurements of small consideration and no record. As only the brave, strong and proficient survived and reproduced, Nature really set the standard for the original stock of the Soft-Coated Wheaten Terrier.

This has evolved a very attractive, well-made dog of medium size, quick-witted and responsive. The demands of his function required steadiness and discrimination, which have been retained, while preserving the joy in living and the stamina associated with a terrier.

It has produced a dog whose natural attributes have been maintained and whose appearance has not been artificially altered.

It has provided a dog whose mature coat is abundant throughout, giving protection from the elements and the enemy. This coat is very soft, wheaten in color, and from it the breed takes its name. The coat goes through a natural progression of change from puppyhood to maturity, but should be clear wheaten by 18 to 24 months of age.

In the standard for the breed, the quality of moderation is emphasized; in fact, lack of exaggeration anywhere has seemed to be the hallmark of the breed.

Sponsored by Dr. G. J. Pierse, the Soft-Coated Wheaten Terrier was campaigned to registration with the Irish Kennel Club and on March 17th, 1937, a most fitting day for Irish dogs, made its debut in the Irish Kennel Club Championship Show. For many years this breed was required to qualify in both major and minor field trials over rat, rabbit and badger before attaining Championship registration with The Kennel Club of Great Britain came in 1943.

The history of the Soft-Coated Wheaten in the United States must begin with a quote from the *Boston Globe Post,* dated November 24, 1946:

"With a cargo which included several hundred tons of choice Scotch and Irish whiskey, seven pedigreed pups (one was lost over the side on the trip) and 18 homing pigeons, the freighter *Norman J. Colman* arrived yesterday after a 12-day voyage from Manchester, Liverpool and Belfast."

Two of the fortunate dogs who survived the passage were consigned to Miss Lydia Vogel of Springfield, Mass., and were, as far as we know, the first to come to our side of the Atlantic. They were shown at Westminster in February 1947, and seventeen puppies were whelped. However, American Kennel Club registration was not achieved at that time.

Ten years later in March of 1957, the O'Connors of Brooklyn imported Holmenocks Gramachree. Shown in the Miscellaneous Class in Staten Island in 1961, she took her first ribbon. Encouraged by the enthusiasm of exhibitors and spectators, a search was initiated by letter, telephone and cable for other Wheaten owners. Only the Arnolds of Connecticut were interested in actively promoting the breed.

In 1962, on St. Patrick's Day—again that most appropriate date—the Soft-Coated Wheaten Terrier Club of America was founded when a small group of interested fanciers met in Brooklyn and agreed on a common goal, namely to preserve and protect the Wheaten in the United States and to promote the breed to public interest and American Kennel Club registration. First officers were elected—Margaret O'Connor, Eileen Jackson, Ida Mallory and Charles Arnold.

Also present at that meeting were three Wheatens destined to pioneer the breed in the show rings—Holmenocks Gramachree, Gads Hill and Holmenocks Hallmark, better known as "Irish" (O'Connor), "Liam" and "Maud" (Arnold). On July 4, 1962, four puppies were whelped—Irish the dam and Liam the sire. These were the first in the United States in more than ten years.

Since that time, each year has seen substantial gains in stud book registrations, in Club memberships, and in public interest. And each year showing has increased in breed competition and in obedience exhibition.

The Soft-Coated Wheaten Terrier was admitted to registration in The American Kennel Club Stud Book on May 1, 1973, and to regular show classification in the Terrier Group at AKC shows October 3, 1973.

Official Standard for the Soft-Coated Wheaten Terrier

General Appearance—The Soft-Coated Wheaten Terrier is a medium-sized, hardy, well-balanced sporting terrier covered abundantly with a soft, naturally wavy coat of a good clear wheaten color. The breed requires moderation in all points and any exaggerated features are to be shunned. The head is only moderately long, is well balanced and should be free of any coarseness; the back is level with tail set on high and carried gaily; legs straight in front and muscular behind with well-laid-back shoulders and well-bent stifles to provide a long graceful stride. The dog should present an overall appearance of a hardy, active and happy animal, strong and well-coordinated.

Head—Well balanced and moderately long, profusely covered with coat which may fall forward to shade the eyes.

Skull flat and not too wide with no suggestion of coarseness. Skull and foreface about equal length.

Cheeks clean and stop well defined.

Muzzle square, powerful and strong, with no suggestion of snipiness. Lips are tight and black.

Nose is black and large for size of the dog.

Eyes—Dark hazel or brown, medium in size and well protected under a strong brow; eye rims black.

Ears—Break level with the skull and drop slightly forward close to the cheeks rather than pointing to the eyes; small to medium in size.

Teeth—Large, clean and white with either level or scissors bite.

Neck—Medium in length, strong and muscular, well covered with protective coat.

Shoulders—Well laid back, clean and smooth.

Body—Body is compact; back strong and level. Ribs are well sprung but without roundness to provide a deep chest with relatively short coupling.

Length of back from point of withers to base of tail should measure about the same as from point of withers to ground.

Tail is docked and well set on, carried gaily but never over the back.

Legs and Feet—Forelegs, straight and well boned; hind legs well developed with well bent stifles; hocks well let down, turned neither in nor out.

Feet are round and compact with good depth of pad. Nails dark.

Dewclaws on forelegs may be removed; dewclaws on hind legs should be removed.

Coat—Abundant, soft and wavy, of a good clear wheaten color; may be shaded on the ears and muzzle.

The Soft-Coated Wheaten Terrier is a natural dog and should so appear. Dogs that appear to be overly trimmed should be penalized.

Coat on ears may be left natural or relieved of the fringe to accent smallness.

Coat color and texture do not stabilize until about 18-24 months and should be given some latitude in young dogs.

For show purposes the coat may be tidied up merely to present a neat outline but may not be clipped, plucked or stylized.

Size—Dogs should measure 18-19 inches at the withers and should weigh between 35-45 pounds, bitches somewhat less.

Movement—Free; gait graceful and lively having reach in front and good drive behind; straight action fore and aft.

Temperament—Good tempered, spirited and game; exhibits less aggressiveness than is sometimes encouraged in terriers in the show ring; alert and intelligent.

Major Faults—Overshot. Undershot. Coat texture deviation. Any color save wheaten.

Approved June 12, 1973

Staffordshire Bull Terrier

THE STAFFORDSHIRE BULL TERRIER had its beginnings in England many centuries ago when the Bulldog and Mastiff were closely linked. Bull baiting and bear baiting in the Elizabethan era produced large dogs for these sports and later on the 100-120 pound animal gave way to a small, more agile breed of up to 90 pounds.

Early in the nineteenth century the sport of dog fighting gained popularity and a smaller, faster dog was developed. It was called by names such as "Bulldog Terrier" and "Bull and Terrier." The Bulldog bred then was a larger dog than we know today and weighed probably about 60 pounds. This dog was crossed with a small native terrier which appears in the history of the present-day Manchester Terrier. This dog, averaging between 30 and 45 pounds, became the Staffordshire Bull Terrier.

Mr. James Hinks, in about 1860, crossed the Old Pit Bull Terrier, now known as the Staffordshire Bull Terrier, and produced the all-white English Bull Terrier.

The Bull Terrier obtained recognition by The Kennel Club in England in the last quarter of the nineteenth century, but the Staffordshire Bull Terrier, due to its reputation as a fighting dog, did not receive this blessing.

In 1935 the Staffordshire Bull Terrier was recognized by The Kennel Club in England and enthusiasts were able to conduct conformation matches. The aggressive attitude of the Royal Society for the Prevention of Cruelty to Animals had long previously been able to restrict the sport of dog fighting and thus the Staffordshire Bull Terrier has evolved as a pet, companion and of such temperament as can be treated in every sense as a show dog.

The Staffordshire Bull Terrier was admitted to registration in The American Kennel Club Stud Book effective October 1, 1974, with regular show classification in the Terrier Group at AKC shows available on and after March 5, 1975.

Official Standard for the Staffordshire Bull Terrier

Characteristics—From the past history of the Staffordshire Bull Terrier, the modern dog draws its character of indomitable courage, high intelligence, and tenacity. This, coupled with its affection for its friends, and children in particular, its off-duty quietness and trustworthy stability, makes it a foremost all-purpose dog.

General Appearance—The Staffordshire Bull Terrier is a smooth-coated dog. It should be of great strength for its size and, although muscular, should be active and agile.

Head and Skull—Short, deep through, broad skull, very pronounced cheek muscles, distinct stop, short foreface, black nose. Pink (Dudley) nose to be considered a serious fault.

Eyes—Dark preferable, but may bear some relation to coat color. Round, of medium size, and set to look straight ahead. Light eyes or pink eye rims to be considered a fault, except that where the coat surrounding the eye is white the eye rim may be pink.

Ears—Rose or half-pricked and not large. Full drop or full prick to be considered a serious fault.

Mouth—A bite in which the outer side of the lower incisors touches the inner side of the upper incisors. The lips should be tight and clean. The badly undershot or overshot bite is a serious fault.

Neck—Muscular, rather short, clean in outline and gradually widening toward the shoulders.

Forequarters—Legs straight and well boned, set rather far apart, without looseness at the shoulders and showing no weakness at the pasterns, from which point the feet turn out a little.

Body—The body is close coupled, with a level topline, wide front, deep brisket and well sprung ribs being rather light in the loins.

515

Hindquarters—The hindquarters should be well muscled, hocks let down with stifles well bent. Legs should be parallel when viewed from behind.

Feet—The feet should be well padded, strong and of medium size. Dewclaws, if any, on the hind legs are generally removed. Dewclaws on the forelegs may be removed.

Tail—The tail is undocked, of medium length, low set, tapering to a point and carried rather low. It should not curl much and may be likened to an old-fashioned pump handle. A tail that is too long or badly curled is a fault.

Coat—Smooth, short and close to the skin, not to be trimmed or de-whiskered.

Color—Red, fawn, white, black or blue, or any of these colors with white. Any shade of brindle or any shade of brindle with white. Black-and-tan or liver color to be disqualified.

Size—Weight: Dogs, 28 to 38 pounds; bitches, 24 to 34 pounds. Height at shoulder: 14 to 16 inches, these heights being related to weights. Non-conformity with these limits is a fault.

DISQUALIFICATIONS

Black-and-tan or liver color.

Effective March 5, 1975

516

Welsh Terrier

JUDGING from the old paintings and prints of the first known terriers, the Welsh Terrier is a very old breed, for these prints show us a rough-haired black-and-tan terrier.

In old times this dog was more commonly known as the Old English Terrier or Black-and-Tan Wire Haired Terrier, and as late as 1886 the English Kennel Club allotted one class for "Welsh or Old English Wire Haired Black and Tan Terriers." Even to this day the color of the Welsh is as it was over a hundred years ago.

In other respects, also, the Welsh Terrier has changed very slightly. He is, as he was then, a sporting dog extensively used in his native home, Wales, for hunting the otter, fox, and badger, and he possesses the characteristic gameness that one naturally looks for in such a dog. Although game, he is not quarrelsome, in fact, he is well mannered and easy to handle.

The first record of Welsh Terriers having a classification of their own in England was in 1884–85 at Carnavon where there were twenty-one entries, but even at this time it was not uncommon for dogs to be shown as Old English Terriers and also as Welsh Terriers. As late as 1893 Dick Turpin, a well-known show dog of those days, continued in this dual role. Welsh Terriers were first brought to this country by the late Mr. Prescott Lawrence in 1888, when he imported a dog and a bitch, T'Other and Which, and showed them at the old Madison Square Garden in the Miscellaneous Class. No other Welsh, however, were imported for some time, Ch. Red Palm making his debut over here some years later. But about 1901 classification was offered for Welsh at Westminster, and four or five dogs were shown; from then on their popularity has steadily increased.

Welsh Terriers should stand about fifteen inches and weigh about twenty pounds. Black and a rich tan in color, they should be built like a cleverly made hunter, with plenty of bone and substance. The head should be broader than that of the Fox Terrier, but the skull should be very flat and the eyes set fairly far apart to give that intelligent, unmistakably Welsh expression, so different from other terriers and so characteristic of the breed.

Official Standard for the Welsh Terrier

Head—The skull should be flat, and rather wider between the ears than the Wirehaired Fox Terrier. The jaw should be powerful, clean-cut, rather deeper, and more punishing—giving the head a more masculine appearance than that usually seen on a Fox Terrier. Stop not too defined, fair length from stop to end of nose, the latter being of a black color. *Ears*—The ear should be V-shaped, small, not too thin, set on fairly high, carried forward and close to the cheek. *Eyes*—The eye should be small, not being too deeply set in or protruding out of skull, of a dark hazel color, expressive and indicating abundant pluck.

Neck—The neck should be of moderate length and thickness, slightly arched and sloping gracefully into the shoulders.

Body—The back should be short, and well-ribbed up, the loin strong, good depth, and moderate width of chest. The shoulders should be long, sloping, and well set back. The hindquarters should be strong, thighs muscular and of good length, with the hocks moderately strraight, well let down, and fair amount of bone. The stern should be set on moderately high, but not too gaily carried.

Legs and Feet—The legs should be straight and muscular, possessing fair amount of bone, with upright and powerful pasterns. The feet should be small, round and catlike.

Coat—The coat should be wiry, hard, very close and abundant.

Color—The color should be black and tan, or black grizzle and tan, free from black penciling on toes.

Size—The height at shoulder should be 15 inches for dogs, bitches proportionately less. Twenty pounds shall be considered a fair average weight in working condition, but this may vary a pound or so either way.

Head and jaws 10   Legs and feet 10
Ears 5   Coat 15
Eyes 5   Color 5
Neck and shoulders 10   Stern 5
Body 10   General appearance 15
Loins and hindquarters 10   TOTAL 100

DISQUALIFICATIONS

(1) Nose: white, cherry or spotted to a considerable extent with either of these colors.

(2) Ears: prick, tulip or rose.

(3) Undershot jaw or pig-jawed mouth.

(4) Black below hocks or white to an appreciable extent.

West Highland White Terrier

IT IS PROBABLE that the West Highland White Terrier and all the terriers of Scotland came from the same stock; the Scotties, Cairns, Dandie Dinmonts, and West Highland Whites are branches from the same tree and its roots.

The West Highland White Terrier, according to notable authors and the Malcolm family of Poltalloch, Scotland, originated at Poltalloch, where they had been bred and maintained for more than 100 years prior to their appearance at dog shows. In 1916 Colonel Malcolm said that his father and grandfather both kept them. It is probable that the lineage of the Malcolm dogs goes back to the time of King James I, who asked for some "earth-dogges" out of Argyleshire.

Years ago the breed was known as the Rosencath Terrier, also as the Poltalloch Terrier. The name Roseneath was taken from the Duke of Argyll's place in Dumbartonshire, Scotland. The first show held for the breed was at Crufts in London.

Mr. Robert Goelet, among the early fanciers to import the West Highlander to the United States, paid heavy money for the importation of British champions such as Kiltie of Glenmere and Rumpus of Glenmere, both grand dogs in their time. Today the breed is widely known and justly popular.

The West Highland is all terrier—a large amount of Scotch spunk, determination, and devotion crammed into a small body. Outdoors they are truly sporty, good hunters, speedy and cunning, with great intelligence. In the house they are all that can be desired of a pet; faithful, understanding, and devoted, yet gay and light-hearted.

One of the reasons West Highland White Terriers are such delightful little dogs to own is their hardiness. They need no pampering. They love to romp and play in the snow and will follow skaters or walkers for miles across frozen lakes and harbors. They are also easy to show and handle as they require very little trimming and, indeed, look better and more characteristic when in their natural state. Of course, there are always a few hairs which should be pulled out just to smarten the dog up a bit, but there is no prettier sight than a well-kept West Highland White Terrier shown in full coat.

The West Highland's outer coat is hard and stiff and should be kept so by proper grooming and dry-cleaning rather than by washing. There are people who think a white dog hard to keep clean, but this is not so. A little time spent each day with a brush and comb keeps him always in the pink of condition.

Official Standard for the West Highland White Terrier

General Appearance—The West Highland White Terrier is a small, game, well-balanced, hardy-looking terrier, exhibiting good showmanship, possessed with no small amount of self-esteem, strongly built, deep in chest and back ribs, straight back and powerful hindquarters on muscular legs, and exhibiting in marked degree a great combination of strength and activity. The coat should be about 2 inches long, white in color, hard, with plenty of soft undercoat. The dog should be neatly presented. Considerable hair should be left around the head to act as a frame for the face to yield a typical Westie expression.

Color and Pigmentation—Coat should be white, as defined by the breed's name. Nose should be black. Black pigmentation is most desirable on lips, eye-rims, pads of feet, nails and skin. *Faults*—Any coat color other than white and nose color other than black are serious faults.

Coat—Very important and seldom seen to perfection; must be double-coated. The outer coat consists of straight hard hair, about 2 inches long, with shorter coat on neck and shoulders, properly blended. *Faults*—Any silkiness or tendency to curl is a serious fault, as is an open or single coat.

Size—Dogs should measure about 11 inches at the withers, bitches about one inch less. *Faults*—Any specimens much over or under height limits are objectionable.

Skull—Should be fairly broad, being in proportion to his powerful jaw, not too long, slightly domed, and gradually tapering to the eyes. There should be a defined stop, eyebrows heavy. *Faults*—A too long or too narrow skull.

Muzzle—Should be slightly shorter than the skull, powerful and gradually tapering to the nose, which should be large. The jaws should be level and powerful, the teeth well set and large for the size of the dog. There shall be six incisor teeth between the canines of both lower and upper jaws. A tight scissors bite with upper incisors slightly overlapping the lower incisors or level mouth are equally acceptable. *Faults*—Muzzle longer than skull. Teeth much undershot or overshot are a serious fault, as are teeth defective or missing.

Ears—Small, carried tightly erect, set wide apart and terminating in a sharp point. They must never be cropped. The hair on the ears should be short, smooth and velvety, and trimmed free of fringe at the tips. *Faults*—Round-pointed, drop, broad and large ears are very objectionable, as are mule-ears, ears set too closely together or not held tightly erect.

Eyes—Widely set apart, medium in size, dark in color, slightly sunk in the head, sharp and intelligent. Looking from under heavy eyebrows, they give a piercing look. *Faults*—Too small, too full or light-colored eyes are very objectionable.

Neck—Muscular and nicely set on sloping shoulders. *Faults*—Short neck or too long neck.

Chest—Very deep and extending at least to the elbows with breadth in proportion to size of the dog. *Faults*—Shallow chest.

Body—Compact and of good substance, level back, ribs deep and well arched in the upper half of rib, presenting a flattish side appearance, loins broad and strong, hindquarters strong, muscular, and wide across the top. *Faults*—Long or weak back; barrel ribs; high rump.

Legs and Feet—Both forelegs and hind legs should be muscular and relatively short, but with sufficient length to set the dog up so as not to be too close to the ground. The shoulder blades should be well laid back and well knit at the backbone. The chest should be relatively broad and the front legs spaced apart accordingly. The front legs should be set in under the shoulder blades with definite body overhang before them. The front legs should be reasonably straight and thickly covered with short hard hair. The hind legs should be short and sinewy; the thighs very muscular and not set wide apart, with hocks well bent. The forefeet are larger than the hind ones, are round, proportionate in size, strong, thickly padded, and covered with short hard hair; they may properly be turned out a slight amount. The hind feet are smaller and thickly padded. *Faults*—Steep shoulders, loaded shoulders, or out at the elbows. Too light bone. Cowhocks, weak hocks and lack of angulation. A "fiddle-front" is a serious fault.

Tail—Relatively short, when standing erect it should never extend above the top of the skull. It should be covered with hard hairs, no feather, as straight as possible, carried gaily but not curled over the back. The tail should be set on high enough so that the spine does not slope down to it. The tail must never be docked. *Faults*—Tail set too low; tail too long or carried at half mast or over back.

Movement—Should be free, straight and easy all around. In front, the leg should be freely extended forward by the shoulder. The hind movement should be free, strong and fairly close. The hocks should be freely flexed and drawn close under the body; so that when moving off the foot the body is thrown or pushed forward with some force. *Faults*—Stiff, stilty or too wide movement behind. Lack of reach in front, and/or drive behind.

Temperament—Must be alert, gay, courageous and self-reliant, but friendly. *Faults*—Excess timidity or excess pugnacity.

Approved December 10, 1968

GROUP V: TOYS

Affenpinscher

PROGENITOR of the more familiar Brussels Griffon, the Affen-pinscher, or Monkey Dog, was well known on the European continent as far back as the seventeenth century. This quaint little dog's popularity has been overshadowed by the Griffon, but more recently he is enjoying a return to favor. The breed was admitted to the American Kennel Club's *Stud Book* and to dog show classification in 1936.

A game, alert, intelligent, and sturdy little "terrier type," the Affen-pinscher is characterized by his "monkeyish" expression, derived from a prominent chin with hair-tuft and mustache. This expression is further accentuated by his bushy eyebrows, shadowing black-bordered eyelids and large, piercing dark eyes. The entire coat is stiff and wiry in texture, and with his cropped ears and docked tail he is every inch a real dog, despite his small size. The ideal Affenpinscher should measure no more than ten and a quarter inches at the shoulder, and weigh no more than seven to eight pounds.

Official Standard for the Affenpinscher

General Appearance—Small, but rather sturdy in build and not delicate in any way. He carries himself with comical seriousness and he is generally quiet and a very devoted pal. He can get vehemently excited, however, when attacked and is fearless toward any aggressor.

Coat—A very important factor. It is short and dense in certain parts and shaggy and longer in others, but should be hard and wiry. It is longer and more loose and shaggy on the legs and around the eyes, nose and chin, giving the typical monkey-like appearance from whence comes his name. The best color is black, matching his eyes and fiery temperament. However, black with tan markings, red, gray and other mixtures are permissible. Very light colors and white markings are a fault.

Head—Should be round and not too heavy, with well-domed forehead. *Eyes* —Should be round, of good size, black and very brilliant. *Ears*—Rather small, set high, pointed and erect, usually clipped to a point. *Muzzle*—Must be short and rather pointed with a black nose. The upper jaw is a trifle shorter than the lower jaw, while the teeth should close together; a slight undershot condition is not material. The teeth, however, should not show.

Neck—Short and straight.

Body—The back should be straight with its length about equal to the height at the shoulder. Chest should be reasonably deep and the body should show only a slight tuck-up at the loin.

Legs—Front legs should be straight as possible. Hind legs without much bend at the hocks and set well under the body. *Feet*—Should be round, small and compact. Turned neither in nor out, with preferably black pads and nails.

Tail—Cut short, set and carried high.

Size—The smaller dog, if of characteristic type, is more valuable, and the shoulder height should not exceed 10¼ inches in any case.

Approved September 15, 1936

Brussels Griffon

THE BRUSSELS GRIFFON is not a dog of beauty as measured by accepted standards, but one teeming with personality, hence it is not surprising that he makes lasting friends wherever he is known. He comes of neither exalted nor ancient lineage, yet is one of the most distinctive and unusual of all dogs. Although classified as a toy, there is nothing of the pampered pet in this bundle of jaunty good nature whose keynote is insouciance from his very turned up nose to the tip of his gaily carried tail. No matter what change of fortune the years may bring, he promises to remain the delightful little Belgian street urchin to the end of time.

The German Affenpinscher and the Belgian street dog, combined, were the true foundation from which our Griffons emanated, and there is only meager data available on both of these seventeenth-century breeds. To all accounts, in Belgium there was a strong conformity to a distinct type in the peasants' dogs of that epoch. These dogs were nearly as large as our Fox Terriers, but heavily built, as are most Belgian animals. Covered with a shaggy, rough, muddy-colored coat and unlovely of feature, but intelligent and interesting in disposition, they were popularly termed Griffons D'Ecurie, Stable Griffons, and they paid for their keep by killing the stable vermin. It is not uncommon to run across mention of these loyal companions as *"chiens barbus"* in the old folk songs and tales of the period, for they were to be found in nearly every household.

On the other hand, the Affenpinscher may be said to resemble the Yorkshire Terrier in many particulars, the likeness being particularly noticeable in head properties as well as in the length of body and leg. Doubtless it was felt that the injection of Affenpinscher into the then Griffons would serve to further increase the ratting ability of the Belgian dogs, although for lack of definite proof, this last must remain a conjecture.

At some later date, the smooth-coated Pug, already established in neighboring Holland, was used as a cross with the Griffon. This crossbreeding was responsible for the two types of coat which we have even in our present-day litters.

Whether there was any definite reason for adding the Ruby Spaniel to this combination, we cannot say. At any rate this breed was also brought into the picture and is largely responsible for the facial characteristics and impression which are so much a part of our present-day dog, but which have made it impossible for him to do the work to which he was once well suited.

And so we come to the twentieth-century Brussels Griffon, a small, compact dog with a harsh coat similar to that of the Irish Terrier (or else a smooth coat traceable to the Pug and termed Brabancon), with a short upturned face best described as a "speaking countenance" and a gay carriage.

The Griffon's super intelligence causes him to be sensitive, and it is not uncommon for a young dog, when in the presence of strangers, to display the same self-consciousness as a child in its awkward teens. Although obedient and easily managed, Griffons are sometimes difficult to break to the leash, hence this training should always be begun at a very early age. Strange as it may seem, the Brabancons display a marked stubbornness when on leash, although in all other respects they are every bit as tractable as their rough brothers.

As a young puppy, the Griffon must be given the same intelligent care necessary for a puppy of any of the smaller breeds. The average sized Griffon becomes very sturdy as he matures, and he develops into a real comrade, capable of holding his own on hikes and in swimming.

Official Standard for the
Brussels Griffon

General Appearance—A toy dog, intelligent, alert, sturdy, with a thick-set short body, a smart carriage and set-up, attracting attention by an almost human expression.

Head—*Skull*—Large and round, with a domed forehead. *Ears*—Small and set rather high on the head. May be shown cropped or natural. If natural they are carried semi-erect. *Eyes*—Should be set well apart, very large, black, prominent, and well open. The eyelashes long and black. Eyelids edged with black. *Nose*—Very black, extremely short, its tip being set back deeply between the eyes so as to form a lay-back. The nostrils large, the stop deep. *Lips*—Edged with black, not pendulous but well brought together, giving a clean finish to the mouth. *Jaws*—Chin must be undershot, prominent, and large with an upward sweep. The incisors of the lower jaw should protrude over the upper incisors, and the lower jaw should be rather broad. Neither teeth nor tongue should show when the mouth is closed. A wry mouth is a serious fault.

Body and Legs—Brisket should be broad and deep, ribs well sprung, back level and short. *Neck*—Medium length, gracefully arched. *Tail*—Set and held high, docked to about one third. *Forelegs*—Of medium length, straight in bone, well muscled, set moderately wide apart and straight from the point of the shoulders as viewed from the front. Pasterns short and strong. *Hind legs*—Set true, thighs strong and well muscled, stifles bent, hocks well let down, turning neither in nor out. *Feet*—Round, small, and compact, turned neither in nor out. Toes well arched. Black pads and toenails preferred.

Coat—There are two distinct types of coat—rough and smooth. The rough coat should be wiry and dense, the harder and more wiry the better. On no account should the dog look or feel woolly, and there should be no silky hair anywhere. The coat should not be so long as to give a shaggy appearance, but should still be distinctly different all over from the smooth coat. The head should be covered with wiry hair slightly longer around the eyes, nose, cheeks, and chin, thus forming a fringe. The smooth coat is similar to that of the Boston Terrier or Bulldog, with no trace of wire hair.

Color—In the rough-coated type, coat is either 1. reddish brown, with a little black at the whiskers and chin allowable, or 2. black and reddish brown mixed, usually with black mask and whiskers, or 3. black with uniform reddish brown markings, usually appearing under the chin, on the legs, over the eyebrows, around the edges of the ears and around the vent, or 4. solid black. The colors of the smooth-coated type are the same as those of the rough-coated type except that solid black is not allowable. Any white hairs in either the rough or smooth coat are a serious fault, except for "frost" on the black muzzle of a mature dog, which is natural.

Weight—Usually 8 to 10 pounds, and should not exceed 12 pounds. Type and quality are of greater importance than weight, and a smaller dog that is sturdy and well proportioned should not be penalized.

SCALE OF POINTS

Head
 Skull 5
 Nose and stop 10
 Eyes 5
 Chin and jaws 10
 Ears 5 35
Coat
 Color 12
 Texture 13 25

Body and General Conformation
 Body (brisket and rib)
  15
 Legs 10
 Feet 5
 General Appearance (neck,
  topline, and tail carriage)
  .... 10 40
 TOTAL   100

DISQUALIFICATIONS

Dudley or butterfly nose.
White spot or blaze anywhere on coat.
Hanging tongue.
Jaw overshot.
Solid black coat in the smooth type.

Approved February 6, 1960

530

Chihuahua

(Chih-wah-wah)

Smooth Coat Chihuahua

Long Coat Chihuahua

WHILE LITTLE or nothing is known of the previous history of the Toltecs, it has been established that they existed in what is now Mexico as early as the ninth century A.D., and that during their several centuries of occupancy they had a breed of dog called the Techichi. This dog was small, although not tiny, and of heavy-boned structure. His coat was long, while his most distinctive feature was muteness.

The Techichi, regarded as indigenous to Central America, is the progenitor of the Chihuahua that now enjoys popularity throughout the United States, where he has been bred to his greatest perfection. No records of the Techichi are, so far, available prior to the ninth century, but it seems probable that his ancestors were in the locality prior to the advent of the Maya tribes about the fifth century.

The evidence firmly establishing the Techichi to the Toltec period is found in pictures carved on stones—they may be found today in the Monastery of Huejotzingo, on the highway from Mexico City to Puebla. This monastery was constructed by the Franciscan Monks around 1530 from materials of the existing Pyramids of Cholula, built by the Toltecs. The carvings give a full-head view and a picture of an entire dog that closely approximates the Chihuahua of modern times. There also are remains of pyramid constructions and some pointers to the early existence of the Techichi at Chichen Itza in distant Yucatan.

Toltec civilization was centered principally around Tula, which is close to the present Mexico City, and there one finds the most

531

abundant relics of this ancient breed. For that reason, there always has been speculation regarding the discovery of the earliest specimens of the modern breed in the State of Chihuahua. The dogs were found, about 1850, in some old ruins close to Casas Grandes, said to be the remains of a palace built by Emperor Montezuma I.

The conclusions of K. de Blinde, a Mexican breeder and authority who spent years traversing sections of the country on horseback, were that the present form of Chihuahua evolved from crossing the Techichi with the small hairless dog brought from Asia to Alaska over the land bridge where the Bering Strait now runs. This hairless dog, similar to the one found in China, was responsible for the reduction in size.

The Aztec conquerors of the Toltecs flourished for several centuries, and just prior to the coming of Hernando Cortés civilization was at a high state and the wealth prodigious. Dogs of the rich were highly regarded, and the blue-colored ones were held as sacred. Paradoxical as it seems, the common people found little use for this same breed, and there are even tales that they were eaten.

The stormlike career of Cortés in Mexico during 1519–20 left little of either Aztec wealth or civilization. Practically all Montezuma's possessions were wrung from his dying hands, and it is only natural that his dogs became lost for several centuries.

While the Techichi's principal home was Mexico, there is a historic letter written by Christopher Columbus to the King of Spain that adds a curious note to knowledge of the breed. Reporting on the seizure of the present island of Cuba, Columbus stated that he found: "A small kind of dogs, which were mute and did not bark, as usual, but were domesticated." These dogs could not have been taken to Cuba by the Aztecs, who were not a seafaring people.

Legend and history are rich in tales of the ancestors of the present Chihuahua. He is described as a popular pet, as well as a religious necessity, among the ancient Toltec tribes and later among the Aztecs. Archaeologists have discovered remains of this breed in human graves in Mexico and in parts of the United States.

The phenomenon is believed due to the part the dog played in the religious and mythological life of the Aztecs. He was employed in connection with the worship of deities, with the voyage of the soul in the underworld, and in relation to the human body. With the sacrifice of a dog with a red skin, burning it to ashes with the corpse of the deceased, the sins of the human were supposed to be transferred to the dog, and the indignation of the deity thus averted. The dog also was credited with guiding the human soul through the dark regions of the underworld, fighting off evil spirits and leading the soul of the deceased safely to its ultimate destination.

The modern Chihuahua is quite different from his early ancestors, with his variegated colors ranging from snow white to jet black. Mexico favors the jet black with tan markings, and the black and white spotted. The United States prefers the solid colors.

American breeders have produced a diminutive dog that has few comparisons, even among other breeds, in size, symmetry, and conformation, as well as intelligence and alertness. Curiously, the Chihuahua is clannish, recognizing and preferring his own kind, and, as a rule, not liking dogs of other breeds. The smooth-coated are the most numerous in the United States, and the most clannish, but the long-coated Chihuahua is rapidly increasing. It has all the characteristics of the smooth.

Official Standard for the Chihuahua

Head—A well-rounded "apple dome" skull, with or without molera. Cheeks and jaws lean. Nose moderately short, slightly pointed (self-colored, in blond types, or black). In moles, blues, and chocolates, they are self-colored. In blond types, pink nose permissible.

Ears—Large, held erect when alert, but flaring at the sides at about an angle of 45 degrees when in repose. This gives breadth between the ears. In *Long Coats*, ears fringed. (Heavily fringed ears may be tipped slightly, never down.)

Eyes—Full, but not protruding, balanced, set well apart—dark ruby, or luminous. (Light eyes in blond types permissible.)

Teeth—Level or scissors bite. Overshot or undershot bite or any distortion of the bite should be penalized as a serious fault.

Neck and Shoulders—Slightly arched, gracefully sloping into lean shoulders, may be smooth in the very short types, or with ruff about neck preferred. In *Long Coats*, large ruff on neck desired and preferred. Shoulders lean, sloping into a slightly broadening support above straight forelegs that are set well under, giving a free play at the elbows. Shoulders should be well up, giving balance and soundness, sloping into a level back. (Never down or low.) This gives a chestiness, and strength of forequarters, yet not of the "Bulldog" chest; plenty of brisket.

Back and Body—Level back, slightly longer than height. Shorter backs desired in males. Ribs rounded (but not too much "barrel-shaped").

Hindquarters—Muscular, with hocks well apart, neither out nor in, well let down, with firm sturdy action.

Tail—Moderately long, carried sickle either up or out, or in a loop over the back, with tip just touching the back. (Never tucked under.) Hair on tail in harmony with the coat of the body, preferred furry in *Smooth Coats*. In *Long Coats*, tail full and long (as a plume).

Feet—Small, with toes well split up but not spread, pads cushioned, with fine pasterns. (Neither the hare nor the cat-foot.) A dainty, small foot with nails moderately long.

Coat—In the *Smooth*, the coat should be soft texture, close and glossy. (Heavier coats with undercoats permissible.) Coat placed well over body with ruff on neck, and more scanty on head and ears. In *Long Coats*, the coat should be of a soft texture, either flat or slightly curly, with undercoat preferred. Ears fringed (heavily fringed ears may be tipped slightly, never down), feathering on feet and legs, and pants on hind legs. Large ruff on neck desired and preferred. Tail full and long (as a plume).

Color—Any color—solid, marked or splashed.

Weight—A well-balanced little dog not to exceed 6 pounds.

General Appearance—A graceful, alert, swift-moving little dog with saucy expression. Compact, and with terrierlike qualities.

SCALE OF POINTS

Head, including ears	20
Body, including tail	20
Coat	20
Legs	20
General Appearance and Action	20
TOTAL	100

DISQUALIFICATIONS

Cropped tail, bobtail.
Broken down or cropped ears.
Any dog over 6 pounds in weight.
In Long Coats, too thin coat that resembles bareness.

Approved November 14, 1972

English Toy Spaniel

SINCE the spread of civilization has been from East to West, it is only natural that most of our oldest breeds of dog should trace their origin to the eastern countries. Such is the case of the English Toy Spaniel, an affectionate, intelligent little dog that captivated royalty, aristocrats, and the wealthy for at least three centuries.

It has been a widespread fallacy that the Toy Spaniel made its first appearance in England during the reign of King Charles II, in the seventeenth century, for it was in honor of this sovereign that the black-and-tan variety took its name. Yet the Toy Spaniel had been known in England and in Scotland more than a hundred years before.

Just how long the Toy Spaniel had been known in Europe, particularly the south of Europe, before it was carried to England, must remain a matter of doubt. Yet most authorities are agreed that it goes back to Japan, and possibly China, of very ancient times.

According to Leighton, the English Toy Spaniel had its origin in Japan, was taken from there to Spain, and thence to England. Yet the extremely short nose of the breed might constitute evidence that it went from Spain to Japan, where it developed its present characteristics. There is a story, also, that specimens of this toy breed were brought from Japan by Captain Saris, a British naval officer, in 1613. They were presents from the Emperor of Japan—every Japanese royal present always included dogs—to King James I.

The tale of Captain Saris seems a logical one, but it cannot be accepted as marking the debut of the Toy Spaniel into England and Scotland. The breed was known in England long before that, for Dr. Johannes Caius, celebrated professor and the physician to Queen

Elizabeth, included it in his work *Of Englishe Dogges*. He refers to it as the "Spaniell Gentle, otherwise called the Comforter." His other references stamp it as almost the identical dog of today.

It is difficult to associate the Toy Spaniel with the austere Elizabeth; evidence that the breed was the favorite of the warmer-hearted Mary, Queen of Scots, in the same century is much more acceptable. The early years of Mary, during the first third of the sixteenth century, were spent in France. When she returned to Scotland as Queen, she brought specimens of the breed with her, and these dogs remained her favorites up to the time of her execution. In fact, her especial pet refused to leave her, even on the scaffold.

All Toy Spaniels up to the time of King Charles II appear to have been of the black-and-tan variety, later called the King Charles. This king's favorites were brought over from France by Henrietta of Orleans, and one is described as a black and white.

The development of the other varieties, the Prince Charles, which is a tricolor of white, black, and tan; the Ruby, which is chestnut red; and the Blenheim, which is white and chestnut red; occurred at later times. All are identical in their characteristics, with the exception of color. For a long time they were bred without any reference to color. Often the same litter would produce dogs of several varieties. It is only in modern times that the science of color breeding set the different varieties apart.

The history of the Blenheim variety seems rather more definite than that of the King Charles, although in some ways incompatible with other data. The development of the Blenheim, or red and white, is credited to John Churchill, the first Duke of Marlborough. Churchill, famous soldier and diplomat, was made an Earl in 1689, and became a Duke in 1702. At that time he acquired Blenheim, which has been the family seat of the Marlboroughs ever since.

It is said by Ash that the first Duke received as a present from China a pair of red-and-white Cocker Spaniels, and that these dogs were the basis of his subsequent breeding. The Chinese origin of the breed is mentioned also by Lady de Gex, who claims that during the fifteenth and sixteenth centuries there were carried from China to Italy numerous specimens of both red-and-white and black-and-white spaniels. These dogs subsequently were crossed with Cockers and Springers, intensifying the sporting instincts which the Toy still retains.

The Dukes of Marlborough bred the Blenheim variety for many generations, and apparently they did so without the infusion of much outside blood—unless it were that of the Cocker and other varieties of spaniel. It was said by Scott in 1800 that the Duke of Marlborough's Blenheims were the smallest and best Cockers in England. They were used very successfully for woodcock shooting. And writers of a still later period describe the dogs found at Blenheim as larger than other specimens of the red and white. Also, the Marlborough strain did not have such exaggerated short noses.

Regardless of the early history of the English Toy Spaniel, it seems certain that many specimens of modern times trace their origin back to various small spaniels of England. Selective breeding has reduced them down to the limits of nine to twelve pounds, but it has not altogether erased their natural hunting instincts.

Official Standard for the English Toy Spaniel

KING CHARLES, PRINCE CHARLES, RUBY AND BLENHEIM

Head—Should be well domed, and in good specimens is absolutely semi-globular, sometimes even extending beyond the half-circle, and absolutely projecting over the eyes, so as nearly to meet the upturned nose. *Eyes*—The eyes are set wide apart, with the eyelids square to the line of the face—not oblique or foxlike. The eyes themselves are large and dark as possible, so as to be generally considered black, their enormous pupils, which are absolutely of that color, increasing the description. *Stop*—The stop, or hollow between the eyes, is well marked, as in the Bulldog, or even more so; some good specimens exhibit a hollow deep enough to bury a small marble in it. *Nose*—The nose must be short and well turned up between the eyes, and without any indication of artificial displacement afforded by a deviation to either side. The color of the end should be black, and it should be both deep and wide with open nostrils. A light-colored nose is objectionable, but shall not disqualify. *Jaw*—The muzzle must be square and deep, and the lower jaw wide between the branches, leaving plenty of space for the tongue, and for the attachment of the lower lips, which should completely conceal the teeth. It should also be turned up or "finished," so as to allow of its meeting the end of the upper jaw, turned up in a similar way as above described. A protruding tongue is objectionable, but does not disqualify. *Ears*—The ears must be long, so as to approach the ground. In an average-sized dog they measure 20 inches from tip to tip, and some reach 22 inches or even a trifle more. They should be set low down on the head and hang flat to the sides of the cheeks, and be heavy-feathered.

Size—The most desirable size is from 9 pounds to 12 pounds. *Shape*—In compactness of shape these Spaniels almost rival the Pug, but the length of coat adds greatly to the apparent bulk, as the body, when the coat is wetted, looks small in comparison with that dog. Still, it ought to be decidedly "cobby," with strong, stout legs, short broad back and wide chest.

Coat—The coat should be long, silky, soft and wavy, but not curly. There should be a profuse mane, extending well down in the front of the chest. The feather should be well displayed on the ears and feet, and in the latter case so thickly as to give the appearance of being webbed. It is also carried well up the backs of the legs. In the Black and Tan the feather on the ears is very long and profuse, exceeding that of the Blenheim by an inch or more. The feather on the tail (which is cut to the length of about 1½ inches) should be silky, and from 3 to 4 inches in length, constituting a marked "flag" of a square shape, and not carried above the level of the back.

COLORS OF THE TWO VARIETIES

King Charles and Ruby—The King Charles and Ruby types which comprise one show variety are solid-colored dogs. The King Charles are black and tan (considered a solid color), the black rich and glossy with deep mahogany tan markings over the eyes and on the muzzle, chest and legs. The presence of a few white hairs intermixed with the black on the chest is to be faulted, but a white patch on the chest or white appearing elsewhere disqualifies. The Ruby is a rich chestnut red and is whole-colored. The presence of a few white hairs intermixed with the red on the chest is to be faulted, but a white patch on the chest or white appearing elsewhere disqualifies.

Blenheim and Prince Charles—The Blenheim and Prince Charles types which comprise the other show variety are broken-colored dogs. The Blenheim is red and white. The ground color is a pearly white which has bright red chestnut or ruby red markings evenly distributed in large patches. The ears and cheeks should be red, with a blaze of white extending from the nose up the forehead and ending between the ears in a crescentic curve. In the center of the blaze at the top of the forehead, there should be a clear "spot" of red, the size of a dime. The Prince Charles, a tri-colored dog, is white, black and tan. The ground color is a pearly white. The black consists of markings which should be evenly distributed in large patches. The tan appears as spots over the eyes, on the muzzle, chest and legs; the ears and vent should also be lined with tan. The Prince Charles has no "spot," that being a particular feature of the Blenheim.

SCALE OF POINTS

King Charles, or Black and Tan.
Prince Charles, White, with Black and Tan Markings.
Ruby, or Red.

Symmetry, condition, size and		Eyes	10
soundness of limb	20	Ears	15
Head	15	Coat and feathering	15
Stop	5	Color	10
Muzzle	10	TOTAL	100

Blenheim, or White with Red Markings.

Symmetry, condition, size and		Eyes	10
soundness of limb	15	Ears	10
Head	15	Coat and feathering	15
Stop	5	Color and markings	15
Muzzle	10	Spot	5
		TOTAL	100

DISQUALIFICATIONS

King Charles and Ruby: A white patch on the chest, or white on any other part.

Approved July 14, 1959

Italian Greyhound

THE ITALIAN GREYHOUND is the smallest of the family of gazehounds (dogs that hunt by sight). The breed is believed to have originated more than 2,000 years ago in the Mediterranean basin, possibly in the countries now known as Greece and Turkey. This belief is based on the depiction of miniature Greyhounds in the early decorative arts of these countries and on the archaeological discoveries of small Greyhound skeletons. Though never excessively popular, by the Middle Ages the breed had become distributed throughout Southern Europe and was a favorite of the Italians of the sixteenth century with whom miniature dogs were much in demand. Thus they became known as "Italian Greyhounds". As a breed it has survived many centuries, prized for its beauty, small size and sweet disposition. They were frequently included in the Renaissance paintings of such artists as Giotto, Carpaccio, Memling, Van der Weyden, Gerard David, Hieronymus Bosch and others.

The breed was a favorite of various royal families of Europe including the consort of England's James I, Anne of Denmark; Mary Beatrice d'Este of Modena, the Italian consort of James II; Frederick the Great of Prussia; Catherine the Great of Russia and, more recently, Queen Victoria.

The first volume of the English Kennel Club's stud book listed 40 of the breed. Volume III of the American Kennel Club's Stud Book (1886) contains the first Italian Greyhound registration in this country.

However, it was not until 1950 that as many as 50 were registered in the United States in a single year and 1957 before an equal number was registered in Great Britain.

Following both World Wars, when the breed was in danger of extinction, fresh stock was imported into England from the United States, giving evidence of the high quality to be found in America. The last twenty years have seen the breed enjoying its greatest recorded popularity ever. Italian Greyhounds have competed successfully in all parts of the country in dog shows and obedience trials with a number of Best-in-Show awards to its credit.

The Italian Greyhound is a true Greyhound in miniature. There is some difference of opinion as to whether he was originally bred for hunting small game or was meant to be simply a pet and companion. It seems most likely that he filled both roles, and for this reason he is very adaptable to both city and country living. He is rather luxury loving and enjoys the comforts of an apartment; at the same time being a true hound, he likes exercise and outdoor activities.

The Italian Greyhound can weigh as little as 5 lbs. or as much as 14 or 15 lbs., but the average weight is about 8 lbs. His coat is short and smooth and requires little grooming. He is odorless and sheds little. Though he gives the impression of fragility, the breed is hardy, seldom ill, and thrives in such northern countries as Sweden and Scotland. The bitches are easy whelpers and good mothers.

Perhaps the most outstanding characteristic of the Italian Greyhound is his affectionate disposition. He thrives best when this affection is returned, and is happiest with his owner and immediate family though he may sometimes seem a trifle aloof with strangers. He is sensitive, alert and intelligent and remains playful until long past puppyhood. He adapts to most households and gets along well with children and with other pets.

While very similar in appearance to the Greyhound, the Italian Greyhound is considerably smaller and more slender in all proportions. He differs also from his larger relative in his characteristic and elegant gait, high stepping and free. He may be any color including all shades of fawn, cream, red, blue or sometimes black or with a black facial mask; the coat may be either solid or with various degrees of different colors mixed with white markings except that dogs with the black-and-tan pattern such as found in other breeds and brindle markings are subject to disqualification in the show ring. The coat is fine, smooth and glossy.

Official Standard for the Italian Greyhound

Description—The Italian Greyhound is very similar to the Greyhound, but much smaller and more slender in all proportions and of ideal elegance and grace.

Head—Narrow and long, tapering to nose, with a slight suggestion of stop.

Skull—Rather long, almost flat.

Muzzle—Long and fine.

Nose—Dark. It may be black or brown or in keeping with the color of the dog. A light or partly pigmented nose is a fault.

Teeth—Scissors bite. A badly undershot or overshot mouth is a fault.

Eyes—Dark, bright, intelligent, medium in size. Very light eyes are a fault.

Ears—Small, fine in texture; thrown back and folded except when alerted, then carried folded at right angles to the head. Erect or button ears severely penalized.

Neck—Long, slender and gracefully arched.

Body—Of medium length, short coupled; high at withers, back curved and drooping at hindquarters, the highest point of curve at start of loin, creating a definite tuck-up at flanks.

Shoulders—Long and sloping.

Chest—Deep and narrow.

Forelegs—Long, straight, set well under shoulder; strong pasterns, fine bone.

Hindquarters—Long, well-muscled thigh; hind legs parallel when viewed from behind, hocks well let down, well-bent stifle.

Feet—Harefoot with well-arched toes. Removal of dewclaws optional.

Tail—Slender and tapering to a curved end, long enough to reach the hock; set low, carried low. Ring tail a serious fault, gay tail a fault.

Coat—Skin fine and supple, hair short, glossy like satin and soft to the touch.

Color—Any color and markings are acceptable except that a dog with brindle markings and a dog with the tan markings normally found on black and tan dogs of other breeds must be disqualified.

Action—High stepping and free, front and hind legs to move forward in a straight line.

Size—Height at withers ideally 13 inches to 15 inches.

DISQUALIFICATION

A dog with brindle markings. A dog with the tan markings normally found on black and tan dogs of other breeds.

Approved December 14, 1976

Japanese Chin

THAT THE JAPANESE CHIN is a very old Toy breed is attested to by the fact that dogs closely resembling them have been noted on the old Chinese temples as well as on ancient pottery and embroideries. Presumably these dogs originated in China, centuries ago, since it is reported that one of the Chinese emperors gave a pair to the emperor of Japan. They were kept in the hands of the nobility and frequently used as gifts of esteem to diplomats and to foreigners who had rendered some outstanding service to Japan.

When in 1853 Commodore Perry steamed into the harbor of Wraga and opened the country's trade to the world, he was presented with some of these dogs; then he in turn gave a pair to Queen Victoria. In time, specimens came to America, but there remains no record as to their final destination here. Others gravitated to this country as a result of thieving among Japanese kennels, when ships took the dogs all over the world. Every ship from the Orient carried several to ready buyers. Unfortunately, the dogs were not long-lived; World War I cut off the supply to America to such an extent that we had to use what we had to maintain and improve the breed. Japan, too, suffered losses among her prized Chin when earthquakes played havoc among her breeders. Since then Japanese fanciers have taken up other breeds and the supply of Chin has diminished. However, Japanese Chin are widely distributed, with breeders in England, France, Switzerland, Austria and Germany, where the high quality of the dogs has been maintained.

542

From its introduction until August 9, 1977, the breed was known and registered by the AKC as the Japanese Spaniel. Effective with that date, its name officially became the Japanese Chin.

There are different types of Japanese Chin. Essentially, though, the characteristic specimen must look Oriental; must be aristocratic in appearance, stylish in carriage. The larger dog is apt to lack these features, therefore only the small dog is considered of show type. Some specimens carry profuse coats, others shorter and coarser-textured coats; either is correct, but a woolly coat is not favored.

The majority of dogs are black-and-white, although there are whites with lemon or red markings, including all shades from pale lemon to deep red as well as brindle. In each case the nose color must match the markings, with dark eyes regardless. Colors may be mixed within the litter in cases where the sire or dam is of other than pure black-and-white inheritance. Frequently a lemon-and-white produces only black-and-white offspring, and it may require several generations before the colors revert. Years ago, when a black-and-white dog had too much black on the body, a lemon-and-white mate was used in the hope of breaking the color in the next generation. The lemon-and-whites often had more profuse coats, so these were used to improve hair quantity as well as texture. It seems more difficult to produce a good lemon-and-white than a good black-and-white.

A Japanese Chin is a good companion, bright and alert. Naturally clean and game, too, he makes an ideal pet that can thrive in almost any climate. He is sensitive, though, with definite likes and dislikes, but rarely, if ever, does he forget friend or foe.

Official Standard for the Japanese Chin

General Appearance—That of a lively, high-bred little dog with dainty appearance, smart, compact carriage and profuse coat. These dogs should be essentially stylish in movement, lifting the feet high when in action, carrying the tail (which is heavily feathered, proudly curved or plumed) over the back. In size they vary considerably, but the smaller they are the better, provided type and quality are not sacrificed. When divided by weight, classes should be under and over 7 pounds.

Head—Should be large for the size of the dog, with broad skull, rounded in front.

Eyes—Large, dark, lustrous, rather prominent and set wide apart.

Ears—Small and V-shaped, nicely feathered, set wide apart and high on the head and carried slightly forward.

Nose—Very short in the muzzle part. The end or nose proper should be wide, with open nostrils, and must be the color of the dog's markings, *i.e.* black in black-marked dogs, and red or deep flesh color in red or lemon-marked dogs. It shall be a disqualification for a black and white Japanese Chin to have a nose any other color than black.

Neck—Should be short and moderately thick.

Body—Should be squarely and compactly built, wide in chest, "cobby" in shape. The length of the dog's body should be about its height.

Tail—Must be well twisted to either right or left from root and carried up over back and flow on opposite side; it should be profusely covered with long hair (ring tails not desirable).

Legs—The bones of the legs should be small, giving them a slender appearance, and they should be well feathered.

Feet—Small and shaped somewhat long; the dog stands up on its toes somewhat. If feathered, the tufts should never increase in width of the foot, but only its length a trifle.

Coat—Profuse, long, straight, rather silky. It should be absolutely free from wave or curl, and not lie too flat, but have a tendency to stand out, especially at the neck, so as to give a thick mane or ruff, which with profuse feathering on thighs and tail gives a very showy appearance.

Color—The dogs should be either black and white or red and white, *i.e.* parti-colored. The term red includes all shades of sable, brindle, lemon and orange, but the brighter and clearer the red the better. The white should be clear white, and the color, whether black or red, should be evenly distributed patches over the body, cheek and ears.

SCALE OF POINTS

Head and neck	10	Tail	10
Eyes	10	Feet and legs	5
Ears	5	Coat and markings	15
Muzzle	10	Action	5
Nose	5	Size	10
Body	15	TOTAL	100

DISQUALIFICATION

In black and whites, a nose any other color than black.

Maltese

THE MALTESE is known as "ye ancient dogge of Malta," which for more than twenty-eight centuries has been an aristocrat of the canine world.

Malta has been prominent in history from earliest times. Though settled by the Phoenicians about 1500 B.C., we know that other Mediterranean races lived there as far back as 3500 B.C. Many writers of old have spoken in glowing terms of the fame and opulence of Malta, so justly celebrated for proficiency in the arts and crafts of peace and war as well as for the high state of civilization of its people. Amid these surroundings, among these people, the tiny Maltese lived.

At the time of the Apostle Paul, Publius, the Roman governor of Malta, had a Maltese named Issa of which he was very fond. In this connection the poet Marcus Valerius Martialis (Martial), born in A.D. 38 at Bilbilis in Spain, made this attachment famous in one of his celebrated epigrams:

> Issa is more frolicsome than Catulla's sparrow. Issa is purer than a dove's kiss. Issa is gentler than a maiden. Issa is more precious than Indian gems . . . Lest the last days that she sees light should snatch her from him forever, Publius has had her picture painted.

This last referred to a painting of Issa said to have been so lifelike that it was difficult to tell the picture from the living dog.

Besides Martial, other ancient authors discoursed on the beauty, intelligence, and lovable qualities of Maltese dogs, among them

Callimachus the Elder (384–322 B.C.); Strabo (*c.* B.C.–A.D. 24); Pliny the Elder (23 B.C.–A.D. 79); Saint Clement of Alexandria in the second century; and others equally celebrated.

The Greeks erected tombs to their Maltese, while from the fifth century on Greek ceramic art shows innumerable paintings of these dogs. A fine model of one was dug up in the Fayum, in Egypt—it is not unlikely that this was the kind of dog worshipped by the Egyptians. And it is said that queens of old served the choicest foods out of golden vases to their Maltese.

Dr. Caius (1570), physician to Queen Elizabeth, wrote in Latin:

> There is among us another kind of highbred dogs, but outside the common run those which Callimachus called Melitei from the Island of Melita . . . That kind is very small indeed and chiefly sought after for the pleasure and amusement of women. The smaller the kind, the more pleasing it is; so that they may carry them in their bosoms, in their beds and in their arms while in their carriages.

Aldrovanus, who died in 1607 and who also wrote in Latin, says he saw one of these dogs sold for the equivalent of $2000. Considering the value of the dollar in the time of Queen Elizabeth, the price paid would be equal to a five-figure sum in this day. Since the time of Good Queen Bess the Maltese has often been mentioned, writers invariably drawing attention to its small size. In 1607 E. Topsell said they were "not bigger than common ferrets." Almost 200 years later, in 1792, Linnaeus referred to them as being "about the size of squirrels," while Danberton in his *History Naturelle* writes that "ladies carried them in their sleeves."

The fact that for so many centuries Maltese have been the household pets of people of culture, wealth, and fastidious taste may account for their refinement, fidelity, and cleanliness. It should be remembered that they are spaniels, not terriers, and that, as history has long recorded them, they are healthy and spirited even though tiny.

Official Standard for the Maltese

General Appearance—The Maltese is a toy dog covered from head to foot with a mantle of long, silky, white hair. He is gentle-mannered and affectionate, eager and sprightly in action, and, despite his size, possessed of the vigor needed for the satisfactory companion.

Head—Of medium length and in proportion to the size of the dog. *The skull* is slightly rounded on top, the stop moderate. *The drop ears* are rather low set and heavily feathered with long hair that hangs close to the head. *Eyes* are set not too far apart; they are very dark and round, their black rims enhancing the gentle yet alert expression. *The muzzle* is of medium length, fine and tapered but not snipy. *The nose* is black. *The teeth* meet in an even, edge-to-edge bite, or in a scissors bite.

Neck—Sufficient length of neck is desirable as promoting a high carriage of the head.

Body—Compact, the height from the withers to the ground equaling the length from the withers to the root of the tail. Shoulder blades are sloping, the elbows well knit and held close to the body. The back is level in topline, the ribs well sprung. The chest is fairly deep, the loins taut, strong, and just slightly tucked up underneath.

Tail—A long-haired plume carried gracefully over the back, its tip lying to the side over the quarter.

Legs and Feet—Legs are fine-boned and nicely feathered. Forelegs are straight, their pastern joints well knit and devoid of appreciable bend. Hind legs are strong and moderately angulated at stifles and hocks. The feet are small and round, with toe pads black. Scraggly hairs on the feet may be trimmed to give a neater appearance.

Coat and Color—The coat is single, that is, without undercoat. It hangs long, flat, and silky over the sides of the body almost, if not quite, to the ground. The long head-hair may be tied up in a topknot or it may be left hanging. Any suggestion of kinkiness, curliness, or woolly texture is objectionable. Color, pure white. Light tan or lemon on the ears is permissible, but not desirable.

Size—Weight under 7 pounds, with from 4 to 6 pounds preferred. Over-all quality is to be favored over size.

Gait—The Maltese moves with a jaunty, smooth, flowing gait. Viewed from the side, he gives an impression of rapid movement, size considered. In the stride, the forelegs reach straight and free from the shoulders, with elbows close. Hind legs to move in a straight line. Cowhocks or any suggestion of hind leg toeing in or out are faults.

Temperament—For all his diminutive size, the Maltese seems to be without fear. His trust and affectionate responsiveness are very appealing. He is among the gentlest mannered of all little dogs, yet he is lively and playful as well as vigorous.

Approved March 10, 1964

Official Standard for the
Manchester Terrier (Toy)

The Standard for the Manchester Terrier (Toy Variety) is the same as for the Manchester Terrier except as regards weight and ears.

Miniature Pinscher

THE MINIATURE PINSCHER has existed for several centuries. Germany, of course, is its native land, but it has been bred as well in the Scandinavian countries for a long time. Real development of the breed abroad began in 1895 when Germany's Pinscher Klub was formed. This club, now called the Pinscher-Schnauzer Klub, gave the breed its initial standard.

From the time of the Pinscher Klub's formation, the breed improved both in type and popularity, but more rapid headway was evident from 1905 up until World War I. That war of course handicapped progress in almost everything. Following it, or in about 1919, fanciers abroad once more started to advance the Miniature Pinscher, and as a result of importations to the United States, breeding was undertaken here to a limited extent.

There were few Miniature Pinschers seen at American dog shows prior to 1928, the impetus to breed advancement dating from 1929 when the Miniature Pinscher Club of America, Inc., was formed. Previously the breed had been shown in the Miscellaneous Class. The little dog's popularity has increased steadily. Many entries appear at the shows with imported and American-bred specimens winning the toy group on several occasions.

Although the Miniature Pinscher is similar to a Doberman on a smaller scale, it has a nature and way about it suggestive of a much larger dog. It is especially valuable as a watchdog, sometimes keener even than a dog twice its size. It is a born show dog, too, noted for its lively temperament and intelligence, while it is often used on the stage because of its style, smartness, and pep. The close, slick coat requires scant attention, hence always looks neat and clean. And last but not least, the "Minpin's" fondness for home and master is exceptional.

Official Standard for the Miniature Pinscher

General Appearance—The Miniature Pinscher was originated in Germany and named the "Reh Pinscher" due to his resemblance in structure and animation to a very small specie of deer found in the forests. This breed is structurally a well-balanced, sturdy, compact, short-coupled, smooth-coated toy dog. He is naturally well groomed, proud, vigorous and alert. The natural characteristic traits which identify him from other toy dogs are his precise Hackney gait, his fearless animation, complete self-possession, and his spirited presence.

Faults—Structurally lacking in balance, too long- or short-coupled, too coarse or too refined (lacking in bone development causing poor feet and legs), too large or too small, lethargic, timid or dull, shy or vicious, low in tail placement and poor in action (action not typical of the breed requirements). Knotty over-developed muscles.

Head—In correct proportion with the body. *From Top*—Tapering, narrow with well-fitted but not too prominent foreface which should balance with the skull. No indication of coarseness. *From Front*—Skull appears flat, tapering forward toward the muzzle. Muzzle itself strong rather than fine and delicate, and in proportion to the head as a whole; cheeks and lips small, taut and closely adherent to each other. Teeth in perfect alignment and apposition. *From Side*—Well-balanced with only a slight drop to the muzzle, which should be parallel to the top of the skull. *Eyes*—Full, slightly oval, almost round, clear, bright and dark even to a true black; set wide apart and fitted well into the sockets. *Ears*—Well-set and firmly placed, upstanding (when cropped, pointed and carried erect in balance with the head). *Nose*—Black only (with the exception of chocolates, which may have a self-colored nose).

Faults—Too large or too small for the body, too coarse or too refined, pinched and weak in foreface, domed in skull, too flat and lacking in chiseling, giving a vapid expression. *Jaws and teeth* overshot or undershot. *Eyes* too round and full, too large, bulging, too deep-set or set too far apart; or too small, set too close (pig eyes). Light-colored eyes not desirable. *Ears* poorly placed, low-set hanging ears (lacking in cartilage) which detract from head conformation. (Poorly cropped ears if set on the head properly and having sufficient cartilage should not detract from head points, as this would be a man-made fault and automatically would detract from general appearance.) *Nose* any color other than black (with the exception of chocolates which may have a self-colored nose).

Neck—Proportioned to head and body. Slightly arched, gracefully curved, clean and firm, blending into shoulders, length well-balanced, muscular and free from a suggestion of dewlap or throatiness. **Faults**—Too straight or too curved; too thick or too thin; too long or short; knotty muscles; loose, flabby or wrinkled skin.

Body—*From Top*—Compact, slightly wedge-shaped, muscular with well-sprung ribs. *From Side*—Depth of brisket, the base line of which is level with the points of the elbows; short and strong in loin with belly moderately tucked up to denote grace in structural form. Back level or slightly sloping toward the rear. Length of males equals height at withers. Females may be slightly longer. *From Rear*—High tail-set; strong, sturdy upper shanks, with croup slope at about 30 degrees; vent opening not barreled. *Forequarters*—Forechest well-developed and full, moderately broad, shoulders clean, sloping with moderate angulation, co-ordinated to permit the true action of the Hackney pony. *Hindquarters*—Well-knit muscular quarters set wide enough apart to fit into a properly balanced body.

Faults—*From top*—Too long, too short, too barreled, lacking in body development. *From side*—Too long, too short, too thin or too fat, hips higher or considerably lower than the withers, lacking depth of chest, too full in loin, sway back, roach back or wry back. *From rear*—Quarters too wide or too close to each other, overdeveloped, barreled vent, underdeveloped vent, too sloping croup, tail set low. *Forequarters*—Forechest and spring of rib too narrow (or too shallow and underdeveloped), shoulders too straight, too loose, or too short and overloaded with muscles. *Hindquarters*—Too narrow, undermuscled or overmuscled, too steep in croup.

Legs and Feet—Strong bone development and small clean joints; feet catlike, toes strong, well-arched and closely knit with deep pads and thick blunt nails. *Forelegs and Feet*—As viewed from the front straight and upstanding, elbows close to body, well-knit, flexible yet strong with perpendicular pasterns. *Hind Legs*—All adjacent bones should appear well-angulated with well-muscled thighs or upper shanks, with clearly well-defined stifles, hocks short, set well apart turning neither in nor out, while at rest should stand perpendicular to the ground and upper shanks, lower shanks and hocks parallel to each other.

Faults—Too thick or thin bone development, large joints, spreading flat feet. *Forelegs and Feet*—Bowed or crooked, weak pasterns, feet turning in or out, loose elbows. *Hind legs*—Thin undeveloped stifles, large or crooked hocks, loose stifle joints.

Tail—Set high, held erect, docked to ½ to 1 inch. **Faults**—Set too low, too thin, drooping, hanging or poorly docked.

Coat—Smooth, hard and short, straight and lustrous, closely adhering to and uniformly covering the body. **Faults**—Thin, too long, dull; upstanding; curly; dry; area of various thickness or bald spots.

Color—1. Solid red or stag red. 2. Lustrous black with sharply defined tan, rust-red markings on cheeks, lips, lower jaw, throat, twin spots above eyes and chest, lower half of forelegs, inside of hind legs and vent region, lower portion of hocks and feet. Black pencil stripes on toes. 3. Solid brown or chocolate with rust or yellow markings. **Faults**—Any color other than listed; very dark or sooty spots. **Disqualifications**—Thumb marks or any area of white on feet or forechest exceeding one-half ($^1/_2$) inch in its longest dimension.

Size—Desired height 11 inches to 11$^1/_2$ inches at the withers. A dog of either sex measuring under 10 inches or over 12$^1/_2$ inches shall be disqualified. **Faults**—Oversize; undersize; too fat; too lean.

SCALE OF POINTS

General appearance and movement		Neck	5
—(very important)	30	Body	15
Skull	5	Feet	5
Muzzle	5	Legs	5
Mouth	5	Color	5
Eyes	5	Coat	5
Ears	5	Tail	5
		TOTAL	100

DISQUALIFICATIONS

Color—Thumb marks or any area of white on feet or forechest exceeding one-half ($^1/_2$) inch in its longest dimension.

Size—A dog of either sex measuring under 10 or over 12$^1/_2$ inches.

Approved May 13, 1958

Papillon

(Pah-pee-yown)

THE PAPILLON, known in the sixteenth century as the dwarf spaniel, is the modern development of those little dogs often seen pictured in rare old paintings and tapestries. Rubens, Watteau, Fragonard, and Boucher all depicted them, and their popularity was so great that noble ladies of the day did not consider their portraits complete unless one of these elegant little dogs was pictured with them. Madame de Pompadour was the proud possessor of two, Inez and Mimi by name. Marie Antoinette was another ardent admirer, while as early as 1545 there is record of one having been sold to a lady who later ascended the throne of Poland.

It is Spain that we have to thank for the Papillon's primary rise to fame, though Italy, particularly Bologna, probably developed the largest trade. Many were sold to the court of Louis XIV, who had his choice among those brought into France. Prices ran high, and the chief trader, a Bolognese named Filipponi, developed a large business with the court of France and elsewhere. Most of the dogs were transferred from one country to the other upon the backs of mules.

As time went on, a change developed in the dwarf spaniel which gave rise to the present-day name, Papillon. During the days of Louis the Great, the dwarf spaniel possessed large, drooping ears, but gradually there came into being an erect-eared type, the ears being set obliquely on the head and so fringed as to resemble the wings of a butterfly, from which the present breed derives its name. The causes of this change remain largely theoretical, but whatever they may be, we now have a toy dog whose type of body and coat is about the same as that of the original dwarf spaniel of Spain and Italy, but whose ears may be either erect or drooping. Both types may, and often do, appear in the same litter. In continental Europe, as well as Great Britain, the drop-eared variety is called Epagneul Nain, although the breed as a whole carries the nomenclature of Papillon, as it does in this country. Here both types are judged together and with equality. Another change concerns color. Originally, almost all were of solid color. Today white predominates as a ground color, with patches of other colors, and solid-colored dogs are disqualified.

Papillons are hardy dogs. It is unnecessary to coddle them in winter; and they do not suffer particularly in severe hot weather. They delight in country activities and are equally contented in apartments. As ratters, they are extremely useful. Too small to kill a rat outright, they will worry it until it is exhausted, then dispatch it quickly. As a rule the bitches whelp easily and give little trouble when rearing puppies.

Although they have been exhibited for many years in the United States, it was not until 1935 that Papillons were represented in The American Kennel Club by their own breed club, the Papillon Club of America.

Official Standard for the Papillon

General Appearance—The Papillon is a small, friendly, elegant toy dog of fine-boned structure, light, dainty and of lively action; distinguished from other breeds by its beautiful butterfly-like ears.

Head—Small. The skull of medium width, and slightly rounded between the ears. A well-defined stop is formed where the muzzle joins the skull. The muzzle is fine, abruptly thinner than the head, tapering to the nose. The length of the muzzle from the tip of nose to stop is approximately one third the length of the head from tip of nose to occiput.

Nose—Black, small, rounded and slightly flat on top.

Eyes—Dark, round, not bulging, of medium size and alert in expression. The inner corner of the eyes is on a line with the stop. Eye rims black.

Mouth—Lips are tight, thin and black. Teeth meet in a scissors bite. Tongue must not be visible when jaws are closed. *Fault*—Overshot or undershot.

Ears—The ears of either the erect or drop type should be large with rounded tips and set on the sides and toward the back of head.
  (1) Ears of the erect type are carried obliquely and move like the spread wings of a butterfly. When alert, each ear forms an angle of approximately 45 degrees to the head. The leather should be of sufficient strength to maintain the erect position.
  (2) Ears of the drop type, known as Phalene, are similar to the erect type, but are carried drooping and must be completely down.

Faults—Ears small, pointed, set too high, one ear up or ears partly down.

Neck—Of medium length.

Body—Must be slightly longer than the height at withers. It is not a cobby dog. Topline straight and level. The chest is of medium depth with well-sprung ribs. The belly is tucked up.

Forequarters—Shoulders well developed and laid back to allow freedom of movement. Forelegs slender, fine-boned and must be straight. Removal of dewclaws on forelegs optional.

Hindquarters—Well developed and well angulated. Hocks inclined neither in nor out. The hind legs are slender, fine-boned, and parallel when viewed from behind. Dewclaws, if any, must be removed from hind legs.

Feet—Thin and elongated (harelike), pointing neither in nor out.

Tail—Long, set high and carried well arched over the body. The plume may hang to either side of the body. *Fault*—Low-set tail, one not arched over back or too short.

Coat—Abundant, long, fine, silky, flowing, straight with resilient quality, flat on back and sides of body. A profuse frill on chest. There is no undercoat. Hair short and close on skull, muzzle, front of forelegs and from hind feet to hocks. Ears well fringed with the inside covered with silken hair of medium length. Backs of the forelegs are covered with feathers diminishing to the pasterns. Hind legs are covered to the hocks with abundant breeches (culottes). Tail is covered with a long flowing plume. Hair on feet is short but fine tufts may appear over toes and grow beyond them forming a point.

Size—Height at highest point of shoulder blades, 8 to 11 inches. Weight is in proportion to height. *Fault*—Over 11 inches. Over 12 inches disqualifies.

Gait—Free, quick, easy, graceful, not paddle-footed, or stiff in hip movements.

Color—Always parti-color, white with patches of any color. On the head color other than white must cover both ears, back and front, and extend without interruption from the ears over both eyes. A clearly defined white blaze and noseband are preferred to a solidly marked head. Symmetry of facial markings is desirable. The size, shape, placement or absence of patches on the body are without importance. Papillons may be any parti-color, provided nose, eye rims and lips are well-pigmented black. Among the colors there is no preference.

The following faults shall be severely penalized:
(1) Nose not black.
(2) Color other than white not covering both ears, back and front, or not extending from the ears over both eyes. A slight extension of the white collar onto the base of the ears or a few white hairs interspersed among the color, shall not be penalized provided the butterfly appearance is not sacrificed.

Disqualification—An all white dog or a dog with no white.

DISQUALIFICATIONS

Height—Over 12 inches.
An all white dog or a dog with no white.

Approved February 8, 1975

Pekingese

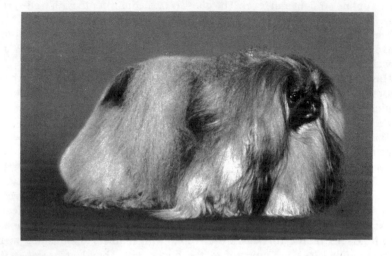

FASCINATING by reason of its Oriental background and distinctive personality, the Pekingese holds honored place in the dog world. In ancient times it was held sacred in China, the land of its origin, and intricately carved Foo Dog idols of varying sizes, ranging in materials from ivory to bronze and jewel-studded wood, have been handed down.

The exact date of origin is debatable, the earliest known record of its existence being traceable to the Tang Dynasty of the eighth century. However, the very oldest strains (held only by the imperial family) were kept pure, and the theft of one of the sacred dogs was punishable by death.

The characteristics we seek to retain and perfect today were in evidence in the earliest Pekingese as shown by three of the names by which they were designated in ancient China. Some were called Lion Dogs, evidently because of their massive fronts, heavy manes and tapering hindquarters. We find a second group termed Sun Dogs because of their strikingly beautiful golden red coats. Since those early days many other darker red shades have become identified with certain strains, but even today we see numerous Sun Dogs at our shows. A third name was Sleeve Dog, this being given only to those diminutive specimens which were carried about in the voluminous sleeves of the members of the imperial household.

Introduction of Pekingese into the western world occurred as a result of the looting of the Imperial Palace at Peking by the British in 1860. It is a matter of history that four were found behind some draperies in the apartments of the aunt of the Chinese emperor. Apparently they were her particular pets—she committed suicide on the approach of the British troops. It is said that throughout the palace the bodies of many of these dogs were found, the Chinese having killed them rather than have them fall into the hands of the Caucasians. The four Pekingese found by the English were of different colors; a fawn and white part-color was the one presented to Queen Victoria on the return to Great Britain. Lord Hay and the Duke of Richmond kept the remainder and bred them.

Pekingese were not exhibited in England until 1893, when Mrs. Loftus Allen exhibited one at Chester. However, the undeniable beauty and interesting history of the breed placed it in the foreground where it has since remained. The three dogs which were outstanding in the breed's earliest development in the Occident were Ah Cum and Mimosa, termed the "pillars of the stud book" in England, followed by a large black-and-tan specimen named Boxer, so-called because he was obtained by Major Gwynne during the Boxer uprising in 1900. Curiously enough, Boxer had a docked tail and so was never exhibited. He undoubtedly did more for the breed in the early part of the century than any other Pekingese.

That the Oriental dog took quick hold of the American fancy is evidenced by the age of the Pekingese Club of America, which became a member of The American Kennel Club in 1909. So much for the introduction of the Pekingese to the Occident.

The transplanting of the Pekingese into Western soil has in no way changed his personality. He combines marked dignity with an exasperating stubbornness which serves only to endear him the more to his owners. He is independent and regal in every gesture; it would be a great indignity to attempt to make a lap dog out of him. Calm and good-tempered, the Pekingese employs a condescending cordiality toward the world in general, but in the privacy of his family enjoys nothing better than a good romp. Although never aggressive, he fears not the devil himself and has never been known to turn tail and run. He has plenty of stamina, much more in fact than have a number of the larger breeds, and he is very easy to care for.

Since he has been brought down from his pedestal in Chinese temples, the Pekingese has but one purpose in life, to give understanding companionship and loyalty to his owners. It may be truly said that the Pekingese fulfills his mission to perfection.

Official Standard for the
Pekingese

Expression—Must suggest the Chinese origin of the Pekingese in its quaintness and individuality, resemblance to the lion in directions and independence and should imply courage, boldness, self-esteem and combativeness rather than prettiness, daintiness or delicacy.

Skull—Massive, broad, wide and flat between the ears (not dome-shaped), wide between the eyes. *Nose*—Black, broad, very short and flat. *Eyes*—Large, dark, prominent, round, lustrous. *Stop*—Deep. *Ears*—Heart-shaped, not set too high, leather never long enough to come below the muzzle, nor carried erect, but rather drooping, long feather. *Muzzle*—Wrinkled, very short and broad, not overshot nor pointed. Strong, broad underjaw, teeth not to show.

Shape of Body—Heavy in front, well-sprung ribs, broad chest, falling away lighter behind, lionlike. Back level. Not too long in body; allowance made for longer body in bitch. *Legs*—Short forelegs, bones of forearm bowed, firm at shoulder; hind legs lighter but firm and well shaped. *Feet*—Flat, toes turned out, not round, should stand well up on feet, not on ankles.

Action—Fearless, free and strong, with slight roll.

Coat, Feather and Condition—Long, with thick undercoat, straight and flat, not curly nor wavy, rather coarse, but soft; feather on thighs, legs, tail and toes long and profuse. *Mane*—Profuse, extending beyond the shoulder blades, forming ruff or frill round the neck.

Color—All colors are allowable. Red, fawn, black, black and tan, sable, brindle, white and parti-color well defined: black masks and spectacles around the eyes, with lines to ears are desirable. *Definition of a Parti-Color Pekingese*—The coloring of a parti-colored dog must be broken on the body. No large portion of any one color should exist. White should be shown on the saddle. A dog of any solid color with white feet and chest is not a parti-color.

Tail—Set high; lying well over back to either side; long, profuse, straight feather.

Size—Being a toy dog, medium size preferred, providing type and points are not sacrified; extreme limit 14 pounds.

SCALE OF POINTS

Expression	5	Shape of body	15
Skull	10	Legs and feet	15
Nose	5	Coat, feather and condition	
Eyes	5		15
Stop	5	Tail	5
Ears	5	Action	10
Muzzle	5	TOTAL	100

FAULTS

Protruding tongue, badly blemished eye, overshot, wry mouth.

DISQUALIFICATIONS

Weight—over 14 pounds.
Dudley nose.

　　　　　　　　　　　　　　　　　Approved April 10, 1956

Pomeranian

A MEMBER of the family of dogs known unofficially as "the spitz group," the Pomeranian has descended from the sled dogs of Iceland and Lapland, if we are to consider type as indicative of heritage. The name, of course, traces to Pomerania, not, however, as a point of origin, but possibly because the breed may have been in process of being bred down to size there. At any rate, in its larger form the dog served as an able herder of sheep. In fact, when it first came into notice in Britain about the middle of the preceding century, some specimens are said to have weighed as much as thirty pounds and to have resembled the German wolf spitz in size, coat, and color.

The Pomeranian was not well known until 1870, when the Kennel Club (England) recognized the so-called spitzdog. Probably the nearest to original type and size of the Poms exhibited in England was the somewhat large sable dog Ruffle, shown by Mrs. Barrett and later brought to this country by Mrs. Smythe. Specimens of the breed were shown in the United States in the Miscellaneous Class as far back as 1892, but regular classification was not provided until 1900 at New York. In 1911 the American Pomeranian Club held its first specialty show.

The majority of early American winners were heavier in bone, larger in ear, and they usually weighed under six pounds. Geneally speaking, they had type and good coat texture, although they lacked the profuseness of coat in evidence today. American-breds show marked improvement over those early winners, as the patient efforts of fanciers have brought them closer to the Standard. Indeed, American-breds have held their own with the best from anywhere; for instance Ch. Pall Mall His Majesty went to Europe and on several occasions defeated all toys for the coveted Best in Show. Over here as well, home-bred Pomeranians have contended successfully for highest honors at all-breed fixtures.

Diminutive size, docile temper, and a vivacious spirit plus sturdiness have made Pomeranians great pets and companions.

Official Standard for the Pomeranian

Appearance—The Pomeranian in build and appearance is a cobby, balanced, short-coupled dog. He exhibits great intelligence in his expression, and is alert in character and deportment.

Head—Well-proportioned to the body, wedge-shaped but not domed in outline, with a foxlike expression. There is a pronounced stop with a rather fine by not snipy muzzle, with no lippiness. The pigmentation around the eyes, lips, and on the nose must be black, except self-colored in brown and blue.

Teeth—The teeth meet in a scissors bite, in which part of the inner surface of the upper teeth meets and engages part of the outer surface of the lower teeth. One tooth out of line does not mean an undershot or overshot mouth.

Eyes—Bright, dark in color, and medium in size, almond-shaped and not set too wide apart nor too close together.

Ears—Small, carried erect and mounted high on the head, and placed not too far apart.

Neck and Shoulders—The neck is rather short, its base set well back on the shoulders. The Pom is not straight-in-shoulder, but has sufficient layback of shoulders to carry the neck proudly and high.

Body—The back must be short and the topline level. The body is cobby, being well ribbed and rounded. The brisket is fairly deep and not too wide.

Legs—The forelegs are straight and parallel, of medium length in proportion to a well balanced frame. The hocks are perpendicular to the ground, parallel to each other from hock to heel, and turning neither in nor out. The Pomeranian stands well-up on toes.

Tail—The tail is characteristic of the breed. It turns over the back and is carried flat, set high. It is profusely covered with hair.

Coat—Double-coated; a short, soft, thick undercoat, with longer, coarse, glistening outer coat consisting of guard hairs which must be harsh to the touch in order to give the proper texture for the coat to form a frill of profuse, standing-off straight hair. The front legs are well feathered and the hindquarters are clad with long hair or feathering from the top of the rump to the hocks.

Color—Acceptable colors to be judged on an equal basis; any solid color, any solid color with lighter or darker shadings of the same color, any solid color with sable or black shadings, parti-color, sable and black & tan. Black &

tan is black with tan or rust, sharply defined, appearing above each eye and on muzzle, throat, and forechest, on all legs and feet and below the tail. Particolor is white with any other color distributed in even patches on the body and a white blaze on head.

Movement—The Pomeranian moves with a smooth, free, but not loose action. He does not elbow out in front nor move excessively wide nor cowhocked behind. He is sound in action.

Size—The weight of a Pomeranian for exhibition is 3 to 7 pounds. The ideal size for show specimens is from 4 to 5 pounds.

Trimming and Dewclaws—Trimming for neatness is permissible around the feet and up the back of the legs to the first joint; trimming of unruly hairs on the edges of the ears and around the anus is also permitted. Dewclaws, if any, on the hind legs are generally removed. Dewclaws on the forelegs may be removed.

Classifications—The Open Classes at Specialty shows may be divided by color as follows: Open Red, Orange, Cream & Sable; Open Black, Brown & Blue; Open Any Other Allowed Color.

Approved March 9, 1971

Official Standard for the
Poodle (Toy)

The Standard for the Poodle (Toy variety) is the same as for the Standard and the Miniature varieties except as regards height.

Pug

THE PUG, one of the oldest breeds, has flourished true to his breed down through the ages from before 400 B.C. He has always been domesticated and has endeared himself to mankind.

The truth of how the Pug came into existence is shrouded in mystery, but authorities are agreed that he is of oriental origin with some basic similarities to the Pekingese. China, where the breed was the pet of the Buddhist monasteries in Tibet, is its earliest known source. It next appeared in Japan, and then in Europe, where it became the favorite for various royal courts.

In Holland the Pug became the official dog of the House of Orange after one of the breed saved the life of William, Prince of Orange, by giving alarm at the approach of the Spaniards at Hermingny in 1572. An effigy of the monarch with his Pug at his feet is carved over William's tomb in Delft Cathedral. Later, when William II landed at Torbay to be crowned King of England, his retinue included his beloved Pugs and they became the fashionable breed for generations.

By 1790 the Pug's popularity had spread to France where Josephine, wife of Napoleon, depended on her Pug "Fortune" to carry secret messages under his collar to her husband while she was imprisoned at Les Carmes. "Fortune" must have had a possessive nature, for it is said that he bit the future Emperor when he entered the bedchamber on his wedding night.

Called the "Mopshond" (from the Dutch word "to grumble") in Holland, "Mops" in Germany and "Carlin" in France, the origin of the name "Pug Dog" has a variety of explanations. The most likely is that which likens the dog's facial expression to that of the marmoset monkeys that were popular pets of the early 1700s and were known as Pugs; hence "Pug Dog" to distinguish dog from monkey. The appellation of "Pug Dog" has endured to this day.

Credit for the acclaim with which the Pug was received in England must go to two well-known fanciers. Lady Willoughby de Eresby of Greenthorpe, near Lincoln, was one of the breed's sponsors; the dogs of her kennel were distinguished by their silver-fawn coloring. Mr. Morrison of Walham Green was also a sponsor; the dogs of his kennel were a brighter golden color. There was nothing to distinguish the two strains other than color and as they were interbred, a claim that a dog of the breed is now pure in either strain would be spurious.

The now popular black Pug made its advent in England years later, seemingly introduced by Lady Brassey, a well-known traveler who returned from a round-the-world cruise in 1877 with a number of black Pugs. However, the existence of black and dark Pugs, liberally marked with white, had been noted in writing and pictures prior to this time.

This lovable and staunch little dog is well described by the motto *Multum in Parvo*— "a lot of dog in a small space." His appearance is always that of being well-groomed and ready for the show ring. He is small but requires no coddling and his roguish face soon wiggles its way into the hearts of men, women and especially children—for whom this dog seems to have a special affinity. His great reason for living is to be near his "folks" and to please them. The Pug is at home in a small apartment or country home alike, easily adaptable to all situations.

Official Standard for the
Pug

Symmetry—Symmetry and general appearance, decidedly square and cobby. A lean, leggy Pug and a dog with short legs and a long body are equally objectionable.

Size and Condition—The Pug should be *multum in parvo*, but this condensation (if the word may be used) should be shown by compactness of form, well-knit proportions, and hardness of developed muscle. Weight from 14 to 18 pounds (dog or bitch) desirable.

Body—Short and cobby, wide in chest and well ribbed up.

Legs—Very strong, straight, of moderate length and well under.

Feet—Neither so long as the foot of the hare, nor so round as that of the cat; well-split-up toes, and the nails black.

Muzzle—Short, blunt, square, but not up-faced.

Head—Large, massive, round—not apple-headed, with no indentation of the skull.

Eyes—Dark in color, very large, bold and prominent, globular in shape, soft and solicitous in expression, very lustrous, and, when excited, full of fire.

Ears—Thin, small, soft, like black velvet. There are two kinds—the "rose" and "button." Preference is given to the latter.

Markings—Clearly defined. The muzzle or mask, ears, moles on cheeks, thumb mark or diamond on forehead, back-trace should be as black as possible.

Mask—The mask should be black. The more intense and well defined it is the better.

Trace—A black line extending from the occiput to the tail.

Wrinkles—Large and deep.

Tail—Curled tightly as possible over the hip. The double curl is perfection.

Coat—Fine, smooth, soft, short and glossy, neither hard nor woolly.

Color—Silver or apricot-fawn. Each should be decided, to make the contrast complete between the color and the trace and the mask. Black.

SCALE OF POINTS

	Fawn	Black		Fawn	Black
Symmetry	10	10	Eyes	10	10
Size	5	10	Mask	5	...
Condition	5	5	Wrinkles	5	5
Body	10	10	Tail	10	10
Legs and feet	5	5	Trace	5	...
Head	5	5	Coat	5	5
Muzzle	10	10	Color	5	10
Ears	5	5	TOTAL	100	100

Shih Tzu
(Sheed-zoo)

THE LEGEND of the Shih Tzu has come to us from documents, paintings, and objets d'art dating from A.D. 624. During the Tang Dynasty, K'iu T'ai, King of Viqur, gave the Chinese court a pair of dogs, said to have come from the Fu Lin (assumed to be the Byzantine Empire). Mention of these dogs was again made in A.D. 990-994 when people of the Ho Chou sent dogs as tribute.

Another theory of their introduction to China was recorded in the mid-seventeenth century when dogs were brought from Tibet to the Chinese court. These dogs were bred in the Forbidden City of Peking. Many pictures of them were kept in *The Imperial Dog Book*. The smallest of these dogs resembled a lion, as represented in Oriental art. In Buddhist belief there is an association between the lion and their Deity. Shih Tzu means Lion. The dogs for court breeding were selected with great care. From these the Shih Tzu known today developed. They were often called *"the chrysanthemum-faced dog"* because the hair grows about the face in all directions.

These dogs were small, intelligent, and extremely docile. It is known that the breeding of the Shih Tzu was delegated to certain court eunuchs who vied with each other to produce specimens which would take the Emperor's fancy. Those which were selected had their pictures painted on hangings or tapestries, and the eunuchs, responsible for the dogs, were given gifts by the Emperor.

It is known that the Shih Tzu was a house pet during most of the Ming Dynasty and that they were highly favored by the royal family. At the time of the Revolution a large number of dogs were destroyed and only a few escaped the invader's knives.

Around 1930, Lady Brownrigg, an English woman living in China, was fortunate to find a few of these dogs, which she imported to England. These, with a few salvaged by an English officer on duty in China, made up the stock which was responsible for the continuation of the breed in Europe.

From England, dogs of this breed were sent to the Scandinavian countries, to other countries in Europe, and to Australia. During World War II, members of the Armed Forces stationed in England became acquainted with the breed and on their return brought some back to the United States, thus introducing them to this country. Since then many have been imported.

The Shih Tzu was admitted to registration in The American Kennel Club Stud Book in March 1969, and to regular show classification in the Toy Group at AKC shows September 1, 1969.

Official Standard for the
Shih Tzu

General Appearance—Very active, lively and alert, with a distinctly arrogant carriage. The Shih Tzu is proud of bearing as befits his noble ancestry, and walks with head well up and tail carried gaily over the back.

Head—Broad and round, wide between the eyes. Muzzle square and short, but not wrinkled, about one inch from tip of nose to stop. *Definite Stop. Eyes*—Large, dark and round but not prominent, placed well apart. Eyes should show warm expression. *Ears*—Large, with long leathers, and carried drooping; set slightly below the crown of the skull; so heavily coated that they appear to blend with the hair of the neck. *Teeth*—Level or slightly undershot bite.

Forequarters—Legs short, straight, well boned, muscular, and heavily coated. Legs and feet look massive on account of the wealth of hair.

Body—Body between the withers and the root of the tail is somewhat longer than the height at the withers; well coupled and sturdy. Chest broad and deep, shoulders firm, back level.

Hindquarters—Legs short, well boned and muscular, are straight when viewed from the rear. Thighs well rounded and muscular. Legs look massive on account of wealth of hair.

Feet—Of good size, firm, well padded, with hair between the pads. Dewclaws, if any, on the hind legs are generally removed. Dewclaws on the forelegs may be removed.

Tail—Heavily plumed and curved well over the back; carried gaily, set on high.

Coat—A luxurious, long, dense coat. May be slightly wavy but *not* curly. Good woolly undercoat. The hair on top of the head may be tied up.

Color—All colors permissible. Nose and eye rims black, except that dogs with liver markings may have liver noses and slightly lighter eyes.

Gait—Slightly rolling, smooth and flowing, with strong rear action.

Size—Height at withers—9 to 10½ inches—should be no more than 11 inches nor less than 8 inches. Weight of mature dogs—12 to 15 pounds—should be no more than 18 pounds nor less than 9 pounds. However, type and breed characteristics are of the greatest importance.

FAULTS

Narrow head; overshot bite; snipiness; pink on nose or eye rims; small or light eyes; legginess; sparse coat; lack of definite stop.

Approved May 13, 1969

Silky Terrier

THE SILKY TERRIER is a native of Australia, where it has long found favor with the flat or cottage dwellers. Unlike other Australian breeds, it has been a dog not solely of the bush country but, for the most part, a companion in suburban homes. For years it was called the Sydney Silky in honor of its city of origin, but in 1955 it became known abroad as the Australian Silky Terrier. Since the late 1920s, it has been regarded in its homeland as a distinct breed, with stud-book records maintained by both the Royal Agricultural Society Kennel Club and the Kennel Control Council.

It was first exhibited in Australia in 1907, the period which climaxed years of development. A Standard was drawn up in 1909, after which it went into India and to somewhat smaller extent into Britain. It was admitted to registry in this country as the Silky Terrier in 1959.

The Silky Terrier derives mainly from the Australian Terrier crossed with the Yorkshire. Whether those early breeders of the preceding century planned deliberately to produce a dog different from the then existing Australian Terrier, or whether the Silky was a by-product, a sport perhaps, we do not know. Thus we can but surmise on something less than purely factual basis.

At any rate, by crossbreeding and subsequent development the Australians evolved an appealing toy dog of eight to ten pounds, with a silky-textured coat of blue and tan. Lightly built and rather low-set, the dog is pronounced in terrier character and spirit. The head especially shows strong terrier influence, with its flat skull, scissors bite, and small, dark eyes.

The erect ear, devoid of sidewise flare, is one of the later-fixed characteristics effected by Australian breeders, since up until the 1940s both prick and pendant ears were sanctioned. The double ear carriage may have been a holdover from an old Skye Terrier heritage acknowledged to be part and parcel of Australia's terrier family. Likewise the all-soft coat of the Silky Terrier may be accounted for by an influence due not wholly to the Yorkshire cross, for deep within the Skye lay dormant a factor for silkiness. Ash, it will be recalled, mentions "bonnie wee Skyes with long, silky hair." These things, among others, attest to the skill with which early breeders produced and by patient selection developed the Silky Terrier.

The Silky is friendly, and forceful as only a terrier can be. He is agile and light-footed, and he looks out on the world with a curious air which would seem to denote a degree of intelligence seldom encountered in a dog so small. A toy, designed no doubt as a pet, still he has done his share of worthwhile work, for it is told that he has helped to control rodents on many an Australian poultry farm.

Official Standard for the Silky Terrier

The Silky Terrier is a lightly built, moderately low-set toy dog of pronounced terrier character and spirited action.

Head—The head is strong, wedge-shaped, and moderately long. The skull is a trifle longer than the muzzle, in proportion about three-fifths for the skull, two-fifths for the muzzle. *Skull*—Flat, and not too wide between the ears. *Stop* —Shallow. *Ears*—Small, V-shaped and pricked. They are set high and carried erect without any tendency to flare obliquely off the skull.

Eyes—Small, dark in color, and piercingly keen in expression. Light eyes are a fault. *Teeth*—Strong and well aligned, scissors bite. A bite markedly undershot or overshot is a serious fault. *Nose*—The nose is black.

Neck and Shoulders—The neck fits gracefully into sloping shoulders. It is medium long, fine and to some degree crested along its topline.

Body—Low-set, about one fifth longer than the dog's height at the withers. A too short body is a fault. The back line is straight, with a just perceptible rounding over the loins. Brisket medium wide, and deep enough to extend down to the elbows.

Tail—The tail is set high and carried erect or semi-erect but not over-gay. It is docked and well coated but devoid of plume.

Forequarters—Well laid back shoulders, together with good angulation at the upper arm, set the forelegs nicely under the body. Forelegs are strong, straight and rather fine-boned.

Hindquarters—Thighs well muscled and strong, but not so developed as to appear heavy. Legs moderately angulated at stifles and hocks, with the hocks low and equidistant from the hock joints to the ground.

Feet—Small, cat-like, round, compact. Pads are thick and springy while the nails are strong and dark colored. White or flesh-colored nails are a fault. The feet point straight ahead, with no turning in or out. Dewclaws, if any, are removed.

Coat—Flat, in texture fine, glossy, silky; on matured specimens the desired length of coat from behind the ears to the set-on of the tail is from five to six inches. On the top of the head the hair is so profuse as to form a topknot, but long hair on face and ears is objectionable. Legs from knee and hock joints to feet should be free from long hair. The hair is parted on the head and down over the back to the root of the tail.

Color—Blue and tan. The blue may be silver blue, pigeon blue or slate blue, the tan deep and rich. The blue extends from the base of the skull to the tip of the tail, down the forelegs to the pasterns, and down the thighs to the hocks. On the tail the blue should be very dark. Tan appears on muzzle and cheeks, around the base of the ears, below the pasterns and hocks, and around the vent. There is a tan spot over each eye. The topknot should be silver or fawn.

Temperament—The keenly alert air of the terrier is characteristic, with shyness or excessive nervousness to be faulted. The manner is quick, friendly, responsive.

Movement—Should be free, light-footed, lively, and straightforward. Hindquarters should have strong propelling power. Toeing in or out is to be faulted.

Size—Weight ranges from eight to ten pounds. Shoulder height from nine to ten inches. Pronounced diminutiveness (such as a height of less than 8 inches) is not desired; it accentuates the quality of toyishness as opposed to the breed's definite terrier character.

Approved April 14, 1959

Yorkshire Terrier

THE YORKSHIRE TERRIER became a fashionable pet in the late Victorian era and even before. But in its beginnings it belonged to the working class, especially the weavers. In fact, it was so closely linked to them that many facetious comments were made regarding the fine texture of its extremely long, silky coat, terming it in the ultimate product of the looms.

The Yorkshire Terrier made its first appearance at a bench show in England in 1861 as a "broken-haired Scotch Terrier." It became known as a Yorkshire Terrier in 1870 when, after the Westmoreland show, Angus Sutherland—the reporter for *The Field*—stated, "They ought no longer to be called Scotch Terriers, but Yorkshire Terriers for having been so improved there." For a number of years thereafter classes were offered for the breed as Yorkshire Terriers, as well as Broken-haired Scotch Terriers. Often members of the same litter were shown in classes of both designations.

The Yorkshire Terrier traces to the Waterside Terrier, a small longish-coated dog, bluish-gray in color, weighing between 6 and 20 pounds (most commonly 10 pounds). A breed common in Yorkshire since early times, the Waterside Terrier—crossed with the old rough-coated Black and Tan English Terrier (common in the Manchester area) and with the Paisley and Clydesdale Terriers—was brought to Yorkshire by the Scotch weavers who migrated from Scotland to

England in the middle of the nineteenth century. All these breeds were bred together to make what is now known as the Yorkshire Terrier.

The earliest record of a Yorkshire Terrier born in the United States dates to 1872. Classes for the breed have been offered at all shows since 1878. At early shows, these classes were divided by weight— under 5 lbs., and 5 lbs. and over. However, the size soon settled down to an average of between 3 and 7 lbs. Only one class was offered when it became apparent from records that the class for larger dogs was rarely filled as well as the one for smaller dogs.

Modern specimens of the Yorkshire Terrier breed true to type and their characteristics are well fixed. Coloring is distinctive, with their metallic colors being a dark steel-blue from the occiput to the root of the tail, and a rich golden tan on head, legs, chest and breeches. Puppies that will develop to correct adult colors are always born black with tan markings.

While a Toy, and at various times a greatly pampered one, the Yorkshire is a spirited dog that definitely shows its terrier strain. Although the length of the show dog's coat makes constant care necessary to protect it from damage, the breed is glad to engage in all the roistering activities of the larger terrier breeds.

Official Standard for the Yorkshire Terrier

General Appearance—That of a long-haired toy terrier whose blue and tan coat is parted on the face and from the base of the skull to the end of the tail and hangs evenly and quite straight down each side of body. The body is neat, compact and well proportioned. The dog's high head carriage and confident manner should give the appearance of vigor and self-importance.

Head—Small and rather flat on top, *the skull* not too prominent or round, *the muzzle* not too long, with *the bite* neither undershot nor overshot and teeth sound. Either scissors bite or level bite is acceptable. *The nose* is black. *Eyes* are medium in size and not too prominent; dark in color and sparkling with a sharp, intelligent expression. Eye rims are dark. *Ears* are small, V-shaped, carried erect and set not too far apart.

Body—Well proportioned and very compact. The back is rather short, the back line level, with height at shoulder the same as at the rump.

Legs and Feet—*Forelegs* should be straight, elbows neither in nor out. *Hind legs* straight when viewed from behind, but stifles are moderately bent when viewed from the sides. *Feet* are round with black toenails. Dewclaws, if any, are generally removed from the hind legs. Dewclaws on the forelegs may be removed.

Tail—Docked to a medium length and carried slightly higher than the level of the back.

Coat—Quality, texture and quantity of coat are of prime importance. Hair is glossy, fine and silky in texture. Coat on the body is moderately long and perfectly straight (not wavy). It may be trimmed to floor length to give ease of movement and a neater appearance, if desired. The fall on the head is long, tied with one bow in center of head or parted in the middle and tied with two bows. Hair on muzzle is very long. Hair should be trimmed short on tips of ears and may be trimmed on feet to give them a neat appearance.

Colors—Puppies are born black and tan and are normally darker in body color, showing an intermingling of black hair in the tan until they are matured. Color of hair on body and richness of tan on head and legs are of prime importance in *adult dogs*, to which the following color requirements apply:

BLUE: Is a dark steel-blue, not a silver-blue and not mingled with fawn, bronzy or black hairs.

TAN: All tan hair is darker at the roots than in the middle, shading to still lighter tan at the tips. There should be no sooty or black hair intermingled with any of the tan.

Color on Body—The blue extends over the body from back of neck to root of tail. Hair on tail is a darker blue, especially at end of tail.

Headfall—A rich golden tan, deeper in color at sides of head, at ear roots and on the muzzle, with ears a deep rich tan. Tan color should not extend down on back of neck.

Chest and Legs—A bright, rich tan, not extending above the elbow on the forelegs nor above the stifle on the hind legs.

Weight—Must not exceed seven pounds.

Approved April 12, 1966

GROUP VI: NON-SPORTING DOGS

Bichon Frise
(Bee-shahn Free-zay)

THE BICHON, like his cousin the Caniche, descended from the Barbet or Water-Spaniel, from which came the name "Barbichon", later contracted to "Bichon." The Bichons were divided into four categories: the Bichon Maltais, the Bichon Bolognais, the Bichon Havanais and the Bichon Teneriffe. All originated in the Mediterranean area.

Appreciated for their dispositions, the dogs traveled much through antiquity. Frequently offered as items of barter, they were transported by sailors from continent to continent. The dogs found early success in Spain and it is generally felt that Spanish seamen introduced the breed to the Canary Island of Teneriffe. Most sources agree that in this period the name "Teneriffe" was retained mainly because of its slightly exotic nature and the enhanced commercial value the name gave the common Bichon.

In the 1300s, Italian sailors rediscovered the little dogs on their voyages and are credited with returning them to the Continent, where they became great favorites with Italian nobility, and as with other dogs of that era, were often cut "lion style."

The "Teneriffe" or "Bichon" made its appearance in France under Francis I, the patron of the Renaissance (1515-1547). However, its greatest success was in the court of Henry III (1574-1589), where it was pampered, perfumed, and beribboned. The breed also enjoyed considerable success in Spain as a favorite of the Infantas, and painters of the Spanish school often included them in their works. One finds such a dog in several of the paintings of Goya.

After a brief renewal of interest under Napoleon III, the fate of this aristocratic dog took a new turn. In the late 1800s, it became the "common dog", running the streets, accompanying the organ grinders of Barbary, leading the blind and doing tricks in circuses and fairs.

At the end of World War I, a few fanciers recognized the potential of the dogs and in France four breeders began establishing their lines through controlled breeding programs. On March 5, 1933, the official Standard of the Breed (as written by the then President of the Toy Club of France, in conjunction with the Friends of the Belgian Breeds) was adopted by the Societe Centrale Canine of France. As the breed was known by two names, "Teneriffe" and "Bichon," the president of the International Canine Federation, Madame Nizet de Leemans, proposed a name based on the characteristics that the dogs presented and the name "Bichon Frise" (plural: Bichons Frises) was adopted. On October 18, 1934, the Bichon was admitted to the stud book of the French Kennel Club. The International Canine Federation recognizes the Bichon Frise as "a French-Belgian breed having the right to registration in the Book of Origins from all countries." The breed is recognized in France, Belgium and Italy.

In 1956, Mr. and Mrs. Francois Picault immigrated to the United States and settled in the Midwest where Etoile de Steren Vor whelped the first Bichon litter born in the United States (sired by Eddie White de Steren Vor.) In 1959 and 1960, two breeders in different parts of the United States acquired Bichons, thus providing the origins for breed development in this country.

Accepted for entry in the Miscellaneous Class, September 1, 1971, the Bichon Frise was admitted to registration in the American Kennel Club Stud Book in October, 1972, and to regular show classification in the Non-Sporting Group at AKC shows April 4, 1973.

Official Standard for the
Bichon Frise

General Appearance—A sturdy, lively dog of stable temperament, with a stylish gait and an air of dignity and intelligence.

Color—Solid white, or white with cream, apricot, or gray on the ears and/or body.

Head—Proportionate to the size of the dog. Skull broad and somewhat round, but not coarse; covered with a topknot of hair.

Muzzle—Of medium length, not heavy or snipy. Slightly accentuated stop.

Ears—Dropped, covered with long flowing hair. The leather should reach approximately halfway the length of the muzzle.

Eyes—Black or dark brown, with black rims. Large, round, expressive, and alert.

Lips—Black, fine, never drooping.

Nose—Black, round, pronounced.

Bite—Scissors.

Neck—Rather long, and gracefully and proudly carried behind an erect head.

Shoulders—Well laid back. Elbows held close to the body.

Body—Slightly longer than tall. Well developed with good spring of ribs. The back inclines gradually from the withers to a slight rise over the loin. The loin is large and muscular. The brisket, well let down.

Tail—Covered with long flowing hair, carried gaily and curved to lie on the back.

Size—The height at the withers should not exceed 12 inches nor be under 8 inches.

Legs and Feet—Strong boned; forelegs appearing straight, with well-knit pasterns. Hindquarters well angulated. Feet, resembling cat's paws, are tight and round.

Coat—Profuse, silky and loosely curled. There is an undercoat.

Grooming—Scissored to show the eyes and give a full rounded appearance to the head and body. Feet should have hair trimmed to give a rounded appearance. When properly brushed, there is an overall "powder puff" appearance. Puppies may be shown in short coat, but the minimum show coat for an adult is two inches.

Faults—Cowhocks, snipy muzzle, poor pigmentation, protruding eyes, yellow eyes, undershot or overshot bite.

Serious Faults—Corkscrew tail, black hair in the coat.

Approved November 14, 1972

Boston Terrier

ONE OF OUR very native American breeds, the Boston Terrier was the result of a cross between an English Bulldog and a white English Terrier, later considerably inbred. Incidental peculiarities of the first dogs used as sires are partly responsible for the present type.

About the year 1870 Mr. Robert C. Hooper of Boston came into the possession of an imported dog named Judge, which he purchased from Mr. William O'Brien of the same city. Judge, commonly known as Hooper's Judge and destined to be the ancestor of almost all true modern Bostons, was a cross between a Bulldog and an English Terrier, and in type he resembled the former. He was a well-built, high-stationed dog of about thirty-two pounds, in color dark brindle with white blaze. His head was square and blocky and his mouth nearly even. Judge was mated to "Gyp or Kate," as the name appears on old-time pedigrees. This white bitch, owned by Mr. Edward Burnett of Southboro, Mass., weighed around twenty pounds; she was low- and square.

From the mating of Judge and Gyp descended Wells' Eph, a dog of strong build and, like his dam, low-stationed. He was dark brindle with even white markings and had a nearly even mouth. Eph was bred to Tobin's Kate, a comparatively small twenty-pound female with fairly short head and straight three-quarter tail. She was golden brindle in color. From these dogs in the main evolved the Boston Terrier breed.

In the year 1889 about thirty fanciers in and around Boston organized what was known as the American Bull Terrier Club, and they exhibited the dogs as Round Heads or Bull Terriers. As time went on, these fanciers met with considerable opposition from Bull Terrier breeders, who did everything possible to discourage them. The Boston Terrier fanciers, however, refused to be discouraged, and in 1891 formed the Boston Terrier Club of America. As their dog was bred in Boston, they changed the name to Boston Terrier. After two years of sustained effort to have the Boston recognized as a pure-bred, they succeeded in persuading The American Kennel Club to admit the breed to the stud book in 1893 and the club to membership.

Up to this time, of course, the Boston Terrier was only in its infancy. There was hard work ahead to standardize the breed and to make the Bostons of that day into a more even lot. Great progress has been made, however, since 1900 in developing different strains by careful, selective breeding which included a certain amount of inbreeding. The result is a clean-cut dog, with short head, snow-white markings, dark, soft eyes, and a body approximating the conformation of the terrier rather than the Bulldog.

The Boston, while not a fighter, is well able to take care of himself. He has a characteristically gentle disposition that has won him the name of the American gentleman among dogs. As a companion and house pet, he is eminently suitable.

Official Standard for the
Boston Terrier

General Appearance—The general appearance of the Boston Terrier should be that of a lively, highly intelligent, smooth-coated, short-headed, compactly built, short-tailed, well-balanced dog of medium station, of brindle color and evenly marked with white. The head should indicate a high degree of intelligence, and should be in proportion to the size of the dog; the body rather short and well knit, the limbs strong and neatly turned; tail short; and no feature be so prominent that the dog appears badly proportioned. The dog should convey an impression of determination, strength and activity, with style of a high order; carriage easy and graceful. A proportionate combination of "color" and "ideal markings" is a particularly distinctive feature of a representative specimen, and a dog with a preponderance of white on body, or without the proper proportion of brindle and white on head, should possess sufficient merit otherwise to counteract its deficiencies in these respects. The ideal "Boston Terrier expression" as indicating "a high degree of intelligence," is also an important characteristic of the breed. "Color and markings" and "expression" should be given particular consideration in determining the relative value of "general appearance" to other points.

Skull—Square, flat on top, free from wrinkles; cheeks flat; brow abrupt, stop well defined. *Eyes*—Wide apart, large and round, dark in color, expression alert, but kind and intelligent. The eyes should set square in the skull, and the outside corners should be on a line with the cheeks as viewed from the front. *Muzzle*—Short, square, wide and deep, and in proportion to skull; free from wrinkles; shorter in length than in width and depth, not exceeding in length approximately one third of length of skull; width and depth carried out well to end; the muzzle from stop to end of nose on a line parallel to the top of the skull; nose black and wide, with well defined line between nostrils. The jaws broad and square, with short regular teeth. Bite even or sufficiently undershot to square muzzle. The chops of good depth but not pendulous, completely covering the teeth when mouth is closed. *Ears*—Carried erect, either cropped to conform to the shape of head, or natural bat, situated as near the corners of skull as possible.

Head Faults—Skull "domed" or inclined; furrowed by a medial line; skull too long for breadth, or *vice versa*; stop too shallow; brow and skull too slanting. Eyes small or sunken; too prominent; light color or walleye; showing too much white or haw. Muzzle wedge-shaped or lacking depth; down-faced; too much cut out below the eyes; pinched or wide nostrils; butterfly nose; protruding teeth; weak lower jaw; showing turn-up, layback, or wrinkled. Ears poorly carried or in size out of proportion to head.

Neck—Of fair length, slightly arched and carrying the head gracefully; setting neatly into shoulders. **Neck Faults**—Ewe-necked; throatiness; short and thick.

580

Body—Deep with good width of chest; shoulders sloping; back short; ribs deep and well sprung, carried well back to loins; loins short and muscular; rump curving slightly to set-on of tail; flank very slightly cut up. The body should appear short but not chunky. **Body Faults**—Flat sides; narrow chest; long or slack loins; roach back; swayback; too much cut up in flank.

Elbows—Standing neither in nor out. *Forelegs*—Set moderately wide apart and on a line with the point of the shoulders; straight in bone and well muscled; pasterns short and strong. *Hind Legs*—Set true; bent at stifles; short from hocks to feet; hocks turning neither in nor out; thighs strong and well muscled. *Feet*—Round, small and compact and turned neither in nor out; toes well arched. **Leg and Feet Faults**—Loose shoulders or elbows; hind legs too straight at stifles; hocks too prominent; long or weak pasterns; splay feet.

Gait—The gait of the Boston Terrier is that of a sure-footed, straight-gaited dog, forelegs and hind legs moving straight ahead in line with perfect rhythm, each step indicating grace with power. **Gait Faults**—There shall be no rolling, paddling or weaving when gaited and any crossing movement, either front or rear, is a serious fault.

Tail—Set-on low; short, fine and tapering; straight; or screw; devoid of fringe or coarse hair, and not carried above horizontal. **Tail Faults**—A long or gaily carried tail; extremely gnarled or curled against body. (Note—The preferred tail should not exceed in length approximately half the distance from set-on to hock.)

Ideal Color—Brindle with white markings. The brindle to be evenly distributed and distinct. Black with white markings permissible but brindle with white markings preferred. *Ideal Markings*—White muzzle, even white blaze over head, collar, breast, part or whole of forelegs, and hind legs below hocks. **Color and Markings Faults**—All white; absence of white marking; preponderance of white on body; without the proper proportion of brindle and white on head; or any variations detracting from the general appearance.

Coat—Short, smooth, bright and fine in texture. **Coat Faults**—Long or coarse; lacking luster.

Weight—Not exceeding 25 pounds, divided by classes as follows: lightweight, under 15 pounds; middleweight, 15 and under 20 pounds; heavyweight, 20 and not exceeding 25 pounds.

SCALE OF POINTS

General appearance	10	Forelegs	5
Skull	10	Hind legs	5
Eyes	5	Gait	10
Muzzle	10	Feet	5
Ears	2	Tail	5
Neck	3	Color	4
Body	15	Ideal markings	5
Elbows	4	Coat	2
		TOTAL	100

DISQUALIFICATIONS

Solid black; black and tan; liver or mouse colors.
Dudley nose.
Docked tail or any artificial means used to deceive the judge.

Approved April 9, 1957

Bulldog

TO THE BEST of our knowledge the Bulldog had its origin in the British Isles, the name bull being applied because of the dog's use in connection with bullbaiting.

Exactly when this old English sport first started is hardly possible to say, but in *The Survey of Stamford* the following reference is made to its probable origin:

> William Earl Warren, Lord of this town in the reign of King John (1209), standing upon the walls of his castle at Stamford, saw two bulls fighting for a cow in the castle meadow, till all the butchers' dogs pursued one of the bulls, which was maddened by the noise and multitude, through the town. This so pleased the Earl that he gave the castle meadow where the bulls combat began, for a common to the butchers of the town after the first grass was mowed, on condition that they should find a "mad bull" on a day six weeks before Christmas for the continuance of that sport for ever.

Anyone who has read about the sport of bullbaiting must have been conscious of its extreme cruelty. From this we can gather that the original Bulldog had to be a very ferocious animal. Beauty and symmetry of form were in no way desirable, the appearance of the dog counting for nothing. The extraordinary courage possessed by these dogs is hardly believable. Bred from a long line of fighting ancestors, they grew to be so savage, so courageous as to be almost insensitive to pain. Such was the Bulldog of British sporting days.

Then came the year 1835, when dogfighting as a sport became illegal in England. To all intents and purposes, therefore, the English Bulldog had outlived his usefulness; his days were numbered. However, there were dog lovers who felt a deep disappointment at the passing of so fine a breed, so forthwith they set themselves the task of preserving it. Though ferocity was no longer necessary or desirable, they wished to retain all the dog's other splendid qualities. With this idea in mind, they proceeded to eliminate the undesirable characteristics and to preserve and accentuate the finer qualities. Scientific breeding brought results, so that within a few generations the English Bulldog became one of the finest physical specimens, minus its original viciousness. Now he was regarded as a dog which anyone could exhibit with pride.

This is the Bulldog we know today; a breed of dog of which we may be justly proud. At the same time we must express our gratitude to our British cousins who realized the value of the English Bull sufficiently to preserve him for posterity.

Official Standard for the Bulldog

General Appearance, Attitude, Expression, etc.—The perfect Bulldog must be of medium size and smooth coat; with heavy, thick-set, low-swung body, massive, short-faced head, wide shoulders and sturdy limbs. The general appearance and attitude should suggest great stability, vigor and strength. The disposition should be equable and kind, resolute and courageous (not vicious or aggressive), and demeanor should be pacific and dignified. These attributes should be countenanced by the expression and behavior.

Gait—The style and carriage are peculiar, his gait being a loose-jointed, shuffling, sidewise motion, giving the characteristic "roll." The action must, however, be unrestrained, free and vigorous.

Proportion and Symmetry—The "points" should be well distributed and bear good relation one to the other, no feature being in such prominence from either excess or lack of quality that the animal appears deformed or ill-proportioned. *Influence of Sex*—In comparison of specimens of different sex, due allowance should be made in favor of the bitches, which do not bear the characteristics of the breed to the same degree of perfection and grandeur as do the dogs.

Size—The size for mature dogs is about 50 pounds; for mature bitches about 40 pounds.

Coat—The coat should be straight, short, flat, close, of fine texture, smooth and glossy. (No fringe, feather or curl.)

Color of Coat—The color of coat should be uniform, pure of its kind and brilliant. The various colors found in the breed are to be preferred in the following order: (1) red brindle, (2) all other brindles, (3) solid white, (4) solid red, fawn or fallow, (5) piebald, (6) inferior qualities of all the foregoing. *Note:* A perfect piebald is preferable to a muddy brindle or defective solid color. Solid black is very undesirable, but not so objectionable if occurring to a moderate degree in piebald patches. The brindles to be perfect should have a fine, even and equal distribution of the composite colors. In brindles and solid colors a small white patch on the chest is not considered detrimental. In piebalds the color patches should be well defined, of pure color and symmetrically distributed.

Skin—The skin should be soft and loose, especially at the head, neck and shoulders. *Wrinkles and Dewlap*—The head and face should be covered with heavy wrinkles, and at the throat, from jaw to chest, there should be two loose pendulous folds, forming the dewlap.

Skull—The skull should be very large, and in circumference, in front of the ears, should measure at least the height of the dog at the shoulders. Viewed from the front, it should appear very high from the corner of the lower jaw to the apex of the skull, and also very broad and square. Viewed at the side, the head should appear very high, and very short from the point of the nose to occiput. The forehead should be flat (not rounded or domed), neither too prominent nor overhanging the face. *Cheeks*—The cheeks should be well rounded, protruding sideways and outward beyond the eyes. *Stop*—The temples or frontal bones should be very well defined, broad, square and high, causing a hollow or groove between the eyes. This indentation, or stop, should be both broad and deep and extend up the middle of the forehead, dividing the head vertically, being traceable to the top of the skull. *Eyes and Eyelids*—The eyes, seen from the front, should be situated low down in the skull, as far from the ears as possible, and their corners should be in a straight line at right angles with the stop. They should be quite in front of the head, as wide apart as possible, provided their outer corners are within the outline of the cheeks when viewed from the front. They should be quite round in form, of moderate size, neither sunken nor bulging, and in color should be very dark. The lids should cover the white of the eyeball, when the dog is looking directly forward, and the lid should show no "haw." *Ears*—The ears should be set high in the head, the front inner edge of each ear joining the outline of the skull at the top back corner of skull, so as to place them as wide apart, and as high, and as far from the eyes as possible. In size they should be small and thin. The shape termed "rose ear" is the most desirable. The rose ear folds inward at its back lower edge, the upper front edge curving over, outward and backward, showing part of the inside of the burr. (The ears should not be carried erect or prick-eared or buttoned and should never be cropped.)

Face—The face, measured from the front of the cheekbone to the tip of the nose, should be extremely short, the muzzle being very short, broad, turned upward and very deep from the corner of the eye to the corner of the mouth. *Nose*—The nose should be large, broad and black, its tip being set back deeply between the eyes. The distance from bottom of stop, between the eyes, to the tip of nose should be as short as possible and not exceed the length from the tip of nose to the edge of under lip. The nostrils should be wide, large and black, with a well-defined line between them. Any nose other than black is objectionable and a brown or liver colored nose shall disqualify. *Chops*–The chops or "flews" should be thick, broad, pendant and very deep, completely overhanging the lower jaw at each side. They join the under lip in front and almost or quite cover the teeth, which should be scarcely noticeable when the mouth is closed. *Jaws*–The jaws should be massive, very broad, square and "undershot," the lower jaw projecting considerably in front of the upper jaw and turning up. *Teeth*–The teeth should be large and strong, with the canine teeth or tusks wide apart, and the six small teeth in front, between the canines, in an even, level row.

Neck—The neck should be short, very thick, deep and strong and well arched at the back.

Shoulders—The shoulders should be muscular, very heavy, wide-spread and slanting outward, giving stability and great power.

Chest—The chest should be very broad, deep and full.

Brisket and Body—The brisket and body should be very capacious, with full sides, well-rounded ribs and very deep from the shoulders down to its lowest part, where it joins the chest. It should be well let down between the shoulders and forelegs, giving the dog a broad, low, short-legged appearance. The body should be well ribbed up behind with the belly tucked up and not rotund.

Back—The back should be short and strong, very broad at the shoulders and comparatively narrow at the loins. There should be a slight fall in the back, close behind the shoulders (its lowest part), whence the spine should rise to the loins (the top of which should be higher than the top of the shoulders), thence curving again more suddenly to the tail, forming an arch (a very distinctive feature of the breed), termed "roach back" or, more correctly, "wheel-back."

Legs and Feet—*Forelegs*—The forelegs should be short, very stout, straight and muscular, set wide apart, with well developed calves, presenting a bowed outline, but the bones of the legs should not be curved or bandy, nor the feet brought too close together. *Elbows*—The elbows should be low and stand well out and loose from the body. *Hind Legs*—The hind legs should be strong and muscular and longer than the forelegs, so as to elevate the loins above the shoulders. Hocks should be slightly bent and well let down, so as to give length and strength from loins to hock. The lower leg should be short, straight and strong, with the stifles turned slightly outward and away from the body. The hocks are thereby made to approach each other, and the hind feet to turn outward. *Feet*—The feet should be moderate in size, compact and firmly set. Toes compact, well split up, with high knuckles and with short stubby nails. The front feet may be straight or slightly out-turned, but the hind feet should be pointed well outward.

Tail—The tail may be either straight or "screwed" (but never curved or curly), and in any case must be short, hung low, with decided downward carriage, thick root and fine tip. If straight, the tail should be cylindrical and of uniform taper. If "screwed" the bends or kinks should be well defined, and they may be abrupt and even knotty, but no portion of the member should be elevated above the base or root.

586

SCALE OF POINTS

General Properties
  Proportion and symmetry
  5
  Attitude 3
  Expression 2
  Gait 3
  Size 3
  Coat 2
  Color of coat 4   22
Head
  Skull 5
  Cheeks 2
  Stop 4
  Eyes and eyelids 3
  Ears 5
  Wrinkle 5
  Nose 6

  Chops 2
  Jaws 5
  Teeth 2   39
Body, Legs, etc.
  Neck 3
  Dewlap 2
  Shoulders 5
  Chest 3
  Ribs 3
  Brisket 2
  Belly 2
  Back 5
  Forelegs and elbows 4
  Hind legs 3
  Feet 3
  Tail 4   39
        TOTAL 100

DISQUALIFICATION

Brown or liver colored nose.

Approved July 20, 1976

Chow Chow

DUE IN GREAT measure to the ruthlessness with which Chinese emperors destroyed the works of art and the literature of their predecessors, it is difficult to secure evidence of the antiquity of that lordly, aloof dog, the Chow Chow. Still, a bas-relief was discovered not so very long ago, dating back to the Han dynasty, about 150 B.C., that definitely places the Chow as a hunting dog in that period. While this establishes the breed as more than 2000 years old, it is believed by many authorities that the Chow goes back much farther; that it is, indeed, one of the oldest recognizable types of dog.

The theory has been advanced that the Chow originated through a crossing of the old Mastiff of Tibet and the Samoyed, from the northern parts of Siberia. Certainly the Chow evinces some of the characteristics of both breeds. Refutation lies in the fact that the Chow is the only breed in the world possessing a blue-black tongue. On this score, some maintain that the Chow is one of the basic breeds, and that he may have been one of the ancestors of the Samoyed, the Norwegian Elkhound, the Keeshond, and the Pomeranian, all of which are of somewhat similar type.

In modern times the Chow Chow has become a fashionable pet and guard dog, but there is plenty of evidence available in China to prove that for centuries he was the principal sporting dog. Perhaps the most unusual and lavish kennel in all history was the one maintained by a T'ang emperor about the seventh century A.D. It was so extensive that the emperor could not have availed himself of a fraction of the facilities for sport it afforded. It housed 2500 couples of "hounds" of the Chow type, and the emperor had a staff of 10,000 huntsmen.

Apparently the Chow has been an unusually gifted breed of dog, since his uses have run the gamut of work done by nearly all recognized breeds. He is credited with great scenting powers, with staunchness on point, and with cleverness in hunting tactics. He is used frequently on Mongolian pheasant, and on the francolin of Yunnan, and on both has received great praise for his speed and stamina.

Undoubtedly the Chow Chow is of far northern origin, but he has always been found in greatest number in the south of China, particularly in the district centering about Canton. In that region of China where he is considered indigenous, he is usually called the "black-tongue," or the "black-mouthed" dog. In the north, as in Peiping, he is called *lang kou* (wolf dog), *hsiung kou* (bear dog) or, the more sophisticated *hei she-t'ou* (black-tongued) or Kwantung *Kou*, *i.e.* the dog of Canton.

The name Chow Chow has little basis for its origin in China; it is believed that expression evolved from the pidgin-English term for articles brought from any part of the Oriental empire during the latter part of the eighteenth century. It meant knickknacks or bric-a-brac, including curios such as porcelain and ivory figurines, and finally what is described today as "mixed pickles," whether of the edible variety or not. It was far easier for the master of a sailing vessel to write "chow chow" than it was to describe all the various items of his cargo. So, in time, the expression came to include the dog.

The first Occidental description of the Chow Chow was penned by the Reverend Gilbert White, rector of Selborne, England, and this was published later in the *Natural History and Antiquities of Selborne*. The description, which is a most complete one, indicates that the dogs were not very different from specimens of modern times. It was a neighbor of the rector who in 1780 brought a brace of Chows from Canton on a vessel of the East India Company.

The importation of Chows into England did not begin, however, until about 1880, and the breed started toward its present popularity after Queen Victoria took an interest in it. The first specialty club was formed in England in 1895; the dog was exhibited for the first time in the United States in 1890 when a specimen named Takya, owned by

Miss A. C. Derby, took a third prize in the Miscellaneous Class at the Westminster Kennel Club show in New York. Since 1901 the Chow Chow has made steady progress, and today it is one of America's firmly established breeds.

Official Standard for the Chow Chow

General Appearance—A massive, cobby, powerful dog, active and alert, with strong, muscular development, and perfect balance. Body squares with height of leg at shoulder; head, broad and flat, with short, broad, and deep muzzle, accentuated by a ruff; the whole supported by straight, strong legs. Clothed in a shining, offstanding coat, the Chow is a masterpiece of beauty, dignity, and untouched naturalness.

Head—Large and massive in proportion to size of dog, with broad, flat skull; well filled under the eyes; moderate stop; and proudly carried. *Expression*—Essentially dignified, lordly, scowling, discerning, sober, and snobbish—one of independence. *Muzzle*—Short in comparison to length of skull; broad from eyes to end of nose, and of equal depth. The lips somewhat full and overhanging. *Teeth*—Strong and level, with a scissors bite; should neither be overshot, nor undershot. *Nose*—Large, broad, and black in color. (Disqualification—Nose spotted or distinctly other color than black, except in blue Chows, which may have solid blue or slate noses.) *Tongue*—A blue-black. The tissues of the mouth should approximate black. (Disqualification—Tongue red, pink, or obviously spotted with red or pink.) *Eyes*—Dark, deep-set, of moderate size, and almond-shaped. *Ears*—Small, slightly rounded at tip, stiffly carried. They should be placed wide apart, on top of the skull, and set with a slight, forward tilt. (Disqualification—Drop ear or ears. A drop ear is one which is not stiffly carried or stiffly erect, but which breaks over at any point from its base to its tip.)

Body—Short, compact, with well-sprung ribs, and let down in the flank.

Neck—Strong, full, set well on the shoulders.

Shoulders—Muscular, slightly sloping.

Chest—Broad, deep, and muscular. A narrow chest is a serious fault.

Back—Short, straight, and strong.

Loins—Broad, deep, and powerful.

Tail—Set well up and carried closely to the back, following line of spine at start.

Forelegs—Perfectly straight, with heavy bone and upright pasterns.

Hind Legs—Straight-hocked, muscular, and heavy boned. *Feet*—Compact, round, catlike, with thick pads.

Gait—Completely individual. Short and stilted because of straight hocks.

Coat—Abundant, dense, straight, and off-standing; rather coarse in texture with a soft, woolly undercoat. It may be any clear color, solid throughout, with lighter shadings on ruff, tail, and breechings.

DISQUALIFICATIONS

Nose spotted or distinctly other color than black, except in blue Chows, which may have solid blue or slate noses.

Tongue red, pink or obviously spotted with red or pink.

Drop ear or ears.

Approved March 11, 1941

Dalmatian

No BREED has a more interesting background or a more disputed heritage than that dog from long ago, the Dalmatian. His beginning is buried so deep in the past that researchers cannot agree as to his origin. As to the great age of the breed, and the fact that it has come through many centuries unchanged, investigators are in complete agreement.

Models, engravings, paintings, and writings of antiquity have been used with fair excuse but no certainty to claim the spotted dog first appeared in Europe, Asia, and Africa. Perhaps some of the divergencies in opinion as to the original home of the Dalmatian can be accounted for by the fact that the dog has frequently been found in bands of Romanies, and that like his gypsy masters, he has been well known but not located definitely in any one place. Authoritative writers place him first as a positive entity in Dalmatia, a province of Austria on the Eastern shore of the coast of Venice. Though he has been accredited with a dozen nationalities and has as many native names—he is nicknamed by the English, the English Coach Dog, the Carriage Dog, the Plum Pudding Dog, the Fire House Dog, and the Spotted Dick—it is from his first proved home that he takes his correct name, the Dalmatian. We find references to him as Dalmatian in the middle eighteenth century. There is no question whatsoever that his lineage is as ancient and his record as straight as that of other breeds.

His activities have been as varied as his reputed ancestors. He has been a dog of war, a sentinel on the borders of Dalmatia and Croatia. He has been employed as draft dog, as shepherd. He is excellent on rats and vermin. He is well known for his heroic performances as fire-apparatus follower and fire-house mascot. As a sporting dog he has been used as bird dog, as trail hound, as retriever, or in packs for boar or stag hunting. His retentive memory has made him one of the most dependable clowners in circuses and on the stage. Down through the years the intelligence and willingness of the Dalmatian have found him in practically every role to which useful dogs are assigned. Most important among his talents has been his status as the original, one-and-only coaching dog.

The imaginative might say that his coaching days go back to an engraving of a spotted dog following an Egyptian chariot! Even the practical minded will find no end of proof, centuries old, of the Dalmatian, with ears entirely cropped away and padlocked brass collar, plying his natural trade as follower and guardian of the horse-drawn vehicle.

He is physically fitted for road work. In his make-up, speed and endurance are blended to a nicety. His gait has beauty of motion and swiftness, and he has the strength, vitality, and fortitude to keep going gaily till the journey's end. The instinct for coaching is bred in him, born in him, and trained in him through the years. The Dalmatian takes to a horse as a horse takes to him, and that is to say, like a duck to water. He may work in the old way, clearing the path before the Tally Ho with dignity and determination, or following on with his ermine spottings in full view to add distinction to an equipage. He may coach under the rear axle, the front axle, or, most difficult of all, under the pole between the leaders and the wheelers. Wherever he works, it is with the love of the game in his heart and with the skill which has won him the title of the only recognized carriage dog in the world. His penchant for working is his most renowned characteristic, but it in no way approaches his capacity for friendship.

There is no dog more picturesque than this spotted fellow with his slick white coat gaily decorated with clearly defined round spots of jet black, or, in the liver variety, deep brown. He does not look like any other breed, for his markings are peculiarly his own. He is strong-bodied, clean-cut, colorful, and distinctive. His flashy spottings are the culmination of ages of careful breeding.

His aristocratic bearing does not belie him, for the Dalmatian is first of all a gentleman. He is a quiet chap, and the ideal guard dog, distinguishing nicely between barking for fun or with purpose. His courtesy never fails with approved visitors, but his protective instinct is highly developed and he has the courage to defend. As a watchdog he is sensible and dependable. He is not everyone's dog—no casual admirer will break his polite reserve, for he has a fine sense of distinction as to whom he belongs. Fashion has not distorted the Dalmatian. He is born pure white, develops quickly and requires no cropping, docking, stripping, or artifices of any sort. He is all ready for sport or the show ring just as nature made him. He is extremely hardy, an easy keeper, suited to any climate. He requires only the minimum of care, for he is sturdy and neat and clean.

Official Standard for the Dalmatian

The Dalmatian should represent a strong, muscular, and active dog; poised and alert; free of shyness; intelligent in expression; symmetrical in outline; and free from coarseness and lumber. He should be capable of great endurance, combined with a fair amount of speed.

Head—Should be of a fair length, the skull flat, proportionately broad between the ears, and moderately well defined at the temples, and not in one straight line from the nose to the occiput bone as required in a Bull Terrier. It should be entirely free from wrinkle. *Muzzle*—Should be long and powerful—the lips clean. The mouth should have a scissors bite. Never undershot or overshot. It is permissible to trim whiskers. *Eyes*—Should be set moderately well apart, and of medium size, round, bright, and sparkling, with an intelligent expression; their color greatly depending on the markings of the dog. In the black-spotted variety the eyes should be dark (black or brown or blue). In the liver-spotted variety they should be lighter than in the black-spotted variety (golden or light brown or blue). The rim around the eyes in the black-spotted variety should be black; in the liver-spotted variety, brown. Never flesh-colored in either. Lack of pigment a major fault.

Ears—Should be set rather high, of moderate size, rather wide at the base, and gradually tapering to a rounded point. They should be carried close to the head, be thin and fine in texture, and preferably spotted. *Nose*—In the black-spotted variety should always be black; in the liver-spotted variety, always brown. A butterfly or flesh-colored nose is a major fault.

Neck and Shoulders—The neck should be fairly long, nicely arched, light and tapering, and entirely free from throatiness. The shoulders should be oblique, clean, and muscular, denoting speed.

Body, Back, Chest and Loins—The chest should not be too wide, but very deep and capacious, ribs well sprung but never rounded like barrel hoops (which would indicate want of speed). Back powerful; loin strong, muscular and slightly arched.

Legs and Feet—Of great importance. The forelegs should be straight, strong, and heavy in bone; elbows close to the body; feet compact, well-arched toes, and tough, elastic pads. In the hind legs the muscles should be clean, though well defined; the hocks well let down. Dewclaws may be removed from legs. **Nails**—In the black-spotted variety, black or white; or a nail may be both black and white. In the liver-spotted variety, brown or white; or a nail may be both brown and white.

Gait—Length of stride should be in proportion to the size of the dog, steady in rhythm of 1, 2, 3, 4 as in the cadence count in military drill. Front legs should not paddle, nor should there be a straddling appearance. Hind legs should neither cross nor weave: judges should be able to see each leg move with no interference of another leg. Drive and reach are most desirable. Cowhocks are a major fault.

Tail—Should ideally reach the hock joint, strong at the insertion, and tapering toward the end, free from coarseness. It should not be inserted too low down, but carried with a slight curve upwards, and never curled.

Coat—Should be short, hard, dense, and fine, sleek and glossy in appearance, but neither woolly nor silky.

Color and Markings—Are most important points. The ground color in both varieties should be pure white, very decided, and not intermixed. The color of the spots in the black-spotted variety should be dense black; in the liver-spotted variety they should be liver brown. The spots should not intermingle, but be as round and well defined as possible, the more distinct the better. In size they should be from that of a dime to a half-dollar. The spots on the face, head, ears, legs, and tail to be smaller than those on the body. Patches, tricolors, and any color markings other than black or liver constitute a disqualification. A true patch is a solid, sharply defined mass of black or liver that is appreciably larger than any of the markings on the dog. Several spots that are so adjacent that they actually touch one another at their edges do not constitute a patch.

Size—The desirable height of dogs and bitches is between 19 and 23 inches at the withers, and any dog or bitch over 24 inches at the withers is to be disqualified.

MAJOR FAULTS

Butterfly or flesh-colored nose. Cowhocks. Flat feet. Lack of pigment in eye rims. Shyness. Trichiasis (abnormal position or direction of the eyelashes).

FAULTS

Ring or low-set tail. Undersize or oversize.

SCALE OF POINTS

Body, back, chest and loins	10	Legs and feet	10
Coat	5	Neck and shoulders	10
Color and markings	25	Size, symmetry, etc.	10
Ears	5	Tail	5
Gait	10	TOTAL	100
Head and eyes	10		

DISQUALIFICATIONS

Any color markings other than black or liver.
Any size over 24 inches at the withers.
Patches.
Tri-colors.
Undershot or overshot bite.

Approved December 11, 1962

French Bulldog

WHILE THERE has been a difference of opinion as to the origin of the French Bulldog, it seems pretty well established that one ancestor must have been the English Bulldog—probably one of the toy variety, of which there were a great number in England around 1860. These toy Bulldogs, not finding favor with the English, were sent in large numbers into France. There they were crossed with various other breeds, and finally became popular in fashionable circles, particularly with women. It was then that they were given the name Boule-Dog Français, although later on England scoffed at the idea of applying the word *Français* to a breed so clearly showing a strong strain of English Bulldog. At that time there was little uniformity of type, and one found dogs with rose ears, while others had bat ears which have since come to be recognized as an outstanding feature of the French Bulldog.

There are two distinctive features in French Bulldogs: one, the bat ear, as above mentioned; the other, the skull. The correctly formed skull should be level, or flat, between the ears, while directly above the eyes, extending almost across the forehead, it should be slightly curved, giving a domed appearance. Both of these features add much to the unusual appearance of the French Bulldog.

The preservation of the bat ear as a distinct feature has been due to the persistent efforts of American fanciers, since in the early days of breeding these dogs in Europe the tendency was toward the rose ear. Had this movement not been opposed by America, the breed would eventually have lost the feature that so strongly accentuates its individuality, and the result would have been practically a miniature English Bulldog.

This controversy over type was directly responsible for the formation of the French Bulldog Club of America, the first organization in the world devoted to the breed. Fanciers gave a specialty show in the ballroom of the Waldorf-Astoria in 1898, this being the first of its kind to be held in such de luxe quarters. The affair proved a sensation, and it was due, no doubt, to the resulting publicity that the quaint little chaps became the rage in society. Show entries increased until the peak was reached about 1913, when there were exactly 100 French Bulldogs benched at Westminster, while the following specialty shows had even more.

Unquestionably the dog that did the most toward the establishment of the breed in America was Ch. Nellcote Gamin, imported in 1904 by Mr. and Mrs. Samuel Goldenberg. With the addition of Gamin to the splendid stock already in this country, we were made independent of further importation in order to produce the finest Frenchies in the world. To Gamin goes credit for the greatest influence in molding the breed that can be attributed to any one dog. He was a famous sire, and today it is almost impossible to find a Frenchie that does not have Gamin inheritance.

An ideal French Bulldog should be a well-balanced, compactly built, *sound* dog, having the appearance of an active, intelligent, muscular dog of heavy bone, with a smooth coat, and medium or small stature. The weight may vary (anything up to twenty-eight pounds being permissible under the American Standard), but it is generally conceded that the ideal, or most popular, size is between nineteen and twenty-two pounds. A "Frenchie" may be any color except black (meaning without trace of brindle), black and white, black and tan, liver, or mouse color. Of the allowed colors no one is considered preferable.

In expression, the sour, pugnacious expression of the English Bulldog is not desired; a French Bulldog should have a bright, alert look which gives it the appearance of always being ready for fun and frolic, as it is.

While bred principally as pets and companions, Frenchies are remarkably intelligent and serve as good watchdogs. They are affectionate, sweet-tempered, and dependable. While alert and playful, they are not noisy and, as a rule, bark very little. Their size is another advantage in considering them as indoor pets, while the smooth, short coat is easily kept clean.

Official Standard for the
French Bulldog

General Appearance—The French Bulldog should have the appearance of an active, intelligent, muscular dog, of heavy bone, smooth coat, compactly built, and of medium or small structure. *Proportion and Symmetry*—The points should be well distributed and bear good relation one to the other, no feature being in such prominence from either excess or lack of quality that the animal appears deformed or poorly proportioned. *Influence of Sex*—In comparison of specimens of different sex, due allowance should be made in favor of the bitches, which do not bear the characteristics of the breed to the same marked degree as do the dogs.

Weight—A lightweight class under 22 pounds; heavyweight class, 22 pounds, and not over 28 pounds.

Head—The head should be large and square. The top of the skull should be flat between the ears; the forehead should not be flat but slightly rounded. The stop should be well defined, causing a hollow or groove between the eyes. The muzzle should be broad, deep and well laid back; the muscles of the cheeks well developed. The nose should be extremely short; nostrils broad with well defined line between them. The nose and flews should be black, except in the case of the lighter-colored dogs, where a lighter color nose is acceptable. The flews should be thick and broad, hanging over the lower jaw at the sides, meeting the underlip in front and covering the teeth which should not be seen when the mouth is closed. The underjaw should be deep, square, broad, undershot and well turned up. *Eyes*—The eyes should be wide apart, set low down in the skull, as far from the ears as possible, round in form, of moderate size, neither sunken nor bulging, and in color dark. No haw and no white of the eye showing when looking forward.

Ears—The ears shall hereafter be known as the bat ear, broad at the base, elongated, with round top, set high on the head, but not too close together, and carried erect with the orifice to the front. The leather of the ear, fine and soft.

Neck—The neck should be thick and well arched, with loose skin at throat.

Body—The body should be short and well rounded. The chest, broad, deep and full, well ribbed with the belly tucked up. The back should be a roach back, with a slight fall close behind the shoulders. It should be strong and short, broad at the shoulders and narrowing at the loins.

Legs—The forelegs should be short, stout, straight and muscular, set wide apart. The hind leg should be strong and muscular, longer than the forelegs, so as to elevate the loins above the shoulders. Hocks well let down. *Feet*—The feet should be moderate in size, compact and firmly set. Toes compact, well split up, with high knuckles and short, stubby nails; hind feet slightly longer than forefeet.

Tail—The tail should be either straight or screwed (but not curly), short, hung low, thick root and fine tip; carried low in repose.

Color, Skin and Coat—Acceptable colors are: All brindle, fawn, white, brindle and white, and any color except those which constitute disqualification. The skin should be soft and loose, especially at head and shoulders, forming wrinkles. Coat moderately fine, brilliant, short and smooth.

SCALE OF POINTS

General Properties			
Proportion and symmetry		Jaws 6	
.... 5		Teeth 2	40
Expression 5		*Body, Legs, etc.*	
Gait 4		Shoulders 5	
Color..................... 4		Back 5	
Coat 2	20	Neck 4	
Head		Chest 3	
Skull 6		Ribs 4	
Cheeks and chops 2		Brisket 3	
Stop 5		Belly 2	
Ears 8		Forelegs 4	
Eyes 4		Hind legs 3	
Wrinkles 4		Feet 3	
Nose 3		Tail 4	40
		TOTAL	100

DISQUALIFICATIONS:

Other than bat ears.

Black and white, black and tan, liver, mouse or solid black (black means black without any trace of brindle).

Eyes of different color.

Nose other than black, except in the case of the lighter-colored dogs, where a lighter color nose is acceptable.

Hare lip.

Any mutilation.

Over 28 pounds in weight.

Approved February 11, 1947

Keeshond

(Caze-hawnd)

IT TOOK a national political turnover in Holland to bring the Keeshond (*pl.* Keeshonden) to wide attention in the latter part of the eighteenth century, but the breed had been one of the favorite dogs of the Dutch people for several hundred years before that. Never a hunter, and never used for any of the specialized forms of work that have characterized so many other breeds, the Keeshond had managed by the very force of his personality to win a high place in the affections of a nation.

The events leading up to the recognition of the Keeshond as the national dog of Holland were concerned with the social unrest that seemed to be spreading like a prairie fire throughout the world in the years immediately preceding the French Revolution. Holland was divided into two great camps, the Prinsgezinden, or partisans of the Prince of Orange, and the Patriotten, or Patriots.

The Patriots, consisting principally of the people of the lower and upper middle classes, were led by a man named Kees de Gyselaer, who lived in Dordrecht. Like most of his race, de Gyselaer was a dog lover, and at the time he owned a little dog that he called Kees. This dog gave the breed its name, for it became the symbol of the Patriots. It appeared in countless pictures and cartoons made in those days of civil strife. The men who composed the party were firmly of the opinion that their own spirit was typified in the dog. He was a dog of the people.

Histories are rather vague as to what name the Keeshond bore prior to its adoption as a symbol by the Patriots, but it was known mainly as the barge dog. The breed had served for countless years on the *rijnaken,* or small vessels that were found in great numbers on the Rhine River. These vessels seldom were larger than 200 tons at the time when the Keeshond enjoyed its greatest popularity in Holland, and consequently would not accommodate a very large dog. There probably were more of this breed of dog kept as pets and watchdogs throughout the Netherlands than there were dogs on the barges. It was only natural that the dogs of the barges became better known, for they were continually moving up and down the river, coming in contact with more people.

The origin of the Keeshond undoubtedly is Arctic, or possibly Sub-Arctic, and it is of the same strains that produced the Samoyed, the Chow Chow, the Norwegian Elkhound, the Finnish Spitz, and the Pomeranian. It seems the most closely related to the Pomeranian. Some authorities believe that the Pomeranian was produced by selective breeding of the Keeshond.

The Keeshond has changed little in the past two centuries, for the earliest descriptions represent it as nearly identical with the dog of today. There also are a number of old paintings and drawings that prove how well the old Keeshond type has been preserved. A drawing, made in 1794, shows the children and the dog of a burgomaster mourning beside his tomb. The dog clearly resembles today's Keeshonden. Other evidence is found in the paintings of that famous Dutch artist, Jan Steen.

The close link between the Keeshond and the Patriots in the latter part of the eighteenth century almost proved the dog's undoing. He was so much in the public eye as the symbol of the Patriots that when the Prince of Orange established his party as the dominant one, few people wanted the dog that stood for the opposition. Many who owned Keeshonden disposed of them quietly; and only the most loyal maintained the breed. And then, the type of vessel used on the rivers gradually changed. Each year they seemed to get larger, until, eventually, they were quite pretentious and had plenty of room for large dogs. This affected the popularity of the Keeshond considerably.

The breed was at very low ebb until 1920, at which time the Baroness van Hardenbroek became so interested in the old breed that she undertook an investigation to see how much of the old stock still survived. The results of this search were very surprising. Whereas the breed had passed from public attention, it was still kept in its original form by certain captains of riverboats, by farmers, and by truckmen. There were many excellent specimens. Some owners even had maintained their own crude stud books.

The Baroness van Hardenbroek began breeding Keeshonden and spreading their story throughout Europe. In ten years she brought the breed to such a solid position that in 1933 De Raad van Beheer op Kynologisch Gebied in Nederland accepted the standard and the points for judging the breed. Also, there was formed the Dutch Keeshond Club. Prior to this the breed had invaded England, where it made a very good impression as early as 1925.

Alert and intelligent, the Dutch called the Keeshond the ideal companion dog. People in his native land list among his qualities the fact that he has no desire to hunt; that he would much rather remain with his master or mistress.

The whole appearance of the Keeshond gives evidence of his alertness. A wolf-gray in color, he has a stand-off coat that always looks as if it had just been brushed and trimmed.

Official Standard for the Keeshond

General Appearance and Conformation—The Keeshond is a handsome dog, of well-balanced, short-coupled body, attracting attention not only by his alert carriage and intelligent expression, but also by his luxurious coat, his richly plumed tail, well curled over his back, and by his foxlike face and head with small pointed ears. His coat is very thick round the neck, fore part of the shoulders and chest, forming a lionlike mane. His rump and hind legs, down to the hocks, are also thickly coated forming the characteristic "trousers." His head, ears and lower legs are covered with thick short hair.

The ideal height of fully matured dogs (over 2 years old), measured from top of withers to the ground, is: for males, 18 inches; bitches, 17 inches. However, size consideration should not outweigh that of type. When dogs are judged equal in type, the dog nearest the ideal height is to be preferred. Length of back from withers to rump should equal height as measured above.

Head—*Expression*—Expression is largely dependent on the distinctive characteristic called "spectacles"—a delicately penciled line slanting slightly upward from the outer corner of each eye to the lower corner of the ear, coupled with distinct markings and shadings forming short but expressive eyebrows. Markings (or shadings) on face and head must present a pleasing appearance, imparting to the dog an alert and intelligent expression. **Fault**— Absence of "spectacles."

Skull—The head should be well proportioned to the body, wedge-shaped when viewed from above. Not only in muzzle, but the whole head should give this impression when the ears are drawn back by covering the nape of the neck and the ears with one hand. Head in profile should exhibit a definite stop. **Fault**

—Apple head, or absence of stop.

Muzzle—The muzzle should be dark in color and of medium length, neither coarse nor snipy, and well proportioned to the skull.

Mouth—The mouth should be neither overshot nor undershot. Lips should be black and closely meeting, not thick, coarse or sagging; and with no wrinkle at the corner of the mouth. **Faults**—Overshot or undershot.

Teeth—The teeth should be white, sound and strong (but discoloration from distemper not to penalize severely); upper teeth should just overlap the lower teeth.

Eyes—Eyes should be dark brown in color, of medium size, rather oblique in shape and not set too wide apart. **Fault**—Protruding round eyes or eyes light of color.

Ears—Ears should be small, triangular in shape, mounted high on head and carried erect; dark in color and covered with thick, velvety short hair. Size should be proportionate to the head—length approximating the distance from outer corner of the eye to the nearest edge of the ear. **Fault**—Ears not carried erect when at attention.

Body—*Neck and Shoulders*—The neck should be moderately long, well shaped and well set on shoulders; covered with a profuse mane, sweeping from under the jaw and covering the whole of the front part of the shoulders and chest, as well as the top part of the shoulders. *Chest, Back and Loin*—The body should be compact with a short straight back sloping slightly downward toward the hindquarters; well ribbed, barrel well rounded, belly moderately tucked up, deep and strong of chest.

Legs—Forelegs should be straight seen from any angle and well feathered. Hind legs should be profusely feathered down to the hocks—not below, with hocks only slightly bent. Legs must be of good bone and cream in color. **Fault**—Black markings below the knee, penciling excepted.

Feet—The feet should be compact, well rounded, catlike, and cream in color. Toes are nicely arched, with black nails. **Fault**—White foot or feet.

Tail—The tail should be set on high, moderately long, and well feathered, tightly curled over back. It should lie flat and close to the body with a very light gray plume on top where curled, but the tip of the tail should be black. The tail should form a part of the "silhouette" of the dog's body, rather than give the appearance of an appendage. **Fault**—Tail not lying close to the back.

Action—Dogs should show boldly and keep tails curled over the back. They should move cleanly and briskly; and the movement should be straight and sharp (not lope like a German Shepherd). **Fault**—Tail not carried over back when moving.

Coat—The body should be abundantly covered with long, straight, harsh hair; standing well out from a thick, downy undercoat. The hair on the legs should be smooth and short, except for a feathering on the front legs and "trousers," as previously described, on the hind legs. The hair on the tail should be profuse, forming a rich plume. Head, including muzzle, skull and ears, should be covered with smooth, soft, short hair—velvety in texture on the ears. Coat must not part down the back. **Fault**—Silky, wavy or curly coats. Part in coat down the back.

604

Color and Markings—A mixture of gray and black. The undercoat should be very pale gray or cream (not tawny). The hair of the outer coat is black tipped, the length of the black tips producing the characteristic shading of color. The color may vary from light to dark, but any pronounced deviation from the gray color is not permissible. The plume of the tail should be very light gray when curled on back, and the tip of the tail should be black. Legs and feet should be cream. Ears should be very dark—almost black. Shoulder line markings (light gray) should be well defined. The color of the ruff and "trousers" is generally lighter than that of the body. "Spectacles" and shadings, as previously described, are characteristic of the breed and must be present to some degree. There should be no pronounced white markings. **Very Serious Faults**—Entirely black or white or any other solid color; any pronounced deviation from the gray color.

SCALE OF POINTS

General conformation and appearance		20	Tail 10	
Head			Neck and shoulders 8	
Shape 6			Legs 4	
Eyes 5			Feet 3	35
Ears 5			*Coat*	15
Teeth 4	20		*Color and markings*	10
Body				
Chest, back and loin 10			TOTAL 100	

Approved July 12, 1949

Lhasa Apso

BEYOND the northern boundary of India, where the mighty Mount Everest stands like a guardian sentinel, is the mysterious land of Tibet. It is a country of huge mountains and deep valleys, with a climate of intense cold and great heat, a country where conditions are hard on man and beast. This is the home of the Lhasa Apso, known in that land as Abso Seng Kye, the "Bark Lion Sentinel Dog." Small wonder, then, that these members of dogdom should be of such hardy and vigorous constitution.

There are four breeds native to this country: The Tibetan Terrier; the Tibetan Spaniel, a beautiful toy dog; the fierce and powerful Tibetan Mastiff; and the Lhasa Apso, which is raised in the lamaseries and villages around the sacred city of Lhasa. The dogs of Tibet have two characteristics in common, namely, the heavy coat of hair to protect them from the rigors of the climate, and the tail upcurled over the back.

Since danger threatens from without and within in this strange land, a huge Mastiff is chained to a post beside the outer door to prevent intruders from entering, while Lhasa Apsos are kept as special guards inside the dwellings. For this work the little dogs are peculiarly adapted by their intelligence, quick hearing, and finely developed instinct for distinguishing intimates from strangers.

The crude manner of breeding among the Tibetans is doubtless responsible for the fact that colors are not fixed; that is, if one breeds a black-and-white dog to a honey-colored bitch, he may get a brown or brown-and-white puppy as a result.

The two original dogs brought from Asia to this country were Taikoo, a black-and-white male, and Dinkie, a female the color of raw silk. Both were beautiful specimens of the breed, and from them came offspring colored black and white, grizzle and white, honey, golden, and brown and white. No doubt, under the influence of more scientific western breeding, color inheritance will become more certain.

The little Lhasa Apso has never lost his characteristic of keen watchfulness, nor has he lost his hardy nature. These two features should always be developed, since they are of outstanding merit. We have found that these dogs are easily trained and responsive to kindness. To anyone they trust they are most obedient, and their beautiful dark eyes are certainly appealing as they wait for some mark of appreciation for their efforts.

Official Standard for the
Lhasa Apso

Character—Gay and assertive, but chary of strangers.

Size—Variable, but about 10 inches or 11 inches at shoulder for dogs, bitches slightly smaller.

Color—All colors equally acceptable with or without dark tips to ears and beard.

Body Shape—The length from point of shoulders to point of buttocks longer than height at withers, well ribbed up, strong loin, well-developed quarters and thighs.

Coat—Heavy, straight, hard, not woolly nor silky, of good length, and very dense.

Mouth and Muzzle—The preferred bite is either level or slightly undershot. Muzzle of medium length; a square muzzle is objectionable.

Head—Heavy head furnishings with good fall over eyes, good whiskers and beard; skull narrow, falling away behind the eyes in a marked degree, not quite flat, but not domed or apple-shaped; straight foreface of fair length. Nose black, the length from tip of nose to eye to be roughly about one-third of the total length from nose to back of skull.

Eyes—Dark brown, neither very large and full, nor very small and sunk.

Ears—Pendant, heavily feathered.

Legs—Forelegs straight, both forelegs and hind legs heavily furnished with hair.

Feet—Well feathered, should be round and catlike, with good pads.

Tail and Carriage—Well feathered, should be carried well over back in a screw; there may be a kink at the end. A low carriage of stern is a serious fault.

Approved July 11, 1978

Poodle

FEW DOGS have climbed to such high favor in so many different countries as has the Poodle, but it appeared so early in various parts of the world that there is some doubt as to the land of its origin.

It is supposed to have originated in Germany, where it is known as the *Pudel* or *Canis Familiaris Aquatius*. However for years it has been regarded as the national dog of France, where it was commonly used as a retriever as well as a traveling-circus trick dog. In France it was and is known as the *Caniche*, which is derived from *chien canard* or duck dog. Doubtless the English word poodle comes from the German *pudel* or *pudelin*, meaning to splash in the water. The expression "French" Poodle was in all probability a somewhat later cognomen, bestowed as a result of the dog's great popularity in France.

At any rate, the Poodle undoubtedly originated as a water retriever. In fact the unclipped Poodle of today bears strong resemblance in type to the old Rough-haired Water Dog of England as painted by Reinagle at the beginning of the nineteenth century; and except that the Irish Water Spaniel is born with short hair on its face and tail, there is little difference between this ancient Irish dog and the Poodle.

Authorities concede that the large, or Standard, Poodle is the oldest of the three varieties, and that the dog gained special fame as a water worker. So widely was it used as retriever that it was shorn of portions of its coat to further facilitate progress in swimming. Thence came the custom of clipping to pattern which so enhanced the style and general appearance that its sponsors, particularly in France, were captivated by it.

All of the Poodle's ancestors were acknowledged to be good swimmers, although one member of the family, the truffle dog (it may have been of toy or miniature size), it is said, never went near the water. Truffle hunting was widely practiced in England, and later in Spain and Germany, where the edible fungus has always been considered a great delicacy. For scenting and digging up the fungus, the smaller dogs were favored, since they did less damage to the truffles with their feet than the larger kinds. So it is rumored that a terrier was crossed with the Poodle to produce the ideal truffle hunter.

Despite the Standard Poodle's claim to greater age than the other varieties, there is some evidence to show that the smaller types developed only a short time after the breed assumed the general type by which it is recognized today. The smallest, or Toy variety, was known in England in the eighteenth century, when the White Cuban became popular there. This was a sleeve dog attributed to the West Indian island of Cuba, whence it traveled to Spain and then to England.

Standard Poodle

Miniature Poodle

Queen Anne, we are told, admired a troupe of performing dogs that danced to music in almost human fashion. And this penchant, by the way, Poodles of all sizes have carried down the years intact.

But the Continent had known the Poodle long before it came to England. Drawings by the German artist, Albrecht Dürer, establish the breed in the fifteenth and sixteenth centuries. How long the dog had been known in Spain is problematical, but it was the principal pet dog of the latter eighteenth century, as shown by the paintings of the Spanish artist, Goya. And France had Toy Poodles as pampered favorites during the reign of Louis XVI at about the same period.

There is scarcely a pure-bred dog of this day that can claim so many references in art and literature going back into time. Bas-reliefs dating from the first century, found along the shores of the Mediterranean, portray the Poodle very much as it is in this twentieth century. Clipped to resemble the lion, it is not unlike some of the specimens seen at the earliest dog shows. Possibly long ago there was a link between the dog attributed to the Island of Melita—now known as the Maltese—and the Toy Poodle. Similarly there may have been a relationship between the Poodle and the dog of Spain—the spaniel. If they do not come from the same progenitor, at least the paths of their ancestors must have crossed at some remote time.

The universal esteem in which the Poodle has been held since the beginning of modern history is attested by its interesting variations in size and color. In accordance with present-day show classification, we have three sizes—Standard Poodles, Miniature Poodles, Toy Poodles —as well as an array of colors to suit almost anyone's taste. We have white ones, black ones, brown, cream, and blue ones, gray, apricot and so on; any solid color is allowed. Some are pink-skinned, some blue- or silver-skinned, others cream-skinned. Hence he who fancies a Poodle is never at a loss: he may choose a big dog to guard and protect, a medium-sized one to fit into restricted quarters, or a tiny tot to serve only as "comforter." And he can pick a color to match whatever his décor may happen to be. Surely such an unusual selection may have played at least some part in the Poodle's continued rise to fame. But beyond that, the dog's innate intelligence and his ability to learn are considered exceptional.

It should be kept in mind that the words, *Standard, Miniature*, and *Toy* are used to denote size only. The Standard or large Poodle must be over fifteen inches at the shoulder; the Miniature must be fifteen inches or under, but over ten inches at the shoulder, and the Toy ten inches or less. All are one breed, governed by the same standard of perfection.

In addition to differences in size and color, the Poodle enjoys another characteristic unique among doggy kinds, namely, a coat which lends itself to a choice of hair styling. The top coat is very

611

profuse indeed, wiry in texture and composed of thick, close curls, and the undercoat is woolly and warm. If allowed to grow unhindered the top coat forms thin, cylindrical mats which form a mass of ropelike cords: thus the curly Poodle becomes what used to be known in the old days as the Corded Poodle. This style, though, went out long ago; it was impractical for everyday living and difficult to keep in condition.

The various clips are of course a matter of taste insofar as the average owner is concerned. If he plans to exhibit in the show ring, however, he must choose between the Continental and the English Saddle clips for a dog that is over a year old. In the Continental clip the hindquarters are shaved bare with rosettes optional on the hips, while in the English Saddle clip a short-clipped blanket of hair covers the hindquarters. Dogs under one year of age may be shown in naturally long coat except for the face, feet, and base of tail, which is shaved.

Official Standard for the Poodle

General Appearance, Carriage and Condition—That of a very active, intelligent and elegant-appearing dog, squarely built, well proportioned, moving soundly and carrying himself proudly. Properly clipped in the traditional fashion and carefully groomed, the Poodle has about him an air of distinction and dignity peculiar to himself.

Head and Expression—(a) *Skull*—Moderately rounded, with a slight but definite stop. Cheekbones and muscles flat. Length from occiput to stop about the same as length of muzzle. (b) *Muzzle*—Long, straight and fine, with slight chiseling under the eyes. Strong without lippiness. The chin definite enough to preclude snipiness. Teeth white, strong and with a scissors bite (c) *Eyes*—Very dark, oval in shape and set far enough apart and positioned to create an alert intelligent expression. (d) *Ears*—Hanging close to the head, set at or slightly below eye level. The ear leather is long, wide, and thickly feathered; however, the ear fringe should not be of excessive length.

Neck and Shoulders—Neck well proportioned, strong and long enough to permit the head to be carried high and with dignity. Skin snug at throat. The neck rises from strong, smoothly muscled shoulders. The shoulder blade is well laid back and approximately the same length as the upper foreleg.

Body—To insure the desirable squarely-built appearance, the length of body measured from the breastbone to the point of the rump approximates the height from the highest point of the shoulders to the ground. *(a) Chest*—Deep and moderately wide with well sprung ribs. *(b) Back*—The topline is level, neither sloping nor roached, from the highest point of the shoulder blade to the base of the tail, with the exception of a slight hollow just behind the shoulder. The loin is short, broad, and muscular.

Tail—Straight, set on high and carried up, docked of sufficient length to insure a balanced outline.

Legs—*(a) Forelegs*—Straight and parallel when viewed from the front. When viewed from the side the elbow is directly below the highest point of the shoulder. The pasterns are strong. Bone and muscle of both forelegs and hindlegs are in proportion to size of dog. *(b) Hindlegs*—Straight and parallel when viewed from the rear. Muscular with width in the region of the stifles which are well bent; femur and tibia are about equal in length; hock to heel short and perpendicular to the ground. When standing, the rear toes are only slightly behind the point of rump. The angulation of the hindquarters balances that of the forequarters.

Feet—The feet are rather small, oval in shape with toes well arched and cushioned on thick firm pads. Nails short but not excessively shortened. The feet turn neither in nor out. Dewclaws may be removed.

Coat—

(a) Quality—(1) curly: of naturally harsh texture, dense throughout. *(2) corded:* hanging in tight even cords of varying length; longer on mane or body coat, head, and ears; shorter on puffs, bracelets, and pompons.

(b) Clip—A Poodle under 12 months may be shown in the "puppy" clip. In all regular classes, Poodles 12 months or over must be shown in the "English Saddle" or "Continental" clip. In the Stud Dog and Brood Bitch classes and in a non-competitive Parade of Champions, Poodles may be shown in the "Sporting" clip. A Poodle shown in any other type of clip shall be disqualified.

(1) "Puppy": A Poodle under a year old may be shown in the "Puppy" clip with the coat long. The face, throat, feet and base of the tail are shaved. The entire shaven foot is visible. There is a pompon on the end of the tail. In order to give a neat appearance and a smooth unbroken line, shaping of the coat is permissible.

(2) "English Saddle": In the "English Saddle" clip, the face, throat, feet, forelegs and base of the tail are shaved, leaving puffs on the forelegs and a pompon on the end of the tail. The hindquarters are covered with a short blanket of hair except for a curved shaved area on each flank and two shaved bands on each hindleg. The entire shaven foot and a portion of the shaven leg above the puff are visible. The rest of the body is left in full coat but may be shaped in order to insure overall balance.

(3) "Continental": In the "Continental" clip the face, throat, feet and base of the tail are shaved. The hindquarters are shaved with pompons (optional) on the hips. The legs are shaved, leaving bracelets on the hindlegs and puffs on the forelegs. There is a pompon on the end of the tail. The entire shaven foot and a portion of the shaven foreleg above the puff are visible. The rest of the body is left in full coat but may be shaped in order to insure overall balance.

(4) "Sporting": In the "Sporting" clip a Poodle shall be shown with face, feet, throat, and base of tail shaved, leaving a scissored cap on the top of the head and a pompon on the end of the tail. The rest of the body and legs are clipped or scissored to follow the outline of the dog, leaving a short blanket of coat no longer than one inch in length. The hair on the legs may be slightly longer than that on the body.

In all clips the hair of the topknot may be left free or held in place by no more than three elastic bands. The hair is only of sufficient length to present a smooth outline.

Color—The coat is an even and solid color at the skin. In blues, grays, silvers, browns, cafe-au-laits, apricots, and creams the coat may show varying shades of the same color. This is frequently present in the somewhat darker feathering of the ears and in the tipping of the ruff. While clear colors are definitely preferred, such natural variation in the shading of the coat is not to be considered a fault. Brown and cafe-au-lait Poodles have liver-colored noses, eye rims and lips, dark toenails and dark amber eyes. Black, blue, gray, silver, cream and white Poodles have black noses, eye rims and lips, black or self-colored toenails and very dark eyes. In the apricots while the foregoing coloring is preferred, liver-colored noses, eye rims and lips, and amber eyes are permitted but are not desirable.

Parti-colored dogs shall be disqualified. The coat of a parti-colored dog is not an even solid color at the skin but is of two or more colors.

Gait—A straightforward trot with light springy action and strong hindquarters drive. Head and tail carried up. Sound effortless movement is essential.

Size—
The Standard Poodle is over 15 inches at the highest point of the shoulders. Any Poodle which is 15 inches or less in height shall be disqualified from competition as a Standard Poodle.
The Miniature Poodle is 15 inches or under at the highest point of the shoulders, with a minimum height in excess of 10 inches. Any Poodle which is over 15 inches or is 10 inches or less at the highest point of the shoulders shall be disqualified from competition as a Miniature Poodle.
The Toy Poodle is 10 inches or under at the highest point of the shoulders. Any Poodle which is more than 10 inches at the highest point of the shoulders shall be disqualified from competition as a Toy Poodle.

Value of Points—
General appearance, temperament, carriage and condition 30
Head, expression, ears, eyes, and teeth 20
Body, neck, legs, feet and tail 20
Gait 20
Coat, color and texture 10

Major Faults—Any distinct deviation from the desired characteristics described in the Breed Standard with particular attention to the following:
Temperament—Shyness or sharpness.
Muzzle—Undershot, overshot, wry mouth, lack of chin.
Eyes—Round, protuding, large, or very light.
Pigment—Color of nose, lips and eye rims incomplete, or of wrong color for color of dog.
Neck and Shoulders—Ewe neck, steep shoulders.
Tail—Set low, curled, or carried over the back.
Hindquarters—Cow hocks.
Feet—Paper or splayfoot.

DISQUALIFICATIONS
Clip—A dog in any type of clip other than those listed under Coat shall be disqualified.
Parti-colors—The coat of a parti-colored dog is not an even solid color at the skin but of two or more colors. Parti-colored dogs shall be disqualified.
Size—A dog over or under the height limits specified shall be disqualified.

Approved November 14, 1978

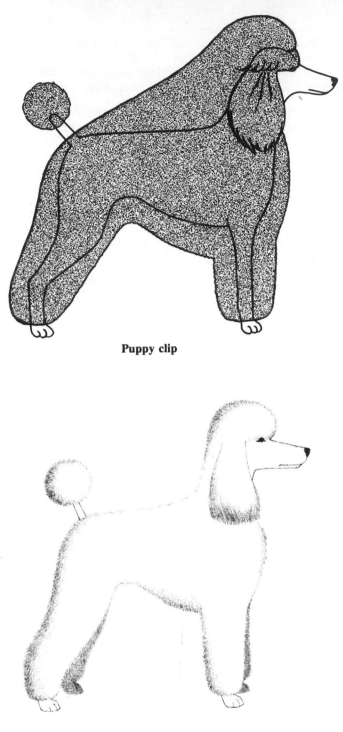

Puppy clip

Sporting clip

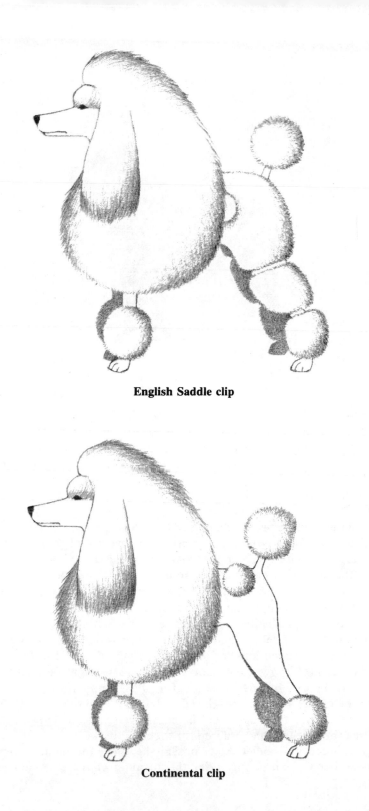

English Saddle clip

Continental clip

Schipperke

THE SCHIPPERKE originated in the Flemish provinces of Belgium and is sometimes erroneously described as a Dutch dog, due perhaps to a misconception regarding the location of Flanders, a part of which extends into northern France, and to the fact that previous to 1832 Belgium and Holland were at times united. Mr. Charles Huge, the Belgian judge, says: "The Schipperke is not derived from the Spitz or Pomeranian but is really a diminutive of the black sheepdog commonly called the 'Leauvenaar' which used to follow the wagons along our old highways in the provinces. The proof of this is that those specimens that are born with a tail carry it like the Groenendael."

In the mid-nineteenth century some of these forty-pound sheepdogs were still herding sheep in the neighborhood of Louvain, and from these both the Schipperke and the Groenendael have descended. The herd dog was gradually bred larger, and the Schipperke bred down to become that "excellent and faithful" little watchdog that we know. The breed has been known for several hundred years; in fact, it may claim the first known "specialty show," as it might be called, given for any breed. In 1690 a show for the Schipperkes of the Guild workmen was held in the Grand Palace of Brussels; the men were invited to bring their dogs and the hammered brass collars which even at that time custom had ordered for the Schipperke.

The breed was called Spits or Spitske then, the name Schipperke having been given it only after the forming of the specialty club in

1888, when it was chosen as more distinctive, and, as a compliment to Mr. Renssens, known as "the father of the Schipperke" because of his efforts to gain recognition for the breed. He was the owner of a canalboat line operating between Brussels and Antwerp and had observed that there were many Schipperkes used as guards on these boats. The name is Flemish for "little captain" and is properly pronounced "skeep-er-ker" (the last r almost silent). Though called a canalboat dog, the Schipperke was as popular with shoemakers and other workmen as it was on the canals.

The "legend of the Schipperke" relates that the custom of cutting the tails arose in 1609, and it tells the story of a shoemaker who, angered by the repeated thieving of his neighbor's dog, cut off his tail—thereby showing the improved appearance soon copied by others and continued to this day. There is no evidence that the breed was ever born tail-less; in fact, it seems that more dogs are born without tails now than earlier in their history. The Belgian Schipperkes Club has an amusing etching illustrating the legend "The Tail of the Schipperke."

The Schipperke has a close undercoat which keeps it warm even in American winters—the latter are far colder than those of its native land; and it sheds water and needs very little attention to keep in order. The dogs have been used to hunt, and at least one American, Mr. Culbertson, a well-known breeder of the past, wrote that he used them with great success on coons and possums in Minnesota.

The general appearance of the Schipperke is very distinctive, resembling no other breed closely. It has a short and thick-set body with foxy head, intelligent, keen expression, but not at all mean; is rather mischievous, the whole suggesting a dog with plenty of coat and an outstanding ruff and long culotte.

The career of the Schipperke as a fashionable pet began in 1885 when Queen Marie Henriette, wife of Leopold II, saw a Schipperke at a Brussels show and acquired it. Before this time it had been the companion of the lower classes.

The first dog in America was supposed to have been imported in 1888 by Mr. Walter J. Comstock of Providence. A few years later Mr. Frank Dole began showing Schips in the Miscellaneous Class. There was a specialty club, founded here about 1905, which died out during World War I. After 1918 there was little interest until, after several years of effort by a few fanciers, the present Schipperke Club of America was founded in 1929. The Schipperke Club Standard insists on the distinctive ruff and fairly heavy body coat, to prevent the breed from degenerating into the "black wire-haired terriers" described by Ash's dog book as undesirable. The dog must not resemble a small black Bull Terrier with the tail cut off. While usually an excellent ratter, the Schip is not a powerful fighter, though he can hold his own with most dogs of his weight and will tackle anything in defense of his household or of his master. He is not aware of the limitations of his size. As Caesar said: "the bravest of these were the Belgians."

Temperament is considered important in judging this breed in France and Belgium and means what we in America would call pep—a Schip without this is not true to type. A judge of the breed for fifty years has said that the most important thing in judging is the correct silhouette: "I first look to see if the dog has the correct silhouette. If not, he is nothing and I look no further. If he has, I look into further details beginning with the bone structure."

This breed is usually long-lived for a small one, many instances of dogs living to be fifteen and sixteen years old being recorded; one dog, bred in Rothesay, Scotland, was reputed to have lived twenty-one years. Schips are very fond of children and in some cases have served as guards; and they have taken the place, to some extent, of human nurses, so devoted are they to their small charges.

The Schipperke is often called "the best house dog" *(le meilleur chien de maison)*.

Official Standard for the Schipperke

Appearance and General Characteristics—Excellent and faithful little watchdog, suspicious of strangers. Active, agile, indefatigable, continually occupied with what is going on around him, careful of things that are given him to guard, very kind with children, knows the ways of the household; always curious to know what is going on behind closed doors or about any object that has been moved, betraying his impressions by his sharp bark and upstanding ruff, seeking the company of horses, a hunter of moles and other vermin; can be used to hunt, a good rabbit dog.

Color—Solid black.

Head—Foxlike, fairly wide, narrowing at the eyes, seen in profile slightly rounded, tapering muzzle not too elongated nor too blunt, not too much stop.

Nose—Small and black. *Eyes*—Dark brown, small, oval rather than round, neither sunken nor prominent. *Expression*—Should have a questioning expression: sharp and lively, not mean or wild. *Ears*—Very erect, small, triangular, placed high, strong enough not to be capable of being lowered except in line with the body. *Teeth*—Meeting evenly. A tight scissors bite is acceptable.

Neck—Strong and full, slightly arched, rather short.

Shoulders—Muscular and sloping.

Chest—Broad and deep in brisket.

Body—Short, thick-set and cobby. Broad behind the shoulders, seeming higher in front because of ruff. Back strong, short, straight and level or slightly sloping down toward rump. Ribs well sprung. *Loins*—Muscular and well drawn up from the brisket but not to such an extent as to cause a weak and leggy appearance of the hindquarters. *Forelegs*—Straight under body, with bone in proportion, but not coarse. *Hindquarters*—Somewhat lighter than the foreparts, but muscular, powerful, with rump well rounded, tail docked to no more than 1 inch in length. *Feet*—Small, round and tight (not splayed), nails straight, strong and short.

Coat—Abundant and slightly harsh to the touch, short on the ears and on the front of legs and on the hocks, fairly short on the body, but longer around neck beginning back of the ears, and forming a ruff and a cape; a jabot extending down between the front legs, also longer on rear where it forms a culotte, the points turning inward. Undercoat dense and short on body, very dense around neck making ruff stand out. Culotte should be as long as the ruff.

Weight—Up to 18 pounds.

FAULTS

Light eyes; large round prominent eyes; ears too long or too rounded; narrow head and elongated muzzle; too blunt muzzle; domed skull; smooth short coat with short ruff and culotte; lack of undercoat; curly or silky coat; body coat more than three (3) inches long; slightly overshot or undershot; swayback; Bull Terrier shaped head; straight hocks. Straight stifles and shoulders; cowhocks; feet turning in or out; legs not straight when viewed from front. Lack of distinction between length of coat, ruff and culotte.

DISQUALIFICATIONS

Any color other than solid black.
Drop or semi-erect ears.
Badly overshot or undershot.

Approved May 12, 1959

Tibetan Terrier

As THE NAME indicates, Tibetan Terriers came from the land of Tibet where, so it is said, they were bred and raised in the monasteries by the lamas almost 2,000 years ago. Originating in the Lost Valley ("lost" when the access road was destroyed in the 14th century by a major earthquake) they were prized as companions and "luck bringers" for those fortunate enough to own them.

So inaccessible was the Lost Valley, so hazardous the journey to and from it, that the occasional visitor was often given a dog to safeguard him on the return trip to the outside world. No dog of this kind was ever sold, as no family would tempt fate by selling part of their "luck", but they were presented as a mark of esteem or a measure of gratitude for favors or services rendered.

Thus it came about that the late Dr. A.R.H. Greig, a practising physician in India in the 1920s, was given a dog by a grateful Tibetan whose ailing wife she had treated. Dr. Greig subsequently bred and raised a number of Tibetan Terriers in India, many of them descended from puppies sent to her by His Holiness the Dalai Lama in appreciation of her interest in their cherished breed. When Dr. Greig returned to England, she established the famous Lamleh Kennel there. Recognized in India in the 1920s and in England in 1937, the breed is now exhibited at shows almost the world over.

Dr. and Mrs. Henry S. Murphy of Great Falls, Virginia, brought the first "official" Tibetan Terrier to the United States in 1956, an import from the Lamleh Kennel in England with a Kennel Club (London) pedigree. Since then the breed has attracted fanciers from Canada to Florida, and from coast to coast.

The Tibetan Terrier is not actually a "terrier". He does not have the terrier disposition, nor does he burrow into the earth ("la terre" in French) as terriers were originally expected to do. This breed was called "terrier" because it was of a size widely associated with terriers. The Tibetan people called them "Luck Bringers" or "Holy Dogs", neither of which seemed suitable as a breed name in the Western world of dogs.

Tibetan Terriers were neither guard dogs nor herding dogs in Tibet. They were valued as companions, and were treated like children of the family. Like the children, they eagerly assisted in taking care of the family's property, their flocks and their herds, but these dogs were not raised for utilitarian purposes. The breed was kept pure-bred, as any mismating might bring bad luck to the family and might even be blamed for any village misfortune.

This is an exceptionally healthy breed, probably as a result of the rigorous natural selection process in their recent homeland. Tibet has one of the most difficult populated terrains in the world, and one of the most dramatic climates. Lhasa, for example, is exceedingly cold in the winter but often reaches 85° F. in the summer. The Tibetan Terrier is prepared to enjoy a blizzard, thanks to his profuse double coat, facial fur to protect his eyes from snow, and "snowshoe" feet, well furnished and suited for walking on the crust. Surprisingly, they do not seem to be at all upset by a hot, humid summer—simply relaxing for a nap during the worst part of such days.

The people of Tibet made no effort to eliminate any of the many colors found in this breed, believing that good health and a delightful temperament were far more important than coat color. It is hoped that Western breeders will continue this sensible breeding program, and that the Tibetan Terrier will continue to be an exceptional companion and friend of man — healthy, gay, intelligent and affectionate.

The Tibetan Terrier was admitted to registration in The American Kennel Club Stud Book on May 1, 1973, and to regular show classification in the Non-Sporting Group at AKC shows October 3, 1973.

Official Standard for the
Tibetan Terrier

Skull and Head—Skull of medium length, not broad or coarse, narrowing slightly from ear to eye, not domed but not absolutely flat between the ears. The malar bones are curved, but should not be overdeveloped so as to bulge. There should be a marked stop in front of the eyes, but this must not be exaggerated. The head should be well furnished with long hair, falling forward over the eyes. The lower jaw should carry a small but not over-exaggerated amount of beard. Jaws between the canines should form a distinct curve. The length from the eye to tip of nose should be equal to that from eye to base of skull, not broad or massive.

Nose—Black. Any color other than black shall disqualify.

Eyes—Large, dark, neither prominent nor sunken; should be set fairly wide apart. Eyelids dark.

Ears—Pendant, not too close to the head, "V" shaped, not too large; heavily feathered.

Mouth—Level by preference but a slight undershot should not be penalized.

Forequarters—Legs straight, heavily furnished.

Body—Compact and powerful. Length from point of shoulder to root of tail equal to height at withers. Well ribbed up. Loin slightly arched.

Hindquarters—Heavily furnished, hocks well let down.

Feet—The feet should be large, round, and heavily furnished with hair between the toes and pads. The dog should stand well down on its pads.

Tail—Medium length, set on fairly high and carried in a gay curl over the back. Very well feathered. There is often a kink near the tip.

Coat—Double-coated. The undercoat fine wool, the top coat profuse, fine, but not silky or woolly; long; either straight or waved.

Color—Any color or colors including white.

Weight and Size—Average weight 22 to 23 pounds, but may be 18 to 30 pounds. Height from 14 to 16 inches.

Faults—Poor coat; mouth very undershot or overshot; a weak snipy foreface.

DISQUALIFICATION

Nose any color other than black.

Approved June 12, 1973

Dandie Dinmont Terrier — *Allen*

Skye Terrier — *Goodman*

Cairn Terriers — *Cumbers*

Staffordshire Bull Terriers — *Cumbers*

West Highland White Terriers — *Cumbers*

Australian Terrier — *courtesy, Purina*

Affenpinscher — *Anderson*

Papillon — *Ashbey*

Toy Manchester Terrier — *Gilbert*

Chihuahua — *courtesy, Purina*

Brussels Griffons — *Cumbers*

Pekingese — *Thompson*

Miniature Pinschers — *Dakan*

Italian Greyhounds — *McCauley*

631

Maltese — *Allen*

Japanese Chin - *Cumbers*

Pomeranians

Pug — *Allen*

Shih Tzu — *Allen*

Yorkshire Terrier puppies — *Cumbers*

Chow Chow — *Anderson*

Bulldog — *Anderson*

635

Keeshonden — *Allen*

French Bulldog — *Allen*

Bichon Frises — *Cumbers*

Boston Terrier — *Thompson*

Lhasa Apso

Standard Poodles

— Ludwig

— Ashbey

Dalmatian — *Callea*

Tibetan Terriers — *Cumbers*

The Miscellaneous Class

AUTHORITIES acknowledge that in total throughout the world there are several hundred distinct breeds of pure-bred dog. Those officially recognized for registration in the Stud Book of the American Kennel Club are presented in the body of this book.

The AKC does not, per se, encourage the admittance of "new" breeds to the Stud Book. However, it does provide for a regular method of development which may result in such recognition.

Briefly stated, the requirement for admission to the Stud Book is clear and categorical proof that a substantial, sustained nationwide interest and activity in the breed exists. This includes an active parent club maintaining a breed registry, with serious and expanding breeding activity over a wide geographic area.

When in the judgment of the Board of Directors such interest and activity exists, a breed is admitted to the Miscellaneous Class. Breeds in the Miscellaneous Class may compete in AKC obedience trials and earn obedience titles. They may also compete at conformation shows, but here are limited to competition in the Miscellaneous Class and are not eligible for championship points.

When the Board of Directors is satisfied that a breed is continuing a healthy, dynamic growth in the Miscellaneous Class, it may be admitted to registration in the Stud Book and the opportunity to compete in regular classes.

Presently, the breeds in the Miscellaneous Class are:

Australian Cattle Dogs
Australian Kelpies
Border Collies
Cavalier King Charles Spaniels
Miniature Bull Terriers
Pharaoh Hounds
Spinoni Italiani

Caring for Your Dog

How to Keep A Dog Alive,
Healthy, Happy, and Well-Behaved

This special section has been prepared in cooperation with faculty members of the New York State College of Veterinary Medicine at Cornell University and the School of Veterinary Medicine at the University of Pennsylvania. Members upon whose studies information has been based include (in alphabetical order):

From Cornell—Dr. Gustavo D. Aguirre (now at the University of Pennsylvania); Dr. Max J. G. Appel; the late Dr. James A. Baker, director of the Cornell Research Laboratory for Diseases of Dogs; Dr. Leland E. Carmichael; Dr. Lisle George; Dr. Frederick B. Hutt; Dr. George Lust; Dr. Ben E. Sheffy; and Dr. Hadley C. Stephenson.

From the University of Pennsylvania—Ruth E. Blank, D.V.M.; M. Josephine Deubler, V.M.., Ph.D.; Peter J. Felsburg, V.M.D., Ph.D.; David H. Knight, D.V.M.; David S. Kronfeld, B.V.Sc., M.V.Sc., Ph.D.; Donald F. Patterson, D.V.M., Ph.D.; and David F. Senior, B.V.Sc.

The section on Nutrition and Feeding was prepared by Dr. Sheffy. The section on Genetic Diseases represents portions excerpted from an article, "New Developments in Canine Medical Genetics" by Dr. Patterson that appeared in *Pure-Bred Dogs —AK Gazette,* October 1975.

SIXTY-THREE DAY WHELPING TABLE

	1	2	3	4	5	6	7	8	9	10	11	12	13	14	15	16	17	18	19	20	21	22	23	24	25	26	27	28	29	30	31
Service January	1	2	3	4	5	6	7	8	9	10	11	12	13	14	15	16	17	18	19	20	21	22	23	24	25	26	27	28	29	30	31
Whelping March	5	6	7	8	9	10	11	12	13	14	15	16	17	18	19	20	21	22	23	24	25	26	27	28	29	30	31	Apr. 1	2	3	4
Service February	1	2	3	4	5	6	7	8	9	10	11	12	13	14	15	16	17	18	19	20	21	22	23	24	25	26	27	28			
Whelping April	5	6	7	8	9	10	11	12	13	14	15	16	17	18	19	20	21	22	23	24	25	26	27	28	29	30	May 1	2			
Service March	1	2	3	4	5	6	7	8	9	10	11	12	13	14	15	16	17	18	19	20	21	22	23	24	25	26	27	28	29	30	31
Whelping May	3	4	5	6	7	8	9	10	11	12	13	14	15	16	17	18	19	20	21	22	23	24	25	26	27	28	29	30	31	June 1	2
Service April	1	2	3	4	5	6	7	8	9	10	11	12	13	14	15	16	17	18	19	20	21	22	23	24	25	26	27	28	29	30	
Whelping June	3	4	5	6	7	8	9	10	11	12	13	14	15	16	17	18	19	20	21	22	23	24	25	26	27	28	29	30	July 1	2	
Service May	1	2	3	4	5	6	7	8	9	10	11	12	13	14	15	16	17	18	19	20	21	22	23	24	25	26	27	28	29	30	31
Whelping July	3	4	5	6	7	8	9	10	11	12	13	14	15	16	17	18	19	20	21	22	23	24	25	26	27	28	29	30	31	Aug. 1	2
Service June	1	2	3	4	5	6	7	8	9	10	11	12	13	14	15	16	17	18	19	20	21	22	23	24	25	26	27	28	29	30	
Whelping August	3	4	5	6	7	8	9	10	11	12	13	14	15	16	17	18	19	20	21	22	23	24	25	26	27	28	29	30	31	Sept. 1	
Service July	1	2	3	4	5	6	7	8	9	10	11	12	13	14	15	16	17	18	19	20	21	22	23	24	25	26	27	28	29	30	31
Whelping September	2	3	4	5	6	7	8	9	10	11	12	13	14	15	16	17	18	19	20	21	22	23	24	25	26	27	28	29	30	Oct. 1	2
Service August	1	2	3	4	5	6	7	8	9	10	11	12	13	14	15	16	17	18	19	20	21	22	23	24	25	26	27	28	29	30	31
Whelping October	3	4	5	6	7	8	9	10	11	12	13	14	15	16	17	18	19	20	21	22	23	24	25	26	27	28	29	30	31	Nov. 1	2
Service September	1	2	3	4	5	6	7	8	9	10	11	12	13	14	15	16	17	18	19	20	21	22	23	24	25	26	27	28	29	30	
Whelping November	3	4	5	6	7	8	9	10	11	12	13	14	15	16	17	18	19	20	21	22	23	24	25	26	27	28	29	30	Dec. 1	2	
Service October	1	2	3	4	5	6	7	8	9	10	11	12	13	14	15	16	17	18	19	20	21	22	23	24	25	26	27	28	29	30	31
Whelping December	3	4	5	6	7	8	9	10	11	12	13	14	15	16	17	18	19	20	21	22	23	24	25	26	27	28	29	30	31	Jan. 1	2
Service November	1	2	3	4	5	6	7	8	9	10	11	12	13	14	15	16	17	18	19	20	21	22	23	24	25	26	27	28	29	30	
Whelping January	3	4	5	6	7	8	9	10	11	12	13	14	15	16	17	18	19	20	21	22	23	24	25	26	27	28	29	30	31	Feb. 1	
Service December	1	2	3	4	5	6	7	8	9	10	11	12	13	14	15	16	17	18	19	20	21	22	23	24	25	26	27	28	29	30	31
Whelping February	2	3	4	5	6	7	8	9	10	11	12	13	14	15	16	17	18	19	20	21	22	23	24	25	26	27	28	March 1	2	3	4

Breeding, Whelping, and Care of Newborn Puppies

THE SUCCESSFUL BREEDING of dogs is both an art and a science requiring a fundamental knowledge of anatomy and physiology (the functions of living organisms or their parts). There are a number of principles which must be followed to avoid major problems.

Male Reproductive Physiology

Male puppies become fertile after six months of age and reach mature fertility by 12–15 months of age. Healthy stud dogs usually remain sexually active and fertile up to eight to ten years old. During the period of fertility, the adult male dog is able to mate at any time; however, fertility will be reduced if breeding is more frequent than twice weekly.

Female Reproductive Physiology

Bitches first have *estrus* (also known as "season" and "heat"), sometime after six months of age; however, this can occur as late as 18 months of age. Estrus will recur at intervals of between four and eight months until late in life. The intervals vary with breeds and individuals.

During estrus the female will accept the male and is fertile. The bitch's estrus cycle is much slower than most species. The cycle has been divided into four periods:

(1) During *proestrus* (approximately nine days), the female is attractive to the male, has a bloody vaginal discharge and the external genitalia are swollen. However, the female will not accept the male in breeding.

(2) During *estrus* (approximately nine days), the female will accept the male. Ovulation usually occurs in the first 48 hours; however, this is extremely variable. Fertilization takes place during estrus, three days after ovulation.

(3) *Diestrus* (60–90 days) follows estrus when the reproductive tract is under control of the hormone progesterone. This occurs whether the dog becomes pregnant or not. Pseudocyesis (false pregnancy) is often seen during diestrus.

(4) *Anestrus* follows diestrus and is the period of no sexual activity, which lasts between three and eight months.

Breeding

If a bitch is not intended for breeding, various forms of contraception are available. Surgical removal of the ovaries and uterus (spay) is 100% effective and permanent. Oral contraceptives recently made available have the advantage of maintaining fertility if subsequent breeding is desired. The advantages and disadvantages of each method should be discussed with a veterinarian.

Contraception can be achieved by isolating the bitch during estrus; however, constant vigilance is necessary to prevent breeding. Estrogens can prevent pregnancy after unwanted breeding, but their use is inadvisable if the bitch is to be preserved for breeding at future heats.

The decision to breed and raise dogs should not be taken lightly. America faces a massive loose dog problem, so the breeder must be certain of a market for the progeny. The sire and dam should be chosen carefully to avoid genetic faults. This ensures the highest quality of progeny.

To avoid the stress of pregnancy and lactation in a young, growing dog, it is customary to not breed at the first heat. To allow sufficient time for recuperation between pregnancies, bitches usually are not bred on consecutive heats. Breeding at the first heat and on consecutive heats is possible; however feeding and management must be excellent to avoid problems.

Prior to breeding, the bitch should be vaccinated against distemper, hepatitis, leptospirosis, and PI_3 virus. The body condition should be good but not overweight. Some nutritionists believe that steady weight increase for three weeks, beginning just prior to breeding, may increase fertility. A control program for internal (worms) and external (fleas and ticks) parasites should be enforced at all times. Prior to breeding the bitch should be tested for parasites and treated accordingly.

The bitch should be tested for brucellosis prior to breeding. It is impractical to test a male dog prior to breeding each female if he breeds many. If the stud is kept separate from pregnant, whelping, or nursing bitches and tested twice yearly, this should be sufficient.

Breeding management varies among breeders and breeds. Most commonly, dogs are bred between the tenth and fourteenth day after the onset of estrus. Breeding is repeated two or three times, two to three days apart. In some dogs, the signs of heat are less obvious. In these cases, microscopic examination of vaginal smears can be a useful guide to the peak fertile period.

Females are usually less inhibited by a new environment, so the bitch is best taken to the stud. The first time a young male is used, breeding will be less tedious if the bitch is experienced.

646

Artificial insemination is a relatively simple procedure which can be used if a natural breeding is impractical. Under special circumstances, artificial insemination is approved by the American Kennel Club when performed by a veterinarian under controlled conditions. The recent development of frozen semen and the possibility of semen banks may soon facilitate breeding between dogs separated by great distances.

Gestation

Gestation (pregnancy) in the bitch lasts about 63 days. Pregnancy diagnosis can be made by abdominal palpation three to four weeks after breeding. The special feeding requirements of the pregnant bitch is described in the section on nutrition.

Milk may be expressed from the breasts a day or two prior to whelping. There should be mild enlargement of the vulva and a slight drop in body temperature. The bitch may refuse to eat and commence nest building.

A whelping box should be prepared which is sufficiently large for the bitch to stretch out comfortably. It should have low sides and be placed in a warm, dry, draft-free, secluded place. Newspapers make good bedding material.

Whelping

A normal, healthy bitch can give birth to puppies easily, with no help required. Each puppy is contained in a placental membrane, which must be removed before the puppy can begin to breathe. The mother usually does this by eating these membranes, then promptly cleaning up the puppy, keeping it warm, allowing it to suckle, and, by licking the puppy, which stimulates its excretory organs. Without this stimulation, the puppy cannot defecate or urinate easily and will not do so well.

The situation should, of course, have been discussed with your veterinarian, and if anything at all seems abnormal during or after the whelping, you will want to telephone for advice.

Usually all goes well, and after all of the puppies are born, cleaned, and are nursing, the bitch will be happy, proud, and resting. Feeding her properly during lactation is described under Nutrition. The veterinarian may wish to give her an injection of oxytocin to contract the uterus and initiate involution.

Abnormal conditions which signify trouble are: indications of extreme pain, trembling, shivering, collapse, vomiting, and straining in labor longer than three hours over one pup.

If the mother seems unwilling or unable to care for her newborn puppy, it may have to be rescued by the owner. First in importance is breathing: each puppy is inside a placental sac, and, after it is born, has no supply of oxygen. It can remain for eight minutes—no longer—before enclosing membranes must be removed from the face region, at least if the mother has not done this already. If the entire procedure of taking care of the puppy or puppies must be attempted by the owner, membranes must be removed, the umbilical cord tied (dental floss is fine for this) and cut about two inches from the abdomen, and iodine applied to the cut end. Circulation should be stimulated by drying the puppy with a towel, rubbing briskly. (See also the coverage of Hand Feeding in the Nutrition Section.)

The newborn puppy is unable to control its body temperature and should be kept in an environmental temperature of 85°F. Chilling during these early days of life will stress a puppy and predispose it to infectious disease. The environmental temperature can be controlled using a towel-covered warm water bowl, a well insulated electric pad, or an electric light bulb.

Until the bitch can nurse puppies properly, those born first may have to be given some fluids by hand. If hand-feeding or other care of newborn puppies is necessary, refer to the section under Nutrition in which it is described in detail.

Some bitches may simulate pregnancy and show all of the typical signs of lactation (false pregnancy or pseudocyesis). This condition is thought to be induced by both progesterone and prolactin.

Colostrum

Colostrum is the first milk produced by the bitch after whelping. Every puppy should have colostrum as early as possible after birth, and certainly during the first 24 hours of life. Colostrum contains a number of substances, including immunoglobulins that will protect the puppy against all of the infectious diseases to which the mother is immune. The absorption of intact immunoglobulins decreases and becomes impossible within a few days following birth.

Food for the puppy and the mother during weaning is discussed in detail under Nutrition.

Eclampsia is an uncommon but serious condition that may occur in lactating bitches if there is an excessive loss of calcium. It is discussed under Nutrition.

CANINE IMMUNIZATION PROGRAMS

VACCINE	AGE TO VACCINATE
Canine Distemper Virus	First vaccination at 6 to 8 weeks; second vaccination at 12 to 16 weeks; revaccinate annually. Ideally, start at 6 to 8 weeks; second vaccination at 10 to 12 weeks; third vaccination at 14 to 16 weeks; revaccinate annually.
Measles Virus	Vaccinate at 6 to 8 weeks. Important dog is vaccinated with canine distemper vaccine between 12 to 16 weeks. Do not use in adult dogs or pregnant bitches.
Infectious Canine Hepatitis Virus (Canine adenovirus 1; CAV1)	Usually given in combination with canine distemper vaccine (same schedule).
Infectious Canine Laryngotracheitis Virus (Canine adenovirus 2; CAV2)	New vaccine. Vaccination with infectious canine hepatitis vaccine will protect against clinical disease with CAV2. Now CAV2 vaccine used as CAV1 vaccine.
Canine Parainfluenza Virus	Usually given in combination with canine distemper and cinine infectious hepatitis vaccine. If given alone, at least two doses are recommended at 4 week intervals. Revaccinate annually.
Rabies Virus (NASPHV Recommendations)	*Modified live vaccines:* If first vaccination between 3 to 12 months of age, revaccinate in 1 year, then every 3 years. If over 1 year of age at first vaccination, revaccinate every 3 years. *Inactivated vaccines:* Trimmune—same as above. Others—first vaccination at 3 to 4 months, revaccinate annually.

VACCINE	AGE TO VACCINATE
Canine Leptospirosis	Usually given in combination with canine distemper—canine infectious hepatitis vaccine.
Canine Herpesvirus	No vaccine available.
Canine Brucellosis	No vaccine available.

Housing and Sanitation

DOGS adapt surprisingly well into many environments. They are found in small apartments of large cities, where the dog's bed, food, and water all are kept in the apartment and exercise and elimination are with a leash, or, in suburbs or country, where the dog may have a house of its own and a yard for exercise.

If a new puppy is brought into a home or apartment as a house pet, the situation will be different from that of a puppy bought as an addition to a large breeding kennel or to an established pack of hunting dogs. Such kennels are usually in separate quarters, and may be under the supervision of personnel. The word "kennel" may refer to one dog house or to housing accommodations for many dogs.

Puppies generally are not sold until they are old enough to be weaned. Until that time they need to be kept at a warmer temperature than do older dogs. This is discussed fully in the section concerning orphan puppies under Nutrition. No puppy, even though it belongs to a hardy breed, should be taken suddenly from a warm whelping pen and the body warmth of other puppies and its mother, to be placed suddenly outside in a bitter cold environment. It needs to be acclimated gradually, and some breeds never could survive being kept out of doors in a cold climate. This should be determined before the puppy is obtained.

All dogs should be kept at comfortable temperatures in surroundings that permit cleanliness and that are as free as possible from annoying insects, such as mosquitoes and flies. Ideally, this is done in a special building screened against pests, to prevent transmission of such parasites as heartworm in regions where they exist by protecting dogs against mosquito bites. Of course, the large areas necessary for large dogs to run cannot be screened easily or inexpensively.

From the sanitary point of view, excreta must be removed daily, or intestinal parasites and microorganisms may flourish to cause disease. The greatest aid to good sanitation is to be able to wash the dog's living quarters with hot water. Those planning construction of new kennel facilities should see that specifications include runs pitched one-fourth inch to the foot in order that excreta can be flushed away more efficiently.

Wherever the dog is kept, consideration should be given to its environment. Near a busy highway, exhaust fumes from passing vehicles could be dangerous, especially if there is exposure to carbon monoxide or leaded gasoline. Gas leaks or noxious fumes in the air could be a source of trouble. If chewed by an exploring, curious puppy or dog, lead paint, old bits of lead, or exposed electric wires all can be dangerous. Constant dampness or exposure to full burning sun or to penetrating winds should be avoided. In order to avoid dampness or a heavy runoff of rain, an outdoor doghouse should be raised somewhat above the ground. It could be placed upon a platform, or sturdy runners could be used at each side.

Especial caution should be taken to protect the puppy—and all dogs for that matter—from antifreeze (ethylene glycol) poisoning. Containers of antifreeze should be securely shut and stored in a place inaccessible to your dogs. Also, make certain that the dogs are not in the vicinity when antifreeze is being drained.

Before a young puppy is brought into its new home, some arrangements already should have been made for its reception. At first, the new puppy might be more comfortable with a bed made temporarily in a box or carton. Washable or disposable clean bedding could be provided by the use of old sheets, towels, or newspapers. A ticking alarm clock is said to help pacify a lonely puppy, as is a hot water bottle with water that never is hot enough to burn the skin.

When the puppy grows larger, its own basket, with a washable blanket or cushion, should be obtained. This should be kept out of drafts and not placed close to a stove or radiator that may become too hot. The puppy may graduate in time to its own dog house. Single kennels are available that can be heated electrically and have swinging doors to permit the dog freedom of attached runs. In kennels out of doors, bedding can be excelsior or newspapers.

Many types of portable and folding kennels are available for dogs that are taken to shows.

Nutrition and Feeding

INTRODUCTION

NUTRITION, the act of being nourished, is named from the Latin word *nutritio,* meaning feeding. In order to obtain the energy necessary to maintain life and to reproduce itself, each living plant and animal must take food materials into its system and must be able to utilize these nutriments, as well as to eliminate the waste products. Men and animals must obtain their food from eating plants, or from eating other animals which have eaten plants.

From soil, water, and air, plants receive (through their roots, stems and leaves) the chemicals which they can convert into carbohydrates, proteins, and fats. These nutrients are found in various plants in the forms of starches, sugars, legumes, seeds, nuts, berries, fruits, fibers, and other diverse substances.

Atoms of the original chemical elements utilized by plants reappear in numerous chemical combinations or compounds. These are seen first in various cells that make up the plant and then are found in cells that compose all of the tissues and organs, bones, and blood, that make up man and animals which have eaten these plants.

The chemical elements utilized by plants are important to all forms of animal life. Some of these elements include: carbon, with the chemical symbol C, and oxygen, O, taken from air in the form of carbon dioxide, CO_2, the chemical formula that implies two atoms of oxygen, or dioxide, and one of carbon; hydrogen, H, and oxygen, O, form water, H_2O, the first chemical formula learned by most persons.

Dissolved in water, which carries them into the plant, are chemicals from the soil: nitrogen, N; phosphorus, P; potassium, K, for *kalium*; as well as various minerals, such as copper, Cu for *cupric*; iron, Fe for *ferrous*; calcium, Ca; salt, NaCl, for the compound sodium chloride, *natron* and chloride.

In nature, the food-chain consists of taking chemicals from air, earth, and water, of using them for perpetuating the life cycles of various living species, and eventually, of returning them in forms that allow them to be reused, or as it is termed today, recycled. Biodegradable substances will decompose through bacterial action. The nitrogen and phosphorous content of soil in cultivation rapidly can be depleted unless nitrogen-fixing bacteria are present. To make or keep soil fertile, fertilizers are added that contain properly balanced amounts of the chemicals nitrogen, phosphorous, and potassium, and other components necessary for a particular crop.

Cells of man and animals similarly can become depleted unless the proper amounts of the right chemicals are added under the right physical circumstances.

To believe, as some are being taught, that "all foods which contain chemicals are poisonous" is not fully to understand that every substance on earth, whether it be a fluid, solid, or gas, is chemical in nature. The problem is to have the right chemical in the right proportion at the right time and place to allow normal development.

METABOLISM, taken from the Greek *metaballein,* meaning to change or alter, describes transformation of materials contained in food into substances needed for energy to produce living cells in the body, to maintain these cells in their many diverse functions, to destroy worn out or damaged cells at the proper time, and to dispose of waste products. The two main processes of metabolism are: **anabolism,** or building up of tissues, and **catabolism,** breaking down of tissues.

A person speaks of feeding a dog, or a family. In reality, each one of the billions of different cells that make up the body of a person or a dog must receive the correct amount of the proper nutrients in order to remain healthy and to function efficiently. For example, each red blood cell must be replaced in 120 days, and to maintain the proper number of 6,000,000 per cubic millimeter, about 5,000,000 must be produced every second.

In nature, three principal types of food are available, in addition to minerals and vitamins which are essential:

1. Carbohydrates. In plants, the carbohydrates can be stored as starches and sugars. When carbohydrates are oxidized, energy and heat are obtained. In animals, excess carbohydrate is stored, first as glycogen in the liver and muscles, and, if there is still an excess, as fat for future use.

2. Fats. These are made up of carbon, hydrogen, and oxygen, with glycerin and certain fatty acids. They are classified as **hard fats,** found in beef and mutton; **soft fats,** found in lard and butter; and **liquid fats,** in oils of seeds, nuts, and olives. Fats can supply more than twice as much energy as carbohydrates or protein because carbon and hydrogen give off great heat when burned. Fats have a fuel value of 4,040 calories per pound. Most fats contain some vitamin A, necessary for growth, while vitamin D is found in butter, cream, or fish liver oils.

Table I

NUTRIENT REQUIREMENTS OF DOGS[1]
(Amounts per pound or kilogram of body weight per day)

WEIGHT OF DOGS lb	Kg	MAINTENANCE Total Kcal per day[2]	GROWTH Total Kcal per day[2]
5	2.3	260	520
10	4.5	440	880
15	6.8	585	1170
30	13.6	990	1980
50	22.7	1450	2900
75	34.1	1950	3900
100	45.5	2450	4900

	Per lb	Per Kg	Per lb	Per Kg
Protein (gm)	2.25	5.0	4.5	10.0
Fat (gm)	0.70	1.5	1.4	3.0
Linoleic acid (gm)	0.1	0.22	0.2	0.44
Carbohydrate[3]	—	—	—	—
Minerals				
Calcium (mg)	120	265	240	530
Phosphorus (mg)	100	220	200	440
Potassium (mg)	65	144	130	288
Sodium chloride (mg)	91	200	182	400
Magnesium (mg)	6.4	14	12.8	28
Iron (mg)	0.6	1.32	1.2	2.64
Copper (mg)	0.07	0.16	0.14	0.32
Manganese (mg)	0.05	0.11	0.10	0.22
Zinc (mg)	1.0	2.2	2.0	4.4
Iodine (mg)	0.015	0.033	0.03	0.066
Selenium (ug)	1.1	2.42	2.2	4.84
Vitamins				
Vitamin A (IU)	50	110	100	220
Vitamin D (IU)	5	11	10	22
Vitamin E (ug)	0.55	1.2	1.1	2.4
Thiamin (ug)	11.0	24	22	48
Riboflavin (ug)	22.0	48	44	96
Pyridoxine (ug)	11.0	24	22	48
Pantothenic acid (ug)	100	220	200	440
Niacin (ug)	114	250	228	500
Folic acid (ug)	1.8	4	3.6	8
Vitamin B_{12} (ug)	0.5	1.1	1.0	2.2
Biotin (ug)	1.0	2.2	2.0	4.4
Choline (mg)	11.8	26	23.6	52

1976 modification by Cornell Research Laboratory for Diseases of Dogs of data taken from NAS-NRC Publication No. 8, Nutrient Requirements of Dogs, revised, 1974.

[1]Symbols: Kg = kilogram; gm = gram; mg = milligram; ug = microgram; IU = International Unit.
[2]Values listed are for gross or calculated energy. Biologically available energy is ordinarily 75–85 per cent of the calculated kilocalories, referred to as kcalories.
[3]Carbohydrates as such have not been shown to be required. As a common ingredient of most dog foods it serves as an excellent source of energy.

3. Proteins. A daily intake of proteins is necessary to furnish a constant supply of amino acids to living cells. Unlike carbohydrates and fats, very little protein is stored in the body in a form readily available for future use.

4. Minerals. Those important for nutrition are listed in Table I. Minerals found in soil come naturally from the crushing or dissolving of various types of rocks.

5. Vitamins. Vitamin, from the Latin *vita* for life and *amine,* meaning an organic compound formed from living organs and containing nitrogen, is a term used to denote a variety of organic substances found in foods of many types and which are necessary for normal metabolic processes. Some vitamins are water-soluble, others are fat-soluble. Those necessary in the diet of dogs are listed in Table I.

Food is taken into the body through the mouth, where, in man, the first process of digestion begins. Saliva contains the enzyme **ptyalin,** which changes some cooked carbohydrates into dextrin and maltose.

The dog does not chew its food to any extent, but usually swallows it rapidly. Thereafter, the process in man and dog is similar. Food passes through the esophagus to the stomach, where contractions of muscles mix it with gastric juice. Gastric juice contains enzymes and acids, especially hydrochloric acid. These substances curdle milk, soften albumen, and help break down fibers and tissues. They also help destroy harmful bacteria which may be present on or in the food, unless the contamination is too heavy or the bacteria are particularly resistant.

Digestion of proteins, such as found in lean meats, egg white, peas, and beans, begins in the stomach. The food is changed into a thick liquid called **chyme,** and in this form passes to the small intestine.

Digestive fluids, including pancreatic juice from the pancreas, intestinal juice from the walls of the small intestine, and bile from the liver stored in the gall bladder, mix with the food in the small intestine. A number of specific enzymes are elaborated. The enzyme **trypsin** breaks down proteins into various amino acids, and others change starches into simple sugars or split fats into fatty acids and glycerins.

When completely digested, the absorbable nutrient substances pass into the body through the walls of the small intestine. Undigestible materials pass into the large intestine and are eliminated.

Medically speaking, the mouth, nasal and air passages, and other natural openings of the body, with the stomach, intestines, and organs into which they lead, are extensions of the skin, and, technically, are considered external surfaces, because there is continuous passage throughout. On the other side of the mucosa that line these passages

Table II

RECOMMENDED NUTRIENT CONTENT OF DRY DOG FOODS
(In percentage or specific amounts per pound or kilogram)

NUTRIENT	DRY MATTER BASIS Per cent		DRY TYPE DOG FOOD Per cent	
Dry matter	100.0		90.0	
Water	0.0		10.0	
Protein	26.6		24.0	
Fat	9.0		8.0	
Linoleic acid	1.1		1.0	
Fiber[1]	4.0		3.6	
Minerals				
Calcium	1.1		1.0	
Phosphorus	0.9		0.8	
Potassium	0.9		0.8	
Sodium chloride	0.8		0.64	
Magnesium	0.1		0.09	
	Mg/lbs of food	Mg/Kg of food	Mg/lbs of food	Mg/Kg of food
Iron	26.00	57.20	23.40	51.48
Copper	3.30	7.20	2.97	6.48
Manganese	2.20	4.80	1.98	4.32
Zinc	55.00	121.00	49.50	108.90
Iodine	0.70	1.50	0.63	1.35
Selenium	0.05	0.11	0.045	0.10
Vitamins				
Vitamin E (Alpha Tocopherol)	23	50	20.4	45
Thiamin	0.45	1.00	0.41	0.90
Riboflavin	1.00	2.20	0.90	1.98
Pyridoxine	0.45	1.00	0.41	0.90
Pantothenic acid	4.55	10.00	4.09	9.00
Niacin	5.00	11.00	4.50	9.90
Folic acid	0.08	0.18	0.07	0.16
Biotin	0.045	0.10	0.04	0.09
Vitamin B_{12}	0.010	0.022	0.009	0.02
Choline	545.40	1200.00	490.90	1080.00
	IU/lbs of food	IU/Kg of food	IU/lbs of food	IU/Kg of food
Vitamin A	2273	5000	2046	4500
Vitamin D	227	500	204.3	450

[1]Not an essential dietary constituent. May facilitate alimentation, however a maximum figure is recommended.

Table III

RECOMMENDED NUTRIENT CONTENT
OF CANNED AND SEMI-MOIST DOG FOODS
(In percentage or specific amounts per pound or kilogram)

NUTRIENT	CANNED DOG FOOD *Per cent*		SEMI-MOIST DOG FOOD *Per cent*	
Dry matter	25.00		75.00	
Water	75.00		25.00	
Protein	12.0		19.95	
Fat	9.725		6.75	
Linoleic acid	0.275		0.825	
Fiber[1]	1.00		3.00	
Minerals				
Calcium	0.30		0.825	
Phosphorus	0.25		0.675	
Potassium	0.25		0.675	
Sodium chloride	0.22		0.60	
Magnesium	0.028		0.075	
	Mg/lbs of food	*Mg/Kg of food*	*Mg/lbs of food*	*Mg/Kg of food*
Iron	7.00	15.40	19.50	42.90
Copper	0.91	2.00	2.48	5.45
Manganese	0.60	1.30	1.65	3.63
Zinc	14.00	30.8	41.25	90.75
Iodine	0.02	0.04	0.53	1.17
Selenium	0.013	0.028	0.38	0.083
Vitamins				
Vitamin E (Alpha Tocopherol)	6.30	13.70	17.00	37.50
Thiamin	0.13	0.28	0.34	0.75
Riboflavin	0.30	0.60	0.75	1.65
Pyridoxine	0:13	0.28	0.34	0.75
Pantothenic acid	1.25	2.75	3.41	7.50
Niacin	1.36	3.00	3.75	8.25
Folic acid	0.20	0.05	0.06	0.135
Biotin	0.10	0.027	0.03	0.075
Vitamin B_{12}	0.003	0.006	0.009	0.020
Choline	150.00	330.00	409.05	900.00
	IU/lbs of food	*IU/Kg of food*	*IU/lbs of food*	*IU/Kg of food*
Vitamin A	625	1375	1705	3750
Vitamin D	62.5	137	170.5	375

[1]Not an essential dietary constituent. May facilitate alimentation, however a maximum figure is recommended.

are the true internal or parenteral regions of the body. After food substances are circulated by the blood and are either utilized by various cells or stored, waste materials must be eliminated. The kidney and urinary system are used for the purpose of excreting all waste products from the inner parts of the body, including all excess protein.

General Rules in Feeding

Food and water are the two most essential items in a dog's life. Each dog wants his own food dish, and a dish of fresh water always should be available. Cleanliness is necessary, not only of the dishes but of the utensils such as can openers. Regularity is important. Regular times, regular amounts, and a relatively stable, uniform diet will be most satisfactory.

Feeding Young Puppies for Growth and Development

Puppies usually are ready for weaning at five to seven weeks of age if, at three to four weeks after whelping, they have received solid food as a supplement to their diet. Good food is important at any stage of the life cycle, but this is especially true during the growth period. Rate of growth is the principal criterion used to evaluate sufficiency of almost all the known nutrients required by dogs.

The nutrient requirements of puppies are double those for adults on the basis of units of body weight. Quality is as important as quantity, especially during the period just after weaning. Food such as eggs, milk, meat, and cottage cheese are desirable. They are palatable, digestible, and contain protein of good quality. Food with a high content of fiber is not desirable during the period of rapid growth.

Because the total daily intake of food must be high, four feedings a day may be preferred for the first month, although three feedings a day can be adequate. The common tendency at this stage is to oversupplement. Caution must be taken not to replace more than 10 to 25 per cent of the daily total with supplements. Not only the total amount, but the proper ratio of calcium and phosphorous must be maintained.

An increasing amount of clinical evidence indicates that attempts to attain a maximum weight for age of young dogs by feeding excessive amounts of food high in energy may precipitate problems in later life because of disproportionate development of the skeleton and muscle mass. An exceedingly high caloric intake, even of a well-balanced dog food, serves no useful purpose, although it may result in the reaching of maturity at a somewhat earlier stage and at a heavier weight. It is important to know that a partial restriction of food intake, particularly during the period after weaning, is not harmful to future proper

659

development. If a balanced diet is fed, the puppy will reach the maximum size and conformation genetically possible, with only a slight delay in reaching full maturity. The dog should be weighed at weekly intervals and the rate of growth compared with published charts for its breed. The amount of food should be adjusted to conform with that for an average rate of growth rather than a maximum one. Plenty of exercise is important at this time.

Feeding twice a day may be initiated after the dog reaches five to six months of age. The stomach does not empty rapidly. Only about one-fourth of the food leaves the stomach four hours after feeding, and even after six hours nearly one-half still remains. Milk leaves the stomach much more rapidly than do solid foods, even when adequate water is given.

Most dogs of small breeds approach maturity during the period of seven to ten months of age, at which time their total nutrient requirements will begin gradually to decrease. Be alert for this change. Needs at this time are only slightly more than those for maintenance. This period will arrive later for large breeds, which develop more slowly. Snacks between meals should be avoided except for an occasional "treat," or milk, as a reward for meritorious behavior.

Do not be alarmed if your dog skips an occasional meal or eats only a part of it. It could signify that a feeding could be eliminated or the quantity reduced. Most dogs should finish their meal in twenty minutes, although this is not necessary. Water, still the least expensive nutriment, always should be available, even if food is fed moist or if foods with high moisture are fed.

Feeding Healthy Adult Dogs

The primary purpose of careful feeding is to meet the nutritional needs of the dog at each stage of life. Proper feeding simply means supplying daily an adequate quantity in correct proportions of all nutriments known to be needed.

Dogs are known to require at least 43 different nutriments, and a great amount of technical scientific literature has been published on this subject. Qualitatively, the dog requires essentially the same nutriments as man.

The dog's owner wants to know in non-technical language, what to feed and how much to feed. If one has sufficient knowledge, training, and time, and either enjoys or can hire the labor involved in preparing nutritious diets expertly and correctly, this can be done in the home or in a kennel kitchen.

Table IV

CALORIC REQUIREMENTS (MAINTENANCE) AND RECOMMENDED DAILY FOOD INTAKES OF AVERAGE ADULT DOGS OF VARIOUS BODY WEIGHTS[1]

Dog's Weight in lbs	Kcal Needed/lb Body Weight	Daily Rations of Dog Food in Ounces		
		Dry Type	*Semimoist*	*Canned*
2	65	1.3	1.7	3.4
5	52	2.5	3.2	7.00
10	44	4.3	5.5	10.75
15	39	6.1	7.8	15.25
20	37	7.5	9.7	18.75
30	33	10.0	12.8	25.0
45	30	14.0	18.0	35.0
75	26	20.4	26.2	51.0
110	24	25.0	32.2	62.5
in Kg	**Per Kg Body Weight**	**Daily Rations of Dog Food in Grams**		
1	143	1.4	2.0	3.7
2	122	2.2	2.8	6.2
5	96	4.7	6.0	11.8
7	86	6.2	8.0	15.7
10	81	8.2	10.7	20.6
15	72	11.0	14.0	27.5
20	66	14.2	17.6	34.5
35	57	21.0	26.8	52.5
50	53	250.0	32.2	62.5

[1]Based on nutrient composition of respective foods as recommended in Tables II and III.
Needs for growth may be estimated by multiplying adult requirements by 2.
Working or lactating dogs may require 2–3 times more food than is required for similar dogs at maintenance (CRLDD).

The majority of dog owners are delighted to have easily available a variety of excellent modern dog foods prepared by reputable manufacturers. Such foods should contain, in the proper proportions, all of the essential carbohydrates, fats, protein, minerals, and vitamins that are needed. Much technical knowledge has gone into formulating these products. They are the simplest and most economical way to feed a dog correctly.

The proper amount for each dog is often a question. Because each individual varies in basic requirements, it is difficult to make one general statement that can cover all dogs under all situations. Such things as size and other breed differences, basal metabolism, nervous temperament, amount of exercise or work done, and requirements during periods of growth, pregnancy or old age will change the quantity of food needed. Even littermates of the same weight may need different quantities of food. The owner should judge the correct amount to give each dog by its own response and condition. An old saying is true, "The eye of the master feeds his dog."

This is especially so in the case of the extremely small toy breeds and of the very large breeds. Scientific analyses have been made of the precise nutritional requirements for breeds of medium size. The basic nutritional requirements for toy breeds and for large breeds are presumed to be identical in every respect to those of the medium breeds, except for appropriate adjustments of volume in relation to size.

Without adequate caloric intake, there cannot be proper digestion and assimilation of essential nutriments; and on the other hand, too many calories will cause obesity. If a chosen diet is balanced properly with reference to calories, protein, minerals, and vitamins, then establishment of the proper relationship between a weighed quantity of dog food and the weight of each dog should bring about optimal nutrition.

Many persons prefer to serve adult dogs a good dry food, served dry, one or two times each day. If fed several times a day, as to females in the last weeks of gestation or to very young puppies, it can be moistened with warm water.

After the dog is a year of age, feeding once daily may be convenient, especially in a large kennel. Most dogs seem more content if fed twice daily. The heavier meal should be at night, if you wish the dog to sleep quietly, or if it will have to work hard early the next morning on a hunting or field trip; the lighter meal is given at night if the dog is used at that time primarily as a watchdog.

While quantity may have to be adjusted somewhat, according to individual size, activity, temperament, or variability of each dog, a simple rule is:

For growing puppies, one-half to one ounce of dry dog food per pound body weight each day.
For adult dogs, one-fourth to one-half ounce of dry dog food per pound body weight each day.

An adult dog that weighs 10 pounds should require 42 kcalories for each pound of body weight, or a total of 420 kcalories per day, while a dog from 50-70 pounds may need only 26 kcalories per pounds body weight, or 1300 to 1820 total calories each day. *Kcalories* is a term now used to indicate 1,000 small calories, equal to 1 Calorie (spelled with a capital c.) Thus, 1 kcal = 1,000 calories = 1 Calorie.

In spite of the fact that a demand schedule or a self-feeding program may be most efficient, particularly during the growth and development stages of life, it is better to establish a regular multiple feeding schedule designed to adapt the dog to living habits of its master and coordinated with any program of social training which is being used. This suggests considerable flexibility, but once a feeding schedule has been selected, it should be followed regularly each day.

Feeding Pregnant and Lactating Bitches

Correct feeding of a pregnant bitch should antedate conception; it should have begun while she was a puppy herself. As a young growing dog, she never should be fed for maximum weight but rather for optimum ideal size for age, as prescribed for her particular breed. Before breeding she should be in a good state of nutrition, have good eating habits, and be well exercised. This should give a firm, vigorous, but not overly fat bitch, that receives routinely a complete dog food or other balanced diet at the same level recommended for maintenance of an adult dog, and with particular regard for protein, minerals, and vitamins.

When signs of heat first are noted, her daily feed intake should be increased slightly from 5 to 10 per cent, or milk or meat could be offered at a period well spaced from the regular feeding time.

After breeding is accomplished, return at once to the same amounts and type of diet to which she was accustomed before first signs of estrus. A bitch in good condition should continue into pregnancy with the same caloric intake that she had during adult maintenance. Her food intake should be increased only as her body weight increases until about the last five weeks before whelping. In later stages of gestation, an increase in weight no longer will indicate correctly her increased need for energy and essential nutriments. Daily food intake gradually should be increased until at time of whelping she may be eating 25 per cent, and sometimes as much as 50 per cent, more than the amount of food she consumed before breeding.

It is important to remember that she should be in good condition before breeding time. The gestation period is not a proper time to attempt rebuilding depleted body reserves of a bitch. Nutritional excesses during the entire gestation period will be channeled to the fetuses, and may result in complications at time of whelping.

If a modern, well-balanced diet of good quality has been fed consistently, no supplementation of any kind is required during gestation. This fact is contrary to cherished folklore of the past, and many breeders have their own ideas on the subject. Therefore, if one feels happier by supplying a supplement, choose a balanced food, such as evaporated milk, small quantities of lightly cooked eggs, tidbits of meat, or raw liver. These supplements never should represent more than 10 per cent of her daily food intake. As her weight and food intake increase, begin dividing and spacing her feeding more frequently in order to avoid the discomfort larger meals might cause, especially in a small dog.

Some bitches may consume little food for the first 24-48 hours after whelping. Then her appetite and need for all nutrients, particularly energy and protein, should rise sharply and reach a peak in about three weeks. During this entire period, adequate calcium, phosphorus, and vitamin D must be fed, and a favorable dietary calcium-phosphorus ratio maintained. Failure to do so leads to eclampsia.

Eclampsia is a temporary derangement of the calcium metabolism. It usually occurs about three weeks after whelping and begins with nervousness, whimpering, an unsteady gait, and spasms. Toy breeds are more commonly affected. The condition can be cured readily by proper treatment if caught in time, and can be prevented in subsequent lactations.

After whelping, the bitch ideally should be at about the same weight as she was when bred, or not more than 5 to 10 per cent heavier. For three weeks after whelping she will need two to three times the food intake that was necessary for maintenance. In the majority of cases, this can be accomplished simply by an increase of her daily diet of dog food.

"Physiological hunger" stimulates her appetite. Coaxing her appetite by mixing tasty supplements with her food is not necessary and may contribute to finicky eating habits later. It is good, however, to offer either fresh or evaporated milk daily during her period of lactation. Milk is a complete food, and even large amounts will not upset the nutritional balance of the feeding program. In addition, it is an excellent source of readily available calcium and phosphorus already in correct proportions. Milk is best fed between regularly spaced meals of her normal diet. The multiple feeding practiced during late gestation should be continued during lactation. Many breeders find a self-feeding regimen very convenient, but close attention must be paid to her actual intake and to the progress of her litter in order to be assured that she is receiving adequate nutrition.

Nursing puppies should be encouraged to eat some food other than the bitch's milk as soon as possible after they have normal sight and locomotion. As weaning progresses, start limiting food intake of the bitch so that she will have fewer problems at time of complete weaning.

The following program will help decrease milk production and help prevent problems in the udder:

On the first day of weaning, do not offer the bitch any food at all, although plenty of water always should be available. On the second day, feed one-fourth of her normal maintenance diet; on the third day, one-half; on the fourth day, three-fourths; and then return to the diet to which she was accustomed before breeding.

Even if recommended feeding practices during gestation and lactation have been followed, many bitches will have depleted partially some of their nutritional reserves during lactation. Lactating females are almost always in a negative calcium balance, and the same is partially true for other nutriments. Beginning several weeks after weaning, therefore, the bitch again should be carefully observed and fed back to the point of optimal nutrition that she enjoyed just before breeding.

Feeding Stud Dogs

No special diets or feeding schedules are necessary for the stud dog. He should be fed in a manner similar to that described for bringing a bitch into peak condition for breeding. Plenty of exercise and careful feeding of a good quality dog food in order to maintain a full but firm body condition is all that is required. Vigor is more important than reserves.

Hand Feeding Orphan or Rejected Puppies, Weaning

Hand rearing puppies is a responsibility, but it need not demand the almost unceasing day and night vigilance and attention formerly thought essential for success, unless one enjoys it. In a large kennel, simplified but effective methods are welcomed.

There are several reasons why puppies may need hand rearing. A common one is the birth of an exceptionally large litter, which means that either several puppies must be selected for hand rearing or that it may be impossible to save all of the puppies. Sometimes after the first one or two puppies are born, the bitch will ignore additional puppies.

Even with a small litter, the bitch may have no milk, or insufficient milk, or may not want to nurse the puppies. Sometimes a bitch dies, but the orphaned puppies still may be saved if someone is willing to hand rear them.

In many cases, even with a normal litter, the bitch herself will discard one or more puppies and, for no detectable reason, will put them deliberately apart from the others. If they are replaced with the mother, by someone who thinks they merely have strayed blindly away from the others, she will continue to reject them. If this fact is realized in time by the owner, such puppies may be rescued and hand reared successfully, provided they are found before they have become chilled. But, if they have been discarded during the night and have lain too long alone in the cold, probably nothing can be done to save them. Few newborn puppies ever can recover from an initial chilling. They feel clammy to the touch, whine, and then, within a few days, will die.

With any newborn puppy, chilling seems to be the greatest single danger. If ever a puppy becomes thoroughly chilled, it seems unable to recover.

Individual owners can have greater success if a few basic necessities are understood. There must be: (1) a suitable environment for the puppies, (2) a formula that is nutritionally adequate, and (3) a satisfactory management and feeding program.

A Suitable Environment: Constant warmth, constantly maintained with no chilling or drafts, is essential. A temperature kept between 85° and 90° F. is most desirable during the period from birth to the fifth day. From the seventh to tenth day, temperature can be reduced gradually to 80°, with further gradual reductions to 75° by the end of the fourth week. To accomplish this, an incubator or brooder, fitted with a source of thermostatically controllable heat, is necessary. A chick brooder element fitted onto the cover of a whelping box may be used, or a homemade incubator may be fitted with infra-red heat lamps. Some veterinary hospitals may have incubators for rent.

Individual compartments in the incubator are desirable for several reasons. Unless orphaned puppies are separated during the first two or three weeks of life, they will suckle or perhaps chew and mutilate one another. All newborn puppies should be kept as free as possible from any disturbance or handling. The bottom of each individual compartment should be lined with a soft, clean, folded diaper. These should be changed whenever necessary, and examined for evaluation of quantity and quality of each puppy's feces.

The formula: In order to make a good puppy formula, the natural composition of bitches' milk must be understood. A comparison of bitches' milk, whole cows' milk, and 20 per cent solids evaporated milk is presented in Table V.

Bitches' milk is more concentrated than cows' milk and has twice the level of protein, almost double the caloric content, and more than twice the content of calcium and phosphorus. Undiluted evaporated cows' milk, as it comes from the can, contains 24 per cent total solids. This formula is too concentrated for puppies and does not provide a

666

Table V

A COMPARISON OF BITCHES' MILK, WHOLE COWS' MILK, AND 20 PER CENT SOLIDS EVAPORATED MILK

	BITCHES' MILK	20% SOLIDS EVAPORATED MILK	COWS' MILK
Protein	7.50%	5.80%	3.50%
Fat	8.30%	6.60%	3.90%
Lactose	3.70%	8.20%	4.90%
Calcium	0.28%	0.20%	0.12%
Phosphorus	0.24%	0.16%	0.09%
Total Solids	22.60%	20.00%	13.00%
Calories	36 calories *per ounce*	35 calories *per ounce*	21 calories *per ounce*

sufficient intake of water. Evaporated milk, if diluted to 20 per cent solids (five parts of evaporated milk plus one part of hot water from the tap), is nearer the composition of bitches' milk than is fresh cows' milk. In our experience, evaporated milk, reconstituted to 20 per cent solids, as mentioned above, with added calcium and phosphorus (one teaspoon of dicalcium phosphate per quart of formula) is comparable to any formula tested. A good formula should supply at least 30 calories for each ounce of formula, with 20 to 25 per cent of these total calories in the form of a high quality protein.

Diluting ordinary cows' milk does not result in a good formula. It can be improved if fortified with fat and protein, such as egg yolk, but the indiscriminate addition of sugars, particularly sucrose or lactose, to increase its caloric content is not recommended.

Although homemade formulas have been used with complete success, for greater ease and certainty the use of commercial formulations is recommended.

Management and Feeding Program: The caloric content and nutritive quality of the formula selected dictates in turn the feeding schedule. If a formula that is too diluted is used, either larger quantities will have to be consumed by the puppy at each feeding or the puppies will have to be fed more frequently; otherwise, poorer than average growth must be expected. On the other hand, overfeeding can be even more undesirable. In hand feeding, a good policy is to underfeed slightly during the period when the puppy is most susceptible to digestive disturbances, then to increase the caloric intake gradually to near full feeding after three weeks of age. To simplify the feeding program, the following caloric intakes are recommended:

1st week: 60-70 calories per pound body weight per day
2nd week: 70-80 calories per pound body weight per day
3rd week: 80-90 calories per pound body weight per day
4th week: 90+ calories per pound body weight per day

The daily needs of formula for a ten-ounce puppy of an average sized breed during its first week of life would be determined as follows:

Because the recommended caloric intake is 60 calories per pound body weight per day, for a 10-ounce or 2/3 pound puppy, 2/3 of 60, or 40 calories, would be needed. If the formula supplies 30 calories per ounce, the amount needed would be approximately 1.5 ounces of formula.

Not more than three feedings a day are necessary if a formula is fed that approaches the composition of bitches' milk in the amounts just outlined. Thus, for a 10-ounce puppy, the daily allowance of 1.5 ounces of formula could be divided into three feedings of one-half ounce each, fed at exactly eight hour intervals.

Common sense is still the most important ingredient in any workable feeding schedule. Start the above puppy with one-fourth to one-half ounce each feeding on the first day, then increase the amount gradually so that it is eating one-half ounce per feeding the fourth and fifth day. Continue to increase this as he gains weight and responds favorably to feeding. The puppy's steady gain in weight and a firm condition of its feces are the best evidence of satisfactory progress. If diarrhea develops, immediately reduce solids intake to one-half the amount previously fed, then gradually increase it again to the recommended level. As mentioned, separate compartments with clean diapers allow careful fecal observations for individual puppies.

The equipment required for preparation and feeding is not extensive and can be simple. This consists of:

1. A sensitive scale
2. Measuring cup marked in ounces
3. Pans and spoons for making formula
4. Pyrex baby-nursing bottles and nipples
5. Data book to record weight and observations on the puppies
6. 20 cc plastic disposable syringe
7. 1 No. 8 French infant feeding tube

Cleanliness and proper sanitary conditions must prevail at all times. Milk is a wonderful medium for bacterial growth. Do not prepare more formula than is required for any 48 hour period. Divide it into portions approximately the size required for each feeding. Keep it refrigerated. Before feeding, warm the formula to about 100° F., or near body temperature. Hold the bottle in such a manner that the puppy does not ingest air; do not let him nurse too rapidly. The hole in the nipple should be enlarged slightly with a hot needle, in order that milk will slowly ooze from the nipple when the bottle is inverted. Reasonably vigorous sucking is required by the puppy, however.

Tube Feeding

For puppies of small breeds or for puppies of all breeds that may be born weak or chilled, or where the sucking reflex is weak, the use of a French infant tube, or *gavage*, is recommended. Even when attempted by the inexperienced, it is completely safe, saves time, and assures proper artificial feeding during critical periods. Follow the same schedule and use the same quantity of the same formula as recommended above for bottle feeding. The procedure of tube feeding is as follows:

> Mark the feeding tube by taping or marking it with a ballpoint pen at a point three-fourths of the distance from the puppy's nose to its last rib. This shows depth for insertion of the tube to assure passage of formula directly into the stomach. Attach the feeding tube to the tip of the syringe. Draw up the previously warmed formula through the tube, filling the syringe. Pick the puppy up with your hand just as you would for bottle feeding, gently pass the tube over the tongue and insert it up to the mark. Then slowly release the required amount of milk. Withdraw and proceed to the next puppy.

An additional important advantage of tube feeding is its adaptability to supplemental feeding of weak puppies born normally and sucking the bitch. The practice of daily weighing all the puppies in a litter and selectively tube feeding those not gaining normally can result in a thriving litter. Frequently, what would be "fading puppies" can be saved by this method.

Puppies can be trained to eat Pablum mixed with their formula at two to three weeks of age. Pan feeding can be started after three weeks of age, at which time the puppies may be weaned from the bottle completely, and meat or a good-quality canned dog food may be offered in addition to the Pablum and formula. At five weeks, Pablum can be discontinued and formula replaced with evaporated milk mixed 1:1 with water. In addition to the meat and canned food, a good commercial dry or moist dog food can be introduced into the feeding program at this time. All changes in feed or feeding schedules should be made gradually.

Daily Habits, Exercise and Grooming:

During the first five to seven days of life, when the puppy relies almost entirely upon instinct, even some of his instincts first must be stimulated. Ordinarily, of course, this is done naturally by the mother in her care of the young, but if the mother is unable to take care of the puppy for any reason, the owner must substitute for her. Many persons do not realize that for the first few days of life both defecation and urination *must* be stimulated after each feeding. This can be accomplished by gentle massage of the anal region with a piece of cotton that has been dipped in warm water. Observe the puppies' daily habits, and stimulate only as may be necessary. By keeping the puppies separated and on diapers, this can be accomplished more easily.

Regular gentle massage is quite beneficial in the daily routine of a hand reared puppy. This is a form of passive exercise, stimulating circulation and thoroughly awakening it, and best may be accomplished by gentle stroking of the sides and back with a folded soft diaper. The best time for such treatment seems to be during the awakening period, just before feeding, while the formula is being warmed.

Simple grooming also is best done at feeding time and should be done only as deemed necessary. At first, grooming consists only of wiping the puppies' eyes with boric acid solution and occasionally rubbing the skin with baby oil because conditions in an incubator may tend to dry the coat. Grooming or handling should not be overdone at an early age. When newborn puppies are not eating, they should be sleeping.

Feeding the Older Dog

Nutritional requirements for adult dogs listed in Table I often must serve only as guides. Commercial foods patterned after these requirements are most acceptable for growth, are satisfactory for reproduction, but tend to be somewhat excessive for maintenance, particularly as a dog grows older. In older dogs, feeding often becomes an individual matter. In aging generally, a gradual but constant reduction of cells and tissues takes place. Not only are the numbers of individual cells of a specific tissue reduced, but they also become progressively smaller. Total enzymatic activity of these tissues is reduced and metabolism is slowed. Even cardiac output and renal function are lower than at an earlier age. The general level of physical activity is decreased to a point at which, in advanced age, moderate exercise must be enforced. Older dogs spend much time sleeping.

A marked reduction in caloric intake is necessary. Only sufficient fat to meet the dog's requirement for essential fatty acids is recommended. Although the amount of nutrient requirements clearly are lower now than are those for growing puppies, they are more nearly alike qualitatively. Protein should be of a high biological value. Milk again becomes a valuable food. Many older dogs suffer from chronic nephritis and must be fed only enough protein to meet metabolic needs, because excess protein must be excreted by the kidneys each day. Such dogs should be under the supervision of your veterinarian.

Feeding Sick Dogs

Feeding the sick dog is truly an individual matter and can be dictated only by the condition of the patient and the cause of sickness. A suitable feeding program must be prescribed by your veterinarian after his tests and diagnosis of the disease. Feeding sick dogs has been simplified by availability of several well-known prescription diets which can be purchased already prepared. The correct listing of ingredients on the label is mandatory, and, as with other commercially canned foods, is done subject to inspection. The particular diet should be one that is recommended by your veterinarian.

Nutritional Deficiencies

With the exception of the apparently ownerless, wandering, neglected dog, the incidence of clinical nutritional deficiencies in dogs has all but disappeared. This is due in part to increased knowledge concerning nutrition. Great credit is due to the availability of good quality, nutritionally-balanced, commercial dog foods. Competition between many reputable manufacturers has resulted in a large number of palatable and nutritionally sound rations.

Many of the nutritional deficiencies that still exist are caused by overly anxious dog owners, who may dilute a carefully balanced diet by adding meat or eggs, resulting in too much protein and a deficiency in calcium. Another common mistake is to add extra fats in order to increase the energy intake or to improve palatability of a diet. Too much fat will cause caloric needs to be met before enough balanced food is consumed to provide the protein, minerals, or vitamins necessary for good health.

A frequent source of difficulty is the practice of oversupplementation with additional mineral and vitamin preparations, especially during the periods of growth and reproduction. An excess of minerals and vitamins, or imbalances that result from simple excesses, may cause clinical signs similar to those of a deficiency. The following table

671

lists minerals and vitamins needed by dogs and the common sources of each, as well as the more frequent clinical signs of deficiency.

Table VI

MINERALS AND VITAMINS NEEDED BY DOGS

**Why They Are Needed . . . and How They are
Supplied in Commercial Dog Foods**

MINERALS AND VITAMINS	CONDITIONS CAUSED BY A DEFICIENCY	PRINCIPAL SOURCES OF SUPPLY
Calcium	Rickets; bowed legs and other bone malformation in puppies; osteomalacia in adults; hyperirritability of muscle and nerves; reduced lactation.	Meat and bone meal Dried skim milk Dicalcium phosphate
Phosphorus	Essentially the same as for calcium deficiency.	Meat and bone meal Dicalcium phosphate Dried skim milk Soybean oil meal
Potassium	Impaired growth; nervous restlessness; poor muscle tone; paralysis.	Soybean oil meal Dried skim milk Animal liver meal Expanded wheat
Sodium and Chlorine	Reduced appetite; fatigue and exhaustion.	Trace mineralized salt Fish meal Meat and bone scraps Animal liver meal
Magnesium	Hyperirritability; convulsions.	Meat and bone meal Soybean oil meal Expanded wheat
Iodine	Goiter.	Trace mineralized salt
Iron	Anemia; fatigue; sometimes diarrhea.	Trace mineralized salt Meat and bone meal Animal liver meal Fish meal

MINERALS AND VITAMINS	CONDITIONS CAUSED BY A DEFICIENCY	PRINCIPAL SOURCES OF SUPPLY
Copper	Same as for iron, plus bone weakness.	Trace mineralized salt Animal liver meal Fish meal Expanded wheat
Cobalt*	Growth impairment; anemia; reproduction impairment.	Trace mineralized salt Animal liver meal
Manganese*	Poor growth; low reproductive efficiency.	Trace mineralized salt Expanded wheat
Zinc*	Depressed growth; skin disorders.	Trace mineralized salt Fish meal Animal liver meal

VITAMINS:

A	Growth failure in puppies; ophthalmia; tendency of mucous membranes to develop lowered resistance against infections of ears, mouth, respiratory, digestive, and urogenital tracts; complete reproductive failure.	Vitamin A oil (stabilized) Animal liver meal Expanded corn Corn gluten meal
D	Rickets; bowed legs and other bone malformation; poor teeth; loss of muscle tone; failure to assimilate calcium and phosphorus.	Vitamin D-activated plant sterol Cod liver oil
E	Impairment of growth; breeding failure; muscle degeneration; abnormal lactation.	Alpha tocopherol (highest vitamin E activity) supplement Expanded whole wheat Expanded corn

*Experimental proof of the precise need for these in dogs is lacking, although need for them is recognized.

MINERALS AND VITAMINS	CONDITIONS CAUSED BY A DEFICIENCY	PRINCIPAL SOURCES OF SUPPLY
K	Failure of blood properly to clot.	Dogs are able to synthesize vitamin K in the digestive tract
Thiamine, B$_1$	Loss of appetite; failure to grow; nervous disorders; paralysis; impaired gastric secretion.	Brewer's dried yeast Expanded wheat Expanded corn Dried skim milk Soybean meal
Riboflavin, B$_2$	Growth failure in puppies; weakness; diarrhea; watery bloodshot eyes; collapse and death in acute deficiency.	Animal liver meal Brewer's dried yeast Dried skim milk Meat and bone meal Fish meal
Niacin	Black tongue—a disease similar to pellagra in man; nervous disorders; loss of appetite and emaciation.	Animal liver meal Brewer's dried yeast Dried skim milk Expanded wheat
Pyridoxine	Anemia; nerve degeneration; loss of appetite; growth failure; emaciation.	Animal liver meal Fish meal Dried skim milk Expanded wheat Soybean meal
Pantothenic acid	Erratic appetite; growth failure; collapse; convulsions; coma in acute deficiency.	Brewer's dried yeast Animal liver meal Dried skim milk Crystalline calcium pantothenate Expanded wheat
Choline	Growth failure in puppies; fatty livers and cirrhosis.	Soybean meal Animal liver meal Fish meal Brewer's dried yeast
Folic acid	Loss of appetite and growth failure in puppies; reduced antibody production.	Animal liver meal Meat and bone meal Soybean meal Brewer's dried yeast

MINERALS AND VITAMINS	CONDITIONS CAUSED BY A DEFICIENCY	PRINCIPAL SOURCES OF SUPPLY
Vitamin B_{12}	Growth failure; anemia; reproductive disorders.	Animal liver meal Fish meal Meat and bone meal Dried skim milk
Vitamin C		In dogs this vitamin is synthesized in the liver.

Administration of Medicine

MEDICINE is not difficult to administer to most dogs, but occasionally an animal is encountered that is extremely reluctant. Here are a few hints which often make the job easier. Some medicines are tasty, or at least tasteless, and can be conveniently included in the dog's food or milk. Cod liver oil, mineral oil, and milk of magnesia can often be given this way. Many pills can often be administered in this manner, too. However, if a dog bites down on a piece of meat and encounters a hard object (such as the pill) he will immediately spit it out. Accordingly, it is better to crush the pill into a powder (by rolling it under the bowl of a spoon) and mixing it with the food.

A much more positive and effective method of giving medications orally is to force the dog to take them. Capsules, pills, and other solid forms can be given by standing along the dog's right side, grasping his muzzle over the top of his nose so that the fingers of the left hand press in on the lips and squeeze them against the teeth. This will usually cause the dog to start to open his mouth. As he does so the lips are curled inward around the points of the teeth. If the dog attempts to close his mouth, he will bite his own lips. The capsule is held in the fingers of the right hand and pushed deeply into the dog's throat. The hand is quickly withdrawn, the mouth closed, and the animal's head elevated while the throat is stroked. Usually the dog will lick his nose when he has swallowed the capsule. If he should spit it out, merely repeat the process of giving it again.

Liquid medicines are more difficult to administer, as the dog may move his head and cause the medicine to be spilled. Liquids are best administered from a vial or small bottle—a spoon is an awkward, clumsy implement to use. It is essential to have someone hold the dog's head steady and just slightly elevated. Insert two fingers inside the corner of the lips and pull the lips outward away from the teeth. This forms a funnel-like pouch into which the medicine may be poured. It will trickle between the teeth and as the animal tastes it, he will usually swallow. Some dogs clench the teeth and do not allow the medicine to enter between them; to overcome this, insert the handle of a spoon between the teeth. Once the dog starts to swallow, he usually takes the medicine satisfactorily.

Care and Grooming

At a dog show, any well-trained, well-groomed dog is a pleasure to watch. Dogs in a show do not look beguiling by accident. Their beauty is intrinsic. First of all, it comes from good structure and then it is determined by good health and by good care.

The Coat

Care of the dog's coat will influence greatly its general appearance. Each breed varies somewhat as regards hair coat and the best method of caring for it. Short-haired dogs should be brushed, while terrier-type dogs require periodic plucking to remove dead hair and to give them a trim appearance, with brushing and combing needed between pluckings. Longer-coated dogs usually are carefully combed and then may be brushed for additional luster.

Brush all the way down to the skin, for the massaging action stimulates circulation of blood and also helps loosen and remove flakes of dandruff. Brushing several times a week will keep the average dog neat and clean, although daily attention is better.

In places with a cold climate and deep snow, the dog may enjoy frisking and plunging through the snow like a small snow plow, but may suffer later from chunks of ice that form between the claws and in other places where hair gets wet and then freezes. This must be attended to carefully in order to avoid causing pain. On city sidewalks, boots and a coat may help keep much of the hair from coming in direct contact with ice, snow, and salt. Towels at the door to catch the drip and to soak up melting ice are a necessity in some localities. A hair dryer could be of help, but should not be turned to hot.

Somewhat similar problems are encountered in various localities from mud, tar, sap from evergreens, cockleburrs, seedpods, or sandburrs.

Mats in the hair are often difficult to remove. Sometimes they can be teased apart using only one or two teeth of the comb. Occasionally they must be cut out. You must be careful here, as it is easy to cut the skin, too. Cutting also leaves a bare, gouged area in the animal's coat. This can be disastrous for a show dog. If the mat must be removed by cutting, try to work the comb all the way through the mat but close to and parallel to the skin, then cut the mat off outside the comb. Mats are most often found as solid masses of hair behind the ears or under the legs.

Shedding

Vigorous and frequent grooming is important when the dog is shedding, as it helps to remove dead hair. Some dogs shed once or twice yearly, and at these times it is desirable to help complete the process by plucking or removing dead-hair tufts. Some dogs, especially those kept indoors most of the time, seem to shed almost constantly. Continual brushing and grooming may be helpful in reducing the quantities of hair which are left about the house.

Baths

A dog should be bathed as seldom as possible, and usually only when excessively dirty or contaminated with something of offensive odor or appearance. Frequent washing removes natural oils and causes the coat to become dry and harsh. When necessary, bathing should be done with a mild soap or coconut-oil shampoo. Stand the dog in a tub or basin, plug its ears with cotton, and place a bland ophthalmic ointment or a few drops of mineral oil in his eyes. Wet the dog with water, apply soap, and work up a good lather. Rinse well when finished, and try to get a towel around the dog before the first shaking begins. If the weather is chilly or windy, the dog should be kept indoors until thoroughly dry. This process may be hastened by vigorously rubbing the dog with rough towels. Once it is clean, the dog can best be kept that way by regular brushing and combing.

Nails

Part of the grooming routine includes care of the nails, eyes, and ears. Nails should be cut periodically so that they just clear the floor. If allowed to grow long, they may cause the foot to splay or spread, or may even grow around in a circle and back into the dog's skin. This is most apt to happen to dogs with the dewclaws, which are not in wear, and which are often covered by long hair so they may not be observed readily.

With most breeds it is advisable to have the dewclaws removed. This should be done surgically, by a veterinarian, during the first days of life, before there is any pain associated with the operation. Note, however, that some breed standards (notably the Briard and Great Pyrenees) require that the dewclaws be left on the dogs.

Ordinary scissors should not be used to cut the nails. Specially designed nail trimmers can be purchased at pet stores. The cut should be made just outside the pink blood line that can be seen on white nails. In pigmented nails, the cut should be judged by noting curvature of the underside of the nail. Only the hook-like projection is removed. Frequency of cutting depends upon the type and amount of exercise the dog receives and the type of surface upon which it walks. Usually once every two months is adequate.

Eyes

Eyes need regular care. Breeds with large protruding eyes are especially predisposed to injuries, foreign bodies, and other accidental scratches or bruises. Constant irritation may produce a chronic infection, and the dog may appear red-eyed, with a slight discharge from the corner. Washing the eye with a warm boric acid solution or a salt solution composed of one teaspoonful of table salt per pint of water, may help. After the eyes are thoroughly cleaned, cotton or cloth patches can be soaked in warm water and held in place over the eyes for five to ten minutes. This treatment is beneficial for mild irritations, but a discharge of any character should indicate the need for professional examination.

(Caution: Boric acid is poisonous if taken internally. Bottles should be labeled plainly, and, like all poisons, kept in a safe place.)

Foreign particles in the eye can cause damage. So can eyelashes that turn in; these may have to be removed by excision of the follicles by electrolysis or surgery. Trouble, too, can be caused by excessive turning in or turning out of drooping eyelids.

If eyes of newborn pups have not opened by the normal time of ten to fifteen days, veterinary advice must be sought, or a form of ophthalmia may develop. Never try to force them open.

Edema of eyelids from insect bites can be helped by cold compresses three to four times a day.

A sty, from bacterial infection, may be helped by hot, but not burning hot, compresses three to four times a day.

Abnormal conditions may be found secondary to infectious diseases, such as Infectious Canine Hepatitis (ICH), Canine Distemper (CD), fungal diseases, septicemia, and migration of worm larva.

679

Ears

Ears are delicate areas. Ear trouble starts usually from an irritation of the lining inside of the ear. This can be caused by soap, water, ear mites, foreign objects (such as weed seeds), or, by an excess secretion of wax. Some owners call this kind of irritation canker, or *otorrhea*. The affected animal will shake its head, scratch, hold the affected ear down, show evidence of pain, and usually present an ear which smells offensive, with a pasty, dark-colored discharge. Treatment of a well-established case is difficult, and response is slow.

Never wash the ears with water, alcohol, or peroxide. Unless used for a specific purpose by your veterinarian, they may further increase irritation.

Dogs with lop ears or hair-filled ear canals are predisposed to more ear troubles than those with erect ears. Because better circulation of air is possible, open ears dry out better than do covered ears. In severe or chronic ear infections, a surgical procedure may be performed which will open the ear canal and allow it to drain and dry. Some cases heal quickly following such surgery. Professional advice should be sought if there is evidence of pain.

Surgical Procedures

Surgical modification or removal of certain hereditary and congenital abnormalities can obscure, disguise or eliminate an undesirable characteristic in a dog. The following guidelines for veterinarians, as to when such surgical operations should or should not be done, are from a report published in the official magazine of the American Veterinary Medical Association, May 15, 1976.

Such surgical operations may be done when an animal's health, comfort and welfare require them, but such operations should not be done to conceal an animal's genetic potential or to deceptively or artificially enhance the value of an animal intended for sale, for breeding purposes, or for showing in competition.

It is unethical for a veterinarian to perform a surgical procedure in a purebred dog for the purpose of concealing a congenital or hereditary abnormality which sets the dog apart from the normal as described in the standard for the breed. Listed are some examples of surgical procedures that would be unethical:

1. Removal of a congenital skin blemish.
2. Procedures to cause erection of ears.
3. Changing set or carriage of ears.
4. Alteration of the location of the testes.
5. Increasing or decreasing dewlap.

6. Setting or altering carriage of the tail.
7. Altering the natural dental arcade.
8. Correcting entropion or ectropion.
9. Correction of stenotic nares, elongated soft palate, and other congenital impediments to air flow.
10. Correction of harelip.
11. Correction of cleft palate.
12. Correction of orthopedic deformities.
13. Removal of excessive skin folds in any body area.
14. Correction of preputial deformities.
15. Correction of umbilical or other hernias of genetic origin.
16. Alteration of body conformation or coloration.

A veterinarian performing any of these procedures should advise the owner that the dog should be sterilized.

Parasites,
External and Internal

PERSONS try to protect themselves against parasites by sanitation, such as drainage, and by isolation, such as screening, and by destruction, through the use of parasiticides. To control or eliminate parasites, a means must be found by which their life cycle can be broken at some point. As more and more is learned about the life cycles of internal and external parasites of dogs, efforts to control them become more successful.

External parasites

The most frequently encountered external parasites encountered by dogs are fleas, lice, ticks, and mites.

Fleas. Fleas are wingless, small, compact insects, especially adapted to sucking blood. Fleas are classified as *Arthropoda,* from words that mean jointed foot. The genus to which the dog and cat fleas belong has a formidable looking but descriptive name, *Ctenocephalides,* pronounced Té-no-se-fól-i-dēs meaning "comb head." Several different genera of fleas, primarily of rodents, can transmit plague and other serious diseases to man and animals.

The flea most common to dogs and cats is undoubtedly a pest and it causes much annoyance and discomfort, but at least it does not transmit disease from dog to dog or from dog to man. The dog tapeworm spends a part of its life cycle in the dog flea and the dog is infected by eating the infected flea. Fleas can spread from filaria also.

Defleaing a dog is not the final answer. The flea's eggs may be laid in bedding, in grass, in the dog's favorite chair, in automobiles, or any other place the dog goes. The use of flea soaps, shampoos, sprays, and powders can result in the death of all of the fleas that come in contact with the product, but new eggs probably will hatch eight to ten days later. In addition to defleaing the dog, areas where eggs have been laid must be cleaned by vacuuming, and by using flea powders.

Lice. The true lice which infect mammals belong to the suborder *Anoplura*, meaning unarmed tail. They are an order of insects, the sucking lice, characterized by absence of wings, and with mouths adapted for piercing and sucking blood and tissue fluids. True lice

682

found upon mammals are classified by entomologists into several suborders. Those found upon man have been studied extensively, because they are visible, they cause discomfort, and because some varieties can carry and transmit infectious organisms, such as typhus fever. Lice have been found in mummies, showing long association with man. Lice found on man include *Pediculus humanus*, variety *capitis*, or head louse; *corporis*, body or clothes louse, *Phthirus pubis*, a crab louse, which lives in hair. Other mammals have many different varieties of lice. Each variety is highly specific as to its nutritive requirements.

A louse from a dog may be transferred on to a person, but would not wish to remain because blood from a human being would not meet its requirements. The heavy infestations of lice now being reported in schools and colleges all over the country do not originate in dogs, but in people.

The specific dog lice are classified as *Linognathus setosus* and as *L. piliferus*. Pronounced li-nóg-na-thus, the word refers to structure of the mouth, while setosus refers to bristles and piliferus to hair.

Bird lice and certain others belong to a still different order which bite rather than suck.

Mites are small animals related to spiders and, as parasites on man and domestic animals, produce irritations of the skin called **acariasis.** *Acarus*, plural *acari*, means mite. Many varieties are found, including a special mite on onions that can cause dermatitis to some persons.

The **otodectes mite** causes otorrhea or canker in the ear of dogs, cats, and domestic rabbits. In some dogs this parasitic inflammation may cause such irritation to nerve endings in the bottom of the external ear canal that running fits may occur. Professional attention is needed.

Sarcoptic Mange is caused by mites that are microscopic in size, live in the skin, and develop burrows. This causes severe itching and thickening of the skin. Somewhat characteristic of the condition is an odor, called "mouse odor," given off by the skin. With professional attention, a positive diagnosis can be made by microscopic examination of deep skin scrapings. The condition can spread rapidly from dog to dog. Complete coverage of the skin of infected dogs is necessary for cure, and extended treatment always is necessary.

Follicular Mange. This condition is caused by a particular mite, *Demodex canis*, which is microscopic in size and lives in the hair follicles. Hairs drop out, the skin reddens, eventually thickens, and hair follicles become infected, with resulting formation of pustules. This kind of mange sometimes is called "red mange." In young puppies, the first sign noted is a loss of hair, in small patches, around the forehead, eyes, muzzle, and forepaws. Diagnosis is confirmed by microscopic examination of hair roots and skin scrapings. The condition calls for extended treatment, which is more likely to result in a cure if started before the pustular symptoms appear. If bitches become affected, special attention is necessary to prevent infestation of her puppies.

Many skin problems are caused by conditions other than mange. An accurate diagnosis should be sought.

Ticks are an order of insects classified as *Ixodidae,* a group of insects that are parasites on man and beasts. The hard ticks have a *scutum,* Latin for shield, which makes them hard to destroy. Much of their complicated life cycle is spent off of the dog. They are very prevalent in wooded lands of the interior and also are abundant along sandy beaches of many of our ocean resorts. Immature ticks rest on the branches of trees and shrubs in the areas, and, when an animal passes by, will drop off onto the animal and obtain the blood meal for completion of their life cycle. An occasional dog has developed general paralysis, which disappears after removal of the tick. Ticks also infest houses and buildings, and in such infested places may be found crawling up the walls.

Dogs have several diseases transmitted by ticks or other vectors. These are described in the section "Rickettsial Diseases."

Dermacentor, meaning to pierce the skin, is used to refer to several ticks which affect dogs. *D. variabilis* is the common dog tick of North America. In the Atlantic states, this tick occasionally can transmit the rickettsial disease of man, Rocky Mountain spotted fever, as well as tularemia, caused by a pastuerella.

D. Andersoni is described, by entomologists, as "a handsome reddish brown species of wood-tick responsible for transmitting Rocky Mountain spotted fever to man and for causing tick paralysis and tularemia. Its first and second hosts are rodents, especially squirrels, while its third hosts are domestic animals and man. *D. venustus* is the same. *D. marginatus* and *D. modestus* also transmit."

Rocky Mountain spotted fever has been found occasionally in all of the states. In man, especially children, it seems to result from picking infected ticks off a dog with the bare hands, and squeezing them. The infectious organisms are inside the tick, pass in its ova from generation to generation, and are shed in its feces. The ticks should be removed carefully, wearing gloves, or by using tweezers or paper.

Textbooks warn against scratching a tick bite, but do not suggest any method for explaining this to the dog. The disease in dogs is so rare that it has not been defined, but is known to occur, and in man it can be fatal. With warnings about it in mind, not many cases seem to have occurred in recent years.

684

Internal Parasites

Worming is a subject open to much controversial opinion. It is undoubtedly true that at least as much damage is done to dogs from improper worming or overworming as is done by the worms themselves. If worms are not the trouble, and there is a good chance that they are not, indiscriminate worming is the worst possible treatment that could be administered to the dog; furthermore, if the dog is sick or run-down, what might be a reasonable amount of worm medicine for a healthy dog becomes a lethal dose for the sick dog.

Dogs may be infested with at least four common types of intestinal parasites. Parasites of any type can be suspected if there is unthriftiness, but can be determined accurately only by identifying worms in the stool or vomitus or by microscopic examination of the stool.

Because remedies effective against one type may be ineffective against others, a microscopic examination of a specimen of the dog's stool is necessary to determine what type of parasite is present in order to use the correct medicine. A worm medicine is intended either to destroy the worms without injuring the stomach and intestines or to stupefy the worms so that they will release their hold and be passed out in the stool. An ideal worm medicine would affect only the worms and never upset the dog. Your veterinarian will advise you on the type and quantity of worm medicine you should use and will tell you how to use it.

Toxacaris canis is the common **roundworm** of dogs. Roundworms, or ascarids, are very common in puppies. Their eggs hatch in the intestines, young microscopic embryos enter the blood stream, and after a period of development while still microscopic in size, migrate into the intestines, where they develop to maturity, lay eggs, and start the cycle again. A dog that has been treated for ascarids when young seldom will have a heavy infestation when older. Because of a hormonal change in the pregnant bitch, the microscopic worm embryos traveling around in her blood stream cannot re-enter her own intestines, but they can go by the blood stream into her unborn puppies. Some puppies are born with roundworms.

Ascarids may be passed periodically in the stool. They look like strips of thin spaghetti about one to three inches long, are white, firm, and round, and often are curled or coiled like springs. Affected pups may eat excessively, be potbellied, have diarrhea, and hiccup occasionally. Treatment depends upon the medication used, and this may depend upon the condition of the dog. As dogs grow older, they may become tolerant or immune to ascarids so that they are no longer as injurious to the animal's health.

Hookworms. These also commonly are encountered in puppies, but dogs of any age can be infested seriously. This worm, too, may be passed to puppies before birth or at an early age. Debilitated animals are easy prey, and a heavy infestation may cause death. These worms are tiny, white, hair-like parasites, which have hook-like mouth parts for chewing and attaching themselves to the intestinal lining. A heavily parasitized dog may be weak and anemic from loss of blood. It may have thin, mucoid bowel movements that always seem diarrheal-like and often contain blood. Worming such animals is a delicate procedure. Often they need blood transfusions to build them up before worming. Mild infestations may produce unthriftiness, loss of weight, poor coat, chronic diarrhea, and other symptoms.

Whipworms. These worms are white in color, with the head being at the small thread-like end. They inhabit the large intestine and the *coecum,* or appendix, of dogs. Symptoms may be vague and include intermittent diarrhea, generally poor condition, and dry, harsh coat. Most cases respond to treatment of medicine by mouth.

Heartworms. Infestation is becoming widespread. Dogs, especially in the coastal plain areas of the Atlantic and the Gulf of Mexico, harbor this parasite, and it is being recognized in states as far north as Minnesota and in the New England states. Mature worms infest the right side of the heart and the pulmonary arteries. In advanced cases, pulmonary hypertension may lead to right sided congestive heart failure. Young worms, called *microfilariae,* are born alive. These microfilariae circulate in the dog's blood stream. If a mosquito feeds upon such a dog, some of its microfilariae are sucked up into the mosquito's body where they mature to the infectious stage within two weeks. The infective larvae gain access to a dog's body through the puncture wound caused by the mosquito's bite. This intermediate larval stage is capable of developing into a mature heartworm. Six to seven months are required for a new generation of microfilariae to appear in the blood. Symptoms and sometimes death are brought about by obstruction of blood flow through the lung caused by tissue reactions to the adult worms. The dog tires easily, has chronic coughing, and shows loss of weight. The diagnosis usually can be made by finding the microfilariae in the blood, but they may be absent, particularly in advanced cases. Drugs to destroy the adult worms must be given intravenously. Oral medications are effective in eliminating the microfilariae and preventing reinfestation by infective larvae. Screening dogs against mosquitoes and daily oral administration of the preventative drug are effective methods of protection.

Tapeworms. Often found in older or mature dogs, two species of tapeworms can claim the dog as their host for a part of their life cycles. These are *dipylidium,* which spends part of its cycle in the flea, with ingestion of an infected flea necessary before the dog in turn becomes infected; and *taenia,* which spends part of its cycle in the rabbit or mouse, so that ingestion of viscera of one of these animals is necessary before a dog can become infected. The head end, or scolex, of these worms attaches to the intestinal linings, and the rest of the parasite streams out into the lumen of the intestine like a rope floating in a river. As the parasite is flat and segmented, and as new segments all are produced at the scolex, the whole worm becomes longer and longer. Eventually some of the segments break off and appear in the stool. Unless the scolex itself is removed, the parasite will grow again.

Often segments passed out in the dog's stool will become attached to hair around the anus. These segments may dry and fall off. Finding such segments or seeing fresh ones in the stool are indicative of tapeworm infestation. The eggs of the tapeworm are contained within the segment, and, unless the segment breaks before passage, a microscopic examination does not reveal the presence of these worms. Special tapeworm vermicides given orally will bring about removal of the complete worm. Reinfestation can occur again in about three months if infected fleas, rabbits, or mice are eaten.

Diseases

SOME GENERAL KNOWLEDGE about disease is essential in order that owners may help keep their dogs as healthy as possible. In almost every instance, the owner will be the first to notice that something is wrong and that the dog is in need of help.

Classically, all of the possible causes of disease have been grouped into two large categories: environmental and genetic. To the environmental group belong the bacteria and viruses, parasites, nutritional deficiencies, toxic chemicals and trauma, all agents which disarrange the normal functions of the body but originate external to it. Genetic diseases, on the other hand, involve the genetic material itself, the "blueprint for life", and are thus intrinsic to the animal.

However, it is becoming clear that diseases in general often cannot be categorized as being wholly environmental or wholly genetic, but might be better thought of as occurring on a continuous scale between environmental on one end and genetic on the other.

The body of each dog is composed of a number of functional systems: *skin* for protection; *respiratory* for breathing; *digestive* for digestion and absorption of food; *cardiovascular* for transport of food and oxygen within the body; *excretory* for elimination of wastes; *muscular* for movement; *skeletal* for support; *reproductive* for propogation; *nervous* for control of movement and sensation; *sensory* for sight, hearing and smell; and *endocrine organs* to produce hormones for chemical regulation of various activities in the body.

Diseases may cause impairment of one or more of these systems. The system affected and degree of impairment are reflected by symptoms seen in a sick dog.

Symptoms

Distinct from external wounds or injuries which can be seen, a bewildering number of symptoms may occur as the result of various diseases. Owners always should be alert for any deviation from the normal. Watch for *constipation, diarrhea, shivering, fever, watery eyes, runny nose, dry hot nose, coughing, lack of appetite, ravenous appetite without a gain in weight, vomiting, increased urination, restlessness* and, of course, any indication of *pain* or *nervous symptoms*.

Obviously, proper treatment depends first upon proper diagnosis and then upon doing what should be done at the right time. Diagnosis is made by careful analysis of the system affected. To be able to do this accurately, a modern doctor of veterinary medicine studies in college for at least six years or more in order to understand functions of the various systems of organs, relationships between impaired function and symptoms, appropriate technical tests and methods used for determining causes and proper treatment for abnormal conditions.

INFECTIOUS DISEASES

In order to understand disease caused by infectious organisms, there must be some knowledge of how the agent enters the dog's body to cause infection; where it multiplies and how fast it multiplies; the damage it causes; how it escapes to infect other dogs; and probably most important, how the dog responds to infection. Once these variables are known, appropriate therapeutic regimens and control measures may be instituted.

Infections and Immunity

The dog's immune system regulates the body's response to an infectious disease agent, or for that matter, any substance foreign to the body. When the immune system functions properly, a state of *Immunity* or protection to a specific agent is conferred on the dog.

The dog's immune response consists of two principal parts—the humoral and cell-mediated immune systems. Each part has its own distinct functions with both contributing to the rapid response to foreign substances and immunity against infectious agents.

The only function of the humoral immune system is the production of antibody; whereas, the cell-mediated immune system mediates a variety of events whose role in infectious disease is still largely unknown. Historically, the body's immune response to infectious agents has been evaluated by its ability to produce antibody against that agent. These antibodies function primarily by neutralizing the agent in the bloodstream and preventing their ability to infect other cells in the body. Thus, the immune status of a particular individual animal is determined by the presence or absence of antibody to a particular infectious agent.

The first contact a dog has with an infectious organism stimulates the production of antibody which appear between 7 to 10 days following infection. In addition, this contact imparts some memory so that the immune system is effectively prepared to repel any later invasion by that organism. A second contact with the agent usually results in antibody production within the first several days after infection.

Vaccination uses this principle by employing a relatively harmless form of the agent as the primary stimulus to impart memory. The dog's defenses are then alerted and any subsequent contact with the agent will result in an early and explosive production of antibody which will usually prevent the infection from taking hold.

Vaccines are prepared by rendering the infectious agent harmless without destroying its ability to stimulate an immune response. Vaccines can be killed or live. Killed vaccines are "dead" in the sense that their infectivity has been destroyed. Most of the current veterinary vaccines are attenuated or modified-live vaccines. In these vaccines the infectious organisms are attenuated or altered to produce no symptoms (or trivial ones), but they are not so altered that they can't multiply in the dog. The ability to multiply in the dog, leading to a prolonged stimulus of the immune system of a similar kind and magnitude to that occurring in natural infections, gives rise to a substantial immunity.

Because killed vaccines contain no live organisms to become established in the body and provide periodic stimulation, the antibodies produced die out in about six months. They must be reinforced, and, after a booster injection, antibodies then are effective for a somewhat longer time, from six to nine months. In contrast, antibodies produced following vaccination with modified-live vaccines persist for 12 months or more, although the duration varies in individual animals.

Viral Diseases

Classified as viral diseases are those known to be caused by the infectious agents called viruses. All viruses are of a relatively small size, cannot be detected by ordinary microscopic examination, and fail to multiply naturally except in the presence of living cells. Different pathogenic viruses have been studied and classified according to the disease each causes in man and animals. Only one viral disease of dogs, rabies, is known to affect both man and dog. Man has hepatitis, which means inflammation of the liver, and man has herpesviruses, which cause fever blisters and other conditions, but, although the names are similar, the causative organisms show differences when studies, compared, and classified in the laboratory. Man does not get canine infectious hepatitis from dogs, nor canine herpesvirus.

Canine Distemper Virus. Of all infectious disease in dogs, the most common is distemper. It is so universal that, except for rabies, distemper once was thought to be the only infectious disease of dogs. It is the disease from which most dogs have died throughout the ages. Before accurate procedures for vaccination were developed, and the virus of distemper was distinguished from the different virus that causes infectious canine hepatitis, both diseases were thought to be the same. Nearly all dogs had distemper sooner or later, and about 50 per cent of dogs that had distemper died. It still is the principal cause of disease and death in unvaccinated dogs. The virus remains an ever present hazard, and constant exposure is almost a certainty.

Distemper virus can be carried from one dog to another or a dog can contract the infection from a contaminated environment, but, generally, distemper virus spreads as an airborne infection, as do the viruses of influenza of human beings. Actual bodily contact is not necessary for this virus to spread. A susceptible dog does not have to be even near an infected one.

After exposure, usually by inhalation of infected air, virus first begins to multiply in lymphatic tissues of a susceptible, unimmunized dog. From six to nine days after exposure, virus appears in the bloodstream and spreads thereby to other organs of the body, especially lungs, intestinal tract, and surface tissues. At this time, each individual's own intrinsic ability quickly to develop protective antibodies, affects future course of infection. If antibody fails to develop, epithelial surface structures and glands become highly infected, and 14 to 16 days after exposure the dog first begins to show visible symptoms that may be notices, such as loss of apetite and weight, eye and nose discharges, and diarrhea. In other cases, epithelial structures become infected before sufficient antibody can be made, and, although virus disappears later from lymphatic tissues, it may persist in cells where it cannot be reached easily by antibodies carried in the blood stream, especially epithelial tissues in the footpads, which then become hardened, or in the brain, where the virus can cause epileptiform convulsions, called "encephalitis", or "chomping fits". If antibody can develop before virus can reach epithelial tissues, virus no longer is found, and the dog recovers with only slight symptoms.

Because visible clinical signs of canine distemper do not appear until two weeks or more after initial exposure, dogs that develop these symptoms within the first two weeks after vaccination, undoubtedly before the time selected for vaccination, already must have become exposed to the highly prevalent airborne virus of distemper.

Distemper can be prevented if a susceptible dog is kept completely isolated from exposure to any infected wild animals or stray animals, as well as to air or any other material that contains distemper virus, such as clothing or shoes of visitors. Because such rigid isolation cannot be assured easily, dependence must be placed in trying to create within each dog a state of protective immunity by vaccination.

A dog is considered immune if it has circulating within its blood stream enough antibodies to destroy all virulent distemper virus to which it may be exposed. A dog remains immune to distemper just as long as it continues to have sufficient antibodies circulating in its blood. While the dog continues to have antibodies formed by activity on the dog's own body, the term active immunity is used.

Nature provides a means for passive transfer of antibodies from a mother to her newborn offspring in her first milk, called colostrum, that contains antibodies, against all of the infectious diseases to which the individual mother is immune. This varies from mother to mother and varies in the same mother from time to time. This method of conferring passive immunity was so named because a dog immunized in this manner does not actively produce these antibodies itself, but merely receives them for temporary protection. The amount of antibody a puppy receives from the bitch through the colostrum is directly proportional to the amount of antibody present in the bitch.

After a puppy has received passive antibodies in colostrum, they begin to fade away and disappear at a regular mathematical rate which can be calculated. Passive antibody disappears from most pups by 12 weeks of age and is absent at 14 weeks of age. Until the distemper antibodies are gone, the puppy is immune to the virus and cannot be vaccinated against distemper with a vaccine that contains distemper virus.

Various vaccination schedules have been proposed for distemper, but they all include at least two vaccinations with the first at approximately 8 weeks of age and the last between 14 to 16 weeks of age.

An alternative to the usual distemper vaccination programs for puppies is the use of measles vaccine. Measles, a human virus, is closely related to the canine distemper virus. Measles vaccine will protect pups from distemper. The protection is of particular interest since maternal distemper antibodies do not interfere with the immunizing effect of the measles vaccine. The resistance induced by measles vaccine does not interfere with the distemper immune response following the administration of distemper vaccine after the disappearance of maternal antibody. In dogs fully susceptible to canine distemper vaccine, measles vaccination has no advantage. Puppies 4 to 6 weeks of age can be vaccinated with measles, but *must* be vaccinated with canine distemper at 16 weeks of age. Measles virus should *not* be used in adult dogs, especially bitches, because of the problem of conferring on puppies passive immunity to not only distemper but also to measles.

Rabies. This disease has been feared throughout history. Not every dog, person, or animal bitten by a rabid one develops the disease, but if the rabies virus should start to reproduce in the body, recoveries are not to be expected. Rabies is caused by a virus which is transmitted by contact with infected saliva, usually from the bite of a rabid animal or bat. Once the dog was thought to be the host that harbored this virus, with man and other animals accidental hosts. Later, it was learned that every mammal is susceptible to rabies, and wild animals have been found to be the reservoir hosts. Of especial importance in maintaining this virus in nature in the continental United States are the skunk, the fox, the raccoon, and bats, some species of which migrate seasonally from other countries.

Vaccination against rabies was one of the earliest preventive measures sought. Over 100 years ago Pasteur made a successful vaccine of a type that still is being produced in some parts of the world. Within recent years new methods and vaccines have been developed and programs initiated which greatly have reduced the incidence of rabies in dogs. Formerly about 6000 dogs and cats in the United States were diagnosed as having rabies each year, but following vaccination campaigns the disease steadily has declined. During this same time, the incidence of diagnosed cases of rabies in wild animals has risen.

Dogs still are the primary direct source of rabies in man. Dog bites in man are common, and whenever a person has been bitten by an unknown dog or wild animal there always is the fear that perhaps it could be rabid. Any dog or other animal that bites a person should be identified as soon as possible and kept under professional observation until tests can be made to determine whether or not it actually has rabies. Knowing that the dog is immune to rabies is of some comfort to the person bitten.

If a dog is bitten by another dog or animal the same information will be wanted, of course, and professional advice should be sought as soon as possible.

New rabies vaccines are currently available which confer protection to dogs for up to 3 years.

Canine Adenovirus I (Infectious Canine Hepatitis Virus). Contained in secretions of the body, especially urine, feces, and saliva, this virus usually enters the body of a susceptible dog by way of the mouth. An elevated temperature will occur three or four days later, its eyes will be reddened, and if the infection is severe, the dog will stop eating, and may enter a coma. Within six to ten days after infection, the dog either dies or has a quick recovery. After recovery, some dogs show a temporary opacity of the eye ("Blue Eye"). Whenever this is seen, it is an indication that the dog has had infectious hepatitis. In a few instances, this condition appears, temporarily, following vaccination, but the disease is prevented.

Infectious canine hepatitis vaccine and distemper are usually combined into a single vaccine, and sometimes these further are combined with different leptospiral components. The problem with maternal antibody is the same as with distemper vaccination. The same vaccination schedule as for distemper should be followed.

Kennel Cough Syndrome. Respiratory disease is one of the most important problems in the dog. Although the majority of cases exhibit signs of a mild upper respiratory disease with nasal discharge and intermittent coughing as the main feature, some cases do subsequently develop a more serious, sometimes fatal, pneumonia.

Kennel cough, or *infectious canine tracheobronchitis,* is a highly contagious respiratory disease in dogs. It is not life-threatening in itself—dogs usually recover within a few days or weeks.

There appear to be two forms of kennel cough.

1. The first is usually seen in dogs known to be vaccinated against distemper and hepatitis. This type is usually caused by canine parainfluenza virus alone or in combination with a bacteria, *Bordetella bronchiseptica.*

2. The second type is a more severe form of the disease seen in dogs with uncertain vaccination histories, such as dogs from pet shops, and dog shelters. Agents which may be isolated in this form include canine distemper virus, canine adenovirus 2, canine parainfluenza virus, and/or *Bordetella bronchiseptica.*

Canine Adenovirus 2 (Infectious Canine Laryngotracheitis Virus). Canine adenovirus 2 (CAV2) is closely related to canine adenovirus 1 (CAV1). Dogs vaccinated against infectious hepatitis (CAV1) are protected from CAV2. For this reason, CAV2 is primarily important in the unvaccinated dog population. CAV2 infection is restricted to the respiratory tract and is one of the infectious agents involved in the "Kennel cough" syndrome. The typical clinical sign in the uncomplicated case is a dry, hacking cough.

Canine Parainfluenza Virus. This is the primary virus in the "Kennel cough" syndrome, not only in unvaccinated dogs, but also in dogs vaccinated against distemper and hepatitis. The virus spreads very rapidly from dog to dog by aerosol inhalation or contact. The infection

694

is restricted to the respiratory tract and the typical clinical signs in the uncomplicated case is a dry, hacking cough.

Recently a vaccine has been produced to protect dogs from parainfluenza infection. This vaccine may be given alone or in combination with the distemper-hepatitis vaccines.

Canine Herpesvirus. Fatal infections of newborn pups are caused by a variety of viral and bacterial agents. Because of the suddenness with which death occurs and the diversity of possible causes, they are among the most difficult of all diseases to diagnose and treat. Among the viral infections that cause death of infant puppies, a canine herpesvirus was discovered. It seems to cause illness and death only in puppies less than one month old, generally in those one to three weeks of age. The virus may cause mild vaginitis in adult bitches or slight nasal discharge in older dogs, but only the young puppy suffers severe or fatal infection. Features of the neonatal illness consists of the sudden death of apparently healthy puppies after only a brief period of illness, usually lasting less than 24 hours.

Although the herpesvirus disease may resemble bacterial septicemia, a characteristic pathological change may be seen that distinguishes it from bacterial and other viral diseases, such as hepatitis. This change consists of speckled kidneys, caused by death of cells in the kidney cortex. They create a pale background, upon which are superimposed bright red hemorrhages or red spots. No other disease of dogs has similar lesions. Other characteristic changes are pneumonia and hemorrhages in various organs of the body.

Abortion has been seen occasionally of pups that have been infected while still in the uterus. The majority of pups probably are infected by their mother, who was coincidentally infected at the time of whelping. Infection may occur during passage through the birth canal or by infective saliva. Herpesvirus infection in adult dogs is usually so mild it is not noticed. Present evidence suggests that this virus is an uncommon cause of puppy deaths, although the exact number is not known, nor, of course, the number of abortions it may cause.

The observation has been made that bitches who have lost one litter of puppies from this infection later gave birth to normal puppies. No vaccine is available.

Infectious Canine Enteritis. In March 1978, an outbreak of severe hemorrhagic gastro-enteritis occurred among show dogs. The disease was characterized by a sudden onset of a bloody, foul-smelling diarrhea and vomiting which resulted in dehydration. The causative agent was isolated and identified as a canine coronavirus similar to one reported in 1971 following an outbreak of diarrhea in military dogs. Experimentally infected dogs recover spontaneously after 7 to 10 days. The severity of the 1978 outbreak may be related to stress since most of the cases appeared in show dogs. The virus appears to be highly contagious and is probably spread by contact with infectious feces.

At the present time there is no vaccine available. Dogs suspected of having the disease should be treated symptomatically for the diarrhea and vomiting *without delay*.

Infectious Papillomatosis (or Warts). Papillomas occur in various species of animals and are most prevalent in the young. These warts are caused by a virus which is highly specific for each host species. They are benign tumors, and usually are found either around the lips and in the mouths of young dogs, where they may cause considerable inconvenience, or in superficial layers of the skin. Warts usually are multiple in pups; in older dogs they generally occur as individual papillomas. Warts are highly contagious and often spread throughout a litter of puppies or even affect an entire kennel. They appear as a pedunculated, cauliflower-like, gray fibrous projection and may be very small, less than one-eighth of an inch in diameter, or reach a size of nearly two inches. Warts do not invade the skin or spread to other parts of the body in the manner of malignant cancers. They usually clear up spontaneously with time, but if they cause discomfort, or are slow to regress, surgical removal should be considered. Treatment by means of wart vaccines also has been successful. Most success has been obtained with an autogenous vaccine made directly from a suspension prepared from warts of the particular animal affected. Dogs that recover are rarely, if ever, infected again.

Canine Venereal Granulomata. This disease, characterized by soft tumors, has been found only in the mucous membranes of the genital tract of dogs. Both sexes of all breeds seem susceptible. It seems to spread readily, either by coitus from one sex to the other, or by a susceptible one licking an infected one, of either sex. Mucous membranes of the mother may help transmit infection, but it has not been transmitted conclusively by cell-free filtrates of tumor material, according to present records. The viral nature of this infection has not been proven beyond doubt.

The incubation period is about 40 days. Sometimes the tumors disappear spontaneously, and, occasionally, have been removed by skillful surgery.

Bacterial Diseases

A number of bacterial diseases of dogs, especially of young puppies, may result in serious illness or death. In contrast to man, remarkably few specific bacterial diseases affect dogs. Bacterial and fungal diseases may be caused by presence in the body of these microorganisms and products of their growth, as in septicemia, or by production of potent toxins circulated by the blood from a restricted focus of infection, as in tetanus. Examples of septicemic disease are seen in leptospirosis, salmonellosis, or various other pathogenic bacteria. Any condition, such as malnutrition, parasitism, concurrent infections, or various chronic diseases, such as nephritis, that lowers the resistance of a dog will predispose it to the development of certain bacterial infections. Some bacteria are found almost invariably as a component of mixed infections.

Leptospirosis is an infectious disease of man, dogs, cattle, pigs, horses, rodents, and certain other mammals. This disease is caused by living organisms called *leptospira*. The descriptive name comes from Greek words meaning "thin spiral". The three species listed below are considered the only ones of great importance to dogs in the United States:

L. icterohemmorrhagiae was named for symptoms it produces, including icterus, or jaundice. It is maintained in rodents. Their infected urine spreads the disease to other rodents, to dogs, other animals, and sometimes to man.

L. pomona, named for the section of Australia where it first was recognized as a febrile disease of dairy farmers, now has been found in cows, calves, swine, deer, and in dogs, especially those associated with infected animals or fed raw milk from infected cattle.

L. canicola, as the name indicates, is the species associated principally with dogs. It is maintained in dogs, and spreads, primarily in the urine of infected dogs, to other dogs, and to man, cattle, cats, and silver foxes. The fever it causes in human beings may be called "canicola fever". It tends to cause more nephritis in both dogs and in man, and more meningitis in man than do the other species mentioned. It usually is more serious in children than in adults.

There must be actual contact between leptospira and a susceptible animal. Unlike many bacteria and some viruses, these organisms seem able to penetrate unbroken skin and mucosa, the substance that lines the mouth, nose, digestive tract, or genital organs of all animals. To reproduce, they need only to divide, or split. Thus one becomes two and two become four, until within only a day there may be literally millions of leptospira present in the body. Damage follows destruction of cells and tissues, especially those of the liver and kidney. Eventually, they localize in the kidney and pass out of the body in urine, which infects susceptible animals. Leptospira have been found in saliva.

Leptospirosis is a disease of sudden onset. Dogs may refuse to eat, have elevated temperatures, vomiting, and congestion of the conjunctiva, symptoms which resemble those of infectious canine hepatitis. In the latter disease, a characteristic feature is failure of the blood to clot normally, a sign not seen in leptospirosis, and valuable as a diagnostic aid. Dogs are usually weak, reluctant to move, and show abdominal pain. In fatal cases, death usually occurs five to ten days after onset of symptoms. Mortality seldom exceeds ten per cent, deaths being much more common in the young animal. Recovery never is rapid because of damage to digestive tract, liver, and kidneys. Convalescence usually requires a week to ten days. During the acute period of illness dogs may have scant, highly colored urine and little or no feces. There may be trembling or even convulsions.

More common than the acute form of the disease is a chronic illness, characterized by progressive damage to the kidneys. In such instances, death may occur long after initial illness has subsided. Kidney function, which may be poor during acute illness, usually returns to normal within four months, and there is no conclusive proof that any lasting residual effects occur, although the familiar disease of older dogs called "chronic interstitial nephritis" has been attributed to leptospiral damage.

Unlike viral diseases, leptospiral infections will respond to intense therapy with antibiotics, and the carrier state will be prevented.

Vaccination of young dogs with killed leptospiral bacterins is recommended, although the immunity is of short duration, and it should be understood that vaccinations should be repeated at intervals of every six months to a year for adequate protection. One species of leptospira does not give immunity against another.

Bordetella bronchiseptica. Bordetella appears to play a major role in canine respiratory disease. Originally, it was thought to be important only as a secondary invader in viral infections. Recently, it has been shown it alone can preduce mild respiratory disease, primarily coughing, however, the clinical signs are more severe in conjunction with viral infections. There is no bacterin (vaccine) for the disease. Antibiotic therapy is difficult due to the location of the bacteria in the respiratory tract.

Canine Brucellosis. Caused by *Brucella canis,* this recently recognized disease of dogs has been found in dogs of many breeds. It was first reported in Beagles, and this led to some rumors that only Beagles were susceptible, but this is not true. Both sexes are equally susceptible, and there is no age preference. Many breeds in addition to Beagles have been found infected, and the disease now has been identified in all of the states, including Alaska.

Common signs of infection in bitches have been abortion, failures to whelp, and enlarged lymph nodes. Male animals may have *epididymitis,* swelling of the testicle or scrotum, and, in some instances, atrophy of one or both testes. Bacteria may circulate in the blood of infected animals for longer than a year, and organisms are shed in great numbers from aborted discharges and vaginal excretions. Vaginal discharge may persist more than a month after an abortion. These materials are highly infective. Great care should be taken not to touch such material with bare hands, for it can spread to human beings, especially owners and veterinarians.

Generally there are no signs of impending abortion and bitches may appear normal before and following expulsion of dead or live pups. To the careful observer, dogs have been noted to have poor hair coats. They appear slightly depressed and may fail to hunt in their usual manner. Some males suffer loss of libido. The disease often is insidious, and infected animals may appear normal but serve as a source of infection to other dogs in the kennel.

A serological test now has been developed to assist in diagnosis of canine brucellosis. If an abortion occurs, all dogs in the kennel should be blood tested. Positive reactors should be removed. Infectious abortions should be expected if apparently healthy bitch aborts approximately two weeks before term, or if one fails to whelp after two or three matings. Males associated with females that have aborted should be examined for genital health, enlarged lymph nodes, especially those in the neck region, and fertility. A semen examination may reveal abnormal or low numbers of sperm. Infected males have been found to transmit the infection via their semen. Bacterins and antibiotics tested thus far have not proved effective. Control consists of serological tests and removal of animals found infected.

Salmonellosis is caused by a bacterium similar to the one that produces typhoid fever in humans. As a disease in dogs, it tends to affect only the young and debilitated animals. The clinical signs of vomiting, bloody, explosive diarrhea, and dehydration from fluid loss, indicate an infection of the intestinal tract, as ingestion of spoiled food containing the Salmonella organism is the route of infection. In young animals, death can result from septicemia when the organism gains entrance to the blood from the intestine and affects the liver and other internal organs. Older dogs usually experience a severe case of gastroenteritis. Intravenous fluids to combat the shock of fluid loss, antibiotics to kill the bacteria, antispasmodics and intestinal protectants are all needed for treatment. Isolation of affected animals and disinfection of the premises are necessary to prevent the spread of infection via contaminated feces.

Tetanus is not as common in dogs as in man or farm animals, but its occurrence is not rare. It should be considered in all cases of muscle stiffness, especially if there are characteristic spasms. When the tetanus bacillus, *Clostridium tetani,* multiplies in animal tissues, it produces a potent toxin which affects the nervous system and produces typical signs of this painful disease. Tetanus is characterized by generalized muscular stiffness that commences with spasms of the jaw and temporal muscles and progresses to a stiff "sawhorse" gait. There is difficulty in swallowing; often the tail will become rigid. Spasms increase in severity until exhaustion occurs, accompanied by difficult breathing. Death from tetanus is due to exhaustion, respiratory failure, or pneumonia.

Soil, feces, and putrifying material may contain spores of the bacillus. These enter the body through puncture wounds or can follow surgical operations if wounds are not allowed proper circulation of air. Tetanus may occur as a complication following a broken leg should a cast become too tightly fixed, allowing spores to germinate in wound tissue. If signs of tetanus occur, the animal should receive prompt treatment to relieve painful muscle spasms, counteract the effects of the dangerous toxin, and remove its source. The dog should be kept in a dark and quiet room. If it lives for more than a week after onset of tetanus, chances for recovery improve. This generally requires from two to four weeks. Hospitalization is imperative at this time.

Neonatal and "Fading Puppy Syndrome". Mortality of young puppies may be as high as 20–30% per litter, a problem very serious to some breeders. Bacterial diseases, rather than viruses, are the most common cause of death of puppies under three weeks of age. Infection of the umbilicus by Staphylococcus or Streptococcus bacteria can cause fatal septicemia. Pseudomonas, the bacillus of green pus, or E. coli, a common intestinal bacterium, can cause severe hemorrhagic enteritis. Affected individuals often isolate themselves from the rest of the litter, cry intermittently and die within several days after birth. Fever is not a characteristic as puppies do not regulate their temperatures well.

Puppies may acquire these infections from infected milk, contamination of the whelping area with feces of other animals, or from a low grade infection within the dam's uterus.

Treatment is often unsuccessful as pups die before therapy can be initiated. Temperature is an important factor and pups should be kept at 80–85°F after signs of disease are noticed. To prevent the spread of infection, stricken puppies should be removed from the mother, placing them in an incubator when possible. Treatment with antibiotics and supplemental fluids should be begun immediately. Recovery rates are good in puppies that survive more than two days. Because the diseases are acquired from the environment, cleaning and disinfecting the whelping area and treating any bitches which have lost previous litters is often helpful. Other factors which lower the puppies' resistance, such as coccidia, roundworm, or hookworm burdens, impair the ability to fight off infections and complicate the situation.

Rickettsial Diseases

Salmon Poisoning. Salmon disease results from ingestion of raw salmon and some species of trout that carry larvae of the salmon fluke. The fluke larvae harbor a small microorganism, *Neorickettsia helminthoeca,* which actually causes the disease. Infected dogs often die within seven to ten days after initial signs of illness, which generally begin about one week after ingestion of parasitized fish. Affected dogs have high fever, 104° to 107°F, which gradually decreases for six to eight days, after which temperatures become subnormal. There is severe depression and dogs refuse food. Extreme thirst is common and dogs vomit frequently. Lymph nodes usually are enlarged and diarrhea becomes progressively severe until the time of death. There frequently is blood in the stool, and dogs become rapidly emaciated and dehydrated. The mortality rate has been estimated to 50 to 90 per cent. When the above signs are seen in areas where the disease is indigenous, salmon disease should be suspected. The disease is reported, thus far, only from the Pacific Northwest in streams and rivers where salmon spawn. Atlantic salmon and eastern trout have not been found similarly infected.

Vaccines for this rickettsial disease are not available, but dogs that recover are solidly immune. Prevention is best accomplished by not allowing ingestion of fresh salmon and trout. Cooking or freezing inactivate the flukes and prevents transmission of the disease. Vigorous treatment has proved effective, if initiated early in the course of the disease.

701

Canine Ehrlichiosis, also known as tropical canine pancytopenia, is a disease caused by the rickettsia-like organism, *Ehrlichia canis.* It is characterized by *pancytopenia,* a decrease in the number of red blood cells, white blood cells, and platelets to critical levels where anemia, hemorrhage and fatal susceptibility to other disease can occur.

There are two phases of the disease, seemingly related to the breed affected, as the German Shepherd is highly susceptible to the chronic phase. In the acute phase, just after inoculation of the organism into the dog via a tick bite, there is mild disease of two-four weeks' duration. Fever, decreased food consumption, discharges from the eyes and nose, and weight loss occur. In most dogs other than the German Shepherd, infection persists but the signs abate. In the chronic phase a tremendous decrease in the red blood cells and platelets causes bleeding from the nose, mouth and intestinal tract. Other infections occur more easily in these dogs as the lowered number of white blood cells cannot fight off infections. Often edema of all four legs develop and there is moderate to severe weight loss two to three months after initial infection with *Ehrlichia canis.* The lymph nodes of the body are moderately enlarged.

Diagnosis is accomplished by finding the organism within affected cells on a blood smear. Carrier dogs can be determined by a serum test for antibodies to the organism. Treatment is often curative in the acute form of the disease, while in the chronic form, blood transfusions and intravenous fluids are often needed to maintain life. The pancytopenia of the chronic phase may persist for months after eradication of the organism from the body.

Fungal Diseases

Ringworm is a disease of dogs and other animals caused by at least three species of fungi that parasitize the skin. These fungi are referred to as *dermatophytes,* meaning skin plants, and may cause severe infections, especially in animals less than one year of age. Short-haired breeds appear to be more commonly affected than long-haired ones. In addition to skin lesions, ringworm fungi may cause infections of hair and nails.

The most common fungus causing ringworm in dog is *Microsporum canis.* This microorganism is spread by contact from infected animals to other animals and to man. Children who associate with affected dogs frequently become infected, and the converse probably is true.

Dogs with ringworm may occasionally appear normal, but the majority of affected animals have characteristic lesions that appear as circular scaly areas where hair has been lost. Stubby bits of broken grayish hair often are found within and at the periphery of these areas. Sometimes there are pustules and small vesicles at the edges of denuded areas. Severely affected dogs sometimes have scaling, redness, and loss of hair over large areas of the body. Heavy crust formations may be seen, especially in young dogs.

Ringworm generally can be recognized by the characteristic changes noted above; a definite diagnosis can be made only by laboratory tests of skin scrapings and examination under ultraviolet light.

Excellent methods for treating ringworm have been developed. Veterinary advice should be sought as soon as signs of ringworm appear. All old bedding and litter should be removed and burned immediately, because fungi are extremely hardy organisms and reinfection of dogs may occur as well as human infections. Cages and kennel areas should be disinfected thoroughly with an antifungal preparation.

Fungi of various kinds are found in widely scattered sections of the country. The majority are specific in certain localities only, where the soil may be contaminated. Particles of dust from such soil may carry the infection to man and animals by inhalation.

Fungal pneumonias are usually seen as a part of more generalized infections. They are characterized by enlarged lymph nodes, coughing, and varying degrees of respiratory distress. Dogs usually show a chronic intractable cough and there may be diarrhea. Most fungal infections terminate fatally, even with treatment, in contrast to bacterial pneumonias, which generally respond to antibiotics. Animals with any form of pneumonia should receive prompt medical treatment and be placed in warm dry quarters. *Nocardia asteroides* causes generalized purulent nodules in the lungs, lymph nodes, and in other organs. This fungal disease is serious for animals and man. Other important fungal diseases that cause pneumonia as a principal sign of illness are *histoplasmosis, coccidioidomycosis, cryptococcis,* and *blastomycosis*. These fungi are considered highly infectious to man and some animals through contaminated dust. Coccidioidomycosis is found only in dry low areas of the Southwest, while histoplasmosis is much more common in the Midwest, Missippi Valley, and South. Blastomycosis occurs most frequently in the Southwest, Midwest, and West coast of the United States. Cryptococcal infections, though uncommon, are more widely distributed.

703

Protozoan Diseases

Canine Hemobartenollosis. This infectious anemia of dogs is caused by *Hemobartonella canis,* a protozan parasite which attaches to the surface of the red blood cells. It is known to be carried by the brown dog tick, *Rhipiphalus sanguineus,* but other modes of transmission are thought to exist. This disease is very rare except in those dogs which have had their spleen removed for another reason.

Affected animals may experience a slight fever but the most common signs of the disease are pale gums, lips, and ears, and dark brown urine. The protozoa changes the red blood cell membrane to the extent that many of the cells rupture in the blood vessles, causing anemia, jaundice and hemoglobonuria. A blood transfusion is often necessary to save the life of the dog before specific antibiotics can be started to kill the infection.

Babesiosis is an infection of the red blood cells by *Babesia canis,* a protozoa carried from dog to dog by the brown dog tick. There are two forms of the disease, both characterized by anemia and jaundice. In the acute form, so many red blood cells are destroyed that the dog becomes feverish, develops tremendous jaundice and dies. The urine is often stained to the color of coffee from the hemoglobin of destroyed red blood cells. In the chronic form, marginal anemia and mild jaundice may be the only signs present. Treatment for babesiosis is not entirely effective, and blood transfusions may be needed to save a dog with the acute form.

Coccidiosis is an infection of the intestinal tract with the one-celled protozoa of the Isospora family. As there are three individual protozoa, infection with one does not confer immunity to the other two and a dog may have coccidiosis up to three times in its life. Diarrhea, often bloody, and dehydration are the two most common signs seen. Anemia, depression, and weight loss may also occur. Puppies seem to be the hardest hit, as coccidia can be found in the stool of mature dogs without any sign of illness.

The disease is acquired through the ingestion of the infective form, named oocytes, so improper sanitary conditions do much to maintain the disease in a kennel. As the signs are very similar to those seen in other forms of intestinal parasitism, a stool sample must be examined by a veterinarian to diagnose coccidiosis. The treatment is with an oral antibiotic, and an antispasmodics and intestinal protective agents help alleviate the straining often associated with the diarrhea.

Toxoplasmosis. This common protozoan disease of dogs and other warm-blooded animals is prevalent throughout the world. It can be transmitted from some affected animals to man, and thus the family's health must be considered when a diagnosis of toxoplasmosis is made. The parasite, *Toxoplasma gondii,* invades virtually all multiplying cells in the body. It may be transmitted congenitally to the fetus by infected mothers. Sputum, nasal secretions, and feces may be infectious.

Toxoplasmosis in dogs occurs in all parts of world, but the majority of infections are either inapparent or have very mild symptoms of a vague nature. Animals that become clinically ill usually are those whose resistance has been lowered by simultaneous distemper infection. Young animals are the most commonly and seriously affected. Severe or fatal primary toxoplasmosis is rare.

Signs of illness are not characteristic, but include fever, apathy, depressed appetite, cough, difficult and labored breathing, enteritis, emaciation, and disturbances such a tremor of the nervous system, incoordination, and paralysis. Toxoplasmosis should be considered in dogs under one year of age, with unexplained severe gastrointenstinal, respiratory, or nervous system illness that accompanies or follows other infectious diseases, such as distemper or hepatitis. Definitive diagnosis can be made only by demonstration or isolation of the organism or by serological tests. Because toxoplasmosis can cause human illness, even though actual transmission from dog to man has not been shown, it is believed wise to destroy proved infected animals that are proven to be clinically ill.

NON-INFECTIOUS DISEASES

In addition to nutritional deficiencies and genetic defects discussed under those headings, dogs develop some diseases without infection.

Factors that operate within the body can cause cell destruction or failure of cells normally to function. Hormonal imbalances produce a variety of patterns in disease, as does lack of certain enzymes. Allergies may affect some dogs seriously, as well as the condition called auto-immune reaction, in which the dog has developed a hypersensitivity to its body's own protein, which has been altered chemically and assumes the role of an allergen.

Genetic defects are not always apparent at birth but may, later in life, appear as dysplastic hips, PRA or other eye problems, inability to form a number of essential enzymes, or other conditions.

Neoplasms, those tumorous growths that seemingly appear spontaneously, must have a basic cause, or perhaps result from two causes working together.

Many skin abnormalities, termed eczemas by some, are of as yet unknown origin. Some are caused by allergies of various kinds and some from insects and other parasites, or irritating substances or infections. Some, such as papillomas or warts, are caused by viruses and are infectious diseases. Others are calluses, caused by external conditions.

Allergies

Allergic reactions usually are manifested by sneezing and coughing, intense itching, dermatitis, or diarrhea. Materials, termed allergens, that cause such reactions may be protein, carbohydrate, lipids, or simple inorganic chemicals. They cause a reaction whether applied by contact, in food and drugs, or inhaled. Reactions occur whenever a dog that can react is brought into contact with material that causes the reaction. The reaction apparently is brought about by combination of the allergen, or antigen, with antibody. The combination releases a substance that resembles histamine, or perhaps other substances, to produce the clinical reaction.

If an allergen is not brought into contact with a sensitized dog, no reaction occurs. Or if the dog loses its sensitivity, there is no reaction. Some allergens, such as plant pollens, occur only at certain times of the year. Such variables lead to situations of seasonal affliction, which may occur one year because of sensitization, but not another year if the dog no longer is sensitized. In making a determination of the allergen, a good history helps. Skin or food tests that can remove or add a suspected cause may reveal the specific offender, which can be avoided henceforth, or treated in some cases.

Auto-Immune Diseases

The major activity of the immune system is to process and destroy foreign substances which enter the body, such as viruses, bacteria and fungi. An auto-immune disease occurs when the immune system reacts against tissue in the body as though it were a foreign substance.

Auto-immune Hemolytic Anemia. In auto-immune hemolytic anemia, the red blood cell is the target for destruction. Signs include pale ears and gums, fast heart rate, weakness, fever, dark yellow-brown urine, dark brown stool and increased respiratory effort. A specific blood test, the Coombs test, confirms the diagnosis.

Immune-Mediated Thrombocytopenia Purpura. The platelet is the cell under attack in this disease. Signs are referrable to a severe decrease in the platelet count which causes a bleeding tendency. Bruises and hematomas occur after minimal trauma and appear on the skin where the hair coat is thin—belly, groin, armpit. Hemorrhage into the mouth, intestinal tract, urinary tract and eyes can occur. Blood tests are necessary to differentiate the condition from rat poisoning and other diseases.

Rheumatoid Arthritis. This disease causes swelling and tenderness of many of the joints of the paws and lower legs. The joints close to the body, hip and shoulder, are usually spared. Morning stiffness which decreases on exercise is common. Pain may become so severe that the dog carries a leg. The joints in the same location on both front or hind legs are often affected simultaneously; radiographs of the joints often reveal erosion and destruction of bone adjacent to the joints. A positive rheumatoid factor test is helpful for diagnosis.

Pemphigus Vulgaris. The skin is the target for destruction in pemphigus vulgaris, with lesions commonly occurring in the tongue, gums, lips, eyelids, anus, vulva, nailbeds and around the nose. Ulcers, erosions and blisters often develop, then become encrusted.

Systemic Lupus Erythematosus (SLE). In this disease, many organs are affected because the immune reaction is against genetic material within cells. An animal with lupus commonly develops signs of the other auto-immune diseases including anemia, bleeding tendencies and swollen joints. In addition, skin lesions similar to those in pemphigus have been noted. Organs involved may include skin, bone marrow, liver and kidney. Other degenerative changes within the kidneys can lead into acute renal failure. The diagnosis of SLE is accomplished by blood tests demonstrating antibodies to genetic material within cells. The tests for the other auto-immune disease are often positive.

The young female dog between the age of two and eight years has a greater risk of developing an auto-immune disease, as roughly 75% of the affected individuals fit those two categories. All breeds are equally susceptible. Treatment is based on suppression of the immune response with certain drugs, the most common one being a form of cortisone. In those cases with life-threatening anemia or bleeding, stronger drugs have been used. Blood transfusions may be necessary in critical cases, but are not used routinely.

Large doses of immunosuppressive drugs are initially needed to control the disease, after which the amounts can be tapered, and even discontinued. Exacerbations are commonly seen and any episode can result in death if treatment is delayed.

Hormone Imbalance

Hormones are the chemical compounds that cause cellular activity of a most basic nature. They are produced by various glands in the body and generally are carried by the blood to their target organ where they either stimulate or depress activity. Control of hormone production or secretion is usually determined by the substance the target organ secretes or metabolizes in such a way that a negative feedback system exists. If the level of hormone in the body rises, so does the amount of substance released by the target organ. This increased level has an inhibitory effect on the endocrine gland, causing a lowering of hormone production which then allows for a diminished amount of substance produced. Disease states occur when there is insufficient production of hormone or when the negative feedback mechanism no longer functions and excessive hormone is elaborated.

Diabetes Mellitus. Diabetes mellitus is caused by the relative or absolute lack of insulin production from cells within the pancreas. Insulin normally causes a lowering of the blood glucose level after a meal by allowing the glucose to enter fat tissue in the body where the sugar is then stored for slow release between meals. In the absence of insulin, sugar accumulates in blood and is eliminated from the body in the urine, causing an increase in the amount of urine produced as water is used to dilute the sugar passed by the kidneys. There is a compensatory increase in the water consumption to balance the increase in urination thereby preventing dehydration. As there is insufficient storage of sugar in the body for release between meals, the body begins to break down the protein stores to release the glucose required for energy. This can cause weight loss despite an increase in appetite. There is actually starvation of the body in the midst of plenty, for although the blood glucose level rises, the body cells receive little glucose, for insulin is required to transport it into the cells.

The typical diabetic dog is a middle-aged female who shows a gradual increase in urine production, water consumption and possibly weight loss. On occasion, loss of vision may be the most noticeable symptom as cataracts are very common in the diabetic and cause reduced vision.

When the body begins to break down protein excessively, metabolic waste products can build up in the blood in the form of ketone bodies. Nausea and vomiting occur and dehydration develops quickly as the dog is no longer able to balance an increase in urine production with an increase of water consumption. This form of diabetes, called ketoacidosis, is very dangerous and dogs can go into hyperglycemic coma very quickly and die. Intravenous fluids, insulin administration and control of acidosis are necessary to prevent death.

The non-ketotic diabetic must be treated with insulin every day or two for the remainder of its life. An intact female *must* be spayed or the diabetes will go out of control with every heat cycle. A constant diet and daily exercise are necessary to keep energy requirements and food intake constant so there are few fluctuations in the blood glucose level from day to day.

Insulinoma. This condition is caused by a functional tumor of the beta cells of the pancreas, resulting in excess insulin production. Insulin is released in excessive amounts after a meal and causes the blood glucose to drop to a level where weakness, muscle twitching, incoordination, and convulsions occur. Insulinomas have been reported in many breeds of dogs; older dogs have a higher risk of developing the tumor although the tumor has been found in dogs as young as 3½ years.

Diagnosis is accomplished by finding a lower than normal blood glucose level after a 12–24 hour fast. The fact that feeding honey or karo syrup to an affected individual causes a reversal of the neurologic signs is suggestive of a hypoglemic condition. The majority of the tumors are malignant, and if they have not spread before surgery, surgical treatment may be successful.

Pancreatic Insufficiency. Beside the production of insulin, the pancreas also elaborates most of the enzymes necessary for the proper digestion of food in the intestinal tract. Repeated bouts of inflammation or infection of the pancreas cause blockage of the secretory ducts, and the enzymes destroy functional tissue of the organ itself. This results in scarring of the tissue and loss of secretory ability. Strangely, the cells which manufacture insulin are often spared. Due to the lack of enzymes, food is passed through the digestive tract without proper digestion and absorption. The body stores of fat, then muscle, are broken down and weight loss ensues. The appetite is increased tremendously and these dogs will eat whatever is offered them. The stool is characteristically light in color and may appear oily and greasy due to the high amounts of undigested fats and proteins present. Larger amounts of water are present in the feces causing a soft to liquid appearance. The absolute volume of stool produced per day is increased.

Clinical signs such as these are highly suggestive of enzyme insufficiency but tests are necessary to substantiate the diagnosis. Supplementation with oral forms of pancreatic enzymes is the treatment, along with a low fat, moderate protein diet. As the enzymes are destroyed in the high acid environment of the stomach, large amounts of enzyme are often necessary to insure enough enzyme reaches the small intestine where absorption and digestion take place. The destruction of the pancreas must be nearly complete for an insufficiency state to develop as only 5-10% of the organ is needed for adequate enzyme production. Therapy must be continued for the dog's entire life span.

Diabetes Insipidus. Excessive urine production and water consumption are hallmarks of diabetes insipidus. The lack of antidiuretic hormone, ADH, causes the kidneys to lose the ability to produce a concentrated urine. This rare condition in dogs needs to be differentiated from the other causes of increased water consumption and urine production such as chronic kidney disease and diabetes mellitus. Injections of synthetic ADH can be given to enable the dog to control the concentration of its urine and bring the water intake back to normal.

Addison's Disease and Cushing's Syndrome. The adrenals are two of the major glands in the body that control functions necessary for everyday life and stressful emergency situations. Cortisol and aldosterone are the two most important hormones elaborated by the adrenal glands, each by a different zone of the outer portion of the gland. Aldosterone is intimately interconnected with the maintenance of body fluid volume and is produced in the outermost layer of the gland. Cortisol is manufactured in the middle layer, and is responsible for converting normal metabolism to the metabolism necessary for prolonged stressful situations. Two different diseases exist, one of inadequate hormone synthesis, the other of excessive synthesis.

Addison's disease is caused by inadequate production of aldosterone and cortisol. Female dogs are more frequently affected than males and the usual age of onset is between 2 and 7 years.

As the adrenals lose their function slowly, the signs of the disease come on slowly and do not become noticeable until a stressful situation occurs. Insufficient cortisol levels cause vomiting, abdominal pain and decreased appetite. The body is unable to produce sufficient intermediates for metabolism and lethargy and confusion can be seen. The lack of aldosterone leads to excessive electrolyte and water loss from the kidneys, and when coupled with the already present vomiting and anorexia, weight loss and dehydration can develop within days. Blood pressure drops and the heart rate becomes slower and weaker. All of these can snowball to cause irreversible shock and death after an event that normally would be handled without a problem. Such events include minor surgery, infections or heavy exercise.

Blood tests are the only way to definitively diagnose the condition as many other diseases mimic the clinical signs of Addison's disease. Intravenous fluids are necessary to restore the fluid and electrolyte loss and to combat the shock before organs become permanently damaged. Administration of synthetic cortisol and aldosterone can quickly restore the body's level of these hormones. When the situation is no longer critical, a maintenance dose of aldosterone can be formulated. As the damage to the adrenal glands is rarely reversible, replacement therapy is necessary for the remainder of the dog's lifespan. This can be in one of three forms: an oral tablet for daily use; an injection given by a veterinarian every three to four weeks; or a pellet placed under the skin of the back every six to ten months. Cortisol rarely needs to be given as the body seems to adjust to the deficiency once aldosterone has been replaced.

Cushing's Syndrome. When an excessive amount of cortisol is produced in the body, there are three possible causes for the condition. A tumor can exist within the portion of the brain responsible for the stimulation of the adrenal glands. If a portion of the adrenal gland itself turns into a tumor, it may excrete cortisol in larger amounts than normal. Thirdly, the zone of the glands which manufactures the cortisol may enlarge and produce excessive amounts of hormone when normally stimulated. The condition which develops, Cushing's syndrome, is characterized by various signs and symptoms. Increased urine production, thirst and appetite are very commonly seen. A "pot-bellied" appearance develops due to enlargement of the liver and weakening of the muscles of the belly wall. The hair coat is lost gradually over the prominences and wear areas of the body such as the flanks and neck, but these areas quickly enlarge to include the back and both sides of the body. The skin itself becomes thin, scaly and dry with an increase in pigmentation. Calcium can be deposited in the skin of the groin, neck and back. Affected individuals are more susceptible to infections, the skin, respiratory tract and urinary tract being the most common sites involved.

Although the combination of many of these signs is suggestive of Cushing's syndrome, blood tests are often required to differentiate the three causes of the condition. A tumor of the brain is not surgically removable and often grows within the brain to cause other neurologic signs. The treatment of choice for a tumor of one adrenal is surgical removal. With hyperactivity of both glands, there is both a surgical and a medical treatment. Removal of both glands creates an individual with Addison's disease, necessitating lifelong therapy. Medical treatment uses a drug which destroys the zone responsible for cortisol synthesis. Just enough drug is given to shrink the size of the zone to a more normal size, thereby lowering the production of cortisol. Individual sensitivity to the drug may cause more destruction than anticipated, causing a temporary or permanent Addisonian state.

Hypothyroidism. The thyroid glands secrete a hormone which controls the basic metabolic rate of the entire body. Inadequate hormone levels reset the body to function at a lower metabolic level. Dogs put on fat easily on a normal diet, become sluggish and seek a warm place to sleep even in the summer months. Hair changes are most noticeable and include loss of hair from the flanks and back, increased pigmentation of the skin, scaling and seborrhea. Secondary bacterial infection of the skin is common. The ears can be affected by seborrhea to such an extent that the canals become filled with thick, yellow greasy scales. Females cease to have heat cycles and males lose libido.

There are several specific blood tests available to determine the level of thyroid function. Tablets of thyroxine, the thyroid hormone, are used to treat the condition. Improvement of the animal's condition is generally noted within 3 to 4 months, although the seborrhea and hair loss may take several months to resolve.

Other Non-Infectious Diseases

Acute Gastric Dilation-Torsion (Bloat) is a life-threatening process in the dog. The condition occurs most frequently in large, deep-chested breeds. The typical history is recent ingestion of a large meal followed by exercise. The etiology of G-D-T is unknown but the anatomic changes are easily recognized. Restlessness and unproductive attempts to vomit are usually the first signs. The abdomen becomes severely distended with a drum-like sound on tapping. Depending on the duration of the syndrome, various degrees of shock may be seen. The element of time is the most important in the treatment of Gastric-Dilatation-Torsion. With the onset of the syndrome, numerous changes take place within the body which, if not stopped, become irreversible. Death may result in hours. Immediate surgery provides the best chance for survival. The stomach must be decompressed and the torsion corrected by repositioning the stomach.

Epilepsy is a disease characterized by repetitive seizures or convulsions. The causes of epileptic fits include viral, bacterial and fungal infections of the brain, blood clot formation, lead poisoning, trauma to the head and brain tumors. Low blood sugar or irregular heart beat can also cause episodes that look like convulsions. If no cause for the seizures can be found, the condition is called idiopathic epilepsy. Certain breeds, including the German Shepherd, St. Bernard, Irish Setter, Poodle and Beagle have a higher incidence of epilepsy than other breeds.

When a dog is having a seizure, the safest thing to do is leave it alone and remove any objects nearby that might injure the animal. Trying to awaken the dog is futile as it is not sleeping. After having a seizure, a dog is often confused and bewildered. He should be placed in a quiet, dark room to recover completely.

Treatment with oral anti-epileptic drugs helps prevent the seizures or make them milder. There are many types of medication available and administration of several drugs simultaneously may be necessary to control the seizures. When the dog is having continuous convulsions or seizures so frequently that recovery between episodes is impossible, coma and death may occur. Emergency treatment with intravenous drugs is necessary to stop the convulsions and sedate the dog.

713

Cystic Calculi. Bladder stones are a fairly common entity in both male and female dogs. Except for the Dalmatian, there is no true breed predisposition. The Dalmatian dog is more prone to develop urate stones due to an inherited enzyme difference; they can develop the other three types of stones as well. Any breed of dog can develop any of the three types of bladder stones.

The location of the stones in the female is nearly always in the bladder. In the male, small stones which develop in the bladder may be passed into the urethra, become lodged and cause blockage. The female dog has a wider, shorter urethra and rarely suffers from blockage.

Signs indicative of bladder stones include straining to urinate, urinating small amounts of urine frequently, bloody urine and increased water consumption. Inability to pass urine while straining or dribbling suggests blockage. Infection is encountered in association with bladder stones and must be treated if present. This is particularly important as one type of stone seems to form in the presence of infection.

Surgical removal of all stones in the bladder and urethra is the only successful treatment. Compounds which increase or decrease the acidity of the urine are used to help prevent the formation of additional stones. The exact substance used depends on the type of stone present. Salting the food to increase water consumption and simultaneously urine production helps decrease the concentration of minerals in the urine, thereby reducing the rate of stone formation.

Neoplasms

Tumors have been reported from virtually every location in the body. Benign and localized tumors may do little damage, unless pressure from their size interferes with function of certain organs, or if their location predisposes them to external injury and consequent bacterial infection.

Not all tumors are benign. Many are characterized by malignancy, and some of these can spread, or *metastasize*. If a malignant tumor thus spreads it establishes new foci, and, if this continues, death must ensue eventually. Determining the nature of a neoplasm requires microscopic examination of cellular tissue obtained by biopsy. Based upon the findings, decisions are made as to the type of treatment necessary.

DEGENERATIVE DISEASE

When vital organs are damaged beyond repair by progressive degenerative changes, signs of disease occur. Several such organs are the heart and kidney.

Congestive Heart Failure. The heart pumps blood throughout the body, providing nutrients and oxygen to the tissues and carrying waste products to the excretory organs. There are four chambers in the heart; valves between the chambers insure the flow of blood from the body to the heart, into the lungs, back to the heart and then to the body. As the valves become thickened and irregular, blood leaks back into the heart chambers, decreasing the flow of blood into the lungs and the general circulation. The blood which should be sent to the body backs up into the lungs, and the blood which should be circulating in the lungs backs up into the general circulation. The fluid portion of the blood escapes into the lung tissue and air passages, organs of the body and the abdominal cavity.

Signs of heart failure are referrable to sites of fluid accumulation. Coughing after resting or sleeping, decreased exercise tolerance and difficult breathing come from fluid in the lungs. Enlargement of abdominal organs, swelling of the abdomen and edema in the legs are caused by backup of fluid into the general circulation. A pounding heart beating against the chest wall can be felt in some cases. When a veterinarian examines the dog, he usually finds a loud heart murmur and fluid sounds within the lungs. Radiographs can determine the degree of heart enlargement and an EKG can diagnose how severe the enlargement may be, and if an irregular heart beat is present.

Digitalis and diuretics are necessary to strengthen the contraction of the heart and to promote excretion of excess fluid respectively. Feeding a low salt diet helps prevent fluid retention. Limiting the animal's exercise helps reduce the stress on the heart also.

Cardiomyopathy. Canine congestive cardiomyopathy is a disease which affects the large and giant breeds of dogs. It usually develops between the first and fifth year. The condition is characterized by degeneration and weakening of the heart muscle which permits stasis of blood in the lungs and abdomen, similar to heart failure. The size of the heart itself is greatly enlarged and predisposes to irregularities in the heart rate. The pulse rate is sometimes only one-quarter or one-fifth the heart rate.

Signs of cardiomyopathy include fatigue, cough, distended abdomen, swollen legs and collapse. The pulse and heart beat are both very irregular. Prompt treatment with digitalis to strengthen the heart and diuretics to reduce the fluid is imperative. Other drugs to lessen the irregularity of the heart are often used. Life expectancy is short once the condition is diagnosed (6 to 15 months) as the drugs used in treatment cannot reverse the changes in the heart muscle itself.

Chronic Kidney Failure. The two kidneys comprise the clearing house for many of the metabolic waste products of the body. Their functional reserve is high. Indeed, if one kidney is removed, the other can handle all the excretory functions normally. It is not until 70% or more of the kidney tissue is damaged that signs of renal failure develop. These signs include increased water consumption and urine production, weight loss, inappetence, vomiting and diarrhea. If the disease is slowly progressive, a non-responsive anemia develops and the gums and lips become white. When the kidneys fail completely, there is little or no urine produced and vomiting becomes very severe. Dehydration develops rapidly and death is imminent.

It is important to recognize the signs of kidney failure early as dietary changes lessen the production of metabolic waste products that worsen the vomition and diarrhea. Many dogs live comfortable lives with marginal kidney function if they are allowed free access to clean water and never experience limitation of their water intake.

All breeds are affected equally, males in equal proportion to females. Contrary to popular belief, this is not a disease of older adult dogs. When degeneration starts early in life, signs of disease can develop at the age of three to five years.

Aging Process. The reasons are not precisely understood, but with advancing years there is progressive loss of normal cellular function in vital organs. Eventually, a stage is reached when an organ is unable to perform its normal activity. These conditions can include disturbed kidney function, liver derangement, circulatory disturbances and heart disease, respiratory difficulty, or digestive upsets. Although these inevitable changes are irreversible, an accurate diagnosis should be made in order to alleviate discomfort for as long as possible.

GENETIC DISEASES

All genetic diseases are fundamentally due to abnormalities in *deoxyribonucleic acid* (DNA), the material of which genes are made.

DNA in mammals, such as man or the dog, occurs primarily in the chromosomes of the cell, where it provides the genetic message that directs cellular metabolism. It is estimated that mammals have 10,000 to 100,000 pairs of genes.

DNA has two unique biologic properties:

1. Through the process of replication, it accurately reproduces itself — thereby insuring transmission of the genetic material from one generation to the next.

2. Through a sequence of reactions, the genetic message of DNA is first transcribed as messenger RNA (mRNA), which then serves as a template for construction of a protein molecule. Each structural gene produces a different protein molecule.

All differences between individuals due to the effect of genes are the result of differences in the concentration or structure of specific protein molecules.

Abnormalities in DNA result in defective synthesis of one or more of the thousands of protein molecules produced in the body's cells. Genetic disorders can be classified according to the type of underlying abnormality in chromosonal DNA, as follows: (1) Diseases due to single mutant genes; (2) Polygenic defects; (3) Diseases due to chromosonal anomalies.

Diseases Due to Single Mutant Genes

In a disease due to a single mutant gene, only one of the 10,000 or so pairs of genes has been altered. Since in higher organisms genes occur in pairs (one inherited from the mother and one from the father), abnormalities (mutations) in a particular gene may involve one or both members of the pair. Individuals having one mutant gene and one normal gene are called *heterozygous*. Individuals in which both genes are of the same type, whether normal or mutant, are *homozygous*.

Recessive Inheritance: In diseases that have a recessive pattern of inheritance, both genes of the pair must be abnormal to produce the disease state (the individual is homozygous). Dogs with one mutant gene and one normal member of the pair are heterozygous carriers, who are outwardly normal but can pass the abnormal gene to their offspring. Pedigree patterns for these diseases indicate that:

In matings between two heterozygous carriers, 25% of the offspring will be affected, 50% will be carriers, and 25% will be homozygous normal.

In matings between homozygous affected and carrier dogs, 50% of the offspring will be affected and the remaining 50% will be carriers.

In matings between two affected dogs, 100% of the offspring will be affected.

In all matings, the risk to male and female offspring is equal.

A dog with a recessively inherited defect has usually inherited one mutant gene of the pair from *each* of its parents, who are themselves outwardly normal carriers.

Recessive mutant genes can be passed through many generations before coming to light in the offspring of two dogs who carry the same gene mutation. Since the chance that two dogs will carry the same rare mutation is greater when they are related to each other, recessively inherited diseases tend to increase with inbreeding. However, it should be made clear that it is not inbreeding in itself that causes the increase in recessively inherited disease—inbreeding merely exposes deleterious recessive gene mutations that are being carried in the bloodline.

A well known example of a recessively inherited disease in dogs is the *gray collie syndrome*. Pups that receive a double dose of genes for this condition have an unusual silvery gray coat color pattern and a defect in the production of white blood cells, the blood cells that normally combat infection. While the pups appear healthy at birth, at about 10–12 weeks of age they begin to have episodes of fever, diarrhea and sore joints. Periods of illness last three to four days, and recur regularly at 12 to 13 day intervals. Blood counts show that during periods of illness, the white cells almost disappear from the circulating blood. This apparently produces an increased susceptibility to infection that is responsible for the signs of illness. An infected pup may survive to maturity if treated repeatedly with antibiotics, but periods of illness continue to occur at regular intervals and the animals are sterile. The exact biochemical basis for this disease is as yet unknown, but it is clear that inheritance is as a simple recessive trait. Carriers are outwardly normal and there is as yet no means of detecting them except through test matings.

Dominant Inheritance: In diseases that have dominant pattern of inheritance, only one member of a pair of genes need be of the mutant type to produce the disease. Pedigree patterns of dominantly inherited disorders indicate:

Affected individuals are usually heterozygotes.

Heterozygous affected mated with normal produces 50% affected offspring.

Mating of two heterozygous affected (rare) produces 75% affected offspring.

In animals with dominantly inherited disorders, usually one of the parents is affected and transmission of the condition is observed from one generation to the next. Some individuals may be very mildly affected and difficult to detect without careful examination. In such cases, the condition can mistakenly be thought to "skip generations."

An example of a dominantly inherited defect in dogs is *congenital hereditary lymphedema*. In this condition, pups are born with a variable amount of fluid (edema) in the soft tissues of the body, due to a defect in the development of lymphatic vessels. The rear limbs are usually most severely affected, and occasionally pups are completely edematous. Mildly affected pups usually survive to adulthood and appear otherwise healthy, while pups with extensive edema often die before weaning. This condition, which was first observed in a mixed dog, has also been found in German Shepherd Dogs and Siberian Huskies.

Genetic studies have shown that congenital hereditary lymphedema is dominantly inherited. Some affected individuals have only slight edema when born and appear outwardly normal by three months of age. However, special studies show abnormal development of the lymph vessels of the rear legs, and subsequent breeding tests demonstrate that the mildly affected dogs can transmit the condition to their offspring as readily as dogs with the severe form. This example points out the importance of careful examination of all members of the family in identifying and controlling a hereditary disease.

Polygenic Defects

Polygenic disorders result from the cumulative action of a number of different genes rather than from an abnormality in a single pair. The exact number of genes involved and their individual functions are difficult to determine, and the pattern of inheritance tends to vary from family to family. Polygenic inheritance can sometimes mimic either dominant or recessive inheritance on superficial examination, and this feature may lead to erroneous conclusions regarding the type of underlying genetic abnormality.

The polygenically inherited disorder most familiar to dog breeders is *hip dysplasia,* an abnormality in development of the hip joint occurring particularly in larger breeds. As a result of a poorly fitting hip joint, severely affected animals suffer lameness and develop arthritis later in life.

Controversies concerning the mode of inheritance of hip dysplasia raged for many years. Some observers believed the condition to be

719

recessively inherited because they sometimes observed dysplastic offspring in litters from normal parents. Others noted that parents with hip dysplasia when bred to non-dysplastic dogs frequently had a high proportion of dysplastic offspring, suggesting dominant inheritance. Due largely to the research of investigators in Sweden, working with a large population of German Shepherd Dogs used in the Armed Forces, the weight of evidence now overwhelmingly supports the concept that hip dysplasia is neither a simple recessive nor a simple dominant condition, but is due to the cumulative effects of a number of genes affecting the development of the hip joint.

A simplified model to aid in understanding this type of inheritance can be conceived of as a balance in which one pan contains "good genes" (promoting normal development of the hip joint), while the other contains "bad genes" (tending to produce the ill-fitting joint of hip dysplasia). The actual conformation of the hip joint in the mature animal will depend on the relative numbers of the two types of genes a pup receives from its parents. If there are enough genes predisposing to hip dysplasia, the balance will be tipped in that direction and the hips will develop abnormally. If there are a large number of bad genes, the balance will tip entirely to that side and a severe degree of dysplasia will be present.

It should be noted that in our balance model a state can exist in which the pans are exactly balanced. This will correspond to the condition in which the individual has normal, or marginally normal, hips by X-ray examination, but has a large number of dysplasia promoting genes. Such individuals, though themselves outwardly within normal limits, can transmit hip dysplasia-predisposing genes to their offspring. If two such "balanced" individuals are mated, the chances are great that at least some of the offspring will receive enough dysplasia producing genes to tip the balance toward the hip dysplasia side.

Breeding studies have supported the view that hip dysplasia is inherited in a way that is anticipated from this type of model. The more severely affected dogs tend to produce the highest percentage of affected offspring. Likewise, the more severely affected parents, the more severe is the degree of hip dysplasia in the offspring.

Polygenic defects are especially subject to modification by the environment. Observations by Dr. W. H. Riser of the University of Pennsylvania Veterinary School indicate that the incidence of hip dysplasia in German Shepherd Dog pups is greatest in those which show early rapid growth and weight gains, suggesting that nutrition might have some influence on the disease—the heavier the dog, the greater the degree of biochemical inbalance.

720

Chromosomal Anomalies

In recent years, methods have been developed that allow the direct observation of chromosomes from animal cells. Each species has a characteristic chromosome number. The cat has 19 pairs, humans 23, and the dog 39 pairs.

Although we know that genes are located in the chromosomes, defects in single genes and polygenic defects cannot be identified by existing methods of observing the chromosomes because the changes are too small to be visible. It has been recognized, however, that major abnormalities in chromosome number and structure do occur in dogs, often producing serious defects in the individual. Only one example will be given here.

Normal male dogs have 78 chromosomes (39 pairs) including an X and a Y chromosome. Through a rare accident of chromosome separation during cell division, an extra X chromosome may be incorporated when the sperm or egg is formed. If this abnormal germ cell fuses with a normal germ cell of the other sex at the time of fertilization, the resulting individual will have an extra X chromosome. Animals that normally have the XY sex chromosome constitution of normal males will become XXY individuals. This abnormal chromosome constitution has been found in man, cats, sheep, mice, and recently has been found to occur in dogs. In all cases, affected individuals have the physical characteristics of males, but have small testes and are sterile.

Determining Whether the Condition is Hereditary

When confronted with a new defect or disease, breeders concerned about the future of their bloodlines frequently ask whether the condition is hereditary. If it is one of the approximately 100 disorders in dogs whose hereditary nature is well-established, it is usually possible for the veterinarian to give a definite answer to this question. However, because many disorders in dogs have not been carefully studied from the genetic standpoint, there is still a great deal to learn, particularly about defects and illnesses in the period before weaning. The breeder is usually the first to recognize abnormalities in this period and is often in a better position to see their repeated occurrence within a family or line than is the veterinarian. Alertness and careful observation on the part of the breeder is of vital importance to further progress in identifying and controlling genetic diseases of dogs.

Discovery comes most easily to the prepared mind. These are some lines of evidence that should make the breeder suspect that a particular condition has a major genetic component:

1. *The condition occurs more frequently within groups of related individuals than among other dogs.* This of course refers to the fact that hereditary diseases tend to run in families, a fact we are all aware of. The principle also applies on a larger population scale. A particular condition may be observed with higher frequency in members of the same line than in less closely related members of the breed. Or, as is often the case, the condition may occur more frequently in one breed than in another.

The unusual breed distribution of particular forms of *congenital heart disease* was the original clue to their genetic basis. Examination of a large population of dogs presented to the University of Pennsylvania Veterinary Clinic showed that certain breeds were predisposed to defects in certain parts of the heart. *Patent ductus arteriosus,* a condition in which a blood vessel near the heart that normally closes at the time of birth remains open, was found to be significantly more common in Poodles, Collies and Pomeranians than in other breeds. Breeding experiments with affected dogs later proved that these conditions are polygenic defects, inherited in a manner similar to hip dysplasia.

2. *The condition increases in frequency with inbreeding.* Inbreeding is broadly defined as the mating of related individuals. The most severe form of inbreeding involves parent-offspring or brother-sister matings. Linebreeding is a form of inbreeding which usually involves mating a prominent sire to a more distantly related relative such as a granddaughter or niece.

The effect of inbreeding is to increase the chance of homozygosity. If there is a rare mutant gene within a line, mating of close relatives will increase the chance that a pup will receive the gene in double dose. As a result, defects that are due to single recessive genes or are polygenic tend to increase in frequency when inbreeding is practiced. A variety of defects in dogs, including *cleft palate, cryptorchidism, congenital heart defects* and *progressive retinal atrophy* can be expected to increase in frequency when inbreeding occurs in lines carrying the offending genes.

3. *The disease has a characteristic age of onset and course.*

Some genetic disorders behave as if the course of the disease were "programmed." That is, individuals with the same genetic defect vary within very narrow limits in the age of onset and the progression of the disease process.

First Steps in Training

THERE ARE a certain number of basic things a civilized dog should do when you tell him to, to make your life and his easier. They are: walking at your side in the streets, called "heeling" in the jargon of training, sitting, and lying down on command, staying where you tell him to, coming when you call him, and standing and holding his position at your command. The fact that these "exercises" are exactly those included in the requirements for the C.D. (Companion Dog) title awarded in obedience competition by the AKC is by no means a coincidence. We feel that they are the minimum requirements of a civilized dog—sufficient to make him easy to live with and a pleasure to own, a true companion as the title implies.

A fair amount of precision in their performance is required in obedience competition. While we recommend that you train your dog to do properly whatever he is doing, there is of course no necessity for the perfection in home training that is striven for in the competition ring. There is, however, one absolute requirement identical in ring and home—your dog must learn to obey you instantly, with one and only one command or order. The truest sign of the poorly trained dog is the repeated command or commands, quite generally given in a rising voice, and only reluctantly complied with by the dog.

Background to Training

Dogs are not unlike children. They are curious and investigative, and with no ill will in the world they will try various modes of behavior and ways of doing things. It is up to you to channel these natural attempts at coping with their world into the paths you desire—those acceptable to you, and later those actually useful and helpful. A dog, like a child, has certain wants and needs. He will experiment with different methods of attracting your attention to them (once he has learned you are the fount and source of most of his requirements in this world) until he finds one or several which work. Dogs are basically pragmatists. Having little or no moral sense, they use the methods which result in the maximum results combined with the minimum discomfort to them.

Thus if your dog learns that he gets what he wants by constant whining (the child analogy holds remarkably well here), he will whine. If he learns that he gets attention through refusal to eat, he will refuse to eat. If he learns that relieving himself on your Aubusson carpet (a considerable convenience as compared to waiting until he is let outside) brings less discomfort by way of discipline than the discomfort of waiting, he will happily shower the carpet. But if he learns from his first contact with you that your ways of doing things result in praise and comfortable relations, while other ways result in firm, unvarying correction, he is simply going to take the easier way out. Making the right way (your way) the easier way is a fair definition of training.

The foundation stone of training is confidence. It is a two-way thing, meaning your dog's confidence in you, and yours in him. First, he must have confidence that you are fair and trustworthy, which may come as a surprise to you, and although dogs most assuredly don't think in such terms, they operate using the principles. He must have confidence that a certain action is always greeted with the same reaction. In training this means that certain actions are always prohibited, and certain others always encouraged. That way he can live in a secure world, without worrying about how you will react to what he does. Vacillation is the deadly enemy of good training, undercutting security completely. And security is of the utmost importance to any puppy or dog.

Praise and Correction

Under confidence comes the subheading, a vitally important one, of praise and correction. Praise means what it implies, obvious approval when your dog has done something right, which is easy enough. But it also means praise after you have corrected or disciplined your dog. This is not so obvious, but it is important, because of the desirability of maintaining smooth and happy relations with your dog. One of the basic mistakes made by many home trainers is that of continued anger at a dog that has misbehaved, or has been seemingly unable to absorb a training lesson. This has no effect on a dog except a harmful one. He cannot remember, after only a few minutes, what it was he did, or didn't do, and he only knows you are displeased with him. All of which teaches him nothing except that you're not as easy to get along with as might be.

Of course you should never have been angry with him in the first place, but humans are human, and the best trainers lose their tempers once in a while. The reason they are the best trainers is that they show it as little as possible, and have learned to control it.

Therefore, rule: *when you have corrected your dog for either omission or commission, praise him at once.* Let him know that the point has been made, but nonetheless you are still friends. Do this no matter how many times you've had to make the identical correction. It takes a few times for any correction to sink in. Your praise afterward won't lessen the impact of the correction, but it will reassure him that all is well between you, and the training can progress without hard feelings on either side.

As to corrections themselves, they are with one exception, mild and non-violent. We recommend as strongly as possible that you do not strike your dog, ever, or at least hardly ever. The exception is that in which your dog actually threatens to bite, which does happen, although rarely. In this circumstance you will have to judge, from your knowledge of your own dog, how to handle it. You may have to hit him. But even then, once it is over, remember to praise and comfort him afterward, for he wants to get along.

In any other situation, don't hit him. And this includes with your hand, with a rolled-up newspaper, with a stick; in short, with anything at all. And don't threaten to hit him, which is almost worse than actually hitting him. That is what makes dogs "hand shy," cringing at an upraised hand or even a hand near them. If when he sees a hand raised near him he has good reason to expect that someone is going to swing at him, he has every reason in the world to try to skitter away.

In the lines of hitting, it should be obvious why you shouldn't hit him with a stick, but the rolled-newspaper myth is widespread enough to deserve a paragraph of discussion. The idea, generally is that it doesn't hurt a dog—it is simply the loud whack that scares him and punishes him. This is faulty thinking from several angles. First, if you're thinking along lines of scaring him into doing what you want him to, or desisting from what you don't want, you're on the wrong track already. And second, deliberately teaching a dog to be frightened of sudden loud noises comes close to criminal behavior. Third and perhaps most important, it is unlikely that you will have a rolled newspaper in your hand at all times, or even close to hand. This is the really fatal flaw in the fabric, for a correction, to be effective at all, must be administered immediately, not in ten seconds' time.

The main point of good and positive corrections is that they must be immediate and somehow connected with the act. If they are constructive corrections, they must show the dog instantly what he ought to be doing. For example, if you are teaching your dog to sit, and he does not, you must instantly show him what he ought to be doing by guiding him to a sitting position with your hands. And if it is a disciplinary correction, it must be as fast as humanly possible, and as closely as possible connected with the misdeed. As an example—when you are teaching your dog not to jump up on people, the knee which throws him off balance at the moment of his jump is an excellent disciplinary correction. Note that neither of these involves any unpleasantness from you to him, no shouting, no hitting or beating, no recriminations. And note also that there is no mention anywhere here of "punishment." A dog is never punished; he is corrected. This may seem to you a fine point, but it is in such fine points that lies the difference between good and bad training.

One further point before we go on to actual details of training and housebreaking. Never, under any imaginable circumstances, correct or discipline your dog when you have called him to you, or when he has come to you of his own accord. The dog has a mind which makes direct and short-term connection. If he comes to you and you correct or discipline him, he will not connect it with whatever he was doing before, but with the fact that he came—the most recent thing he did before the roof fell in. After a few times, he'll be a little reluctant about coming, and perhaps soon he won't come at all. You have only to put yourself in his position (a very good idea when considering any aspect of training, incidentally), imagining a friend asking you to come to him, then shouting at you or hitting you when you arrive. Very soon you'd get very cautious about approaching him. Your dog feels much the same way. Don't ever do it. If he has done something wrong at a distance, either get to where he is for your correction, or forget about it until you have the opportunity to do it right.

Housebreaking

There are two basic housebreaking situations: one in which housebreaking can be accomplished directly, and another in which paper-breaking is an intermediate stage. Direct housebreaking is by far the more preferable, but your ability to do this will be dictated by your living accommodations. If you have a yard of any sort directly outside your door, then it is not only possible but best to housebreak directly. If you live in a city apartment, as many dog owners do, the intermediate paper-breaking may be called for.

Direct housebreaking is simple. Basically, it means taking the puppy outside frequently, allowing him to relieve himself, and then returning him to the house. When he is in the house, confine him either in a large sleeping-living box or crate or, if you are able to keep a close watch on him, keep him tied on a short leash or rope (six feet or so) in the kitchen. In either case, the puppy will be restricted to a small area in which he must play and sleep, and he will be very reluctant to soil that area.

If he does inadvertently soil it—and these accidents will happen—chastise him mildly and take him outside immediately to the area he has used before, to remind him that the only permissible place is there. But be fair to him. A young puppy has to eliminate quite often, so in the early days before he has had a chance to build up any sort of control, take him out often. Do definitely take him out about an hour after each feeding. As he grows older, he will be able to contain himself for longer periods and the necessary outings will be reduced to around four a day, but let him work up slowly to that.

Don't worry about the close confinement inside. The novice dog owner tends to think that it is unfair to the new pup to keep him in close quarters, but experienced owners and trainers know that it is, if anything, a kindness to the puppy because it allows him to get the housebreaking done with efficiently and over with. Most of the housebreaking trouble you may have heard of results from "kind" owners who let an unhousebroken pup have the run of the house. The pup gets into the habit of soiling the floors, and for years after he may have to be corrected constantly. As between two weeks or so of close confinement and efficient housebreaking, and possibly years of dissatisfaction and continual corrections, there seems an obvious choice. If you make a point of playing with your pup in his confinement area, and when you are outside with him, your future relations won't suffer either. Do what needs to be done, with firmness, kindness, and love.

The housebreaking problem in an apartment is somewhat more difficult. Your vet may advise you not to take the puppy out into city streets until his shots protect him against diseases he might pick up there. And it may simply be physically inconvenient to make many trips from a high-floor apartment to the busy street. In this case, set up a paper-breaking room, preferably the kitchen, in which the pup is to be confined. Cover the entire floor with several thicknesses of newspaper, and wait for the pup to use them. Pick up the soiled papers and replace them, and continue in this fashion for a day or two. Then leave a small corner of the room bare, and hope he doesn't use it. If he does, chastise him mildly and put him on the papers, letting him know that it is there and only there he is to go.

As the days go by and he seems to come to understand the paper idea, widen the bare area until you have a papered area equivalent to about two full newspaper sheets. Until he is old enough to go to the street, keep him using that area, replacing the soiled papers as they are used. Then begin street walks with him until he learns that the street is the place to go, and remove the papers. At that point, watch carefully for any indication of need for relief—he may search frantically for the papers—and take him out promptly.

As with direct housebreaking, keep him absolutely confined, in this case to the paper-breaking room, until he has completely learned his lesson. It won't hurt him.

At nighttime in either city or country, make it easier for him by exercising a bit of caution on the water intake—it will help him control the outgo. Don't give him water for at least two hours before his bedtime, and make sure he is taken out, or allowed access to the papers, just before the household retires. You'll be surprised how long even quite a young puppy can hold it if he has relieved the immediate pressures of eating and drinking.

The Collar and Leash

When it comes to the serious training of your dog, we recommend that you wait until he is about six to eight months old before beginning. Until then he will have little power of concentration, and concentrated lessons will only confuse him. In any case, he deserves to enjoy his brief puppyhood before going on to serious life, so don't push him too hard at first. On the other hand, if you read this with an older dog in mind, don't hestitate to start a dog of any age in training. Despite the old adage, a dog can be trained if he can still move around.

While heeling is not the most important of the exercises, it is the first that should be taught, for it forms the foundation on which the others are built. In preparation for this training, you should have a training collar and leash. The collar to use is the metal chain-link variety, with metal rings at each end. Get the right size for your dog (about one inch longer than the measurement around the largest part of his head) and learn to put it on properly for training. Slip the chain through one of the rings so the collar forms a sort of loop, sliding through one ring, with the other ring left for attachment to the leash. This training collar has been found to be the most effective one for its purpose, which is to control the dog during training—to exert as much control as you need, or as little. When you use it, bear in mind that in the wrong hands it can be harmful to the dog; in really thoughtless hands it can be an instrument of torture. You must never, repeat *never,* use the training collar to exert a constant pull on your dog's neck, for that will only choke and damage him. Like nearly every other useful device, the training collar can be misused, but when properly used it is of great help in training.

The proper method of use is: when you want to get your dog's attention, or urge him into a desired position or in some direction, give a light, quick snap or tug on the leash, which *momentarily* tightens the collar about his neck. Then release the pressure instantly, and the correction will have been made. Use it this way and you will have no problems; misuse it and the harm can be great. We can only leave it to your good judgment and sense to use it properly.

The proper way of putting the collar on your dog is with the loose ring at the right of the dog's neck, the chain attached to it having come over the neck and through the holding ring, rather than under the neck. It seems a small point, but as the dog is at your left during most of training, this arrangement is what makes the collar effective, as it allows the collar to loosen instantly when you have finished the quick snap on the leash. With the proper training leash (leather or webbing, six feet long and half to full inch wide), you are ready to begin.

Introduce him gently to the apparatus. Put the collar on and let him wear it for a day before trying anything else. Then snap the leash onto the collar and let him drag that around for a while to get used to it, being careful that he doesn't get it tangled with something and get panicky. Then when he is used to the leash being on, take up your end of it and walk around with him, putting little or no pressure on. Gradually, over a short period, increase your control until he learns that, while it restrains him, it is nothing to be afraid of. When you have reached the point where you can persuade him to come along in the general direction you want to go by gentle snaps of the leash, you are ready to begin with heeling proper.

Heeling

From this point on, you should establish regular training periods, of about fifteen minutes to half an hour in length, once or twice a day. Any longer will be fatiguing for him, and you too, and training will suffer unless his mind is fresh and alert. Nothing is worse for training than boredom, either on his part or yours, from overlong sessions. During each training session, keep everything quite businesslike, but don't of course, leave out the praise and friendliness. Then after each session, take a little time to play and romp with him, just to ease off the pressure and make sure your relations are friendly and good.

To begin heeling, get him more or less at your left side, then start off walking, giving him the command, "Mike, heel!", using his name, followed immediately by the command word. Give the command just as you take the first step, and simultaneously give him a light snap with the leash to persuade him to come along. Use only as much force as is necessary to get him moving with you. As you are walking along, continue to urge him to walk just at your left side, with his head about opposite your left leg and level with it, by snapping the leash as you go to urge him forward or back, right or left, into position. Each time give the command "Heel!" as you snap. And each time you snap and command, follow it with praise. It need only be a brief word or two, as "That's it, good boy!" It will take a good deal of work before he understands what is going on, for this is the first time he has had to perform at command, but if you are kind and patient and skillful, he will soon learn, and without rancor.

The entire secret of successful heel training is learning the art of the snap of the leash. The training collar is not meant for choking a dog, although you will hear it called "choke collar." And it will indeed choke him if you use it to tow him along with a steady pull. The proper method is the quick snap and equally quick release pressure, the snap being nothing more than a quick tug which tightens the chain collar momentarily around his neck to get his attention, and at the same time urges him in the proper direction. If you will remember *always* to use the collar and leash for quick snaps and releases, never hard enough really to hurt him, and especially never maintaining continual pressure, you will be well along in training skills.

Equally important is the praise you give him after each snap correction. However mild your corrections, each is a discomfort to him, and if you praise him immediately, it will take the sting out without removing the lesson.

Work on the heeling until you are able to give him only one command, "Mike, heel!", as you start walking, and do not have to use the leash for correction at all. From walking largely in a straight line, begin to make circles and corners, turnabouts and other maneuvers, keeping him at your side with continual snaps and praise, until you are confident that he is walking with you of his own accord. Then you are ready to begin teaching the sit.

Sit

The sit is taught by having your dog sit when you stop walking while he is heeling. It can be begun quite early. When you stop, give the command, "Sit!", and while your left hand guides his rear down to a sitting position, your right hand holds his head up and in position with the leash. With your hands and the leash, make him stay in the sitting position a moment, then give the heel command and start up. Again stop, give the sit command, guide him into position, and have him stay seated a little longer.

Gradually, as he gets the idea, you will be able to abandon first the command, and finally the leash and hand correction. He will sit automatically when you come to a stop, waiting either for you to start up again or for his release through an established release command, such as "Okay!"

Finally, when he has learned quite fully the meaning of sit, and learned to do it when you stop walking, you are ready to teach the sit from any position. Put the collar and leash on and give him the "Sit!" command, guiding him into position just as you did before. Concentrate on this phase, continuing the pure sit training until he will sit on command with no corrections, and then begin to introduce the "Stay."

Stay

In the stay, your dog is simply required to stay in his sitting position until released by you. To teach it, sit him, on leash, and immediately tell him "Stay!", repeating the command in a coaxing but firm voice, keeping your hands on him if necessary to reinforce the command. The first few times, don't try to make him stay more than ten or twenty seconds, then release him. But slowly increase the time, cutting down on the continued commands, until he will stay on one command for at least three minutes. You'll find it's a handy bit of training.

At this point it might be well to reinforce our earlier statements on "one command and one only." The truly trained dog will do what he is told the first time he is told. Otherwise he cannot be called trained. This should not be taken to mean that you should not use second and third and however many commands you may need during the initial training, but you must arrive at the point where you need only say "Heel" once to get him started, or "Sit" just once to get him sat. Once he has the idea of what you want him to do, give the command only once, in a firm but pleasant tone, and then use the leash and collar to be sure he does what he told. There is never any need to be rough; simply be firm and unequivocal. The command means the action, and nothing else. It is absolutely fatal to training to have to give a command a second time, whether pleading or shouting furiously, once your dog knows what the command is about. Don't do it.

Stand-Stay

Once he has mastered heeling and sitting, and sitting and staying, he is ready to learn the stand-stay. The usefulness of this may escape you at first, but you will find it indeed a very valuable thing. As only one example, you will find brushing and grooming far and away easier if your dog will stand firmly in position when told to.

This, too, is taught from the heel. As you are heeling along with him, and as you slow down to come to a halt, give him the command, "Stand!" As you do so, stop his forward motion with the leash, and before he has a chance to sit as he has learned to, block the forward and downward motion of his rear with your left hand, fingers extended, just in front of the top of his right hind leg. Don't grab him, just block him. If he still attempts to sit, don't chastise him, for he's only trying to do what you've first taught him. Simply start up again with the "Heel!" command and after a few steps, stop again, using your left hand more firmly to prevent his sitting. He will probably be a little confused at this point, but your praise will reassure him. As he is standing, give him the "Stand!" command repeatedly, to let him know you want him to stay in that position, and also give him the "Stay!" command. This command he will know from the sit-stay training, and he will soon get the idea of what you want him to do.

Continue this training until he will stand firmly at your side until you start up heeling again. If he tries to sit, simply start up heeling again with the command, then stop after a step or two and again give the stand-stay command. Mix this training in with normal sits when you stop walking. He may at first be quite confused, and you may have to reinforce the sit with commands again for a short while. Soon it will become clear to him that he is to sit unless there is a command to the contrary, and to stand when he hears the word.

Now you can begin to leave him a little while he is either sitting or standing at the stay. Whichever position he is in, give him a firm command, "Stay!" At the same time, bring your right hand around, fingers extended, and hold it just in front of his nose, palm to him, for a second, as a "stay" signal. With the leash still in your hand, take a step away from him. If he attempts to move or follow you, give him a firm "No!" and then repeat the "Stay!", if necessary guiding him back into position with your hands and leash. Here again be prepared for natural confusion, for up to now you have wanted him to go with you when you started walking. Keep at it until he learns that he is now to stay unless given a countercommand to heel, or is released. Step away again and move slowly until you are at the distance of the leash. Stay there only a few seconds before coming back to praise him and release him. As the training sessions go on, slowly increase the time you are away from him until you can stay away for at least a minute while he holds the stand position, and three minutes while he holds the sit. Then you can begin to move around him while he is sitting or standing. Still holding the leash, walk away from him and circle around him, being careful that the leash neither tugs on him nor drags across his face. Continue this until he will stay quietly and confidently for the times listed above, during which you can walk away from him to the front or back or sides and circle him several times. Don't try to stop him from turning his head to watch you, but deal with any breaks from position gently and firmly, giving the correction and then praise when he has resumed his position, then reinforcing it with the command again, and leaving once more.

Here again we will remind you of the necessity of praise for your dog after every correction, and whenever he does something right by himself. It is to gain your praise that he works and learns. We haven't said "Praise him" after every sentence, for it would be boring and repetitious for you as you read this. But praise is never boring to your dog. So read each of these paragraphs as though after every sentence we wrote: *"Praise him!"*

Down

Teaching the down comes naturally at this point, for he has learned the meaning of commands—that there is something he must do either actively or passively, at your commands—and another item is simply further accomplishment along the same lines. Sit him at your side, then kneel beside him and reach over his back with your left arm, taking hold of his left front leg near his body with your left hand, and his right front leg similarly with your right hand. Tell him "Down!" and as you do so, lift him gently into the down position by lifting his front feet off the floor or ground and easing his body down until he is indeed lying down.

We recommend this method because it involves no struggle between you and your dog. He is comforted by the fact that you are there with your arm around him, and there is no pressure of leash or hand for him to fight by bracing his front legs, and his rear is already on the ground.

When he is down, release your grasp on him slowly, sliding your left hand around and leaving it on his back, continually telling him "Down, *stay!*" and keep him in position for a few seconds. Then release him and get him into sitting position, by command, for another try. Continue this until he goes down at command without your having to lift him, and will stay quietly until released, without any pressure of your left hand on his back. Then give the command without putting your hands into the ready position. Soon, by gentle and steady progress over a period of days, you will be able to stand erect and give only the one command, "Down!" to have him flop at your side. From this you can improvise until he goes down when several feet away from you, still on leash.

When he has learned the down, leave him at the stay, as before with the sit and stand, first walking away only briefly and then for longer periods and then circling him. You will find it will be easier this time, for he knows now what "Stay!" means.

Come

Once your dog has mastered all these, it is time to teach him to come to you on command. While this is perhaps the most important thing your dog should learn, it is placed here in the training schedule for several very good reasons. Among them are: he has learned to work at command, just as in the down, and more important, he has acquired the abilities to heel and sit, both of which are used in the preliminary "come" training.

This is how it is done: after all the preceding training, when you are heeling one day, suddenly take a step backward and tell him, "Mike, *come!"* As you give the command, give a snap on the leash to turn him around to his right as he is walking, and get him headed back toward you. When he is turned around, keep walking backward, urging him to come toward you with continued gentle snaps of the leash and repetitions of the "Come!" command. And remember to praise him, for this is a confusing turn of events for him. Then, when he is in full stride toward you, stop, and as he reaches you, give the command, "Sit!" It may be necessary to guide him into a sitting position directly in front of you, but there is a very good chance you won't have to. Get him into a sitting position directly in front of you and facing you, and the first "recall" is completed. Tell him "Stay!" and walk around into position, then start up at heel again for another try.

Continue working in this vein until you have only to step backward and give the command with no leash urging, and he turns and walks to you, sitting in front without further command. From this, the progression to the recall from a sitting position at a distance is simple. Get him sat, and step away from him to the end of the leash, then give the "Come!" command. If he hesitates, give him a slight snap on the leash to let him know what you want, and he will get up, come to you, and sit again in front.

The entire idea behind this method is that there is never a brute strength contest between you and him. He is already in motion when you first give him the "Come!" while heeling, and there is no tugging on him with the leash to get him up from a sit or down when he hasn't the slightest idea what "Come!" means. By the time you do introduce the ordinary recall, he does know what it means, and will respond to the command, so there is only a reminder snap to get him in motion.

These, the heel, sit, stand, stay, down, and recall, are the basic lessons, and once these are firmly learned on leash, you are ready for the final step, which is obedience without a controlling leash in your hand. In preparation for this, you must be absolutely, totally sure that he obeys your commands without hesitation on leash. Work on them for a while until there is no slightest doubt in your mind. This is a crucial point in training, and the one at which training often breaks down. Many home trainers give the on-leash work a lick and promise, barely getting their dogs to do what they tell them, and then trying it without leash control. It is invariably fatal to the training, and we cannot recommend more strongly that you have the on-leash work down firmly and confidently before taking the leash off and giving a command.

But once you are sure of yourself and your dog, go ahead. Get him seated at your side as you have been doing. Take off the leash and start up with the heel command. You will probably be greatly surprised to find that he heels with you, but it is no surprise at all if the previous training has been good. Go through the whole routine, the stands, downs, stays and recalls, just as if he still had the leash on. In most cases, if all has gone well before, all will go well now. If not, put the leash back on for correction of whatever parts he is unsure about. Work on that part until you both have it properly, and then take the leash off and try it again. It will work, and you will have a trained dog, which is what this is all about. One point of caution, though: when trying the recall off leash, don't do it from a great distance at first. Do it from only six feet or so, and work up to a distance slowly. It is like everything else in training: slow, gradual progress is the way.

To close this section, we will repeat that the moving force of training is confidence. Your confidence in yourself as a trainer, and in your dog as an intelligent being. And your dog's confidence in you as a kind, fair, and firm master and owner. Through patience and the application of the methods we have outlined here, you can and will have a well-trained dog. It isn't done in a day or a week or a month, but doing it can be fun and not work if you go about it right. And the result will be a trained dog, a joy to own and a true companion.

First Aid

FIRST AID is important in many situations, in order to prevent further complications of injuries already sustained, to alleviate pain, or to save life. First aid is a first step taken, if necessary, prior to proper diagnosis and treatment by a veterinarian. When veterinary services are not available immediately, one should be prepared to give emergency aid.

Problems probably will arise from one of the following situations or conditions: shock, bleeding, cuts, burns, fractures, dislocations, heatstroke, poisoning, convulsions, porcupine quills, skunks, and fish hooks. Seemingly, it is possible for a dog to get into as many unexpected accidents and situations as can any child or any adult.

If one of these situations should occur, knowing and practicing in advance an easy method of restraint, a method of transporting the dog, application of a properly positioned tourniquet, and design and application of a simple splint, may be essential. This might make a club project, with an invited speaker to demonstrate and explain methods.

Restraint

Some means of restraint are needed in handling any injured dog, for even a well-loved pet may become frantic or panic-stricken while help is being given. Muzzling a dog is the quickest and easiest way to prevent biting. A cotton bandage, a necktie, or a piece of rope about two feet long will make such a muzzle. Tie a loose knot in the middle, leaving a large loop. Slip the loop over the dog's nose, pull the knot tight over the nose, bring the ends down under the chin, tie a knot there, then bring the ends around back of the ears, and tie again. If the dog is short-nosed, take one of the ends from behind the ears, pass it over the forehead, slip it under the noose around the nose, bring it back over the forehead, and tie firmly with the remaining end. The muzzle then will not interfere with breathing.

Carrying

An injured dog must be carried in such a way as not to cause further injury. A large dog can be carried on your shoulders around your neck, holding the feet in front. Preferably, the injured dog can be placed on a blanket, with the four corners brought together to form a sling. Smaller dogs may be carried by slipping one hand under the chest, and steadying the head with the other hand.

Shock

A dog in shock will be completely prostrated. The breathing will be shallow, its eyes have a glassy look, its pupils probably wide open, its legs and ears cold and its gums pale. If the weather is cool, cover the dog to keep it warm. Administration of intravenous fluids or a blood transfusion may be needed as soon as possible, and the dog should be taken immediately to the hospital.

Internal Bleeding

Internal bleeding brings on shock, and frequently follows automobile accidents; gentle handling is a must. Visible bleeding from cuts may be controlled by bandaging and direct pressure; even a tourniquet may be necessary until professional attention can be obtained. Tourniquets should be loosened every fifteen or twenty minutes if there is any delay in reaching the hospital.

Fractures

Fractures and dislocations usually are self-evident. The affected limb will be held in an unnatural position. The sooner the fracture is set or the dislocation corrected the less injurious aftereffects will be. If a leg bone is severely out of line, a temporary splint or support would be helpful. Transportation to the hospital should be done with as little change as possible in the position of the affected limb or joint.

Poisoning

Poisoning presents special problems. First advice is that you contact the nearest Poison Control Center. All owners should make themselves aware of the address and phone number of the nearest center for such emergencies. If the exact poison can be identified, better treatment can be given. Try to determine whether the dog had an opportunity to swallow ant poison, mouse poison, poisoned bait for foxes, various plant and flower sprays, or to eat rats, mice, or other rodents or vermin that have been poisoned perhaps with warfarin. Strychnine poisoning results in very rigid extensions of the limbs, and neck. Forcing the dog to vomit is very dangerous to the dog if it has been poisoned by strychnine.

If the dog actually has been observed swallowing poisoned bait, then forcing it to vomit may be valuable. To do so, give it a strong salt solution of six teaspoonfuls to a glass of water, mustard mixed with water, or even a couple of teaspoonfuls of salt on the back of its tongue. After vomiting occurs give it egg whites or milk, but have a veterinarian see it as quickly as possible.

Again here, because of the high incidence of dogs being poisoned by consuming antifreeze, owners are cautioned to keep dogs out of the vicinity where antifreeze is being poured.

Heatstroke

The most frequent cause of heatstroke is the confining of a dog in an automobile that is exposed to the sun. Breathing is difficult and very rapid. The dog is in a state of collapse. Reducing the dog's temperature by immediately placing it under a cold shower is a good first-aid treatment. Many dogs, and young children, too, die each summer from being locked in a car inadequately ventilated, left in a hot parking lot, while the owner or parent shops in air-conditioned comfort.

Porcupine Quills

If dog and porcupine meet, the porcupine wins, and the dog comes away with innumerable quills in its face, neck, and front legs. Removal of these quills is painful. Pain may be lessened somewhat if vinegar is applied to the quills to soften them. Quills must be pulled out gently, using a pair of pliers. Many cases will need professional care if the quills are to be removed without excessive pain.

Fish Hooks

If a fish hook is caught in a dog's foot or mouth, it usually cannot be withdrawn because of the barbed hook. The barbed section must be pushed through and cut off with wire-cutting pliers before the shaft can be withdrawn. In some cases the eye of the hook must be cut off and then the remainder of the hook pushed on through. To avoid further unnecessary injury and pain you may need professional help.

Skunks

The standard method of ridding a dog of skunk odor is promptly to give him a bath with soap and water, after first thoroughly rubbing the entire hair coat with a large can of tomato juice or catsup. A repeat may be necessary. Tomato soup or catsup also are used for this purpose.

Foreign Bodies in the Intestinal Tract

Dogs swallow bones, stones, and sometimes even golf balls. Persistent vomiting is the most constant sign of such a foreign body lodged in the intestinal tract. There is no home method of first aid for this situation; the dog should be taken to the hospital. Dogs grab at sticks, long bones, or roots which may, sheared off by the molars, become lodged in the roof of the mouth. It will paw at the mouth in an attempt to dislodge the object. Pull the dog's tongue out and look in. If you can see the object, pull it out with your fingers or a pair of pliers. It may be imbedded so firmly that the dog will have to be taken to the hospital.

Burns

Simple burns, such as occur from hot water, grease, or hot irons, etc., usually can be handled by applying a sterile antibiotic ointment which is soothing, protects the burned surface, and serves to keep air away from it. Larger burns should also have a light bandage for additional protection. Burns are not only painful, slow-healing, and prone to infection, but they may also leave ugly scars which as hairless areas will detract from your dog's appearance or may spoil it for show purposes. Burns from acids or alkalies should first be flushed with diluted baking soda or diluted lemon juice solutions respectively, and then treated as regular burns.

Owners often try to apply turpentine or kerosene to remove paint, tar, or grease spots from their dogs. These produce painful burns. Treatment by the application of a vegetable cooking oil, followed by gentle washing with mild soap and water and further application of oil is often soothing and healing. You can remove the paint by clipping the hair in involved areas. Small spots are best just allowed to wear off.

Dogs that are very seriously burned may also go into shock, and, of course, they require hospital treatment if they are in pain.

Electric Shock

Electric shock is occasionally encountered, as puppies often play with electric outlet cords. The pup usually chews into the cord, suddenly stiffens, and falls over in a rigid manner. *Always pull the plug from the wall before touching the dog.* If you can feel the dog's heart beating, but it is not breathing, initiate artificial respiration at once and have someone call your veterinarian for further instructions. Artificial respiration is given by placing the dog on its side and alternately depressing and releasing the chest by pressing gently on the rib cage at its most posterior margin. Aromatic inhalants are beneficial in some cases.

Convulsions

This symptom is very startling and rather awesome. One's first reaction is sympathy. However, if the dog already has fallen down, and is not apt to become tangled in furniture, fall down the stairs, or otherwise injure itself, the best course is to leave it alone. The convulsion will pass and the dog then can be handled more easily. If the dog is in a situation where it might injure itself, it may be advisable to hold it down. If this is done, be careful to keep the fingers away from its mouth, as severe bite wounds may result. During convulsions the dog will not be vicious or attempt to attack you, for usually it is oblivious to what is going on.

Convulsions are most commonly caused by a virus infection that has reached the brain, especially distemper. However, other irritating factors may influence the condition. Ear infections, parasite infestations, epilepsy, or other conditions may be involved. Do not worm dogs that have convulsions. This may be exactly the wrong thing to do and may even cause death.

IMPORTANT: *First aid is emergency aid. In a serious emergency, first aid can never replace the need for professional attention.*

Glossary

AKC: American Kennel Club.

Albino: Animal deficient in pigmentation.

Almond eyes: The eye set in surrounding tissue of almond shape.

Amble: A relaxed, easy gait in which the legs on either side move almost, but not quite, as a pair. Often seen as the transition movement between the walk and the faster gaits.

Angulation: The angles formed by a meeting of the bones; mainly, the shoulder, upper arm, stifle, and hock.

Apple head: An irregular roundedness of topskull, in greater or less degree humped toward its center.

Apron: Longer hair below the neck on the chest. Frill.

Babbler: The hound that barks when not on the trail.

Back: Variable in meaning depending upon context of the standard. In some standards defined as the vertebrae between the withers and the loin.

Bad mouth: Crooked or unaligned teeth; bite over or undershot in excess of standard specifications.

Balanced: A consistent whole; symmetrical, typically proportioned as a whole or as regards its separate parts; i.e., balance of head, balance of body, or balance of head and body.

Bandog: A dog tied by day, released at night. Tiedog.

Bandy legs: Having a bend of leg outward.

Barrel: Rounded rib section.

Barrel hocks: Hocks that turn out, causing the feet to toe in. Also called "spread hocks."

Basewide: Wide footfall, resultant of "paddling" movement, causing body to rock from side to side. *See:* Puddling.

Bat ear: An erect ear, rather broad at the base, rounded in outline at the top, and with orifice directly to the front. (French Bulldog.)

Bay: The prolonged bark or voice of the hunting hound.

Beard: Thick, long hair growth on the underjaw.

Beauty spot: A distinct spot, usually round, of colored hair, surrounded by the white of the blaze, on the topskull between the ears. (Blenheim Spaniel, Boston Terrier.)

Beefy: Overheavy development of the hindquarters.

Belton: A color designation. An intermingling of colored and white hairs, as blue belton, lemon, orange, or liver belton. (English Setter.)

Bench show: A dog show at which the dogs competing for prizes are "benched" or leashed on benches.

Best in show: A dog-show award to the dog adjudged best of all breeds.

Bevy: A flock of birds.

Bilateral cryptorchid: See Cryptorchid.

Bird dog: A sporting dog trained to hunt birds.

Bitch: A female dog.

Bite: The relative position of the upper and lower teeth when the mouth is closed. *See* Level bite, Scissors bite, Undershot, Overshot.

Blanket: The color of the coat on the back and upper part of the sides, between the neck and the tail.

Blaze: A white stripe running up the center of the face usually between the eyes.

Blinker: A dog that points a bird and then leaves it, or upon finding a bird, avoids making a definite point.

Blocky: Square or cubelike formation of the head.

Blooded: A dog of good breeding; pedigreed.

Bloom: The sheen of a coat in prime condition.

Blue merle: Blue and gray mixed with black. Marbled.

Bluies: Colored portions of the coat have a distinct bluish or smoky cast. This coloring is associated with extremely light or blue eyes and liver or gray eye rims, nose and lip pigment. (Pembroke Welsh Corgi.)

Board: To feed, house, and care for a dog for a fee.

Bobtail: A naturally tailless dog or a dog with a tail docked very short. Often used as a name for the Old English Sheepdog.

Bodied up: Mature, well-developed.

Bolt: To drive or "start" an animal out of its earth or burrow.

Bone: The relative size (girth) of a dog's leg bones. Substance.

Bossy: Overdevelopment of the shoulder muscles.

Brace: Two dogs of a kind. A couple.

Breastbone: Bone in forepart of chest. (Pointer).

Breed: Pure-bred dogs more or less uniform in size and structure, as produced and maintained by man.

Breeder: A person who breeds dogs. Under AKC rules the breeder of a dog is the owner (or, if the dam was leased, the lessee) of the dam of the dog when the dam was bred.

Breeding particulars: Sire, dam, date of birth, sex, color, etc.

Brick-shaped: Rectangular.

Brindle: A fine even mixture of black hairs with hairs of a lighter color, usually tan, brown, or gray.

Brisket: The forepart of the body below the chest, between the forelegs, closest to the ribs.

Brock: A badger.

Broken color: Self color broken by white or another color.

Broken-haired: A roughed-up wire coat.

Broken-up face: A receding nose, together with a deep stop, wrinkle, and undershot jaw. (Bulldog, Pekingese.)

Brood bitch: A female used for breeding. Brood matron.

Brush: A bushy tail; a tail heavy with hair.

Brushing: A gaiting fault, when parallel pasterns are so close that the legs "brush" in passing.

Bullbaiting: An ancient sport in which the dog baited or tormented the bull.

742

Bull neck: A heavy neck, well-muscled.

Burr: The inside of the ear; i.e., the irregular formation visible within the cup.

Butterfly nose: A parti-colored nose; i.e., dark, spotted with flesh color.

Buttocks: The rump or hips.

Button ear: The ear flap folding forward, the tip lying close to the skull so as to cover the orifice, and pointing toward the eye.

Bye: At field trials, an odd dog remaining after the dogs entered in a stake have been paired in braces by drawing.

Camel back: Arched back, like that of one-hump camel.

Canine: A group of animals—dogs, foxes, wolves, jackals.

Canines: The two upper and two lower sharp-pointed teeth next to the incisors. Fangs.

Canter: A gait with three beats to each stride, two legs moving separately and two as a diagonal pair. Slower than the gallop and not as tiring.

Carpals: Bones of the pastern joints.

Castrate: To remove the testicles of the male dog.

Cat-foot: The short, round, compact foot like that of a cat. The foot with short third digits.

Catch dog: A dog used to catch and hold a hunted animal, so the huntsman can take it alive.

C.D. (Companion Dog): A suffix used with the name of a dog that has been recorded a Companion Dog by AKC as a result of having won certain minimum scores in Novice Classes at a specified number of AKC licensed or member obedience trials.

C.D.X. (Companion Dog Excellent): A suffix used with the name of a dog that has been recorded a Companion Dog Excellent by AKC as a result of having won certain minimum scores in Open Classes at a specified number of AKC licensed or member obedience trials.

Champion (Ch.): A prefix used with the name of a dog that has been recorded a Champion by AKC as a result of defeating a specified number of dogs in specified competition at a series of AKC licensed or member dog shows.

Character: Expression, individuality, and general appearance and deportment as considered typical of a breed.

Cheeky: Cheeks prominently rounded; thick, protruding.

Chest: The part of the body or trunk that is enclosed by the ribs.

China eye: A clear blue eye.

Chippendale front: Named after the Chippendale chair. Forelegs out at elbows, pasterns close, and feet turned out. *See:* Fiddle front, French front.

Chiseled: Clean-cut in head, particularly beneath the eyes.

Choke collar: A leather or chain collar fitted to the dog's neck in such a manner that the degree of tension exerted by the hand tightens or loosens it.

Chops: Jowls or pendulous flesh of the lips and jaw. (Bulldog.)

Chorea: A nervous jerking caused by involuntary contraction of the muscles, usually affecting the face or legs.

Clip: The method of trimming the coat in some breeds, notably the Poodle.

Clipping: When pertaining to gait, the back foot striking the front foot.

Cloddy: Low, thickset, comparatively heavy.

Close-coupled: Comparatively short from withers to hipbones.

Coarse: Lacking refinement.

Coat: The dog's hair covering.

Cobby: Short-bodied, compact.

Collar: The marking around the neck, usually white. Also a leather or chain for restraining or leading the dog, when the leash is attached.

Condition: Health as shown by the coat, state of flesh, general appearance and deportment.

Conformation: The form and structure, make and shape; arrangement of the parts in conformance with breed-standard demands.

Corky: Active, lively, alert.

Couple: Two hounds.

Coupling: The part of the body between the ribs and pelvis; the loin.

Coursing: The sport of chasing the hare by Greyhounds.

Covering ground: The ratio of the distance between the ground and brisket and the distance between front and rear legs. As in "covers too much ground."

Cow-hocked: When the hocks turn toward each other.

Crabbing: Dog moves with his body at an angle to the line of travel. Also referred to as "sidewinding", "sidewheeling" or "yawing."

Crank tail: A tail carried down and resembling a crank in shape.

Crest: The upper, arched portion of the neck.

Cropping: The cutting or trimming of the ear leather for the purpose of inducing the ears to stand erect.

Crossbred: A dog whose sire and dam are representatives of two different breeds.

Crossing over: Unsound gaiting action which starts with twisting elbows and ends with crisscrossing and toeing out. Also called "knitting and purling" and "weaving."

Croup: The back part of the back, above the hind legs.

Crown: The highest part of the head: the topskull.

Cry: The baying or "music" of the hounds.

Cryptorchid: The adult whose testicles are abnormally retained in the abdominal cavity. Bilateral cryptorchidism involves both sides; that is, neither testicle has descended into the scrotum. Unilateral cryptorchidism involves one side only; that is, one testicle is retained or hidden, and one descended.

Culotte: The longer hair on the back of the thighs.

Cur: A mongrel.

Cushion: Fullness or thickness of the upper lips. (Pekingese.)

Cynology: The study of canines.

Dam: The female parent.

Dappled: Mottled marking of different colors, no one predominating.

Deadgrass: Tan or dull straw color.

Derby: Field-trial competition for young, novice sporting dogs usually between one and two years of age.

Dewclaw: An extra claw or functionless digit on the inside of the leg; a rudimentary fifth toe.

Dewlap: Loose, pendulous skin under the throat.

744

BROKEN-UP FACE, LAY BACK   SNIPY MUZZLE

DOWN FACE   DISH FACE   CHEEKY

DOMED HEAD   BUMPY SKULL   FROG FACE

LEVEL MOUTH   OVERSHOT MOUTH   UNDERSHOT MOUTH

Diagonals: Right front and left rear legs constitute the right diagonal; left front and right rear constitute the left diagonal. In the trot the diagonals move together.

Diehard: Nickname of the Scottish Terrier.

Dish-faced: When the nasal bone is so formed that the nose is higher at the tip than at the stop; or, a slight concaveness of line from the stop to the nose tip.

Disqualification: A decision made by a judge or by a bench show committee following a determination that a dog has a condition that makes its ineligible for any further competition under the dog show rules or under the standard for its breed.

Distemper teeth: Teeth discolored or pitted as a result of distemper or other enervating disease or deficiency.

Divergent hocks: Hocks that turn out. *See* barrel hocks.

Dock: To shorten the tail by cutting.

Dog: A male dog; also used collectively to designate both male and female.

Dog show: A competitive exhibition for dogs at which the dogs are judged in accordance with an established standard of perfection for each breed.

Dog Show, All Breed: See Dog Show, Conformation.

Dog Show, Conformation (Licensed): An event held under AKC rules at which championship points are awarded. May be for *all breeds,* or for a single breed (Specialty Show).

Dog Show, Specialty: See Dog Show, Conformation.

Domed: Evenly rounded in topskull; convex instead of flat. Domy.

Double coat: An outer coat resistant to weather and protective against brush and brambles, together with an undercoat of softer hair for warmth and waterproofing.

Down-faced: The muzzle inclining downwards from the skull to the tip of the nose.

Down in pastern: Weak or faulty pastern (metacarpus) set at a pronounced angle from the vertical.

Drag: A trail prepared by dragging along the ground a bag impregnated usually with animal scent.

Drawing: Selection by lot of dogs to be run, and in which pairs, in a field-trial stake.

Drive: A solid thrusting of the hindquarters, denoting sound locomotion.

Drop ear: The ends of the ear folded or drooping forward, as contrasted with erect or prick ears.

Dropper: A bird-dog cross.

Dry neck: The skin taut; neither loose nor wrinkled.

Dual champion: A dog that has won both a bench show and a field trial championship.

Dudley nose: Flesh-colored.

Elbow: The joint between the upper arm and the forearm.

Elbows out: Turning out or off from the body; not held close.

Even bite: Meeting of front teeth at edges with no overlap of upper or lower teeth.

PRICK EAR

BUTTON EAR

SEMI PRICK EAR

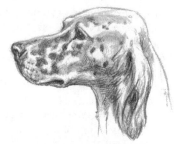

HANGING EAR

ROSE EAR

BAT EAR

Ewe neck: Concave curvature of the top neckline.

Expression: The general appearance of all features of the head as viewed from the front and as typical of the breed.

Eyeteeth: The upper canines.

Faking: To change the appearance of a dog by artificial means with the objective of deceiving the onlooker as to its real merit.

Fall: Hair overhanging the face.

Fallow: Pale cream to light fawn color; pale; pale yellow; yellow-red.

Fancier: A person especially interested and usually active in some phase of the sport of pure-bred dogs.

Fangs: See Canines.

Fawn: A brown, red-yellow with hue of medium brilliance.

Feathering: Longer fringe of hair on ears, legs, tail, or body.

Feet east and west: The toes turned out.

Fetch: The retrieve of game by the dog; also the command to do so.

Fiddle front: Forelegs out at elbows, pasterns close, and feet turned out. French front.

Field Champion (Field Ch.): A prefix used with the name of a dog that has been recorded a Field Champion by AKC as a result of defeating a specified number of dogs in specified competition at a series of AKC licensed or member field trials.

Field trial: A competition for certain Hound or Sporting Breeds in which dogs are judged on ability and style in finding or retrieving game or following a game trail.

Flag: A long tail carried high; usually referring to one of the Pointing Breeds.

Flank: The side of the body between the last rib and the hip.

Flare: A blaze that widens as it approaches the topskull.

Flat bone: The leg bone whose girth is elliptical rather than round.

Flat-sided: Ribs insufficiently rounded as they approach the sternum or breastbone.

Flat withers: A fault that is the result of short upright shoulder blades that unattractively join the withers abruptly.

Flews: Upper lips pendulous, particularly at their inner corners.

Flicking pasterns: Extremely loose movement of the lower forelegs.

Floating rib: The last, or 13th rib, which is unattached to other ribs.

Fluffies: A coat of extreme length with exaggerated feathering on ears, chest, legs and feet, underparts and hindquarters. Trimming such a coat does not make it any more acceptable. (Pembroke Welsh Corgi.)

Flush: To drive birds from cover, to force them to take flight. To spring.

Flying ears: Any characteristic drop ears or semi-prick ears that stand or "fly."

Flying Trot: A fast gait in which all four feet are off the ground for a brief second during each half stride. Because of the long reach, the oncoming hind feet step beyond the imprint left by the front. Also called Suspension Trot.

Forearm: The bone of the foreleg between the elbow and the pastern.

Foreface: The front part of the head, before the eyes. Muzzle.

Foster mother: A bitch or other animal, such as a cat, used to nurse whelps not her own.

Foul color: A color or marking not characteristic.

Foxy: Sharp expression; pointed nose with short foreface.

French front: See Fiddle front.

Frill: See Apron.

Fringes: See Feathering.

Frogface: Extending nose accompanied by a receding jaw, usually overshot.

Front: The forepart of the body as viewed head on; i.e., forelegs, chest, brisket, and shoulder line.

Frontal bone: The skull bone over the eyes.

Furnishings: The long hair on the foreface of certain breeds.

Furrow: A slight indentation or median line down the center of the skull to the stop.

Futurity Stake: A class at dog shows or field trials for young dogs which have been nominated at or before birth.

Gait: The pattern of footsteps at various rates of speed, each pattern distinguished by a particular rhythm and footfall. The two gaits acceptable in the show ring are walk and trot.

Gallop: Fastest of the dog gaits, has a four-beat rhythm and often an extra period of suspension during which the body is propelled through the air with all four feet off the ground.

Game: Hunted wild birds or animals.

Gay tail: The tail carried up.

Gazehound: Greyhound or other sight-hunting hound.

Geld: See Castrate.

Genealogy: Recorded family descent.

Goose rump: Too steep or sloping a croup.

Grizzle: Bluish-gray color.

Groom: To brush, comb, trim, or otherwise make a dog's coat neat.

Groups: The breeds as grouped in six divisions to facilitate judging.

Guard hairs: The longer, smoother, stiffer hairs which grow through the undercoat and normally conceal it.

Gun dog: A dog trained to work with its master in finding live game and retrieving game that has been shot.

Guns: Sportsmen who do the shooting at field trials.

Gun-shy: When the dog fears the sight or sound of a gun.

Hackles: Hair on neck and back raised involuntarily in fright or anger.

Hackney action: The high lifting of the front feet, like that of a hackney horse—a waste of effort.

Ham: Muscular development of the hind leg just above the stifle.

Handler: A person who handles a dog in the show ring or at a field trial. *Also see* Professional handler.

Hard-mouthed: The dog that bites or marks with his teeth the game he retrieves.

Harefoot: A foot whose third digits are longer; hence, an elongated foot.

Harlequin: Patched or pied coloration, usually black on white. (Great Danes.)

Harness: A leather strap shaped around the shoulders and chest, with a ring at its top over the withers.

Haw: A third eyelid or membrane in the inside corner of the eye.

Heat: Seasonal period of the female. Estrum.

Heel: See Hock; also a command to the dog to keep close beside its handler.

Height: Vertical measurement from the withers to the ground; referred to usually as shoulder height. *See* Withers.

Hie on: A command to urge the dog on; used in hunting or in field trials.

High standing: Tall and upstanding, with plenty of leg.

Hindquarters: Rear assembly of dog (pelvis, thighs, hocks and paws).

Hock: The tarsus or collection of bones of the hind leg forming the joint between the second thigh and the metatarsus; the dog's true heel.

Hocks well let down: Hock joints close to the ground.

Hocking out: Spread hocks.

Holt: The lair of the fox or other animal in tree roots, banks, drains or similar hideouts. Lodge.

Honorable scars: Scars from injuries suffered as a result of work.

Hound: A dog commonly used for hunting by scent or sight.

Hound-marked: A coloration composed of white, tan, and black. The ground color, usually white, may be marked with tan and/or black patches on the head, back, legs, and tail. The extent and the exact location of such markings, however, differ in breeds and individuals.

Hound jog: The usual pace of the hound.

Hucklebones: The top of the hipbones.

Inbreeding: The mating of closely related dogs of the same standard breed.

Incisors: The upper and lower front teeth between the canines.

In-shoulder: Shoulders point in, not parallel with backbone, a fault found in dogs with shoulder blades too far forward on chest.

Interbreeding: The breeding together of dogs of different varieties.

Isabella: Fawn or light bay color.

Jowls: Flesh of lips and jaws.

Judge: The arbiter in the dog show ring, obedience trial, or field trial.

Kennel: Building or enclosure where dogs are kept.

Kink tail: The tail sharply bent.

Kiss marks: Tan spots on the cheeks and over the eyes.

Knee joint: Stifle joint.

Knitting and purling: See Crossing over.

Knuckling over: Faulty structure of carpus (wrist) joint allowing it to double forward under the weight of the standing dog; double-jointed wrist, often with slight swelling of the bones.

Landseer: The black-and-white Newfoundland dog, so-called from the name of the famous painter who used such dogs as models.

Layback: The angle of the shoulder blade as compared with the vertical.

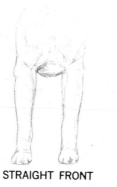

STRAIGHT FRONT

STRAIGHT FRONT

FIDDLE FRONT

NARROW FRONT

OUT AT ELBOW

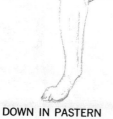

DOWN IN PASTERN

KNUCKLED OVER

"WOLF" SHOULDER

CORRECT HIND END

MODERATELY
ANGULATED HINDQUARTER

COW-HOCKED

STRAIGHT STIFLED

CAT FOOT　　　　HARE FOOT　　　　SPLAY FOOT　　　　PAPER FOOT

Lead: A strap, cord, or chain attached to the collar or harness for the purpose of restraining or leading the dog. Leash.

Leather: The flap of the ear.

Level bite: When the front teeth (incisors) of the upper and lower jaws meet exactly edge to edge. Pincer bite.

Level gait: Dog moves without rise or fall of withers.

Liam: Leash.

License: Formal permission granted by AKC to a non-member club to hold a dog show, obedience trial, or field trial.

Line breeding: The mating of related dogs of the same standard breed, within the line or family, to a common ancestor, as, for example, a dog to his granddam or a bitch to her grandsire.

Lion color: Tawny (Ibizan Hound).

Lippy: Pendulous lips or lips that do not fit tightly.

Litter: The puppy or puppies of one whelping.

Liver: A color; i.e., deep, reddish brown.

Loaded shoulders: When the shoulder blades are shoved out from the body by overdevelopment of the muscles.

Loin: Region of the body on either side of the vertebral column between the last ribs and the hindquarters.

Lower thigh: See Second thigh.

Lumber: Superfluous flesh.

Lumbering: An awkward gait.

Lurcher: A crossbred hound.

Lymer: A hound of ancient times led by a liam.

Mad dog: A rabid dog.

Mane: Long and profuse hair on top and sides of the neck.

Mantle; Dark-shaded portion of the coat on shoulders, back, and sides. (St. Bernard.)

Mask: Dark shading on the foreface. (Mastiff, Boxer, Pekingese.)

Match show: Usually an informal dog show at which no championship points are awarded.

Mate: To breed a dog and bitch.

Median line: See Furrow.

Merle: A coloration, usually blue-gray with flecks of black.

Milk teeth: First teeth.

Miscellaneous Class: A competitive class at dog shows for dogs of certain specified breeds for which no regular dog show classification is provided.

Mismarks: Self colors with any area of white on back between withers and tail, on sides between elbows and back of hindquarters, or on ears. Black with white markings and no tan present. (Pembroke Welsh Corgi.)

Molars: Dog has 4 premolars on each side of the upper and lower jar. There are two true molars on each side of the upper jaw, and three on each side of the lower jaw. Upper molars have three roots, lower have two roots.

Molera: Incomplete, imperfect or abnormal ossification of the skull.

Mongrel: A dog whose parents are of mixed-breed origin.

Monorchid: A unilateral cryptorchid. *See* Cryptorchid.

Moving close: When the hocks turn in and pasterns drop straight to the ground and move parallel to one another, the dog is "moving close" in the rear. Action places severe strain on ligaments and muscles.

Moving straight: Term descriptive of balanced gaiting in which angle of inclination begins at the shoulder, or hip joint, and limbs remain relatively straight from these points to the pads of the feet, even as the legs flex or extend in reaching or thrusting.

Music: The baying of the hounds.

Mute: To run mute, to be silent on the trail; i.e., to trail without baying or barking.

Muzzle: The head in front of the eyes—nasal bone, nostrils, and jaws. Foreface. Also, a strap or wire cage attached to the foreface to prevent the dog from biting or from picking up food.

Muzzle band: White marking around the muzzle. (Boston Terrier.)

Neck well set-on: Good neckline, merging gradually with strong withers, forming a pleasing transition into topline.

Nick: A breeding that produces desirable puppies.

Non-slip Retriever: The dog that walks at heel, marks the fall, and retrieves game on command; not expected to find or flush.

Nose: Organ of smell; also, the ability to detect by means of scent.

Obedience Trial (Licensed): An event held under AKC rules at which a "leg" toward an obedience degree can be earned.

Obedience Trial Champion (O.T. Ch.): A prefix used with the name of a dog that has been recorded an Obedience Trial Champion by the AKC as the result of having won the number of points and First Place wins specified in the current Obedience Regulations.

Oblique shoulders: Shoulders well laid back. The ideal shoulder should slant at 45 degrees to the ground, forming an approximate right angle with the humerus at the shoulder joint.

Occiput: Upper, back point of the skull.

Occipital protuberance: A prominently raised occiput characteristic of some gun-dog breeds.

Open bitch: A bitch that can be bred.

Open Class: A class at dog shows in which all dogs of a breed, champions and imported dogs included, may compete.

Orange belton: See Belton.

Organized competition: Competition governed by the rules of a club or society, such as the AKC, organized to promote the interests of pure-bred dogs.

Otter tail: Thick at the root, round, and tapering, with the hair parted or divided on the underside.

Out at elbows: Elbows turning out from the body as opposed to being held close.

Out at shoulder: With shoulder blades loosely attached to the body, leaving the shoulders jutting out in relief and increasing the breadth of the front.

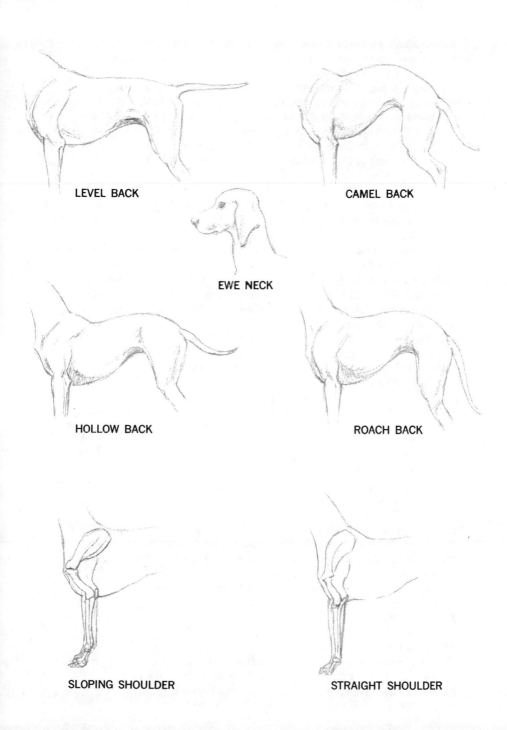

LEVEL BACK

CAMEL BACK

EWE NECK

HOLLOW BACK

ROACH BACK

SLOPING SHOULDER

STRAIGHT SHOULDER

Out at walk: To lease or lend a puppy to someone for raising.

Outcrossing: The mating of unrelated individuals of the same breed.

Oval chest: Chest deeper than wide.

Overhang: A heavy or pronounced brow. (Pekingese.)

Overreaching: Fault in the trot caused by more angulation and drive from behind than in front, so that the rear feet are forced to step to one side of the forefeet to avoid interfering or clipping.

Overshot: The front teeth (incisors) of the upper jaw overlap and do not touch the front teeth of the lower jaw when the mouth is closed.

Pace: A gait which tends to promote a rolling motion of the body. The left foreleg and left hind leg advance in unison, then the right foreleg and right hind leg.

Pack: Several hounds kept together in one kennel. Mixed pack is composed of dogs and bitches.

Padding: A compensating action to offset constant concussion when a straight front is subjected to overdrive from the rear; the front feet flip upward in a split-second delaying action to coordinate stride of forelegs with longer stride from behind.

Paddling: A gaiting fault, so named for its similarity to the swing and dip of a canoeist's paddle. Pinching in at the elbows and shoulder joints causes the front legs to swing forward on a stiff outward arc. Also referred to as "tied at the elbows."

Pads: Tough, shock-absorbing projections on the underside of the feet. Soles.

Paper foot: A flat foot with thin pads.

Parent club: National club for the breed. Listing with name and address of secretary can be obtained from American Kennel Club, 51 Madison Avenue, New York, N.Y. 10010.

Parti-color: Variegated in patches of two or more colors.

Pastern: Commonly recognized as the region of the foreleg between the carpus or wrist and the digits.

Peak: See Occiput.

Pedigree: The written record of a dog's descent of three generations or more.

Penciling: Black lines dividing the tan on the toes. (Manchester.)

Pied: Comparatively large patches of two or more colors. Piebald, parti-colored.

Pigeon-breast: A chest with a short protruding breastbone.

Pigeon-toed: Toes pointing in.

Pig jaw: See Overshot.

Pile: Dense undercoat of soft hair.

Pincer bite: See Level bite.

Pitching: Severe rocking of the haunches as the rear legs swing forward in a wide arc, rather than flexing normally at the stifle and hock.

Plume: A long fringe of hair hanging from the tail as in Setters.

Poach: When hunting, to trespass on private property.

Point: The immovable stance of the hunting dog taken to indicate the presence and position of game.

CORRECT MOVEMENT
FRONT

PADDLING

WEAVING

GOOD MOVEMENT
REAR

POOR MOVEMENT
REAR

Points: Color on face, ears, legs, and tail when correlated—usually white, black or tan.

Poke: To carry the neck stretched forward in an abnormally low, ungainly position, usually when moving.

Police dog: Any dog trained for police work.

Pompon: A rounded tuft of hair left on the end of the tail when the coat is clipped. (Poodle.)

Pounding: Gaiting fault resultant of dog's stride being shorter in front than in the rear; forefeet strike the ground hard before the rear stride is expended.

Premium list: An advance-notice brochure sent to prospective exhibitors and containing details regarding a forthcoming show.

Prick ear: Carried erect and usually pointed at the tip.

Professional handler: A person who shows dogs for a fee.

Pump handle: Long tail, carried high.

Put down: To prepare a dog for the show ring; also used to denote a dog unplaced in competition.

Puppy: A dog under twelve months of age.

Pure-bred: A dog whose sire and dam belong to the same breed, and are themselves of unmixed descent since recognition of the breed.

Quality: Refinement, fineness.

Racy: Tall, of comparatively slight build.

Ragged: Muscles appear ragged rather than smooth. (English Foxhound.)

Rangy: Long-bodied, usually lacking depth in chest.

Rat tail: The root thick and covered with soft curls; at the tip devoid of hair, or having the appearance of being clipped. (Irish Water Spaniel.)

Reach of front: Length of forward stride taken by forelegs without wasted or excessive motion.

Register: To record with the AKC a dog's breeding particulars.

Retrieve: A hunting term. The act of bringing back shot game to the handler.

Ribbed up: Long ribs that angle back from the spinal column (45 degrees is ideal); last rib is long.

Ringer: A substitute for; a dog closely resembling another dog.

Ring tail: Carried up and around almost in a circle.

Roach back: A convex curvature of the back toward the loin. Carp back.

Roan: A fine mixture of colored hairs with white hairs; blue roan, orange roan, lemon roan, etc. (English Cocker Spaniel.)

Rocking horse: Both front and rear legs extended out from body as in old-fashioned rocking horse.

Rolling gait: Swaying, ambling action of the hindquarters when moving.

Roman nose: A nose whose bridge is so comparatively high as to form a slightly convex line from forehead to nose tip. Ram's nose.

Rose ear: A small drop ear which folds over and back so as to reveal the burr.

Rounding: Cutting or trimming the ends of the ear leather. (English Foxhounds.)

Rudder: The tail.

Ruff: Thick, longer hair growth around the neck.

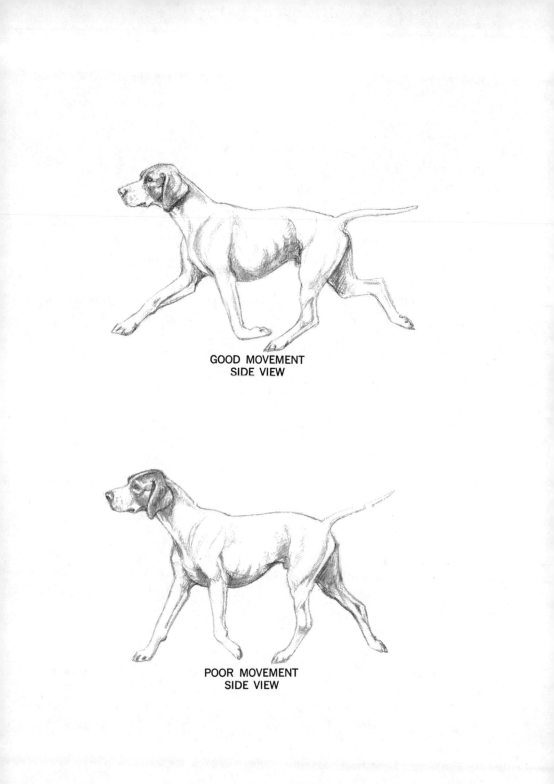

GOOD MOVEMENT
SIDE VIEW

POOR MOVEMENT
SIDE VIEW

RING TAIL

SICKLE TAIL

SQUIRREL TAIL

CRANK TAIL

SCREW TAIL

GAY TAIL

PLUME

OTTER TAIL

SABER TAIL

Saber tail: Carried in a semi-circle.

Sable: A lacing of black hairs over a lighter ground color. In Collies and Shetland Sheepdogs, a brown color ranging from golden to mahogany.

Saddle: A black marking over the back, like a saddle.

Saddle back: Overlong back, with a dip behind the withers.

Scent: The odor left by an animal on the trail (ground scent), or wafted through the air (air-borne scent).

Scissors bite: A bite in which the outer side of the lower incisors touches the inner side of the upper incisors.

Screw tail: A naturally short tail twisted in more or less spiral formation.

Second thigh: That part of the hindquarter from the stifle to the hock, corresponding to the human shin and calf. Lower thigh.

Sedge: See Deadgrass.

Self color: One color or whole color except for lighter shadings.

Seeing Eye dog: A dog trained by the institution, The Seeing Eye, as guide for the blind.

Semi-prick ears: Ears carried erect with just the tips leaning forward.

Septum: The line extending vertically between the nostrils.

Set up: Posed so as to make the most of the dog's appearance for the show ring.

Shelly: A shallow, narrow body, lacking the correct amount of bone.

Shoulder-height: Height of dog's body as measured from the withers to the ground. *See* Withers.

Sickle hocked: Inability to straighten the hock joint on the back reach of the hind leg.

Sickle tail: Carried out and up in a semicircle.

Sidewheeling: See Crabbing.

Sight hound: See Gazehound.

Single tracking: All footprints falling on a single line of travel. When a dog breaks into a trot, his body is supported by only two legs at a time, which move as alternating diagonal pairs. To achieve balance, his legs angle inward toward a center line beneath his body, and the greater the speed, the closer they come to tracking on a single line.

Sire: The male parent.

Skully: Thick and coarse through skull.

Slab sided: Flat ribs with too little spring from spinal column.

Sled dogs: Dogs worked usually in teams to draw sleds.

Slew feet: Feet turned out.

Sloping shoulder: The shoulder blade set obliquely or "laid back."

Smooth coat: Short hair, close-lying.

Snatching hocks: A gaiting fault indicated by a quick outward snatching of the hock as it passes the supporting leg and twists the rear pattern far in beneath the body. The action causes noticeable rocking in the rear quarters.

Snipy: A pointed, weak muzzle.

Soundness: The state of mental and physical health when all organs and faculties are complete and functioning normally, each in its rightful relation to the other.

Spay: To perform a surgical operation on the bitch's reproductive organs to prevent conception.

Speak: To bark.

Spectacles: Shadings or dark markings over or around the eyes or from eyes to ears.

Spike tail: Straight short tail that tapers rapidly along its length.

Splashed: Irregularly patched, color on white or white on color.

Splayfoot: A flat foot with toes spreading. Open foot, open-toed.

Spread: Width between the forelegs when accentuated. (Bulldog.)

Spread hocks: Hocks pointing outward.

Spring: *See* Flush.

Spring of ribs: Curvature of ribs for heart and lung capacity.

Squirrel tail: Carried up and curving more or less forward.

Stacking: *See* Set up.

Stake: Designation of a class, used in field trial competition.

Stance: Manner of standing.

Standard: A description of the ideal dog of each recognized breed, to serve as a word pattern by which dogs are judged at shows.

Standoff coat: A long or heavy coat that stands off from the body.

Staring coat: The hair dry, harsh, and sometimes curling at the tips.

Station: Comparative height from the ground, as high-stationed, low-stationed.

Stern: Tail of a sporting dog or hound.

Sternum: Breastbone.

Stifle: The joint of the hind leg between the thigh and the second thigh. The dog's knee.

Stilted: The choppy, up-and-down gait of the straight-hocked dog.

Stop: The step up from muzzle to skull; indentation between the eyes where the nasal bone and skull meet.

Straight-hocked: Lacking appreciable angulation at the hock joints. Straight behind.

Straight in pastern: Little or no bend between joint and foot.

Straight shoulders: The shoulder blades rather straight up and down, as opposed to sloping or "well laid back."

Stud book: A record of the breeding particulars of dogs of recognized breeds.

Stud dog: A male dog used for breeding purposes.

Substance: Bone.

Superciliary arches: The ridge, projection, or prominence of the frontal bone of the skull over the eye; the brow.

Suspension trot: *See* Flying trot.

Swayback: Concave curvature of the back line between the withers and the hipbones.

Symmetry: Pleasing balance between all parts of the dog.

Tail set: How the base of the tail sets on the rump.

T. D. (Tracking Dog): A suffix used with the name of a dog that has been recorded a Tracking Dog as a result of having passed an AKC licensed or member tracking test. The title may be combined with the U.D. title and shown as U.D.T.

Team: Usually four dogs.

Terrier: A group of dogs used originally for hunting vermin.

Terrier front: Straight front, as found on Fox Terriers.

Thigh: The hindquarter from hip to stifle.

Throatiness: An excess of loose skin under the throat.

Thumb marks: Black spots on the region of the pastern.

Ticked: Small, isolated areas of black or colored hairs on a white ground.

Tied at the elbows: See Paddling.

Timber: Bone, especially of the legs.

Tongue: The barking or baying of hounds on the trail, as to give tongue, to open or speak.

Topknot: A tuft of longer hair on top of the head.

Topline: The dog's outline from just behind the withers to the tail set.

Toy dog: One of a group of dogs characterized by very small size.

Trace: A dark stripe down the back of the Pug.

Trail: To hunt by following ground scent.

Triangular eye: The eye set in surrounding tissue of triangular shape; three-cornered eye.

Tri-color: Three-color; white, black, and tan.

Trim: To groom the coat by plucking or clipping.

Trot: A rhythmic two-beat diagonal gait in which the feet at diagonally opposite ends of the body strike the ground together; i.e., right hind with left front and left hind with right front.

Trumpet: The slight depression or hollow on either side of the skull just behind the orbit or eye socket, the region comparable with the temple in man.

Truncated: Cut off. (Old English standard calls for jaw that is square and truncated.)

Tuck-up: Characterized by markedly shallower body depth at the loin. Small-waisted.

Tulip ear: Ears carried with a slight forward curvature.

Turn-up: An uptilted foreface.

Twisting hocks: A gaiting fault in which the hock joints twist both ways as they flex or bear weight. Also called "rubber hocks."

Type: The characteristic qualities distinguishing a breed; the embodiment of a standard's essentials.

U.D. (Utility Dog): A suffix used with the name of a dog that has been recorded a Utility Dog by AKC as a result of having won certain minimum scores in Utility Classes at a specified number of AKC licensed or member obedience trials. The title may be combined with the T.D. title and shown as U.D.T.

Undershot: The front teeth (incisors) of the lower jaw overlapping or projecting beyond the front teeth of the upper jaw when the mouth is closed.

Unilateral cryptorchid: See Cryptorchid.

Upper arm: The humerus or bone of the foreleg, between the shoulder blade and the forearm.

Varminty: A keen, very bright or piercing expression.

Vent: The anal opening.

Walk: Gaiting pattern in which three legs are in support of the body at all times, each foot lifting from the ground one at a time in regular sequence.

Walleye: An eye with a whitish iris; a blue eye, fisheye, pearl eye.

Weaving: See Knitting and purling.

Weedy: An insufficient amount of bone; light-boned.

Well let down: Having short hocks.

Wet neck: Loose or superfluous skin; with dewlap.

Wheaten: Pale yellow or fawn color.

Wheel back: The back line arched markedly over the loin. Roached.

Whelps: Unweaned puppies.

Whip tail: Carried out stiffly straight, and pointed.

Whisker: Longer hairs on muzzle sides and underjaw.

Whitelies: Body color white with red or dark markings. (Pembroke Welsh Corgi.)

Wind: To catch the scent of game.

Winging: A gaiting fault where one or both front feet twist outward as the limbs swing foward.

Winners: An award given at dog shows to the best dog (Winners Dog) and best bitch (Winners Bitch) competing in regular classes.

Wirehair: A coat of hard, crisp, wiry texture.

Withers: The highest point of the shoulders, immediately behind the neck.

Wrinkle: Loose, folding skin on forehead and foreface.

Wry mouth: Lower jaw does not line up with upper jaw.

Index

765